Rome: An Empire of Many Nations

The center of gravity in Roman studies has shifted far from the upper echelons of government and administration in Rome or the Emperor's court to the provinces and the individual. The multidisciplinary studies presented in this volume reflect the turn in Roman history to the identities of ethnic groups and even single individuals who lived in Rome's vast multinational empire. The purpose is less to discover another element in the Roman Empire's "success" in governance than to illuminate the variety of individual experience in its own terms. The chapters here, reflecting a wide spectrum of professional expertise, range across the many cultures, languages, religions and literatures of the Roman Empire, with a special focus on the Jews as a test case for the larger issues. This title is also available as Open Access on Cambridge Core.

JONATHAN J. PRICE is the Fred and Helen Lessing Professor of Ancient History at Tel Aviv University and the author of many studies on Greek and Roman historiography, and Jewish history and epigraphy of the Roman period. His publications include *Jerusalem under Siege: The Collapse of the Jewish State, 66–70 C.E.* (1992), *Thucydides and Internal War* (Cambridge, 2001), and editions of about 3,000 Jewish inscriptions in *Corpus Inscriptionum Iudaeae/Palaestinae*, Volumes I–V (2010–21).

MARGALIT FINKELBERG is Professor of Classics (emeritus) at Tel Aviv University and a member of the Israel Academy of Sciences and Humanities. She has authored *The Birth of Literary Fiction in Ancient Greece* (1998), *Greeks and Pre-Greeks: Aegean Prehistory and Greek Heroic Tradition* (2005), *Homer* (2014; Hebrew), *The Gatekeeper: Narrative Voice in Plato's Dialogues* (2019), *Homer and Early Greek Epic: Collected Essays* (2020), and numerous scholarly articles. She is the editor of *The Homer Encyclopedia* (3 vols.; 2011).

YUVAL SHAHAR is Senior Lecturer in Jewish History at Tel Aviv University. His published studies on the history, historiography and historical geography of Palestine in the Hellenistic, Roman and Byzantine periods include *Josephus Geographicus: The Classical Context of Geography in Josephus* (2004).

T0370783

This volume was conceived and produced in honor of our dear colleague Benjamin H. Isaac, the Fred and Helen Lessing Professor of Ancient History Emeritus at Tel Aviv University, as well as, inter alia, an Israel Prize laureate, and a member of the Israel Academy of Sciences and Humanities and of the American Philosophical Society. Some but not all of the articles were first presented in May 2015 in a conference at Tel Aviv University on the occasion of his retirement and seventieth birthday. We wish him many more fruitful years of scholarship.

Jonathan Price, Yuval Shahar, Margalit Finkelberg

Rome: An Empire of Many Nations

New Perspectives on Ethnic Diversity and
Cultural Identity

Edited by

JONATHAN J. PRICE
Tel Aviv University

MARGALIT FINKELBERG
Tel Aviv University

YUVAL SHAHAR
Tel Aviv University

CAMBRIDGE
UNIVERSITY PRESS

CAMBRIDGE
UNIVERSITY PRESS

University Printing House, Cambridge CB2 8BS, United Kingdom

One Liberty Plaza, 20th Floor, New York, NY 10006, USA

477 Williamstown Road, Port Melbourne, VIC 3207, Australia

314–321, 3rd Floor, Plot 3, Splendor Forum, Jasola District Centre,
New Delhi – 110025, India

79 Anson Road, #06–04/06, Singapore 079906

Cambridge University Press is part of the University of Cambridge.

It furthers the University's mission by disseminating knowledge in the pursuit of
education, learning, and research at the highest international levels of excellence.

www.cambridge.org
Information on this title: www.cambridge.org/9781009256223
DOI: 10.1017/9781009256193

© Cambridge University Press 2021
Reissued as Open Access, 2022

When citing this work, please include a reference to the DOI 10.1017/9781009256193

First published 2021

A catalogue record for this publication is available from the British Library.

Library of Congress Cataloging-in-Publication Data
Names: Price, Jonathan J., editor. | Finkelberg, Margalit, editor. | Shaḥar, Yuval, 1953– editor.
Title: Rome : an empire of many nations : new perspectives on ethnic diversity and cultural identity / edited by
Jonathan J. Price, Margalit Finkelberg, Yuval Shahar.
Other titles: Rome, an empire of many nations : new perspectives on ethnic diversity and cultural identity
Description: Cambridge, United Kingdom : New York, NY : Cambridge University Press, 2021. | Includes
bibliographical references and index.
Identifiers: LCCN 2020057804 (print) | LCCN 2020057805 (ebook) | ISBN 9781108479455 (hardback) | ISBN
9781108785563 (ebook)
Subjects: LCSH: National characteristics, Roman. | Romans – Ethnic identity. | Ethnicity – Rome. | Jews –
Rome – History. | Religious pluralism – Rome. | Group identity – Rome.
Classification: LCC DG78 .R5838 2021 (print) | LCC DG78 (ebook) | DDC 937/.06–dc23
LC record available at https://lccn.loc.gov/2020057804
LC ebook record available at https://lccn.loc.gov/2020057805

ISBN 978-1-009-25622-3 Paperback

Contents

Figures

Contributors

Cédric Brélaz
Professor of Ancient History, University of Fribourg, Switzerland

Angelos Chaniotis
Professor of Ancient History and Classics, School of Historical Studies, Institute for Advanced Study, Princeton

Daniela Dueck
Associate Professor of Ancient History, Bar Ilan University

Werner Eck
Professor of Ancient History (emeritus), University of Cologne

Margalit Finkelberg
Professor of Classics (emeritus), Tel Aviv University

Erich S. Gruen
Gladys Rehard Wood Professor of History and Classics (emeritus), University of California, Berkeley

Benjamin Isaac
Fred and Helen Lessing Professor of Ancient History (emeritus), Tel Aviv University

Ido Israelowich
Senior Lecturer in Classics, Tel Aviv University

Aharon Oppenheimer
Sir Isaac Wolfson Professor of Jewish Studies (emeritus), Tel Aviv University

Jonathan J. Price
Fred and Helen Lessing Professor of Ancient History, Tel Aviv University

Youval Rotman
Associate Professor of History, Tel Aviv University

John Scheid
Professor of Religion, Institutions and Society of Rome (emeritus), Collège de France

Yuval Shahar
Senior Lecturer in Jewish History, Tel Aviv University

Brent D. Shaw
Andrew Fleming West Professor in Classics (emeritus), Princeton University
Dr. Yotam Tepper
Archaeologist, Israel Antiquities Authority
Dr. Shlomit Weksler-Bdolah
Archaeologist, Israel Antiquities Authority
Alexander Yakobson
Associate Professor of Ancient History, Hebrew University of Jerusalem

Acknowledgments

The editors would like to thank those who provided the funding for the conference in honor of Benjamin Isaac, held in Tel Aviv in May 2015, that gave rise to the present volume: first of all, Joan C. Lessing, whose continuing, generous support is invaluable to historical research and advanced study of history in Tel Aviv University. Within Tel Aviv University, we are grateful to the Rector's office, the Dean of Humanities, the Zvi Yavetz School of Historical Studies, the Shirley and Leslie Porter School of Cultural Studies and the Goldstein-Goren Diaspora Research Center. Our talented graduate student in ancient history, Noam Rytwo (Ritbo), prepared the bibliography and the indices; we thank him, as well as the Zvi Yavetz School of Historical Studies for underwriting his work.

Abbreviations

AE	*L'Année Épigraphique* (see Cagnat et al. 1888–)
BCTH	*Bulletin archéologique du Comité des Travaux historiques et scientifiques* (see Cagnat et al. 1892)
BMC	*British Museum Catalogue* (see Hill)
BMCRE	*British Museum Catalogue of Coins of the Roman Empire* (see Poole et al.)
BRGK	*Bericht der römisch-germanischen Kommission des deutschen archäologischen Instituts* (see Deutsches Archäologisches Institut)
CCL	see CCSL
CCSL	*Corpus Christianorum, series Latina* (see Dekkers et al.)
CIIP	*Corpus Inscriptionum Iudaeae/Palaestinae* (see Ameling et al.)
CIL	*Corpus Inscriptionum Latinarum* (see Mommsen et al.)
CJ	*Classical Journal*
CPG	*Corpus Paroemiographorum Graecorum* (see Leutsch and Scheidewin)
CPJ	*Corpus Papyrorum Judaicarum* I–III (see Tcherikover et al.)
CSEL	*Corpus Scriptorum Ecclesiasticorum Latinorum* (see Vahlen et al.)
FHG	*Fragmenta Historicorum Graecorum* (see Müller et al.)
GV	*Griechische Vers-Inschriften* 1: Grab-Epigramme (see Peek)
IAM	*Inscriptions antiques du Maroc* (see Galand et al.)
IG	*Inscriptiones Graecae* (see Deutsche Akademie der Wissenschaften zu Berlin)
IGBulg	*Inscriptiones Graecae in Bulgaria repertae* (see Mihailov)
IGLS	*Inscriptions grecques et latines de la Syrie* (see Jalabert et al.)
IGR	*Inscriptiones Graecae ad res Romanas pertinentes* (see Cagnat et al. 1906–)
IJO	*Inscriptiones Judaicae Orientis* (see Noy et al.)
ILAlg	*Inscriptions latines de l'Algérie* (see Gsell et al.)
ILB	*Les inscriptions latines de Belgique* (see Deman et al.)
ILS	*Inscriptiones Latinae Selectae* (see Dessau)
ILTun	*Inscriptions latines de la Tunisie* (see Merlin)

IvO	*Die Inschriften von Olympia* (see Dittenberg and Purgold)
LSAM	*Lois sacrées de l'Asie Mineure* (see Sokolowski)
MAMA	*Monumenta Asiae Minoris Antiquae* (see Calder et al.)
P. Lond	*Greek Papyri in the British Museum* (see Kenyon and Bell)
PIR	*Prosopographia Imperii Romani Saeculi* I, II, III (see Klebs et al.)
PLRE	*Prosopography of the Later Roman Empire* (Jones et al.)
RGZM	*Jahrbuch des Römisch-Germanisches Zentralmuseum*
RIB	*The Roman Inscriptions of Britain* (see Collingwood et al.)
RIL	*Recueil des inscriptions Libyques* (see Chabot)
RMD	*Roman Military Diplomas* (see Roxan and Holder)
RPC	*Roman Provincial Coinage* (see Burnett et al.)
SEG	*Supplementum epigraphicum Graecum* (see Chaniotis et al.)
SNG München	*Sylloge Nummorum Graecorum München*
SNG von Aulock	*Sylloge Nummorum Graecorum von Aulock*
TAD	*Textbook of Aramaic documents from Ancient Egypt* (see Porten and Yardeni)
TAM	*Tituli Asiae Minoris* (see Kalinka et al.)
TAPA	*Transactions of the American Philological Association*

This title is part of the Cambridge University Press *Flip it Open* Open Access Books program and has been "flipped" from a traditional book to an Open Access book through the program.

Flip it Open sells books through regular channels, treating them at the outset in the same way as any other book; they are part of our library collections for Cambridge Core, and sell as hardbacks and ebooks. The one crucial difference is that we make an upfront commitment that when each of these books meets a set revenue threshold we make them available to everyone Open Access via Cambridge Core.

This paperback edition has been released as part of our Open Access commitment and we would like to use this as an opportunity to thank the libraries and other buyers who have helped us flip this and the other titles in the program to Open Access.

To see the full list of libraries that we know have contributed to *Flip it Open*, as well as the other titles in the program please visit https://www.cambridge.org/core/services/open-research/open-access/oa-book-pilot-flip-it-open/flip-it-open-acknowledgements

Introduction

When Greek historians turned their attention to the Roman Empire, the main question they sought to answer, which they displayed prominently in their introductions, was the reason for the success of the Empire. Success was defined in terms of acquisition, extent, stability and duration of conquest. Polybius, although not the first Greek historian of Rome, was perhaps the first to formulate the question, which he stated like a banner in the introduction to his complex work: his purpose was to explain 'by what means and under what system of government the Romans succeeded in less than fifty-three years in bringing under their rule almost the whole of the inhabited world, an achievement which is without parallel in human history'.[1] A century later, Dionysius of Halicarnassus did Polybius one better by adding duration of rule to Rome's achievement: 'the supremacy of the Romans has far surpassed all those that are recorded from earlier times, not only in the extent of its dominion and in the splendor of its achievements – which no account has as yet worthily celebrated – but also in the length of time during which it has endured down to our day';[2] and his long preface is filled with other such proclamations. In the second century CE, Appian of Alexandria wrote the same idea in less florid prose: 'No ruling power up to the present time ever achieved such size and duration',[3] after stating that he embarked on a long proof. These three historians are representative of a prevailing trend.[4]

Polybius introduced the notion, which was maintained and developed with necessary adjustments for centuries, that the Roman Empire was contiguous, or nearly so, with the entire habitable world. Rome's universal rule was widely (but, of course, not unanimously) accepted as stable and lasting. This was also the official, well-propagated view, as can be seen abundantly in official Roman art, especially from the establishment of the Principate (e.g. the breastplate of the statue of Augustus at Prima Porta), many coin series and literature. As Ovid wrote in Fasti 2.683–4: *Gentibus est aliis tellus data limite certo: / Romanae spatium est urbis et*

---

[1] Polyb. 1.1.5, trans. I. Scott-Kilvert.   [2] Dion. Hal. AR 1.2.1, trans. E. Cary.
[3] Appian, *Praef.* 29.
[4] See the discussion of these three historians and other authors, including Aelius Aristides, in Price 2020 in *The Future of Rome*.

orbis idem.[5] This was a perceived fact to which conquered peoples, both disgruntled subjects and enthusiastic converts, learned to adjust, as several chapters in the present collection demonstrate. If any defects in Roman rule were perceived, the analysis focused on causes of instability; the main dichotomy in these analyses was between internal and external causes, with Roman writing in Latin especially keen about internal decay, a theme carried over from the Republic. It is true that there were principled objections to Roman rule throughout the history of the Empire, especially from Greek intellectuals; historians such as Polybius (at first), Dionysius, Appian, Josephus (*mutatis mutandis* for a Jewish audience) and others wrote to answer them.[6]

It could be said that the modern study of the Roman Empire has generally followed, openly or implicitly, and in modern fashion, the main question driving – or prefacing – the Greek panoramic histories of the Empire. Naturally, modern explanations for the Roman Empire's wide extent and unusual longevity employ different methods, theories and even evidence from those of the ancients. An obvious example is the voluminous contemporary knowledge and refined analytical tools for studying economy and demography, which were not available in antiquity and therefore only crudely enlisted or omitted by ancient authors, who focused on more accessible factors like morals and ethics, methods of government and army.[7]

It should also be emphasized that analysis of the *reasons* for success does not presuppose the same *attitudes* toward empire, which certainly have shifted considerably not only from antiquity to the present but from the late nineteenth to the early twenty-first century. An interesting intellectual history of the last 150 years could be written by following the vicissitudes of the attitudes towards the Roman Empire in Western scholarship. The modern *wissenschaftliche* study of Rome, employing a wide range of literary and epigraphic sources, may be said to have begun with Mommsen,[8] for

---

[5] Further insight is afforded by the honorand of this volume, Benjamin Isaac, in a classic essay, 'Roma Aeterna', now republished in his collected papers, Isaac 2017a.

[6] Other responses are discussed in various chapters here; see esp. Shaw, Finkelberg, Brélaz and Scheid.

[7] Economic explanations of the Roman Empire range from Marxist to Capitalist, but trends change fast; see Dmitriev 2009.

[8] Gibbon's methods and style were substantially different, cf. James Rives: 'Just as Edward Gibbon was in many ways the first modern historian of the Roman Empire, so too was he one of the last who framed his work almost entirely in terms of the literary sources', Rives 2006, 100. What follows is not a systematic survey but opportunistic use of certain (but far from all) key works in historical scholarship on the Roman Empire, for the sake of illustrating a process. A brilliant survey of trends in Roman scholarship, covering issues beyond the 'success' of the Empire, is provided by David Potter (2006), projecting in 2006 that the 'thrust of work for the future seems to me to be the interaction between different groups' in the Roman world.

whom the Roman Empire had been acquired through 'defensive imperialism' and was governed well and securely by virtue of a broad and fairly uniform 'Romanization' of the provinces, based on constitution and law, so stable that it was able to endure unstable emperors in Rome. The idea of Romanization as defining and securing the entire Empire was adopted to varying degrees by British historians of the nineteenth century, whose main modification was to add archaeological evidence as a support. To us, from the distance of more than a century, it seems clear, almost too clear, why British historians then tended to view the Roman Empire as a single and unified civilizing force, although this view persisted well into the twentieth century.[9]

It may also seem clear to us, again almost too obvious, why during the twentieth century seminal works questioned not only the nineteenth-century understanding of Rome's motives in acquiring and maintaining empire but also the very nature of imperial rule and the reasons for the Empire's 'success' in ancient terms. In the gloom of crumbling empires, two world wars and seemingly endless proxy wars, assessments of Rome's achievement and the very nature of its government and empire turned darker, both on the European continent and in North America. We may omit here a decade-by-decade review of the twentieth century and skip to William Harris' epochal work of 1979, *War and Imperialism in Republican Rome, 327–70 BC*, arguing vigorously (if not really for the first time) that Roman territorial expansion was aggressive and motivated by social, political and economic ambitions of the Roman élite, as well as certain non-élite sectors, for whom continuous war and expansion was singularly profitable. This book may have been a decade late in the American context in which it was written. Most of the voluminous work on Roman power written in the twenty to thirty years that followed was a reaction to Harris' thesis, even if he did not address the problems of empire during the Principate, when Rome is conventionally viewed as trying to maintain and administer its conquests with relatively little further expansion.[10] Yet the ancient question persisted in that and subsequent studies. Even Harris' latest book on Roman power, *Roman Power: A Thousand Years of Empire* (2016), sets out inter alia to determine, 'Why in the first place did Roman power spread so widely and last so long?' (p. 2); the book asks how Rome managed the

---

[9] See Freeman 1997. On Classicists in the British civil service, see Murray 2000. The textbooks of H. H. Scullard may be mentioned as persisting in nineteenth-century attitudes, although they linger even in E. Badian's critical *Roman Imperialism in the Late Republic* (1968).

[10] This conventional construction is critiqued by Isaac 1990 already on his first page.

Empire during the Principate and Late Antiquity, and the reasons for disruptions and eventual collapse.

In that same decade, Edward Luttwak, in a derivative work that both excited and annoyed Classicists, opened a parallel stream of research and debate by proposing that Rome had a 'grand strategy', much like twentieth-century empires about which he was an expert;[11] this was yet another approach to Rome's 'success'. The most effective answer to this thesis was Benjamin Isaac's thorough demonstration of the lack of such a strategy or even of the ability and tools to formulate one, the undefined nature of extreme boundaries (*limes*) and the importance of motives for expansion such as emperors' greed for glory.[12] Isaac's book, deemed 'heretical' by one of his Israeli colleagues,[13] is situated within *limes* studies, but in its minute analysis of places, local inscriptions and individuals, it anticipated, in a way, Isaac's next *magnum opus*, a pioneering study of racism in antiquity, which itself was part of a significant turn in the study of the Roman Empire.[14]

This is a turn which we are currently living through, and the link between scholarly interests and contemporary issues is fully acknowledged, at the risk of crude determinism. In a recent, controversial book reflecting the latest intellectual and academic trends, David Mattingly openly embraces the notion that each generation should interpret the Roman Empire self-reflectively, according to its own concerns.[15] In totally rejecting Romanization as a useful or accurate concept for explaining Rome's influence and long rule in the provinces, he adopts post-colonialism as a workable model, focusing on the relations between ruler and ruled: the historian must be particularly sensitive to the feelings and thoughts of the ruled and their diverse experiences as subjects; in this way, Rome's rule is interpreted as 'a manifestation of elite negotiation and native agency', even if that 'negotiation' was regularly delineated by violence. Naturally, the term 'post-colonialism' can be used only as a mode of thought and inquiry: it should not be suggested that the multi-ethnic continental Roman Empire was similar in structure and function to modern colonial empires.[16]

The demolition of the prevailing idea of Romanization (although still defended as a useful concept by Harris in his 2016 book) began earlier,

---

[11] Luttwak 1976/2016.   [12] Isaac 1990.

[13] Shatzman 1994; he agreed, however, with many of Isaac's central points.   [14] Isaac 2004.

[15] Mattingly 2011, 3: 'It is generally agreed that the Roman Empire was one of the most successful and enduring empires in world history' (p. 3). On the same page, he quotes J. S. Wacher, 'The endurance of the Roman Empire is one of the success stories of history. That it survived so long is a sign of its principal achievement, whereby a heterogeneous mixture of races and creeds were induced to settle down together in a more or less peaceful way under the Pax Romana.'

[16] Cf. again Isaac 1990.

particularly in France, where studies of Rome's rule in Africa and elsewhere starkly pointed out the violence and coerciveness of Roman rule, and different forms of resistance. Romanization was rejected as an imperialist perspective, and serious attention was given to the native experience.[17] This shift in focus to Rome's human subjects continued during the following decades, proceeding through models and theories from the social sciences (e.g. World Systems Theory, acculturation theory and the very popular core-periphery model),[18] leading to post-colonialism in different guises, with detailed attention given to local cultures and priority to other kinds of evidence than canonical texts.[19] The nineteenth-century notion of Romanization has dwindled to a faint evanescence.[20] In the present book, among the seventeen chapters, the word 'Romanization' appears only once (Cédric Brélaz referring to an attitude of Apollonius of Tyana).

Other twenty-first-century interpretations of the Roman Empire seem almost like late-breaking news, for example globalization,[21] micro-ecology,[22] comparative imperialisms,[23] creolization[24] and cultural plunder and appropriation.[25] This overview of scholarship could be extended in many ways; the literature is broad, ever-expanding, if not always deep.

Whatever one may think of post-colonialism, its early forerunners and current advocates, its impact as stated has been to encourage attention to the individual (i.e. the identity and inner lives of persons and groups), and in doing so, shake the main impetus of understanding the Roman Empire from the ancient question of 'success' in terms of extent and longevity to the human experience of the Empire, and of empire in general. In this, it may prove to be one of the more productive turns in Roman history. The present generation has produced a plethora of studies of identity, ethnicity, multi-cultural structures in the Roman Empire, asking not primarily Why and How but What and Who. The conference that gave rise to this volume – held in Tel Aviv University in honor of Benjamin Isaac on

---

[17] See, e.g., the seminal Bénabou 1976. Ronald Syme had attacked Romanization as 'ugly and vulgar' on other grounds; see Mattingly 2011, 22.

[18] This last idea, put forward by I. Wallerstein, and its application to the Roman Empire have been astutely critiqued by B. Isaac 2017b.

[19] For an efficient survey, see Rothe 2012.

[20] Although a recent, forceful defense of the concept is offered by Ando 2000, who avers that 'The stability of the Roman empire requires substantial and specific explanation', and argues for *ideology*, i.e., 'on a slowly realized consensus regarding Rome's right to maintain social order and to establish a normative political culture'.

[21] Hingley 2005 and Sweetman 2007.

[22] See Horden and Purcell 2000 with Isaac 2017b, 117–21.

[23] Scheidel 2009; Morris-Scheidel 2009; Mutschler/Mittag 2008; Alcock et al. 2001.

[24] J. Webster 2001.   [25] Loar et al. 2018.

26–27 May 2015 – is just one of many such academic gatherings in recent years; this volume as a whole is dedicated to Ben Isaac, in celebration of a distinguished life of scholarship and his seminal contributions to the multiple topics and disciplines in Roman history represented here. The center of gravity in Roman studies has shifted far from the upper echelons of government and administration in Rome or the Emperor's court to the provinces and the individual. As Veyne noted, 'in a multinational empire whose makeup was multiple, heterogeneous, unequal, and sometimes hostile and badly integrated, the identity of each individual was inherently complex'.[26] And Greg Woolf, whose work in this area has been both originary and instrumental, notes that the focus of 'identity politics' has been 'not on the emergence of vast imperial identities, but rather on how imperial regimes have shaped local experiences; on the emergence of newly self-conscious peoples and nations; on diasporas and displacements; and on how the experience of migration has impacted on the lives of countless individuals'.[27] Indeed, from the perspective of our own time, this turn in Roman studies reflects the sharpened focus in contemporary politics, education, social relations and legislation on individual identity, ethnicity and the problems of a multi-cultural society. Future generations will decide whether this has in fact added to our knowledge and understanding of the Roman Empire.

Naturally, the turn in Roman studies was preceded by developments in other academic fields, such as the study of ethnic groups and boundaries in anthropology and the dynamics of individual identity against the larger collective, in psychology. Such developments set the stage for Youval Rotman's chapter in this volume, 'The Boundaries of Being a Jew'. The investigation of the variety of identities – multiple identities could overlap in one individual, as in Paul, or as Brent Shaw shows in his study here, of a certain individual in Africa – and the products of ethnic expression and suppression have not usually aimed to illuminate Roman policy or methods of control. While it is true that some of these studies have continued the old agenda of explaining the extent and longevity of Rome's dominance, this does not seem to be the prevailing reason of most, and certainly not of the present collection.

The study of ethnicity and identity in the Roman Empire is more often than not collaborative, given the wide range of languages, territories and specialties required for such a many-faceted topic. The turn toward identity

---

[26] Veyne 2005, 237.

[27] From the chapter titled 'Imperial Identities' in Woolf 2012, 227. His path-breaking work in this direction was Woolf 1998.

and ethnicity has been the result of both new investigations of the old materials and the greater emphasis placed on other sources: private and local epigraphy, letters and private documents on papyri, local narratives, non-Roman literatures including those in languages other than Greek, regional art.[28] These non-canonical materials play a large role in the chapters in this volume, as well.

The chapters here are organized under four rubrics. The first includes studies on *ethnicity and identity*. One matter that set Rome apart as imperialists was their extensive granting of citizenship. This practice not only turned the possible incorporation as a Roman into an incentive for peaceful acceptance of Rome's dominance but also created interesting cases of multiple identity.[29] This was as true at the pinnacle of Roman society and government as it was in the army and provincial societies. As Werner Eck shows in his chapter, 'The Imperial Senate: Center of a Multinational Empire', the Senate in the first to third centuries CE was composed of individuals from thirty provinces. The provincial senators were considered Roman in every respect, but they did not shed their former identity completely. That is, while they lost their *origo*, they were allowed to keep the *dignitas*, their reputation and rank, from their homeland. The many different *patriae* represented in the Senate made it a working symbol of a multi-national empire. Senators enjoyed the rights and privileges as citizens of their places of origin and as Roman citizens. As Eck writes, 'it is hard to doubt the fundamental awareness of their [the senators'] diverse origins among most members of the Senate'. This does not mean that ethnic stereotypes and prejudices did not affect even senators; it was what the Emperor Claudius, in his famous speech, railed against, and what Daniela Dueck, in her chapter, 'Ethnic Types and Stereotypes in Ancient Latin Idioms', shows persisted stubbornly in patterns of language and thought. Once a prejudice is formulated in a proverb, it is nearly impossible to uproot, even when the proverb transmits demonstrably false conceptions and information.

Outside the Senate, multiple identities could reside more easily in the same person. Brent Shaw, 'Keti Son of Maswalat: Ethnicity and Empire', presents a fascinating example of this: a certain Gaius Iulius Gaetulus, a high-ranking Roman citizen and soldier in the Roman army, who was

---

[28] Some of the original, foundational work was done in epigraphy, pioneered by Louis Robert. 'Robert's ability to integrate realia of all sorts to recreate the social imagination of residents of Roman Asia Minor has done more than anything to lay the foundation for contemporary work on Rome's relationship with its subjects', Potter 2006.

[29] See now the papers in Berthelot-Price 2019.

at the same time Keti son of Maswalat from the tribe of the Misiciri, from the subtribe of the S'RMMi. After explaining the individual case in detail, Shaw gets to the main point, relevant to the purpose of this collection, videlicet, 'to see this divided composite of identity as potentially running internally through individual subjects all the way down to the ground level of any given locale. There is every reason to believe that the empire was filled with persons of such divided identity.' The empire can thus be seen as a kind of composite of composite identities, since the cases of multiple identities similar to that of Keti were widespread throughout the various provinces and persistent through generations: not only complex personal identities but parallel civic apparatuses continued to exist across generations. Or in Shaw's memorable formulation, it was an 'ever-changing, every-adapting social schizophrenia that was maintained over many generations in not a few of the provincial families in the empire'.

In the third part of this volume, the specific test-case of the Jews is explored in six chapters which reflect not only the venue of the conference but also the particularly plentiful, if troublesome, evidence for this one small people living in practically every province of the empire, and beyond it. The Jews are perhaps the most extensively self-documented ethnic minority in the Empire ('the Greeks' are ill-defined as a single group), but their literature is notoriously difficult to use as historical evidence, and the Jews themselves were unusual as an ethnic minority who could be considered both a religion and a nation or ethnos and maintained their strong identity as both while living in transplanted communities throughout the provinces for many generations. As a *religion*, Erich Gruen, in 'Religious Pluralism in the Roman Empire: Did Judaism Test the Limits of Roman Tolerance?', finds that the Jews (at least before 70 CE) enjoyed unexceptional Roman acceptance as a foreign cult, this general acceptance being 'a longstanding ingredient of Roman identity'. Judaism as a religion was comfortably incorporated into Rome's 'pluralistic religious universe'.

The kind of natural Roman religious 'pluralism' that Gruen sees does not, of course, contradict Dueck's finding of prejudice implanted deep in the Latin language, nor does it illuminate the Romans' attitude toward the Jews as a political problem. This question is taken up by Alexander Yakobson, 'Rome's attitude to Jews after the Great Rebellion – beyond Raison d'état', who sets out to demolish the widely held idea of an especially harsh Roman policy against the Jews after 70 CE. The Flavians presented their suppression of the Jewish rebellion not as conquest over a foreign god or demonic enemy but as the restoration of peace in a divided empire. The special Jewish tax (soon alleviated) answered financial needs; leaving the

Jewish temple in ruins was a political and military decision. Thus the treatment of the Jews after the rebellion did not depart from the Romans' ecumenical treatment of non-Roman religions in their vast empire.

Yet defining the Jews still defied paradigms. After treatments of Jews as a religion and as a nation (one capable of rebelling), Youval Rotman explores the question of Jewish identity further in 'Between *Ethnos* and *Populus*: the Boundaries of Being a Jew'. Rotman's innovation is to focus on how the Jews defined themselves within their Graeco-Roman context, since their self-definition as 'sons of Israel' did not exactly fit any of the other terms available: *ethnos, genos, laos, dēmos, populus, natio, polis, civitas*. Rotman's main conclusion is that markers that we would consider ethnic and religious were viewed and used by the Jews themselves, especially in the context of rabbinic conversion, as delineating political, social and civic boundaries. 'At the basis of all cases we find a political objective: a group of people who insists on defining themselves as a civic entity in order to become one, and to portray themselves as active agents, no matter what the circumstances are.' This general idea is borne out by Price's study of Jewish micro-communities (i.e. synagogal communities) in 'Local Identities of Synagogue Communities in the Roman Empire: The Evidence from Inscriptions'. In a manner that was more internally self-assertive than defiant of Rome's power and integrative tendencies, the inscriptions from synagogues across the Empire connect each community to the general Jewish, self-defining story, rather than to the local non-Jewish community, much less the Empire as a global enterprise.

The last two case studies of the Jews delve even further into 'rabbinic literature'. One impediment to investigating ethnic or religious communities within the Roman Empire is the lack of internal literatures. Papyri and inscriptions shed some light on the inner workings of cults and even the thoughts of their members, but in most cases there is no creative literary product. The biggest exceptions to this are, of course, the Jews and the Christians. Their literatures are very different in nature and purpose. Rabbinic literature, consisting of the two Talmuds, midrashim and other works, is the most difficult for the historian to penetrate. The task Yuval Shahar sets in 'The Good, the Bad, and the Middling: Roman Emperors in Talmudic Literature' is not to extract empirical data about Roman emperors from rabbinic texts – the old standard approach – but to read rabbinic stories sensitively, against parallels in classical literature, for how the rabbinic authors processed the memory of emperors who impinged closely on their own history. There is no single blanket judgment about the Roman leaders, but attitudes differed according to the state of relations between the Jews and the Roman authorities, so that, for example, the contrasting positive portraits of Caracalla ('Antoninus') in rabbinic texts and the negative portraits of him in classical sources, which stress his violent hostility toward Roman senators, bring home that the historical memory of emperors depended on who was remembering. Similarly, Aharon Oppenheimer, 'The Severans and Rabbi Judah haNasi', examining the life of the most famous Jewish patriarch in the period that Shahar defines as the most positive in Jewish memory, examines the Talmudic stories of the friendship between Caracalla and Rabbi Judah. The historicity of these stories is not important (and in some cases is impossible, such as the tradition that the emperor used a secret tunnel between Rome and Palestine to travel every day to consult Rabbi Judah); what is important is the historical memory of good relations during that small period of time. Oppenheimer proposes that this is not something that the rabbinic memory would have recorded and perpetuated vainly, without reason. Accordingly, he links the Severans' policy of urbanization with Rabbi Judah's various favorable halakhic rulings in relation to the cities.

Identity involves not just ethnicity or individual or group definition in legal, civic and social frameworks but also a formative historical narrative, as well as religious beliefs and practices, education, and personal experiences such as dreams. All of these elements of identity are addressed in the second group of papers on *culture and identity* in the Roman Empire. As Margalit Finkelberg shows in 'Roman Reception of the Trojan War', the foundational story identifying Romans as Trojan refugees underwent a fundamental change in the Augustan era, when Troy and the Romans' Trojan antecedents were lionized to the detriment of the reputation of the Greeks. This was revisionist history to suit imperial needs, and it had a remarkably strong and long afterlife. Dio of Prusa even claimed that the Greeks lost the war (!). The idea of Troy's superiority, promoted most importantly by Vergil, 'was the one that suited best the new geopolitical reality and the imperial ambitions of Rome'.

What was a proud Greek to do under Roman domination? As Dio observed, 'the situation has changed ... for Greece is subject to others and so is Asia'. One successful strategy, which had profound if paradoxical effects on identity, was to promote Roman–Greek kinship or, even more radically, embrace Roman pretensions entirely and, in defiance of previous historical traditions, invent a Roman origin for Greeks to promote imagined Roman origins for themselves. This is the subject treated in some detail by Cédric Brélaz in 'Claiming Roman Origins: Greek Cities and the Roman Colonial Pattern'. The changes in the narrative were not imposed by Rome. Naturally, not all or even most Greek cities participated or approved, but those cities that incorporated the imperial cult worshipped Roma, even adopted Roman colonial symbols and became 'honorary colonies', reaped the awards in privileges and status. One might claim that these strategies were devised insincerely for diplomatic and political advantage, but they were 'an aspect of cultural interaction' and could have long-term effects in ideology, personal and collective identity.

From history and myth to religion. John Scheid, 'Roman Theologies in the Roman Cities of Italy and the Provinces', looks at something purely Roman, Roman deities and rites, with solely Roman connotations and watches how they spread and were adapted to other regions after Roman conquest. The adoption of Roman gods and rites was not total. Nuances in theology and mythology elude, but close examination of the specific cases of Trier, Cologne, and the Batavi and the Tungri reveals that public religion developed differently in each place, according to local culture and history. Roman deities with strictly local origins and context were transplanted in far-flung, foreign places as those places became part of the Roman collective identity. As Scheid observes, the mechanism of this transplantation, *mutatis mutandis*, 'made it possible to extend the domain of the gods of a Roman city. Somewhat like the provincial government extended, without too much distortion, the jurisdiction of the magistrates of the city of Rome. As the law, which was intended only to regulate relations between citizens in Rome, theology and sacred law were extended by a sort of legal fiction to divinities that were not Roman, but henceforth had a vocation to act in a Roman context.'

As with history and religion, so with education and even the inner private lives of imperial subjects. Ido Israelowich, 'The Involvement of Provincial Cities in the Administration of School Teaching', points out that, since the expanding Roman imperial government required literate bureaucrats at the local level throughout the provinces, the demand for teachers rose accordingly, which led provincial cities to grant teachers immunity from certain civic obligations in order to encourage the profession. But teachers' skill was needed for practical reasons; they weren't elevated to cultural icons. The teacher remained an artisan, whose inglorious profession, like that of the archivist, the shorthand writer, the accountant or the ledger-keeper, was much required throughout the cities of the High Roman Empire. 'Cities endowed schoolteachers with privileges because they needed to pay for their practical skills, not as a token of appreciation for the culture they represented.'

On the premise that the Empire generated social, cultural and legal (policing) forces that could have brought a kind of commonality to the experience of nighttime in diverse places, Angelos Chaniotis, 'Many Nations, One Night? Historical Aspects of the Night in the Roman Empire', searches for a 'nocturnal koine'. Shared developments are discovered particularly in the cities: nightlife characterized by voluntary associations and nocturnal religious celebrations. 'The unprecedented connectivity created by the Empire favored the diffusion of cults, religious practices, and religious ideas and can, therefore, be regarded as an important factor for the frequency of nocturnal rites,' Chaniotis writes.

The volume closes with two studies that rely on material remains in archaeological sites to understand certain aspects of the Roman army's presence in the province of Iudaea/Palaestina. Yotam Tepper, 'The Roman Legionary Base in Legio-Kefar 'Othnay – The Evidence from the Small Finds', documents the largest Roman military base from the second to third centuries CE discovered so far in the eastern Roman Empire. It served Legio II Traiana and Legio VI Ferrata. Such a base is important not only for questions of Roman imperial and military policy but also on the basis of small finds such as coins and tiles, for the details of commercial and social ties between the occupying army and the local populations.

The extensive excavations of Jerusalem afford an unusually close look at a city, a highly developed urban cult center, that underwent destruction, occupation by a legion, reconstruction as a Roman colony and transformation into a Christian urban center. The significance of practically every stone turned up in the excavations over the past 150 years has been examined and debated. Shlomit Weksler-Bdolach, 'The Camp of the Legion X Fretensis and the Starting Point of Aelia Capitolina', puts the pieces together in a way that will not satisfy every opinion but suggests that the camp of Legio X Frentensis was imposed on the city without regard for local conditions; but this was unusual, and it should be remembered that the Roman soldiers acted as a garrison after a prolonged and costly revolt. Weksler-Bdolach's excavations also have far-reaching implications for the timing of the foundation of Aelia Capitolina and the later development of the city.

Rome remained an 'Empire of many nations' even after the transfer of the capital to the East and the humiliations suffered by the city founded by Romulus near the Tiber. As Benjamin Isaac points out, in his own contribution to the volume – 'From Rome to Constantinople', placed first in his honor – 'Emperors who called themselves Roman continued to reign in the

East over subjects who called themselves Romans, although Greek was their language, until the fifteenth century, a thousand years longer than in the Western Roman Empire'. Ben Isaac will have the last word here: 'Rome was not a capital city. It was not supposed to be one. It was the state, the Empire, the collective citizenship, all in one.'

Jonathan Price

PART I

Ethnicity and Identity in the Roman Empire

1 | From Rome to Constantinople[*]

BENJAMIN ISAAC

The transfer of an imperial capital seems a drastic step, but conceptually simple. Indeed, we know about capitals. They are permanent, having been there if not forever, then for many centuries: London, Paris and Lisbon, for instance. Others, such as Washington, DC, and Brasilia, have been created in more recent periods. They could be transferred from one city to another, as in the case of Bonn and Berlin, St Petersburg and Moscow. Or things may be a little more ambiguous: Amsterdam is capital of the Netherlands, but The Hague ('s Gravenhage) is seat of the government and, most of the time but not always as a matter of principle, royal residence. In the case of Rome, things are even more complicated.

Rome was no state; it was no people; it was not the capital of an Empire. It was a city, but it was also far more than that. Rome *was* the Empire, and that is what it remained until the fifteenth century, for the Byzantine Empire is a modern appellation. Those we often call 'the Byzantines' called themselves citizens of the Roman Empire, and the Byzantine Emperors were called Roman Emperors until the fall of Constantinople in the fifteenth century.[1] In its classical age there was hardly a straightforward name

---

[*] This chapter is based on a lecture in honour of the late Martin Ostwald, given on 26 May 2015. Martin was a great scholar, a generous friend of many, and a regular visitor whose contribution to ancient history at Tel Aviv University is recalled here with profound gratitude. I am grateful to Joan Lessing and Jonathan Price for inviting me to speak in memory of Martin. This is also a fitting occasion to express my deep appreciation of the fact that I was elected to act as Fred & Helen Lessing Professor of Ancient History from 1995 until 2015, successor to Zvi Yavetz, a fine scholar and excellent friend. It has been an honour and a pleasure to be allowed to submit this paper as part of the proceedings of a remarkable conference organized by Margalit Finkelberg, Aharon Oppenheimer, Jonathan Price and Yuval Shahar at Tel Aviv University on 26 and 27 May 2015. I am grateful to my colleagues Avi Laniado and Yuval Shahar for useful suggestions and references.

[1] Mango, 1980: 1: 'The Byzantine Empire, as defined by the majority of historians, is said to have come into being when the city of Constantinople, the New Rome, was founded in 324 AD . . . As for the epithet 'Byzantine,' serious objections could be and have often been raised concerning its appropriateness. For better or for worse, this term has, however, prevailed . . . . In reality, of course, there never existed such an entity as the Byzantine Empire.'

for the Roman state, for *civitas* was a fluid term that could simply indicate any tribe or city, but could also refer to its citizens. The expression that most often is used for the 'Roman state' in Latin is *nomen Romanum*, the Roman name. It indicated all that was Rome: the people, the state, the Empire and its reputation.

Cicero is the first to use this term frequently: 'For so great is the dignity of this empire, so great is the honour in which the Roman name is held among all nations.'[2] Here it can still be interpreted as merely a term for 'reputation'. That is no longer the case when Cicero says: 'Who has such a hatred, one might almost say for the Roman name, as to despise and reject the *Medea* of Ennius or the *Antiope* of Pacuvius, and give as his reason that though he enjoys the corresponding plays of Euripides he cannot endure books written in Latin?'[3] Another clear instance is: 'Plans have been formed in this state, O judges, for destroying the city, for massacring the citizens, for extinguishing the Roman name.'[4] Here *civitas, urbs, cives* and *nomen Romanum* are used in one and the same sentence in four different meanings, all designating essential aspects of Rome.[5] The expression *nomen Romanum* occurs quite frequently in Augustan literature, notably in the work of Livy, where I count more than twenty instances. It is found again in phrases that may indicate 'the Roman reputation' or 'fame',[6] but also in the sense of 'power': 'Go, and with the help of the gods, restore the unconquerable Roman name!'[7] It is encountered frequently as well as a term for 'the Roman people': 'But, they added, the immortal gods, taking pity upon the Roman name [i.e. the people], had spared the innocent armies.'[8] It can be used in a more abstract sense for 'the existence' or 'identity' of Rome: 'the Volsci, their ancient foes, had armed for the purpose of extinguishing the Roman

---

[2] Cic. *Ver.* 2.5.150 : *tanta enim huius imperi amplitudo, tanta nominis Romani dignitas est apud omnis nationes ut ista in nostros homines crudelitas nemini concessa esse videatur.*

[3] Cic. *Fin.* 1.4.6: *quis enim tam inimicus paene nomini Romano est, qui Ennii Medeam aut Antiopam Pacuvii spernat aut reiciat, quod se isdem Euripidis fabulis delectari dicat, Latinas litteras oderit?*

[4] Cic. *Mur.* 80.6: *Inita sunt in hac civitate consilia, iudices, urbis delendae, civium trucidandorum, nominis Romani extinguendi.*

[5] See also Cic., *Phil.* 2.20.13

[6] E.g., Livy 4.33.5: *nominis Romani ac uirtutis patrum uestraeque memores*; 10.36.12: *numen etiam deorum respexisse nomen Romanum uisum*; 35.58.5; also, in a similar sense: Tac. *Ann.* 4.24.6.

[7] Livy 7.10.4: *perge et nomen Romanum inuictum iuuantibus dis praesta*; also: 25.38.10.

[8] Livy 27.33.12 (208 BC, senators speaking): *ceterum deos immortales, miseritos nominis Romani, pepercisse innoxiis exercitibus.* Also: 10.11.12. Similarly: Sall. *Cat.* 52.24; Plin. *NH* 17.2.2; Nepos, *Vit. Han.* 7.3.

name.'[9] In the fourth century the Isaurians are described as inhabiting a region 'in the middle of "the Roman name"'.[10] Here, of course, it refers to the Roman Empire in a territorial sense.

All the same it is telling that there was no more concrete term for the Roman state or the Empire. Rome was eternal, of course.[11] It still is. However, nowadays we think of Rome as a city being eternal. Cicero, when he called Rome eternal, thought of the Roman Empire being eternal, but he never distinguished between city and Empire.[12]

And yet, the capital of the Empire was transferred from Rome to Constantinople in the fourth century. That might seem a conceptual impossibility, but it happened. It was part of a major eastward shift of power, economic and military. That, however, is not the subject of this short chapter, which discusses the historical background to the transformation of the city of Byzantium into Constantinople.

When this happened there had been in fact a tradition of about four centuries suggesting that it might occur. There was a rumour to that effect at the time of the rule of Julius Caesar:

> Nay, more, the report had spread in various quarters that he intended to move to Ilium or Alexandria, taking with him the resources of the state, draining Italy by levies, and leaving the charge of the city to his friends.[13]

The fact that there was such a rumour does not mean, of course, that Caesar actually contemplated it, but it proves that the idea, or rather the fear, existed. It was thinkable to transfer the essence of what was the city of Rome to another city.

The second case arose not long after Caesar's death: few stories are as familiar as that of Antony and Cleopatra, at least in one seventeenth-century version. There were rumours among the Romans that Antony, if victorious, intended to bestow their city upon Cleopatra and transfer the seat of power to Egypt.[14] Here we might notice already that the element of

---

[9] Livy 6.2.2: *hinc Uolsci, ueteres hostes, ad exstinguendum nomen Romanum arma ceperant*; also: 6.17.4; 23.26.3. Sall. *Iug.* 58.3.3.

[10] HA *Tir. Tryg.* 26: *in medio Romani nominis solo regio eorum.*

[11] See my paper 'Roma Aeterna' in Isaac 2017.

[12] For a different emphasis: van Dam 2010: Ch. 1.

[13] Suet. *Iul.* 79.5: *Quin etiam varia fama percrebuit migraturum Alexandream vel Ilium, translatis simul opibus imperii exhaustaque Italia dilectibus et procuratione urbis amicis permissa.* Also: Nic. Dam. *Life of Augustus* 20: 'Some said that he had decided to establish a capital of the whole empire in Egypt, and that Queen Cleopatra had lain with him and borne him a son, named Cyrus, there. This he himself refuted in his will as false. Others said that he was going to do the same thing at Troy, on account of his ancient connection with the Trojan people.'

[14] Dio 50.4.1; Nic. Dam. *Life of Augustus* 68.

an East–West antagonism is clearly perceived, an antagonism which ultimately, more than four centuries later, led to the division of the Empire into an eastern and a western half. It is remarkable to note that Horace was worried when Augustus financed buildings in Ilion.

> Yet, warlike Roman, know thy doom,
> Nor, drunken with a conqueror's joy,
> Or blind with duteous zeal, presume
> To build again ancestral Troy.
> Should Troy revive to hateful life,
> Her star again should set in gore.[15]

Rumours like those in the times of Caesar and Antony were spread as well during the reign of Caligula (AD 38–41):

> and within four months he perished, having dared great crimes and meditating still greater ones. For he had made up his mind to move to Antium, and later to Alexandria, after first slaying the noblest members of the two orders.[16]

Again, in the reign of Nero, in 68, there were reports that Nero planned to kill the senators, burn down the city and sail to Alexandria.[17] At a less sensational level Tacitus reports what Nero actually did: 'Eager to make a brilliant name as learned and eloquent, Nero successfully backed Ilium's application to be exempted from all public burdens, fluently recalling the descent of Rome from Troy and of the Julii from Aeneas and other more or less mythical traditions.'[18]

In the early third century, after the death of Septimius Severus there is said to have been a plan to divide the Empire into two parts, the West going to Caracalla with Rome as capital; the Propontis would serve as boundary and Byzantium as military frontier city. Geta, the younger son, would obtain the East with Antioch or Alexandria as capital and Chalcedon as frontier city.[19]

There was then a definite anxiety concerning the central role of Rome as the essence of its Empire attested from the early years of the principate

---

[15] Hor. *Carm.* 3.3 (trans. John Conington): *sed bellicosis fata Quiritibus | hac lege dico, ne nimium pii | rebusque fidentes avitae | tecta velint reparare Troiae. Troiae renascens alite lugubri | fortuna tristi clade iterabitur | ducente victrices catervas | coniuge me Iovis et sorore.*

[16] Suet. *Cal.* 49.2.5: *intraque quartum mensem periit, ingentia facinora ausus et aliquanto maiora moliens, siquidem proposuerat Antium, deinde Alexandream commigrare interempto prius utriusque ordinis electissimo quoque.*

[17] Dio, *Ep.* 63.27.2.   [18] Tac. *Ann.* 12.58.1.

[19] Hdn. 4.3.4–9. Caracalla visited the Troad in 214: Dio 77.16.7. Unlike other senior Romans he identified with the Greek side in the Trojan conflict. He dedicated a bronze statue to Achilles and honoured him with sacrifices; he also had his freedman Festus cremated there, with a great *tumulus* constructed over his bones, in imitation of the burial of Patroklos.

onward. In most cases these rumours focused on rulers who were hated (or slandered) in particular and who died a violent death: Antony, Caligula, Nero, but not, for instance, Augustus or Claudius. At another level, Tacitus' observation has been quoted often:

> Welcome as the death of Nero had been in the first burst of joy, yet it had not only roused various emotions in Rome, among the Senators, the people, or the soldiery of the capital, it had also excited all the legions and their generals; for now had been divulged that secret of the empire, that emperors could be made elsewhere than at Rome.[20]

For clarification of these long-standing ideas about the place of Rome within the empire, we might recognize traditions about the origins of the city of Rome in the far distant past. The foundation myths of Rome emphasized a Trojan origin, most famously celebrated by Vergil in the reign of Augustus, but already attested in poetry of the third–second centuries BC.[21] Not only Rome but the house of Caesar also claimed to be of Trojan origin.

Well before the reign of Augustus, in the days of the republic, Troy already played a special role as the ancestral home of the Romans. Pyrrhus, who claimed to be a descendant of Achilles, regarded this tradition as an indication that he would defeat Rome, a Trojan colony.[22] Scipio Africanus visited Troy in 190 BC, emphasizing that the Romans were descendants of the Trojans.[23] A century afterward, Sulla honoured the city. Subsequently, Caesar visited it:

> Then marvelling at their ancient fame, he seeks / Sigeum's sandy beach and Simois' stream, / Rhoeteum noble for its Grecian tomb, / And all the hero's shades, the theme of song. / Next by the town of Troy burnt down of old / Now but a memorable name, he turns / His steps, and searches for the mighty stones / Relics of Phoebus' wall.[24]

---

[20] Tac. *Hist.* 1.4: *finis Neronis ut laetus primo gaudentium impetu fuerat, ita varios motus animorum non modo in urbe apud patres aut populum aut urbanum militem, sed omnis legiones ducesque conciverat, evulgato imperii arcano posse principem alibi quam Romae fieri.*

[21] In Enn. *Ann.* (Ennius c. 239 BC–c. 169 BC), cf. Fabrizi 2012. It is also found in Plut. *Rom.* 1.1.7 where it is asserted that the city was named after Roma, a woman among the refugees from Troy (cf. *Aeneid* 5.604–99).

[22] Paus. 1.12.1. For an account of the development of the tradition of Rome's Trojan origins: Gruen 1992: 6–51.

[23] Livy 37.37. It could be argued that Livy, writing in the age of Augustus, invented this statement attributed to Scipio. However, this is not a very likely assumption and, clearly, Scipio's visit was a recorded fact for which no other motive can easily be advanced.

[24] Luc. *Phars.* 9.964–99 (trans. Ridley): *Sigeasque petit famae mirator harenas et Simoentis aquas et Graio nobile busto Rhoetion et multum debentis uatibus umbras. circumit exustae nomen memorabile Troiae magnaque Phoebei quaerit uestigia muri.* Cf. Sage 2000: 211–32.

Augustus visited Troy,[25] and afterward Claudius again honoured the city in a manner typical of the astute, but somewhat pedantic historian that he was.

> He allowed the people of Ilium perpetual exemption from tribute, on the ground that they were the founders of the Roman people, reading an ancient letter of the senate and people of Rome written in Greek to king Seleucus, in which they promised him their friendship and alliance only on condition that he should keep their kinsfolk of Ilium free from every burden.[26]

It will be clear from this little survey that there are two kinds of reports: those concerning historical leaders who were regarded as bad news and who are described as intending to abandon Rome and move power eastward. Then there are the more responsible characters who are reported as having merely paid their respect to the old city of Roman origins.

The rumours did not disappear. In the third–fourth centuries the Christian author Lactantius (c. 250–c. 325) predicted that what previously wicked rulers had only planned eventually and inevitably would happen in fact.[27]

> The cause of this destruction will be that the Roman Empire which now rules all the earth – it is a terrible thing to say, but I will say it because it will happen – that the Roman Empire will be destroyed and that power will return to Asia, that the Orient will rule and the West will be reduced to slavery.

---

[25] Dio 54.7: Augustus visited when he was in the area in 20 BC. See Frisch 1975: 83: Augustus stayed in the house of a leading citizen, Melanippides son of Euthydikos. Following his visit, he financed the restoration and rebuilding of the sanctuary of Athena Ilias, the *bouleuterion*, and the theatre. After work on the theatre was completed in 12/11 BC, Melanippides dedicated a statue of Augustus in the theatre to record this benefaction.

[26] Suet. *Claud.* 25.3: *Iliensibus quasi Romanae gentis auctoribus tributa in perpetuum remisit recitata uetere epistula Graeca senatus populique R. Seleuco regi amicitiam et societatem ita demum pollicentis, si consanguineos suos Ilienses ab omni onere immunes praestitisset.*

[27] Lactant. *Div. Inst.* 7.15.11: *Cujus vastitatis et confusionis haec erit causa, quod Romanum nomen, quo nunc regitur orbis (horret animus dicere: sed dicam, quia futurum est) tolletur de terra, et imperium in Asiam revertetur, ac rursus Oriens dominabitur, atque Occidens serviet.* For this passage, see also Olbrich 2006: 488–9 with note 31. Olbrich sees this passage as referring to the end of the city of Rome and suggests that such predictions led to the transfer of the capital of the Empire. If Rome, the city, would fall, the Empire would continue to exist if Rome was no longer the capital. I do not find this likely. Myth and solemn predictions seem a frivolous reason for the transfer of an imperial capital. More specifically, *nomen Romanum* can hardly refer to the city as such, and the somber tone of the passage does not suggest that the transfer of the capital is the subject of the prediction. Similarly I find Olbrich's interpretation of *Cod. Theod.* 16.10.1 (of 17 December 320) rather speculative. I am not persuaded by the argument that Constantinople was founded out of fear for the end of the city of Rome – with the end of the Empire as a concomitant result – and that oracles and myth played a central role in defining an ideology which steered Constantine's decisions (Olbrich 2006: 490–1).

We may note, incidentally, that Lactantius was close to Constantine. It will be appropriate here to refer to a text written more than four hundred years earlier, namely Polybius' *History*, where he recalls Scipio Aemilianus' famous tears at the destruction of Carthage.[28] Scipio is said to have mentioned the fall of earlier empires and then, crying, to have quoted, 'The day shall be when holy Troy shall fall and Priam, lord of spears, and Priam's folk.'[29] When asked 'what he meant by these words, he did not name Rome distinctly, but was evidently fearing for her, from this sight of the mutability of human affairs'.[30] Thus we find ruminations about the end of Rome in two authors as far apart as Polybius and Lactantius. Rome may fall one day like Troy in the past, besides other empires – the ones mentioned by Scipio, according to Polybius, are mostly in the East: Assyrians, Medes, Persians, besides Macedonia. The explicit idea that power will return to the Orient did not occur, of course, to Polybius, who wrote before Rome conquered the Near East. The idea of an east–west clash developed after Rome expanded farther east, to Anatolia, Syria and Egypt.

Eventually it happened. In 330 Constantine founded Constantinople.[31] Yet there are reports that the choice of Byzantium for the purpose had been far from certain. There were rumours that the first location had been closer to the traditional location of Roman origin, namely at Troy. We see this in Zosimus (c. 500):

> Since he could not bear to be blamed, so to say, by everybody, he sought a city which could be a counterweight to Rome and where he had to build a palace. When he found himself between Sigeion in the Troad and ancient Ilion he found a suitable place to build a city. He laid the foundations and built part of the wall, high enough so that those who sail to the Hellespont even today can see it. However, he changed his plans, left this project unfinished and went to Byzantion.[32]

---

[28] On this passage, see Momigliano 1975: 22–3: 'How many tear-drops are implied in the simple Greek word ἐδάκρυεν "he wept"?'

[29] Polyb. 38.22: ἔσσεται ἦμαρ ὅταν ποτ' ὀλώλῃ Ἴλιος ἱρὴ καὶ Πρίαμος καὶ λαὸς ἐϋμμελίω Πριάμοιο.

[30] φασὶν οὐ φυλαξάμενον ὀνομάσαι τὴν πατρίδα σαφῶς, ὑπὲρ ἧς ἄρα ἐς τἀνθρώπεια ἀφορῶν ἐδεδίει.

[31] Olbrich 2006: 483–509; Melville-Jones 2014: 247–62.

[32] Zos. 2.30.1: Οὐκ ἐνεγκὼν δὲ τὰς παρὰ πάντων ὡς εἰπεῖν βλασφημίας πόλιν ἀντίρροπον τῆς Ῥώμης ἐζήτει, καθ' ἣν αὐτὸν ἔδει βασίλεια καταστήσασθαι· γενόμενος δὲ Τρωάδος μεταξὺ <Σιγείου> καὶ τῆς ἀρχαίας Ἰλίου καὶ τόπον εὑρὼν εἰς πόλεως κατασκευὴν ἐπιτήδειον, θεμελίους τε ἐπήξατο καὶ τείχους τι μέρος εἰς ὕψος ἀνέστησεν, ὅπερ ἄχρι τοῦδε ὁρᾶν ἔνεστι τοῖς ἐπὶ τὸν Ἑλλήσποντον πλέουσιν· ἐλθὼν δὲ εἰς μετάμελον καὶ ἀτελὲς τὸ ἔργον καταλιπὼν ἐπὶ τὸ Βυζάντιον ᾔει. Also: Zonar. 13.3.1ff., who asserts that Constantine began to build his city on the promontory of Sigeum before he decided that it was going to be Byzantium.

Also, extensively in Sozomen (400–50):

> The Emperor [Constantine] always intent on the advancement of religion
> erected splendid Christian temples to God in every place – especially in
> great cities such as Nicomedia in Bithynia, Antioch on the Orontes, and
> Byzantium. He greatly improved this latter city, and made it equal to
> Rome in power and influence; for when he had settled his empire as he
> was minded, and had freed himself from foreign foes, he resolved on
> founding a city which should be called by his own name, and should equal
> in fame even Rome. With this intent he went to the plain at the foot of
> Troy on the Hellespont, above the tomb of Ajax, where, it is said, the
> Achaians entrenched themselves when besieging Troy; and there he laid
> out the plan of a large and beautiful city, and built gates on a high spot of
> ground, whence they are still visible from the sea to mariners. But when he
> had proceeded thus far, God appeared to him by night and bade him seek
> another site for his city. [Trans. Edward Walford (Bohn)][33]

Constantine is reported first to have thought of Serdica (Sofia),[34] Chalcedon[35] and perhaps even Thessaloniki. It is probably significant that the two really major cities of the East are not mentioned: Antioch and Alexandria. There is disagreement about the historical truth of these reports, but the least that can be said is that they reflect an idea that had been around for over almost four centuries.

In this connection it is important – as has been observed frequently – that in the third century the emperors frequently resided for long periods in various cities. According to Herodian, referring to the second century, 'Rome is wherever the Emperor is' (addressed to Commodus).[36] Diocletian, Maximian and the other tetrarchs instead travelled between – and resided in – a series of smaller but still sizable cities nearer the frontiers, which were aggrandized with major public building projects such as palaces and hippodromes (often side by side as though they were little Romes), basilicas and baths: these included Trier, Milan, and Aquileia in the west; Spalato, Sirmium, Thessalonica and Serdica in the Balkans; Nicomedia and

---

[33] Sozom. *Hist. eccl.* 2.3.2: ἔγνωκεν οἰκίσαι πόλιν ὁμώνυμον ἑαυτῷ καὶ τῇ Ῥώμῃ ὁμότιμον. καταλαβὼν δὲ τὸ πρὸ τοῦ Ἰλίου πεδίον παρὰ τὸν Ἑλλήσποντον ὑπὲρ τὸν Αἴαντος τάφον, οὗ δὴ λέγεται τὸν ναύσταθμον καὶ τὰς σκηνὰς ἐσχηκέναι τοὺς ἐπὶ Τροίαν ποτὲ στρατευσαμένους Ἀχαιούς, οἵαν ἐχρῆν καὶ ὅσην τὴν πόλιν διέγραψε· Sozomenus thus emphasizes the original Christian nature of the project and the dominant element of Constantine's enormous personal ambition. Neither must be accepted without question.

[34] Dio Continuatus, frg. 15 (*FHG* 4: 199); Zonar. 13.3.1–4 (Bonn 3. pp. 13–14).

[35] Cedrenus (Bonn 1. p. 496); Zonar. 13.3.1–4 (Bonn 3. pp. 13–14) and further references in Dagron 1984: 29–30, n. 3.

[36] Hdn. 1.6.5: ἐκεῖ τε ἡ Ῥώμη, ὅπου ποτ' ἂν ὁ βασιλεὺς ᾖ.

Antioch in the east. It is therefore conceivable that Constantine at first saw his foundation as belonging to this category.[37]

Why Byzantium was chosen over more important cities is a matter of speculation. Before Constantine made his decision, there was no particular reason to believe Byzantium was destined for this particular greatness and centrality.[38] It has been called 'the key to the Pontus'.[39] It is well known that the site had important strategic advantages, but also problems, described briefly and to the point by Polybius: 'The Byzantines occupy a site, as regards the sea, more favourable to security and prosperity than any other city in the world, but as regards the land it is in both respects more unfavourable than any other.'[40] He then describes how it controls access to the Black Sea and occupies fertile land. The currents in the Bosporus supplied it with excellent fish.[41] However, it was hard to defend on the west side. The site was being surrounded by Thracians with whom the Byzantines were engaged in constant warfare. The prevailing winds made it difficult to approach and supply by sea from the South. It had no natural fresh water supply. A factor not emphasized in the ancient sources, but undoubtedly important as well and relevant for Constantine's choice, was its controlling position on one of the two land bridges between Europe and Asia Minor.[42] The history of the city before the fourth century is a subject of great interest but less immediately relevant for the present discussion.[43]

Recent studies have suggested modifications in the traditional interpretation of claims, made first by Christian authors, that Constantine's city was

---

[37] Bréhier 1915: 243–345; Alföldi 1947: 10–16. Alföldi argues that at first Constantinople was not conceived as a rival to Rome, but as a residence, just as Milan, Sirmium, Trier, Cologne, Antioch, and Nicomedia. Great building projects do not mean that a city is intended to be a rival to Rome. According to Dagron 1984: 46–7, the sources agree on one point: Constantine conceived a city after the image of Rome. He wanted that Constantinople would have the same power as Rome and share with Rome the leadership of the Empire. See also Melville-Jones 2014: 248; Grig and Kelly 2012: 7. For tetrarchic imperial residences: Millar 1977: 40–53. For the city of Rome from late antiquity to the Middle Ages: Krautheimer 1980.

[38] van Dam 2010: 50–2.   [39] HA *Gall.* 6.8.2: *claustrum Ponticum.*

[40] Polyb. 4.38.1: Βυζάντιοι κατὰ μὲν θάλατταν εὐκαιρότατον οἰκοῦσι τόπον καὶ πρὸς ἀσφάλειαν καὶ πρὸς εὐδαιμονίαν πάντη τῶν ἐν τῇ καθ᾿ ἡμᾶς οἰκουμένῃ, κατὰ δὲ γῆν πρὸς ἀμφότερα πάντων ἀφυέστατον.

[41] Strabo 7.320.

[42] Darius crossed the Bosporos not far from Byzantion on his way to Scythia (Hdt. 4.87). See also the sources cited by Merle 1916: 10. There was also the road from Byzantium to the Strymon: Thuc. 2.97.

[43] Dagron 1984: Ch. 1: 'La foundation de Constantinople: Byzance avant Constantin', with sources and literature in note 1; van Dam 2010: 50–1. For Byzantium as a Greek settlement, see Isaac 1986: 215–37; for the advantages of the site: 215–16. See also Malkin and Shmueli 1988: 21–36. Byzantium was granted the status of a Roman citizen colony only in the reign of Septimius Severus: Hsch. 38 (Praeger p. 16); Chron. Paschale (Bonn p. 495); cf. Dagron 1984: 17 and n.6.

conceived from the start as the new or second Rome and also as a purely Christian city.[44] Regarding its Christian character, it should be noted that Byzantium before Constantine had no distinguished history as a Christian city.[45] It is not even mentioned in the New Testament. These later Christian authors offer their own perspective which ignores the fact that there were both secular and non-Christian sacred buildings in the city.[46]

The claim that, from the start, it was intended to replace Rome is not conclusively confirmed, given the relatively slow development of Constantinople as imperial capital. There is no contemporary evidence that Constantine always conceived his new foundation as the eastern capital of the empire, or that he intended that it should replace Rome.[47] It has been argued that Constantine may not have had a fully formed plan already in 324.[48] True, there are claims that Constantine decided in 324 to found it as 'the new Rome'[49] or 'the second Rome',[50] but these sources are of a later date. In fact, the name that stuck was Constantinople.[51] The city actually took time to develop into an imperial capital.[52] A *praefectus urbi* as existed in Rome was not appointed until 359.[53] The city became the undisputed centre of the Late Roman Empire only in the reign of Theodosius I. This has been demonstrated by an analysis of the *subscriptiones* of imperial constitutions, preserved in the *Codex Theodosianus*, showing that over 240 laws had been issued at that time, out of a total of more than 600 included in this compilation, which were enacted from Constantinople.[54] Half a century after its foundation Constantinople formally became 'the New Rome',[55] even though Rome, in the fourth century and during the first half of the fifth, retains a privileged position in the literary documents of the time that mention it, especially those produced by pagan, Latin-writing authors.[56] Eutropius is a relatively early historian who mentions the ascent of Constantinople:

---

[44] The first time reservations on this point were expressed was not so recent: Bréhier 1915: 256–7. For Constantine's Christian buildings there: Euseb. *Vit. Const.* 3.47.4–49 with comments by Cameron and Hall, 297–9 and Melville-Jones 2014: 257. Oros. 7.28; August. *de Civ. D.* 5.25.

[45] Bréhier 1915: 257–8.   [46] Bréhier, 1915: 258–66.   [47] See n. 39.

[48] Melville-Jones 2014: 249, who also discusses the coinage, 250–1 with note 6.

[49] Them. *Or.* 3.42, for which see Melville-Jones 2014: 252. See also Theophanes, *Chron.* AM 5821 with the comments by Mango and Scott 1997: 46.

[50] A possible early exception might be Publilius Optatianus Porphyrius, *Carmina* 4.5–6, for which see Melville-Jones 2014: 6. The later sources are Socrates, *HE* 1.16; Sozom. *HE* 2.3.5.5 (c5); Novella 655 (c6).

[51] Melville-Jones 2014: 249.

[52] For the expansion of the city and its population and the consequences of this expansion in the period following the foundation as Constantinople, see Van Dam 2010: 52–3.

[53] Socrates 2.41; *CTh* 1.6.1.   [54] Cañizar Palacios 2014: 280–310.

[55] Cañizar Palacios 2014: 281–2.   [56] Cañizar Palacios 2014: 286–93.

> He [Constantine] was the first that endeavoured to raise the city named after him to such a height as to make it a rival to Rome.[57]

That still is a somewhat ambiguous, rhetorical assertion. Eutropius had a vested interest, for he was *magister memoriae* in Constantinople in the second half of the fourth century.

Conclusions

Reality trumped ideology again and again. Old fears became reality.

Rome was not a capital city. It was not supposed to be one. It was the state, the Empire, the collective citizenship, all in one. In theory it could not be duplicated or transferred. Paradoxically, there was fear and there were rumours for centuries that precisely this would happen, even at a stage when there was no such danger. Eventually it happened indeed, and when it did – another paradox – this may not have been the intention from the start. Before Constantinople was founded, there had been fears for more than three centuries that a new capital was to be located at or near the mythic cradle of Rome: Troy. These fears were combined with a pronounced view of an East–West antagonism which, somehow, was translated over time into the actual split of the Empire into an eastern and a western part, a Latin-speaking and a Greek-speaking half. Not so long before this took place, the new capital was planted on a suitable site without Roman historical significance, replacing an old Greek city.

Although the sources have been interpreted along different lines, it now seems very likely that Constantine did not declare from the start that he was founding a 'New Rome' or 'Second Rome', a city to replace Rome. Also, *not* having declared that he was in fact doing so, it did not become a reality in his days, but only under his successors. Like so many foundations, at first it was just another city on an important site, although an old and venerable one, renamed after the man who refounded it. Yet Constantine's decision had drastic results: it initiated the transfer of the centre of the Empire eastward, to the Greek-speaking part of the Roman Empire, even though it took more than a generation before this became a reality, whatever had been intended. It is conceivable, although a matter of speculation, that Constantine, in selecting Byzantium for his new city of Constantinople, consciously avoided the antagonism that would have been the result if he

---

[57] Eutr. *Brev.* 10.8.1 (trans. H. W. Bird): *primusque urbem nominis sui ad tantum fastigium evehere molitus est, ut Romae aemulam faceret.*

had truthfully declared that he was establishing a New Rome or an alternative Eastern Rome on or near the site of Roman origins. Christians later claimed he had founded a Christian city – that was only partially true. Again, it is possible that Constantine avoided fierce conflict by refraining from establishing a fully Christian, second Rome.

The fear that Rome would come to an end never materialized (Rome is still there),[58] but the shift of the centre of power eastward took place, not as the result of a one-time decision by a ruler, but through historical dynamics and preceded by centuries of suspicion and tension. The decision rather reflected a development that occurred, inevitably, over time. Emperors who called themselves Roman continued to reign in the East over subjects who called themselves Romans, although Greek was their language, until the fifteenth century, a thousand years longer than in the Western Roman Empire, where the last Emperor, Romulus Augustu(lu)s, abdicated in 476.[59]

---

[58] For the city from the fourth century until the fourteenth, see Krautheimer 1980. Phantasies of reviving the Roman Empire belong in recent history to fascist rule in Italy. These have left their depressing imprint on the modern city.

[59] The sad figure of Romulus Augustulus as last Emperor of the Roman West has attracted a good deal of attention in the scholarly literature, e.g., Momigliano 1973: 409–28; Croke 1983: 81–119; Nathan 1992: 261–71.

2 | The Imperial Senate

Center of a Multinational Imperium

WERNER ECK

Philip V of Macedon already recognized one of the decisive political strategies through which Rome strengthened the basis of its rule.[1] In a letter to the inhabitants of the city of Larissa he talks of the fact that the Romans have recognized that there is an advantage in not being possessive about their citizen rights; rather, they try to expand the number of citizens by accepting foreigners, in this particular case freed slaves, and thereby to increase Rome's power. This characteristic feature of Roman politics is referred to also by Dionysius of Halicarnassus, according to whom this practice was implemented in Rome as early as the days of King Servius Tullus.[2] Philip V was probably too idealistic in his view of Rome's attitude, but he recognized one of the basic principles of Roman politics. In his eyes, Rome did not see membership in the *res publica populi Romani* as exclusive; rather, Rome saw the necessity of accepting other people from the outside into the Roman citizen body – of course under certain conditions and for the advantage of the *res publica*.

This basic axiom can be traced in different ways in Rome's history, starting in the days of the Republic; it becomes more prominent under Caesar, and even more so from Augustus on, when a single individual could make the essential political decisions in Rome.[3] The goal of this political and legal openness was primarily to create a strong commitment to Rome and its ruler; the policy was intended to strengthen the loyalty of people to Rome, or to create integration, as we would probably say today.

Not all members of the political ruling class saw this granting of Roman citizen rights as appropriate and useful for Rome. Moreover, the effect was not always what those who granted the *civitas* had hoped for. What took

---

[1] IG IX 2, 517, ll. 28 ff.: "It is also possible to observe others employing similar enfranchisements, among whom are also the Romans, who receive into their citizen body even their slaves when they free them, giving them even a share in the offices" (translation by Burstein 1985: 87). For the English version, I wish to thank Ofer Pogorelski and Jonathan Price.

[2] Dion. Hal. 4, 22, 3 f.

[3] Still of fundamental importance is Sherwin-White 1973; Vittinghoff 1952; id. 1994; and now, focusing on viritane grants of citizenship, Marotta 2009. For a new model calculating the increase of roman citizenship, see Lavan 2016: 3–46.

place in AD 9 in Germania east of the Rhine, namely the clash with the Cherusci and the annihilation of the Roman army under the command of Varus, was not normal. Arminius, the chieftain of the Cherusci who led the Germanic uprising, had not only received Roman citizenship from Augustus but even had become a member of the *equester ordo* – nevertheless, he broke his loyalty and friendship with Rome.[4] But in most cases the effect of granting the *civitas Romana* was what one could expect, at least, so far as can be known from our sources. The integration was strengthened, and the affiliation to Rome and its fundamental interests became more or less natural, for the majority of the new citizens and even more so for their descendants. When the soldiers of the Danube armies saved the Empire during the severe crisis of the second half of the third century AD, it was partly a consequence of the continuous granting of *civitas Romana* to hundreds of thousands of soldiers and their descendants, mainly from the Balkan provinces. We can see this process from the time of Claudius to the beginning of the third century through numerous military diplomas.[5] Long before the Constitutio Antoniniana, the extensive granting of Roman citizenship to the auxiliary soldiers, mostly born in the Danube provinces, created the decisive require-ments for a profound integration of an essential part of the local societies. The affiliation to Rome via Roman citizenship led by and large to stability in the provinces and ultimately contributed to the fact that at the end of the third century, after the long crisis, the former stability was temporarily restored. The positive effect of this integration through Roman citizenship is thus evident.

The integration of the formerly conquered peoples, however, did not occur only through service in the Roman army. Perhaps more important was the integration of the ruling classes of cities and tribes. Participation in public matters in these societies, being usually timocratic and hierarchical, was open in general only to the leaders and not to all members to the same degree. But via the hierarchical structures the majority of the lower popu-lation was also integrated even if they could not gain independent political stature. Many ruling families of the Roman commonwealth obtained the Roman citizenship at an early stage, through viritane grants, through procedural actions like the granting of the *ius Latii* in some provinces of the West, or by establishing *municipia*, in which the previous socioeco-nomic leaders of single cities were incorporated into the Roman citizen

---

[4] Vell. Pat. 118, 2: *iure etiam civitatis Romanae decus equestris consecutus gradis.*

[5] Altogether more than 1,200 diplomas are now known. Around 150 diplomas issued to praetorians or the *urbaniciani* do not grant full citizenship but only the *conubium* with *feminae iuris peregrini*; but the huge majority of the diplomas grant *civitas Romana*.

body. Even in the new Roman colonies, local *principes* were often integrated into the new citizen body.[6]

The road to integration, however, did not end there; rather, it led in different ways from the provincial cities to Rome, via families whose members became part of the two empire-wide groups, the *equester ordo* and finally the *ordo senatorius*. This process had already begun before Caesar; the first nonethnic Roman who became consul was L. Cornelius Balbus, who received Roman citizenship from Pompeius after the war against Sertorius and advanced to a consulship in 40 BC.[7] That was still unusual at that time and was also an effect of a time of massive changes; however, it marked very clearly what could be achieved through the decision of the Roman political elite and the ambition of the people, who until that point were excluded from the inner core of Roman society. But even after the turmoil of the civil wars, in which the loyalty to a powerful figure was the decisive criterion by which one could be accepted into the political elite, the admission of former *peregrini* to the *ordo senatorius* or the *equester ordo* did not end.[8] During his more than forty years of rule, Augustus developed a policy that was decisive also for his successors.[9] Claudius made it very clear in his speech in AD 48 regarding the request of the *primores Galliarum* to be admitted to the Senate with the following famous words:[10] *sane novo m[ore] et divus Aug[ustus av]onc[ulus] meus et patruus Ti[berius] Caesar omnem florem ubique coloniarum ac municipiorum bonorum scilicet virorum et locupletium in hac curia esse voluit*. This statement did not refer only to the *coloniae* and the *municipia* in Italy but also to Romans already living in *coloniae* and *municipia* in the surrounding provinces. Hence, Claudius continued by saying: *quid ergo non Italicus senator provinciali potior est? iam vobis, cum hanc partem censurae meae adprobare coepero, quid de ea re sentiam, rebus ostendam, sed ne provinciales quidem, si modo ornare curiam poterint, reiciendos puto*. The rhetorical question that Claudius addressed to himself shows that not all members of the Roman ruling class were in favor of expanding their sociopolitical group with people from the provinces; rather, they opposed the intention of the emperor more or less openly. However, Claudius' decision, which he secured by a *senatus consultum*, overruled this resistance.

Claudius' fundamental approach was a constant feature of all later emperors. And naturally, to the criterion *si modo ornare curiam poterint*

---

[6] See now Eck 2016c: 237 ff., cf. 238 ff. on citizenship through the foundation of colonies and *municipia*, and 255 ff. on the grant of citizenship to the local ruling classes.

[7] See Alföldi 1976: passim.

[8] The most comprehensive treatment of this is still Wiseman 1971. On the political process in general, Syme 1939: 78 ff. 349 ff. On the *ordo equester*, Nicolet 1966 and 1974; Demougin 1988.

[9] See Syme 1939: 349 ff.; Kienast 2014: 151 ff. with extensive literature.

[10] CIL XIII 1668 = D. 212.

a second criterion was added: loyalty toward the ruling emperor. An example is the conduct of Vespasian, who after Nero and the civil wars was forced to restore the decimated Senate to its former size.[11] He included especially people who joined his side during the civil wars of 69/70. Among the senators who entered the Senate for the first time under his rule, one can find C. Caristanius Fronto from Antioch in Pisidia, *consul suffectus* in the year 90;[12] Ti. Iulius Celsus Polemaeanus from Sardis/Ephesus, *suffectus* in the year 92; and C. Antius A. Iulius Quadratus from Pergamon, *suffectus* in 94.[13] Catilius Longus came from Apameia in Bithynia; he had served as prefect of an auxiliary unit in Iudaea under Vespasian, just like Caristanius Fronto.[14] From the Iberian Peninsula came L. Baebius Avitus, L. Antistius Rusticus and Q. Pomponius Rufus; the last two were consuls under Domitian just like Polemaeanus and Iulius Quadratus.[15] The homeland of Iavolenus Priscus was probably the province of Dalmatia,[16] and the two brothers Pactumeius Fronto and Pactumeius Clemens were born in Cirta in Africa.[17]

This short list shows that already from the Flavian period the Senate was occupied by individuals from quite a few provinces. This trend intensified under the subsequent emperors, so that at the end of the second and the beginning of the third centuries, the senators whose original homeland was in the provinces already formed a clear majority in the Senate. The second volume of the congress "Epigrafia e Ordine Senatorio" (EOS) from 1981, published in 1984, presents all the information regarding the background of the members of the Senate known in that year.[18] That information is still valid and nearly complete, as is evident from the two new volumes of the "Epigrafia e Ordine Senatorio 30 anni dopo," published in 2014.[19] Therefore it is possible to use the results of 1984 in analyzing the background of the senatorial families from the first to the third centuries.

The proportion of senators of Italian origin was never negligible during the imperial period, but that number declined slowly at first, during the first half of the first century, and then more sharply from the beginning of the second century. From the articles in EOS we know that, apart from the Italian senators, the members of the Senate came from thirty provinces. Only a few provinces are missing in this list (i.e., provinces that did not provide any senators at all) – at least as far as we now know; new inscriptions may change this picture in the future. To this group of missing provinces belong Britannia and Germania Inferior, from which we know

---

[11] See the general treatment of this in Eck 1991a: 73 ff. = id. 1995: 103 ff.   [12] PIR² C 423.
[13] PIR² J 260 und 507; H. Halfmann 1979: 111 ff.   [14] Eck 1981: 227 ff., esp. 242 ff.
[15] Caballos 1990.   [16] PIR² J 14.   [17] PIR² P 36. 38.   [18] Panciera 1982 [1984].
[19] Caldelli and Gregori 2014.

of only one senator who came possibly from either of the two provinces.[20] The three small provinces of the Alps did not have representatives in the Senate before the later third century or perhaps only from the beginning of the fourth: The two Moesian provinces were not represented in the Senate even in the later period, unless one wishes to take into account some of the so-called soldier emperors, who have little to do with the normal process of entering the Senate.[21] The island of Cyprus records no senator, nor does Sardinia.[22] The same is true regarding Iudaea/Syria Palaestina, although since 1984 more members of the *equester ordo* from there have become known.[23] At least one senator, M. Valerius Maximianus, came from Pannonia; he was born in Poetovio and was appointed *consul suffectus* around 186.[24] From Egypt, namely from Alexandria, we know of two senators, a P. Aelius Coeranus and his homonymous son, both of whom were consuls after the death of Septimius Severus.[25] Altogether, the senators from the end of the first century BC to the third century AD who can be identified with some certainty as provincial came from cities located in the following provinces:[26]

Hispania citerior	Baetica	Lusitania
Gallia Narbonensis	Gallia Lugdunensis	Gallia Aquitania
Britannia or Germania Inf.	Germania Superior	Raetia
Noricum	Dalmatia	Pannonia Superior
Thracia	Macedonia	Achaia
Asia	Pontus-Bithynia	Lycia-Pamphylia
Galatia	Cappadocia	Cilicia
Syria	Arabia	Aegyptus
Creta-Cyrenae	Africa proconsularis	Numidia
Mauretania Caesariensis	Mauretania Tingitana	Sicilia

[20] Birley 1982: 531 ff.; Eck 1982: 539 ff.   [21] Šašel 1982: 553 ff.
[22] Bowersock 1982b: 669 f.; Zucca 2014: 341 ff.   [23] Bowersock 1982a: 651 ff.; Eck 2007: 236 ff.
[24] CIL VIII 4600; AE 1956, 124.
[25] See Reynolds 1982: 673 f. and J. d'Arms 683, who mention Coeranus' possible descent from an imperial freedman; consequently, he of course could be designated Egyptian only in a "marginal sense," as both authors note. But in the final analysis this is irrelevant, since for example even the senators from the provinces of Asia Minor were not each classified as belonging to a specific ethnic sector of the local population. Descendants of an imperial freedman were after several generations part of the citizens of a city, which was probably the decisive element in determining their origin.
[26] See EOS II. Cf. now N. Hächler 2019, 128ff.

The list shows that the majority of provinces of the *Imperium Romanum* sent members to the central governing organ of the empire. But the implementation was not equal across these provinces. The number of provincial cities from which we can identify senators with reasonable certainty is just over 200.[27] This is only a fraction of all the autonomous cities in the provinces. The number of cities is divided very differently among the separate provinces. Not in all provinces, however, are the numbers of senators known to us always representative. Only four senators altogether are known from the sixty-four communities of the tres Galliae with their large territories. This is a very minimal representation, whereas Belgica, according to our current knowledge, is completely missing. This low number, however, probably does not reflect reality but can be explained by the epigraphic documentation, or paucity thereof, in the province of Aquitania, the Lugdunensis and the Belgica. The number of senators and their home cities from these provinces may have been in fact higher, especially since Gaul provided the requisite economic base for senators.[28]

The number of cities in the two Hispaniae, the Tarraconensis and the Baetica, is quite high, but the many known senators from these provinces come from a very limited number of communities: Eleven cities from the Baetica and fourteen from the Tarraconensis sent senators to Rome according to our current knowledge. The highest number of cities represented in the Roman Senate belong to the provinces that also occupy the top places in a senatorial career: Africa (proconsularis) and Asia. About thirty communities from Asia and at least forty-seven communities from Africa sent senators to Rome.[29] A few cities are notable for the number of senators coming from them. In Asia, Pergamon and Ephesus stand out in this regard;[30] Pergamon also had its first consul, C. Antius A. Iulius Quadratus, by the end of the first century and hence it is represented among the leading groups of the Senate.[31] Surprisingly, the first consul from Ephesus took office around the end of the second century;[32] Ti. Iulius Celsus Polemaeanus, who is almost automatically associated with Ephesus because he was buried there, in the basement of his library – hence the name Celsus-Library – was originally from Sardis. But the number of senators from the capital of Asia is the highest we

[27] On the basis of the data in Panciera 1982.   [28] Eck 1991b: 73 ff.
[29] Halfmann 1982: 603 ff.; Corbier 1982: 685 ff.; Le Glay 1982: 755 ff.
[30] Halfmann 1982: 625ff, 627 ff.   [31] Halfmann 1979: (n. 13) 112 ff.
[32] Ti. Claudius Severus, Inschr. Ephesus III 648; Halfmann 1982: 628.

know from all cities in the provinces.[33] In Africa there are also several cities that stand out in this respect: Bulla Regia, Lepcis Magna, Hippo Regius.[34] However, it appears that until the end of the third century Carthage, the *caput provinciae*, is missing among these cities known for their high number of senatorial families – notwithstanding that Carthage had many aristocratic families. That seems to have changed in the fourth or even the fifth century, when we know many *viri clarissimi* from that city, attested by newly found inscriptions from Carthage.[35] They got senatorial rank and title through their occupation in the *officia* of the imperial administration, but they most probably had nothing to do anymore with the Senate in Rome.

Not a few families were represented in the Senate by members over the course of several generations. We know of the first senator from the *familia Silia* from Lepcis Magna as early as the beginning of the rule of Marcus Aurelius, and the last known member of this family was the governor of Germania Superior in 240.[36] The earliest consul from the *Cuspii* of Pergamon was appointed in AD 126 under Hadrian;[37] therefore, their senatorial status goes back at least to the time of Trajan. The last known member of this family was one of the *consules ordinarii* of the year 197 during the Severan period.[38] Among other families, which however came from Italian cities, the membership in the Senate was even much longer. The Neratii from Saepinum had a seat in the Senate from the second half of the first century, and they were represented there at least until the end of the fourth;[39] the same is true for the Bruttii Praesentes, who came from the region of Brutti in the south of Italy.[40]

From the middle of the first century AD, the Senate, while it met in Rome, appears to have turned more and more into a mixed assembly, when one considers the provinces of the empire from which the individual members and their families came. From a legal point of view and with respect to *origo*, there was no difference among the individual senators, since all of them had the same *origo*: Rome itself. Ideologically, it could not

---

[33] Halfmann 1982: 627 ff.; the high number is probably due also to the very abundant inscriptional evidence surviving from there, but it corresponds well with the size of the city and above all its function as *caput provinciae*, by which the contacts of the Ephesians with Roman magistrates were facilitated to a significant degree. It was thus one of the most important requirements for the rise of the imperial aristocracy.

[34] Corbier 1982: 711 ff.; 720 f.; 721 ff.   [35] Mastino and Ibba 2014: 355.

[36] Corbier 1982: 725 and Weiß 2015: 23 ff.   [37] RMD IV: 236; RGZM 29; AE 2005: 1714.

[38] Halfmann 1982: 626.   [39] PIR² N p. 341 ff.; PLRE I p. 615, with the names of the Naeratii.

[40] The first Bruttius is attested in the reign of Titus (AE 1950: 122); for the last, see PLRE I Praesens and AE 1978: 262.

have been otherwise: whoever represents Rome must be a Roman, in all respects. The fact that Rome was the *origo* of all the senators is stated very clearly in the *liber primus* of the *Sententiae* of Paulus:[41] *Senatores et eorum filii filiaeque quoquo tempore nati nataeve, itemque nepotes, pronepotes et pronepotes ex filio origini eximuntur, licet municipalem retineant dignitatem.* Senators lost, so to speak, their old *origo* and were associated with it at the most so far as they kept the *dignitas*, the reputation and the rank that they had acquired in their homeland. Other sources confirm this legal bond to Rome.[42] The members of the *ordo senatorius* were not connected anymore to their original community. Moreover, a senator and his relatives did not have any legal duties regarding their place of origin, and no one could oblige them to *munera* there. Rome was to be their base.

Beyond the legal aspects, the separation of the senators from their homeland was a matter of course also for practical reasons:[43] They had their duties in Rome itself; above all, they had to take part in the meetings of the Senate and in other gatherings, for example the meetings of the *fratres Arvales*, which are well attested.[44] This separation from the homeland was reinforced by official tasks required of officeholders. These official tasks were carried out partly in Rome, but mostly outside the capital in different provinces and sometimes in Italy. The emperor sent a senator to his home province very seldom, for a special reason or from carelessness.

If senators wanted to visit their home province,[45] apart from Sicily and the Narbonensis, then they needed specific permission, which was issued at first by the Senate but soon by the emperor.[46] This rule of requesting leave (*commeatus*) did not apply for Italy; only senators who were bound to Rome due to a magistracy had to ask. When Pliny the Younger was *praefectus aerarii Saturni*, he asked Trajan for a month's leave so that he could settle some matters of one of his estates near Tifernum Tiberinum, located more than 150 miles from Rome.[47] For most of the senators, however, regular personal contacts with their home cities in the provinces were not so simple, even under the relatively good travel conditions of the early and high empire. We can assume that many senators who accomplished many discernible things in their home city did so through

---

[41] Dig. 50, 1, 22, 5.   [42] Dig. 50, 1, 22, 4; Dig. 50, 1, 23.   [43] Talbert 1984: 66 ff.

[44] See the *Acta fratrum Arvalium* in the new editon of Scheid 1998.

[45] The requirement that all senators live in Rome affected the mobility of both the senators themselves and many others, on which see Eck 2016d.

[46] Tac. *Ann.* 12, 23, 1: *Galliae Narbonensi ob egregiam in patres reverentiam datum ut senatoribus eius provinciae non exquisita principis sententia, iure quo Sicilia haberetur, res suas invisere liceret*; Cass. Dio, 60, 25, 6 f.; cf. Talbert 1984: (n. 43) 138 ff.

[47] Plin. *Ep.* 10, 8.

letters.[48] It is enough to consider Cuspius Rufus, a senator from Pergamon in the period of Pius, whose ties to his family's home city were extremely close.[49] Nevertheless, when we consider all the factors and circumstances of senatorial life, it is not surprising that many scholars have thought that the contact of most of the provincial senators with their home cities was broken off quite abruptly. This seems to be confirmed by the fact that senators were relatively seldom magistrates in their home-towns, despite the fact that it was still legally possible for them, as Hermogenianus stated in his *liber primus iuris epitomarum* written at the end of the third century.[50] In practice, of course, this was almost impossible to do *in persona*, since no senator could have been absent from Rome for a whole year for nonofficial reasons. But it would have been possible for a senator to take care of the financial duties of a local office while the concrete functions were taken care of by a local *praefectus*.

On the other hand, we know of not a few examples of senators who time and again – at least when they reached the age of 65 and were no longer obliged to take part in Senate meetings and normally had no tasks as magistrates – retired to their home communities or at least made sure that they were present there.[51] When the city of Carthage wanted to honor Minicius Natalis Quadronius Verus, *cos. suff.* in AD 139, with a *quadriga*, after his proconsulate in Africa, he decided that the monument would be set up not in Rome but in Barcino in Tarraconensis, the city where the Natalis family originated. The *quadriga* with the senator's statue stood in the center of the baths, which had been built by the senator and his father around the year 123.[52] Such an act is understandable only if the aging senator himself had retired to Barcino, or at least felt himself emotionally connected with the city.[53] Similar is the case of C. Antius A. Iulius Quadratus, who saw to it that a great number of honorary statues would be set up for him in his home city, Pergamon. He seems actually to have returned to Pergamon personally as well.[54] On the other hand, we can see that the home cities of senators in the provinces were rarely selected for honorary statues, which were erected by provincial communities for their former governors. Ti. Claudius Candidus, a legate of Pannonia Superior in the Severan period, was honored in his hometown Rusicade in Africa by a prefect of a fleet who served under his command at the middle Danube.[55]

---

[48] Pliny gives many examples how he is involved in various matters in Comum – only by sending and receiving letters.

[49] On this, see Krieckhaus 2006: 131 ff.   [50] Dig. 50, 1, 23 praef.; Eck 1980: 283 ff.

[51] See some examples in Krieckhaus 2006: n. 49.   [52] CIL II 4509 = 6145 = Dessau 1029.

[53] Eck and Navarro 1998: 237 ff.   [54] Eck 2010: 89 ff., esp. 101.   [55] Erkelenz 2003, 245.

Likewise P. Iulius Geminius Marcianus, legate of the province of Arabia under Marcus Aurelius, saw to it that some cities of his administrative district would erect statues in his honor in his hometown Cirta, even with inscriptions in Greek.[56] Apart from the cities of Italy, such honorary statues in the provincial home cities of governors are only sporadically attested.[57] This could indicate a weak relationship of many senators to their natural *origo*.

Less frequent are the cases in which senators were buried "at home," like Celsus Polemaeanus, whose burial place in the basement of his library in Ephesus has already been mentioned.[58] C. Iulius Quadratus Bassus, *consul suffectus* in 105, who died in Dacia at the beginning of Hadrian's rule during a battle against the empire's enemies, was buried in Pergamon, in his home province Asia, by an order of Hadrian.[59] Herodes Atticus lived during the last years of his life in Marathon on the east coast of Attica because of tensions between him and Marcus Aurelius. He found his last resting place in Attica.[60] The majority of senatorial graves, without regard for where the senators came from, have been found near Rome or cities in the vicinity,[61] in other words where normally the nonofficial life of the senators and their families took place.

All these observations seem to show, as indicated earlier, that the former home communities of the Senate members did not play an essential role in their lives and that the contacts with them were reduced or even broken off. Through this interpretation of our relevant material one decisive aspect of senatorial existence is not being taken into account: the economic basis of all these families. Each senator had to prove that he had a minimum fortune of one million sestertii, although many, if not the majority, had much more than that.[62] Otherwise many of them would have been classified as *pauper senator*. Plentiful evidence attests to far greater fortunes and respective incomes, not only for Seneca but also for many other people like Q. Vibius Crispus.[63] The larger part of these fortunes consisted, as was general in Roman society, of landed property, which produced income directly through farming or by other forms of land use, from which the Roman families could make a living.[64] We know that in the time of Trajan, each new senator had to invest a third of his fortune in Italian landed property, because – as Pliny writes in one of his letters – in this way it could be

---

[56] Ibid. (n. 55) 269.   [57] See, in general, the lists in Erkelenz 2003: (n. 55) 239 ff.
[58] See Eck 2010: (n. 54) 106 ff.   [59] Habicht 1969: No. 21.   [60] Philostr. VS. 565 f.
[61] See the dissertation of Th. Knosala, Die Grabrepräsentation der ritterlichen und senatorischen Bevölkerungsgruppe in Lazio. Beginn der Republik – spätseverische Zeit, which will be published at Propylaeum Heidelberg 2021.
[62] For this topic, see Talbert 1984: (n. 43) 47 ff.
[63] PIR² V 543; cf., in general, Duncan-Jones 1982: 17 ff.   [64] Andermahr 1998.

guaranteed that the senators would not look at Italy merely as *hospitium aut stabulum*.[65] Under Marcus Aurelius this Italian requirement was evidently lowered to one quarter.[66] This means two things: On the one hand, the relationship to Rome – at least among the *homines novi* – was still weak, while the connection to the home communities was stronger. On the other hand, this indicates more than anything else that the larger part of the productive land, despite the partial transfer to Italy, still remained in the provinces. If the majority of the landed property of the senatorial families stayed in their former homelands, then the members of these families were in one way or the other necessarily present there, via administrators (*procurators*) or maybe also via close relatives, who represented the interests of the senator at home. Moreover, the revenues from the lands must have gone to Rome, in kind or as cash value. Such close connections to the home cities are illustrated, for example, by the letter of Septimius Severus from AD 204, by which he conveyed to an unknown recipient – perhaps a proconsul from Asia – that a *senator populi Romani* according to a *senatus consultum* should not tolerate any billeting in his house against his will. Nine copies of this letter on marble slabs have been found in the territory of the provincia Asia; senators probably fixed the text publicly on their properties, in order to protect their houses in the cities of the province.[67] The same is evident from a decree of Valerian and Gallienus,[68] who verify in writing to a senator named Iulius Apellas that he should not tolerate any billeting in his house, which was probably in Smyrna. All the senators who posted such imperial documents not only had property in their home cities but also were carefully trying to protect the value of their property. These documents signify that the provincial senators – just like their colleagues from Italy – had to maintain economic contact with their places of origin. This contact could consist not only in impersonal connections involving merely the "transfer" of the revenues to Rome but also perforce in a real relationship with the citizenry of the communities, who were directly involved in the senators' transactions; as

---

[65] Plin. *Ep.* 6, 19, 4: *eosdem patrimonii tertiam partem conferre iussit in ea quae solo continerentur, deforme arbitratus – et erat – honorem petituros urbem Italiamque non pro patria sed pro hospitio aut stabulo quasi peregrinantes habere.*

[66] HA. *Marc.* 11, 8.

[67] CIL III 14203,9; IG XII 5, 132; Inschriften von Ephesus II 207. 208; AE 1977, 807; TAM V 1, 607 = Drew-Bear et al. 1977: 365: *Exemplum sacrarum litterarum Severi et Antonini Augustorum videris nobis senatus consultum ignorare qui si cum peritis contuleris scies senatori populi Romani necesse non esse invito hospitem suscipere subscripsi datum pridie Kalendas Iunias Romae Fabio Cilone II et Annio Libone conssulibus.*

[68] CIL III 412 = IGR IV 1404 = Drew-Bear et al. 1977: 367 n. 53 = SEG 27, 763 = Petzl 1987, no. 604.

a result, in turn, the senators retained knowledge of the situation in their cities, quite the opposite to the prevailing opinion about the relations of provincial senators to their places of origin.

In addition, many senators were also the patrons of their home cities, to whom the inhabitants, especially from the ruling classes, could turn and seek consultation.[69] Cornelius Fronto, a senator from Cirta in Africa and a rhetoric teacher of Marcus Aurelius, is a clear example of continuing commitment to one's home city,[70] just as Pliny the Younger is with respect to his *patria* Comum. We can therefore assume that many senators, if not all, were kept informed about the situation of their home city and hence also about the situation of the province of their city.[71] It is surely no accident that Pactumeius Fronto is called *consul ex Africa primus* on an inscription of his daughter from Cirta.[72] The Superaequani said of their fellow citizen Q. Varius Geminus: *primus omnium Paelign(orum) senator factus est.*[73] A *centurio* of the *legio III Augusta* honors his commander Ti. Claudius Gordianus and points to the fact that he, the commander, came from *Tyana ex Cappadocia.*[74] Other texts also mention occasionally the origins of senators.[75] The connection between a senator and his provincial city or an entire province was seen therefore as something absolutely real and accepted.

When we look at the origins of individual senators, it is undeniable that the Senate was the center of a multinational empire. Multinational is, of course, understood here not in the modern sense of nations but in the sense of different *patriae*, with which specific citizen rights were connected, which stood originally on the same level as Roman citizen rights. One can assume that the members of the Senate were aware that they came from different regions of the empire and that their cultural background was not the same; but most of them did not see these differences as multinational,

---

[69] Engesser 1957; Eilers 2002; Nicols 2014.

[70] Champlin 1980. Several inscriptions from Messene in Achaia yield a strikingly clear case of a senator's strong ties to his home city; see Eck 2017.

[71] This is true above all for senators who were patrons of cities, with whom personal contact had to be maintained. See, for example, for M. Sedatius Severianus, legate of Dacia Superior and patronus of Sarmizegetusa: when he became *consul suffectus* five *legati* of Sarmizegetusa came to Rome to congratulate the patron: CIL III 1562 = Dessau 3896 and Dessau 9487, AE 1933, 249.

[72] CIL VIII 7058 = 19427 = Dessau 1001 = ILAlg II 1, 644.   [73] CIL IX 3306 = Dessau 932a.

[74] AE 1954, 138.

[75] See, e.g., AE 1956, 124: *M(arco) Valerio Maximiano M(arci) Valeri Maximiani quinq(uennalis) s[ac(erdotalis)] f(ilio) pont(ifici) col(oniae) Poetovionens(ium)* . In a *titulus honorarius*, which was installed under a statue for P. Cornelius Anullinus in Illiberis, the residents of the city explicitly mention that he came from their city, CIL II 2075 = Dessau 1139. That was not normal. But in this case, the widespread custom in Baetica of adding a mention of one's home city to one's name in inscriptions, played a role.

namely as reflecting different *patriae*, but rather in a much simpler way: senators from Italy versus senators from the provinces. This is at least what the rhetorical question in Claudius' speech assumes: *non Italicus senator provinciali potior est.*[76] It seems that by this expression Claudius meant the notion of a majority in the Senate, with which of course he did not want to agree. In any case, it is hard to doubt the fundamental awareness of their diverse origins among most members of the Senate. These observations raise a further question: Did the knowledge and the consciousness of the different geographical and hence diverse cultural backgrounds have implications, either in the collective decisions of the Senate itself or in the decisions of individual senators? The question is legitimate and interesting, but answering it will require a wide-ranging investigation, which will be carried out in the future.[77]

---

[76] See n. 3.

[77] On the possible consequences of the origin of senators from certain provinces, cf. now Kirbihler 2014: 279 ff.

| Ethnic Types and Stereotypes in Ancient Latin Idioms[*]

DANIELA DUECK

Ethnic and racial prejudice and xenophobia occur in every society, but in widely differing degrees, social settings, and moral environments. They are the result of the human tendency to generalize and simplify, so that whole nations are treated as a single individual with a single personality (Isaac 2004, 3).

The Nature of Idioms and Proverbial Expressions

This study is a search for cultural insights through common linguistic structures. More specifically, it is an attempt at gleaning some knowledge of ancient Classical views of foreigners from Latin idioms and proverbial expressions. Let us simply start with the basic definition of idioms as words or phrases that have a figurative meaning which is different from the literal meaning of the individual word(s) composing them. The characteristics of idioms, their social and linguistic functions, and their research are closely related and partially similar to those of proverbs.[1] Like idioms, proverbs, in any culture, contain generalizations or approximate truths originating in real-life experience. Often they turn actual and factual realities into exaggerated and inaccurate assertions. In all their aspects, proverbs, proverbial expressions and single-word idioms, usually emerge from popular experience and are based on impressions of ordinary people. These become maxims reflecting common, sometimes prejudiced, concepts of situations, people, places and other details related to human encounters with the

---

[*] I have never been a registered student of Benjamin Isaac but he was kind enough to comment on some of my earlier studies, always offering precise and illuminating suggestions, and his own publications are a constant inspiration for me. I warmly greet him on his birthday and wish him many more healthy years of productivity and satisfaction.

I thank the participants in the conference for their helpful comments and in particular Walter Ameling, Joseph Geiger, Erich Gruen, Benjamin Isaac and Irad Malkin.

This chapter is part of a larger on-going research project on Greek and Roman proverbs.
[1] On general discussions of idioms, see Everaert et al. 1995; Glucksberg 2001: 68–89. On proverbs, see Mieder and Dundes 1994; Mieder 2004. Specifically on Greek and Roman proverbs, see Kindstrand 1978; Huxley 1981; Russo 1997.

world. The humble origin of idioms and proverbs does not always mean that they do not hold facts and verifiable truths or that they cannot express educated ideas, but rather that they are not the result of scientific and informed observations. While their origin and initial transmission are both oral, they often penetrate learned and literary texts so that, specifically for ancient societies, we have some record of this popular and oral world of ideas preserved throughout generations.

The Greek *paroimia, gnome* or *apophthegma* and the Latin *proverbium, sententia, elogium* or *dictum*, were usually prose or metric phrases, concise, witty, and sometimes enigmatic or allegorical. They expressed experience and common sense, universal truths and popular wisdom. At times they held even moral and didactic values. In our present study we broaden the scope to include also more flexible proverbial expressions and single-word idioms. As we shall see, unlike strict proverbs in their traditional sense, not all of the idioms and phrases we discuss have moral implications as lessons to be learned or implicit advice or guidance, but all carry ethnic connotation and meaning.

Because of their popular origin, proverbs and idioms regularly reflect ancient times and preserve traces of past events and periods. Many sayings refer to specific regions and peoples. Accordingly, place names or mere ethnonyms, even when detached from a whole sentence as single-word idioms, become proverbial for particular situations, human characteristics and natural conditions. Furthermore, unique events and individual character traits are generally applied and often exaggerated to denote collective local and personal types.

The popularity of idioms and proverbs and their antiquity turn them into a first-rate source of interest for historians and anthropologists. They preserve various facts sometimes through generations after the original circumstances have long changed or after a certain phenomenon has disappeared. They are remains of the past undamaged by time. Their historical value is especially precious because they contain unbiased information and not such that was consciously and deliberately inserted for tendentious historiographical purposes. In this sense they are pieces of 'oral archaeology'[2] in the same sense as material archaeology is straightforward and unequivocal. Still, being an oral testimony, these linguistic phrases may have gone through changes and adjustments in the course of their transmission. But, unlike lengthy and detailed pieces of originally oral evidence, such as tales, fables and poems, which are more flexible and more prone to

---

[2] Huxley 1981: 339.

changes, it seems that proverbs and idioms are more stable. This has to do with their encapsulated and dense nature. As we shall see later, sometimes we can tell the approximate age of idioms through the dates of the written sources that quote them. Based on theories of the social and linguistic nature of proverbs and idioms, it is assumed that such phrases penetrate literary sources when they are already prevalent for long. Accordingly, they are generally older than the definite date of the quoting source we possess. If, then, we are fortunate enough to have evidence for another, later, use of the same proverbial expression, then we can be rest assured both of its old age and of its consistent durability over the ages.

Finally, the value of proverbs and idioms increases because they are one of the rare avenues that enable an access to the knowledge and concepts of popular, uneducated and illiterate sectors of Greek and Roman societies. Both their simple origin and their oral transmission emphasize their significant role within the public domain, unlike many written sources, which were kept within the narrower sectors of the educated elite.

Latin Ethnic Idioms

The following discussion intends to offer a brief study of mainly Latin ethnic idioms, meaning bywords and phrases that apply collective names of ethnic groups and associate them with fixed attributes. In analyzing the ethnic aspect of these idioms it is not always possible to separate places from their inhabitants and vice versa, because certain geographical regions prescribe in the popular mind certain human traits. In the present study this is apparent, for instance, with regard to Abdera, its air and its effect on the inhabitants' stupidity, or to Campania, its riches and the resulting arrogance of its residents (see following discussion). Despite this occasional overlap between 'geographical' and 'ethnic' proverbs, I have tried to focus mainly on proverbs that apply strictly to ethnic denominations.

Such proverbial phrases in their specific ethnological aspect usually derive from an initial encounter with foreigners that frequently becomes exaggerated and distorted through oral transmission and rumour. One may easily imagine how someone – a merchant, a soldier, an administrator – visited a certain region where he met local inhabitants or where he met people from other places; a first impression was made by physical looks or on the basis of an act or unique behaviour; this impression was shaped – immediately or eventually – into a generalization pertaining to all local inhabitants or to all people belonging to the same *ethnos* or region. In this way, proverbs and idioms repeatedly transmitted stereotypic concepts – not necessarily bad ones – in the perhaps unfair belief that all people with a particular characteristic or ethnic origin were the same.

To begin this study I have used the modern collection of A. Otto, *Die Sprichwörter und sprichwörtlichen Redensarten der Römer*.[3] This collection is arranged alphabetically and includes some references to the main occurrences of each phrase and a brief explanation. On the basis of this valuable selection, and with frequent consultation of the *CPG* (*Corpus Paroemiographorum Graecorum*),[4] I have expanded the discussion by including parallel issues and by directing the inquiry toward the topic of ethnographic beliefs and prejudices. The subsequent survey demonstrates the theme by dividing the extant Latin proverbials into groups according to types of ethnic traits displayed in them.

Physical Traits

The primary encounter with foreign and unknown nations is clearly and always made through sight. Even if one does not talk to, or trade with, or fight, or approach, other people, a visual impression is made. Accordingly, we find several proverbial expressions related to physical appearance. In Plautus' *Poenulus* ('the little Punic') Antamonides, a soldier in love with one of two Carthaginian girls, exclaims:

> Now that I'm angry I'd like my girlfriend to meet me: with my fists I'll make sure that she's black as a blackbird this instant, I'll fill her with blackness to such an extent that she's much blacker than the Egyptians (*atrior . . . quam Aegyptini*) who carry the bucket round the circus during the games. (Plaut. *Poen.* 1288–91)[5]

Egyptians thus are presented as a standard for blackness, even if the image is based not on an actual visit to Egypt but on the appearance of Egyptians who were brought to Rome and performed or worked in the circus. Perhaps these implied circumstances emphasized even more the physical difference between locals (Roman city dwellers who attended the theatre) and foreigners (Egyptian slaves). But Egyptians were not the usual symbol of dark complexion. Based on what we have available in writing, other North

---

[3] Otto 1962 [1890] reprinted in Hildesheim 1962.
[4] Leutsch and Scheidewin 1965 (reprint of 1839).
[5] Translations of Greek and Roman texts are based on the *Loeb Classical Library* ones when available, unless otherwise indicated.

Africans were more commonly used as proverbial illustrations of black or dark skin.

In the so-called Priapic erotic epigrams, a certain very repulsive girl is said to be 'no whiter than a Moor' (*non candidior puella Mauro*) (46.1). In another Priapic epigram the Moors represent elaborately curly hair when mocking a feminine male who 'primp[s] his hair with curly irons so he'd seem a Moorish maiden' (*ferventi caput ustulare ferro, ut Maurae similis foret puellae*) (45.2–3).[6] The Latin *Mauri*[7] sometimes referred specifically to the inhabitants of the region defined in ancient geographies as Mauritania, or Maurousia in Greek, which is more or less parallel to parts of modern Morocco and Algeria.[8] However, we often find the same terminology applied, especially in poetic works, to Africans in general.[9] Accordingly, the proverbial association of *Mauri* with dark skin could be understood as pertaining to the inhabitants of north-western Africa or to the inhabitants of the continent as a whole. It seems that even if the crowds had no precise geographical idea of peoples and places, the popular notion of certain groups who have black skin must have been established and transmitted.

The Latin references to Egyptians and *Mauri* as people with a darker complexion combine to form the traditional and most well-known use of *Aethiops* as the symbol of black skin already in Greek proverbial applications. The very etymology of the Greek word Αἰθίοψ, denoting a 'burnt face' (αἴθω, ὄψ), as well as the Greek idiom 'to wash an Aethiops white,'[10] must have fixed this image in the minds of the crowds, even those who had never met any person from the relevant African regions. This is quite clear, for instance, in Juvenal's contrast between 'white' and 'Aethiops' (*derideat Aethiopem albus*, Juv. 2.23).

Another unique physical trait was proverbially associated with the people of the island of Myconos. According to this popular notion, all people on the island of Myconos were bald. Strabo commented that 'some call bald men Myconians (Μυκόνιοι), from the fact that baldness is prevalent in the island' (10.5.9 and cf. Plin. *HN* 11.130). Lucilius through Donatus on verse 440 in Terence's *Hecyra*, alluding to a person from Myconos, also says: 'all young men in Myconos are bald' (*Myconi calva omnis iuventus*).[11] This notion, or image, perhaps explains another early Greek proverb related to Myconos. When Plutarch discussed the sitting order in a symposium, he commented that it is not rational to 'make no

---

[6] Translation by Hooper 1999.   [7] Lewis and Short, s.v. *Mauri*.
[8] Sall., *Jug*. 18.10; Strabo 17.3.2–8; Mela 1.4.4.   [9] Hor. *C*. 2.6.3; Juv. 10.148.
[10] Luc. *Adv. Ind*. 28; *CPG*, Zen. 1.46.   [11] Donatus ad Ter. *Hecyr*. Act 3, Scene 4, l. 440.

difference in their seats, at the first dash making the whole company one Myconos (μία Μύκονος) as they say' (*Quaest. Conv., Mor.* 2.616b), meaning, in this context, treating all as one, all alike. Why and how did Myconos of all places gain such an attention in Greek and Latin proverbs? There seems to be no historical reason, and we must leave it at that.

Character Traits

Beside ethnic proverbials for physical appearances, the largest group of Greek and Latin ethnic idioms clearly and perhaps unsurprisingly relates to character traits, and mostly unfavourable ones. So enter the typically stupid.

First, and already in earlier Greek tradition,[12] is Abdera in Thrace, which became typically proverbial for its foolish inhabitants. In several Latin contexts there is not even a need for explanation, and the mere locality indicates its prejudiced reputation; for instance, when Cicero says, *Hic Abdera non tacente me* (*Att.* 4.16.6), while reporting on some commotion in the senate when Cicero could not hold his tongue in front of what he considered sheer stupidity. Or when he says, using the Greek adjective, *id est* Ἀβδηριτικόν (*Att.* 7.7.4), commenting on some silly intentions of Pompey and his advisors. Similarly, Martial bluntly snaps at one Mucius and says: 'You have the intelligence of Abdera's rabble' (*Abderitanae pectora plebis habes*) (Mart. 10.25.4). And Juvenal says of the philosopher Democritus of Abdera that 'his wisdom shows us that men of high distinction and destined to set great examples may be born in a dense air, and in the land of fools' (Juv. 10.48–50). This fixed image prevailed even in the supposedly scientific works of Galen, who commented that '[i]n Scythia there has been only one philosopher, but in Athens many; in Abdera there are many stupid people, but in Athens few' (*Scripta Minora* 2.79). This prejudice toward the Abderitans originated in Greek discourse, but there is no hint of any special place Abdera had in Roman life. Therefore, while Abdera was not a central point on Roman routes and in imperial activities, this is a clear case of inherited proverbial expression, which carries with it inherited prejudice. The contexts and the meaning remained the same for both languages and societies.

The Boeotians were also typed as quite thick. In Cornelius Nepos' biography of Alcibiades we find this comment: 'all Boeotians devote

---

[12] Dem. 17.23 and later Luc. *Hist. Cons.* 2.

themselves to body strength more than to mental power' (*omnes enim Boeotii magis firmitati corporis quam ingenii acumini inserviunt*) (Nepos, *Alc.* 11.3). And when Horace discusses popular taste and judgment, he says:

> Call that judgment, so nice for viewing works of art, to books and to these gifts of the Muses, and you'd swear that he'd been born in Boeotia's heavy air (*Boeotum in crasso . . . aere*) (Hor. *Epist.* 2.1.241–4).

Along similar theories of deterministic environments, this idea wears a pseudoscientific robe in Cicero's *On Fate*:

> We see the wide difference between the natural characters of different localities: we notice that some are healthy, others unhealthy, that the inhabitants of some are phlegmatic and as it were overcharged with moisture, those of others parched and dried up; and there are a number of other very wide differences between one place and another. Athens has thin air, which is thought also to cause sharpness of wit above the average in the population (*acutiores putantur Attici*); at Thebes the climate is dense (*crassum*), and so the Thebans are dull and strong (*pingues et valentes*). (Cicero, *De fato*, 7)

The idea of stupid Boeotians features also in the earlier Greek expression of 'Boeotian ear' (Βοιώτιον οὖς), or, in other variations, 'Boeotian mind' (Βοιώτιον νοῦς) or 'Boeotian pig' (Βοιωτία ὗς), all pointing at a foolish behaviour.

The ear appears also in the Latin ethnic expression of 'Batavian ear', referring to the ethnos inhabiting the region of the modern Netherlands. Martial describes the reaction of a person he accidentally met in the street:

> Are you, are you really, that Martial, whose lively and naughty jests are known to everyone who has not a Batavian ear? (Mart. 6.82.4–6)

> *Tunees, tune' ait 'ille Martialis,*
> *cuius nequitias iocosque nouit*
> *aurem qui modo non habet Batauam?*

In this context, this means everyone who is not dull, simple, unrefined and graceless.[13]

In the collective and popular mind of the Romans the Abderitans and the Boeotians were stupid, but the Gauls were not so bright either. They

---

[13] Note that Erasmus adopted in the sixteenth century exactly this proverbial expression – *Auris Batava* – as the title of one of his treatises to denote his national pride and to emphasize Dutch honour and industry. See Wesseling 1993.

were depicted mainly as naïve, gullible and unsophisticated. An epigram by Martial addressed at the emperor conveys this idea:

> I will deem that you have read it, and in my pride have the joy of my Gallic trustfulness. (Mart. 5.1.9–10)

> *Ego te legisse putabo*
> *Et tumidus Galla credulitate fruar.*

Here, too, it seems that this Gallic *credulitas* was based on actual experience, as witnessed, for instance, in Julius Caesar's record of his Gallic campaigns:

> Caesar was informed of these events; and fearing the fickleness of the Gauls (*infirmitas Gallorum*), because they are capricious (*mobiles*) in forming designs and intent for the most part on change, he considered that no trust should be reposed in them. It is indeed a regular habit of the Gauls to compel travellers to halt, even against their will, and to ascertain what each of them may have heard or learnt upon every subject; and in the towns the common folk surround traders, compelling them to declare from what districts they come and what they have learnt there. Such stories and hearsay often induce them to form plans upon vital questions of which they must forthwith repent; for they are the slaves of uncertain rumours (*incertis rumoribus serviant*), and most men reply to them in fictions made to their taste. (Caesar, *BG* 4.5)

Such characterization of the Gauls as fickle, impulsive and gullible was not new. Already Polybius alluded to the frivolous nature of this ethnos.[14] If so, perhaps by Caesar's time this image has become a literary *topos* or indeed a proverbial stereotype.[15] Yet Caesar clearly relied on his experience in Gaul. How then can one separate reality from a literary *topos*? It seems to me that Caesar's description was indeed based on actual encounters with the local inhabitants. But, the interpretation of their behaviour was perhaps influenced by a set of preconceived notions deriving from current ideas which were already delivered, for instance, by Polybius. Even if Caesar has not read these sections in Polybius' *Histories*, this probably common prejudice possibly prompted him to notice and emphasize these specific traits among the Gauls.

---

[14] 'The general reputation of the Gauls' (2.7.5); 'their inordinate drinking and gluttony' (2.19.4); 'the Gaulish fickleness' (2.32.8).

[15] There is a very fine line between the nature and application of the two features of *topos* and idiom. In both linguistic structures Gauls, for instance, are fickle, but it seems that they differ in extent: an idiom delivers this idea by the mere ethnic denomination or by a short chain of words; a literary *topos* expands it into a broader image of behaviour and activity.

Then there are the typically arrogant people. Plautus comments on a certain mercenary:

> Where does he come from, do you think?
> Praeneste, probably, to judge from his boasting. (Plautus, *Bacch.* 24)
>
> *Praenestinum opino esse, ita erat gloriosus.*

So were also the people of Capua:

> Did you think you were consul of Capua . . ., a city where arrogance had once her dwelling (*domicilium quondam superbiae fuit*), or of Rome, a state where all consuls before you have bowed to the will of the senate? (Cicero, *Post reditum in senatu*, 7.17)

And again in another speech of Cicero:

> Capua . . . the abode of pride and the seat of luxury (Cicero, *De leg. Agr.* 2.97)
>
> *Capuae in domicilio superbiae atque in sedibus luxuriosis . . .*

Why Praeneste and Capua? The last reference ties this trait with the city's riches and luxury, and both are known to have been prosperous; this probably was explained in the popular concept the arrogance of their residents.

Campanian arrogance was also proverbial. Cicero speaks of *illa Campanorum arrogantia* (*De leg. agr.* 2.33.9), of the *Campanum supercilium* (*De leg. agr.* 34.93) and of the 'always proud Campanians' (*Campani semper superbi*) (*De leg. agr.* 35.95). This specific image and stereotype perhaps resulted from the proverbially very fruitful region of Campania, as it was coined in the proverb denoted as *vulgo dictum*:

> Campania produces more ointments than other countries do oil.
>
> *Plus apud Campanos unguenti, quam apud ceteros olei .* (Plin., *HN* 18.111)

All these arrogant people – the inhabitants of Praeneste, Capua and Campania – lived on the Italian peninsula not very far from Rome; but Latin proverbials typed also the people of Rhodes as symbols of arrogance, perhaps again due to their high economic status. Accordingly, Cato the Elder seems to have relied on such common notions when he commented that 'they say that the Rhodians are proud' (*Rhodienses superbos esse aiunt*) (Gellius, 6.3.50). The *aiunt* here emphasizes the inauthoritative and probably popular provenance of this characterization. Note that Cato went on to say: 'but in what does their pride affect us? Would it become us to impute it to them as a crime that they are prouder than we are?', meaning that in this case Cato has not succumbed to negative notions associated with prejudice. Still dwelling on the arrogance of the Rhodians, we see that in Plautus the association of a certain pompous person specifically with Rhodes seems to be not just a geographical indication. The context reveals that the essence of *Rhodius* contributes to the overall description and portrayal of the man:

> A fellow rolling in wealth, a mighty military man, from Rhodes, a ravager of foemen, a braggart (*magnus miles Rhodius, raptor hostium, gloriosus*). (Plaut. *Epid.* 300–1)

In Latin proverbs there were nations typed as thieves and frauds. First and foremost are the Punics. There is no need to expand here on *Punica Fides* – whole chapters are devoted to stereotyped profiles of this ethnic group in both Isaac's *The Invention of Racism* and Gruen's *Rethinking the Other*.[16] But the Punics were not alone. The people of Crete were conceived as liars and cheaters:

> Well known is that I sing of: Crete, that holds a hundred cities, cannot deny this, liar though she be. (Ov. *AA* 1.297–8)

> *Nota cano: non hoc, centum quae sustinet urbes,*
> *Quamvis sit mendax, Creta negare potest.*

> The Cretans will be my witness – and the Cretans are not wholly false. (Ov. *Am.* 3.10.19)

> *Cretes erunt testes – nec fingunt omnia Cretes.*

Clearly, these two Ovidian citations apply the people of Crete as supporters of truth. But it is the very use of them as a standard that proves the inherent prejudice.

Local Habits

Besides the typing of nations and inhabitants of specific places as having typical character traits, there were bywords alluding to local habits and norms of life as they were grasped in popular and thus proverbial perception. Accordingly, the men of Massilia were somewhat feminine. The servant in Plautus' comedy says to the old man:

---

[16] Isaac 2004: 324–51; Gruen 2011: 115–40.

> Where are you – you who think to practice Massilian customs here?
> (Plautus, *Cas.* 963)
>
> *Ubi tu es, qui colere mores Massilienses postulas?*

We do not know what these Massilian customs, *mores Massilienses*, were. The context in Plautus' comedy implies that his audience did know and understand the pun, but we need Athenaeus' explanation:

> The Iberians go out dressed in elaborate robes that resemble those worn in tragedy, and wear tunics that hang to their feet, although this has no negative effect on their strength in war. The Massaliotes, on the other hand, who wear the same costume as the Iberians, became effeminate. The weakness and addiction to luxury in their hearts, at any rate, has led to them behaving in an ugly way and allowing themselves to be treated like women, hence the proverb 'I hope you sail to Massalia!' (πλεύσειας εἰς Μασσαλίαν). (Athenaeus 12.523 C)

And this, of course, is not a nice wish.

In his biography of Pyrrhus, Plutarch depicts the atmosphere in Tarentum at the time of the Pyrrhic war and describes the behaviour of the inhabitants at these pressing times:

> [T]hey remained at home in the enjoyment of their baths and social festivities . . . as they strolled about, they fought out their country's battles in talk . . . Many therefore left the city, since they were not accustomed to being under orders, and called it servitude not to live as they pleased. (Plut. *Pyrrh.* 16.2)

No wonder then that this city gained the reputation of a spoiled city, the seat of luxury, and was proverbially typed as 'soft Tarentum':

> Small things become small folks: imperial Rome is all too large, too bustling for a home; the empty heights of Tibur, or the bay of soft Tarentum (*molle Tarentum*), more are in my way. (Hor. *Sat.* 2.4.34)

And,

> insolent Tarentum, garlanded and sodden with wine (*coronatum et petulans madidumque Tarentum*). (Juv. 6.297)

Persian splendour too, was famous and stereotypic but all the more hated:

> Persian elegance, my lad, I hate. (Hor. *C.* 1.38.1)
>
> *Persicos odi, puer, apparatus.*

And, the Parthians were proverbially drunk:

> The more the Parthians drank, the thirstier they became. (Pliny, *HN* 14.148)

> *quanto plus biberint, tanto magis sitire Parthos.*

The Good Traits

So far we have seen that all nations included in these examples were typed with certain characteristics, mostly unflattering as contexts and internal intonations reveal: the simplicity of the Gauls is not cute, and the Parthian drunkenness and Massilian femininity are not attractive. Weren't any nations stereotypically and proverbially marked for their good traits? There were, in fact, mainly two.

The Athenians, for instance, were presented as loyal: Velleius Paterculus speaks of the behaviour of the Athenians in Sulla's times:

> So constant was the loyalty (*fides*) of the Athenians towards the Romans that always and invariably, whenever the Romans referred to any act of unqualified loyalty (*sincera fides*), they called it an example of 'Attic faith'. (Vell. Pat. 2.23)

Other proverbial expressions available in Latin texts reveal that the Romans thought the Athenians were also very sharp and clever:

> I'll give you a good six hundred witticisims for a dowry, and all Attic ones, without a single Sicilian quip among them. (Plautus, *Pers.* 394–5)

> *Dabuntur dotis tibi inde sescenti logi,*
> *Atque Attici omnes; nullum Siculum acceperis.*

Or, in Cicero:

> You observe that the old flow of wit and humour (*urbanitas*) has quite dried up, which fully justifies our friend Pomponius in saying: 'Were it not that we, we few, conserve the ancient Attic glory'. (*Ad fam.* 7.31.2)

> *vides enim exaruisse iam veterem urbanitatem, ut Pomponius noster suo iure possit dicere: 'nisi nos pauci retineamus gloriam antiquam Atticam'.*

Martial also speaks of 'witty stories touched with Attic grace' (*lepore tinctos Attico sales*) (Mart. 3.20.9) and of Attic wit, *Cecropius lepos* (Mart. 4.23.6).

Romans were, of course, even more brilliant than the Athenians, but the Attic wit is still the standard for measuring it:

There is your wit, not Attic, but more pungent than that of Attic writers –
the good old city wit of Rome. (Cicero, *Ad fam.* 9.15.2)

*Accedunt non Attici, sed salsiores, quam illi Atticorum, Romani veteres
atque urbani sales.*

And it became a proud coinage that 'A Roman wins while sitting'
(*Romanus sedendo vincit*) (Varro *RR* 1.2.2), perhaps originating in the
delaying policy of Fabius Maximus in the second Punic war but then
becoming the constant praise of the invincible Romans.

Ennius is said to have stated that 'The Roman state stands by its ancient
manners and its men' (*Moribus antiquis res stat Romana virisque*) (Ennius,
Annales, F 500 Vahlen). This Roman manner or character – *mos Romanus /
mos Romanorum* – is mentioned in several contexts which do not allow for
any other understanding than an admirable and honorable one, that of
honesty and integrity:

Cicero, *Ad fam.* 7.5.3 (To Julius Caesar)
I would beg you, dear Caesar, to receive him with such a display of
kindness as to concentrate on his single person all that you can be possibly
induced to bestow for my sake upon my friends. As for him I guarantee –
not in the sense of that stale expression of mine, at which, when I used it in
writing to you about Milo, you very properly jested, but in the Roman
manner (*more Romano*) such as sober men use – that no honester, better,
or more modest man exists.

Cicero, *Ad fam.* 7.16.3 (To C. Trebatius Testa)
Balbus has assured me that you will be rich. Whether he speaks in the
Roman manner (*Romano more*), meaning that you will be well supplied
with money, or according to the Stoic dictum, that 'all are rich who can
enjoy the sky and the earth', I shall know later.

Discussion

Prejudice and idioms should not be confused with each other: one is
a social phenomenon, the other is a mode of expression. Let us explain.
Prejudice originates in reality which, through exaggeration, generalization
and misunderstanding, becomes stereotypical and frequently malicious.
Thus, when Latin sources refer to Jewish missionary tendencies (Hor., *Sat.*,
1.4.142–3), to the credulity of the Jews (Hor., *Sat.*, 1.5.100) or to their
laziness (Tac., *Hist.*, 15.4.3), they promote prejudice.[17] But, in all these

---

[17] For a comprehensive collection of Greek and Latin views of Jews, see Stern 1974–84.

examples, and many others, the assertion of these biases is stylistically fluid, and even if identical or similar details are applied, they do not become part of fixed modes of expression or even proverbs. The mere ethnic denomination *Iudaeus* does not represent a whole set of often intolerant ideas. At the same time, idioms and proverbial expressions, like prejudice, also originate in reality which, through exaggeration, generalization and misunderstanding, become stereotypical and frequently malicious, but this similarity is due to the fact that ethnic idioms simply contain prejudiced notions. Again, the Jews are a point in argument, for there seem to be no idioms or proverbial expressions related to Jews.

The sociological function of ethnic bywords is similar to that of ethnic jokes:

> Ethnic jokes delineate the social, geographical and moral boundaries of a nation or ethnic group. By making fun of peripheral or ambiguous groups they reduce ambiguity and clarify boundaries or at least make ambiguity appear less threatening.[18]

It seems then that the perspective of the society which coins such idioms (or jokes) is aimed primarily from inside out, reflecting how foreigners and outsiders are seen. At the same time, however, this ethnographic gaze may be interpreted as stemming from an upper position downwards, because foreigners are mostly associated with bad traits, and, specifically in Latin proverbs, there are no 'bad' idioms involving the Romans. These observations are perhaps unsurprising, but they show once again that such ethnic idioms are more revealing of the society which coins them than of the ethnic groups reflected in them.

The ethnic groups introduced in Latin idioms, as discussed in the present study, are all inhabitants of the Roman Empire. If we place them on a map, some patterns emerge. Four phrases refer to North African nations including the Egyptians; four refer to the further east: Indians, Arabians, Parthians and Persians; three deal with people of Asia Minor; four deal with dwellers of four Mediterranean islands; but twelve concentrate on the Italian peninsula and eleven refer to the inhabitants of mainland Greece. Clearly, the geo-ethnic centre gains more attention. The farthest nations in these proverbials are the Indians in the East; the Scythians, Gauls and Batavians in the North; the Ethiopians in the South; and the people of Massilia in the West.[19] The

---

[18] Davies 1982: 383.

[19] We have not discussed them in detail, but there are three seemingly self-explanatory idioms related to edge nations: *Indorum gemmae* – jewels of the Indians; *Arabum divitiae* – riches of the Arabians; *Scytharum solitudines* – isolation of the Scythians.

emerging picture is thus a reflection of centre and periphery, the centre composed of the Italian peninsula and mainland Greece together. Then there is a nearer periphery – north Africa, Massilia, Gaul and Asia Minor, and a remote periphery – Scythians, Indians, Parthians and Arabians.

This division between centre and mostly remote periphery represents not only geographical distribution of proverbial nations but also a difference in the essence of proverbial prejudice and image. The nearer nations and inhabitants are typed mostly with personal attributes such as deception, arrogance and stupidity – all qualities which are usually perceived through actual acquaintance and perhaps even specifically through interactions related to trade: one may grasp whether or not the person he transacts with is devious and dishonest, or is too proud about himself or about his merchandise, or is stupid and gullible in handling such transactions.[20] The remote peripheral nations, by comparison, are typed more with exceptional habits or unusual local conditions, which seem extraordinary to the Greek and Roman observers, such as extreme riches, relatively unique skin colour or what is seen as uncivilized customs. In all likelihood, the emergence of such proverbial prejudice is based less on direct and frequent encounters and more on rare visits which produced popular rumours and exaggerated images.

Finally, and although part of a work still in progress, it seems that in comparison to Latin ethnic proverbials, Greek ethnic idioms are, first, more numerous; second – and unsurprisingly – their geographical centre is situated more to the east on mainland Greece and Asia Minor and less on the western Mediterranean and northern Europe. A third point is that, evidently, the Romans inherited from the Greeks some of their world of prejudices but incorporated them in their geographically and ethnically wider world where there was also a slight shift in geographical focus. The old world, so to speak, became integrated with the new world.

Conclusion

The study of idioms and proverbial expressions opens up the gate leading to the ethnic notions of the relatively inaccessible analphabetic or illiterate sectors of ancient society.[21] Thus, from the point of view of the Romans, 'others' were located anywhere in the inhabited known earth. At the same time, ethnographic interest turned either to neighbouring and well-known

[20] Isaac has noted another geographical pattern in this ethnic prejudice: people in northern Italy are depicted as arrogant, while people in the south are conceived as thieves. See Isaac 2004.
[21] On illiterate geography, in proverbs as well, see Dueck 2021.

people or to remote groups dwelling at the fringes of the world. The first, closer, group was so familiar that its members became the focus of mockery and 'familiarity bred contempt' (after Aesop). The second, remote, group was so distant and unknown that its members became typed as strange and eccentric.

The emerging picture is first and foremost revealing of the Roman character; and it becomes clear, even if unsurprising, that, in a typical way of dealing with unknown people, the Romans, too, looked at them from inside out and kept these stereotypes as an integral part of their world view and self-identity.

4 | Keti, Son of Maswalat

Ethnicity and Empire

BRENT D. SHAW

To the extent that an historian can justifiably use the slippery concept of personal identity, it is usually conceded that an amalgam of various social roles and recursive human behaviors is involved. The problems then quickly multiply.[1] How many of these roles or behaviors were available to an individual in any specific circumstance? And how were the given or selected roles mobilized and in what contexts? To begin to answer these questions, we must attempt to determine the range of inherited and arbitrary items assigned to a person as opposed to the number of more voluntarily adopted and assumed cultural roles and resources – elements out of which an individual formed his or her own identity and had it shaped by others. Even where the choice of one element was possible – for example, an adult who embraced the new faith of Christianity – one is still faced with decoding the circumstances governing the salience of this identity over any others. In what circumstances might the new Christian choose or not choose to forefront his or her new religious affiliation? We are then compelled to explain why the particular salience exists in that circumstance.[2] In many cases, especially in complex ones that traverse significant lengths of time, an individual was not always essentially person 'x' or person 'y' but rather, to use one possible example, an adult, a man, a father, a Roman (citizen or not), a Gaul, a Trevir, a soldier, a Christian, a veteran, a farmer, a municipal magistrate, or, more likely, some combination of these by turn. What is being considered here is not some high-flown Barthian theory about ethnic boundaries. What is being envisaged, rather, is a series of more tangible aspects of social existence that allow persons to define themselves and others to identify them.[3] Among these

---

[1] This brief investigation into one man's ethnic identity in the Roman empire is offered in gratitude to Ben Isaac whose research into army and frontiers, into race and ethnicity, and other important facets of Roman imperial history, have been a constant inspiration and an incitement to better scholarship. Above all, it is to the generous and decent man himself that it is dedicated with great affection.

[2] I am thinking, especially, of the arguments of Brubaker 2004, notably but not only in that work; for the specific application of his ideas to the case of Christians in north Africa, see Rebillard 2012.

[3] I forebear from repeating the now massive bibliography on the subject. For an historian's point of view, I find the resume and positions staked out by Halsall 2007: 35–45, to be reasonable,

items, a recent historical analysis relevant to our time has listed the following ones: language, arms and modes of fighting, costume, bodily styles (e.g. hair arrangements), cuisine, and similar cultural attributes.[4] One can easily think of other less material items such as traditional occupation and religious adherence. Given precise contextual factors, only some of these are properly construed as ethnic in nature. Even of this limited number, most usually converge in a configuration that identify one as a specific kind of person, like a centurion in the Roman army as opposed to one who has a linguistic-kinship-locational ethnic identity, like Numidian or Gaetulian. But the two could easily reinforce each other, as when a Musulamian man served in the First Flavian Cohort of the Musulamii. Such restrictive conventions are complicated by the liberal use of metaphor. Christians, for example, conceived of themselves as a 'new race' or *ethnos*.[5] For many persons in the Roman Empire beginning in the later first and early second centuries, but not before, a new potential identity had been created. Further to complicate the metaphor, men and women who were or became Christians began deploying familial models of power and a broad kinship terminology to express their relationship to an all-powerful god who was a father to his children. Christians as Christians became persons who were one another's brothers and sisters. So even salience has problems with it. A restricted emphasis for a person – 'I am (in essence) a Musulamus' – can work if he can front or parade certain aspects of personhood while telling other ones to get lost or at least to hide in the closet for a while. Some given aspects of our personhood, however, are so durable that doing this is difficult. They might not accept the repudiation.

As has been perceptively noted, 'in a multinational empire whose makeup was multiple, heterogeneous, unequal, and sometimes hostile and badly integrated, the identity of each individual was inherently complex'.[6] In making these remarks, Veyne suggests that the forming of personal identity, including civic or ethnic identities, was complicated by the very existence of the Roman Empire. An exemplary case has been provided for Africa by the interrogation of a witness before Zenophilus, the Roman governor of Numidia, in the year 320. Court appearances, after all, were one of the contexts that hailed forth assertions of who one was.

---

although do not think that I am as committed to as purely imaginative a construction of ethnicity as he seems to be.

[4] Pohl 1998: 17–69.

[5] Most forcefully explicated, perhaps, by Buell 2005, with an emphasis on race.

[6] Veyne 1999/2005: 237, although on another culture/identity problematic.

Asked to identify himself, the man declared: 'I am a teacher of Roman literature, a Latin grammarian; my father is a decurion here in the city of Constantina, my grandfather was a soldier who served in the imperial *comitatus*, and our family is descended from Maurian blood.'[7] So: occupational profession, inherited civic status, inherited military status, and ethnic lineage; each of them was an element configured by Roman imperial power. The variations and permutations necessarily proliferate. I would therefore like to focus on a single case of ethnicity that illustrates some of the problems. The man's life is significant because his ethnicity was strongly implicated in the various identities that were created and offered to individuals by the Roman imperial state. His career has already received some attention but, I believe, it still poses a series of interpretive problems that make him deserving of more. His life is a manifest instance where the Roman imperial state, a complex and powerful institution, helped, by the use and application of its cultural and administrative categories, to create new possible identities. Let us first consider the bilingual Latin/palaeo-Tamazight inscription on our man's gravestone found at the town of Thullium (modern Kef beni Feredj), directly north of Madauros in the proconsular province of Africa (see Fig. 4.1).[8]

Latin Text

> C(aius) Iulius Gae[tu]|lus vet(eranus) donis | donatis torqui/bus et armillis | dimissus et in civit(ate) | sua Thullio flam(en) | perp(etuus), vix(it) an(nis) LXXX / h(ic) s(itus) e(st)[9]

> Gaius Julius Gaetulus, veteran soldier, having been awarded the honors/ military decorations of torques (neck bands) and armillae (arm bands), and having received an honorable discharge from the army, held the post of Perpetual Flamen in his own hometown of Thullium. He lived 80 years. He is buried here.

---

[7] *Gesta apud Zenophilum*, 1 (CSEL 26: 185); see Modéran 2004: 264; 2008: 119–20; see Shaw 2014: 537.

[8] For location, see *Atl. arch.* f. 9 (Bône) no. 242; on the name, see Lepelley 1981: 224–5, who prefers to follow Gsell in ILAlg. 1, p. 14, in calling the town Thullio; further on location see: Desanges et al. 2010: s.v. 'Thullio', p. 262, who also prefer Thullio to Thullium, while allowing that 'Thullio parait être l'abl.-loc. d'un typonyme *Thullium*'.

[9] RIL 146 = CIL 8.5209 = ILAlg. 1.137 (Kef beni Feredj, *Atl. arch.* f. 9, no. 242). I have considered this text in the context of an analysis of ethnicity in Africa (Shaw 2014: 531–2). Of necessity, some of the remarks made there will be reprised here.

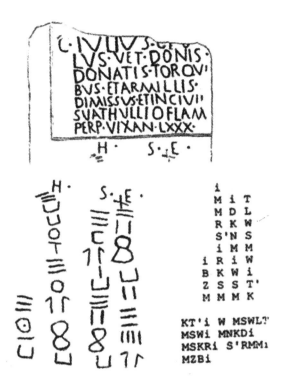

Figure 4.1 Tombstone of Gaius Julius Gaetulus / Keti son of Maswalat. From Chabot, *Recueil des inscriptions Libyques*, no. 146.

Palaeo-Tamazight Text

KT'i W MSWLT | MSWi MNKDi | MSKRi S'RMMi | MZBi[10]

Keti, son of Maswalat, the servant/soldier of the supreme chief/king, from (the tribe of) the Misiciri, from (the subtribe of) the Saremmi, / high priest [?]

The Latin text on the gravestone set up for our man tells us that the deceased named in in the epitaph, Gaius Julius Gaetulus, was a decorated veteran of the Roman army who returned to his home town where he held

---

[10] The script of these inscriptions has conventionally been called 'Libyan' and the language they represent 'Libyan', and so on. Even though this practice has been followed in all publications to the present, I am breaking with it here. The label is somewhat misleading in its implications, both ancient and modern. The indigenous language reflected in these texts is manifestly an early form of the language currently designated as Tamazight – the language of the indigenous inhabitants of North Africa. I shall therefore simply designate the language and the script used to write it as 'palaeo-Tamazight' until some more appropriate term is found. It could equally be called proto- or palaeo-Tifinagh. See Kerr 2008: esp. 46, on the existence of some type of continuity, which must surely be the case, despite the abundance of caution shown by Kerr and others.

the high-ranking priesthood of *flamen perpetuus* in its municipal hierarchy. Gaetulus' military decorations reveal that he received some of the imperial army's most prestigious awards. The *dona militaria* of armbands and neck torcs were awarded only to Roman citizens.[11] Almost certainly a citizen from birth, as indicated by his *tria nomina*, our man probably served in one of the legions of the imperial army, perhaps (but not necessarily) the Legio III Augusta in Africa itself.[12] In the other text on the same stone, which is inscribed in the palaeo-Tamazight script, this same man is called KT'i son of MSWLT, Keti son of Maswalat, an 'imperial servant' or 'soldier of the emperor' from the people of the Misiciri, from the sub-people of the S'RMMi.[13] His personal name and his larger community identity in the African language are completely different from his public face in the Latin text on the same stone. About when did Keti die and to when does his gravestone date? Some think as early as the late first century. Given the rate at which novel elements in the formal language and abbreviated elements in funerary epitaphs developed and then penetrated the more remote highland zones, however, it seems more likely that we are considering a date in the early to mid second century.[14]

[11] Maxfield 1981: 88–91.

[12] Few recruits of the legion are explicitly attested from this region. In all of the recruiting inscriptions known for the III Augusta, only five are known from 'Hippo Regius', which designation probably included the whole *territorium* subject to the colony: see 'Origins of Recruits of Legio Tertia Augusta', Table 2A in Shaw 1983: 145–6; but 'African Recruits for Army Units Outside Africa', Table 3, *ibid.*: 147, reveals only a single case known from the region of Hippo Regius; Le Bohec 1989: 223, agrees that there is no compelling evidence for his service in the III Augusta.

[13] Rebuffat 2005: at 203; the vocalization of the man's name, as well as that of the sub-tribe to which he belonged is somewhat speculative. Chabot 1940: 38, though it should be Kafa son of Maswalat. Maswalat seems to be the closest that we can get to the father's name (so Chabot 1940: 38, based on a Punic transcription). There are also close analogues in neo-Punic texts from the region, such as the Masiwal son of Shal from Henchir Medid: Jongeling 2008: 151, Hr. Meded, no. 18. For the Misiciri, we are reasonably certain from the transcription found in Latin inscriptions. The 'KT' could be Keti, which I have (very provisionally) accepted as a reasonable possibility: see Shaw 2014: 531–2, based on the existence of African ethnonyms like the Ketianoi (Ptolemy, 4.6.6; see also Desanges 2005). But something like Kuti or Kouti/Kouta seems just as likely: there are ethnic group names like Kut/Kout; and Latinized African names in our own highland like Coutz- or Koutz (in Greek). The *gens u-Koutamani* from the mountainous Col de Fdoulès region to the west: CIL 8.20216 (= 8379) and the better edition by Cagnat 1892: 489; cf. Shaw 1991: 40–1 (and notes), probably to be related to the Koidamousioi of Ptolemy, 4.2.5; and the personal name Cotuzan in our sample. I accept Rebuffat's transcription of the final sign of his first name with a lower case –i- rather than an H (Chabot) or an –ʿ- (Galand); see Rebuffat 2006: 267–8, for the justification.

[14] Rebuffat 2005: 194, argues for a late first century CE date; and it very probably dates before Caracalla, when military decorations of the type awarded to our Gaetulus were largely discontinued by the state. The first rather than the second century has been argued based on

Manifestly Gaetulus' identity involved a number of locational factors that can be specified. First among them was his home town of Thullium. Then followed the larger region of the Cheffia, the highland lying to the southeast of Hippo Regius in which Thullium was located (see map Fig. 4.2). Further encapsulating both the Cheffia and Hippo was a larger region lying west of the frontiers of the old republican province of Africa which, for convenience, we might call either eastern Numidia or western Proconsularis.[15] Parts of the latter large region were far western extensions of the Khoumirie (Kroumirie) highlands, while other parts of it stretched further southward and westward, ringing the southern horizon of the Hippo plain.[16] The highlands are sometimes referred to as 'the mountains of the Medjerda'. They are one of the few micro-zones in the Maghrib east of the Atlas in Morocco that boast a higher than average rainfall, indeed among the highest in all of North Africa. An intensive mixed arboriculture has traditionally been the backbone of the rural economy, distinguishing it from the preference for cereal culture in the plains lying below the high-lands. The rural economy in Roman antiquity appears to have shared this same distinction between highland and plains regions in this part of Africa. It is not accidental, I think, that the one detailed epigraphical text suggesting agricultural development in the lands near Thullium concerns a Lucius Arrius Amabilianus, an arboriculturalist. Like our Gaetulus, he was a *flamen perpetuus*, probably in the same municipality of Thullium.[17] The octogenarian Amabilianus boasts of having established his *domus* and having improved its economic well-being. He laid out an orchard with apple trees and provided it with a well, and then he set out a second orchard of fruit trees that he furnished with a water reservoir and a well. Amabilianus was another hard-working *bonus agricola* of the time who rightly boasted of the improvements that he made to his patrimony.[18]

---

the nominative of the name, the absence of DM/S and the formula HSE – for which criteria, see Lassère 1973: chart, p. 120, and 123–9. Mountain areas, however, probably experienced some temporal 'drag' in the taking up of lowland styles.

[15] See Camps 1993b.

[16] Despois and Raynal 1967: 167–72; 236–7; for the western Khoumirie, part of this same forested region, see Bonniard 1934: 103–5; 219–32 (rainfall); 297–302 (forest cover); 393–400 (rural economy); 439–42 (density of population: densest in premodern Tunisia).

[17] *ILAlg.* 1.158 (about 6 km SSW of the site of Thullium); inscription on the cover of a sarcophagus. The text is rather difficult to decipher, perhaps because it was incised by a stoneworker who did not have a good knowledge of Latin. Amabilianus' age is recorded twice, from which it seems reasonably certain that he died at the age of 80 years, 3 months and some days.

[18] The others are considered in Shaw 2013, 66–8; he is very much like the good tree-planting farmer from Uppenna (*ILTun.* 243), also an octogenarian; and another from Biha Bilta (AE 1975: 853), also a digger of wells and cisterns; see Stone 1998: 103–13. Our man, Amabilianus, should be added to his list.

Arboricultural crops appear to have been the ones of which he was especially proud.

Since both Gaetulus and Amabilianus held municipal priesthoods, we might ask when and how the municipalization of the region, and therefore of Gaetulus' home town of Thullium, took place. Far to the northwest an Augustan colony was established at Hippo Regius, and a little further away to the south the Flavian emperors founded a colony of veteran soldiers at Madauros. But these were exceptional Roman settlements made by the direct intervention of the Roman state. Otherwise, Thullium was right in the middle of a zone that was remote in terms of Roman municipal development. The closest municipal centers were located on the periphery of a fifty-mile radius extending outwards from Thullium: Hippo Regius to the northwest, Thuburnica to the southeast, and Thagaste to the southwest. There was no known move to formal Roman municipal status made by any of the towns in the Cheffia highlands throughout the whole period of the high empire. We must therefore suspect that the advancement of Thullium to formal municipal status took place – if it happened at all – in the later empire.[19] Just how far the forming of municipal institutions eventually proceeded and what the process meant in the highlands is difficult to say. A comparable village in a similar highland environment at Henchir Aïn Tella (ancient Castellum Ma [. . .] rensium), in the far western Khoumirie to the north of Thullium, was still governed by *seniores* or a council of elders as late as the age of the Tetrarchs.[20] Generally speaking, then, it seems that the communities in the mountainous highlands from which Gaius Julius Gaetulus came were not as intensely connected with the main patronal resources of the empire. They were not able to develop the costly apparatus of urban Romanity sufficiently to convince governors or emperors that they were worthy of elevation to colonial or municipal status. In this fashion, the political ecology of the region determined elements of the identity of its inhabitants.

If the important colonial harbour city of Hippo Regius was only about forty kilometers from Thullium as the crow flies, the experiential distance was considerable. The accidence of the terrain and the heavily forested environment contributed to a palpable sense of difference from the

---

[19] Gascou 1972 records nothing in these highland regions up to the end of the Severan period; for late municipalization, see Gascou 1982: 270–2 for the region in general and 285–6 for Thullium in particular.

[20] CIL 8.17327 (Hr. Aïn Tella, 209–305 CE); see Shaw 1991: 36–7 for analysis; its local economy was probably based on a similar highland arboriculture economy, as the dedication to Mercury would seem to indicate.

metropolitan world of a well-connected Mediterranean sea port. Even within the Cheffia, Gaetulus' village of Thullium was a satellite outlier, being located towards the northwestern periphery of the region. As such, it was much closer to the outer eastern periphery of the Hippo Regius region than to the subzone of the Bagrada (the modern Medjerda) river valley to the south. If Thullium was most probably still a simple *civitas* at the time that Gaius Julius Gaetulus served in the army, we know that its inhabitants were gradually adopting Roman norms. Formal municipalization was slow, only coming in the later empire when similar small towns were achieving higher status in the flush of what can be called a late imperial rural 'boom economy' in Africa. In the early fifth century, the village was known to Augustine, the Catholic Christian bishop of Hippo. He referred to Thullium and to a man there with the African name of Kurma who was a *curialis* of the municipality.[21] Augustine's words are rhetorically construed (for him, Kurma's unusual life-and-death experience was being used as an example), but they strongly suggest that to be a member of the town council of Thullium and to be in the ranks of its *duoviri* did not require particularly great wealth.

The ethnic group of the Misiciri to which Gaetulus belonged is one of the better-attested 'tribal' entities in Roman-period North Africa.[22] By studying the distribution of inscriptions in both palaeo-Tamazight and Latin, or ones that were bilingual, using both languages simultaneously, it is possible to plot the region in which the people who identified themselves as Misiciri lived. Their distribution on a map (see Fig. 4.3) shows that their region was a zone between the Bagrada valley and hilly lands to the south and the coastal plain inland of Hippo Regius to the northwest. If there were long-term interactions between the inhabitants of the Cheffia and their environment, it is hardly surprising that they came to share common identities. The peoples inhabiting the region would have shared a common distinctive environment in which they lived and worked. The larger montane zone consists of distinctive subzones, and so it is speculatively possible to identify five major subgroups of which the Misiciri were formed and to map their locations in the highlands of the Cheffia.[23] The concentrated location of inscriptions belonging to each subgroup argues in favor of an ecological component in its formation and identity. Each seems to be

---

[21] Aug. *De cura pro mort. gerend.* 12.15 (CSEL 41: 644; conventionally dated to c. 422 CE): *Homo quidam Curma nomine, municipii Tulliensis, quod Hipponi proximum est, curialis pauper, vix illius loci duumviralicius et simpliciter rusticanus* . He appears to have been related to another Curma (of the same name) who was the town blacksmith, a *faber ferrarius*.

[22] Camps 1993a: 113–26; and 'Les Misiciri,' in 1960, 248–50 and maps figs. 26–7.

[23] As argued by Camps 2002: 141–7.

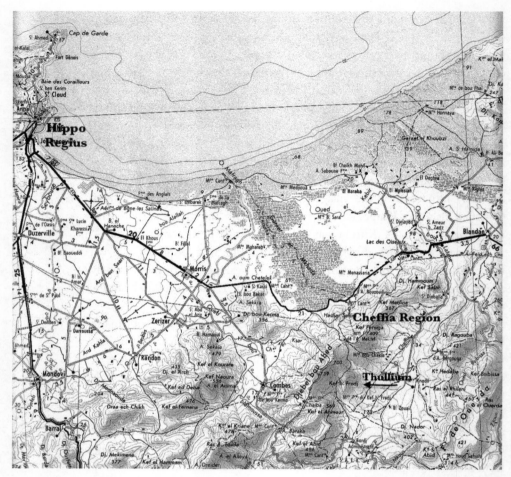

Figure 4.2 The Hippo Regius Region: Hippo Regius and Thullium. Based on IGN 1960 'Carte d'Algérie' 1:200.000.

located within a fairly well-defined territory that was formed by a valley – that is, by distinctive mountain and riverine confines.[24] What is more, if the ecology of these regions in the Roman past resembled that of the later nineteenth and early twentieth centuries (which I have no reason to doubt), then the dense habitation of the mountain highlands was matched by an intense fragmentation of ethnic identity. In addition to the five subgroups of the Misiciri, seven other ethnic groups have been identified in the highlands immediately adjacent to the Cheffia. Most probably, like the

---

[24] Camps 1960: map, fig. 26; argument p. 250; Camps 1993a: map fig. 3: 'Les cinq clans ou fractions des Misiciri.'

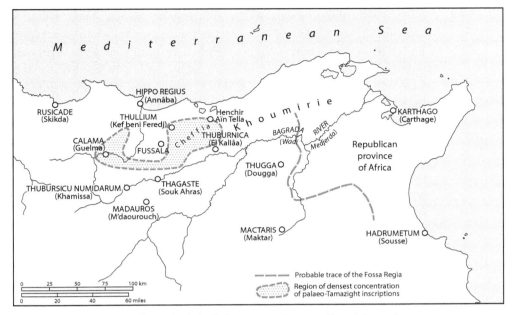

Figure 4.3 Proconsular Africa: The 'Cheffia' Region in Context. Copyright: author.

subsections of the Misiciri, they were local groups of the much larger peoples collectively named the Numidae.[25]

Having been raised in this ecology, who was our Gaetulus? Was he was a high-ranking Roman citizen, a soldier in the Roman army named Gaius Iulius Gaetulus? Or was he Keti son of Maswalat from the tribe of the Misiciri, from the subtribe of the S'RMMi? Almost certainly he was both at the same time. He was like the man from Gaul who boasted on his tombstone found at Aquincum on the Danube: "I am a citizen of the Franks and a Roman soldier under arms.'".[26] Like many Gauls and Germans serving the empire, this man maintained a bifurcated identity. One was local and the other imperial, the second being determined by the existence of the empire and its army. Gaius Julius Gaetulus was like the Roman citizen from Tarsus who called himself Paulus. Several times Paul insisted on his possession of the Roman citizenship before high-ranking

---

[25] Rebuffat 2006: 269–73, has proffered good arguments for the existence of seven additional ethnonyms for groups found in highlands immediately adjacent to the west and south of the Cheffia: the NGRi, NMRSi, NNBYi, NM&Ni, NMGNWi, NZDBi and the NTBBi – all of whom appear to be ethnic subgroups of peoples who were otherwise called Numidae.

[26] CIL 3.3576 = ILS 2814 (Aquincum): *Francus ego cives Romanus miles in armis | egregia virtute tuli bello mea dextera sem(p)er*; see James 1988: 42 (as most often in the citation of this item, however, with the wrong CIL reference; as still in Mathisen (2018), p. 60 n. 39).

officials of the imperial state. At the same time, he was Saul, a man who self-identified before his fellow Jews as Jewish, a descendant of Abraham from the tribe of Benyamîn, and belonging to a family of strict Pharisaic upbringing.[27] A special aspect of Gaius Julius/Keti's split identity is that it was not new to him. It had been maintained over a number of generations. The original citizenship of Gaetulus' remote male ancestor, and hence Keti's own *praenomen* and *nomen* of Gaius Julius, almost certainly dated to the time of Julius Caesar. That ancestor had probably received land and citizenship from the great generalissimo in the mid-40s BCE as a reward for military service. A precise date for our inscription is difficult to specify with any certainty, but we have argued earlier that some point in the early to mid second century makes the most sense of all of the evidence. If so, our Gaetulus was part of a family that had connections with individuals and institutions that were Roman for about two centuries (possibly more if there were Marian antecedents in his line of armed service). But let us say, provisionally, that we are looking at approximately two centuries. Assuming an arbitrary calculation of about thirty years to a generation, our Gaetulus was part of a family whose service connections with Rome (or, at very least, Roman citizen identity) had continued through no less than five to six generations. We are fortunate to have evidence of another man from Thullium who did army service and who also bore the name of Maswalat. Having served in the Roman army, like our Keti, he is similarly called a 'servant of the great chief' (i.e. the Roman emperor). There is a considerable likelihood that his Roman name was also Gaius Julius. If not these names, however, he surely bore the Roman *tria nomina*. But this Maswalat, despite having had the same army service as Keti, had all of his identity recorded solely in his native language and in words taken from his own African tongue to describe his imperial service.[28]

As shown previously all by his army service, our Keti was also a Roman. Indeed, as has been acutely observed, in this respect he could hardly have been more Roman.[29] Yet in his native language he chose to present himself as an African who belonged to an ethnic group, the Misiciri, and more specifically to a smaller subgroup of the Misiciri, the S'RMMi. Such men who performed imperial service, and persons related to them, added the

---

[27] Acts 26.5 (lived as a Pharisee); 22.6 (education under Gamaliel); Romans 11: 1; Philipp. 3: 5; oddly enough, we have no idea what his Roman *tria nomina* were.

[28] There is another inscription in the same cemetery: RIL 148 (Kef beni Feredj), noted by Rebuffat (2005), p. 194: MSWLT W GPNYM S'RRMi MSWi MNKDi (Maswalat son of GPNYM from the (subtribe of the) S'RRMi, servant/soldier of the emperor). Rebuffat thinks it is possible that he might be the father of our man.

[29] Rebuffat 2005: 208.

cognomen Gaetulus, Gaetulicus, or variants to their Roman names and were proud of it.[30] The problems with our Gaetulus, however, are not so easily solved. Without doubt, during all of the years that he served in the army, he would have forefronted his imperial identity. He would ordinarily have spoken Latin and he would have been committed to the military values that enabled him to win the honors that he did. If he enlisted at the usual age of 18 to 20 and received a normal *honesta missio*, Gaius Iulius Gaetulus would have returned to his home town in his mid forties. He died at the age of 80, so more than half of his adult life was lived not in the Roman army but back home in the highland society of the Cheffia. In this context, inherited aspects of his behavior, inculcated from infancy and early childhood, like the native language that he spoke, would have come back into play in his daily interactions with the local people with whom he now lived. Who our man was depends very much on the time when we are considering his personhood. Was army service a usual gateway to imperial membership for men in these highlands? We are fortunate to know of other cases precisely like Keti's. There were, for example, several known men from the same region who bore the name Iasuchthan: from the highlands around Mactaris to the southwest of the Cheffia, but also in the Cheffia itself.[31] A man most probably from our region, also bearing a 'republican' praenomen and nomen, Marcus Porcius Iasucthan was a centurion serving in the Roman army who left record of his service at the distant desert post of *ad Golas* (modern Bu Njem, Libya) in the 220s CE.[32] The long metrical poem erected at Iasucthan's behest is filled with indications that for him Latin was manifestly a second language.[33] At least in terms of language, but probably much else, Iasucthan shared the same kind of double identity as did Keti son of Maswalat, and this some three generations later.

That a culture and therefore a personal identity is confirmed and continued by the inculcation and adoption of a language goes without saying. Language is a verbal and written encoding of the canons of a culture taken on by humans from birth without their assent or permission. What is significant about the region that Keti came from is that it gives all of the appearances of being a particularly strong container of indigenous African cultures and languages. By contrast, the lowlands and plains areas below the Cheffia seem to have been caught up in a series of large-scale economic acculturations led by Punic city-states in Africa that led to the proletarianization or transition to peasant agriculture by the local

---

[30] Gascou 1970: 731: his group # 1, most directly explained by Marian recruiting; and p. 732, groups # 2–3, most readily explained by subsequent phases of army recruiting.

farmers.[31] Through the years of the high empire and into late antiquity, the rural dwellers in these lowlands continued to speak Punic as their primary or first language. In the highlands, however, where this economic shift did not take place, the inhabitants apparently continued to speak various dialects of native African languages that we rather misleadingly call Libyan, but which were most probably distant ancestral forms of Tamazight. The reason that we know this is because of truly striking concentrations of inscriptions. Almost all of them are on funerary stones, written in a script developed to write the local language, as a form of writing that was distinctively different from the Punic and neo-Punic scripts used to write 'Punic' or the Roman script that was used to write Latin.[32]

Better to understand the physical and social context, we might reconsider the position of Thullium in comparison with the small village of Fussala. Fussala was equidistant from Hippo Regius, probably located about 15 to 20 km southwest of Thullium. We know that the first language spoken at Fussala, indeed practically the only one spoken by the majority of the peasant farmers in the region, was some form of what we (and the Romans) call Punic.[33] The palaeo-Tamazight speakers of the highlands, who lived in places like Thullium, had a linguistic buffer zone of non-Latin speakers placed between them and the large imperial urban center of Hippo Regius and the plains region immediately adjacent to that city. It would have been a rather permeable buffer, however, since it is likely that there was a greater linguistic proximity between palaeo-Tamazight and Punic, and related spoken languages, than there was with Latin.[34] Further nuances are evident, even within a small community like Thullium. Two separate cemeteries have been found in the village: one that contains gravestones with the palaeo-Tamazight and bilingual Latin/palaeo-Tamazight epitaphs, and a second one where the writing on the gravestones that do boast epitaphs (admittedly relatively few) is only in Latin.

A basic and simple sign of empire in the highlands around Thullium was the pursuit of what has been called the epigraphic habit. It seems likely that the heyday of the production of epigraphical texts in non-Latin languages tracked the chronological arc of the production of Latin inscriptions for the

[31] My hypothesis only, supported by some evidence and not contravened by any of which I am aware: Shaw 2003: 105–6.

[32] Camps 1993a: 113 estimated that something like three-quarters of all known inscriptions in the so-called Libyan script are concentrated in this region.

[33] For Punic as first language of the peasants at Fussala, see Shaw 2011: 427–33, with full reference to the primary and secondary sources.

[34] Kerr 2008: 58–60, and *passim*, who argues, convincingly to my mind, for a Punic origin (by suggested ideas and forms) of what he calls the Libyco-Berber script.

same purposes, mainly funerary memorialization and the recording of public honors.[35] That writing in this particular script was used demonstrates a type of cultural continuity in which Gaius Julius Gaetulus must have shared. The palaeo-Tamazight script is found widespread across the entire face of Africa. Variants of it are found in distant Mauretania Tingitana far to the west and in the form of casual wall graffiti in lands much further to the east on the desert periphery of Tripolitania, perhaps significantly, in this latter instance, in connection with a Roman army base.[36] Perhaps even more important than the simple use of this script for interpreting Keti's social position is apparent from the distribution of writing in all of the highland regions east of the Guelma/Calama line in North Africa (Table 1). Of all these zones, the subregion of the Cheffia is the only one where Latin/palaeo-Tamazight bilinguals are found. There are few of them, so there is every reason to believe that those who chose to have˙ their final memorials recorded in both languages were themselves rather special cases. They were not special, however, in that they were surrounded by an unusually high number of palaeo-Tamazight inscriptions.

Lowland beliefs and religious institutions inflected the nature of local culture in the highlands of the Cheffia and therefore customs of burial and commemoration. Many of the iconic themes on funerary stelae – crescent moons, rosettes, caducei, crowns, and palm branches – are the same as ones conventionally found on the Saturn stelae of contemporary African cult in the Roman-type transformation of the cult of Ba'al Hammon. However pervasive these signs were on the cultic imagery found in the highlands, it was not for any engagement with the cult of Ba'al Hammon or Saturn that Gaius Julius Gaetulus was noted. Most significant is the fact that he came back to his home municipality of Thullium to hold the position of *flamen perpetuus*, the local priest in charge of the cult of the emperor. He was not alone. The 'good farmer' from this same region, Lucius Arrius Amabilianus, also held the same position, probably also at Thullium. Without large numbers or ways of tracking and quantifying all such ritual adherences, it is still notable that a few of the wealthiest and highest-status men were careful to note their engagement with the imperial cult. The position of *flamen*, which would have engaged the holder of the title in the annual celebration of the emperor's birthday and the administration of public oaths of loyalty, was surely selected to emphasize Gaetulus' Roman

---

[35] Kerr 2008: 61–2.

[36] For the far west, see Galand 1966: 9–77, nos. 1–27; and for the far eastern periphery, at the army base at Bu Ngem, see Rebuffat 1974–5: eleven instances dating to the post-Severan third century.

Table 1 *Location of Inscriptions east of the Rusicade (Skikda) – Calama (Guelma) line*

Region	Latin Inscriptions	Palaeo-Tamazight Inscriptions	Latin-palaeo Tamazight bilinguals
Dougga/Thugga zone	763	18	0
Maktar/Mactaris zone	448	40	0
Ghardimaou region; forest zone of Mrassen and Ouchtat	**6**	**19**	**1**
Forest highlands of NE Algeria	**2**	**52**	**0**
Cheffia region	**38**	**132**	**7**
Chiebna-Bou Larès region	**4**	**176**	**3**
Lamy-Bou Hadjar region	**2**	**92**	**0**
Hippo-Mondovi-Duvivier zone	135	36	0
Region of Ouled Béshiah (heavy forested lands; forests of Mahbouba, Fedj Mechta and Ouled Béshiah)	**22**	**109**	**0**
Souk Ahras zone	155	137	0
Sedrata/Theveste zone	648	29	0
Guelma/Calama zone	362	97	0
Total	951		

Sources: CIL 8 and ILAlg. 1 for Latin inscriptions (CIL 8 numbers are approximate for each region, discounting repeats); RIL for so-called 'Libyan' inscriptions. The counts that would be most likely to change considerably from currently published ones would be neo-Punic texts. In order to keep the figures reflecting similar times of discovery (i.e. co-ordinate with the publication of the RIL), the counts do not include finds later than those in CIL/ILAlg. 1. I do not believe, however, that the additions would substantially alter the *general picture* that I wish to draw here.

identity. He lived before the times when Christian ideas and practices were beginning to have wide influence in Africa. The emergence of Christian institutions at Thullium was probably roughly analogous to the pattern found at Fussala, located in the southeastern borderlands of Hippo Regius. There are some signs of Christian building activities in the Cheffia, including a chapel built at Bar el-Ghoula by a patron of the church, but they are rather few in number and do not seem to betoken anything like the comparatively intense Christian presence at lowland sites in the regions around the Cheffia.[37] From Augustine's words about the ironworker Kurma, there appears to have been no Catholic bishop at Thullium in the first decades of the fifth century. Like the village of Fussala, Thullium

---

[37] ILAlg. 1.159 (Dar el-Ghoula; *Atl. arch.* f. 9, no. 243), about 5 km south of Thullium.

appears to have been nested within the large Christian bishopric of Hippo Regius. Neither the acts of the general conference held at Carthage of 411 nor the *Notitia* of bishoprics of 484 indicate that there was any bishop, Catholic or 'Donatist', in the town. By the late Vandal period, however, Thullium had been able to assert its autonomy from the diocese of Hippo. There was a bishop of the Christian church from the town who was present at the conference at Carthage in 525.[38] From the point of view of the formalities of the Christian church, Thullium, like Fussala, was a late developer. Fussala got its own bishop as early as the 420s, whereas the establishment of a bishopric at Thullium was delayed by as much as eighty or ninety years later.

In the provinces of the early to mid second century, optative identities like being a Roman or, later, being a Christian were largely matters of personal adhesion. But language and kinship were not. You were born and raised with given ones. The largest social group named in inscriptions from the Cheffia, both in Latin and in palaeo-Tamazight texts, was called the Misiciri. They were members of a kinship unit who were present on a geographic and demographic level that covered most of the region. It was the largest African group to which Keti claimed to belong. But he also recognized a subgroup of the Misiciri, called the S'RMMI or Saremmi. Manifestly, they were a smaller and more specific kinship group, to which he also belonged. Arguments have been proffered that there were at least four other similar subgroups of the Misiciri that are attested in the palaeo-Tamazight inscriptions in this same region: the NSFH, NNDRMH, NFZIH, and the NBIBH.[39] Whether these were all the subunits of the Misiciri, and whether or not they confirm the existence in Roman period Africa of the 'five-fifths' segmentary systems found in some modern-day Amazigh groups in the Atlas and Rif far to the west, will need further investigation and discovery to confirm. It is sufficient to note here that the Roman Empire kinship identity in this region was nested in complementary segmentary units that had apparently existed for a fair period of time. These same nesting arrangements of kinship groups are attested for other similar ecologies in the Roman world. An inscription from Rawwâfa in northern Arabia records a temple built by a man, one Sa'dat, who identifies himself as from the Sisthioi, a subgroup of the Thamudenoi (Thamûd), and

---

[38] *Concilia Africae: Concilium Carthaginiense*, 5–6 Februarii 525 (CCL 149: 271, lines 7; cf. 256, line 71; 258, line 143): *Marianus episcopus municipii Tulliensis, legatus provinciae.*

[39] Camps 1993a: 119 (and the pages preceding); for their putative location, see his map, fig. 3, p. 126.

the Sisthoi themselves were from the 'tribe' (phylê) of Rhobathos.[40] Here is found the same trifold nesting of one 'ethnic' unit within another.

Furthermore, a gendered aspect of the public notation of ethnic identity is regularly discernible in the epigraphy of the region. In all the funerary epitaphs from the Cheffia, all of the females are identified with names that look very Latin. Not one of them is memorialized in the palaeo-Tamazight script or in a palaeo-Tamazight/Latin bilingual. No woman in any type of epigraphical text identifies herself as a member of any of the kinship groups in the Cheffia. In the public sphere, it seems that men, but not women, deliberately marked elements of traditional culture and ethnic affiliation. And yet there must surely be a strong presumption that indigenous women, as in many comparable instances in the western provinces of the empire, were special bearers of local identity, such as being a Misiciri or a S'RMMi. Apparently these women, who were surely in the majority, simply did not present themselves in the field of public epigraphy.

There is one strong qualifier to all of these observations on kinship and ethnic identity. Our man boasted the Roman Latin *cognomen* of Gaetulus. In Roman terms, there is no doubt that he was seen and classified as a 'Gaetulian'. The problem is that there was almost certainly no ethnic group defined in terms of kinship (like the Misiciri, for example) that identified itself as Gaetulian. Such a term never appears in the indigenous palaeo-Tamazight script or in any contemporary epigraphical texts as the name of a distinct ethnic group.[41] The name appears to be an external identifier, one of the generic categories of 'Africans' that were used by imperial administrators, and by the geographers and ethnographers who provided them with 'ethnic information'. The name seems to have emerged as a convenient label for a generic class of indigenous persons who happened to engage in armed service for the Roman state. Gaetulians were seen as a grab bag of sometimes southern, sometimes highland, sometimes autonomist, occasionally violent peoples. Various peoples who were occasionally involved in resistance to programs of settlement and integration that were fronted by Mediterranean states with which they came into contact were categorized as 'Gaetulian' regardless of their own self-ascribed ethnic identity. In defeating any people who fell under this external rubric, Roman generals assumed the ethnic name 'Gaetulicus' as

---

[40] Graf 1978, 10.

[41] That is, other than as a part of personal nomenclature or in the naming of auxiliary units of the army (both of these surely being connected); I take ILAlg 2.1.501 (Cirta) that mentions a *tumultus Gaetulorum* not to refer to a specific ethnic group, but rather to a general category of rebellious Africans.

a victory *cognomen*.[42] Many of the specific ethnic groups who fell under this external rubric were subsequently absorbed into the armed forces of the Roman state. Evidence of such armed service dates early into the pre-Roman past of the Carthaginian hegemony in Africa. We are told that Hannibal recruited Gaetulians for service in his army.[43] Men of this extraction formed a pool of potential recruits for armies whether they were Carthaginian, African, or Roman. Marius recruited important elements from ethnic groups called Gaetulian for his African campaigns against Jugurtha.[44] In the civil wars of the 40s, these same Gaetulians, along with Numidae, were recruited by the Pompeiani and served them until Julius Caesar, the descendant of Marius, appeared on African shores. At that point they defected *en masse* to his side.[45] In regions further to the west, around Cirta and Calama, other men of this same background went over to the side of Caesar's self-appointed freelancing baronial ally, the Campanian freebooter Publius Sittius. It is very likely that many of the Africans who later bore the *cognomen* Sittius were among the Gaetulians who were enfranchised by Caesar's man in the west.[46] It is similarly probable that the Gaetuli who loyally served Julius Caesar in the battles in the old Republican province of Africa in 46 BCE account for considerable numbers of men who were enfranchised by him. They later bore the *praenomen* Gaius and the *nomen* Julius, as our man Keti did many generations later. This particular Roman connection with the so-called Gaetulians deserves closer inspection.

In taking over command of the war against Jugurtha, Gaius Marius recruited heavily not just from among newly eligible Roman citizens in Italy but also from, as is often not noted as part of this same process, among 'ethnic' peoples in North Africa. These latter men also provided important additional manpower for the war against Jugurtha. Being well acquainted

---

[42] For just one well known case, see Fishwick and Shaw 1976 on Cn. Lentulus Gaetulicus, the surname being conferred on his son by the victorious father.

[43] Livy, 23.18.1: found serving in his forces in 216 BCE in southern Italy under their own *praefectus* named Isalca.

[44] Ps.-Caes. *Bell. Afr.* 56.3: *namque Gaetuli ex equitatu regio nobiliores equitumque praefecti, quorum patres cum Mario ante meruerant eiusque beneficio agris finibusque donati post Sullae victoriam sub Hiempsalis regis erant dati potestatem . . . perfugiunt in Caesaris castra*; see Gascou 1969: 557–68.

[45] Ps.-Caes. *Bell. Afr.* 32.3: *Interim Numidae Gaetulique diffugere cotidie ex castris Scipionis et partim in regnum se conferre, partim, quod ipsi maioresque eorum beneficio C. Mari usi fuissent Caesaremque eius adfinem esse audiebant, in eius castra perfugere catervatim non intermittunt*; and 56.3 (see the note preceding).

[46] Ps.-Caes. *Bell. Afr.* 25.2: *paucis diebus pugnando capit et praeterea duo oppida Gaetulorum*; cf. ILAlg. 2.1.1705 (Cirta) for a Publius Sitti[us] Gaetu[lus].

with local languages and customs and thoroughly experienced with the climate and terrain, they were perhaps among the most useful of Marius' new recruits. He drew many of them from indigenous peoples living along the frontiers of the Republican province. When the war was over, he arranged land rewards not only for his Roman citizen and Italian veterans but also for his African soldiers. They were settled in towns and in rural regions in the same interstitial zone along the western border of the Roman province.[47] In Roman parlance, these Africans doubtless became his clients and were understood to be so, although surely no Roman technical term would have been necessary in the minds of the Gaetuli themselves to describe the social gratitude that linked them to their benefactor. They had served him, and now he had served them. As was traditional, they assumed close ties of loyalty by kinship and military service with Marius' descendants. In the factionalism of the civil wars that rent Africa in 46 BCE, it was natural that the descendants of Marius' Gaetulian recruits rallied to support Julius Caesar, who was Marius' close familial relation, against his personal enemies, the Pompeiani. In response, Caesar had extended the citizenship to these men and had made grants of land to them.

In consequence we encounter many descendants of these Gaetulians in the high empire who bear the *praenomen* Gaius and the *nomen* Julius.[48] Several generations after the age of Caesar, we find cohorts of Gaetulians in the service of the Roman army. One of them, the *Cohors Prima Gaetulorum*, is reasonably well documented.[49] The geographic distribution of the *cognomen* 'Gaetulicus' reveals heavy concentrations just to the west of the old provincial boundary, the Fossa Regia, one of them in eastern Numidia where Keti's home town of Thullium was located. Most of the other groups of men bearing the *cognomen* of 'Gaetulicus' were connected with various army bases in Africa, including Ammaedara, Theveste, and Lambaesis. Such men are also found concentrated in colonial settlements of veterans, like Madauros and Thubursicu Numidarum.[50] There are good reasons to believe that Marius was responsible for the settlement of his African veterans who would otherwise have been labeled as Gaetulians but who, after their receipt of citizenship, bore the *praenomen* Gaius and the *gentilicium* Marius. Significant numbers of the descendants of such men

---

[47] Gascou, 'Marius et les Gétules,' pt. 4 in 1969: 555–68.   [48] Gascou 1970: 723–36.

[49] Lassère 1994: 244–53; see *ILAlg*. II.1, 665 = CIL 8.7039 (Cirta); *RMD*, 1, no. 3 (Syria, 88 CE); *RMD*, 1, no. 4 (Suhoz, Bulgaria, 91 CE); *RMD*, 2, no. 87 (near Carnuntum, 114 CE); *RMD*, 4, nos. 221, 228, 235, 241, 270 (Pannonia Inferior/Moesia Inferior, c. 99–110-146); *RMD*, 5, nos. 329–31 (Syria, 88 CE).

[50] Gascou 1970: 730–1, and distribution map at 729.

are found in the borderlands of the old republican province in Africa: that is to say, in lands south and east of the Fossa Regia. The distribution manifestly points to the pattern that we would expect from the historical scenario just described.[51] As with the men and women who later have the *cognomen* Gaetulicus, or variants like Gaetulus, those bearing the *praenomen-nomen* Gaius Marius when they are found outside the core area to the west of the republic province in Africa, are also attested in the big army camps or in veteran colonies.

All these facts indicate that army service continued to define who these men were over several generations. Gaetulian was manifestly an external Roman label used to cover such armed servitors. The men themselves, however, had their own local identities: for some of them it was that of belonging to the Misiciri. To use the name of Misiciri, however, only raises further questions of identity and representation. The Misiciri were just one of a number of small ethnic groups lying south and west of the frontier of the old province of Africa from whom the Roman state continued to recruit in the empire. Men from smaller local groups like the Misiciri were usually recruited under larger headings, being considered Gaetuli, Afri, Musulamii, Numidae, or the like, for the administrative purposes of the Roman state. Men in all of these groups continued to contribute manpower to the auxiliary units of the imperial army. Many of the Gaetulians who were already Roman citizens from the days of Marius and Caesar, however, were eligible for direct entry into the legions of the imperial army. This historical background and the claims with the Roman state that could be based on it are significant. In the wider context of the empire, it is manifest that there were firm ethnic prejudices held by the big power holders, against Gauls and Germans and other northerners for example, that were effective barriers to advancement in the imperial system.[52] Even for Gauls and Germans, however, a gateway into the ranks of imperial power – and one that became dominant for excluded northerners from the early third century onward – was through service in the army.

This is the role in which we find our Gaius Julius Gaetulus at Thullium, and most likely not a few of the other men whose gravestones we find in the Cheffia – men like Lucius Postumius Crescens, also from Thullium. Crescens was remembered not just in Latin on his memorial stone, but also in a parallel inscription in palaeo-Tamazight where he self-identified as belonging to the Misiciri, probably assuming that everyone knew that his

---

[51] Gascou 1969, distribution map, fig. 5, 'Carte de répartition des Marii en Proconsulaire et Numidie,' 559; 1970: 732.

[52] Isaac 2004: 411–39; with comments by Shaw 2005: 230–1.

being one of the local S'RMMi was understood.[53] There were others who, like Nabdhsen son of Cotuzan, noted that he was from the *tribus* Misiciri. Perhaps because he died at the age of twenty, Nabdhsen never made it into active army service. This is the only information that appears in Latin in Nabdhsen's epitaph. But the words in Latin are accompanied by a parallel inscription in palaeo-Tamazight which shows that, like Gaetulus, Nabdhsen also identified himself as a member of the S'RMMi.[54] Nabdhsen probably shared a status similar to Sactut son of Ihimir who was also memorialized in a parallel palaeo-Tamazight inscription on his tombstone.[55] Such was probably also the case with Chinidial son of Wisicir from the *tribus* Misiciri from a site just to the southwest of Thullium, whose Latin epitaph is also accompanied by one in palaeo-Tamazight. In this case, interestingly, the text in the indigenous script does not say that he belonged to the Misiciri but rather to the NChPi, who, like the S'RMMi, were most probably a smaller subgroup of the Misiciri.[56] Chinidial therefore preferred to note his membership in the small kinship group, assuming that everyone understood that the NChPi were a subgroup of the Misiciri. On the other hand, one Paternus son of Zaedo, like our Gaetulus, is named as a member of the Misiciri only in the palaeo-Tamazight text on his stone, as is another son of the same father in the same town.[57] Similarly, one Aug[e?] son of Sadavo, Numidian from the *tribus* Misiciri, includes his affiliation with the larger ethnic group as a significant element of his identification.[58] An important ancillary point revealed by the nomenclature of these men is that the default mode of ethnic identity in the highlands of the Cheffia shows no sign of any obvious Punic influences. These personal names are not cast in a formal Roman Latin mode; they are Latin transcriptions of African names. Nabdhsen, Cotuzan, Chinidial, Zaedo, Auge, Sadavo, and so on, are not Punic names but African ones – just like the Kurma from Thullium who was mentioned by Augustine. This much is evident from other regions in Africa, where some locals who also had the *praenomen - nomen* Gaius Iulius, like Gaius Iulius Arish and Gaius Iulius Manulus from

---

[53] RIL 193 = ILAlg. 1.145 (Kef beni Feredj/Thullium)

[54] RIL 145 = CIL 8.5218, cf. 17933 = ILAlg. 1.138 (Kef beni Feredj/Thullium); the cutter cut MISICTRI, but the 'T', if it is the letter that actually appears on the stone, is surely a cutter's error for an 'I'.

[55] RIL 151 = CIL 8 5220 + 17395 = ILAlg. 1.147 (Kef beni Feredj/Thullium).

[56] RIL 252 = CIL 8.5217 = ILAlg. 1.156 (Aïn el-Hofra, c. 10 km SE of Kef beni Feredj; *Atl. arch.* f. 10, no. 24); the WISICIR of line 2 probably should be read as MISICIR, the tribal name being taken as a personal one by the father.

[57] ILAlg. 1.168 (Henchir Ouled Djenborna = *Atl. arch.* f. 10, no. 42); and ILAlg. 1.169 (same location).

[58] ILAlg. 1.174 (Kef Cheb, Rûm es Sûq, southeast of el-Kala).

Calama (modern Guelma), adhered rather to the use of the Punic language and to the worship of Lord Ba'al.[59] They are two examples of Africans from non-highland areas whose culture had become Punicized before becoming Roman.

Through a series of ingenious and insightful parallels, it has been shown that the palaeo-Tamazight on Keti's funerary stone reading MWSi MNKDi probably means something like 'servitor of the supreme chieftain/king'. This was a local Misicirian way, so to speak, of describing Keti's service in the Roman army. Several of the Latin bilingual speakers in the Cheffia, including our man Keti/Gaetulus, Postumius Crescens, and Sactut son of Ihimir, were army veterans.[60] For them and, we must suspect, for many others like them, the army was one of the main instruments of imperial integration and identity. The social and disciplinary regimes in the hot-house of the legion and the auxiliary formations helped to shape an identity vitally linked with the empire.[61] The role of the uniform requirements of a type of a national military service in forming identity was surely as significant here as it has been in many modern instances.[62] While the majority of recruits of the Legio III Augusta in Africa seem to have come from the more densely populated urban centers of the old province of Africa, especially from their urban proletariats, recruiting also continued from 'ethnic zones' of the African provinces. Many of the non-citizen recruits from these social groups probably gained citizenship and the ability to enroll in the legionary forces of the empire through auxiliary service in one of the units of Afri, Mauri, Numidae, or Gaetuli that are well attested in the *auxilia* of the high empire. The recruiting of highland peoples, whether the Ituraeans in the Lebanon, Thracians from the Balkans, or Isaurians from southern Asia Minor, was as normal. It was as typical as it later was for the armies of early modern Europe for whom military service by Scots, Swiss, Auvergnians, Pyrenaeans, or other impoverished highland men was normal. We can therefore say that armed service for the Roman state was a choice that a young man like Keti might make.

---

[59] For Arish, see Jongeling 2008: 186, no. OU N 7 = Jongeling and Kerr 2005: 42; for Manulus, see Jongeling 2008: 232–3, Guelma no. 9 = Jongeling and Kerr 2005: 49; compare the Gaius Iulius whose son Severus set up a stone for him in the Punic language at Mactaris: Jongeling 2008: 101, Hr. Maktar no. 27, in a field of neo-Punic texts where the personal names are overwhelmingly Punic. The exceptional nomenclature surely indicates, again, a special case – probably army service and the early acquisition of Roman citizenship from Julius Caesar.

[60] See Rebuffat 2005: 198–200; 2006: 274–7, 289–90.

[61] MacMullen 1984 investigates the sum of influences in legionary service that conduced to this formation of a Roman soldierly identity; much the same must have applied to the auxiliaries.

[62] See, e.g., Weber 1976: 292–302, only trumped in that case by pervasive systems of modern education of a kind not found in the Roman world.

The rider is that the Roman army as specifically configured in the late Republic and Principate had to exist as a viable institution for men like him to be able to make such a decision. Even given the availability of army service, the degree of freedom of choice is still open to debate. Four or five generations of male ancestors of Keti's had already been in Roman army service. Given the tendency for a behavior like this to be inherited, we might ask how much this element was an embedded element of our man's ethnic identity. Did the peoples of the Misiciri who had performed armed service for the Roman state for generations, like the Nepalese Gorkhas, the Gurkhas of the British army, come to be defined by that service?

The empire consisted of many different types of social and political units. These included kingdoms, principalities, and baronies, followed by city-states of various types, conventionally labeled as 'free and autonomous' or wholly subject to the dictates of the states. There followed ethnic units variously known as *gentes, nationes, tribus,* or *populi.* Since the first of these political units tended gradually to be squeezed out by managers of empire who considered such quasi-autonomous entities to be incompatible with the fact of empire, it became conventional to view the empire, ideally, as an amalgam of 'cities' on the one hand and of 'peoples' on the other. Therefore one way of envisioning the imperial project is to see it as an entity composed of distinct modular units: ethnic peoples on the one side and cities or urban communities on the other. More of some were found in certain regions, and more of the others in others. Such a taxonomy was always complicated by the fact that urban groups were themselves sometimes construed as ethnic groups, as, for example, the Cirtenses, Madaurenses, Thuggenses, and the Capsitani in Africa. A different way of thinking about the same process would be to see this divided composite of identity as potentially running internally *through* individual subjects all the way down to the ground level of any given locale. There is every reason to believe that the empire was filled with persons of such divided identity. The one individual case of Keti son of Maswalat powerfully indicates how moveable and changeable some of the elements were that contributed to ethnic identity in this mix. Mommsen long ago made a fundamental observation that is worth repeating: the empire was a continuous revolution, a thing always in the process of remaking itself. The effects of this continual refashioning were felt at local level. In this hybridity, there are some elements that seem more stable or longer term than others, but change was ever present.

Anchoring one end of this polarity were long-term, almost inherited aspects of identity that surely had a large impact on how the person saw himself or herself. Of these, the inculcation and learning of a native language must be one of the most formative, even in a multi-lingual environment. There is no reasonable doubt that a variant of proto- or palaeo-Tamazight was spoken in the highlands to the east and south of Hippo Regius and that it was in all likelihood Keti's language of birth. Since the region was surrounded and, to some extent, penetrated by native speakers of Punic, we might suspect that Keti might have acquired knowledge of this other language, especially given its closer relationship to his native tongue – that is, when compared to Latin. The odd thing, perhaps, is that the palaeo-Tamazight speakers in the region developed, adopted, and propagated an idiosyncratic script of their own in which to write their language in public. This cannot be accidental. The continued use of a distinctive and peculiar script that first appeared in these regions, broadly speaking, with the first African kings must have been a deliberate choice. Both of these facts distinguished this propensity from the speaking of Latin. Although the inscriptions in the Cheffia highlands belong to a relatively restricted Roman time frame, nonetheless the script has a known time span that had already covered about three centuries or so by the time that Keti's relatives were using it for his funerary epitaph.[63] On the other hand, from prolonged army service, if nothing else, Gaius Julius Gaetulus would surely have acquired a reasonably good command of Latin. Even if learned and even if a second or a third language, the language of empire was present in relatively remote villages and hamlets like those of the Cheffia.

Our Gaius Julius Gaetulus or Keti son of Maswalat belonged to the peoples of the Misiciri and the S'RMMi. And he might even have considered the Gaetuli to be some larger such notional kinship-like entity to which he also belonged by virtue of the fact that the Misiciri were labeled as Gaetulians by the Romans whom he served. But he was also a Roman citizen of a family who had been Roman citizens for many generations. He was a citizen of the great imperial metropolis of Rome as also of the town, perhaps municipality, of Thullium. The managers of empire must have been aware of how normal a circumstance this was in the formation of their state. As we have said, one ideal way of reading the standard claim that the empire was made up of 'cities' and 'peoples' was to stress the existence of different and exclusive categories of social groups out of which the empire was composed: cities on the one hand *and* peoples on the other. The empire

---

[63] Kerr 2010: 63, who, correctly I think, sees the writing system as having emerged in the world formed by Rome's second war with Carthage, and remarks: 'The fact that this writing system survived the millennia shows that it must originally have served a functional purpose, unlike some short-live adoptions of writing systems.'

is made of apples and oranges, chalk and cheese. On the other hand, the concept could be understood as indicating a different sort of composite of which the empire was made in which individuals were simultaneously members of cities and also of peoples, like our Gaius Iulius Gaetulus/Keti son of Maswalat.

Of course, it is not possible finally to sort out something as complex as ethnic identity on the basis of a few inscriptions, some scattered literary references, and a few comparative data. But at least the following seems reasonably certain: even after many generations of integration into the parallel apparatuses of the Roman state, an apparently Roman man who served a lifetime in its army and in its municipal institutions still maintained a separate African identity. And he was not alone. The nomenclature of other persons in the Cheffia, the widespread use of a palaeo-Tamazight script, and the presence of stereotypical units of common ethnicities indicate a general social system of which he was part. Demonstrably in his case, and probably in the others, this local African culture was a living fact over a significant number of generations. This vibrant cultural world and the language in which it functioned was not a choice in the formation of Keti's identity. There were also other elements that were outside free choice, and one of the big ones, surely, was the sea change in shape and structure that the Roman Empire went through in the late third and early fourth centuries. In Africa, as elsewhere, the third-century crisis of the empire was a crisis for ethnic identity. It is an observable phenomenon on the southern frontier of the empire, as well as on and beyond its northern ones. A host of identifiable ethnic groups entered this crisis and then disappeared from view. In the mid third century and at the end of it, new groups and new identities emerge. Very few of the old ones made it through the crisis unscathed.[64] The Gaetuli and Gaetulians, like our Gaius Julius, disappear from the record, as do the Misiciri and, needless to say, the S'RMMi and the other four subgroups of the Misiciri of whom we know from the high empire.[65] In some sense, it seems, these groups had their identities confirmed and maintained by being part of an imperial system that recognized them as being a specific people and that continually underwrote that identity by an administrative computation and by a specific type of integration within the empire – in the case of the Misiciri by armed service. When that system profoundly shifted in structure, so did the ethnic identifiers that were part of it.

---

[64] For the evidence and the process for North Africa, see Modéran 2004 and 2008.

[65] On the disappearance of the Gaetuli, see Fentress 1982: 331; and Desanges 1998.

On the other hand, there is no reason to diminish the Roman parts of Keti's identity: his knowledge of Latin, Roman citizenship, municipal service, and Roman name. All of these elements, and the values associated with them, had also been maintained by his family over several generations. These other Roman elements of his identity, however, required the continued presence of the empire, indeed a particular type of that empire, to sustain them. Without an imperial army that entailed specific kinds of recruitment, integration, training and service, there are serious questions whether much of the imperial identity would have taken hold among the men of the Cheffia in the way that it did. As long as those specific connections existed, however, the case of Keti points to the presence, in non-trivial numbers, and in considerable parts of Africa of persons with this type of split identity. And there are surely good reasons to suspect that Keti son of Maswalat/Gaius Julius Gaetulus was a *typical* figure of empire. Everywhere we look, from the Gaulish noblemen in the west to persons like Saul/Paul in the eastern provinces of the empire, we witness the same inside schism that ran along the internal fault line between local society and central state.[66] The different strands in personal identities ran from the top to the bottom of the social orders of the empire, confirming in reality the ideological claim that the Roman Empire was an empire of cities *and* peoples. Frequently, we must suspect, it was so *within* each person. It was an ever-changing, ever-adapting social schizophrenia that was maintained over many generations in not a few of the provincial families in the empire. It was as essential a characteristic of empire as were the elements of its grander political unity.

---

[66] On the Gauls, see Woolf 1998: 39–40.

PART II

Culture and Identity in the Roman Empire

5 | Roman Reception of the Trojan War

MARGALIT FINKELBERG

Roman reception of Greek cultural tradition was anything but passive or straightforward. After the first wave of translations and adaptations that took place in the third and second centuries BCE, remaking and rethinking Greek sources became the normal practice. This gradually led to their replacement by new literary production cast in the Latin language. Homer was superseded by Vergil; Hesiod by Ovid and Vergil again; Sappho, Pindar, and Callimachus by Catullus and Horace; Sophocles and Euripides by Seneca, and so on.

Still, even when approached against this background, Roman reception of Homer is a special case. On the one hand, it is highly symptomatic that the *Odyssia*, the translation of the Homeric *Odyssey* by Livius Andronicus (third century BCE), was the first literary epic to appear in Latin. On the other hand, at approximately the same time or perhaps even earlier,[1] the Romans, who aspired to acquire a prestigious past by securing a place within Greek heroic tradition, started to identify themselves as descendants of the defeated Trojans. This identification became especially prominent in the middle of the first century BCE, with the rise to power of Caesar and Augustus, who claimed to descend from Aeneas through his son Iulus. The silver denarius of Caesar showing Aeneas leaving Troy, minted in 47/46 BCE, is emblematic in this respect. Aeneas carries his father Anchises on his left shoulder and holds in his right hand the Palladium, the statue of armed Athena from the city of Troy. This was the first time when Aeneas replaced Romulus on a Roman coin. This also signalled the beginning of a new era in the reception of the Trojan War.

Romulus and Aeneas

The starting point of my discussion is an ode that Horace wrote in 27 BCE, the year of Augustus' rise to power. It is usually supposed that the poem refers to the plan of transferring the capital to the East, which was reportedly

---

[1] For the discussion see Gruen 1992: 6–51; Cornell 1995: 63–8; Wiseman 1995: 52–5; Jones 1999: 82–8; Erskine 2001: 16; Hornblower 2015: 97–8.

being considered at the time;[2] it seems, however, that the extensive building program launched by Augustus in the city of Ilion (Troy) just a few years later (more later) should also be taken into account here.

Romulus is being admitted to the circle of the Olympian gods. Juno welcomes a descendant of the 'Trojan priestess' (*Troica ... sacerdos*, i.e. Rhea Sylvia), but she also issues a warning:[3]

> *Dum longus inter saeviat Ilion*
> *Romamque pontus, qualibet exules*
>   *in parte regnato beati;*
>   *dum Priami Paridisque busto*
> *insultet armentum et catulos ferae*
> *celent inultae, stet Capitolium*
>   *fulgens triumphatisque possit*
>   *Roma ferox dare iura Medis.*

'As long as the extensive sea rages between Troy and Rome, let them, exiles, reign happy in any other part of the world: as long as cattle trample upon the tomb of Priam and Paris, and wild beasts conceal their young ones there with impunity, may the Capitol remain in splendor, and may brave Rome be able to give laws to the conquered Medes'.

But if these admonitions were not heeded, the following will be fulfilled:

> *Sed bellicosis fata Quiritibus*
> *Hac lege dico, ne nimium pii*
>   *rebusque fidentes avitae*
>   *tecta velint reparare Troiae.*
> *Trioae renascens alite lugubri*
> *Fortuna tristi clade iterabitur,*
>   *Ducente victrices catervas*
>   *Coniuge me Iovis et sorore.*
> *Ter si resurgat murus aeneus*
> *auctore Phoebo, ter pereat meis*
>   *excisus Argivis, ter uxor*
>   *capta virum puerosque ploret.*

'But I pronounce this fate to the warlike Romans, upon this condition; that neither through an excess of piety, nor of confidence in their power, they become inclined to rebuild the houses of their ancestors' Troy. The fortune of Troy, reviving under unlucky auspices, shall be repeated with lamentable destruction, I, the wife and sister of Jupiter, leading on the

---

[2] Suet. *Jul. Caes.* 79.   [3] Horace *Odes* 3.3.37–44, 57–68. Tr. C. Smart, slightly adapted.

victorious bands. Thrice, if a brazen wall should arise by means of its founder Phoebus, thrice should it fall, demolished by my Greeks; thrice should the captive wife bewail her husband and her children.'

Note that Horace both leaves room for the Romans' self-identification as descendants of the Trojans and keeps the Greek tradition of the Trojan War intact. Troy had gotten what it deserved, but Rome inaugurated an entirely new beginning, represented by the figure of Romulus, and its affinity with Troy should not be overemphasized.

Yet Horace, with his characteristically Republican emphasis on Romulus rather than Aeneas[4] and his idea of a single Graeco-Roman civilization, clearly implied in Juno's warning, was far behind his time. The same can be said of his contemporary Dionysius of Halicarnassus, who also worked in Augustan Rome.[5] In his *Roman Antiquities* Dionysius not only tried to defend the idea of Greek origins of the Romans but also argued that the Trojans were in fact Greeks. This idea, however, obviously did not seem appealing enough to become universally accepted.

When Horace wrote his ode, Vergil was already working on the *Aeneid*, a poem destined radically to transform the Romans' attitude toward the tradition of the Trojan War. Vergil was much better attuned to the spirit of the epoch than Horace or Dionysius. Rather than downplaying the Romans' identification with the Trojans as Horace did or claiming, together with Dionysius, that the Trojans and through them the Romans were in fact Greeks, Vergil chose to present the Greeks as inferior to the Trojans and, by all too obvious extrapolation, to the Romans as well. Consider, for example, the reaction of the ghosts of the Greek participants in the Trojan War at Aeneas' appearance in the Underworld:[6]

> *at Danaum proceres Agamemnoniaeque phalanges*
> *ut videre virum fulgentiaque arma per umbras,*
> *ingenti trepidare metu; pars vertere terga,*
> *ceu quondam petiere rates, pars tollere vocem*
> *exiguam: inceptus clamor frustratur hiantis.*

But the Greek chieftains, and the massed ranks whom Agamemnon had led, trembled in violent panic at the sight of their foe with his armour glittering amid the shadows. Some turned to flee as before they had fled to

---

[4] On the difference between the Republican and the Augustan attitude, see Erskine 2001: 30–6. In *Carmen Saeculare* (17 BCE), Horace pays lavish tribute to the myth of Aeneas and the Trojan descent of Augustus, by whom the ode was commissioned (ll. 40–7, 53–4), without at the same time losing sight of Romulus (48–52).

[5] See Gabba 1991: 212–13.   [6] *Aen.* 6.489–93. Tr. W. F. Jackson Knight.

their ships, while others raised a whispering voice; but their attempt at a battle-cry left their mouths idly gaping.

Greek leaders trembling before a Trojan – such was the perspective on the Troy–Greece relationship that Vergil established.

Above all, however, Vergil's strategies concerning this relationship are revealed in two prophecies that he puts into the mouths of Jupiter and of the ghost of Anchises, respectively:[7]

> Veniet lustris labentibus aetas,
> cum domus Assaraci Phthiam clarasque Mycenas
> servitio premet, ac victis dominabitur Argis.

'Time in its five-year spans shall slip by till an age shall come when the House of Assaracus shall crush to subjection even Phthia and illustrious Mycenae, and conquer Argos, and hold mastery there.'

> Ille triumphata Capitolia ad alta Corintho
> victor aget currum caesis insignis Achiuis.
> eruet ille Argos Agamemnoniasque Mycenas
> ipsumque Aeaciden, genus armipotentis Achilli,
> ultus avos Troiae templa et temerata Mineruae.

'Over there is one who shall triumph over Corinth and drive his chariot to the towering Capitol in glorious victory after the slaying of Greeks. And another, there, shall uproot Argos and Mycenae, Agamemnon's own city, and the Aeacid himself, the descendant of Achilles the mighty in arms; so he shall avenge his Trojan ancestors and Trojan Minerva's desecrated shrine.'[8]

The change of emphasis in the approach to the Trojan myth that these quotations demonstrate found its expression not only in poetry but also in the very topography of the Greek city of Ilion, founded on the site of Troy somewhere at the beginning of the first millennium BCE. Let us dwell briefly on its history.

The Background: Ilion (ca. 670–20 BCE)

Horace's picture of Troy, as well as his plea not to restore the city, may create the impression that Troy had lain in ruins since Priam's times.

---

[7] Aen. 1.283–8, 6.836–40.

[8] The references are to Assaracus son of Tros, grandfather of Anchises, to Mummius the conqueror of Corinth (146 BCE), to Aemilius Paulus the conqueror of Macedonia (168 BCE), and to Perseus, its last Hellenistic ruler.

Nothing could be farther from the truth. The topos of the everlasting ruins of Troy, persistent in both Greek and Latin literary tradition,[9] finds no corroboration in the historical and archaeological record.

By the early archaic period we already find the Greek settlement of the Troad firmly established. The settlers were Aeolian Greeks, who formed the first wave of Greek colonization in Asia Minor. The new settlement incorporated within its precincts what had remained of the Bronze Age Troy.[10] These were the monuments seen by the poets responsible for the formative stage of the Homeric tradition. The new landmarks of the Archaic Troad included the city of Ilion itself (Troy VIII), probably with the temple of Athena Ilias (anachronistically introduced in *Iliad* 6), and the seaport Sigeum, which in the course of the seventh and sixth centuries BCE several times changed hands between the Aeolians from nearby Lesbos and the encroaching Athenians, who sought to establish control over the grain supply from the Black Sea. It is in the context of the fight over Sigeum that the Aeolian settlement of the Troad first emerges in the historical record:

> Sigeum, which city Pisistratus had taken by force of arms from the Mytilenaeans. ... during very many years there had been war between the Athenians of Sigeum and the Mytilenaeans of the city called Achilleum. They of Mytilene insisted on having the place restored to them: but the Athenians refused, since they argued that the Aeolians had no better claim to the Trojan territory than themselves, or than any of the other Greeks who helped Menelaus on occasion of the rape of Helen.[11]

The Athenian political rhetoric aside, note the double perspective on Troy and the Troad that transpires from this episode. For the Asiatic Aeolians, the Troad was first and foremost the place where they had lived for generations now; for the Athenians, it was a theatre of the Trojan War and, therefore, a Panhellenic domain. This early politicization of the Trojan space was highly symptomatic. As we shall see immediately, the Iron Age city of Ilion continued to serve as a playground of competing ideologies in the subsequent centuries as well.

In the Persian Wars the ideological aspect of the site of Troy became even more pronounced. As Xerxes' visit to Ilion on his way to Greece (480

---

[9] See esp. Lycurgus *Against Leocrates* 62 (ca. 330 BCE): 'Who has not heard how, after being the greatest city of her time and ruling the whole of Asia, she was deserted forever when once the Greeks had razed her?' Tr. J. O. Burtt. At the time of Lycurgus' speech, the city of Ilion had been part of the Greek political scene for about four hundred years (see subsequently). Cf. also Aesch. *Ag.* 818–20; Eur. *Tro.* 1317.24 and below, with n. 19.

[10] Hertel 2003: 186–213.   [11] Hdt. 5.94. Tr. G. Rawlinson.

BCE) shows, by treating the sack of Troy as Greek trespass on the territory of Asia, the King of Persia symbolically represented the war that he initiated as an act of just retribution for past wrongs – or at least this is how Herodotus saw it. The visit was accompanied by a magnificent sacrifice to Trojan Athena.[12]

At the time of the Peloponnesian War, Ilion was a tribute-paying member of the Delian League,[13] and it was definitely involved in the naval campaign in the Aegean.[14] After the defeat of Athens, Ilion, along with the other Greek cities of Asia Minor, became Persian as a result of the King's Peace (387 BCE).

The year 334 BCE was a turning point in the history of Ilion. The entry of Alexander's army into the Troad, staged as a symbolic re-enactment of the Trojan War,[15] not only provided a powerful theme for Macedonian imperial propaganda but also inaugurated an unprecedented surge of urban development in the city of Ilion (Troy IX). All of a sudden, Ilion became important. The reason is clear: its existence legitimized Alexander's campaign against Persia, helping to represent it as a new Trojan War, that is, another Panhellenic enterprise aiming to avenge the injury inflicted upon the Greeks by the barbarians of Asia. The subsequent growth and prosperity of Hellenistic Ilion was a direct result of its ideological importance in the eyes of Alexander and his successors.

In the Hellenistic period Ilion greatly gained in political importance. It became an autonomous polis and the religious and administrative centre of a koinon.[16] The temple of Athena Ilias, built under Lysimachus and the Seleucids (the end of the fourth to the third century BCE) is representative of the new status of the city. In material, in structure, in the subjects of the reliefs on the metopes this magnificent edifice deliberately evoked the Parthenon and aimed to establish a meaningful correlation, sanctioned

---

[12] Hdt. 7.43: 'On reaching the Scamander ... Xerxes ascended into the Pergamus of Priam, since he had a longing to behold the place. When he had seen everything, and inquired into all particulars, he made an offering of a thousand oxen to the Trojan Athena, while the Magians poured libations to the heroes who were slain at Troy.'

[13] It appears in the Athenian Tribute Lists for the year 425–424 BCE; see further Bryce 2006: 157 and 205 n. 9.

[14] See Xen. *Hell.* 1.1.4: 'Meanwhile Mindarus [a Spartan admiral], while sacrificing to Athena at Ilion, had observed the battle. He at once hastened to the sea.' The context is the Battle of Abydos, 410 BCE.

[15] Cf. Arr. *Anab.* 1.11: 'It is also said that he went up to Ilion and offered sacrifice to the Trojan Athena; that he set up his own panoply in the temple as a votive offering, and in exchange for it took away some of the consecrated arms which had been preserved from the time of the Trojan war. It is also said that the shield-bearing guards used to carry these arms in front of him into the battles.' Tr. J. Chinnock.

[16] Hertel 2003: 237–59; cf. Bryce 2006: 159–65.

by the tradition of the Trojan War at least since the time of Homer, between Athena Ilias and Athena Polias of Athens. Both temples delivered the same message of an epoch-making confrontation between the Greeks and the barbarians and the eventual triumph of the former. This, however, was not destined to last. A new power arose in the Mediterranean, and it was about to present the Trojan landscape and the Trojan War itself in an entirely new light.

The Transformation: Ilium (20 BCE–ca. 500 CE)

The Roman tendency to approach the site of Troy in the perspective of the Aeneas myth can be traced back to the first entry of Roman troops into Asia at the beginning of the second century BCE.[17] Yet it was not before 27 BCE, the year of Augustus' rise to power, that Ilion was placed in the focus of public attention. As we saw, it is in this same year that Horace wrote the ode in which he pleaded not to rebuild Troy. It is not out of the question that while writing these lines Horace also had in mind the events of the First Mithridatic War, in the course of which Ilion had been heavily damaged by the rebellious Roman legate Fimbria (85 BCE). The destruction, however, was apparently not as devastating as some of our sources would have it.[18] Moreover, the ruins of Troy were evoked in similar terms also by Ovid in 8 CE, after Troy had already been rebuilt on a large scale by Augustus:

> *nunc humilis veteres tantummodo Troia ruinas*
> *Et pro divitiis tumulos ostendit avorum.*

> [Troy was great in wealth and men ... now humbled to the dust, she can but point to her ancient ruins, ancestral tombs are all her wealth.[19]

That is to say, just like their Greek predecessors, Roman poets glorified the imagined ruins of Troy, ignoring the real city that existed in their place.[20]

---

[17] See Erskine 2001: 234–7; Bryce 2006: 164–5.

[18] See the excellent discussion by Erskine in Erskine 2001: 237–45; cf. Bryce 2006: 165.

[19] Ov. *Met.* 15. 424–5. Tr. Mary M. Innes.

[20] See n. 9. It is not out of the question that this double perspective of the contemporary Troy was in the background of a scholarly theory according to which there were in fact two Ilions rather than one. The initiator of the theory, which had for centuries hindered the correct identification of the site of Troy, seems to have been Hestiaea of Alexandria, of whom almost nothing is known, but its most influential exponent was the grammarian and commentator of Homer Demetrius of Scepsis (second century BCE). Demetrius was a native resident of the Troad, a fact that invested his discussion of the Trojan landscape with special authority. He was lavishly quoted by Strabo (see esp. 13.1.35, 40), which accounts for the influence of his theory in the modern period. The theory was conclusively refuted only in the 1870s, as a result of

Politicians were, however, a different matter. In 20 BCE, in the course of his visit to the provinces of Asia and Bithynia, Augustus arrived in Ilion. He stayed in the house of one of the citizens, Melanippides, with whom he had been connected by bonds of ceremonial friendship. A telling testimony of this event is provided by inscriptions on the eastern architrave of the temple of Athena and by the basis of a column representing Augustus' stay in Ilion and bearing an inscription which styles him a 'relative' (*suggenês*) and 'protector' (*patrôn*) of its citizens. (Let me note in passing that the 'Trojans' whom Augustus encountered were of course Greeks, descendants of the Greek colonists who had settled in the Troad at the beginning of the first millennium BCE.) However that may be, the ambitious building program launched in the subsequent years was the direct outcome of Augustus' visit.

The increasing tendency to see Troy as the antecedent of Rome exerted a visible influence on the city and its surroundings. The myth of Trojan origins of Rome reshaped Ilion into *Romana Pergama*[21] and resulted in a thorough reinterpretation not only of the Trojan saga but also of the Trojan landscape itself. The Greek participants in the Trojan War and the monuments associated with them came to be seen in a negative light, whereas the palaces of Assarakos and Priam, the house and the tomb of Hector became firmly established as new landmarks of Roman Ilium. These changes emphasized the image of Troy as the starting point in the history of Rome and legitimized Roman presence in Asia. For all practical purposes, Troy was reborn.

The dramatic turn in the reception of the Trojan landscape that took place in the Roman period is epitomized in an epigram on the tomb of Hector at Ophryneion, composed by Germanicus on the occasion of his visit to the city in 18 CE. The epigram, addressed to Hector, is concluded with the following words:

> *Ilios en surgit rursum inclita, gens colit illam*
> *Te Marte inferior, Martis amica tamen.*
> *Myrmidonas periisse omnes dic Hector Achilli,*
> *Thessaliam et magnis esse sub Aeneadis.*

Schliemann's excavations of Troy. On the travellers who were looking for Troy before Schliemann, see Cook 1973: 14–38; on the history of Schliemann's identification, see Traill 1995: 35–58, esp. 53.

[21] The expression was coined by Lucan, see Luc. 9.998–9: *restituam populos; grata vice moenia reddent | Ausonidae Phrygibus, Romanaque Pergama surgent* (spoken by Caesar).

> Look, the glorious Ilios is raised up again, and though the race that inhabits it is not equal to you in the matters of war, it is still a friend of Mars. Hector, tell Achilles that all the Myrmidons have perished, and Thessaly is subject to the great descendants of Aeneas.[22]

In 53 CE, on the occasion of his marriage to Octavia, the sixteen-year-old Nero delivered an oration whose main subject was Troy:

> Anxious to distinguish himself by noble pursuits, and the reputation of an orator, he advocated the cause of the people of Ilium, and having eloquently recounted how Rome was the offspring of Troy, and Aeneas the founder of the Julian line, with other old traditions akin to myths, he gained for his clients exemption from all public burdens.[23]

Ilion had never been more popular than in the three subsequent centuries. Emperors visited it; it became a major tourist attraction issuing souvenir coins with Trojan heroes and scenes from the Trojan War.[24] And yet, since the fourth century CE, probably because the Christianization of the empire stripped the city of its ideological importance, Ilium's name disappears from the record. This was a signal of its decline. In the middle of the fifth century, the agora began to be used as a cemetery, and after a series of earthquakes circa 500 CE the city was abandoned.[25] Troy returned to what it had always been in the imagination of the poets – a city in ruins. With time, even the ruins disappeared, not to be seen again till the end of the nineteenth century. Yet the image of the Trojan War carved out by poets and politicians of the Augustan era survived much longer.

Rome and Beyond

One of the results of the revision of the Trojan tradition initiated in Augustan Rome was that the Greek participants in the Trojan War came to be presented as inferior to the Trojans not only in Latin but also in Imperial Greek literature. Thus, in his *Trojan Oration*, addressed to the citizens of Ilium, Dio of Prusa (ca. 40 – ca. 115 CE) could already afford to represent Homer as a liar and the Trojans as the victors in the Trojan War. According to the *Trojan Oration*, Troy had never been sacked by the Greeks: in fact, it is the Greeks who had lost the war because of their unprovoked attack on Troy. Dio repeatedly praises the Trojans (read:

---

[22] *Anth. Lat.* 708. My translation.   [23] Tac. *Annales* 12.58.1. Tr. A. J. Church and W. J. Brodribb.
[24] Vermeule 1995; Minchin 2012.   [25] Rose 2011: 904.

Romans) and elevates Aeneas, a hero virtually ignored by other Greek authors. Even if the speech was meant as a rhetorical exercise rather than a serious treatment of the Trojan theme, Dio's pro-Roman orientation is unmistaken, and it is made explicit at the end of the oration, when he asserts that the truth about the Trojan War can now be told because 'the situation has changed ... for Greece is subject to others and so is Asia'.[26]

The *Trojan Oration* was part of a trend.[27] The latter produced not only such acknowledged masterpieces as Lucian's *True Stories* and Philostratus' *Heroicus* but also two accounts of the Trojan War written in Greek prose somewhere between the first and the third centuries CE: the *History of the Destruction of Troy* by 'Dares the Phrygian' and the *Journal of the Trojan War* by 'Dictys of Crete'. Although far from masterpieces, these two compositions were to become the foremost sources on the Trojan War for a millennium and a half. Both are presented as eyewitness accounts and therefore as far superior to Homer. The image of the Greek participants that they communicate, although not invariably negative, is far from flattering.[28] This is especially true of Dictys' *Journal* where, for example, Achilles kills Hector in a night ambush (3.15) and kills Memnon when the latter is already wounded by Ajax (4.6). But it is the Latin translations of Dictys and Dares, apparently made in the fourth and fifth centuries CE, that became overwhelmingly influential in the subsequent centuries.

It is true, of course, that such post-Augustan epics as Statius' *Achilleid* (96 CE) and the *Posthomerica* by Quintus of Smyrna (fourth century CE) displayed an attitude to the Trojan War that did not essentially differ from the tradition bequeathed by Homer.[29] Yet in the late antique, medieval, and early modern West it was Dictys and Dares rather than Statius and Quintus who became, as one scholar put it, 'the foundational texts of Trojan historiography'.[30] The fact that Homer was no longer available was far from being the only reason for the enormous popularity these two texts enjoyed.

More than anything else, the popularity of Dictys and Dares was an outcome of the lasting dialogue with the Roman past that ran deeply in the veins of Western tradition. This dialogue involved both identification with Rome and challenge to its authority: the first found its expression in the myth of Trojan ancestry, the second in the adoption of Hector rather than

---

[26] *Orationes* 11.150.
[27] Merkle 1996: 578–9; Zeitlin 2001; Kim 2010: 179–81; Whitmarsh 2010c: 398–9.
[28] See further King 1987: 140–1, Merkle 1996.   [29] King 1987: 129–38.
[30] Patterson 1991: 114.

Aeneas as a model hero (more later).[31] The earliest attribution of Trojan origins to a northern European people is attested as early as the mid seventh century CE: the people in question were the Franks, with the Britons following them one hundred and fifty years later.[32] Throughout the Middle Ages, more and more peoples, states and dynasties lay claim to Trojan ancestry: Venice, Sicily, Tuscany, Naples, Calabria, the Danes, the Normans, Belgium, the Saxons, the German Emperors, the Capetians, and this is just a partial list.[33]

It should also be taken into account that the idea of the Trojan War promulgated by Dictys and Dares went very well indeed with what could be found in Vergil's *Aeneid* (see aforementioned), and the *Aeneid* continued to be read and imitated throughout the Middle Ages.[34] Last but not least, as Katherine King put it, 'the Trojans were considered to be the ancestors of most European peoples, while Achilles and Odysseus were the representatives of the somewhat untrustworthy Eastern half of Christendom'[35] – so much so that the myth of Trojan ancestry was even mobilized to justify the Latin conquest of Constantinople (1204).[36]

All these created a suitable background for Dictys' and Dares' revisionist attitude towards Homer's picture of the Trojan War not only to be perpetuated but also to be taken further. In 1160, Benoît de Sainte-Maure made the account of Dares and, to a lesser degree, of Dictys the basis for his 30,000-verse-long *Le Roman de Troie*. The poem consistently presented Hector as a supreme hero and the Trojans as unambiguously superior to the Greeks; Achilles, on the other hand, became an object of vilification.[37] The popularity of *Le Roman de Troie* was overwhelming. It was soon translated into Spanish and German, adapted into French prose, and used as the basis for Italian poems. In the East it was translated into Greek as *The War of Troy* (Ὁ Πόλεμος της Τρωάδος), by far the longest medieval Greek romance. Since the early thirteenth century, *Historia destructionis Troiae*, the Latin version of *Le Roman de Troie* by Guido delle Colonne, became no less popular and was adapted as frequently.[38] In

---

[31] On two conflicting tendencies entrenched in the medieval myth of Trojan origins, see Waswo 1995; on the medieval attitudes to Aeneas and Hector, see Engels 1998a and 1998b, respectively.

[32] Waswo 1995: 269–74; cf. Engels 1998b: 140.

[33] Patterson 1991: 90–1; Waswo 1995: 286–7; Engels 1998b: 140. See also Patterson 1991: 84, on the myth of Trojan origins as 'the founding myth of Western history in the Middle Ages'.

[34] On the foundation myths of Trojan origins as 'quite remarkably Virgilian', see esp. Waswo 1995: 272; see also Patterson 1991: 90, 114; Ingledew 1994; Simpson 1998.

[35] King 2011: 721.   [36] Patterson 1991: 93; Engels 1998b: 140.

[37] See King 1987: 160–70; Engels 1998b.

[38] On Guido delle Colonne and his influence on the treatment of the Trojan theme in the late medieval and early modern period, see Simpson 1998; Engels 1998b, 140–1.

the subsequent centuries, the picture of the Trojan War established in *Le Roman de Troie* and *Historia destructionis Troiae* prevailed in both high and popular culture. It influenced Dante, Chaucer and Shakespeare. The popular medieval list of the Nine Worthies featured Hector as one of the three foremost heroes of pagan antiquity, the other two being Alexander the Great and Julius Caesar.[39]

To recapitulate, Vergil's idea of the inferiority of Greece before Rome and its imaginary antecedent Troy enjoyed a much longer life than Horace's and Dionysius' vision of a single Graeco-Roman civilization, a vision which happens also to be our own. The latter re-emerged only in the wake of the cultural transformation effected by the Renaissance and was not firmly established until the seventeenth and the eighteenth centuries.[40] The same would also be true of the picture of the Trojan War found in the poems of Homer, whose authority was re-established at approximately the same period.[41]

Conclusions

Whatever its historical and cultural background, by the time of its being reinvigorated in the mid first century BCE the myth of Trojan origins of the Romans had been universally taken for granted. There was more than one way to negotiate the convoluted relationship between Greece and Rome that it implied. One way was to continue privileging Romulus and the old foundational legend by marginalizing the myth of Trojan origins along with the antagonism between Greece and Rome that inevitably followed from it: this was the way Horace followed. Another way was to neutralize the antagonism by claiming that the Trojans and, consequently, the Romans were in fact of Greek descent: this was what Dionysius tried to accomplish. But it was also possible, rather than avoiding the antagonism, to bring it to the fore by presenting the Trojans and, by implication, the Romans as superior to the Greeks. This was what Vergil did.

On the face of it, Vergil's solution was the least obvious of the three. But it was the one that suited best the new geopolitical reality and the imperial

---

[39] A useful survey of the medieval literary production focused on the Trojan War can be found in Ingledew 1994: 666 n. 6; on the Nine Worthies, see Engels 1998b: 144–5 (I am grateful to Josef Geiger for drawing my attention to the latter).

[40] As late as 1714, the French scholar Nicolas Fréret was imprisoned in the Bastille for presenting the argument according to which the Franks were of South German rather than Trojan origin.

[41] On the problems by which the re-establishment of Homer was accompanied, see Finkelberg 2012.

ambitions of Rome. This transpires not only from the *Aeneid* references to Roman military victories over Greeks or the epigram of Germanicus amounting to much the same but, especially, from those imperial Greek authors who, similarly to Dio of Prusa, overtly recognized that the old narrative of the Trojan War did not suit any longer the world in which they lived. The revised Trojan narrative they promulgated fit to perfection the distribution of power within the Roman Empire. To quote Dio again, 'the situation has changed . . . for Greece is subject to others and so is Asia'. It was this change of situation that was above all responsible for the thorough revision of the Trojan tradition that took place in the Imperial Period.

6 | Claiming Roman Origins

Greek Cities and the Roman Colonial Pattern

CÉDRIC BRÉLAZ[*]

Much of the discourse about the privileged relationship between Rome and the Greek world, in comparison with other nations and cultures, relied on the alleged kinship and the common origin the Romans were claiming to have with Greeks.[1] For this purpose, the Trojan myth, since it was first borrowed from the Greeks in the third century BCE, has been continuously reshaped and reinterpreted by the Romans, depending on the immediate context, in order to support the view of a Greek origin for themselves.[2] But what about the opposite phenomenon? Were there Greek cities explicitly claiming Roman origins? Although most Greeks proved to be quite reluctant to admit that Rome possessed any significant cultural achievement, the acknowledgment of the rise of Roman rule as a shifting point for the Greek world can be observed in various fields. One may mention, for instance, the spread in the Greek world, as early as the beginning of the second century BCE, of the worship of the goddess Roma, as well as of the Roman foundation myths and of the she-wolf iconography, as the consequence of Rome's interference into the Hellenistic world;[3] the deliberate reference made by various Greek cities to the alleged kinship between themselves and Rome in order to support requests of privileges in diplomatic intercourse with the Roman Republic;[4] the celebration by the Greeks themselves of the new era inaugurated by Augustus through his victory at Actium which was supposed to bring happiness and wealth to the entire world according to Augustan ideology;[5] the early launch in the province of Asia, and subsequently the diffusion throughout the Eastern Mediterranean, of the imperial cult as the expression of the loyalty of Greek cities to Roman power;[6] finally, the

---

[*] I am delighted to offer this paper as a tribute to Benjamin Isaac for his crucial contribution to our understanding of Roman colonies, in the Near East of course, but also all over the empire. This study was completed during my Stanley J. Seeger Visiting Research Fellowship in Hellenic Studies at Princeton University. I would like to thank the conveners and attendees of the Tel Aviv conference for their remarks and suggestions, as well as Angelos Chaniotis, Christopher Jones and François Kirbihler for sharing material with me.

[1] Isaac 2004: 381–405. [2] See the chapter by Margalit Finkelberg in this volume.
[3] Salvo 2012. [4] Battistoni 2010. [5] Leschhorn 1993; Thonemann 2015.
[6] Ando 2000; Kirbihler 2012.

enthusiastic – and to some extent paradoxical – assumption made by Aelius Aristides that Roman hegemony, by unifying the Greek world, would have allowed the Greeks to end internal struggles and to live in peace.[7]

In what follows, I will rather focus on the influence of the political and institutional model of a Roman colony on Greek cities and will assess the use which was made by some cities of colonial symbols and status in order to claim Roman origins. The progressive Hellenization of the political institutions of the Roman colonies which had been settled in the Greek-speaking provinces, due to the cultural influence of their Hellenic environment, is a well-known phenomenon.[8] But did Roman colonies in the Greek East have conversely any influence on the surrounding Greek cities? Unlike in the West, there were few Roman colonies in those provinces (around thirty by the time of Augustus),[9] and the Roman municipal model was not widespread in the eastern part of the empire (there were only two *municipia* of Roman citizens in the Greek East,[10] contrasting with the numerous occupational associations gathering Roman businessmen in Greek cities from the second century BCE). On the whole, Greek cities did not introduce public offices borrowed from Roman colonies into their constitutions,[11] and the presence of some Roman colonies in the Greek-speaking provinces did not lead to a Latinization of the surrounding populations, not even at a regional level.[12] Still, some Greek cities adopted various elements specific to Roman colonies or put emphasis on their refoundation by Roman emperors. Having the rank of a Roman colony meant for a local community to be a part of the Roman *res publica* within the provinces. This chapter will examine which cities were ready to comply with the Roman colonial model, why they did so, to what extent, and what the meaning of their claim for Roman origins was. I will argue that the issue of the compliance of Greek cities with the Roman constitutional model of a colony was an aspect of cultural interaction.

1 Celebrating Roman (Re)foundation: Roman Colonial Iconography in Greek Coinage

Greek cities in the Imperial period were allowed to continue to mint bronze coins. While the obverse side of the coins typically showed the portrait of

---

[7] Aristid., *Or.* 26.   [8] Brélaz 2017b.   [9] Sartre 2001b.
[10] Stobi in Upper Macedonia (Papazoglou 1986) and Coila in Thracian Chersonesos (Robert 1948: 44–54).
[11] Dmitriev 2005: 189–217; Brélaz 2011; Heller 2013.   [12] Brélaz 2015.

the reigning emperor (local communities were probably requested to do so, even if the so-called 'pseudo-autonomous' coins suggest that there could have been exceptions),[13] Greek cities were very proud to display on the reverse symbols of their glorious past and their fame. In most cases, reverses depicted the main deities traditionally worshipped in the various cities as well as mythological themes, or referred to the sanctuaries or to the ceremonies and games for which the cities were known. This trend towards celebration of local patriotism in the coinage was so common and the competition between cities was so high that this practice also influenced the Roman colonies which had been settled in the Greek-speaking provinces. By the early third century CE, most of these colonies had replaced the usual Roman symbols which had been found so far in the coinage of every single Roman colony all over the empire with depictions referring to local cults and myths and in some cases showing indigenous deities.[14]

I would like to consider here the opposite phenomenon and to see why some Greek cities chose to show on the reverse sides of their coins Roman colonial symbols instead of local ones, and what the meaning of those depictions was. I will focus on the most distinctive of the Roman colonial symbols, which is the scene depicting the very foundation of the colony with the founder acting as a priest, leading two oxen and plowing the original furrow which would have delimited the sacred area of the new community. Since it represented the ceremony performed during the formal creation of the colony – repeating the rite performed by Romulus himself when he founded the city of Rome – this scene was very common in the coinage of most Roman colonies, in the West as in the East, since colonies were part of the Roman State abroad.[15] Now, a similar depiction can be recognized on coins struck by the Carian city of Tralles under Augustus. The obverse side bears the portrait of Gaius Caesar, while the reverse shows a pair of oxen led by a man plowing.[16] The city of Tralles had been striking coins showing bovines for centuries during the Hellenistic period, and this was still the case under Augustus and even in the second century CE.[17] But those were humped bulls and they were depicted in a way which was similar to Near Eastern iconography.[18] This time, however, the presence of a yoke of oxen led by a man clearly hinted at a Roman model.[19]

---

[13] Johnston 1985.   [14] Katsari and Mitchell 2008.   [15] Papageorgiadou-Bani 2004.
[16] RPC I 2649.
[17] SNG München 23, 695–709; RPC I 2639; RPC Online IV 1591, 1593, 1633, 2890.
[18] Casabonne 2006.
[19] Humped bulls can, however, be depicted in plowing scenes as well, as seen on coins struck by the 'honorary' colony of Tyana (SNG von Aulock 6544, 6548–9, 6553).

The same plowing scene can be seen on coins of the city of Thessalonica. In this case, the choice of such a depiction can be explained by the immediate context. At that time, in 48 BCE during the civil war with Caesar, Pompey was staying in Thessalonica. Ancient sources tell us how Pompey acquired land in the town to convert it into a portion of the Roman soil. Such a legal fiction enabled Pompey and the senators who had joined him in Thessalonica to take *auspicia* and to act in the name of the *res publica* as if they had been in Rome.[20] The presence of the plowing scene on these coins seems to have referred to that precise event, when foreign territory was transformed into a part of the land belonging to the Roman people, as was usually done for the creation of a Roman colony.

The context must have been completely different in the case of Tralles. We know that the city of Tralles was severely damaged by an earthquake in 27 BCE and that the emperor Augustus helped the city recover from the destruction through substantial support. It was argued by Thomas Broughton that Augustus seized the opportunity to send Roman colonists to Tralles and to give them lands taken from the territory of the city.[21] The plowing scene on the coin would have referred to such settlements. This assumption is still the common view on this issue in scholarship.[22] The problem is that we don't have any other evidence for the presence of a group of Roman colonists in Tralles. Tralles was certainly not transformed into a Roman colony on this occasion. As far as we can infer from the epigraphic evidence, the city only had Greek institutions in the Imperial period. The possibility that Tralles could have been an example of a double community – that is, a Roman colony existing next to a Greek city which would have been preserved – [23] should be ruled out, since the coins showing the plowing scene bear a legend in Greek and were struck by the Greek city alone. There was actually a community of Roman citizens in Tralles (οἱ ἐν Τράλλεσι κατοικοῦντες Ῥωμαῖοι), but, as in many cities of Asia Minor, those were gathered into a local association of Roman businessmen run by a *curator* or 'chairman'.[24] The existence of this occupational association in Tralles, even if we consider that it could act as a corporate body along with local Greek institutions, is insufficient to explain why the city chose to have the plowing scene, typical of the colonial foundations, displayed on its coins.

This scene, I think, was intended to stress the symbolic refoundation of the city after the earthquake of 27 BCE. The role of the emperor had been so

---

[20] Touratsoglou 1987: 56.   [21] Broughton 1935.   [22] Magie 1950: 469; Thonemann 2011: 208.
[23] See n. 51.   [24] I. Tralleis und Nysa 19, 77, 80. See Van Andringa 2003; Terpstra 2013.

crucial for the recovery of the city that Tralles was renamed after Augustus.[25] As shown by inscriptions as well as by the legends on the coins struck by the city, the official name of Tralles for several decades after that was Kaisareia.[26] Augustus himself was celebrated as the 'founder' (*ktistes*) of Tralles, as shown by the dedication of a statue in his honor by the city.[27] This points to a wider phenomenon: the use of imperial epithets in order to name Greek cities and the celebration of Roman emperors as founders or refounders of Greek cities. As in the case of Tralles, several other cities also called Kaisareia, like Sardis and Philadelphia, had received help from Tiberius after the big earthquake of 17 CE in the Hermos Valley.[28] We also know of dozens of cities in Asia Minor which were using, at least for a while, denominations patterned after the names *Julius*, *Kaisar*, *Sebastos* or other imperial names.[29] But not all these cities had effectively been founded or even rebuilt by Roman authorities. The cases where an entirely new city was created by an emperor, like Nicopolis in Epirus thanks to the synoecism performed by Octavian after his victory at Actium,[30] were quite rare. Moreover, the honorific title *ktistes* – and in some cases even the deliberately archaizing title *oikistes* – were most of the time given to emperors, not because of their material support or because of their completion of a building program but because of their grant of legal privileges, such as tax immunity or the organization of new games.[31]

The use of an imperial epithet as an official title by a local community could not occur without the emperor's permission. As in the case where Greek cities wanted to give him exceptional honors – like the dedication of a temple – the emperor's consent was probably requested and ambassadors were sent to him for this purpose, as shown by the correspondence between the imperial power and local communities.[32] This means that imperial names such as Kaisareia were not imposed upon Greek cities by the central power, but rather were sought by local communities because of the prestige

---

[25] For an alternative view on the circumstances that led to the grant of the name Kaisareia to Tralles, see Kirbihler 2017.

[26] I. Tralleis und Nysa 39, 41; RPC I 2646–58; RPC II 1094–5, 1099–105. See Magie 1950: 1331–2, n. 7; Thonemann 2011: 238, n. 121; Delrieux 2012: 265, n. 18.

[27] I. Tralleis und Nysa 35. A decree displayed at Olympia and praising Augustus for restoring a city from Asia Minor which was ruined by an earthquake (Dittenberger and Purgold 1896: no. 53), regarded by some scholars as emanating from Tralles, should rather be attributed to Sardes according to Rigsby 2010. Lastly, Jones 2015 has rather argued for Chios.

[28] Delrieux 2012.

[29] Brélaz 2017a. See subsequent text for Pisidian Antioch/Caesarea and Caesarea Maritima.

[30] Guerber 2013.   [31] Pont 2007.   [32] See, e.g., Oliver 1989: 91–4, no. 23.

linked to such denominations.[33] Some Greek cities in Asia Minor were then eager to ask for a name suggesting a Roman origin, thinking it was an appropriate way to show their loyalty to the emperor.

In the case of Tralles, the damages caused by the earthquake of 27 BCE had been so serious and the response of Augustus so prompt (seven senators of consular rank are said to have been sent to Tralles by the emperor to deal with the reconstruction of the city) that the intervention of the emperor was thought to have been a 'second foundation of the city' (δευτέρα κτίσις τῆς πόλεως), as shown by an inscription praising one of the ambassadors who were successfully sent from Tralles to Augustus (who was staying in Spain at that time) to ask for his help after the earthquake. The epigram following the dedication celebrates this man as if he had himself refounded the city.[34] This epigram was later seen and copied by the historian Agathias in the sixth century CE.[35] On this occasion, Agathias wrongly assumed Tralles had been peopled with 'Romans' (Ρωμαῖοι) after the city was refounded thanks to the emperor's support.[36] This was probably, more than five centuries after the event, the only satisfactory explanation he had been able to find for why Tralles changed its name for Kaisareia at that time. In fact, the measures taken by Augustus must have been so massive and decisive in Tralles that the city thought the best way to express its recognition was not only to adopt the name of the emperor but even to display on its coins the distinctive scene of the foundation of a city according to the Roman pattern, in order to show that Kaisareia was now a new city.

The reproduction of the plowing scene on pseudo-autonomous coins minted by Tralles in the late first century, as well as the depiction of the Roman she-wolf together with the twins on coins struck under Gordianus III might be regarded – as in the case of Ilium where the constant presence of the she-wolf on the local coinage was meant to celebrate the kinship between this city and Rome through the Trojan myth – as a further sign of the privileged links the city of Tralles maintained with Rome since its

---

[33] Grant of the imperial epithet (*diuinum cognomen*) as a *donum* from the emperor Constantius II to Laodicea ad Mare in AE 2010, 1699. The city was at that time an 'honorary' colony: see next.

[34] Jones 2011 (AE 2011, 1349).   [35] Agath. 2.17.6–8.

[36] Agath. 2.17.5. The word ἀποικία used by Agathias in this context to describe the city certainly does not refer to any Roman colony settled there but echoes the depiction given by the same author earlier in the text of Tralles as being a former Pelasgian 'colony' (2.17.1: τὸ μὲν παλαιὸν Πελασγῶν γέγονεν ἀποικία). For Agathias' classicizing approach of history, see Cameron 1970, 89–111. For another example of Christian reinterpretation of earlier local history in Phrygian Hierapolis, see Thonemann 2012. Nor can it be inferred from the fact that Brutus threatened the city of Tralles to seize part of its territory in 43 BCE (Jones 2016) that lands were declared *ager publicus* there as in Attaleia (see below).

refoundation.[37] Paradoxically enough, the grant of the status of a free city to Samos by Augustus while the emperor was staying on the island in 20/19 BCE seems to have been commemorated in a similar way, by using the colonial metaphor as a symbol for a new start and a refoundation with the participation of Roman power: Augustus was on this occasion praised as the "benefactor, savior and founder" of the city and an "era of the colony" (ἔτος τῆς κολωνίας), replacing the "era of Caesar's victory" referring to the battle of Actium in 31 BCE which had been used thus far, was introduced from that time on.[38]

2 Using Roman Phraseology: 'Colonists' in Greek Cities from the Hellenistic Past to the Roman Model

As Gellius makes clear in the famous passage of his work where the author makes the distinction between a *colonia* and a *municipium* and where he describes the colonies as 'little Romes', the Latin word *colonia* was a technical term and referred to the communities of Roman citizens settled on provincial ground as a result of a decision of the Roman central authorities.[39] Unlike *municipia*, which had been pre-existing cities provided only afterwards with institutions patterned after the Roman model, colonies were from the beginning parts of the Roman State. Therefore, the term *colonia* could not be used in theory to describe a community which would not have been formally created and founded by Rome.

Now, the word *kolones* transliterated in Greek characters from the Latin *coloni* occurs among the official titles of two cities from Phrygia Paroreius in Central Anatolia, Apollonia and Neapolis. Several inscriptions mention the Ἀπολλωνιᾶται Λύκιοι Θρᾷκες κόλωνες from Apollonia, as well as the Νεαπολῖται Θρᾷκες κόλωνες from Neapolis.[40] The few other instances of the transliterated form of *colonus* in Greek (κόλων) we have in the epigraphical record all refer to citizens of Roman colonies in the East (including

---

[37] Tralles: RPC II 1107 (plowing scene); RPC VII.1 481 (she-wolf); Ilium: RPC I 2318; RPC Online IV 90; RPC VII.1 44–5. For occasional depictions of the she-wolf on the coinage of other Greek cities, see, e.g., Ancyra (RPC Online IV 10469), Ephesus (RPC Online IX 629), Laodicea on the Lycus (RPC II 1295), Nicopolis ad Istrum (RPC Online IV 4351), Philippopolis (RPC Online IV 7475).

[38] IG XII 6/1, 186, 66–7; 187, 8; 400.   [39] Gel. 16.13.8–9.

[40] Apollonia: IGR III 318; MAMA IV 143 A (restitution of this title on the statue basis dedicated to the imperial family on which a copy of the *Res Gestae* was engraved), 147, 150; SEG XXXVII 1100; Roueché 1993: 230–5, no. 91 i.a, ll. 49–50; Neapolis: I. Sultan Dağı 505.

'honorary' colonies).[41] Yet some papyri register *koloneiai* as a category of lands in Egypt.[42] In this specific context, the word *koloneia* might have been used by analogy with the formal Roman colonies involving land allotment to soldiers (if we consider that some of those lands in Egypt seem to have belonged to veterans of the Roman army), or more probably with another meaning of *colonia* in Latin, which can refer as well to land ownership and especially to imperial estates.[43] The fact that Neapolis was located in an area surrounded by several imperial estates,[44] however, does not imply that the term *kolones* in the official title of the city should in any way be related to the nearby presence of imperial peasants or *coloni*, whose internal organization was distinct from the Greek city.

In order to explain the presence of the term *kolones* in Apollonia and Neapolis, it was argued by Stephen Mitchell that Roman colonists had been settled in those cities.[45] Such evidence was considered one of the major arguments supporting the theory of the existence of the so-called 'non-colonial colonies', to use the expression coined by Thomas Broughton in an article published in 1935 I already referred to earlier.[46] According to this theory, there were in several places throughout the Roman Empire groups of Roman citizens which would have been settled by the Roman State on the territory of foreign communities without enjoying the formal status of a Roman colony, hence the oxymoron 'non-colonial colonies'. The problem is that this expression doesn't match any known category in Roman public law. Admittedly Roman citizens, personally or even collectively, could in some cases receive within the territory of foreign local communities land lots which had previously been acquired by the Roman people and declared *ager publicus*. Thanks to the testimony of Cicero,[47] this is known to have been the case, for instance, for Pamphylian Attaleia where the recipients of viritane allotments might then have organized in a corporate body known as συμπολιτευόμενοι Ῥωμαῖοι.[48] This was also the case, as suggested by Benjamin Isaac, in Emmaus near Jerusalem. This place was

---

[41] See, e.g., I. Ephesos 1238 (Pisidian Antioch); AE 1952, 206 (Caesarea Maritima); AE 1998, 1207, 1210 (Dium); AE 2002, 1329 (Syrian Antioch); IGLS XVII/1 551 (Berytus). See also Spaul 1994: 92–3, for κόλωνες being cavalrymen recruited from colonies such as Iconium and Pisidian Antioch and serving in the *ala I Augusta Gemina Colonorum*.

[42] Dietze-Mager 2009.

[43] See, e.g., Colum. 11.1.23; Hauken 1998: 2–28 (petition from the *Saltus Burunitanus*).

[44] Mitchell 1978: 317.   [45] Mitchell 1978.   [46] Broughton 1935.

[47] Cic., *Leg. agr.* 1.2.5; 2.19.50.

[48] SEG VI 646; XVII 578. The same expression occurs also in Pontic Amisos (IGR IV 314) and in Isaura (IGR III 292, 294). For *politeumata* as groups and communities having an internal organization comparable to the institutions of a formal city, see Förster and Sänger 2014.

used by Vespasian to allot land to 800 veterans after the Jewish War.[49] But in none of these instances is it granted that those communities of Roman citizens were called *coloniae*, since they apparently did not form autonomous political entities such as ordinary colonies.[50]

To turn to the specific case of Apollonia and Neapolis, neither of these cities were double communities, with a formal Roman colony coexisting with the Greek city, as Stephen Mitchell has very convincingly demonstrated for Iconium or Ninica and as it might well have been the case for further colonies, such as Sinope and Bithynian Apamea, as well as for Nicopolis in Epirus founded as a Greek city, but also maybe along with a Roman colony at the same time, by Octavian.[51] The word *kolones* was part of the official title of both cities, and no distinction was made between the *kolones*, on one hand, and the local population (*Apolloniatai/Neapolitai*), on the other. We must infer from these expressions that the citizens of Apollonia and Neapolis were at the same time 'Lykians/Thracians' and 'colonists', or even better that they were described as 'Thracian colonists' (in addition to 'Lykians' in the case of Apollonia). Each one of these words, in expanding the city's title, contributed to expressing the identity of the local population. The first two (Λύκιοι Θρᾷκες) were ethnics referring to the alleged origin of the inhabitants of Apollonia. The first settlers of Apollonia in Hellenistic times were thought to have been people who migrated from Lykia to Pisidia and Phrygia, as well as Thracian mercenaries engaged by Seleukid kings. This view is supported by the continued use of Thracian names among local onomastics in Phrygia Paroreius until the Imperial period.[52] In calling themselves 'Lykians' and 'Thracian colonists', the citizens of Imperial Apollonia were consciously remembering the Hellenistic foundation of the city as a military colony. The city of Apollonia even struck coins with the portrait of Alexander the Great celebrated as the 'founder' (*ktistes*) of the city in Severan times, although this was a spurious claim, and a cult to Seleukid rulers was kept – or maybe even rather reactivated – during the Imperial period.[53] Such attention paid to the self-promotion of local identity and of civic pride, as well as to local memories, was very common through Greek cities in the Imperial period, and it even included in some cases the worshipping of Hellenistic rulers.[54]

---

[49] Jos., BJ 7.217. The colonial status of this settlement cannot be inferred from the non-technical name 'Qolonia' which was given later to the place with reference to the Roman soldiers who had been sent there: see Isaac 1992: 347–8, 428.

[50] Brélaz 2016.   [51] Mitchell 1979; Esch 2008; Ruscu 2006; Woytek 2011.

[52] Calder 1956; Le Roy 2000; Dana 2011: 107–9; Bru (in press).

[53] Rebuffat 1986; *SEG* VI 592.   [54] Spawforth 2006; Chankowski 2010.

So, why use the Latin word *kolones* to refer to the military colonists sent to Apollonia by the Seleukids?

The word *kolones* was probably borrowed by the cities of Apollonia and Neapolis from the neighboring Roman colonies which were quite numerous in Pisidia.[55] Pisidian Antioch, which was by far the most influential of those colonies, had common borders with both cities and was linked to them through the Via Sebaste. The colony presented itself in Greek as ἡ Ἀντιοχέων κολώνων Καισαρέων πόλις, Caesarea being one of the other names of Antioch dating back to the time when the king of Galatia Amyntas probably renamed its capital in honor of Augustus.[56] The word *kolones*, used in its official titulature by the powerful colony of Antioch, must have seemed fashionable to the citizens of Apollonia and Neapolis. This can explain why they preferred this terminology to a word like *katoikoi*, which usually described soldiers settled on land by a king in the Hellenistic period.[57] A confirmation of such use of Roman colonial terminology as a reference standard can be found in the Near East. As has been recently pointed out by Maurice Sartre, the same word *kolonia* (or *koloneitai* referring to some people coming from a *koloneia*) in Greek characters occurs in inscriptions from Southern Syria.[58] One of these inscriptions was dated by the era of an unspecified *kolonia*. The area where these inscriptions were discovered is too far from known Roman colonies (either veteran colonies such as Berytus or 'honorary' colonies such as Bosra or Damascus) for us to consider that this word could refer to them. It is more probable that the *koloniai* referred to in this context corresponded to the military settlements founded by King Herod in order to control the region and to fight against brigands. It is well known how deeply influenced by the Roman model the Herodian kingdom was: Herod's army was organized according to the Roman one, and the king renamed his capital Caesarea after the emperor.[59] It is not surprising that Herod would have taken the Latin technical term *colonia* to decribe the military colonies he was founding in his kingdom. Then, in using the word *kolones* next to the ethnics 'Lykians' or 'Thracians', the citizens of Apollonia and Neapolis were seeking to benefit at the same time from the glorious past of their Hellenistic military foundation and from the prestige specific to the most up-to-date Roman terminology as far as colonization was concerned.

---

[55] Anderson 1898: 96; Levick 1967; Labarre 2016.
[56] I. Ephesos 1238; Roueché 1993: 230–5, no. 91 i.a, l. 47–8.
[57] Launey 1949, 1037–85; Schuler 1998: 33–41.　　[58] IGLS XV 62a, 103. See also Sartre 2011.
[59] Sartre 2001a: 514–15, 530–6.

3   Becoming a Part of the Roman State: The Promotion of Greek Cities to Colonial Rank

Some cities not only reused Roman colonial symbols and terminology, thus distorting the original meaning of the word, in order to take advantage of the fame linked to the privileged status of a Roman colony, but they even went further and officially bore the title of a colony. Those cities are usually known as 'honorary colonies' in scholarship. The so-called honorary colonies were foreign cities which had been granted the official title of Roman colony without necessarily being settled with veterans, as was the case with the military colonies founded during the second half of the first century BCE.

The transformation of a Greek city into a Roman colony was sometimes meant to punish local communities which had supported the defeated enemy of an *imperator* or resisted Rome, as shown by the cases of the colonies of Sinope, Buthrotum and, above all, of Aelia Capitolina in Jerusalem.[60] This was never the primary purpose of the creation of a colony, but Roman authorities were encouraged to choose as a place for founding a colony preferably a city which in the past had shown hostility toward them. For most 'honorary colonies', however, the grant of colonial status seems to have been a reward rather than a punishment. This is obvious, for instance, for the cities of Selinous in Cilicia and Halala in Cappadocia which were elevated to colonial rank and renamed Traianopolis and Faustinopolis respectively after Trajan and Marcus Aurelius' wife who died there, as a tribute to the emperor's and to the empress' memory.[61] The same can be said of the birthplace of the emperor Philip, a village of the province of Arabia, which became by decision of the emperor the colony of Philippopolis.[62] Similarly, Benjamin Isaac has argued that Caesarea Maritima, the capital of the Herodian kingdom, could also have been granted by Vespasian the status of a Roman colony (with the subsequent grant of Roman citizenship to its inhabitants) to thank the local population for its support during the Jewish War.[63] The grant under Claudius of the colonial status to Caesarea of Mauretania (modern Cherchell in Algeria), the former capital of king Juba, is another example of early concession of colonial rank to a city which was named

---

[60] Isaac 1980–1/1998a; Sartre 2001b: 127; Rizakis 2004: 81–3.   [61] Guerber 2010: 400–1.

[62] IGLS XV, pp. 467–71.

[63] Isaac 2009: 55–60. For an alternative view regarding Caesarea Maritima as an ordinary military colony implying the settlement of Roman soldiers, see Eck 2009.

after the emperor Augustus by a loyal client king, presumably as a reward in this case too.[64]

Most 'honorary colonies', however, were Near Eastern cities which were given colonial rank after the civil war Severus had won against Pescennius Niger. While Severus deprived the cities which had supported Niger of their privileges and turned them into villages, like Antioch or Byzantium, some cities which joined Severus were awarded colonial rank, such as Laodicea. In the same way, Heliopolis, which had belonged up to this point to the colony of Berytus, gained its autonomy from that colony because Berytus had supported Niger.[65] Some other cities were granted colonial rank in the newly conquered province of Mesopotamia, probably because of their support of Roman troops.[66] It seems then that some cities were actively searching for the official grant of colonial rank by the emperor. The perspective of a general grant of Roman citizenship to the local population and the hope of getting fiscal privileges through the additional concession of the *ius Italicum* that some Eastern colonies were actually enjoying must have been a strong stimulus for those cities to look for the colonial status.[67]

The adoption of the colonial status typically required a Greek city to display the title of *colonia* officially and, since it was the original language of the political entity it was now part of, to use Latin for public purposes, especially for legends on coins.[68] The adoption of the Latin language had been for centuries one of the distinctive characteristics of the integration of a political entity into the Roman State, especially when local communities of Italy were granted the rank of *municipium* after the Social War.[69] Even if, unlike in first-century BCE Italy, the use of Latin does not prove to have been systematic in the cities made Roman colonies in Severan times, these were not just cosmetic changes. The conversion of a city into a Roman colony meant the disappearance of the previously existing political entity and the replacement of most Greek institutions by Roman offices and laws. Colonial by-laws patterned after the Roman model (such as the *lex Ursonensis*)[70] were probably still given in the Severan period to the cities accessing that status. Werner Eck has recently published copies of the colonial law from Ratiaria in Dacia dating to the reign of Trajan and of the municipal law from Troesmis in Lower Moesia issued under Marcus Aurelius, showing that Roman authorities continued to issue colonial and municipal by-laws matching the Roman norms (and, in that case,

---

[64] Leveau 1984: 13–24.   [65] Hošek 2017.   [66] Guerber 2010: 375–416.
[67] Guerber 2010: 376–7.   [68] Millar 1990.   [69] Berrendonner 2002; Cappelletti 2011.
[70] Crawford 1996: I, 393–454, no. 25 with AE 2006, 645.

respectively the examples known from the *lex Ursonensis* and from the Flavian *municipia* in Spain) in the second century CE.[71] Because they were now part of the Roman State, the 'honorary colonies' struck coins not only with legends in Latin, as mentioned earlier, but even with the typical iconography of colonial foundation, especially the plowing scene. Actually, the cities which had been elevated to colonial rank were from a legal point of view full colonies, and no distinction was made, for instance, by the jurist Ulpian between those cities which were given the *ius coloniae* and the military colonies settled in the second half of the first century BCE by Caesar or Augustus.[72] Hence the expression 'honorary colonies', convenient as it can be, does not reflect any legal reality in Roman administrative practice.

Unlike in the case of Tralles, where we have seen that there is no reason to think a formal colony had been settled, the plowing scene on the coins of the so-called 'honorary colonies' should not be simply understood as a metaphor for the promotion of these Greek cities to the rank of Roman colony. Since these cities were effectively given a Roman constitution and integrated into the Roman State, it is perfectly possible and even probable that the creation of those colonies had formally been performed through the plowing ceremony delimiting the borders of the new community according to the Roman rite. What is more, Eduard Dąbrowa has suggested that the *vexilla* depicted on the coins of some of these colonies, mentioning even the numbers of the relevant legions, were certainly referring to the veterans who had actually been settled in these cities after they were granted colonial status. This must have been the case, for instance, in Tyre, in Sidon and in Damascus.[73] The settlement of veterans in the territory of some of these cities must have then led to a deep reorganization of land property. The meaning of *vexilla* for the cities which had been turned into Roman colonies significantly differed from the Roman legion banners which were depicted on the coinage of many other Greek cities through Asia Minor in the Imperial period. In that case, Roman military symbols were simply intended to celebrate the victories of the imperial armies, and they should not be regarded as a clue for any settlement of Roman soldiers on the territory of those cities.[74]

---

[71] Eck 2016a; Eck 2016b.   [72] Ulp. (1 de cens.) *Dig.* 50.15.1.

[73] Dąbrowa 2004; Dąbrowa 2012.

[74] Rebuffat 1997. There is no reason to assume that Roman veterans were settled in Philomelium, Laodicea on the Lycus, Side and Anemurium because *vexilla* were depicted on the coins of these cities, as suggested by Rebuffat 1997: 30–45, since the same author shows that in most other cities of Asia Minor this depiction was instead symbolizing the loyalty of local communities

We can infer from the evidence discussed previously that the promotion to the rank of colony was not simply a matter of honor and, in any case, this was never an insignificant event. Becoming a Roman colony meant a heavy price to be paid by the Greek cities willing to enjoy the prestige of what was considered by them a privileged status. The loss of their centuries-long autonomy was compensated for by the possibility of becoming a part of the hegemonic power. This was for a local community the ultimate stage of integration into the Roman Empire.

Conclusions: Rome – An Empire of Many Cities

Scholarship has so far put much emphasis on the reluctance of most Greeks to acknowledge various aspects of Roman rule, especially with regard to cultural issues. One can mention, for instance, the relatively small number of Greeks who were able to speak Latin fluently;[75] the fact that educated Greeks – such as the orators of the Second Sophistic – deliberately avoided using Latin technical terms in their works even when they were describing Roman institutions; the lack of interest of Greek intellectuals in Roman history – with the exception of Plutarch – even when they were supposed to praise the Roman Empire, as Aelius Aristides in his speech to Rome;[76] finally, the rather harsh judgment of educated Greeks on Roman rule, such as Dio Chrysostom's qualifying it as a 'slavery'.[77]

Despite this, and even if most local communities of the Roman Empire were very jealous of their autonomy, we have seen in this paper that some Greek cities were willing to appropriate the symbolism of Roman colonies and to enjoy the prestige, and even the status, of being a part of the Roman State. If the use of Roman colonial symbols or terminology on coins and inscriptions remained a very limited phenomenon, in each instance due to very specific circumstances – the refoundation of the city after an earthquake thanks to the emperor in Tralles, the regional influence of the colony of Pisidian Antioch on the cities of Apollonia and Neapolis, and possibly the grant of freedom by Augustus in the case of Samos – the promotion of cities to the rank of Roman colony can be noticed on a broader scale, especially in the Severan period.

---

towards the Roman army and the emperor. Compare the occasional depiction of the Senate or the Roman People on coins minted by Greek cities: Martin 2013: 84–102.

[75] Rochette 1997.   [76] Pernot 2008.

[77] Dio Chrys., *Or.* 31.125; 34.51. See also Plut., *Mor.* 813 E; 814 E-F; 824 C; 824 E.

The appetite of Near Eastern cities and of some cities of Eastern Anatolia for the Roman colonial status sharply contrasts with the situation in Greece, where local communities were eager to keep their old privileges and considered the rank of free city the most enviable status. This also differed from the situation in Western Asia Minor, where cities preferred to compete for various honorific titles granted or confirmed by the emperors, such as *neokoros* and *metropolis*, or for becoming the capital of a judicial district or for organizing new games acknowledged by the emperor.[78] While some cities in the Imperial period tried to prove their antiquity and their Greekness by maintaining their centuries-long autonomy or joining the Panhellenion,[79] others were ready to give up their autonomy to adopt the Roman colonial pattern and chose to get fame from their formal integration into the Roman State. This contrast shows the wide diversity of situations prevailing in the Roman Empire with regard to political identities and local traditions.

The way each local community saw its own position and role within what was now a world empire explains why some cities were trying to obtain the grant of colonial status by Roman authorities, while others preferred to preserve their ancient rights or to acquire titles which did not imply the loss of their autonomy as a Greek city. This variety of perceptions might lead in some cases to paradoxical claims, like Samos introducing a 'colonial era' to celebrate the refoundation of the city by Augustus through the grant of the rank of a free city (if my interpretation of the word *koloneia* in this context is correct) or, conversely, like Corinth joining the Panhellenion – that is, the institution representing the pinnacle of Hellenism in the Imperial period – although it was a Roman colony.[80] Significant differences in the way Roman rule was perceived can also be seen between local communities enjoying the same status, such as free cities: the elite of the free city of Rhodes, for instance, had little interest for gladiatorial games and was very reluctant to be designated by Roman names even if it actually was enjoying Roman citizenship (this proves to have matched exactly the attitude towards Romanization recommended by Apollonius of Tyana),[81] while in Aphrodisias the most powerful citizens competed for organizing gladiatorial shows and the reliefs of the Sebasteion celebrated the military victories of the emperor.[82] The same applies for the Western part of the empire: Gellius, in the passage I have already mentioned, reports that the citizens of the *municipium* of Italica in Spain, as the

---

[78] Heller 2006; Guerber 2010.   [79] Doukellis 2009.   [80] Millis 2010.
[81] Bresson 1996. See Ap. Ty., *Ep.* 71–2.   [82] Sion-Jenkis 2010.

birthplace of the emperor, asked Hadrian to concede them the rank of a colony in order to be fully part of the Roman State, but that the citizens of the colony of Praeneste, on the contrary, requested the emperor Tiberius to permit them to regain the status of *municipium* they had enjoyed until Sulla settled veterans there after the civil war against Marius and in a way punished the city by turning it into a veteran colony.[83]

As we can see, the problem for the cities of knowing whether or not they should become a Roman colony, whether or not they should adopt Roman colonial symbols, was not only a technical matter of political institutions. The Greek cities, as local communities, had been challenged by the emergence of the hegemonic power of Rome. They had to renegotiate their relationship with Roman power continuously, as made clear by their correspondence with the imperial authorities in order to get confirmation of their privileges. Though not as widespread as in the Western provinces, the Roman colonial model – among the many other titles and statuses local communities could search for – was one of the elements of the debate. This was also a cultural issue: were the cities ready to cope with the cultural influence of Rome? Paradoxically enough, the adoption of Roman colonial symbols or of colonial rank by Greek cities was used to foster and to assert local identities and patriotism: in celebrating its 'second foundation' through the plowing scene which was characteristic of the creation of Roman colonies, the city of Tralles was implicitly referring to its antiquity and was showing the favor it got from the emperor as a city; in using at the same time as their official denomination ethnics referring to their Seleukid origins and a Latin word borrowed from Roman colonies, the cities of Apollonia and Neapolis were building for themselves a mixed identity, including Hellenistic memories and up-to-date terminology patterned after the Roman model; finally, in choosing themselves to apply for the rank of colony, some cities were showing that they could decide independently what their position within the Roman Empire should be. These were all strategies for local communities to put themselves forward and to position themselves in relation to Roman power, of course, but also to their peers because of the competition between them. One empire, many cities. In this respect, the Roman Empire, despite the unification of the Greek world under its rule, continued to be a multipolar world.

---

[83] Gel. 16.13.4–5. See Talamanca 2006.

7 | Roman Theologies in the Roman Cities of Italy and the Provinces[*]

JOHN SCHEID

In Rome, several theologies existed (i.e., several types of discourse and knowledge concerning the gods), for the Romans' religion had neither revelation nor a Book or a truth set by a god. Only *multiple* truths existed, connected to this or that context or this or that moment. Even when a deity pronounced an opinion, it related to a specific event or answered a specific question. It did not lay down a global revelation as the God of monotheism does. We thus find ancestral theology implicit in the practice of worship, the themes developed by mythology, and philosophers' speculations on the nature of the gods. Each of these types of knowledge and discourse had its own autonomy.

*

1

Usually, research on this knowledge addresses only Rome (i.e., the religion of the Roman People, and Roman families) and not the innumerable colonies, *municipia* or peregrine cities of Italy and the provinces. For the religion of Rome, on the banks of the Tiber, concerned only the Roman State, the *Respublica* of the Roman People, and, of course, the Roman citizen, wherever he was, as a member of that State. But this religion and this theology did not impose themselves on the second homeland of every Roman citizen – the colony or *municipium* in which he was born – and where, for the majority of them, he lived. In the framework of this study, I will not consider the peregrine cities.

When a city became Roman, or when a Roman colony was founded, the totality of the Roman state's religious obligations was not spread. The inhabitants who were already there were not converted, and when a colony was founded by the Romans, they did not install a pure facsimile of the religious system of Rome. Not to mention the fact that these changes did not concern the domestic sects of these cities, which were a matter for each family to decide.

[*] I am very happy to be able to present to Ben Isaac these few reflections on theologies in the cities of the empire, which are but a distant echo of the discussions we have shared in Tel Aviv and Paris.

How then can we understand the theologies of the colonies and *municipia* of Italy and the provinces? Did they show the same theological practices that we observe in Rome itself? And if so, how? For philosophy, the answer is certainly yes, since the elites had the same education as in the metropolis. As for mythology, it is much more difficult because we do not know or understand the local mythology that existed prior to the Roman occupation, to which the inhabitants of the provincial Roman cities allude. I have only to mention the Pillar of the Boatmen in Paris: a mixture of local mythological themes and references to Roman theology, all accompanied by a dedication to Tiberius and Jupiter. This obliges us to wonder how this ensemble functioned: should we imagine it in the Romans' mythology as related to Greek mythology, which became a reservoir from which the Romans drew themes either to link their mythology to certain Greek myths or to construct new Roman myths? Unfortunately, our ignorance of local myths is such that we cannot answer this question.

On the other hand, it is possible to provide some answers for civic and private theologies. I do not wish to enter into the classic subject of the description of Gallic religions by Caesar or Tacitus.[1] I prefer to look at what is expressed on the ground. When a colony or a *municipium* was founded in Gaul or Germania, what took place from a religious point of view? Even if the Romans were not in the habit of converting subjugated peoples or imposing their religion on them, this does not mean that nothing happened. Thus, when the Syllanian colony settled in Pompeii, the altar of the temple of Apollo was redone, which gave rise to a new consecration by the quattuorviri.[2] We can therefore assume that the rites were celebrated according to the rites of the colony. This corresponded, of course, to a system of worship and theology similar to that of Rome. There are, however, differences between the two types of practices. For example, the local deities are enriched by novelties. Venus had long been worshipped in Pompeii, but she was now also the protector of Sylla, and in the days of the Julio-Claudians, the Venus of the Romans and the Iulii. This was to be understood in the prayers – in the invocations of the goddess. Evolution is not usually seen, since no new epiclesis characterized the great gods. It was only from the time of the Empire that divinities could bear the epiclesis "Augustus," which is ambiguous and difficult to interpret but which clearly sets the divinities in a Roman context. But from a theological point of view? Was civic theological thought active in the thoughts and actions of the founders?

---

[1] J. North addresses this question in North 2013: 187–200. [2] Cf. for this Van Andringa 2009.

At Pompeii, I would imagine that, owing to the long relations that had developed between the Osci and the Romans, a code of transposition or translation of the names of the reciprocal divinities had existed for a long time. The Roman colonists had no problem addressing the Pompeian Apollo, Jupiter or Venus. This was certainly more complicated when a remote community became a colony, or a colony was settled there. I would like to examine a number of examples. But let us first take a look at the document I was already inviting to take into account in 1991,[3] namely the municipal laws of the Genetiva colony at Urso.

Those statutes derived from Roman municipal law in the time of Caesar, which was applied to each foundation in perhaps a slightly different context. In chapter 64, we see the provisions of the constitution that interest us: "Those who will be duumvirs after the *deductio* of the colony must, within ten days of beginning their position, pose to the decurions – provided not less than two-thirds are present – the question of which and how many feast days there shall be, which rites must be celebrated publicly, and who is to celebrate these rites. What the majority of the decurions that shall then be present decide shall be legal and ratified, and those sacred rites and feast days shall be in force in this colony."[4] This text is of great importance for our purposes. It proves that the local public calendar was set by the local authorities, year after year, and could therefore be amended during this procedure. The text does not explicitly say that the first magistrates of the colony proceeded in the same manner (i.e., that they established the calendar within ten days after taking office). Article 70, for example, distinguishes between the first magistrates and their successors, and in chapter 69, which concerns the religious budget, the *lex* mentions the first magistrates alongside their successors. Therefore, if the constitution does not mention the first duumvirs here, it is most certainly intentional. This is also J. Rüpke's opinion.[5] Should one infer that the essential features of the calendar were in fact imposed by the founder of the colony? In my opinion, this is impossible because otherwise article 64 would no longer make any sense, since it stipulates that the calendar must be officially established each year without saying in the least that this calendar must not

---

[3] Scheid 1991: 42–57 notably 45 ff.; Id. 1999: 381–423.

[4] Crawford 1996: Vol. I, 393–454, notably 401 (Lex coloniae Genetivae, d'Urso), ch. 64: *IIuiri quicumque post colon(iam) deductam erunt, ii in die|bus X proxumis, quibus eum mag(istratum) gerere coeperint, at | decuriones referunto, cum non minus duae partes | aderint, quos et quot dies festos esse et quae sacra |fieri publice placeat et quos ea sacra facere place|at. quot ex eis rebus decurionum maior pars, qui | tum aderunt, decreuerint statuerint, it ius ratum|que esto, eaque sacra eique dies festi in ea colon(ia) | sunto.*

[5] Rüpke 1995: 535.

change the one that had been established "according to this *lex*." The situation is not the same as in article 66, which refers to the appointment of the first augurs and pontiffs by the person who had founded the colony. We must therefore conclude that chapter 64 either allows more time for the first magistrates or does not concern itself with this aspect of the question. It is sometimes difficult to see the reason for these differences in the wording. In chapter 70, which prescribes Games for the Capitoline Triad and Venus, the first duumvirs are excluded, probably because during the first year of the colony, it was difficult to organize this Games. However, the calendar's construction is not linked to immediate budgetary and organizational issues. In any case, it is certain that the first duumvirs built, shortly after the *deductio*, the essential calendar of the Colonia Genetiva. Additions could be made by their successors, but it was essential that they put the calendar in place at the time of foundation.

What is the scope of all this for our subject? I will pass over the material elements that the choices led to: the places of worship concerned or the location of new places of worship, the choice of an annual date, the financing and the responsibility for worship. Let us focus only on one aspect: the calendar itself and what it immediately implied.

What is the meaning of *quos et quot dies festos esse et quae sacra fieri publice placeat* ("the question of when the feast days shall be, what their number shall be, and what rites must be publicly celebrated")? As Rüpke has rightly pointed out, the text speaks only of *dies festi* ("feast days"), and not of *feriae* ("holidays"), which were in some way the temporal property of the gods, as if these distinctions did apply, or did not apply any more, to the provinces or colonies. However, it is difficult to rely too heavily on this finding. It's clear that a colony did not have to keep to the same calendar as the magistrates, the priests and the Senate of Rome. It was, if you will, an obligation of the Roman citizen in relation to Rome, but here we are speaking of something else: the city where the citizen lived his daily institutional and religious life, far from Rome. The districts of Rome themselves did not have the same festive life as the Forum and temples of Rome.

So, what did this citation mean? That at the beginning of each year (and for our direct interests here, ten days after the founding of a colony), the local senate had to consider a motion from the duumvirs to construct the calendar – the public calendar, as the text states. These are the rites that were celebrated *publice* (i.e., in the name of the *populus* and for it). We should note that nothing was foreseen, if not indirectly, for private religious life, since the domain of public worship was carefully delimited.

We must insert here an aside regarding documents such as the *lex* of Urso, which I have just cited. Much has been written on this subject, and I myself have drawn attention to this document to understand the meaning of the creation of a Roman or Latin colony in the Roman Empire. In an article on this law J. Rüpke quite rightly points out that all these rules apply to the public religion of the colony, and he also notes that the *lex* says little about observed celebrations and rites, called *sacra*, aside from an indication of the Games in honor of the Capitoline Triad and Venus, patron of the Iulii.[6] He cites the passage on the calendar, pointing out that it was not necessarily the same as that of Rome, and he imagines it similar to that of the Fasti of Guidizzolo, near Mantua.[7] In this situation, the individual who had this copy made had available to him, besides the Fasti, a list of the years' festivals. This is possible, but let us not forget that the Fasti of Praeneste, which date from the Augustan period, even include the annual holidays of the great local temple of Fortuna Primigenia in the Fasti's text.[8] There should have been several opportunities to set the local holiday calendar in writing. We shall recall here the arvals' calendar, which adds a second document to the ordinary Fasti that includes the movable dates of the annual sacrifice of Dea Dia. So, in Rome itself, this sort of supplement to the basic calendar could have existed.

Things are actually more complicated. A document like that of Urso shows us the institutional life of a colony in Caesar's time, when the document was written for the first time and then, under Domitian, when it was reexamined and engraved. How were the *sacra* present in public life? For this is indeed what the Romans called public worship. Rüpke considers that this document is ignorant of our concept of religion, but only speaks of *sacra*, of feast days, of funding, of priests and of *magistri*. That's completely correct. But as every Latinist knows, our concept of religion did not exist in ancient cities before Christianization. This disturbs the modern scholar, since the term *religio* exists in Latin, but it means something else: "ritual obligation, care in ritual practice," hence "fear, meticulousness in a given practice," such as spelling, for example. In other words, in the positive sense, *religio* actually means, in an abstract way, the same thing as *sacra*, "rites." It is therefore unnecessary to be surprised by the absence of the modern category of "religion" in this document. It did not exist in the Romans' language or thinking. This did not present as a religious decadence or incapacity, in the modern sense, which would make it possible to seek elsewhere the religious sentiments of the Romans. It is therefore

---

[6] Rüpke 2014: 114–36.   [7] Degrassi 1963 : 235.   [8] Ibid., 129.

necessary to bring together the various rules regarding religious practice through the text's various sections to reconstitute the set of rules concerned. This dispersion is not surprising, as Roman legal documents are never synthetic and reasoned; they often present a series of successive rules, which we modern scholars would set out in a more synthetic fashion. As public worship belonged to the religious duties of the city, their regulations are set out in the same way as the other prescriptions relating to the functioning of the city.

But let us return to the gods. If we are discussing worship and feast days, we must also investigate the target of that worship. In short, we must theologize. Discussing worship and festive days amounted to composing what we call the official pantheon of the city. It was at this time that the decurions also had to make an official decision on the names of their public gods, translating or transposing, adding epicleses or not, including one god and excluding another in accordance with internal political equilibria. We do not know much about this procedure. The law of Urso reveals nothing, except that it provides that the duumvirs celebrate the Games in honor of the Capitoline Triad each year, presumably on September 13, which was in some way an obligation common to all Roman cities;[9] the aediles also provided three days of performances to the circus or scenic games and a day of performances at the circus or at the forum in honor of Venus.[10]

2

The area I have chosen for this survey of local theologies, namely the western provinces of the North, excludes whether the settlers were Romans from Rome or from Italy and whether they had their own religious traditions that they would have potentially taken with them and transplanted into their new city. I will therefore only consider colonies which were "honorary," as is often said, partly to deny the reality of the integration policy of conquered peoples. But this is a legal contradiction, because honorary or not, from a legal point of view, they were real colonies.

---

[9] Crawford 1996 : ch. 70. *IIuiri quicu[m]que erunt, ei praeter eos qui primi | post h(anc) l(egem) [fa]cti erunt, ei in suo mag(istratu) munus lu|dosue scaenicos Ioui Iunoni Mineruae deis deabusq(ue) quadriduom m(aiore) p(arte) diei, quot eius fie|ri <poter>it, arbitratu decurionum faciun|to ... ; ch. 71: aediles quicum(que) erunt in suo mag(istratu) munus lu| dos<ue> scaenicos Ioui Iunoni Mineruae tri|duom maiore parte diei, quot eius fieri pote|rit, et unum diem in circo aut in foro Veneri | faciunto ...*

[10] Ibid., ch. 71.

Therefore, this founding – or re-founding – activity contained a theological activity that was perhaps based on traditions that were already ancient, acquired by these populations over the course of decades of contact with the Romans. The local elites who sat in the colonial senates did not necessarily include Varros and Ciceros, but certain personalities, already Roman knights and charged with public offices of the Empire, may have been largely acquainted with Roman customs and public worship and therefore have been familiar with Roman religion. It was not possible to exercise a command in the Roman army or administration, for example, without being obliged by these functions to fill Roman cult obligations.

How could local senates function when, within ten days of the first magistrates' taking office, they had to define the new colony's public calendar? To attempt to uncover the facts, we must make use of examples, and I shall begin with four cases: Trier, Cologne, and the Batavi and the Tungri. We will discuss public theology, and I will add some elements of private theology, as far as is possible. I am well aware of the hypothetical nature of this reconstruction, which we must deduce from sources, albeit direct, but particularly laconic. And in such an exercise, errors are always possible.

Let us begin with Trier, the Colonia Augusta of the Treveri.

We know the gods of this colony, but more of the private gods than the public gods. We must thus make do with what we have – which is not nothing. We have found some dedications addressed to the Roman deities Aesculapius, Bellona, Apollo and Mars Victor, who probably had temples, chapels, or altars in the city. But these inscriptions and deities cannot be related to the theological activities that were carried out at the time of foundation. Not only because their date is often belated in relation to the origins of the Roman Trier, but precisely because they are deities who were probably not "translated": they represented the Roman part of the colony's theology such as it was purely and simply transferred. We must not forget that the Latin colony of Trier had a dual identity: local and Roman. In this case, this is the Roman side.

A cult that is nevertheless particularly important for our purposes is that of Lenus Mars. He was the god of the great temple located outside the city, where representatives of the colony's pagi also gathered for days of collective worship. There were other local Marses: Intarabus, Gnabetius and Loucetios. First, a detail: in a chapter devoted to gods and worship, Greg Woolf wonders about the epicleses.[11] He wonders, in particular, whether,

---

[11] Woolf 1998: 208.

once the conquest was over, the local deities would not have offered the indigenous peoples the possibility of having their own identity. In Lenus Mars or Hercules Magusanus, does not the presence of the epiclesis suggest the existence of a reserve thus manifested with respect to the Roman gods Mars and Hercules? Why were they not satisfied with Mars or Hercules? G. Woolf's answer is not very clear; he is content to lay out the problem. But it is significant that he cites Hercules Magusanus, which shows that he is influenced by the ideas of N. Roymans, who refused to accept, at the time those lines were written, the idea that the Batavi could have adopted a Roman way of life. It is also significant that he refers in the page I cited to the god of Jews and Christians as though the situations were the same. That is precisely the problem. Even in the Gallo-Roman or Germanic world, religion was not necessarily identical to Judaism or Christianity. We can see beneath this comparison a number of exaggerated positions adopted for a time by G. Woolf on the religion of the Romans themselves.

But let us return to our Treveran gods. Lenus Mars is interesting. He was doubtless the Treveri's great god, who had another great place of worship in the territory near Koblenz, at the Martberg,[12] which was also a public place, considering his importance and historical profundity. Two elements related to this god's chief place of worship immediately attract attention. First is the position of his temple, which was located outside the ramparts. That of the Herrenbrünnchen, which belonged perhaps to Mars Victor, also was located near the rampart, which was built later. Yet this was a Roman rule of worship. As Trier was founded from 17 BC *ex nihilo*, the location of Lenus Mars' temple reflects a clearly theological intention, even though it may have been conveyed by the architects of the Roman army, who were likely involved in the organization of the capital Augusta Treverorum. The fact remains that the members of the elite who were the sponsors apparently saw nothing shocking in the fact that the great local god was located outside the city.

Lenus Mars, whose epiclesis "lenus" is incomprehensible, provides other interesting indications. The first comes from the statue that was found in the temple and represents a young Mars, different from the bearded figure of Mars Ultor used in Mandeure, for example. The personality of the Treveran god from whom Lenus Mars took over is unknown, but the choice of Mars – and Lenus Mars – provides two pieces of information. The territory of Trier has been blessed by archaeology. Its excavators have been excellent professionals for over a century, and to top it all off, the Treveri were great chatterboxes, leaving plenty of inscriptions. Perhaps it is

[12] Nickel et al. 2008.

necessary to add, more prosaically, that the tender sandstone of the Treveran countryside is very easy to carve. In any case, if we were to plot on a map all the places where a dedication to Mars has been found, and assuredly placed, we would see a very particular image emerge. In the capital, there were temples, altars, and dedications made to Lenus Mars and Mars Intarabus, who were, according to the current data, gods of the left bank of the Moselle River. On the other hand, Mars Gnabetius and Mars Loucetios are neither represented on the left bank nor in Trier. Also, these gods were not necessarily small local gods. Take, for example, Mars Loucetios, who had a temple with Nemetona near Mainz,[13] thus on former Treveran territory, cut off from a section after the Roman occupation and various uprisings. And the mention of Aresaces on the first stone refers to the Treveri, since it was during the first c. AD. a local unit of the Treveran people in the Roman Army, the cohors Aresacum, that had been commanded by one of Lenus Mars' flamines. The social level of those who dedicated a second inscription to Nemetona, the *legatus Augusti* A. Didius Gallus Fabricius Veiento and his wife, prove that it was an important place of worship. Another dedication should be mentioned here. It comes from Bath,[14] is addressed to Mars Loucetios and Nemetona, and was placed by a Treveran citizen. Perhaps a Trevir from the Hunsrück or the Mainz region? We also note that the Matronae or Matres, who were apparently removed from the public cults of Trier, received a dedication at Vetera in Germania Inferior, probably from a *ciuis Treuir*.[15]

I would explain the exclusion of Mars Loucetius from the Trier pantheon by the fact that the Hunsrück Treveri had been underrepresented in the colony's *deductio* and had therefore not been able to impose the presence of their local Mars among the public, collective gods, contrary to what the western Treveri did. We may even see in this the effect of an internal conflict, due to the resistance of certain Treveran groups first to the Roman alliance, and then to the course adopted, from 17 BC onwards, to transform the Treveran people into a city of the Mediterranean type. This conflict was expressed in the various uprisings that took place after the conquest. Even though the city did not immediately become a Latin colony – doing so only a generation after its foundation – decisions had to be made that would be given validity on the day it became a colony. It should be borne in mind that archaeological chance can always reverse this type of hypothesis, but for the time being, the number of inscriptions is sufficient to allow it to advance. I would add that, unlike Otzenhausen and

---

[13] CIL XIII, 7252; 7253 (Ober-Holm, Mainz).   [14] RIB 140.
[15] CIL XIII, 8634 (Vetera, Xanten).

Donnersberg, two large *oppida* of the right bank of the Moselle, those of the left bank, the Titelberg and the Martberg (which likely remained a Treveran property even after the diminution of their territory) were not abandoned under the Empire. This tends to suggest certain pro-Roman Treveran groups' seizing power on the left bank of the Moselle from 30 BC onwards.

For our purposes, this means that at the time when it was decided to create a collective pantheon for the city and then for the Augustan colony of the Treveri, a list of the public rites to be performed for this or that god was put together, and the choice of the great god of the city was made, according to local political imperatives.

But we can go further by moving to a more strictly theological level. Why choose, from among the names of available gods, Mars rather than some other god? Why not Jupiter, Apollo or Mercury? A word about the epiclesis: It's a necessity if one wishes to express the local, colonial nature of the god. This was done in the same way in Rome, in neighborhoods and in families, according to historical circumstances, and of course also in Italy. Let us not forget that this was a polytheistic regime, and that there was not a single Roman Mars. To go further, it is necessary to compare the Treveran choice with those made by other cities. Mars, with various epicleses, was chosen by many cities of Gaul: Mars Camulus by the Remi, Mars Mullo by the Redones and by the Aulerci Cenomani. But this was not the case further north, among the Batavi and Tungri. The evidence tends to show that it was Hercules, rather, who was designated there as the great local god. To understand, we must examine the Roman gods involved.

In Rome, Mars was the god of war and of those who made it. What was at issue was violent, brutal war, the violent outbreak of warfare-driven rage, and not the war envisaged from the point of view of the fine strategist's cunningness (a role that would more be that of Minerva, who was the technician of the military art taught by instructors), or the brutal imposition of sovereignty (Jupiter). But, contrary to the traditions of certain Italic peoples, Mars was not the principal god in Rome, even though mythology had made him the father of the city's founder. Thus, when the Treveri adopted Mars as their principal god, it wasn't the figure of the community's supreme leader, of a sovereign (Jupiter) or guide (Apollo) that they sought, but rather a figure close to the one claimed by those who recognized themselves in him, the armed citizens. But this did not preclude a versed dedication offered by the Martberg presenting Lenus Mars in a very Roman manner.[16]

---

[16] CIL XIII 7661 (*Inscriptiones Latinae Selectae* 4569), Martberg, Germania Inferior; cf. Dräger 2004: 185–201.

Let us return to the difference between the Batavi and Tungri and the other Gallic peoples. As T. Derks has shown,[17] the Batavi made another choice, although their intentions were certainly identical. Instead of Mars, they chose Hercules to be their principal god, a god who by myth (and by Roman topography) was tied to livestock farming and especially to adventure, to the victorious return after successfully carrying out exploits in faraway lands. Another difference separates this choice from the one made by the Treveri: Hercules was a known god, but he did not belong to the first rank of the great Roman gods, unlike Mars. This also reveals the fact that the Batavi sought in Hercules special qualities rather than his status in the Roman public pantheon. On the other hand, Mars refers to a structured universe, a city with a defined space to defend with armed citizens collectively fighting; in short, a universe with institutions. Hercules, on the contrary, participates only marginally in these activities, for example, at the celebration of a triumph. His exploits take place in another setting. According to his mythology, they are accomplished even before the birth of cities and their institutions. Mars is a citizen god and Hercules a civilizing god, accomplishing his exploits alone or with a handful of companions. One might say that the Batavi chose the myth of the solitary hero as a source of inspiration. This was also, according to a recent study by G. Ræpsæt, the choice of the Tungri.[18] Ræpsæt studies the ethnogenesis of the Ubii, Batavi and Tungri. He also evokes the cult of Hercules as a principal cult, relying on the example of the Batavi. He first quotes Tacitus, who in his text on Germania, mentions the importance of Hercules.[19] Tacitus also mentions Mars, however. Near Tongeren, a ring was found bearing the inscription, and a bracelet (the *Herculi Magusano* restitution being certain according to similar specimens found in Germania).[20] In Jeuk-Goyer,[21] still in Tongeren country, a series of altars dedicated to Hercules has been discovered, which seem to confirm this fact. What is especially interesting is the dedication made to Hercules and Alcmene, an absolute hapax, which confirms the suspicion that in these regions, the search for a Roman god as a local god's equivalent had passed through the mythology. In addition, in Millingen,[22] in Germania Inferior, near Xanten, on another dedication, we find Hercules Magusanus together

---

[17] Derks 1998: 94–115.   [18] Raepsaet 2013: 111–48.

[19] Tac. *Germ.* 3: *Fuisse apud eos et Herculem memorant, primumque omnium virorum fortium ituri in proelia canunt. ... 9. Deorum maxime Mercurium colunt, cui certis diebus humanis quoque hostiis litare fas habent. Herculem et Martem concessis animalibus placant.*

[20] ILB 6 ILB 139bis=10027, 212a.   [21] ILB 24–8 (Jeuk-Goyer).

[22] CIL XIII, 8706 (Millingen).

with Haeva. It was supposed that it could be a local goddess, elsewhere translated by Alcmene, or rather the misspelled version of Hebe, Heracles' wife, who would be the equivalent of a local goddess, for example Nehalennia, who is connected to a successful journey like those performed by Hercules, and whose certain steles at Colijnsplaat or Domburg also represented Hercules. Finally, on Hadrian's Wall, an inscription placed by the first cohort of the Tungri dedicated an altar to Hercules, Jupiter, and the imperial *numina*;[23] another base had to do with Hercules Magusanus and emanated from a *duplicarius* of the ala Tungrorum.[24] On the territory of the neighboring Cugerni we have also a dedication in Xanten,[25] a ring at Kalkar and a temple in Elfrath, near Krefeld, where the cella is decorated with scenes from the adventures of Hercules.[26]

In this distribution of Mars and Hercules, we also see the opposition between grain-farming regions and livestock-farming ones.

Let's return to Trier with another question: Why choose Mars as supreme god, and not Jupiter or Apollo? The answer is probably that at the time of the transposition of the name of their god to Latin, at the latest at the time of the city's foundation or the colony's *deductio*, the Treveri still saw themselves as warriors, or at least as armed men. They saw themselves less in the forum's *togati*, in civilians, than as men bearing arms. For them, a citizen was essentially an armed man. This was evident in their funerary customs at the beginning of the Empire. Later, apparently, things changed, but the choices made at the beginning of the colony were thereafter definitive and presented as an echo of the past of the Treveran people. The preeminent role of Lenus Mars informs us how the Treveri represented the profession of the citizen, how the city and the colony were founded, and perhaps about the distant political conflicts between clans that the map of the epicleses of Mars hints at in the background. The reflections revealed by these choices suggest that the Treveri were not ignorant of Roman institutions and culture. By having distinguished the role and figure of the god Mars from those of other gods of the Roman pantheon, they revealed their knowledge of Roman theology and religion. In building the temple of Lenus Mars at the gates of the city, they clearly applied a Roman religious rule. They left one more indication that confirms the very conscious way in which their pantheon and their religion were elaborated.

It may be argued that the Gauls perhaps did not have a feminine goddess as their principal deity, like the Junos of Latium and Southern Etruria, or

---

[23] RIB I, 1580.   [24] CIL VII, 1090 (Britannia, Mumerills).   [25] CIL XIII, 8610 (Xanten).
[26] Reichmann 1991: 1–30; Zelle 2006.

the Fortuna of Praeneste. This is an argument that must be qualified, at least in part.

Located next to the Treveri, Tungri and Batavi was Cologne.[27] The city's history is very particular. First, the historical occupants of the space, the Eburones, were largely exterminated by Caesar, notably with the Treveri's help. The survivors, along with Ubian groups transplanted from the other side of the Rhine, settled in the liberated space and founded at the beginning of the first century a city that was to serve as a metropolis for the new province of Germania. As this city, which was the seat of Germania's legate, was closely linked to the Julio-Claudian dynasty, the Emperor Claudius transformed it into a Roman colony, which even received the Italic right, meaning that it was legally considered to be city of Italy. Now, if we were to look at the public worship practiced in Cologne, we would find no evidence of either Mars or Hercules as a great local deity. Of course, the city has left fewer cultual remains than Trier, but one noticeable fact emerges from the epigraphic data: One of the public cults was that of the Matronae. It was a mixture of local cults, found mostly in the Claudian colony and marginally in neighboring cities, as well as cults adhered to by legionaries and veterans who, at the beginning of the Empire, were largely from Cisalpine and Narbonese Gaul, where there were similar godesses. The Matronae and Mothers were, for example, attested to at Glanum and Nîmes. Clearly, this cult of the Matronae had developed from the foundation of this peregrine city of Ara Ubiorum and when the Claudian colony was founded around AD 50, this cult was so well established that it belonged to the religious landscape of the colony. One of its great temples was even in the immediate vicinity of the Legio I Minervia camp in Bonn, which was located inside the colony's territory.

We have thus seen three examples of how public religion developed in new colonies, each of which followed different paths according to their culture and historical context. Of course, these cities also possessed a temple dedicated to the Capitoline Triad, or at least a cult for it, especially on September 13 (the day of the Roman Games), and also other Roman deities, but our purpose here was to follow the way in which they outlined their pantheons.

I have two further remarks to make on this subject. The Treveri's thought was apparently quite advanced. Thus, as T. Derks has shown,[28] one would find parents making votive offerings in Lenus Mars' temple for their children. To explain these rites, Derks refers to those we know from

---

[27] See for this Eck 2004.   [28] Derks 2012: 43–80.

Rome, on the day of the Liberalia, the day when young boys became adults, celebrated with a sacrifice that they offered at the temple of Jupiter. In Trier, the founders, and then gradually the rest of the population, began to celebrate their boys' reaching the age of majority with Lenus Mars, who held the role of supreme god.

There has also been some progress in the interpretation of divinities. In Cologne and in the territory of Colonia Claudia, a series of dedications has been found that mention curiae associated with the cult of the Matronae (i.e., groups and clans that bore the same name as the Matronae). Chr. Rüger notes that most of these curiae's dedications are addressed to male deities and wonders if these gods were not the Matronae's consorts.[29] Thus he brings the famous Matronae Aufaniae together with the epithet of their neighbor in Bonn, Mercurius Gebrinius, and the representation of a mythical animal (three goat bodies with a single head) on an altar of the Matronae Aufaniae. For Rüger, this would be evidence of the theriomorphic stage of the Matronae, who would originally be goat goddesses, and whose husband would be Gebrinius (*gabro-, cf. *caper*). Without further emphasizing the fanciful nature of this combination, powerfully inspired by the modern myth of the mother goddess and primitive representations of divinity, Chr. Rüger's hypothesis poses an additional problem, which also raises the Matronae's identification with their mythical ancestors that he makes. On the one hand, there would be a single god before a group of Matronae: Who represents whom? Why a single god facing a plurality of mothers connected to a clan? It would be more prudent to remember that finding several deities in the same place of worship is commonplace, even supposing that it is indeed a common place of worship. And if we are dealing with two different temples, there is no reason to connect the Aufaniae and Mercury Gebrinius. On the other hand, how did the Matronae represent the clan's female ancestor? Which of the three is that famous ancestor? Would not all three of them be the deified matrons of the lineage or group concerned? Add to this the fact that in representations of the Matronae, two wear headdresses and appear older than the middle one, who does not wear the headdress typical of the other two. There is obviously something missing here, and I would be very careful before interpreting this type of collective divinity further.

T. Derks has once again subjected the whole question to criticism, relying on M. Th. Ræpsæt-Charlier's chronological supplements in particular.[30] He rightly dismantles the schematic reconstructions developed by Rüger, who presupposes an evolution of the Matronae's cult from a pre-anthropomorphic

---

[29] Rüger 1987: 1–30.   [30] Derks 1998: 124–30.

stage to an anthropomorphic stage, the beginning of which would be marked by the beautiful sculptures discovered under the Bonn Minster. Derks has especially pointed out that the very form of the matronal names, which are based on the suffix *-inehae*, meaning "those (f.) of, the women of," quite evidently refers to an anthropomorphic group. Moreover, the absence of images of the Matronae before the AD 160s does not mean that the cult was aniconic before that date, as Chr. Rüger presumes. The earliest dedication addressed to the Matronae in this region comes from Jülich,[31] and it dates from the years between AD 71 and about AD 120, which is in agreement with the archaeological data found in exhumed places of worship, such as in Pesch in the Colonia Claudia's territory.

We are still waiting for a clue that would allow us to decipher the figure of the Matronae or Mothers. Nevertheless, with these cults, we have some evidence of a theological thought that has led us toward clans and groups that seem to belong to the private domain, which are in any case subordinate to the level of the colony. Let us now go further into the theology of individuals.

3

The first example comes from the Altbachtal temple area, the Altbach valley in Trier.[32] This sacred precinct was developed at the same time as the city, since the main axis of the precinct coincides with that of the city. There were perhaps temples of public worship, but the large buildings are unfortunately anonymous. The divinities represented were largely Treveran, and they were also found to be present on the territory of the Colonia Augusta Treverorum. It was obvious that the families brought these gods with them when they settled in Trier. Associations also chose to install their place of worship in this area. And significantly, in the late period, a Mithraic sanctuary was located there. This set can add two interesting pieces of data to our research.

First, Mercury. Two things are interesting. To begin with, the location of the temple, situated at the western entrance to the sacred precinct,[33] or in any case just outside. I won't go into detail. We know that the god Mercury was the god of travelers, of mediation, of commerce. He was therefore often present at borders, at entrances, near gates (in Rome, for example). He was also connected to currency circulation, the production of interest and the reproduction of livestock. There are then inscriptions found in and near the

---

[31] ILS 4806.   [32] See Gose 1972: 19–21.   [33] RIB 140.

temple, which testify to the fact that the Treveri had become quite capable of thinking of the gods in Roman terms, at least in the second century AD. The first,[34] by Securius Severus, does not inform us of much, as it is too laconic. The other two are a bit more talkative. The second,[35] which is later, based on the layers on which the altar was placed (but it may have been displaced), concerns the domain for which the god was best known – commerce – as it comes from an ancient seaman of the fleet of Germania who was a beer trader or brewer and a dyer. The third inscription is the most interesting.[36] It concerns the Mercury of the *peregrini*. What's it about? The god is presented as a sort of patron of the *peregrini*: *deus Mercurius peregrinorum*. The *peregrini* are not pilgrims but foreigners established in the Colonia Augusta Treverorum. They were in all likelihood *incolae*, residents who did not have full local citizenship, and who often formed associations in Roman cities. However, there is no indication that this temple served as the seat of an association, as is the case for other temples in the Altbachtal. In any case, these associations of residents were often directed toward the Genius peregrinorum, venerating the divine double of the association, which is structurally linked to it. The dedicator of our altar made another choice, which denotes his perfect knowledge of Roman theology, since it refers to the domain patronized by the god Mercury: circulation and passage. Even better than the knowledge of the Genius, who was a typically Roman deity, the ability to analyze Mercury's domain to relate it to those who are passing through testifies to a theological knowledge that is not merely superficial.

Even less banal is the following dedication. It reads: *Deo Vertumno siue Pisinto C. Fruendus VSLM* ("To the God Vertumnus, or Pisintus, Gaius Fruendus has fulfilled his vow willingly and properly").[37] Pisintus was a local god about whom we know nothing else. But the dedicator, toward the middle of the second century AD, proposed a Latin translation (and the Latin figure in the first place) of Pisintus' name to Vertumnus. Yet Vertumnus was a well-known Roman god. He was the god of metamorphosis, of change. He was not a very active god in the ritual calendar. He was best known by Varro, Propertius and Ovid. According to certain Roman traditions, there was a desire to make him into an Etruscan god,

---

[34] BRGK 17, 1927, 22: *In h(onorem) d(omus) d(iuinae) Deo | Mercurio | Securius | Seuerus u(otum) s(oluit) l(ibens) m(erito)* (second half–beginning third century).

[35] BRGK 17, 1927, 41 : *[– – – – – –] | | [– – – m]iles clas|sis Germanice //// / ////////// a/// neg| [o]tiator ceruesa|rius artis offec|ture ex u[o]to pro | meritis posuit* (third century, maybe mid second).

[36] BRGK 17, 1927, 23: *Deo Mercurio | peregrinorum | Iulius Iulianus | ex uoto posuit* (mid second century).

[37] BRGK 17, 1927, 3.

based on the fact that during the fall of Volsinii, a local god had been installed in Rome under the name of Vortumnus (probably Voltumnus from Voltumna). Yet other sources say that the god had already existed in Rome before Vortumnus' arrival, who was installed, not on the Forum as Vertumnus, but on Aventine Hill. I refer you to the research that I completed with J. Svenbro on this god.[38] The altar of the Altbachtal is all the more important in that the dedication, in a way, translates the domain, the fundamental identity of the god, with *siue*, "either, or": he's the "or" god. Vertumnus is one whom certain attributes immediately transform into another character or god. His entire domain is there; Propertius and Ovid provide dozens of illustrations of this, in which the cycle of the seasons, in particular, plays an important role, insofar as the god Vertumnus is associated with gardens and the seasons. In Ovid's *Metamorphoses*, he courts Pomona, the goddess who made the fruits of the garden grow. Yet a glance at our altar shows that this characteristic was perfectly known and understood by Fruendus or the Treveri, since the four figures that encircle the altar's crown most likely represent the seasons. We cannot explain the sword or the torch, but perhaps they have to do with other attributes that explain Pisintus' transformation into Vertumnus, or the opposite. The altar stood inside the small enclosure with altars and dedications consecrated to the Dii Casus or Cassus. If this name properly conveys the chance, the accidental or the fortuitous, we can grasp the reason for which Pisintus-Vertumnus was associated with the Dii Casus: The two types of deities were connected with chance, and the appearance of Vertumnus is a function of opportunity and context.

Another element that is no less interesting is that to know all this, one had to be literate, for the god himself, as I have said, was rare even in Rome, and it was only by reading, for example, the poets that someone in Trier could acquire information on this god, who was here assimilated to Pisintus. This literary knowledge, which serves as a theological operator, is attested to by another inscription, which was found in Raetia.

We now leave Belgica to go first to Raetia, to the city of Cambodunum (Kempten), where a lead curse tablet was found with the following inscription:[39] "Silent Mutes! Let Quartus be dumb, or be distraught; he wanders like a fleeing mouse or a bird before a basilisk, let his mouth be

---

[38] Scheid and Svenbro 2004: 176–90; Scheid 2012: 150–71.

[39] AE 1958, 150 = Chapot and Laurot 2001: n° L 78 (Cambodunum, Kempten, Rhétie) : *Mutae tacitae ! ut mutus sit | Quartus agitatus erret ut mus| fugiens aut avis adversus basyliscum | ut e[i] us os mutu(m) sit, Mutae | Mutae [d]irae sint ! Mutae | tacitae sint ! Mutae | [Qu]a[rt]us ut insaniat, // Vt Eriniis rutus sit et | Quartus Orco ut Mutae | Tacitae ut mut[ae s]int | ad portas aureas.* Cf. Cf. R. Egger 1957.

mute, Mutes! Let the Mutes be dread! Let the Mutes remain silent! Mutes! Mutes! Let Quartus go mad, let Quartus be brought to the Erinyes and Orcus. Let the Silent Mutes remain silent near the golden doors." A classic curse tablet, but what is less classic is the invocation made to the *Mutae Tacitae*. This goddess, in the singular, is set by Ovid in the etiological myth of the Feralia, the festival of the dead at the end of February. This is the story that is connected to the birth of the Lares. A talkative nymph, Lara, from Lala, etymologically the "Talkative one," revealed to Juno that her husband Jupiter was going to woo the nymph Juturna. She was punished and sent by the all-powerful to the underworld, to silence. It was Mercury who took her. Mercury, who was also the god of thieves and thugs, rapes her on the way. She clearly remained there and gave birth to two boys, who became the Lares. On our fragment of a curse tablet, Ovid's Tacita Muta has become the Mutae Tacitae, following a relatively conventional practice that will not surprise us. The Eileithyiae, the Furrinae, the Camenae and others attest to this, being sometimes in the plural, sometimes in the singular. What is extraordinary, however, is the fact that Tacita Muta was only known to Ovid.[40] His etiology is a small masterpiece of the kind, to the extent that he could be considered as having invented everything, including the name of the goddess. In addition, we will note the fate reserved for the brave Quartus, sent to Orcus like Lara, and the role attributed to the mouse that already intervenes in the rite as it is described by Ovid (placing incense in a hole dug by a mouse), as if the author of the curse tablet were winking at the poet with these allusions.

But – and this is what interests us – we see the name Mutae Tacitae show up in Raetia! From two things to one. Either Tacita Muta was a real divine figure, or the author of the curse tablet was literate and had composed his invocation according to Ovid, himself creating a specialized goddess intended to silence a rival or an enemy. Which solution to choose? I am inclined toward the first, for the change from the singular to the plural *Tacitae* indicates in my opinion a religious practice known for decades. This was also the case for Furrina, found in the singular in the name of her lucus, until the time of Varro, in the middle of the first century BC, and then it appears in the plural on inscriptions from the end of the second and third centuries AD found in this sacred wood.

∗∗∗

We can thus appreciate the value of this brief survey. In Rome, we almost never know how a cult was born, how a divinity was introduced. Not only

----

[40] Bettini 2006: 149–72.

do the origins explain nothing, as H. Versnel writes, but we never particularly know the origins, especially of the most important divinities. How was the Capitoline Triad installed in Rome? We have at our disposal only myths, and we must deduce the rest of the observations that we can make for the historical period, say in the first century BC and under the Empire. The religious restorations of Octavian/Augustus themselves, for which we have an impressive amount of evidence, are far from clear. Remember the arval brethren and their cult's reinvention. Situations such as these that enable us to see the new cities of the provinces, especially in the colonies or the *municipia*, constitute a very privileged field of experimentation, the importance of which is just beginning to be seen. This is partly because we lack a document that suddenly helps us understand everything.

One of the most interesting lines of research is the following: the Roman deities – that is, those of Rome on the banks of the Tiber – were local and connected with their city and the families. They were not expected to be adopted far away and by foreigners, even if these foreigners became Roman citizens. Yet this is what happened. Those responsible for public religious life, family fathers in the settings of family devotions, and even individuals reflected, at the moment when they came into contact with a new institutional context, on how to reconstruct their collective religions. They chose Roman names for their gods – or sanctioned even older traditions – and gave them epicleses: Lenus, Intarabus, and others. They also adopted, qua members of a Roman collectivity, Roman deities. Seen from the Roman side, this new device made it possible to extend the domain of the gods of a Roman city. Somewhat like the provincial government extended, without too much distortion, the jurisdiction of the magistrates of the city of Rome. As the law, which was intended only to regulate relations between citizens in Rome, theology and sacred law were extended by a sort of legal fiction to divinities that were not Roman but henceforth had a vocation to act in a Roman context. It was, incidentally, the extension, according to strict guidelines, of the great Roman principles to the various cities of the empire that made possible the cohesion and the survival of the whole, as a recent study by Clifford Ando shows.[41] In religion, the question has not hitherto been studied, but it is also more difficult, inasmuch as, when the Roman world was Christianized and then destroyed by the Barbarians, Roman sacred law, the jurisprudence of which perhaps contained important data for this issue, fell into the trash cans of history.

---

[41] Ando 2013.

The Involvement of Provincial Cities in the
Administration of School Teaching

IDO ISRAELOWICH

Schoolteachers in the Roman world were a well-defined professional group.
They were in charge of the first stages of education. In Latin they were called
grammatici and *rhetores*, each designating a particular stage of education.
Another term, *praeceptores*, referred to both groups, and probably held
a vocational rather than scholarly connotation.[1] The first two terms are
transliterations of Greek terms. The *praeceptor*, though a Latin term, followed
a curriculum, which self-consciously found its origin in the Hellenized East.[2]
Schoolteachers flourished during the High Empire.[3] In fact, from the reign of
Vespasian onwards they enjoyed immunity from liturgies. An inscription
from Pergamum contains information about an edict of Vespasian that gave
certain privileges to *grammatici* and sophists, in addition to physicians: κελεύω
μήτε ἐπισταθμεύεσθαι [αὐτοὺς μήτε εἰ] φορὰς ἀπαιτεῖσθαι ἐν μηδενὶ τρόπωι
('I order that they will be not liable to have persons quartering with them or
that they will be imposed with property tax in any fashion').[4] This inscription
corresponds to *Dig.* 50.4.18.30, except for the inclusion of philosophers
amongst those upon whom Vespasian bestowed privileges.[5] It seems that
Vespasian was the first to grant immunity for the whole class of teachers.
A later inscription from Ephesus, which can be dated to the reign of Trajan,
documents some of the financial privileges of grammarians and sophists,
alongside physicians.[6] Knibbe, in his edition of the reconstructed text, argued

---

[1] Plaut. *Ps.* 4, 7, 96; Cic. *De Or.* 3, 15, 57; *Phil.* 2, 6, 14; *Fam.* 5, 13; Petr. 88.
[2] Scholarship on Roman education is vast, but see Bonner 1977; Clarke 1971; Marrou 1977;
Morgan 1998.
[3] *Cf.* Cribiore 2005.
[4] The inscription was printed by Herzog 1935 and later by McCrum and Woodhead 1961: no.
458=*FIR.* 1.77=*TAPA* 86 (1955) 348–9. Oliver 1989: no. 38 offers an authoritative commentary.
[5] *Magistris, qui ciuilium munerum vacationem habent, item grammaticis et orationibus et medicis
et philosophis, ne hospitem reciperent, a principibus fuisse immunitatem indultam et diuus Vesp.
et diuus Hadr. rescripserunt* . ('Both the deified Vespasian and the deified Hadrian issued
rescripts to the effect that teachers who are released from civic *munera* and grammarians and
orators and doctors and philosophers had been granted immunity from billeting by the
emperors.') During the reign of Vespasian the privilege of μὴ κρίνειν was extended to
philosophers, alongside rhetors, grammarians, and physicians; *cf.* Herzog 1935: 983;
Bowersock 1969: 32; Levick 1999: 76.
[6] Knibbe 1981–2: lines, 7–14.

that this rescript recalls an earlier *senatus consultum* or an edict of the trium-virs from the years 42–39 BCE.[7] In addition, their popularity soon became so widespread that Antoninus Pius was forced to restrict the application of immunities for schoolteachers, by setting a quota on the number of teachers each city was allowed to award such immunity.[8] However, the decision as to which teacher merited immunity was left to the cities themselves. This chapter aims to clarify the motives behind this policy, from both imperial and civic perspectives.

The Roman state offered no definition of schoolteachers or a method for evaluating their merits. The Roman legislator assigned civic institutions the right to choose their own schoolteachers, according to each city's particular requirements and needs. The choice of teachers was not merely a choice of curriculum. It was a choice of a set of skills necessary for the city's youth.[9] In order to explore the involvement of provincial cities in the administration of school teaching, this chapter will look into the identity of the teachers and what this reveals about the cities' motives in granting them such expensive privileges. The form of the chapter follows the path paved by historians of health care during the High Roman Empire who examined the modus operandi of select-ing public physicians. Such an analysis entails collecting relevant evidence concerning the identity of the practitioners and the information their commu-nities left regarding their elections. Much like schoolteachers, immunity was also bestowed upon city-elected doctors, who also bore the title 'public'.[10] These public physicians are mentioned in more than sixty papyri and were the recipients of an even larger number of honorary monuments. However, virtually no evidence of this kind exists when it comes to grammarians.

I wish to offer an explanation for this seeming discrepancy. Initially, I will sketch the history of school teaching in the Roman world, its origin, *raison d'être*, and typical personnel. This inquiry will be pertinent not because it necessarily depicts provincial teachers during the High Empire but because it portrays the image of schoolteachers that the Roman jurists must have had when bestowing privileges upon them. I will then proceed to examine the legal mechanism set by Rome for administrating professional activity in the provinces and try to uncover the grid of interests that guided this policy. Next, I will assume the point of view of the cities themselves who chose which schoolteachers to look after their children and conse-quently to receive privileges. Finally, I will ask whether schoolteachers fit into the rubric of intellectuals or artisans.

---

[7] Knibbe 1981: 1–10.   [8] *Dig.* 27.1.6.1–2, 4 (Modestinus).   [9] Cf. *AE* 1940, p. 19 s. n. 46.
[10] Below 1953; Cohn-Haft 1956; Nutton 1977: 191–226; Nutton 1981: 9–46.

School Teaching in the Roman World: Origin, *Raison d'être*, and Personnel

According to Suetonius, grammar as a discipline and as a vocation was introduced into Rome by Livius Andronicus and by Q. Ennius who were teaching both at home and in public (*domi forisque*). Moreover, initially the teaching of grammar was restricted to the explanation of Greek authors and to the public reading of the Latin poems they themselves composed.[11] The prosopography and history of Rome's first *praeceptores* suggests that the discipline of *grammatica* was likely to have emerged out of professional practice. Suetonius himself had noted that Lucius Aelius, Rome's first native *grammaticus*, had a double cognomen. The first cognomen was Praeconius because his father was a *praeco*.[12] Kaster reasonably infers that the elder Aelius must have been a *praeco publicus* in Rome.[13] This position entailed assisting a magistrate as a herald and auctioneer with responsibilities to summon the assemblies of both the senate and the people for the purpose of the sale of state property and the letting of state contracts.[14] The vocational background of Aelius, who composed speeches for the like of Quintus Metellus, Quintus Caepio, and Quintus Pompeius Rufus, is interesting. Like all *apparitores*, the *praecones* received wages (*merces*).[15] Hence, for the purpose of self-promotion, this vocational cognomen must have been emphasized by Aelius himself, in his practice as a teacher, if Suetonius knew about it and deemed it worthy to mention. Aelius' other cognomen was Stilo because he was in the habit of writing beautiful orations for whoever needed one.[16] On the evidence of Cicero's *Brutus* 169, 205–7, it can be inferred that Aelius was a distinguished speechwriter but was not delivering his orations himself. Other protagonists of Suetonius' *DGR* all share two distinctive attributes: a humble background and an aspirational character.

In addition, the growth of the Roman economy and the development of its legal system necessitated literacy, which, in turn, required professionals

---

[11] *initium … nihil amplius quam Graecos interpretabantur, aut si quid ipsi Latine conposuissent praelegebant.* ('At the beginning … nothing more than interpreting the Greek (poets), or to read publically something, if they composed in Latin.') Suet. *DGR* 1.2.

[12] *Praeconius, quod pater eius praeconium fecerat.* (Praeconius, because his father was a herald) Suet. *DGR* 3.2.

[13] Kaster 1995: 74.

[14] For *praecones* see Mommsen 1871–88: I, 286–9 and Purcell 1983: 147–8.

[15] Mommsen 1871–88: I, 261.

[16] *Quod orationes nobilissimo cuique scribere solebat.* ('Because he was in the habit of composing orations beautifully to anyone.') Suet. *DGR* 3.2.

who would teach it. William Harris reasonably infers from Varro's recommendation that the overseer of slaves (who was a slave himself) should be literate and that there was a growing demand for literacy, which was accommodated by professional schooling rather than home teaching.[17] Likewise, Cicero confirms that stipulations like laws and wills were done in writing.[18] Together with loans and debts, which must have been recorded in writing, these comments of Cicero and Varro exemplify how significant literacy, and the ability to acquire it, was in managing large households and in conducting business transactions. Under such conditions 'a pervasive system of schools is a prerequisite for mass literacy'.[19] It is quite possible that lower-class children and even slaves were taught in schools to read and write.[20] While children of an upper-class background received their initial training at home or from a tutor, members of the lower classes must have attended schools, thus making teachers a necessity.[21] This hypothesis is further supported by the comment of Suetonius that between the first century BCE and the time of the composition of *De Grammaticis et Rhetoribus* there were at times more than twenty grammar schools in Rome operating simultaneously: *Posthac magis ac magis et gratia et cura artis increvit, ut ne clarissimi quidem viri abstinuerint quo minus et ipsi aliquid de ea scriberent, utque temporibus quibusdam super viginti celebres scholae fuisse in urbe tradantur.*[22] This claim is reaffirmed by epigraphic evidence from cities throughout Italy, which attests to the activity of schools.[23]

With the decline of the Republic and the foundation of the Principate, literacy became a necessity for the imperial government, as can be attested by the emergence of positions such as *ab epistulis*, and, more generally, 'the attraction to the immediate service of the emperor of men whose qualifications were essentially intellectual, literary or scholastic'.[24] These men attended to the various aspects of governing the empire, both from the Roman side and from the side of local communities.

---

[17] Varro *RR* 1.17.4; Harris 1989: 196–7. *Cf.* Booth 1979: 11–19.   [18] Cic. *Top.* 96.
[19] Harris 1989: 233.   [20] Booth 1979: 11–19.   [21] Harris 1989: 233; Bonner 1977: 165–88.
[22] 'Later on, the esteem and care for the art increased more and more, so that even the most esteemed men did not abstain from it and even they themselves composed something upon it. And it is reported that from that time more than twenty schools flourished in the city'. Suet. *DGR* 3.4.
[23] Harris 1989: 241, with n. 352.   [24] Millar 1977: 83.

Legal Mechanism of Administering Professional Activity in Provincial Cities during the High Empire

In sharp contrast to its Republican precedent, the Principate showed great interest in professional activity. Grammarians, alongside other professional groups, were encouraged by the Roman state to practice their trade in the cities of the Roman Empire. A series of imperial acts of legislation granted grammarians, alongside teachers of rhetoric and doctors, an exemption from tutelage, curatorship, and various other civic duties. Thus, Modestinus wrote in his treatise on exemptions from tutelage: 'Grammarians, teachers of rhetoric and doctors who are known as general practitioners are exempt from tutelage and curatorship just as from other public duties'.[25] However, we understand from the Code of Justinian (10.53.1) that exemptions to professors and physicians were applicable only to those who served the community and were chosen and nominated by its formal institutions. Even more explicitly, Emperor Gordian instructed that 'it is not unknown that grammarians or orators who have been approved by a decree of the decurions, if they should not show themselves to be useful to students, can be rejected again by the same council'.[26] Hence, the imperial government saw the *raison d'être* of these immunities to be practical rather than appreciation of cultural values. The practical aspect of these immunities is emphasized by the explicit exclusion of poets from its recipients.[27] In fact, it was necessary soon after these immunities were initially introduced for Pius to issue an edict restricting the number of such exemptions each city could issue. According to Modestinus, the cities were not at liberty to extend this number: '[F]urther, there are in every city a fixed number who are exempt from public duties, the selection of which is limited by law. This appears from a letter of Antoninus Pius written to the province of Asia, but of universal application.'[28] They were, however, allowed to reduce it 'since this will result in a benefit to the public service'. This exemption from public duties could only be enjoyed by a person whom the city council chose, and as long as he was diligent in his work. By so doing, the Roman legislator

---

[25] *Dig.* 27.1.6.1 (Modestinus) *libro secundo excusationum.* Γραμματικοί, σοφισταὶ ῥήτορες, ἰατροὶ οἱ περιοδευταὶ καλούμενοι ὥσπερ τῶν λοιπῶν λειτουργιῶν οὕτωσὶ δὲ καὶ ἀπὸ ἐπιτροπῆς καὶ κουρατορίας ἀνάπαυσιν ἔχουσιν. Cf. *Dig.* 50.4.18.30 (Archadius Charisius).

[26] *Grammaticos seu oratores decreto ordinis probatos, si non se utiles studentibus praebeant, denuo ab eodem ordine reprobari posse incognitum non est. CJ* 10.53.2.

[27] *CJ* 10.53.3.

[28] Ἔστιν δὲ καὶ ὁ ἀριθμὸς ῥητόρων ἐν ἑκάστῃ πόλει τῶν τὴν ἀλειτουργησίαν ἐχόντων, καὶ αἱρέσεις τινὲς προσκείμεναι τῷ νόμῳ, ὅπερ δηλοῦται ἐξ ἐπιστολῆς Ἀντωνίνου τοῦ Εὐσεβοῦς γραφείσης μὲν τῷ κοινῷ τῆς Ἀσίας, παντὶ δὲ τῷ κόσμῳ διαφερούσης. *Dig.* 27.1.6.2.

circumvented any requirement for a licensing system, as the cities themselves acted as barriers against unskilled professionals and charlatans.

It is noteworthy that the Roman legislator understood grammarians and teachers of rhetoric to be a distinct group, separate from teachers of law. Hence the Roman legislator was aiming exclusively at schoolteachers. In fact, provincial law teachers were explicitly prohibited from being exempted, except for those who taught in Rome.[29] The importance of school teachers to the Roman imperial government is reaffirmed by Ulpian, who emphasized that it is the governor of the province who should settle law suits concerning salaries of teachers of various descriptions, alongside physicians, but not teachers of civil law.[30] The inclusion of this category of disputes under the jurisdiction of the governor confirms the significance Rome attributed to their work. Though Ulpian is silent as to how Rome perceived the value of the teachers' work, it might be possible to infer it by noticing the other groups of professionals who were included in the same category as school teachers and had their disputes settled by the Roman governor. Alongside teachers we find masters of elementary schools who are not teachers (*Ludi quoque litterarii magistris licet non sint professors*), as well as archivists, shorthand writers and accountants or ledger-keepers (*iam et librariis et notariis et calculatoribus sive tabulariis*).[31] More generally, the governor should restrict his jurisdiction to professions involving writing or shorthand. Fergus Millar concluded that 'nothing could show more clearly that the values which informed this system of exemptions were not based on practical considerations of service to the state, but on the prestige within contemporary culture of the various branches of learning'.[32] I would like to suggest an additional interpretation: that special care is given to those who train future bureaucrats, without whom the imperial government as well as local administration could not operate.

The Cities' Point of View

It is clear from the work of Philostratus that sophists expected these privileges to be met. Thus, on his appointment as high priest, Favorinus demanded immunity from liturgies to which he was entitled as a philosopher.[33] A more vivid portrayal is that of Aelius Aristides, who

---

[29] *Dig.* 27.1.6.12.   [30] *Dig.* 50.13.1–5 (Ulpian).   [31] *Dig.* 50.13.1.6.   [32] Millar 1977: 501.
[33] Philostr. *VS* 490.

was ordered at the winter of 153 CE by the Roman governor Severus either to take students or forgo his immunities. Though Aristides succeeded in maintaining his status (and perhaps not without taking students), this demand of Severus indicates that the Roman government had practical (rather than cultural) motives when bestowing immunities from liturgies.[34] Cities must have found the presence of schoolteachers to be attractive. Otherwise there would not have been a need to limit the number of exemptions the cities themselves could have willingly bestowed upon them. Furthermore, as was made explicit by the fourth-century emperor Julian, the imperial government sanctioned local administrative authorities to measure the skills of teachers and professors (*magistros studiorum doctoresque*) who merited immunities.[35] Yet an attempted prosopography of those who practiced it is somewhat baffling. *Grammatici* and *rhetores* seldom appear in inscriptions. When they do, it is almost exclusively a funerary inscription, where the epitaphs *grammaticus* and *rhetor* allude to professional identity. Unlike their equivalent ἀρχιατρόι and δημοσίοι ἰατρόι, the *grammatici* and *rhetores* appear with no official title.[36] The *grammatici* were not the beneficiaries of honorary monuments. For example, an inscription from the city of Rome was erected in memory of a beloved daughter by her *grammaticus* father.[37] A similar inscription, this one from Aquitania, recorded the life of a deceased *doctor* of the *artes grammatices*, whose love for his vocation appears on his tombstone: 'Here lies Blaesianus Biturix, a doctor of the art of language and a teacher of decorum, a constant lover of the Muses, subdued forever by the hands of sleep'.[38] Similar inscriptions were found in Belgica;[39] Hispania citerior;[40] Dalmatia;[41] Baetica;[42] and Mauretania Caesariensis.[43] It is therefore clear that this profession and this form of epitaph existed all over the Latin West (I set aside discussion of the Greek East, where a distinction has to be drawn between *praeceptores* and sophists, as well as other aspects of Greek culture, which existed independently of Rome). In addition to these eight there are five Latin inscriptions recording a *rhetor* from Rome, Hispania citerior, Venetia et Histria (Regio X), Germania inferior, and Dalmatia.[44] These too were all funerary and privately erected.

---

[34] For this episode see Israelowich 2016.   [35] CJ 10.53.7.   [36] See next.

[37] *Carissimae filiae Crispinae | quae vixit annos XV menses | VIIII dies XII Crispinianus | pater grammaticus curavit |Modesto et Harintheo(!) conss(ulibus). AE* 1969/70, 0071.

[38] *Artis < grammatices > | doctor morum(que) mag(is) |ter | Blaesianus Biturix M|usarum semper amator | hic iacet aeterno dev|inctus membra sopore . AE* 1989, 0520=*CIL* 13, 01393.

[39] *AE* 1978, 0503.   [40] *CIL* 02, 03872=*ILS* 7765.   [41] *CIL* 03, 13822=*ILS* 7767. (B)

[42] *CIL* 02, 02236=*ILS* 7766.   [43] *AE* 1994, 1903.

[44] *AE* 1985, 0121 (Rome); *AE* 1946, 0003 (Hispania citerior); *CIL* 05, 01028 (Venetia er Histria); *AE* 2004, 0976 (Germania inferior); *CIL* 03, 02127a add. p. 1509=*ILS* 7774 (Dalmatia).

The humble picture of the *grammatici* and *rhetores*, which emerges from the Latin inscriptions, is consistent with the one drawn by Suetonius in his history of these professions in the Roman world. According to Suetonius, teachers of rhetoric initially arrived from the Greek world and were characterized by their humble, and often foreign, origin.[45] Furthermore, they were artisans teaching for fees.[46] In fact, the discipline of *grammatica* likely emerged out of professional practice. The protagonists of Suetonius are often associated with the *apparitores* of the Roman magistrates in terms of skills and abilities. Scribes (*scribae*), messengers (*viatores*), lictors (*lictores*), and heralds (*praecones*) all needed an adequate level of literacy.

The Provincial *Praeceptor*: Between an Intellectual and an Artisan

Immunities and a widespread demand for education made school teaching a lucrative profession. In fact, Domitian had to issue a severe warning against *praeceptores* and physicians who trained slaves:

> Emperor Caesar Domitian, holding the tribunician power for the thirteenth time, saluted imperator for the twenty-second time, perpetual censor, father of the fatherland, to Aulus Licinius Mucianus and Gavius Priscus. I have decided that the strictest restraints must be imposed on the avarice of physicians and teachers, whose art, which ought to be transmitted to selected freeborn youths, is sold in a most scandalous manner to many household slaves trained and sent out, not in the interest of humanity, but as a money-making scheme. Therefore, whoever reaps a profit from trained slaves must be deprived of that immunity bestowed by my deified father, just as if he were exercising his art in a foreign state.[47]

It is assumed that slave owners who had their slaves trained in medicine and schoolteaching did so because these professions were gainful. These schoolteachers and physicians were artisans, not intellectuals engrossed in *artes liberales*. However, while a prosopography of the medical profession

---

[45] For prosopography, see Suet. *DGR* 1–6.   [46] Ibid.

[47] *[Imp. Caesar Domitia]nus tribuniciae potestatis XIII | [imp. XXII cens. perp. p. p.] A. Licinio Muciano et Gauio Prisco. [Auaritiam medicorum atque] praeceptorum quorum ars, | [tradenda ingenuis adulesc]entibus quibusdam, multis | [in disciplinam cubiculariis] seruis missis improbissime || [uenditur, non humanitatis sed aug]endae mercedis gratia, | [seuerissime coercendam] iudicaui. | [Quisquis ergo ex seruorum disciplin]a mercedem [capiet, ei immunitas a diuo patre meo indulta], proinde ac [si | in aliena ciuitate artem exerceat, adim]enda [est]. AE* 1940, p. 19 s. n. 46.

shows that some physicians habitually were part of the educated upper tier of provincial cities, and a study of the role of physicians who were given immunities indicates that their responsibilities extended beyond offering health care into the realm of forensic medicine, a study of schoolteachers indicates no such thing.[48] Of course, these schoolteachers must be discerned from the protagonists of Philostratus and other so-called sophists who were intellectuals of the highest repute, took part in municipal, provincial and even imperial government, and were recipients of great honours due to their benefactions to their cities. These individuals who were extensively studied were not schoolteachers.

A single papyrus recording a grammarian's complaint and dated to the middle of the third century CE sheds light on the role of those appointed schoolteachers, on the motives of the city in appointing them, and their motives in wishing to be elected. The papyrus deals with an appeal of Lollianus, a public grammarian (δημόσιος γραμματικὸς) of Oxyrhynchus. Lollianus was appointed to this position by the city's *Boule* and expected to receive the customary salary. In reality, Lollianus was rarely paid, and when he was, the wages took the form of commodities rather than money. Lollianus further complained that his duties were all-consuming, allowing him no additional work which would sustain him. It was, therefore, his request that he receive a city-owned orchard within the city walls.

While Lollianus' title is elsewhere unattested, it could not have been unique.[49] As Lollianus himself mentioned, this was the title of grammarians who were bestowed with immunities from the city's *Boule*: οἱ θεοὶ πρόγονοι ὑμῶν κατὰ μέγεθος τῶν πόλεων καὶ ποσότητα δημοσίων γραμματι [ῶ]ν. The decree of the emperor's deified forefathers further instructed that the cities that selected public grammarians should give them wages: προστάξαντες καὶ συντάξεις αὐτοῖς δίδοσθαι. Moreover, Lollianus explained why Vespasian set this position and why wages should be paid. The *grammaticus* should dedicate all his time to educating the city's children: ἡ περὶ τοὺς παῖδας ἐπιμέλεια. According to Lollianus this salary was habitually paid (τὴν σύνταξιν τ(ὴν) εἰωθυῖαν). This demand of Lollianus, which calls to mind a similar petition of a public physician in a Roman court at Alexandria a century earlier, relies on Roman legislation concerning immunities for these professionals. A physician by the name of Psasnis requested in 141 CE that the court restore his immunities, which were currently disregarded by the city of Oxyrhynchus, although he was an

---

[48] For the role of physicians in the cities of the Roman Empire, see above all: Cohn-Haft 1956, Nutton 1977, Israelowich 2015: chap. 1.

[49] *Contra*: Parsons 1976: 413.

acting public physician: ἰατρὸς ὑπάρχων τὴ[ν τέ]χνην τούτους αὐτοὺς οἵτινές με εἰς λειτο[υ]ρ[γ]ίαν / δεδώκασι ἐθεράπευσα (I am a physician by skill and I cured these very men who assigned me to liturgy).[50] The ruling of the Roman court, presided over by Eudaimon, was that his immunity should be honoured, if indeed he is a public physician, which means one of those selected by the city's *boule* and within the quota of permitted immune physicians by Pius' rescript: δῖδαξον τ[ὸν στρα-] / τηγόν, εἰ ἰατρὸς εἶ δημοσ [ιε]ύων ἐπιτη[δειως] / καὶ ἕξεις τὴν ἀλειτουργησιαν (the Strategos answered, if you are a public physician you shall get immunity).[51] These petitions relied on the dual mechanism of Roman legislation and municipal administration, which means that Psasnis and Lollianus did not request that the Roman court recognize him as a public physician and a public grammarian. The status of δημόσιος was the ground of both petitions, and a proof for the common use of this title and institution.

Some Preliminary Conclusions

Schoolteachers like Lollianus were expected to educate the city's young, an all-consuming task and humbly recompensed. The willingness of the Roman government to exempt teachers who practiced in provincial cities from *munera* or λειτουργία, which was reciprocated by cities themselves, requires an explanation. An appreciation of certain cultural institutions could have accounted for this act. However, the fact that other agents of this same culture, such as poets, musicians, or sculptors, were not the beneficiary of such privileges, and the complete absence of schoolteachers from all honorary monuments, work against this hypothesis. A second explanation, one which is based on interest rather than good will, might prove more convincing. Civic, municipal, and imperial government, as well as local businesses and the legal system required widespread literacy. Schoolteachers, like their counterpart physicians, offered an indispensable service to the cities. Like physicians, schoolteachers in residence were needed in the cities. Like physicians, schoolteachers gained a privileged place in their unlicensed professional community due to their election to a civic post. Like physicians, schoolteachers offered a service, which the cities recognized as indispensable. However, unlike physicians, schoolteachers remained anonymous throughout the period of the High

---

[50] For this papyrus, see Youtie 1964, Israelowich 2014.
[51] *P. Oxy.* 1.40 with Youtie 1964 *ad loc.* and cf. *P. Fay.* 106.

Empire. They failed to break the glass ceiling for artisans. Unlike the sophists of either Peter Brunt's *Bubble of the Second Sophistic* or those of Glen Bowersock's *Greek Sophists in the Roman Empire*, Lollianus was not a scholar who also had students. He was a teacher by trade. By escaping the anonymity of his colleagues he merely emphasized the reality of his vocation: an artisan, whose inglorious skill, like that of the archivist, the shorthand writer, the accountant or the ledger-keeper, was much required throughout the cities of the High Roman Empire. Cities endowed schoolteachers with privileges because they needed to pay for their practical skills, not as a token of appreciation for the culture they represented.

9 | Many Nations, One Night?

Historical Aspects of the Night in the Roman Empire

ANGELOS CHANIOTIS

Historicizing Ancient Nights

Forty years have passed since sociologist Murray Melbin published his article "Night as Frontier" drawing attention to historical aspects of the night in the nineteenth and twentieth centuries and thus setting the foundations for a historical research of the night. Observing that nighttime activities increased as the settlement of new regions came to an end in the nineteenth century, he argued that the night was gradually perceived as another kind of frontier, as an area that should be colonized.[1] A few years later (1983), Wolfgang Schivelbusch's *Lichtblicke: Zur Geschichte der künstlichen Helligkeit im 19. Jahrhundert* discussed the dramatic impact of a technological change – artificial lighting that expanded nighttime activities – on the society, culture, and economy of nineteenth-century Europe.[2] In the decades the followed, especially after the turn of the century, historical research has studied significant aspects of the night in medieval and Early Modern Europe, in the Ottoman Empire, and in the modern world,[3] focusing on phenomena such as crime, policing, and the maintenance of order, witchcraft and Christian piety, debating, feasting, and entertaining at the royal courts, the rise of street lighting, differences between city and countryside, the emergence of new forms of entertainment, and the relation between gender and nocturnal activities.[4] Although

---

[1] Melbin 1978. A monographic treatment of the subject in Melbin 1987.

[2] English translation: Schivelbusch 1988.

[3] Delattre 2000; Borchhardt-Birbaumer 2003; Ekirch 2005; Bronfen 2008; Cabantoux 2009; Koslofsky 2011; Bourdin (ed.) 2013; Wishnitzer 2014.

[4] Crime and policing: Delattre 2000: 136–43, 268–324, 454–67; Ekirch 2005: 75–84; Cabantoux 2009: 159–90, 229–44; Koslofsky 2011: 128–56. Magic and religion: Cabantoux 2009: 69–82, 135–7, 191–227; Koslofsky 2011: 28–90, 247–51. Nightlife in royal courts: Ekirch 2005: 210–17; Koslofsky 2011: 90–127. Street lighting, gas, and electricity: Delattre 2000: 79–119; Ekirch 2005: 67–74; Cabantoux 2009: 249–62; Koslofsky 2011: 128–56. City vs. countryside: Cabantoux 2009: 245–9; Koslofsky 2011: 198–235. Entertainment: Schivelbusch 1988: 191–221; Delattre 2000: 147–204; Ekirch 2005: 213–17; Cabantoux 2009: 282–9; Koslofsky 2011: 93–103; Triolaire 2013. Gender: Ekirch 2005: 65–6, 220–2; Koslofsky 2011: 174–97.

certain aspects of the night, such as the *symposion*, dreaming, nocturnal rites, and sexuality, had long attracted the interest of Classical scholars, only in recent years have ancient historians and philologists, and to a much lesser extent archaeologists and art historians, more systematically turned their attention to what happened in the Greco-Roman world between sunset and sunrise, also at dusk and at dawn, and what perceptions and stereotypes are connected with the night.[5] Subjects that have been treated in this process include sleep, sleeplessness, dreaming, and supernatural assaults,[6] religious practices and incubation in sanctuaries,[7] the night as the setting of narratives and images,[8] nocturnal violence and safety measures,[9] artificial light,[10] private and public banquets,[11] and nocturnal writing and epigraphy.[12]

An important methodological issue in the historical study of the night is the fact that the 'night' is a marked word; it is a term that carries special social and cultural connotations, giving emphasis to a statement and enhancing emotional display.[13] The function of the night as an enhancer of emotions influences the representation of the night in texts; certain aspects – especially, sex, danger, violence, and supernatural phenomena – are overrepresented over more mundane subjects such as resting or working (fishing, watering the fields, going to the market, etc.). As a 'marked' interval of time, the night has been enduringly associated with a certain set of perceptions: It is intimately linked with fear, anxiety, and erotic desire; it is associated with death and the communication between mortals and the gods, the living and the dead; and it plays a great part in the creation of a sense of togetherness.[14] Despite the difficulties and distortions emerging from universal and diachronic perceptions of the night, one may still observe changes triggered by a variety of factors. The clearest changes

---

[5] Becker 2013 (night and darkness). Collections of essays: Scioli and (eds.) 2010; Chaniotis 2018a; Ker and Wessels (eds.) 2020.

[6] Sleep: Sorabella 2010; Nissin 2015, 118–9. Sleeplessness: Sacerdoti 2014. Dreaming: Harris 2009; Johnston 2010; Casali 2010; Corbeill 2010; Graf 2010; Kenaan 2010; Näf 2010. Incubation: Renberg 2010 and 2015; Harrison 2013. Supernatural assaults: Spaeth 2010;

[7] Religion: Patera 2010; Paleothodoros 2010; Pirenne-Delforge 2018; Carlà-Uhink 2018; Renberg 2006 and 2017; von Ehrenheim 2015.

[8] Casali 2010 and 2018; Kenaan 2010; Mylonopoulos 2018; De Temmerman 2018.

[9] Dowden 2010; Chaniotis 2017; Casali 2018; Mylonopoulos 2018.

[10] Dossey 2018; Wilson 2018.

[11] Dunbabin 2003; Vössing 2004; Stein-Hölkeskamp 2005; Nadeau 2010; Schnurbusch 2011; König 2012; Wecowski 2014; Donahue 2017.

[12] Writing: Ker 2004 and McGill 2014. Epigraphy of the night: Chaniotis 2019. I note that the evidence for orality in erotic graffiti in Pompeii (Wachter 1998) suggests that they were written during the night.

[13] Detailed discussion in Chaniotis 2017 and 2018b.   [14] Chaniotis 2018b, 2018c, and 2019.

can be detected in the world of the Greek cities from roughly the mid fourth century BCE to the late second century CE. A close study of the documentary evidence – inscriptions and papyri – reveals a significant increase in nocturnal religious activities and 'free time activities' – visiting baths and gymnasia, and attending private and public dinners.[15] The intensive warfare in the period between Alexander and Actium and the increased nighttime activities in cities, often connected with the presence of women in sanctuaries and public spaces after sunset, forced civic authorities to address in a more systematic manner the perennial problem of nocturnal safety. The principal factors that had an impact on how the night was experienced and lived in Hellenistic cities and in the Roman East were the continuous wars, the mobility of persons that contributed to the growth of voluntary associations and their nocturnal conviviality, the popularity of mystery cults, the existence of incubation sanctuaries, and the financial contributions of benefactors.[16] The part played by advancements in technology and science was more limited. This general trend, visible in Hellenistic cities and continually growing in the Imperial period, reached its peak in the big urban centers of Late Antiquity. As Leslie Dossey has argued,[17] one may observe in the cities of the Roman East a clear shift towards late hours for dining, bathing, and routine activities, not only for religious celebrations. This shift increased the awareness of safety issues and ultimately contributed to the spread of street lighting.

Understandably, the attempts to sketch a 'history of the night' in the Hellenistic World, the Roman East, and Late Antiquity that I summarized here do not consider local peculiarities and possible short-term developments. Comparing nighttime cultures in the Mediterranean territories of the Roman Empire is an important task. However, it is severely impeded by the imbalance in the source material. There is no Pompeii in Asia Minor; private documents in papyri and ostraka survive only in Egypt and, in limited numbers, in Israel and Syria; civic honorific decrees for benefactors are a phenomenon connected with the civic traditions of Greece and Asia Minor; we only have limited narrative sources about North Africa, Gaul, or Spain; the evidence from Rome is shaped by its role as an imperial capital and the overwhelming presence of the emperor, and so on. This imbalance renders comparisons a hazardous undertaking. The scope of this chapter, which is not based on a systematic study of all available sources, is very limited. I will examine the extent to which the creation of an empire of many nations contributed to convergences in nightlife.

---

[15] Chaniotis 2018b and 2018c.   [16] Chaniotis 2017 and 2018c.   [17] Dossey 2018.

The Realities behind the Nocturnal Stereotypes

The representation of the night in the textual sources is dominated by stereotypes shaped by diachronic and universal experiences. The darkness challenges vision and alerts other senses, especially listening, touching, and smelling. Emotional responses are no less enhanced than sensory. This was already known to Achilles Tatius (second century CE). In his novel *Leukippe and Kleitophon* he presents the protagonist explaining how all wounds are more painful by night and all our emotions burst out – the grief of those who mourn, the anxieties of those who are troubled, the fears of those who are in danger, and the fiery desire of those who are in love.[18] A man in the Arsinoite nome, a contemporary of Achilles Tatius, describes his torments when his wife abandoned him with these words: 'I want you to know that ever since you left me I have been in mourning, weeping at night and lamenting during the day.'[19] In the late first century CE, Statius addressed his wife in almost exactly the same way – asking her why she sorrows by day and fetches painful sighs in the night, passing it with him in sleepless worry.[20] And a metrical graffito in the domus Tiberiana in Rome describes how the soul finds no peace as burning erotic desire chases sleep away.[21] Because of the night's emotive impact, the explicit reference to the night in a narrative was often intended to magnify emotional arousal.[22] This is why we have direct references to the fact that an earthquake occurred during the night in Greek and Latin inscriptions.[23]

Consequently, references to the night in literary sources, inscriptions, and papyri are likely to be influenced by the function of the night as an

---

[18] Ach. Tat. 1.6.2. Discussed by De Temmerman 2014: 183–4 and 2018: 262.

[19] *BGU* III 846: γινώσκειν σε θέλω ἀφ᾽ ὡς ἐξῆλθες ἀπ᾽ ἐμοῦ πένθος ἡγούμην νυκτὸς κλαίων ἡμέρας δὲ πενθῶν.

[20] *Silvae* 3.5.1–2: *quid mihi maesta die, sociis quid noctibus, uxor, anxia pervigili ducis suspiria cura?* On love-induced insomnia, see De Temmerman 2018, 262–4, 268–72.

[21] *Carmina Latina Epigraphica* 943: *Vis nulla est animi, non somnus claudit ocellos, noctes atque dies aestuat omnes amor.*

[22] Chaniotis 2017 and Casali 2018, for narratives of violence; De Temmerman 2018, for the nocturnal setting of episodes in novels.

[23] *IG* XII.8.92, Imbros, second /first century BCE: ὀρφναίην ἀνὰ νύκτα | τοὺς τρισσοὺς νέκυας σταθμὸς ἔθαψε δόμου. . . . νύκτα δὲ πικροτάτην μεταδόρπιον ὑπνώσαντες | οἰκοῦμεν μέλαθρ[ον Περσεφόνης ζοφερόν] ('in the dark night the roof of the house buried the three dead . . . We slept a bitter night after dinner, and now we inhabit the dark palace of Persephone'); discussed in Chaniotis 2018b: 8. Cf. *CIL* VIII 17970a (*AE* 2009, 1771), Besseriani / Ad Maiores (Numidia), 267 CE: *[post terrae motum] quod [patria]e Pate[rno et] | Arcesilao co(n)s(ulibus) hora noc[tis - - somno fessis contigit]*; cf. *CIL* VIII 2481.

intensifier of empathy. Nevertheless, stereotypes reflect real experiences. References to nocturnal activities in Juvenal's satires of the late first and early second century CE are a case in point. His nocturnal themes cover a limited thematic range that principally concerns sex, danger, and entertainment. There are references to nighttime lovers and the nocturnal escapades of Messalina in brothels;[24] to noisy drunks and to a wealthy woman who goes to the baths at night, keeping her dinner guests waiting and overcome by boredom and hunger; to parasites that party all night long;[25] to a millionaire who, terrified for his valuable belongings, keeps a team of slaves watching all night;[26] and to such a variety of dangers, that

> if you go out to dinner without making a will, you might be regarded as careless, unaware of those tragic events that occur: there are as many opportunities for you to die, as there are open windows watching you, while you walk by at night.[27]

Tiles can fall on one's head from the highest roof; a cracked and leaky pot plunges down, pots are emptied over you – not to mention the thieves.[28] And when the Pontine Marsh or the Gallinarian Forest are temporarily rendered safe by an armed patrol, the ruffian vagabonds skip out of there and head for Rome.[29] Only the wealthy can afford to walk with a long retinue of attendants, and plenty of torches and lamps of bronze; they despise anyone who, like Juvenal, walks by the light of the moon or the flickering light of a lamp.[30] Those who do not fall into the group of the drunk, the oversexed, the terrified, and the dangerous are the literati, whose identity is shaped precisely by their lack of sleep and their nocturnal dedication to letters: They are the poets scribbling sublime verses all night in their tiny attics, and the young men urged by their fathers to quit sleep and turn to their wax tablets and the study of law.[31]

Although Juvenal's verses are clearly dominated by stereotypes, they still evince certain historical dimensions of the night and reflect realities. The night is experienced in a different manner by the poor and the rich, the urbanites and the country folk, the young and the old, the men and the women, the masters and the attendants, the educated and the common people, the owners of wealth and those who want to relieve them of it. The prevailing feelings are those of fear and erotic desire.

[24] Juvenal, *Satire* 3.12; 6.115–32.
[25] Juvenal, *Satire* 3.232–8; 6.419–29; 14.46. On drinking cf. Martial, *Epigrams* 1.28, 11.104, 12.12.
[26] Juvenal, *Satire* 14.305–9.   [27] Juvenal, *Satire* 3.272–5. Cf. 3.197f.
[28] Juvenal, *Satire* 3.268–72, 276–80.   [29] Juvenal, *Satire* 3.302–8.   [30] Juvenal, *Satire* 3.282–8.
[31] Juvenal, *Satire* 7.27–9; 14.189–95. On nocturnal writing see Ker 2004, McGill 2014, and Wilson 2020.

Despite the lack of street lighting in Rome,[32] there is a lot of traffic in Juvenal's verses: people returning from dinner parties or going to the baths, guards patrolling dangerous places, and criminals ambushing inattentive victims. The first impression, that Juvenal's people are mostly engaged in leisurely activities – dining and drinking, visiting the baths, and having sex – is deceiving. Apart from the usual practitioners of darkness – the criminals – we encounter a young man studying the law, slaves guarding private houses and accompanying their masters in the dark streets, and night watches patrolling dangerous places; and of course the dinner parties, the brothels, and the baths presuppose not only those who enjoy themselves but also cooks, musicians, prostitutes, and bath attendants.

Juvenal's references to nighttime activities are shaped by the themes of his poetry, exactly as centuries earlier Sappho's praise of the potential offered by the night for erotic encounters and celebrations was shaped by the themes of her poetry.[33] But they are also shaped by the historical context: As we can judge from other sources, the background of the nocturnal scenes painted by Juvenal is the contemporary awareness that the night is more than the privileged territory of criminals, conspirators, magicians, and uncontrolled, ecstatic, or secretive worshippers as it had been in the Republican period.[34] One generation earlier, in Seneca's times, a certain Sextus Papinius was known as *lychnobius* ('living under the light of the lamp'), because he had reversed the functions of day and night. He went over his accounts in the third hour of the night, exercised his voice in the sixth, went out for a drive in the eighth, visited the baths before dawn, and dined in the early morning.[35] Admittedly, such a behavior was noted as an abnormality, exactly as an imaginary city in Iberia, described by Antonius Diogenes in his novel *The Incredible Things beyond Thoule*, where people could see during the night and were blind during the day.[36] But the *lychnobius*' anomalous timetable still required a bath that was accessible before dawn. Surely, not every bath was accessible in the night,[37] but both Seneca and Juvenal (see note 25) make clear that some

[32] On the scarcity of evidence for street lighting before Late Antiquity, see Dossey 2018: 292–307 and Wilson 2018: 66–72.

[33] See Schlesier 2018.

[34] On the predominantly negative perception of the night in Republican Rome, see Carlà-Uhink 2018.

[35] Seneca, *Epist.* 122.15–16.

[36] A summary is provided by Photius, *Bibl.* 166. On the possible date, see Morgan 1985. I owe this reference to Jonathan Price.

[37] According to the *Historia Augusta*, it was Severus Alexander (222–35 CE) who expanded the opening hours of public baths beyond sunset by supplying them with oil for the lamps (SHA, *Alex. Sev.* 23.7).

were. We can neither generalize from such references nor quantify the evidence because of the imbalances of the source material available. Questions such as 'Were there more people awake during the night in Imperial Rome than in Republican Rome?' or 'Was there more nightlife in the Roman East than, say, in Roman Spain?' are meaningless. The historical question that one can ask with a higher chance of a response is whether the creation of an empire and the social and cultural forces that this process unleashed had an impact on the night and contributed to a nocturnal *koine* in the Roman Empire. In this chapter I will consider two important factors of convergence in the Roman Empire: the emperor and his administration, and the increased mobility of people, cultural practices, ideas, cults, and rites. The establishment of the Principate and the emperor's bundle of powers had an impact on the administration and the society of Imperium. How did it affect the nightlife of the population in Rome and the provinces? With this question I am not concerned with the extreme behavior of some Roman emperors, such as Nero's idea to burn Christians as human torches in 64 CE,[38] or Elagabal's reversal of the functions of day and night, criticized by the author of the *Historia Augusta*.[39] I mean primarily the impetus for policing measures and celebrations after sunset.

Policing the Night

Although night guards are attested as early as our earliest textual sources,[40] the proliferation of evidence for *nyktophylakes* in the eastern provinces, especially in Asia Minor Egypt, and Palestine,[41] and for *vigiles* in the western provinces (see note 50) is likely to be connected, at least in part, with the attention given by Augustus to this matter. In 6 CE he established a regular service of *vigiles*, replacing the earlier system of *tresviri nocturni*,[42] and according to Appian he had already introduced *nyktophylakes* by 36/35 BCE.[43] In a letter to Knidos (6 BCE), the princeps explained his interest in public and private safety during the night. The letter concerns a man accused of the death of an enemy who, alongside some companions, had been harassing the accused man for three nights; when a slave tried to

---

[38] Tac. *Annals* 15.44.2–5.   [39] *SHA*, Elagabalus 28.6.

[40] Chaniotis 2017. On night watches in the Republican period: Nippel 1995: 37, 67.

[41] Greece: Apuleius, *Metam.* 3.3 (*praefectus nocturnae custodiae* in Hypata). Fuhrmann 2012: 57. Asia Minor: Brélaz 2005: 82–3. Egypt: Hennig 2002: 285–8; Homoth-Kuhs 2005: 66–7; Fuhrmann 2012: 77–8, 85–6, 130–1. Palestine: Sperber 1970.

[42] Fuhrmann 2012: 116–18. On *vigiles* in Rome, see Nippel 1995: 96–9; Sablayrolles 1996.

[43] Appian, *BC* 5.132.547; cf. Fuhrmann 2012: 101–2.

empty a chamber pot on the assailants who were besieging the house, the pot fell and killed one of them. Augustus unambiguously expresses his indignation that someone was put on trial for defending his own house during the night.[44]

> I learned that Phileinos son of Chrysippos had attacked the house of Eubulos and Tryphera for three nights in succession with violence and in the manner of a siege . . . I am amazed that you do not show indignation against those who deserved to suffer every punishment, since they attacked another's house three times at night with violence and force and were destroying the common security of all.

Beyond this general interest in security that may be attributed to influence exercised by imperial authority, there were local peculiarities. For instance, a regulation limiting the selling of wine during the night is only attested in Roman Palestine. The *Leviticus Rabba* narrates the following incident:[45]

> It happened once that a certain man, who used regularly to drink twelve xestes of wine a day, one day drank [only] eleven. He tried to go to sleep, but sleep would not come to him. [So] he got up in the dark and went to the wine-shop, and said to [the wine-seller]: 'Sell me one xestes of wine.' [The latter] replied to him: 'I cannot, for it is dark.' He said to him: 'If you do not give [it] me, sleep will not come to me.' [To which the wine-seller] replied: 'Just now the watchmen have passed from here, and I am afraid of the watchmen and can [therefore] not give [it] to you.' [The man] raised his eyes and saw a hole in the door. [So] he said to him: 'Hold the bottle up to this hole; you pour from the inside and I shall drink from the outside.' He was insistent. What did the wine-seller do? He put the spout [of the bottle] through the crack in the door and poured from the inside, while the other drank from the outside. As soon as he finished [drinking], he fell asleep in a corner in front of the door. The watchmen passed by him before the door, and thinking him a thief, beat him.

We cannot always determine whether policing measures were taken on a permanent basis, or only temporarily, in order to meet an emergency. Whether they were effective or not depended on numbers, budget, and competence.[46]

---

[44] *I.Knidos* 34: ἔγνων Φιλεῖνον τὸν Χρυσίππου τρεῖς νύκτας συνεχῶς ἐπεληλυθότα τῆι οἰκίᾳ τῆι Εὐβούλου καὶ Τρυφέρας μεθ' ὕβρεως καὶ τρόπωι τινὶ πολιορκίας . . . ἐθαύμαζον δ' ἄν, πῶς . . . μὴ κατὰ τῶν ἀξίων πᾶν ὁτιοῦν παθεῖν, ἐπ' ἀλλο[τρίαν] οἰκίαν νύκτωρ μεθ' ὕβρεως καὶ βίας τρὶς ἐπεληλυ[θό]των καὶ τὴν κοινὴν ἀπάντων ὑμῶν ἀσφάλειαν [ἀναι]ρούντων ἀγανακτοῦντες. For an analysis of the legal aspects of this text, see Karabatsou 2010.

[45] Sperber 1970: 257–8.

[46] See the complaints of night guards in Oxyrrhynchus: *P.Oxy.* VII 1033 (392 CE); cf. Hennig 2002: 285–9; Fuhrmann 2012: 85–6.

Another area in which impulses for safety came from Imperial Rome was firefighting. The city of Rome had fire squads,[47] and at the time of Cassius Dio, the guards of apartment blocks in Rome carried bells (*kodonophorein*) in order to signal alarm in case of an emergency.[48] Pliny was shocked to find out that when a fire destroyed private houses as well as the Gerousia and the Temple of Isis in Nikomedeia, the city had no fire engines, no buckets, no other implements to fight the fire. It was at his initiative that these would be procured.[49] In his letter to Trajan he alludes to the existence of guilds of firefighters in other cities, admitting that under certain conditions such guilds presented a threat. *Praefecti vigilum* existed in some cities of the western provinces; firefighting duties were also undertaken by *collegia*.[50] Of course, firefighting is not exclusively a matter of nocturnal security, but it is instructive with regard to the impact of imperial authority and administration on security measures in the provinces.

An issue related to public order is the use of water of public facilities by private individuals. An inscription of Stratonikeia (ca. mid first century BCE) lists the people who had acquired the right to use the water of a fountain 'day and night'.[51] Although the management of water resources had been a concern of Greek cities since early times,[52] this is the earliest attestation of a regulation concerning access to water during the night. The aim must have been to avoid the use of water resources without the payment of a fee and also to avoid conflicts. The explicit reference to the night is related not to the possibilities offered by darkness for illicit actions but perhaps rather to the preference to use water for irrigation after sunset. This certainly is the case in two documents of the Imperial period that explicitly refer to nocturnal access to water, showing a similar concern for nocturnal activities. An inscription from Tibur records the water rights of two landowners *ab hora noctis . . . ad horam diei*.[53] A contract of sale in the Babatha Archive (Maoza) determines the exact time of the night that irrigation of a piece of land was allowed (120 CE).[54]

Nocturnal security is a concern as old as humankind. The evidence summarized here reveals, however, an increased awareness of this issue. The similarity of practices and the uniform terminology suggest a certain

---

[47] Fuhrmann 2012: 130–1.   [48] Cassius Dio 54.4.4. Cf. Fuhrmann 2012: 57.

[49] Plin. *Letters* 10.33.

[50] Fuhrmann 2012: 57, note 41. For firefighting duties undertaken by *collegia*, see, e.g., Kneissl 1994 and van Nijf 2002.

[51] *I.Stratonikeia* 1508; *SEG* LV 1145; for the interpretation, see van Bremen 2011.

[52] Collin-Boufriet 2008.   [53] *CIL* XIV 3676; Eck 2008: 229.   [54] *P.Yadin* 7; Eck 2008: 236.

degree of convergence. A variety of factors, ranging from the imperial ideology of security and the existence of an empire-wide administration to the movement of Roman officials and, with them, of experiences and practices (as revealed by Pliny's letters), may have contributed to this.

Emulating the Imperial Generosity and Imperial Afterlife

The display of imperial *munificentia* is another new development with an impact on the nocturnal cityscape. It was thanks to the initiative and generosity of emperors that public banquets and spectacles that in earlier periods ended around sunset now continued into the night. In the capital of the Empire, the emperors organized public banquets that allowed for the participation of representatives of different classes. Although these inclusive events could momentarily create the illusion of equality, they ultimately confirmed social barriers by explicitly referring to the participants' unequal social and legal statuses, making special spatial arrangements, and providing varied portions to different groups.[55]

The secular games in Rome included nocturnal performances. The most magnificent celebration was staged by Augustus in late May/early June of 17 BCE.[56] In accordance with an oracle, the people were to enjoy festivities and banquets 'day and night without interruption'.[57] A sacrifice to the Moirai in the Campus Martius took place in the evening of May 31, followed by torchlight entertainment that was presented on a stage without auditorium seats for the spectators. A select group of 110 wives of citizens held a procession and a ritual banquet symbolically attended by the gods, whose images were placed at the site; young people were allowed to attend if accompanied by an adult relative.[58] This model was followed by later emperors.[59]

Although Domitian's private entertainments were purportedly never prolonged after sunset,[60] the emperor also organized nocturnal banquets that drew large numbers from all *ordines*.[61] Furthermore, his *munera* in Rome included hunts of wild animals and gladiatorial combats that continued into the night, while the circus was illuminated with artificial light (*venationes gladiotoresque et noctibus ad lychnuchos*).[62]

---

[55] D'Arms 1990.   [56] Beacham 1999: 114–19.
[57] Zosimus 2.6: ἤμασι δ᾽ ἔστω | νυξί τ᾽ ἐπασσυτέρῃσι θεοπρέπτους κατὰ θώκους | παμπληθὴς ἄγυρις.
[58] Beacham 1999: 116. For these nocturnal events, see Suet., *Aug.* 31.
[59] For Septimius Severus, see Rantala 2013 and 2017; cf. *CIL* VI 32323 = *ILS* 5050.
[60] Suet., *Domitian* 21.   [61] D'Arms 1990: 309.   [62] Suet., *Domitian* 4.1.

Such imperial events, experienced by huge audiences, talked of and commemorated in texts, may have served as a model for local benefactors, naturally on a smaller scale.[63] Public dinners for the entire population, held in connection with religious festivals, were not a novelty in Greek culture.[64] From the late Hellenistic period on, they were among the events that offered members of the elite an opportunity to show off their generosity by extending invitations to a broad cross section of the population – male citizens, married and unmarried women, freedmen and slaves, foreign residents, and the people of the countryside; this trend continued into the Imperial period.[65] Traditionally, public banquets took place in the afternoon and were completed before sunset, but in the Imperial period, the continuation of festivities into the night was not uncommon.[66] For instance, in second-century CE Bithynia, inscriptions listing benefactors regularly include the purposes for which money had been offered: drinking parties (*oinoposion*) and concerts (*symphonia*). The lighting of lamps (*lychnapsia*) suggests nocturnal feasts.[67] In Stratonikeia (second century CE), a priest and his wife

> offered a complete banquet in the gymnasium to all the citizens, the foreigners, and the slaves and [- -]; they also offered a banquet to all the women, those of citizen status, the free women, and the slaves [- -]; . . . they organized a contest at their own expense, paying for the most celebrated shows, throughout the day and for a large part of the night.[68]

Such services, unattested before the Imperial period and possibly influenced by imperial largesse, remained an extraordinary phenomenon.

An imperial impulse of an entirely different nature is the influence that the apotheosis of the emperor had on the widespread perception of death as an ascent to the skies. In the Imperial period, a significant number of

---

[63] Public banquets in the Roman Empire: Dunbabin 2003: 72–9, 82–4, 89–102; Donahue 2017 (with discussion of the role played by benefactors); Chaniotis 2018b: 17–22.

[64] Schmitt Pantel 1992: esp. 260–89.

[65] Late Hellenistic period: Schmitt Pantel 1992: 380–408. Imperial period: Stavrianopoulou 2009; Chaniotis 2018b.

[66] Stein-Hölkeskamp 2005: 112–16; Chaniotis 2018b: 20–2.

[67] Οἰνοπόσιον: *TAM* IV.1.16 LL. 7, 9; 17 LL. 4, 11, 15, 16, 21; συμφωνία: *TAM* IV.1.16 L. 14; 17 LL. 6, 12; λυχναψία: *TAM* IV.1.16 LL. 4; 17 LL. 5, 21. See Chaniotis 2018b: 21–2, for further evidence.

[68] IStratonikeia 254 lines 4–10: [ἐδεξιώσαντο ἐν τῷ γυμνασίῳ πάντας τούς τε πολείτας καὶ ξένους καὶ δούλο]υς δείπνῳ τελείῳ καὶ τοὺς [- -]αν, ἐδείπνισαν δὲ ὁμοίως [- - τὰς γυναῖκας πᾶσα]ς τάς τε πολειτίδας καὶ ἐ[λευθέρας καὶ δούλας - -] . . . ἐπετέλε[σαν δὲ ἀγῶνα ἐκ τῶν ἰδίων μετὰ] καὶ πρωτευόντων ἀκροαμάτων δι' ὅλης ἡμέρας ἄχρι πολ[λ]οῦ μέρους τῆς νυκτός.

grave inscriptions report that a deceased individual had become a star.[69] An epigram from Albanum in the early third century CE presents a boy addressing his father from the grave:

> Cry no longer, sweetest father, and no longer feel pain, carrying in your heart inconsolable grief. For subterranean Hades is not hiding me under the earth, but instead an eagle, Zeus' assistant, snatched me away, when I was enjoying the fire and the torch, to take my place next to the morning star and the beautiful evening star.[70]

We can imagine the parents turning their gaze to the sky at dusk and dawn, looking for their son or daughter among the stars. Such concepts gave the starry sky a new quality.

Cultural Transfer and the Nocturnal Cityscapes of the Empire

The degree of homogenization and persistence of local peculiarities differed greatly in the Roman Empire, depending on a variety of factors that cannot be discussed here. But all differences notwithstanding, we can still observe certain common features, of which I only mention two that had an impact on the nightlife of urban centers: the diffusion of voluntary associations and nocturnal religious celebrations.

Private clubs are already attested in Athens in the early sixth century BCE, and *sodalitates* are mentioned in the Twelve Tables.[71] But the spread of voluntary associations in every major urban center is a phenomenon first of the Hellenistic period, for the Greek world, and of the Imperial period for the Empire.[72] In the main urban centers of both East and West, guilds became a primary mediator of social and economic interaction. Private cult

---

[69] Imperial apotheosis: Domenicucci 1996. The *katasterismos* of ordinary people: Wypustek 2012: 48–57.

[70] *SEG* XXXI 846: Greek: [οὐ γ]ὰρ ὑποχθόνιος κατὰ γῆς Ἀίδης με κέκευθε, | [ἀ]λλὰ Διὸς πάρεδρος ἀετὸς ἥρπασέ με | [πυρ]σῷ ὁμοῦ καὶ δᾴδι γεγηθότα, ἔνθα σύνεδρος | Φωσφόρῳ ἠδὲ καλῷ Ἑσπέρῳ ὄφρα πέλω. Latin: *seḍ [Iovis satelles] m[e aquila arripuit] facę [atque lampade] simul ga[udentem], hic v[icinus] Phospho[ro et pulcro] Hesperio [uti fiam].* Cf. *GV* 1829 (Miletos, first/second century CE): αἰθέρα δ' ὀκταέτης κατιδὼν ἄστροις ἅμα λάμπεις | πατ κέρας ὠλενίης Αἰγὸς ἀνερχόμενος ('eight years old, you gaze at the Ether, shining among the stars, you rise close to the horn of Capricorn and the elbow of Auriga').

[71] Associations in Solon's laws: Ustinova 2005: 183–5. In the Twelve Tables: *XII tab.* 8.27.

[72] A selection of recent studies for the Imperial period: Kloppenborg and Wilson 1996; van Nijf 1997; Dittmann-Schöne 2001; Egelhaaf-Gaiser 2002; Zimmermann 2002; Harland 2003; Baslez 2004; Nigdelis 2010; Fröhlich and Hamon 2013; Gabrielsen and Thomsen 2015; Verboven 2017. For representative collections of texts from the Roman East, see Kloppenborg and Ascough 2011; Harland 2014. For the Hellenistic period, see Chaniotis 2018c.

associations were also the basis of religious worship for larger groups within the urban populations than before the conquests of Alexander in the East and the Roman expansion in the West. Regular banqueting and convivial drinking were common activities of *koina* and *collegia*.[73] Some of these gatherings occurred after sunset. In Rome, the *leges conviviales* mentioned in literary sources defined rules for nocturnal drinking parties in connection with the Saturnalia. An example of such norms survives in the *lex Tappula* from Vercellae, a parody of a *plebiscitum*. The statutes are stated to have been approved in the eleventh hour of the night in a shrine of Hercules.[74] Hercules was also the divinity to whose worship an Athenian club of the second century CE was dedicated. Its officials, the *pannychistai* ('those who conduct service during the all-night celebration'), were possibly responsible for order during the club's nocturnal gatherings.[75]

As we can infer from member lists of associations, membership was often open to representatives of the lower social strata. Voluntary associations accepted foreigners, craftsmen, slaves, and in some cases women as members; of course, professional *koina* and *collegia* consisted of craftsmen and the representatives of various trades. With the diffusion of private associations, a nighttime activity typically associated with the propertied classes[76] was opened on specific days to larger groups of the population. The diffusion of the regular nocturnal conviviality of the private clubs coincides with – and was probably influenced by – conviviality in the circle of the Roman *nobilitas* and the imperial court.[77]

Although nocturnal religious ceremonies are not an innovation of the Hellenistic period, the Late Republic, or the Principate, their number certainly increased along with the diffusion of cults with a soteriological or initiatory aspect.[78] The main celebrations of a variety of religious groups were either nocturnal – enhancing emotional arousal, engendering feelings of exclusivity and a sense of identity – or took place just before dawn. The unprecedented connectivity created by the Empire favored the diffusion of

[73] E.g. Harland 2003: 57–61, 74–83; Dunbabin 2003: 72–3, 78, 93–100; Reiter 2005; McRae 2011; Harland 2014: 53–4, 271; Chaniotis 2018b: 15–17.

[74] *ILS* 8761 (first/second cent. CE); *AE* 1989, 331; Versnel 1994: 161–2.

[75] *SEG* XXXI 122 LL. 25–6: ἐὰν μὴ ὑπομένῃ ἢ μὴ θέλῃ παννυχιστὴς εἶναι λαχών (121/122 CE). See also *SEG* XXXVI 198.

[76] On the aristocratic nature of pre-Hellenistic symposia in Greece, see most recently Wecowski 2014, esp. 303–36; for Rome, see Stein-Hölkeskamp 2005: 34–111. On the expanded membership, see Harland 2003: 28–53.

[77] Banquets in the imperial court: Vössing 2004; Grandjean et (eds.) 2013. See also D'Arms 1990 and Dunbabin 2003: passim.

[78] Chaniotis 2018b: 23–34 and 2018c.

cults, religious practices, and religious ideas,[79] and can, therefore, be regarded as an important factor for the frequency of nocturnal rites. I cannot present here an inventory of such rites in the Empire, but a few examples may illustrate how cult transfer had an impact on the night.

Mystery cults are a case in point, since they are often associated with nocturnal rites and the conscious use of darkness and artificial light. This is known to have happened in Eleusis, one of the oldest and most revered mystery cults, already in the Archaic and Classical period and continued in later periods.[80] In the mid second century CE, the Eleusinian mysteries served as a model for the mystery cult of Glykon New Asklepios in Abonou Teichos, which included a sacred drama that took place during the night.[81]

The use of lamps was an important feature of Egyptian cults, and Achilles Tatius (second cent. CE) characterizes the Serapis festival of lights as the greatest spectacle that he had ever seen.[82] As the Egyptian cults spread in the Mediterranean, so did their nocturnal celebrations. Processions under torchlight (λαμπαδεία) are attested in Athens, Delos, Priene, and Maroneia,[83] and in the tenth book of the *Metamorphoses* Apuleius describes nocturnal initiation rites associated with Isis.[84] We may attribute the introduction of the office of the *lychnaptria* – the female cult servant who lit the lamps – into the cult of Meter Theon in Leukopetra, near Beroia in Macedonia, and into the cult of Dionysus in Philippopolis to the emulation of Isiac practices.[85] Rites during the night are also attested in Samothrace, a sanctuary that in the Imperial period was visited by initiates from many different regions.[86]

Nocturnal ceremonies of an orgiastic nature were traditionally associated with the worship of Dionysus.[87] When introduced into Italy in the late third century BCE, they were met with suspicion by the Roman authorities and contained by the *senatus consultum de Bacchanalibus* of 186 BCE.[88] By

---

[79] Examples of the trendsetters for rituals in the Roman Empire: Chaniotis 2009.

[80] Light in the Eleusinian mysteries: Parisinou 2000: 67–71; Patera 2010. Nocturnal rites: e.g., *I. Didyma* 216 l. 20: ἐν νυχίοις Φερ[σεφό]νης τελετα[ῖ|ς] (70 BCE); cf. *I.Eleusis* 515: ὄργια πάννυχα (Eleusis, c. 170 CE); cf. *I.Eleusis* 175 (third century BCE); 250 l. 44 (c. 100 BCE); 515–16 (c. 170 CE).

[81] Lucian, *Alexander* 38–9. Discussion: Sfameni Gasparro 1999; Chaniotis 2002a.

[82] Lamps in the Egyptian cults: Aupert 2004; Podvin 2011, 2014, and 2015; Renberg 2016. The festival of Serapis: Ach. Tat. 5.2; Abdelwahed 2016.

[83] On the diffusion of Isiac cults: Bricault 2005. *Lampadeia*: Alvar 2007: 303 with note 389.

[84] Apuleius, *Metam.* XI 1–7, 20–1, 23–4. Cf. Griffiths 1975: 278.

[85] *Lychnaptriai* in the cult of Isis: *IG* II² 4771 (Athens, 120 CE). In Leukopetra: *I.Leukopetra* 39. In Philippopolis: *IGBulg* III 1, 1517 line 30 (ca. 241–4 CE).

[86] Cole 1984: 36–7. On the diverse origin of the initiates: Dimitrova 2008.

[87] Light in nocturnal Dionysiac celebrations: Parisinou 2000: 71–2, 118–23; Paleothodoros 2010.

[88] Pailler 1988. See also Carlà-Uhink 2018: 336–41.

the Imperial period, associations of Bacchic initiates were no longer
regarded as a threat to safety, and were free to perform their nocturnal
rites and celebrations.[89] Philo of Alexandria explicitly attributes to
Dionysiac influence the introduction of nocturnal spiritual activities and
wine consumption among the Jewish *therapeutai* in Egypt in the early first
century CE.[90]

> After the supper they hold the sacred vigil . . . They rise up all together and
> standing in the middle of the refectory (*symposion*) form themselves first
> into two choirs, one of men and one of women . . . Then they sing hymns
> to God composed of many measures and set to many melodies, sometimes
> chanting together, sometimes taking up the harmony antiphonally, hands
> and feet keeping time in accompaniment, and rapt with enthusiasm
> reproduce sometimes the lyrics of the procession, sometimes of the halt
> and of the wheeling and counter-wheeling of a choric dance. Then . . .
> having drunk as in the Bacchic rites of the strong wine of God's love they
> mix and both together become a single choir . . . Thus they continue till
> dawn, drunk with this drunkenness in which there is no shame.

An interesting feature of religiosity in the Imperial period is religious
service at dusk and before sunrise, unattested in earlier periods. The
custom of regular prayer at dawn is attested for the worshippers of Theos
Hypsistos. An oracle of Apollo Klarios, associated with this cult, pronounced 'that aether is god who sees all, gazing upon whom you should
pray at dawn looking towards the sunrise'.[91] An essential feature of the cult
of Theos Hypsistos was the lighting of fire on altars and lamps.[92] For
instance, a family in Magnesia on Sipylos dedicated to Theos Hypsistos
an altar and a candelabra (λυχναψίαι).[93] Numerous bronze objects from the
Roman East dated to the third century CE have been shown to be lamp
hangers used in the cult of Theos Hypsistos (λύχνος κρεμαστός).[94] One of
the few things that Pliny was able to discover about the Christians in the
early second century CE is that they gathered to pray before dawn:

---

[89] A few examples: Lerna (*nyktelia*): Plut., *Moralia* 364 F and Paus. 2.37.5. Physkos (second
century CE): IG IX².1.670 (ἱερὰ νύξ). Thessalonike (first century CE): IG X.2.1.259; Nigdelis
2010: 15–16, 30, and 38 no. 12 (with the earlier bibliography).

[90] *On the Contemplative Life* 83–9 (transl. F. H. Colson, Loeb); quoted by Harland 2003: 72–3.

[91] *SEG* XXVII 933: αἰ[θ]έ[ρ]α πανδερκ[ῆ θε]ὸν ἔννεπεν, εἰς ὃν ὁρῶντας | εὔχεσθ' ἡώους πρὸς
ἀνατολὴν ἐσορῶ[ν]τα[ς]. Busine 2005: 35–40, 203–8, 423, with further bibliography.

[92] Ameling 1999.　　[93] *TAM* V.2.1400.

[94] Franken 2002. On the diffusion of the cult of Theos Hypsistos in the Empire, see most recently
Mitchell 2010; the connection of this cult with the Jewish religion and the association of the
theosebeis with it are still debated.

they were accustomed to meet on a fixed day before dawn and sing responsively a hymn to Christ as to a god, and to bind themselves by oath, not to some crime, but not to commit fraud, theft, or adultery, not falsify their trust, nor to refuse to return a trust when called upon to do so. When this was over, it was their custom to depart and to assemble again to partake of food – but ordinary and innocent food.[95]

Regular ceremonies after sunset and before sunrise are also attested for the sanctuary of Asclepius in Epidaurus through a fragmentary inscription (second or third century CE). In the preserved text, one recognizes references to the services that the torchbearer had to perform in the shrines of the Mother of the Gods and Aphrodite, to duties involving lamps (*lychnoi*) and the 'sacred lamp' (*hiera lychnia*), and to rituals at dusk (ὅταν ἑσπέρας αἱ σπον[δαὶ γίνωνται]) and dawn ([ὁ ἔω]θεν ἀνατέλλων).[96] In early first-century CE Teos, the priest of Tiberius was responsible for rituals that took place when the temple of Dionysus was opened and closed, that is, at dawn and dusk; these rituals included libations, the burning of incense, and the lighting of lamps.[97]

As mystery cults served as trendsetters, nocturnal ceremonies became more common than ever before. Among those which are unattested in early periods and seem to be either new rituals or revivals of old ones as the result of the broader trends of the Imperial period, I mention the embassy sent by Lykian Termessos to the Moon, consisting of members of the city's elite,[98] the cult of the star-god Astros Kakasbos in the same polis,[99] the cult of *Nocturnus* and the *Nocturni* in Pannonia,[100] and the nighttime sacrifices for Saturnus in Numidia.[101]

Euergetic Nights

I have already mentioned the role played by benefactors in the organization of public banquets. A leisurely activity that in the Imperial period took place after sunset more often than before was visiting public baths. Bathing culture was significantly enlarged, diffused, and transformed in the eastern

---

[95] Plin. *Letters* 10.96.   [96] *IG* IV².1.742.   [97] *LSAM* 28 lines 11–13.

[98] *SEG* LVII 1482 (ca. 212–30 CE): δωδεκάκ[ις σὺν | τοῖσδε πρεσ]βευταῖς Θεᾷ Σελήνῃ συνεπρέσβευσεν.

[99] *SEG* LVII 1483 (third century CE).

[100] *Nocturni*: *CIL* III 12539, 13461, 13462. *Nocturnus*: *CIL* III 1956, 9753, 14243(2); V 4287.

[101] *AE* 2006, 1802: *d(omino) S(ancto) S(aturno) | sacrum mag(num) nocturnum | anim[a] pro anima vita pro | vita s[a]ng(uine) pro sang(uine).*

provinces and introduced into the western ones during the Imperial period.[102] Emperors and local benefactors, more than local authorities, made the greatest contribution towards the construction, upkeep, and improvement of bathing facilities in both Rome and the provinces.[103] Although baths were typically visited before sunset and dinner,[104] in large cities like Rome, baths were also accessible after sunset. As cited earlier, Juvenal mentions a lady who visits the baths in the night, keeping her dinner guests waiting. The regulations concerning the operation of a bathhouse at Metallum Vipascense in Lusitania provide for the opening of the facility until the second hour of the night.[105] The operation of public baths during the night was not a common phenomenon in the Roman East, but it is nevertheless attested in connection with festivals and as a result of the public services of benefactors. It was thanks to euergetic generosity that in Stratonikeia the baths of men and women remained open for a significant part of the night during the festivals of Zeus and Hera.[106]

In the Roman East, the bathing facilities were usually associated with gymnasia. Typically, gymnasia were open from sunrise to sunset.[107] For instance, the recently published ephebarchical law of Amphipolis (23 BCE) obliged the *ephebarchos* to make sure that the ephebes did not leave their home before daybreak and returned before sunset; they clearly were not allowed to be at a *gymnasion* after sunset;[108] in Magnesia on Sipylos someone was honored for providing oil to all men, young and old, but *until* the night, not *during* the night.[109] To the best of my knowledge, all evidence for gymnasia that were in operation night and day (νυκτὸς καὶ ἡμέρας) or for a large part of the night (τὸ πλεῖστον/ἐπὶ πολὺ μέρος τῆς νυκτός) concerns the generosity and initiative of wealthy supervisors of gymnasia in Asia Minor (first to third

---

[102] On the spread of Roman bathing in Italy and the provinces, see Nielsen 1999; Fagan 1999: 40–74; Farrington 1999, with earlier bibliography.

[103] Fagan 1999: 104–75.

[104] Fagan 1999: 22–4. Greek inscriptions often state that baths (and gymnasia) were open from sunrise to sunset: e.g., IG IV 597, 606.

[105] Juvenal, *Satire* 6.419–29; CIL II 5181 = ILS 6891 (Hadrian's reign); Fagan 1999: 324–6 no. 282.

[106] I.Stratonikeia 254: [ἔθεσαν ἔλαιον πάσῃ] τύχῃ καὶ ἡλικίᾳ ἐν τοῖς δυσὶν βαλανείοις καὶ ἡμέρας καὶ νυκτὸς τῷ σύνπαντι πλήθει τῶν τε [ἐντοπίων καὶ τῶν ἐπι]δημησάντων ξένων ('they offered olive oil to every property and age class in both baths, both day and night, to all the people, both to the locals and to the foreigners who had arrived as visitors'); I.Stratonikeia 324: [ἐ]θήκαμεν δὲ κ[αὶ] τῶν γυναικῶν π[ά]σῃ τύχῃ καὶ ἡλ[ι]κίᾳ ἐν τοῖς γυναικίοις βαλαν[ί]οις ἀπὸ νυκτό[ς]. Cf. I. Stratonikeia 205, 245, 248, 311, 312, 324.

[107] Aeschines, *Against Timarchos* 10.   [108] Hatzopoulos 2016: 27.

[109] TAM V.2.1367 (Imperial period): θέντα τὰ ἀλείμματα ἐξ ὁλκε[ί]ων μεστῶν τοῖς νέοις καὶ γέρου[σι] καὶ παισὶ καὶ ἀπαλαίστρο<ις> δι' ὅλης ἡμέ<ρ>ας ἄχ<ρι> νυκτός.

century CE).[110] This was not to be taken for granted. But still, the largesse of some men could become a model and inspiration for their successors.

The Night as a Frontier

The phenomena that I briefly discussed in this chapter are but a small part of what filled the nights in the Roman Empire with life. I have intentionally avoided the discussion of evidence whose existence or abundance in the Imperial period might be attributed to the 'epigraphic habit' or to the increased number of inscriptions and papyri. Such evidence, relevant for a comprehensive study of the night but connected with specific methodological problems, includes changes in private dining,[111] Latin inscriptions of the Imperial period that record the time of death as during the night,[112] the custom of setting up dedications in accordance with a divine command received during a dream (κατ' ὄναρ, *ex visu*),[113] and the existence of incubation sanctuaries.[114]

A shared feature of some nocturnal phenomena that can be observed in many parts of the Empire is that activities that typically ended before or at sunset were extended beyond the 'boundary' of darkness: partaking of food and wine, celebrating, bathing, training in athletic facilities, organizing processions. The 'boundary' of darkness was crossed thanks to the human agency of the emperor, local benefactors, and religious officials. This was regarded as a service worthy of mention in honorific inscriptions and, in the case of the emperors, record by historians. We can understand the mentality behind the commemoration of such achievements – offering hunts of wild animals and gladiatorial combats under artificial light, having a contest last 'throughout the day and for a large part of the night', offering

---

[110] *I.Magnesia* 163 (Magnesia on the Maeander, first century CE); *SEG* LVII 1364 (Hierapolis, second century CE); Robert and Robert 1954, 169–70 no. 56 and 190–1 no. 94 (Herakleia Salbake, 73/74 and 124/125 CE); *SEG* LXIII 1344 (Patara, early second century CE); *I.Stratonikeia* 203, 205, 222, 224, 244–8, 281, 311, 312, 345, 1050+1034, 1325A (second to third century CE). See also Chaniotis 2018b: 18–19.

[111] E.g. for the introduction of Roman practices, such as the presence of women in the banquets and the use of the triclinium, in Greek areas, see Nadeau 2010.

[112] E.g. *CIL* VI 28923; VIII 22842: *AE* 1994, 796. Death during one's sleep is occasionally mentioned in grave epigrams: e.g., *IG* X.2.1.719 (Thessalonike, second century CE); *SEG* LIX 286 (Athens, third century CE).

[113] These dedications have been collected by G. Renberg and will be presented in a forthcoming book.

[114] Renberg 2017; for a discussion of problematic cases, see Renberg 2017: 523–64.

olive oil 'to every property and age class in both baths, both day and night', leaving the gymnasia open 'for a large part of the night' and so on – if we compare them with the praise for the pancratiast Tiberius Claudius Rufus: While pursuing victory in Olympia, 'he endured to continue the fight until the night, until the stars came out, as his hope of victory encouraged him to fight more vigorously'.[115] What the emperors and the benefactors did was similar: Displaying motivation and engagement, they crossed a frontier that others hesitated or were not accustomed to cross. This is why their services were extraordinary. But extraordinary services can become trendsetters.

Another group of the phenomena that I discussed – improving the security during the night and improving the communication between mortals and gods – also perceive the darkness of the night as a 'boundary': the boundary of a world that either needs to be tamed and become secure or to be placed in the service of humans, facilitating their communication with divine or superhuman powers. There is a whole range of activities in the Roman Empire that fall under this category and could not be discussed here: going to sanctuaries to dream of the gods, interpreting and inducing dreams, understanding the movement of the stars through astrology, and recruiting the chthonic powers against adversaries through magic. The circulation of handbooks of dream interpretation, astrology, and magic contributed to a certain homogeneity of practices that primarily took place during the night.[116]

Despite their criticism against those who reversed the functions of day and night, intellectuals of the Imperial period reveal a similar attitude towards the night. They regarded it as a frontier that confronts people with challenges and requires efforts in order to place it under control. Seneca's treatise *On Darkness as a Veil for Wickedness* evidences a strong interest in the rational use of the night. After complaining about the fact that some people in contemporary Rome had reversed the functions of light and darkness, passing their evenings amid wine and perfumes and eating dinners of multiple courses, he goes on to advise his readers to lengthen their lives by cutting the night short and using it for the day's business.[117] In his recommendations to orators, Lucian alludes to the necessity of

---

[115] *IvO* 54 (early second century CE): ὅτι μέχρι νυκτός, ὡς ἄστρα καταλαβεῖν, διεκαρτέρησε, ὑπὸ τῆς περὶ τὴν νείκην ἐλπίδος ἐπὶ πλεῖστον ἀγωνίσεσθαι προτρεπόμενος.

[116] *Oneirokritika*: Harris-McCoy 2012; du Bouchet and (eds.) 2012; (ed.) 2015; dream interpreters in the Roman Empire: Renberg 2015, with the earlier bibliography. Magical handbooks and inducement of dreams: Graf 1996: 177; Johnston 2010.

[117] Seneca, *Epist.* 122.1 and 3. Work during the night: Wilson 2018, 75–76.

nighttime work, when he writes that the Classical statues reveal sleepless nights, toil, abstinence from wine, and simple food.[118] The *Paedagogus* of Clement of Alexandria, written around 200 CE, prescribes to Christians a nocturnal behavior that is contrasted to what we must regard as a common practice. Clement recommended to fill the night with activities other than banquets accompanied by music and excessive drinking. His readers should often rise by night and bless God, and devote themselves to literature and art; women should turn to the distaff. People should fight against sleep, in order to partake of life for a longer period through wakefulness.[119] The gradual improvement of artificial lighting, which reached its peak in Late Antiquity with the development of glass lamps and the introduction of street lighting,[120] is part of the same process of facing the challenges of the night.

So, how do we answer the question implied by the title of this chapter: many nations, one night? The diffusion of sources is uneven, reflecting local differences in institutions, cultural practices, the persistence of older traditions, and the levels of literacy and urbanization. Wherever and whenever sufficient numbers of relevant sources survive – especially honorific inscriptions and dedications – we observe the same trend: the night was a frontier that invited the adventurous and the inventive, the generous and the ambitious, the faithful and the hopeful to cross it.[121]

---

[118] Luc., *Rhetorum praeceptor* 9: πόνον δὲ καὶ ἀγρυπνίαν καὶ ὑδατοποσίαν καὶ τὸ ἀλιπαρές.

[119] Clement, *Paedagogus* 2.4 and 2.9.

[120] Lamps made of glass: Engle 1987. Artificial light: Seidel 2012: 108–15; Dossey 2018; Wilson 2018: 63–72.

[121] I am very grateful to Emyr Dakin (City University of New York) and Matthew Peebles (Columbia University) for correcting my English. Studies that appeared after the summer of 2018 could not be considered.

PART III

Ethnicity and Identity in the Roman Empire

The Case of the Jews

10 | Religious Pluralism in the Roman Empire

Did Judaism Test the Limits of Roman Tolerance?[*]

ERICH S. GRUEN

1

Paganism, one would imagine, promoted pluralism by its very nature. It contained multiple gods, with a host of major and minor deities and divine offshoots. The smorgasbord of divinities should have fostered forbearance for a wide spectrum of supernatural beings, a motley crew whose authority and responsibilities may have overlapped confusingly but whose collective presence suggests a broad-mindedness by pagans that monotheistic religions did not possess. In principle at least, pluralism ought to have issued in toleration.

Roman expansionism, however, complicated matters in various ways. As the empire spread, first in Italy, then in both the western and eastern Mediterranean, it encompassed an ever increasing number of peoples, cultures, traditions – and gods. How far would tolerance extend when Romans encountered peoples who worshipped snakes and a wide variety of other animals, whose gods had eunuch priests adept at ecstatic dancing accompanied by clashing cymbals, whose mystery cults involved initiation rites with a bull slaying ceremony, whose celebrants indulged in nocturnal and orgiastic rituals, or who worshipped a single divinity but scorned all images or representations of him?[1]

With so many diverse practices brought under the umbrella of the Roman Empire, how far does one stretch the notion of tolerance for religious pluralism? Some scholars indeed have expressed skepticism about the vaunted open-mindedness of the Romans. A famous fictional speech put by the historian Cassius Dio into the mouth of Maecenas, the close friend and adviser of Augustus, should cause some concern on that score. Maecenas purportedly counseled Augustus on the most effective ways to entrench his monarchy. Among them was the enforcement of a national religion by

---

[*] I offer this essay in honor of my good friend and occasional collaborator, Ben Isaac, from whose works and conversations I have learned much and profited greatly. He and I have occasionally had serious scholarly disagreements, but the differences have never disturbed our mutual respect and warm friendship.

[1] For the variety of religions and cults in the Roman Empire, see the surveys of Ferguson 1970; Turcan 1996. See also Rüpke 2001, 2012; Rives 2007.

compelling others to honor it and punishing those who introduce foreign rites, because new divinities turn people away from traditional practices and promote conspiracies, cabals, and upheavals.[2] That suggests troubling limits to tolerance. How tolerant, in fact, were the Romans?

Our own categories create obstacles. Tolerance or intolerance may not be the best designation of alternatives. The terms are modern rather than ancient. There is no Greek or Latin word for tolerance. Nor did any Greek or Roman writer articulate a policy of toleration, let alone formulate a philosophy advocating freedom of religion. Romans, so some have claimed, engaged in imperialism, not magnanimity. As one scholar put it, "Roman-style polytheism was disposed to expand and to absorb or at least to neutralize other gods, not to tolerate them."[3]

The idea of toleration as policy would have been unintelligible to Romans. And even on the most charitable estimate, tolerance presumes superiority, the greater power's willingness to tolerate the eccentricities of the lesser – a willingness that could at any time be withdrawn. Motives of benevolence and generosity, if they existed at all, are beside the point.

2

A different fact needs emphasis here: Romans could and did import external cults at the public level, making them part of the state apparatus, and welcomed them on the private level, as significant numbers of Romans became adherents of foreign rituals. That experience provides critical insight into the Roman disposition.

The importation of cults from elsewhere to Rome began already in its earliest history. So, at least, the traditions preserved by later literary sources attest. The worship of Herakles came from Greece, according to legend, through the Arcadian king Evander who brought it to the site of Rome in time for Romulus himself to sacrifice at the Ara Maxima.[4] The celebrated summoning of Juno Regina from the great Etruscan city of Veii in 396 BCE turned the tide of the supposed ten-year war between Rome and Veii. The goddess, by moving from Veii to Rome, decided that contest for supremacy between the two powers. The ceremony of this summoning, the *evocatio*, meant that Juno Regina would now have her worship in Rome, on the Aventine Hill, where a temple would be constructed for her, and her cult

---

[2] Dio, 52.36.2.   [3] Garnsey 1984: 8. Similarly, Beard et al. 1998: I, 212–14; North 2000: 63.
[4] Livy, 1.7; Dion. Hal. 1.33.

would forever be a reminder of divine favor for Romans against their foes.[5] *Evocatio*, however, it should be noted, has a character quite different from sheer imperialist expropriation. Juno Regina's transfer to Rome was not abduction or a coerced seizure. As the tale has it, a Roman soldier asked Juno whether she wished to move to Rome, and the statue of the goddess duly nodded. Juno thus shifted her allegiance voluntarily, bringing an Etruscan divine presence to the side of Rome where she would be ministered to by Roman priests and worshipped thereafter as part of the state religious structure.[6] The historicity of that and similar events matters little. The attitude indicates a readiness to embrace principal foreign deities and make them part of Roman public ritual. In a parallel development, Etruscan priests, the *haruspices*, took their place at some point in the fourth or early third century as a priestly college, steeped in Etruscan lore, on whom Rome relied for purposes of divination, particularly the expiation of prodigies.[7] The adoption of alien religious elements was, in short, an integral part of Roman history almost from its beginning.

The process accelerated in the third and second centuries, as Rome drew on cults and traditions from further afield. The worship of Asklepios arrived from Epidauros in 293 BCE; the healing deity was brought to Rome to counteract a dreadful pestilence – and stayed to enjoy a shrine built for him on the Tiber Island. It is not irrelevant that the reaching out to Asklepios came as a consequence of a recommendation found by priests in the Sibylline Books – scrolls that themselves were of Hellenic origin composed in Greek hexameter verse.[8] Sibylline advice also prompted the introduction of the worship of Venus Erycina in 217, a goddess of mixed Greco-Phoenician character in western Sicily.[9] Legend had it that the site of her temple in Sicily was also the place where Aeneas had dedicated a shrine to his mother.[10] Venus Erycina, who trailed echoes of the Trojan legend, would thus enhance Roman morale at a critical time in the Hannibalic war. But her arrival was no mere temporary visit. Venus Erycina received a temple on the Capitoline itself, a place of conspicuous honor. The goddess could thus not only serve as reminder of the national heritage; she also represented yet another foreign deity brought into the very center of Roman public life.[11]

[5] Livy, 5.21–3.
[6] On *evocatio*, see the recent discussions of Gustafsson 2000: 42–82; Ando 2008: 128–38, and Orlin 2010: 36–41, 92–3.
[7] MacBain 1982: 43–59; Orlin 2010: 88–100. In general, Haack 2003.
[8] Val. Max. 1.8.2; Livy, 10.47; *Per.* 11; *Vir. Ill.* 22.1–3. On the Sibylline Books and their consultation in Rome, see Diels 1890; Orlin 1997: 76–115.
[9] Livy, 22.9.7–10, 22.10.10, 23.30.13–14, 23.31.9.   [10] Diod. 4.83.4–7; Vergil, *Aen.* 5.759–60.
[11] Schilling 1954: 248–54; Galinsky 1969: 169–90; Gruen 1992: 46–7; Erskine 2001: 198–205; Orlin 2010: 71–6; Battistoni 2010: 124–7.

A still more dramatic instance of this occurred in 205 BCE, during the final years of the Hannibalic war. Unusual prodigies in that year caused Romans to consult the Sibylline Books once more. The priests produced a prophecy that predicted Hannibal's defeat if the Romans should bring Magna Mater, the Great Mother goddess from Asia Minor, to Rome. The goddess was duly conveyed, in the form of a sacred stone, and was received, as directed by the oracle at Delphi, in solemn ceremony by select representatives of the senate, and installed on the Palatine.[12] The significance of this event for Roman politics, diplomacy, and cultural aspirations has been much discussed.[13] What stands out on any interpretation, however, is an elaborate negotiation to transfer to Rome the cult of this powerful Anatolian deity, serviced by eunuch priests in glaringly colorful garb, with ecstatic gyrations, accompanied by tambourines, flutes, and cymbals.[14] The senate determined that the unseemly character of the celebrations prohibited Romans themselves from serving as participants in the ceremonies.[15] That at least preserved some decorum. But the fact remains that this foreign cult was welcomed upon arrival by eminent Romans and was established on no less a location than the Palatine hill. The *ludi Megalenses* were inaugurated there in honor of the goddess and would be held annually as one of the major festivals on the Roman sacred calendar.

We know of just one notable exception to this welcome parade of pluralistic immigrant cults. It occurred in 186 BCE. At that time Roman authorities notoriously cracked down with punishing harshness on the worship of Dionysus, the so-called Bacchanalian conspiracy. For many, the event serves to define the limits of Roman tolerance for alien religion: Bacchic revels crossed the line of Roman endurance; the senate resorted to persecution of practices inimical to their traditions and threatening state supervision of worship.[16] But that analysis fails to tell the whole story. Indeed the tale of a sudden and threatening arrival of the Bacchic cult,

---

[12] Most important testimony in Livy, 29.10.4–29.11.8, 29.14.5–14; Ovid, *Fasti*, 4.247–348.

[13] See Gruen 1990: 5–33, with much of the older bibliography. More recently, see Burton 1996: 36–63; Orlin 1997: 109–11; Roller 1999: 263–85; Erskine 2001: 205–24; Orlin 2010: 76–82; Battistoni 2010: 87–9.

[14] Lucr. 2.610–28; Catull., 63; Ovid, *Fasti*, 4.193–244; Juv. 6.511–16; Mart. 3.81.

[15] Dion. Hal. 2.19.

[16] The evidence appears in Livy, 39.8–19; ILS, 18. It would be pointless to register the gargantuan bibliography here. See the extensive survey of earlier literature by Pailler 1988: 61–122, supplemented by Pailler 1998: 67–86. Cf. the selection of relevant works in Gruen 1990: 37–8, 49–52, 62–3. Among more recent contributions, mention should be made of Cancik-Lindemaier 1996: 77–96; Beard et al. 1998: 91–6; Takács 2000: 301–10; Flower 2000: 23–35; Pagan 2005: 50–67; Orlin 2010: 165–8, 174–5.

discovered in the nick of time, is vitiated by the fact that Dionysiac worship had been widespread in Italy for a long time before – without engendering any repression.[17] Further, the measures actually taken by the senate in 186 are telling. They aimed to assure control of the cult, not to eradicate it. Secret ceremonies were banned; men were prohibited from holding priesthoods, and neither men nor women could serve as administrative overseers; common funds were prohibited; and initiates could not exchange oaths or vows. At the same time, however, the new regulations allowed for retention of altars and images that had a long history; individual worshippers could maintain their connection to the cult if they made their case to the urban praetor and received permission from the senate, and they could continue to participate in the ritual, so long as no more than five persons were involved. All of this indicates a drive to regulate the activities of the cult and to keep them under senatorial control rather than to eliminate Bacchic worship. The curbing of Dionysiac ritual, in other words, represented social and political management – not an attack on alien imports on grounds of their foreignness. In that essential regard, the crackdown on the "Bacchanalian conspiracy" constitutes no real exception to the rule.

The importation of cults that lacked Roman roots proceeded apace. No need to detail them here. In addition to those actually summoned by the state, others entered the scene through private embrace or individual adherence. The worship of Isis serves as a conspicuous example of widespread popularity. An Egyptian deity in origin but expanded and transformed in the Hellenistic era, she subsequently meandered in the Roman Empire to various points in the west, including, quite prominently, Rome itself. The cult or cults of Mithras enjoyed a comparable following. Mithraic roots may have been Persian, but adherents of Mithras spread successfully to Italy and, largely though not exclusively, through the army, to frontier regions, particularly along the Rhine and Danube, as well as elsewhere in the west. A range of other divinities from abroad found their way to Rome or to Romans elsewhere.[18] Juvenal might sneer about the Orontes pouring its refuse into the Tiber. But worshippers in Rome and Italy, whether foreigners or indigenous, practiced a miscellaneous variety of rituals, with little or no repression or persecution.[19]

---

[17] Bruhl 1953: 58–81; Pailler 1988: 275–324.

[18] For Isis, see Malaise 1972; Sonnabend 1986: 128–42; Takács 1995. For Mithras, see Beck 1984: 2002–115; Clauss 1990; Arcella 2002.

[19] To be sure, the senate more than once took action against the cult of Isis for reasons usually obscure and unexpressed. Most of the actions were bunched within a short period of the late Republic and of no lasting effect. The senate prohibited worship of Isis on the Capitol in 59 BCE and destroyed the altars that had been set up – only to have them restored after a popular

None of this involves tolerance. The term is inapplicable. The state lacked a religious establishment or a centralized apparatus to demand uniformity, even if anyone wished to do so. And the thoroughly pluralistic religious society of the Roman Empire discouraged it. Hence, the very notion of extending or withdrawing tolerance is simply irrelevant. Even the characterization of Romans as broad-minded or liberal may be off the mark. Acceptance and embrace of alien cults was simply a long-standing ingredient of Roman identity.

3

How does Judaism fit into this picture? On the face of it, the community ill suits the profile of the other sects discussed earlier. Jews carried the reputation of an exclusivist, separatist group, rigorously monotheistic, disdainful of other gods, and hostile to their worshippers as misguided idolaters. The attitude, of course, goes back to the Hebrew Bible. The distinctiveness of Israel constitutes a central motif, as in the classic text of Leviticus 18:3 that enjoins the Israelites to set themselves definitively apart from the ways of Egyptians and Canaanites alike.[20] A core value of the nation rests in its self-perception as the Chosen People, with an obligation to follow the Law and resist those who revere false gods and

protest; Varro, *apud* Tertullian, *Ad Nat.* 1.10. A further step took place in 53 when the senate voted to destroy temples to Isis that had been erected by private parties. Here too, however, a reversal of sorts set in, for the worship of Isis and Serapis prevailed, so long as the rites took place outside the *pomerium*; Dio, 40.47.3–4. Valerius Maximus records yet another episode, probably in 50, when the senate ordered the demolition of the shrines of Isis and Serapis but the workmen refused to cooperate, causing the consul Aemilius Paulus to take an axe himself against the doors of the building; Val. Max. 1.3.4; cf. Wardle 1998: 151–2. One more such episode occurred in 48 when, in response to a troubling omen, the augurs recommended that the shrines of Isis and Serapis be rooted out; Dio, 42.26.1–2. The relatively rapid sequence of official actions against the cult, confined within a circumscribed period of time, implies that circumstances rather than hostility to the cult took precedence. And plainly none of the actions had enduring effect. Symbolic moves to reassert senatorial authority in a time of upheaval, with a designated scapegoat, seems a more appropriate interpretation. The fact that a shrine to Isis had been installed on the Capitol in the first place is itself noteworthy. So is the resistance of the populace to senatorial efforts to diminish the cult. The authorities clearly took no action to eradicate it. Five years later, in 43, the triumvirs themselves ordered the erection of a temple to Isis and Serapis; Dio, 48.15.4. See the balanced discussion of Orlin 2010: 204–5. Augustus later decreed that Egyptian rites be practiced outside the *pomerium*, but kept the temples in good repair; Dio, 53.2.4. And Agrippa subsequently directed that the rituals be held still further from the city; Dio, 54.6.6. Obviously they continued to thrive.

[20] See now the analysis of Berkowitz 2012: 24–40.

lead the devout astray.[21] Postbiblical texts reinforced the image of Jewish exclusiveness. The *Book of Jubilees*, for instance, supplies a deathbed speech for Abraham to his children and grandchildren, exhorting them to steer clear of all Gentiles, and to scorn any association with their ways, their food, and, especially, their daughters.[22] And a celebrated passage in the *Letter of Aristeas*, the fictional tale of the translation of the Hebrew Bible into Greek, makes the point unequivocally. It has the Jewish High Priest ridicule Greek idolatry and insist that the laws of Moses erect iron walls and inviolable fences to keep the Jews safely isolated from Gentile taint.[23]

The impression of Jewish separatism prevailed also among Greek and Latin writers of the Roman period who took any notice of them. Diodorus of Sicily maintained that of all people the Jews alone would associate themselves with no other nation and reckoned them all as enemies.[24] Tacitus famously accused the Jews of a malignant hatred toward all people but themselves, refusing to eat or sleep with others, and, although most prone to lust, abstaining from all intercourse with non-Jews.[25] And Juvenal caustically quips that Jews in Rome lead no inquirers to a desired destination unless they are circumcised.[26] It is hardly surprising that scholars regularly cite these and other passages to exhibit pagan denunciation of Jews for their exclusivist ways and their displeasure with Gentiles.[27] All this would seem to make it quite unlikely that the practice of Jewish rites would be readily welcomed under the umbrella of the Roman Empire.

4

Yet the facts on the ground offer a very different picture from literary representations, whether by Jews who stressed their exclusivity or by Romans who focused on Jewish idiosyncrasies. Did Rome marginalize the Jews? Documentary testimony points in other directions. The Jewish historian Josephus preserves a dossier of documents recording pronouncements by Roman leaders and officials that protect the rights and privileges of Jews, mostly in Greek communities of the Roman province of Asia. This

[21] E.g., Gen. 12:1–3; Exod. 6:7, 23:24, 33:16; Lev. 20:26; Num. 23:7–10; Deut. 7:6, 10:15, 12:2–4, 12:31, 14:2. Cf. Cohn 1994: 74–90; Schwartz 1997, 120–42; Lieu 2004: 108–26; Wills 2008: 1–12, 29–34.

[22] *Jub.* 20.4, 22.16–20.   [23] *LetArist.* 131–39.   [24] Diod. 34/5.1; 1–4.   [25] Tac. *Hist.* 5.5.1–2.

[26] Juv. 14.103–4.

[27] See, e.g., Sevenster 1975: 89–96; Feldman 1993: 125–31; Schäfer 1997: 167–79; Berthelot 2003: 80–171.

collection of senatorial decrees, letters by magistrates, municipal declarations, and imperial edicts appears to imply a policy of Roman guardianship of practices and prerogatives belonging to Jews against efforts to restrict or abolish them.[28]

To be sure, one needs to exercise caution here. Josephus' dossier does not add up to a general policy that holds everywhere and throughout. Most of the items he records belong to a relatively brief period at the end of the Roman Republic and the principate of Augustus and refer to events in the circumscribed area of western Asia Minor. The pronouncements by representatives of the government arose in the ad hoc circumstances of the Roman civil war, beginning in 49 BCE between Caesar and Pompey, proceeding through the conflicts that followed the assassination of Caesar between the triumvirs and the "liberators," and the unsettled political and economic circumstances of Asia Minor as the Augustan principate established itself. They do not attest to a sweeping attitude of "toleration" or an active engagement by Rome in support of Jewish priorities. For example, exemption of Jews from military service in the Roman legions by backers of the Pompeian cause aimed at shoring up support against the Caesarians. Similarly, Caesar's own declarations that strengthened the hand of the Jewish High Priest sought to enhance his position in the eastern part of the empire where Pompeian sentiment had previously prevailed. Comparable assertions issued from Augustus and Agrippa, reiterating confirmation for Jewish commitment to matters like observance of the Sabbath and annual contributions to the Temple in Jerusalem. These repeated Roman declarations of backing for Jewish privileges (with little evidence of actual implementation by Roman officials) were episodic, infrequent, and prompted by the conditions of civil conflict in the empire – not a matter of Roman stewardship of Jews.[29]

But there is a broader import here. The very issuance and reissuance of these pronouncements, however conventional they may have become, carry real significance. They indicate that, far from marginalizing Jews as a separatist sect, Roman officialdom found reasons for reasserting their place within the confines of the empire.

---

[28] Such has always been the standard interpretation. The fullest and best study by far, enshrining this viewpoint, is Ben Zeev 1998, with a substantial bibliography.

[29] Detailed arguments in defense of this position can be found in Gruen 2002b: 84–104.

5

The idea of Jewish exclusivity also needs reconsideration. How separatist, in fact, were the Jews? Despite the impression delivered by some sources, Jews welcomed and gained converts in notable numbers in the age of the Roman Empire. Specific figures, of course, elude us. And just what constituted "conversion" in this period is beyond our grasp – if indeed there was any specific formula. The degree of adherence to Jewish laws, customs, and traditions by proselytes doubtless varied by situation, period, and location.[30] Even circumcision need not have been obligatory. Philo maintains that proselytes could forgo physical circumcision, so long as they could circumcise their desires, pleasures, and other passions.[31] In the Jewish novel *Joseph and Aseneth*, Aseneth's conversion required only repentance and a smashing of her idols.[32] The Roman historian Cassius Dio observed that those of alien race who do no more than emulate the customs of the Jews could still be reckoned as *Ioudaioi*.[33] The Jewish openness to conversion, in any case, is undeniable. Both Philo and Josephus boasted that Jewish customs like the Sabbath, dietary laws, and fasts have won adherents from all over the world.[34] Pagan writers also noticed the appeal of Judaism to non-Jews and the burgeoning numbers of those who joined the faith – although the writers were not particularly happy about it.[35] Converts to Jewish ways of life and institutions and those who became, in some fashion, members of Jewish communities were conspicuous in the Roman world. The Jews did not discourage, let alone exclude, them.

Nor was conversion of any sort necessary to become part of a broader Jewish society. The term "godfearers" has become convenient to describe those who belonged to this larger circle. It appears in both literary and epigraphic sources.[36] That it had some recognizable significance is clear from the great donor inscriptions from Aphrodisias that list benefactors with distinguishing labels as Jews, proselytes, or *theosebeis*, as well as a whole separate category of *theosebeis*.[37] The term evidently designates a group of Gentiles closely associated with Jews and operating in a shared society. Their existence further demonstrates the willingness of Jews to

---

[30] Birnbaum 1996: 193–219; Cohen 1999: 129–30, 140–74; Goodman 2007: 160–8.

[31] Philo, *QE*, 2.2.   [32] *Jos. As.* 9–10.   [33] Dio, 37.16.4–17.1.

[34] Philo, *Mos.* 2.17–27; Jos. *CA* 2.282–3.   [35] Tac. *Hist.* 5.5.1–2; Juv. 14.96–106.

[36] E.g., Acts, 10.1–2, 13.16, 16.14, 17.17, 18.4; Jos. *Ant.* 14.110; *IJO*, II, #27, 49; Siegert 1973: 109–64; Wander 1998: 65–73.

[37] *IJO*, II, #14.

bring within their broader compass a range of interested and sympathetic Gentiles. This seriously undermines the idea of deliberate Jewish segregation.

One can go further along these lines. Jews themselves reached out to the wider pagan religious world. Even the worship of Yahweh, fundamental and binding though it was for all Jews, was not altogether restrictive or singular. A famous line in the *Letter of Aristeas*, put in the mouth of a Greek aristocrat but composed by a Hellenistic Jew, states that "the god whom Jews worship, the overseer and creator of all, is the same one worshipped by all people, including us Greeks, only we call him Zeus."[38] This is not a merging or blending of interchangeable deities, as it is often interpreted. Rather, it expresses a Jewish sense that their monotheistic faith can be ascribed without strain to Gentiles as well.

Epigraphic testimony from the Roman Empire bears out the crossovers and intertwinings most persuasively. One might cite as illustrations two funerary epitaphs from different parts of the Roman world, one from Pannonia on the Danube, one from Cirta in North Africa, probably sometime in the second or third century CE. In each case, the deceased, a woman, carries the identifying marker of *Iudea*, but the gravestone is headed by *D.M.* (i.e., *dis manibus*), a standard formula in pagan epitaphs, alluding to the divine spirits of the dead.[39] Not that *dis manibus* occurs all that frequently in Jewish inscriptions. But plainly no prohibition prevented Jews from adopting a Gentile formula alluding to spirits of the dead and interpreting them in their own fashion.

A different sort of illustration with comparable significance deserves mention. Manumission declarations from the Black Sea region show that some Jews at least were conversant with forms and procedures in pagan documents. The emancipations themselves took place in Jewish synagogues, but the proceedings regularly followed Gentile models. In one inscription from Gorgippia in the Bosporan kingdom, dated to 41 CE, the manumitter invokes *theos hypsistos*, "highest god," a phrase commonly employed in Jewish inscriptions, and frees his slave in the synagogue. But he accompanies this with a vow that the liberated slave be under the protection of "Zeus, Earth, and Sun."[40] Evidently the dedicator found no strain or tension between appealing to the Jewish god and simultaneously calling upon the protection of divine powers as framed by Gentiles.

Finally, a recently published document also from Hierapolis, dating to the mid second century CE, illuminates still another corner of this process.

---

[38] *LetArist*, 16.   [39] *IJO* I Pan 4 (Pannonia); Le Bohec 71 (Cirta).   [40] *IJO*, I BS 20 (Gorgippia).

It belongs to the sarcophagus of a certain Hikesios, "also named Judah," whose accomplishments deserved record. The inscription calls him "most famous victor in sacred contests." Indeed it refers to him as "multiple victor."[41] Whether his triumphs came in athletic or musical contests is unspecified. But the fact that a man who carried the name Judah could enter – and win – numerous "sacred contests" (i.e., those consecrated to pagan deities), holds real significance. The text demonstrates not only that gymnasial games were open to Jews but that Jews advertised their participation proudly in these quintessentially pagan competitions.

The evidence as we have it challenges any notion of impenetrable borders between paganism and Judaism. Jews did not retreat into isolationism or separatism. Nor was the distinctive identity of the Jews compromised by participation in the wider religious pluralism of the Roman Empire.

6

Judaism, like other religious communities under the aegis of the imperial power, enjoyed the indifference of the authorities. Jews in the diaspora dwelled all over the Mediterranean. Their synagogues were ubiquitous. Attestations, whether literary or archaeological, place these houses of prayer, in multiple numbers, in Syria, Egypt, Cyrenaica, Cyprus, Anatolia, the Black Sea, Greece, Macedonia, the Aegean islands, and Italy.[42] The institutions had their own officialdom, untrammeled by Roman interference, and provided a setting not only for religious services but also for education, communal dining, celebration of festivals, judicial decisions, gathering of assemblies, and manumission of slaves. Jewish communal life thrived. And it was not cut off from the larger society. Evidence exists from various quarters for Jewish access to the cultural and educational institutions, even the civic institutions, of cities in the empire. Nor should one omit to mention that many Jews in the diaspora possessed Roman citizenship. Paul of Tarsus is only the most celebrated example. However rare the practical exercise of that privilege may have been, it represented a key mark of status.[43]

Jews in fact had a strong representation in the city of Rome itself. If issues arose that involved their interests or those of Jews in general, they

---

[41] *IJO* II, #189 (Hierapolis).   [42] Levine 2000.

[43] On all this, see the discussion of Gruen 2002b, 105–32, with references to sources and scholarship.

could turn out in force. So, for instance, when Roman policy in the east threatened to affect contributions to the Temple in Jerusalem in 59 BCE, the Jews of Rome organized vociferous demonstrations. Indeed, it was not uncommon for them to make their presence felt in Roman *contiones*, gatherings for discussion of public issues, when the matter was of concern to them – and they carried weight.[44] When King Herod, ruler of Judaea under Roman hegemony, died in 4 BCE, and Jewish embassies arrived in Rome to express diverse views over the future of the land, Roman Jews, up to eight thousand of them according to Josephus, gathered to put pressure on the emperor Augustus to grant Judaea independence from the Herodian family.[45] Philo claimed quite plausibly that Augustus interfered not at all with Jewish traditional customs, including their meetings in synagogues and their contribution of tithes to Jerusalem. Moreover, Augustus saw to it that if allocations of grain were scheduled on the Sabbath when Jews could not be present, their portion would be held in reserve, to be distributed on the following day.[46] That form of consideration offers insight into the successful integration of Jews into the social and economic life of the city. Pronouncements by Roman officials and by Roman emperors regularly reiterated affirmation of Jewish prerogatives and the protection of Jewish adherence to the traditions of their ancestors.

There were, to be sure, some bumps in the road. On three separate occasions, so we are told, Jews were expelled from the city of Rome. But those occasions were widely spaced, in 139 BCE, 19 CE, and 49 CE; special circumstances prevailed in each case; the expulsions (as in the case of Isis worshippers) were more symbolic than effective, expressions of the government's need to reassert its commitment to traditional religion; and had no long-term impact upon the Jewish experience in Rome.[47] Sejanus, the ambitious and sinister praetorian prefect of the emperor Tiberius, allegedly plotted (for reasons unknown) against the Jews, slandering those in Rome, and encouraging attacks against others in the provinces. Whatever the truth of those claims, to be found only in Philo, Tiberius himself canceled the efforts after Sejanus' death, denounced the accusations, and instructed

---

[44] Cic. *Pro Flacco*, 66–8.

[45] Jos. *BJ*, 2.14–25, 2.37–8, 2.80–1; *Ant.* 17.219–29, 17.248–9, 17.299– 301.

[46] Philo, *Legat.* 155–8.

[47] 139 BCE: Val. Max. 1.3.3; 19 CE: Jos. *Ant.* 18.65–84; Tac. *Ann.* 2.85; Suet. *Tib.* 36; Dio, 57.18.5a; 49 CE: Suet. *Claud.* 25.4. This is not the place for a detailed dissection of these texts and their implications. The conclusion expressed here receives fuller defense in Gruen (2002b), 15–41. For other views, see, e.g. Smallwood (1981), 128–30, 203–16; Feldman (1993), 300–4; Botermann (1996), 50–102; Slingerland (1997), 39–46, 50–62, 67–9, and passim; Williams (2010), 79–102.

all provincial governors to reassure Jews in their jurisdictions that only those few who were guilty of infractions would be punished, and the nation as a whole should be regarded as a trust under Roman protection.[48] Caligula notoriously sought to install a statue in the Temple, an effort that caused frightful consternation among Jews, thwarted only by Caligula's assassination. But, despite Philo's representation of Caligula's lunatic anti-Semitism, the emperor may have had other purposes in mind than an assault on Jews. And he dropped the effort anyway when the intensity of Jewish objections became clear.[49] Caligula's successors made no comparable attempts. The emperor Claudius indeed, in his famous letter to the Alexandrians, asserted, as had Augustus and Tiberius before him, that the Jews of Alexandria should be permitted to follow their own customs and honor their own god.[50]

The bumps in the road have attracted much of the scholarly attention. But it needs to be emphasized that they were brief, temporary, exceptional, and by no means representative of imperial policy or Jewish experience. Pronouncements by Roman officials and by Roman emperors regularly reiterated affirmation of Jewish prerogatives and the protection of Jewish adherence to the traditions of their ancestors.

7

Rome comfortably incorporated Jews, indeed explicitly safeguarded their privileges, within its pluralistic religious universe. The behavior provides a telling indicator of Roman attitudes toward that universe. But there is a fundamental question that still needs to be confronted. Did the Jews, in the eyes of Rome, fall under the heading of a religious sect at all? Did the Romans not regard Jews as a nation (i.e., an ethnic entity) rather than a religion? In other words, did the empire not treat Jews as part of its collection of nations instead of its assemblage of multiple religions? In that case, attitude to the Jews was a social and political matter, and had nothing to do with worship, ritual, or belief.

The language of our texts does not afford an easy answer. Ancient authors frequently refer to Jews as *ethnos* or *genos* in Greek, *natio* or *gens* in Latin, which would seem to designate ethnicity rather than religion. If so,

---

[48] Philo, *Legat.* 159–61.   [49] See Gruen (2012), 135–47.
[50] *CPJ*, II, #153, 85–8; Jos. *Ant.* 19.283, 19.285, 19.290

relevance to the subject of religious pluralism would be marginal. Jews could be categorized with Syrians or Phoenicians, with Gauls or Spaniards, rather than with worshippers of Isis or Mithras, the reference being to their origins, their location, or their ethnic association, not to beliefs or rituals. The term *Ioudaioi* in Greek or *Iudei* in Latin might apply simply to inhabitants of the land of Judaea, to members of the Jewish state, or to those in the diaspora whose families stemmed from that land. Religious connotations, in principle at least, need not be part of that identity.[51]

But is that how Romans understood the Jews? The question needs to be addressed, and the evidence for Roman perception of Jews deserves closer scrutiny. Key texts for this purpose have for the most part been surprisingly overlooked in the discussion: the letters, senatorial decrees, and edicts by Roman officials, noted earlier, that reaffirmed Jewish privileges. To be sure, we do not have the documents themselves, only Josephus' reproduction of them. But the historian's collection closely parallels the phraseology, content, and formulas to be found in Roman pronouncements on stone, bronze, or papyrus in other contexts. Josephus could certainly have obtained copies of the texts from Jews in diaspora cities. And one can have confidence in the general reliability of his dossier.[52]

What emerges most strikingly is the consistent reference to Jews in terms of their sacred rites, rituals, practices, ceremonies, and observances – in short, their religion. For example, the Roman consul of 49 BCE declared in a letter to Ephesus that Jews who are Roman citizens should be exempt from military service on grounds of their religion, so that they can practice their sacred rites.[53] A subsequent letter from the governor of Asia to Laodicea and other cities sharpened the principle somewhat by stating that Jews have a right to observe the Sabbath and the rest of their sacred

---

[51] See Mason 2007: 457–512. The influential discussion of Cohen 1999: 69–139, argues that *Ioudaios* initially had a strictly geographic or ethnic meaning, but subsequently, in the second or first century BCE, took on a cultural and religious significance. That is a provocative, but altogether too schematic, reconstruction. No sharp change occurred at an identifiable moment – if ever. Buell 2005: 35–49, rightly finds fluidity rather than dichotomy, but goes too far in largely dissolving the differences. She does not differentiate religious identity from ethnic or racial identity but sees religion as a "swing category" within definitions of ethnicity and race and as the engine for ethno-racial transformation. This is not the place to discuss the fraught issue of whether *Ioudaioi* should be translated as "Jews" or "Judaeans." The bibliography on this subject continues to grow. See the extensive annotated bibliographies by Miller 2010: 98–126; 2012: 293–311; 2014: 216–65. Add also Schwartz 2014.

[52] Ben Zeev 1998: 16–21, 357–68, 382–7; Gruen 2002b: 84–6.

[53] Jos. *Ant.* 14.228: ἱερὰ Ἰουδαϊκὰ ... δεισιδαιμονίας ἕνεκα; 14.232, 14.234, 14.237, 14.240. Cohen (1999), 95, oddly sees this as indicating that Romans reckoned Jews as a strictly ethnic-geographic community.

rituals in accord with their traditional laws.[54] Yet another missive expanded on the exemption from military service by specifying that Jews do not bear arms on the Sabbath and that military service would interfere with their dietary restrictions, their ability to assemble in accordance with ancestral customs, and their offerings for sacrifices.[55] Other comparable pronouncements, with similar phraseology, can also be cited.[56] In all of these documents, Jews come under the Roman aegis almost exclusively as a religious group.[57]

The comments of Roman writers and intellectuals, whatever their particular outlook, also repeatedly refer to Jewish ritual, practices, and beliefs, not to ethnicity. So, for example, Cicero, although he recognized that Jews could be an effective pressure group in Rome, sums them up as a *barbara superstitio* and makes reference to the *religio Iudaeorum*.[58] Varro does employ the term *gens Iudaea* but he does so in the context of Jewish worship of the divine without images.[59] Seneca expressed criticism of Jews for their sacred institutions (*sacramenta*), most especially for their observance of the Sabbath, which he reckoned as a colossal waste of time.[60] Petronius sardonically labels Jewish abstinence from pork as worship of a pig-god, and proceeds to heap scorn on the Sabbath and on circumcision.[61] Pliny the Elder refers to the *Iudaea gens* but denotes it as remarkable for contempt of the divine powers.[62] Plutarch's references to Jews concern their opinions on the gods, their adherence to the Sabbath, and their abstinence from pork.[63] Tacitus characterizes the Mosaic laws as

---

[54] Jos. *Ant.* 14.241–2.   [55] Jos. *Ant.* 14.223, 14.226.

[56] Jos. *Ant.* 14.245–6, 14.260–1, 14.263–4.

[57] It does not follow, of course, that the Romans regarded Jews as merely a religious sect. When the term *ethnos* is applied to Jews, even in these documents, it can have a wider connotation, meaning something like the "Jewish people," as Josephus often uses it; e.g. Jos. *Ant.* 14.320, 14.323. See Gruen (2020), 172–180. And the Roman letters directed to the Jewish leader Hyrcanus recognized that his official position (sanctioned by Caesar) was both High Priest and Ethnarch, implying that Jews constituted more than just a religious body: Jos. *Ant.* 14.191, 14.194, 14.196, 14.199. Cf. also Jos. *Ant.* 14.212: Ὑρκανῷ καὶ ἔθνει τῶν Ἰουδαίων. Romans had, after all, had a treaty relationship with the Judean state that dated back to the Hasmonean era. Nonetheless, the religious aspects of Judaism predominated in the eyes of gentiles: Jews did not worship the same gods as they did; Jos. *Ant.* 12.125–6; *CAp.* 2.65, 2.79.

[58] Cic. *Pro Flacco*, 67–8. It is worth noting that Cicero here uses both *religio* and *superstitio* with reference to the Jews, employing the terms essentially as equivalents. Although scholars have commonly seen a positive connotation for the one and a negative one for the other, that is by no means always the case. The designation *superstitio* or *deisidaimonia* is frequently used in a neutral fashion, meaning merely "worship" or "religion." On the complex meanings of *religio*, see the analysis of Barton 2016, 15–52.

[59] Varro, *apud* Aug. *Civ. Dei*, 4.31.   [60] Seneca, *apud* Aug. *Civ. Dei*, 6.11.

[61] Petronius, fr. 37.   [62] Pliny, *NH*, 13.46.

[63] Plut. *De Superst.* 3, 8; *De Stoic. Rep.* 38; *Quaest. Conv.* 4–6.

creating new religious prescriptions different from those of all other mortals, and, among other Jewish traits, he stresses their contributions to the Temple, their beliefs about the underworld, their monotheism, aniconism, and their religious festivals.[64] Juvenal's scorn fastens upon laws handed down in a secret volume by Moses and the Jews' supposed refusal to accommodate anyone who did not share their sacred beliefs.[65] And Apuleius' one reference to the people calls them "superstitious Jews."[66]

It is essential to stress that this collection of offhand remarks that run the gamut from admiration to disapproval to indifference constituted neither racism nor "proto-racism."[67] Romans avoided reference to Jewish ethnic traits, inherited or genetic characteristics, descent, geographic influence, appearance, speech, or any qualities associated with racial origins. Religion almost alone sprang to mind when Romans paid any attention to Jews.[68] The Jews' peculiar practices called forth some caustic comments, puzzlement, and amusement from Roman literary figures. But those comments had no racial overtones.

The laissez-faire attitude that prevailed in the pluralistic world of the Roman Empire comfortably included Judaism within its compass. With only very rare exceptions, Jewish practices and beliefs went unhindered, synagogues flourished, advocacy for Jewish causes was successful, and Jews maintained a network of connections among themselves between Jerusalem and the diaspora all over the Mediterranean.

The very fact that Romans regarded Jews essentially as practitioners of a religion carries significance. Ethnicity was irrelevant. Romans did not speak of Jews in terms of origins, bloodlines, descent, or ethnic attributes that might suggest an alien presence in their midst.[69] Jewish religious

---

[64] Tac. *Hist.* 4.1, 5.1–5.   [65] Juv. 14.100–4.   [66] Apul. *Florida*, 6.

[67] Contra: Sherwin-White 1967: 86–101; Isaac 2004: 440–91.

[68] A rare exception is the obscure historian Ptolemy who wrote a book on Herod, only a single passage of which survives, quoted by the grammarian Ammonius. Ptolemy distinguishes Jews and Idumaeans on the grounds that Jews are such by origin and nature, whereas Idumaeans were originally Phoenicians and Syrians, only subsequently subjugated and amalgamated by Jews; Ptolemy, *FGH*, II, B199, F1 = Stern 1974: 355–6. The historian does appear to set Jews in an ethnic rather than a religious category. But it is noteworthy that, in Ptolemy's view, what made the Idumaeans part of the Jewish *ethnos* was compulsory circumcision – a religious prescription. The influential article of Goodman 1989: 40–4, claiming that only after 96 CE were Jews defined by their religion alone rather than by their birth, flies in the face of most of the evidence discussed here. See the criticisms of Goodman, on other grounds, by Schwartz 2001: 187–8.

[69] To be sure, theories about Jewish origins did circulate in the Greco-Roman world, tracing their beginnings to Crete, Assyria, Egypt, Libya, or Asia Minor; Tac. *Hist.* 5.2. But none of these makes any allusions to ethnic traits, and most are rather flattering to the Jews. Cf. Feldman 1991:

customs, however strange and unusual they might seem, were no more alien than those of the numerous cults and modes of worship that Romans had incorporated into their society almost from the beginnings of their history. The commitment to religious pluralism accommodated Jews without difficulty. Jewish experience in the Roman Empire for the vast proportion of the time, at least until the great war of 66–70 CE, was smooth and untroubled.[70] Jews thrived in the Mediterranean diaspora, even in Rome itself. The Roman government extended favor and support abroad, and found ample space for Jews at home. Increasing numbers of Jews indeed enjoyed Roman citizenship, which was perfectly compatible with Jewish traditions – especially as those traditions became increasingly open to the outside world. It should be underscored that this was not a matter of "tolerance" on the Roman part but an integral part of the Roman mindset. Rome's own legends and history show a receptivity to foreign cults and alien sects of a bewildering variety of types. A receptivity to adherents of Judaism, by comparison, was simply business as usual. It fit a consistent pattern of Roman indifference, religious pluralism – and supreme self-confidence.

331–60. Dio Cassius, writing in the early third century CE, does link the name *Ioudaioi* with the land called *Ioudaia*. That would appear to associate Judaism with a geographic or an ethnic concept. But he swiftly abandons that line by pointing out that the term now applies even to those who live in Rome and to all other people who, though of a different *ethnos*, emulate Jewish customs. Dio then goes further. He elaborates on his understanding of Jews and sets it unequivocally in religious terms: They honor none of the gods worshipped by others but only their own divinity; they allow no statues or images of him; yet they built an extravagantly large and beautiful temple to him; their customs distinguish them from the rest of mankind; Dio, 37.17.1–3. Dio's understanding thus coheres with the rest of our testimony.

[70] Limits of time and space prevent taking this story beyond 70 CE. The destruction of the Temple certainly created a very different situation for Jews in Palestine. How much difference it made for Jews elsewhere is a more difficult question. It is worth stressing, however, that the war of 66–70 did not arise out of religious – let alone ethnic – discontent. And Latin authors like Tacitus and Juvenal who wrote after the war refer to Jews in much the same terms as Seneca and Petronius, who wrote before it. One might also observe the quite striking tale in Tacitus and Josephus that, during the Roman siege of Jerusalem, the doors of the Temple suddenly flew open and a voice was heard exclaiming that the gods were exiting the shrine, thus evidently moving to the side of Rome; Tac. *Hist.* 5.13.1; Jos. *BJ*, 6.300. This is plainly an echo of the ancient Roman practice of *evocatio*, dating to the very early Republic, in which the gods of the enemy were summoned to depart and take up residence in Rome. See earlier. Not that Yahweh became part of the Roman pantheon. But the story accurately reflects Roman expectation that even the divine protectors of their foes could be embraced by the wider religious culture of imperial Rome.

11 | Rome's Attitude to Jews after the Great Rebellion – Beyond *Raison d'état?*

ALEXANDER YAKOBSON

According to an influential thesis set out by Martin Goodman in his *Rome and Jerusalem*,[1] Jews and Judaea were treated with extraordinary harshness in the wake of the Great Rebellion. Goodman refers chiefly to Rome's failure to allow the Temple in Jerusalem to be rebuilt and to the imposition, as well as the continuing retention, of the special tax on Jews throughout the empire. This, he argues, amounted to unusual severity that cannot be explained by ordinary considerations of imperial policy. He suggests that this policy resulted from the new Flavian dynasty's need to base its legitimacy on a victory in a foreign war. Since Vespasian was a usurper of humble origins who had seized power through civil war, and thus deficient in legitimacy, he had to present himself as Rome's saviour from a foreign foe in order to legitimize his rule. In order to drive this point home, the Jews had to be presented and treated as dangerous enemies of Rome. This policy, not originating in religious or ethnic hostility, but imposed by the regime's pressing political needs, amounted to a 'war on Judaism' and 'depicting the religion of the Jews as not worthy to exist'. This was to have fateful repercussions for the relations between Jews and the empire, finally resulting in two rebellions with catastrophic results – in the Diaspora under Trajan and in Judaea under Hadrian.

Despite many valid points, I disagree with the thesis. Vespasian enjoyed considerable legitimacy at the beginning of his reign; he did not need to base his legitimacy on a continuous 'war against the Jews'; nothing he did needs to be explained by attributing this motivation to him. Naturally, the new ruler was anxious to cultivate his public image, and the victory in Judaea played an important part in this. This put the Jews in an unenviable position. The Flavian victory was, for them, a catastrophic and traumatic event; its celebration must have been deeply offensive. But there is no reason to assume that Vespasian needed to defend his legitimacy by extraordinary means. His policy towards Jews and Judaea is perfectly susceptible to rational explanation without such an assumption.

[1] Goodman 2007: 428 ff.

Hostility to Jews in the wake of the rebellion,[2] and perhaps also the political expediency of demonstrating this hostility, cannot of course be ruled out; but there is no reason to attribute decisive importance to this aspect. This applies both to the Jewish tax and to the issue of the Temple. However, what from the Roman viewpoint can easily be accounted for by ordinary considerations of imperial policy must have seemed to many Jews a religious and ethnic insult. This may well have contributed to the final result, as suggested by Goodman.

1 Crisis of Legitimacy?

No doubt, the victory in Judea came in very handy for Vespasian and was used to the full extent in order to enhance the prestige of the new ruler who, indeed, lacked distinguished ancestry. But there is no need to overdramatize Vespasian's deficit of legitimacy at this point, much less to attribute it to his seizure of power in a civil war. The main legitimacy of any victor in a civil war was, surely, the fact that he has extinguished the flames of civil strife and brought internal peace to Rome. Only unsuccessful civil wars are well and truly illegitimate. The inherent illegitimacy of a civil war works, eventually (as had happened with Octavian), in favour of the victor whose victory brings peace; history then tends to be rewritten in order to absolve him of any blame for having started the war in the first place. As regards Vespasian, as we shall see, this task was easy.

For all the undoubted importance of the victory in the Jewish war, it is an exaggeration to present it, as is sometimes done, as the 'foundation myth'[3] of Vespasian's principate and the new dynasty. The main foundation myth was different: it is surely reflected in what Suetonius says in the opening sentence of Vespasian's biography:

> The empire, which for a long time had been unsettled and, as it were, drifting, through the usurpation and violent death of three emperors, was at last taken in hand and given stability by the Flavian family (*rebellione trium principum et caede incertum diu et quasi vagum imperium suscepit firmavitque tandem gens Flavia*). (*Vesp.* 1.1).[4]

---

[2] On Roman attitudes to Jews at that time, see, e.g., Gruen 2002a: 38–9.

[3] See, e.g., Barnes 2005: 129; Rives 2005: 156 ('as many scholars have emphasized').

[4] English translations in this chapter will usually follow the Loeb edition. According to Edmondson 2005: 9, this phrase 'hints at the importance of the suppression of the revolt in Judaea in the official Flavian version of events'. But surely 'taking in hand and stabilizing' the empire means putting an end to its 'drifting' – i.e., civil wars.

Elsewhere (*Vesp.* 8.1), Suetonius says that the state had been 'tottering and almost overthrown' (*prope afflicta nutansque*) before Vespasian's accession. According to Tacitus, the year 69 was 'nearly the last year of the commonwealth' (*rei publicae prope supremus*) (*Hist.* 1.11), 'a period rich in disasters, frightful in its wars, torn by civil strife' (*Hist.* 1.2). *Res publica* here is obviously without 'republican' political connotations. It is the existence of the Roman state that is said to have been threatened – because it was repeatedly torn by civil wars, not, principally, because of the Jewish rebellion.

The Judaean war could never have been presented as having posed anything like an equal danger to Rome. Even the blatantly exaggerated account of the victory in an inscription on the now-disappeared 'Arch of Titus' at the south-east end of the Circus Maximus (erected under Titus) could do no more than falsely claim that Jerusalem had never been conquered, and had mostly been left unmolested, before 70.[5] Taking such a city and 'subduing the race of the Jews', in the words of the inscription, was indeed a glorious victory (of Titus and of his father, the commander-in-chief). But the contest was not one in which the fate of the empire hung in the balance, nor is it described as such. The Jewish enemy had simply not been powerful enough to mark the victor(s) as having 'saved the state by defeating the Jews'[6] – whereas Vespasian was definitely presented as having saved it by ending the civil wars.

In fact, according to Josephus' preface to his *Jewish War*, part of his motivation for writing was that 'some men' had published accounts of the war that sought, out of hostility to Jews, to belittle their stature as a (worthy) enemy, thus presenting the victory as less glorious by implication (*BJ* 1.3). Naturally, we cannot be sure that Josephus presents his rivals' writings fairly.[7] But this line of argument was only possible because the Jews in Judaea were an enemy that, however one managed the delicate balancing act of disparaging them without belittling the importance of the victory, could not in any case be described as having threatened the existence of the empire.[8] Thus, they could not provide the victor with a credible claim of having 'saved' it from them.

Of course, the military achievement involved was considerable. Taking a major well-fortified city by storm after a prolonged siege made 'subduing'

---

[5] *CIL* 6. 944 = *ILS* 264.   [6] Goodman 2005: 171.

[7] Cf. Mason 2005: 258–9. Josephus' own characterization of the importance of the war, in the opening sentence of his book, is wildly exaggerated.

[8] Cf. Gruen 2002a: 38 on the Roman feeling of 'outrage at the idea that this puny and insignificant ethnos' ventured to challenge the power of Rome.

the Jews an outstanding accomplishment, not merely a matter of suppressing a rebellion in a small province. While the Judaean triumph was 'an anomaly' in being the only triumph ever celebrated over a provincial population, the war itself was 'a major event in Roman military history, demanding a massive concentration of forces'; the siege of Jerusalem was 'the longest . . . in the whole of the imperial period' and the forces deployed there were 'significantly larger' than those deployed for the invasion of Britain in 43.[9] Naturally, a victory won by Vespasian and Titus was in any case bound to be presented as a victory in a full-fledged foreign war in order to justify the triumph and other displays of Flavian triumphalism. For the Jews, being advertised as a defeated enemy of Rome was an unenviable position. It is not obvious that to be presented as conquered foreign foes was, in itself, worse than to be portrayed as long-time subjects of the empire who had treacherously rebelled against it.[10] On the other hand, a foreign victory left greater room for advertisement, and the Flavians certainly made the most of it, celebrating and monumentalizing their victory on a grand scale.[11]

While Vespasian was certainly 'portrayed . . . as warrior hero' due to this victory, his claim to be the 'saviour of the state'[12] could not rest wholly or primarily on it but was sustained mainly by the very factor blamed for his alleged deficit of legitimacy – victory in civil war. The horrors brought by this war extending to Rome and to the Capitol itself were such that the man who had ended them could indeed be credibly presented as Rome's saviour. The emphasis on *aeternitas* in Vespasian's coinage may reflect the existential anxieties generated by these events.[13] Pliny the Younger, writing under Vespasian, holds that the relief extended by him to the exhausted state (*fessis rebus subveniens*) – obviously, a state exhausted by civil strife – is paving his way to heaven (*NH* 2.18). The greater the calamity preceding Vespasian's advent to power, the greater the glory brought by ending it.

---

[9] Millar 2005: 101–2.
[10] Cf. Joseph. *BJ* 2.355–7: Agrippa II, trying to dissuade the populace in Jerusalem from rebelling, argues that while defending one's freedom against foreign conquest deserves respect, a nation that has accepted Roman rule for a long time and then rebels 'is rather a refractory slave than a lover of liberty'. Such sentiments were probably shared by many. This does not mean that in actual practice 'defenders of liberty' first conquered by Rome were treated less harshly. According to Gambash 2013, the opposite was generally true. He notes that Judaea was treated by Vespasian and Titus as a full-fledged foreign enemy, with great harshness, throughout their campaign and in its aftermath, and the victory over it was advertised accordingly. This, according to him, resulted from the fact that Judaea had been wholly lost to Roman control at the beginning of the rebellion, and reconquering it required an all-out war, with massive deployment of military power. See also Gambash, Gitler, and Cotton 2013.
[11] See on this Millar 2005.   [12] Goodman 2007: 439.   [13] Levick 1999: 66.

Thus, there is no reason to portray the Flavians as insecure in their legitimacy and implicitly apologetic – 'a government seeking to justify the seizure and retention of power by claiming to have defeated a dangerous enemy'.[14] Vespasian's seizure of power was very probably regarded by many as a major blessing to Rome (not merely presented as such by the regime, which was inevitable in any case). According to Tacitus (*Hist.* 4.3), the senators who voted him the imperial powers were 'filled with joy and confident hope, for it seemed to them that civil warfare, which, breaking out in Gallic and Spanish provinces, had moved to arms first the Germanies, then Illyricum, and which had traversed Egypt, Judaea, Syria, and all provinces and armies, was now at an end, as if the expiation of the whole world had been completed'. Josephus attributes a similar attitude to the people: 'The people, too, exhausted by civil disorders, were still more eager for his [Vespasian's] coming, expecting now at last to obtain permanent release from their miseries, and confident that security and prosperity would again be theirs' (*BJ* 7.66).

Josephus is no doubt echoing Flavian propaganda. But this only goes to show that, far from trying to 'disguise the unpalatable truth of the civil strife' which had brought Vespasian to power,[15] this propaganda was using this fact in order to glorify the new emperor. And indeed, it is not difficult to believe there was a widespread feeling of relief, with high hopes pinned on someone whose victory had brought peace – a man who, for all his lack of distinguished ancestry, was a victorious military commander, with two adult sons holding out a hope for uncontested hereditary succession.[16]

Moreover, unlike others who could claim credit for extinguishing a civil war (including Octavian), Vespasian bore no blame for having fomented it in the first place. He had stepped in only at a late stage, under Vitellius – an unpopular ruler and a usurper in his own right, who inspired little confidence in future stability. At any rate, it was easy to portray Vitellius in this light retrospectively. The man who could be plausibly blamed for burning down the temple of Jupiter on the Capitol ('the saddest and most shameful crime the Roman state had suffered since its foundation', Tac. *Hist.* 3.72) was an easy target.

---

[14] Goodman 2007: 463. The context is Domitian's rule. The alleged deficit of legitimacy extended, allegedly, to the third representative of the dynast; this is unlikely in itself. Similarly, Overman 2002: 216.

[15] Goodman 2005: 171.

[16] Cf. Levick 1999: 92 (on Vespasian's demeanour at the outset of his reign): 'This was a confident man, and one with a good conscience'.

Furthermore, Rome's second dynasty was not haunted by the ghost of the first one. The latter had safely vanished without a remnant, its prestige tarnished by Nero's tyranny (and the collapse of the Augustan peace following it) – though Vespasian had not been disloyal even to Nero.[17]

Unlike the 'usurpation', Vespasian's modest pedigree was, indeed, a handicap. However, his legitimacy was amply enhanced by sundry omens, prophesies and miracles for which the Orient provided wide scope but which included also earlier events interpreted *ex eventu*.[18] This clearly demonstrated that Vespasian had come to power by divine favour – something that in any case could be taken, in Roman terms, as implied by the victory itself: *victrix causa deis placuit*.[19] Having related these things, Suetonius (*Vesp.* 7.2) notes that Vespasian still lacked *auctoritas* and *maiestas*; however, 'these also he obtained' (*haec quoque accessit*); he then relates how Vespasian healed a blind man and a lame one in public in Alexandria.[20] By the time he returned to Rome, Vespasian is described as being at the height of his power and glory: *talis tantaque fama in urbem reversus* (8.1).

Naturally, the new ruler took care to enhance his *auctoritas* and *maiestas* still further; Suetonius proceeds to mention the triumph of *de Iudaeis* and Vespasian's eight consulships. But it is highly unlikely that Vespasian felt that he was facing a 'crisis of legitimacy upon [his] accession'.[21]

Although his rule was duly confirmed by a *senatus consultum* and a subsequent *lex*, Vespasian's decision to make July 1, the date of his military proclamation in Egypt, his *dies imperii* shows him unembarrassed by the legions' role in his advent to power. His two sons were, and were presented as, a guarantee of dynastic continuity and stability,[22] an important element of legitimacy after the experience of the civil war.

Finally, Vespasian 'never tried to conceal his former lowly condition, but often even paraded it. When certain men tried to trace the Flavian family's origins to the founders of Reate and a companion of Hercules ... he laughed at them for their pains' (Suet. *Vesp.* 12). Nevertheless, lack of noble ancestry was, no doubt, felt to call for *auctoritas*-enhancing measures such as Vespasian's accumulation of ordinary consulships and imperial

---

[17] Cf. Tac. *Hist.* 2.76 (Mucianus is urging Vespasian to allow the armies of the East to proclaim him Emperor).

[18] See on this Levick 1999: 67–70.   [19] Luc. 1.128; cf. Dio, *Epitome* 63.13.1.

[20] Cf. Tac. *Hist.* 4.81.   [21] Thus Vasta 2007: 136.

[22] See, e.g., Plin. *NH* 2.18; Joseph. 7.73; Tac. *Hist.* 2.77; 4.8; 4.52; Suet. *Vesp.* 25.1; Dio 66.12.1.

salutations and the assumption of censorship – as well as, probably, putting an even greater emphasis on the Judaean victory. But there is no indication that this deficiency produced a 'crisis of legitimacy'.

Admittedly, the borderline between a 'crisis of legitimacy' and a simple need to cultivate the new emperor's prestige energetically can be blurred. This is a matter of degree. Millar, for example, describes Vespasian's standing in terms that are somewhere between those two poles: 'As a first-generation senator, Vespasian had no inherited social prestige to draw on, and immediate steps needed to be taken to enhance the public standing of the new Flavian dynasty.'[23] This urgent need explains, according to Millar, the intensity with which the victory in Judaea was celebrated in monuments through the city; note that he speaks of a weakness caused by Vespasian's modest descent, not his 'usurpation'.

It is thus an exaggeration to say that, in Vespasian's case, 'the glory of a foreign victory was used, as earlier in Roman history [Octavian is obviously meant; we shall return to him presently – A. Y.] both to justify seizure of political power and to disguise the unpalatable truth of the civil strife though which it had been won'.[24] Rather than the foreign victory's being used to disguise the origins of Vespasian's principate, the two achievements, external and internal, were celebrated together. The Flavian triumphalism and the rhetoric of peace were sending a double message to the public. One triumphed, naturally, over foreign enemies – not over fellow citizens; but internal peace (resulting from the not-to-be-openly-celebrated victory over Roman citizens) was even more important – Vespasian's main claim to have 'saved the state'. The *pax* celebrated by him comprised both aspects. Vespasian was following Octavian's footsteps: Octavian's triple triumph in 29 BCE celebrated, officially, three foreign victories, two of them over Cleopatra (Actium and the conquest of Egypt); but Augustus' main achievement was the peace he brought to the Roman world by ending civil strife.

The prominence given to *pax* under Vespasian,[25] therefore, should not be interpreted exclusively, or mainly, as an allusion to the Judaean victory – still less as a sign that he was waging a 'war on Judaism'. According to Goodman, following the Judaean triumph during which 'a copy of Jewish Law' was displayed as part of the spoils, it became clear that 'this war on Judaism was not to be only a temporary feature of Flavian propaganda'; this is reflected in the regime's building projects, starting with the *Templum*

---

[23] Millar 2005: 102.   [24] Goodman 2005: 171.

[25] On the different aspects of this prominence, including coins, monuments and inscriptions, see Noreña 2003: 27–35.

Pacis.[26] But although the spoils from the Jerusalem Temple, including the famous candelabrum, were indeed displayed there (alongside other master-pieces of painting and sculpture from all over the empire),[27] the peace celebrated by the *Templum Pacis* was surely much more than the victory in Judaea.[28] According to Millar, the intended message of the speedy construction of the *Templum* was the reestablishment of peace – generally, after a period of civil war, and specifically in Judaea.[29]

Moreover, the Roman peace had been challenged by foreigners and restored not just in Judaea. Certainly, Judaea provided the new dynasty with the most dramatic 'peace-bringing' external victory, with which Vespasian and Titus were personally identified. But the external aspect of the peace for which the regime claimed credit, in the *Templum Pacis* and generally, was surely much wider than the peace secured by that victory. It must have been the universal peace dramatically symbolized by the extraordinary step, taken by Vespasian, of closing the temple of Janus;[30] something to be done, according to Augustus in *Res Gestae* (13), when 'peace had been secured by victories throughout the Roman empire by land and sea'.[31] In his account of 68 BCE, Tacitus described Rome's foreign and domestic tribulations together, as part of the same grim picture:

> Four emperors fell by the sword; there were three civil wars, more foreign wars, and often both at the same time. There was success in the East, misfortune in the West. Illyricum was disturbed, the Gallic provinces wavering, Britain subdued and immediately let go. The Sarmatae and Suebi rose against us; the Dacians won fame by defeats inflicted and suffered; even the Parthians were almost roused to arms through the trickery of a pretended Nero. (*Hist.* 1.2)

---

[26] Goodman 2007: 453. [27] Plin. *NH* 34.84; Joseph. *BJ* 7.159–62.

[28] Noreña holds that the peace proclaimed by the *Templum Pacis* was 'military' – the victory in Judaea and, generally, 'pacification of foreign peoples' and Roman military power, rather than 'civilian': 'Vespasian would not have chosen to memorialize the domestic peace that followed the civil war of 68–9, since this would only serve as a permanent reminder of the civil violence that had enabled his ascent to the throne . . . A civil war monument had no place in Verspasianic Rome' (Noreña 2003: 35). But surely the *Templum* was a monument to civil peace, not to civil war.

[29] Millar 2005: 109; cf. 112; similarly, Levick 1999: 126 ('a declaration of normality restored after the civil wars'). On the date of the inauguration see Dio 65.15.1–2. On the wider imperial, 'foreign' significance of the message conveyed by the *Templum* and its exhibits, not confined to the victory in Judaea, see Levick 1999: 127; Vasta 2007: 127.

[30] Orosius 7.3.7–8, citing Tacitus.

[31] Cf. Woolf 1993b: 177: while both Augustus and Vespasian made foreign victories 'the ostensible occasion for promoting the cult of *pax*', including the closing of the temple of Janus, 'the evocation of civil harmony seems an inescapable sub-text'.

The rebellion led by the Batavian auxiliary commander Iulius Civilis, which came to involve Germanic and Gallic tribes in an attempt to set up a 'Gallic Empire', took heavy effort and massive forces to suppress at the beginning of Vespasian's reign.[32] The *Templum Pacis* was surely meant to celebrate the peace throughout the empire, in both its aspects, external and internal.

Moreover, there was a clear connection between the two: foreign enemies were encouraged to challenge the empire because of Roman civil strife. In Tacitus' words (referring to the rebellion led by Civilis), 'nothing had encouraged [the Gauls] to believe that the end of our rule was at hand than the burning of the Capitol ... Now [according to Druids] this fatal conflagration has given proof from heaven of the divine wrath and presages the passage of the sovereignty of the world to the peoples beyond the Alps' (*Hist.* 4.54).[33] This view (reflecting, at any rate, the Rome perception) helps explain how the civil war could be presented as a threat to the very survival of the empire – more so, certainly, than any threat originating in Judaea.

That a victory in civil war could be celebrated implicitly, under the pretext of an external victory, is attested by Tacitus for the beginning of Vespasian's reign, when senators 'gave Mucianus the insignia of a triumph, in reality for civil war, although his expedition against the Sarmatae was made the pretext' (*Hist.* 4.4). Celebrating the victory in Judaea was, of course, of great importance in itself, rather than merely a pretext for something else. Nevertheless, Josephus attests that the Judaean triumph itself was widely regarded as signifying much more than the victory to which it was officially dedicated:

> The city of Rome kept festival that day for her victory in the campaign against her enemies, for the termination of her civil dissentions, and for the dawning hopes of her felicity. (*BJ* 7.157)[34]

All this is not to minimize the obvious importance of the victory in Judaea in the regime's self-presentation. However, making extensive political use of a foreign victory did not have to result in long-term official demonization of the vanquished, dictating the policy towards them. This did not happen after Actium, for all the allegedly fateful character of the confrontation, the virulence of anti-Egyptian propaganda that

---

[32] Levick 1999: 107–13.   [33] Cf. Tac. *Hist.* 4. 57.1; Joseph. *BJ* 7.77–9.

[34] The triumphal procession itself had a wider imperial aspect and celebrated, according to Josephus, 'the magnitude of the Roman Empire' by parading its riches, 'the wonderful and precious productions of various nations' (*BJ* 7.133, see 132–7 for a detailed account); cf. Beard 2003: 551–2.

accompanied it, and its ideological importance for the Augustan principate. The Judaean war was no match for Actium and Cleopatra's alleged schemes to put herself, with Mark Anthony's help, in a position of rendering judgement on the Capitol. Nevertheless, already a few years after Actium, Cleopatra herself could be treated (by Horace, *Carm.* 1.37, while recalling her alleged threat to the Capitol) with a degree of respect: once no longer an active and dangerous foe, she could be given credit for dying bravely, with dignity.[35] Here, admittedly, one can point to the difference between Vespasian's modest pedigree and that of Caesar's (adopted) son: Vespasian, it can be argued, had a greater need to exploit a foreign victory, even if it was a more modest one. However, neither the Jewish tax nor the failure to have the Temple rebuilt need to be accounted for in the way suggested by Goodman.

2   The Jewish Tax – Imposed by Propaganda Needs?

As for the tax imposed on Jews throughout the empire – this was indeed an extraordinary step in Roman terms. However, it was clearly inspired by extraordinary circumstances, and these must have been (mainly) financial rather than propagandistic. It should be viewed above all as a measure aimed at increasing state revenue at a time when this was urgently needed. The finances of the empire had been devastated by the civil wars (following Nero's extravagance); it was widely recognized that extraordinary steps needed to be taken to remedy the situation.[36] Vespasian was notoriously inventive in devising new sources of revenue, above all new and increased taxes (including the famous *pecunia non olet* one). 'Not content with reviving the imposts which had been repealed under Galba, he added new and heavy burdens, increasing the amount of tribute paid by the provinces, in some cases actually doubling it' (Suet. *Vesp.* 16.1);[37] 'he declared at the beginning of his reign that a huge sum [forty billion sesterces; though the manuscript is often amended to make the sum less astronomical] was needed to put the state on its feet financially' (*ut res publica stare posset*). Suetonius assumes that Vespasian's notorious unscrupulousness in financial matters was largely involuntary: he was 'driven by necessity to raise money by spoliation and robbery because of the desperate state of the *aerarium* and the *fiscus*' (16.3). It was one of the great

---

[35] Cf. Goodman 2007: 463 (comparing the Flavian dynasty's attitude to Jews unfavorably to the Augustan precedent).

[36] See Levick 1999: 95–106 on Vespasian's policies that ensured the 'financial survival' (the chapter's title) of the state.

[37] Cf. Dio 65, 8.3–4. *Pecunia non olet*: Suet. *Vesp.* 23.3; Dio 65.14.5.

achievements of his reign that he restored the state to financial health – while carrying out an extensive building programme that included, as a matter of priority, the restoration of the Capitol. But this achievement came at a high price. Part of the price, unsurprisingly in the circumstances, had to be paid by the Jews. This, surely, is the context in which the Jewish tax should be examined. Any additional motivation, while it cannot be ruled out, must have been secondary.

Imposing a tax on a non-territorial ethnic or religious group was, admittedly, unexampled in Roman practice. But from Vespasian's (far from disinterested) viewpoint, this tax had already existed, in a way – in the form of the voluntary contribution paid by Jews to the Temple in Jerusalem. It was now 'diverted' to the Capitoline Jupiter (as the testimony of Josephus and Dio is usually understood)[38] in a greatly aggravated form – the aggravation being perfectly in the spirit of the times. From Vespasian's perspective, the choice was between diverting these sums to Roman uses or allowing the Jews to keep their money and, in that sense, benefit from the war. The latter option must have looked singularly unattractive to him. The question is, needless to say, not one of fairness – of which there was obviously very little in these proceedings – but of motivation.

All this is not to argue that there could not have been an element of deliberate humiliation there – especially if the tax was indeed earmarked for the temple of Jupiter. Appearing to share a widespread prejudice against an unpopular group is something that a ruler might occasionally find useful without any crisis of legitimacy forcing his hand. But there is no need to assume that the desire to humiliate the Jews, and the political need to be perceived as humiliating them, was the main motive for imposing the tax – or for retaining it later on. Once a tax is imposed, whatever the original reason for this, and starts yielding very considerable sums (as was clearly the case with the Jewish tax),[39] it is unfortunately the rule that it will not be abolished unless there are very strong reasons for doing so. The Jews were never in a position to provide the Roman government with a good enough reason to give up the revenue produced by the Jewish tax. Its retention under Domitian does not show that the dynasty still felt, under its third

---

[38] Joseph. 4.218; Dio 65.7.2. Gambash argues that there is no certainty that the Jewish tax was used to finance the building of the new Capitoline shrine; there is a 'plausible possibility' that the money went to the Capitol in the sense of 'one of the branches of the *aerarium* [thought to have been situated on the *mons Capitolinus*]' (Gambash 2013: 191–2).

[39] See Levick 1999: 101. The suggested figure of 5 to 6 per cent of Rome's annual revenue is based on very uncertain estimates, both of the overall state revenue and of the Jewish population of the empire.

emperor, a need to defend its legitimacy by appearing to wage an incessant 'war on Judaism' and the Jews.

It is true that, as Goodman points out, Domitian, at the start of his reign and before he had accumulated his own triumphs, triumphal arches and imperial salutations, lacked, and doubtless envied, his father's and elder brother's military prestige. The fact that he 'was still in 85 issuing coins with the caption JUDAEA CAPTA' may indeed be attributed to his desire to partake in the glory of that victory; but this is not tantamount to feeling the need 'to justify his rule' by ostentatious hostility to Jews.[40] It is far more probable that he regarded the Jewish tax as an important source of revenue which he, so far from giving it up, was determined to exploit to the full. The harshness with which the tax was exacted under Domitian, vividly attested by Suetonius, was not out of tune with the general character of his rule,[41] and with the financial difficulties he faced. The context in which Suetonius mentions this harshness is the financial straits to which Domitian 'was reduced by the cost of his buildings and shows, as well as by the additions which he had made to the pay of the soldiers'; faced with this, he resorted to 'every kind of robbery' (*Dom.* 12). It is, admittedly, likely that his task, in the case of the Jewish tax, was made easier by the fact that an unpopular minority was targeted; the same applies to the original imposition of the tax.

There seems to be no good reason to think that, as Goodman suggests, the tax was abolished by Nerva and reimposed by Trajan. It seems more likely that the phrase *fisci Iudaici calumnia sublata*,[42] inscribed on a coin issued under Nerva, refers not to an abolition of the tax but to putting an end to harsh investigations of people suspected (often unjustly, hence *calumnia*) of evading it. This was presumably more worth taking credit for, before the general public, than any measure of relief benefiting the Jews;[43] all the more so if one assumes that Jews had been relentlessly demonized as dangerous enemies of Rome, but also on general grounds.

---

[40] Goodman 2007: 466–7. On the Flavian IUDAEA CAPTA coins, see Cody 2003: 105–13. See also Lopez (in print). Lopez argues that the IUDAEA CAPTA coins, and various other aspects of Flavian policy that he examines (including the Jewish tax, the celebration of the victory, the treatment of the Temple and the general policy in Judaea following the rebellion), denoted no special hostility to Jews.

[41] Cf. Overman 2002: 218: 'Domitian's own attitude toward the Jews appears to have developed a sharper edge than existed during the reign of his father or brother'. A 'sharper edge' characterized Domitian's reign on more than one issue.

[42] *BMCRE* 3. 15 no. 88, 17 no. 98, 19 nos. 105–6. The testimony of Dio 68.1.2 according to which Nerva did not permit 'to accuse anybody of *asebeia* or of a Jewish way of life' is often cited in this context, on the assumption that Nerva's liberalization benefitted people of non-Jewish origin, and could thus be expected to be popular with the wider public.

[43] Cf. Cotton and Eck 2005: 45–6.

If one assumes that Trajan did reimpose the tax, it seems very unlikely that his main reason for this would have been, as Goodman suggests, that his father had been a legionary commander in Judaea. The main reason would have been, presumably, that Trajan had grand plans of his own and needed a lot of money. Reimposing a tax abolished by Trajan's deified adoptive father (bringing back the *calumnia* he had taken pride in abolishing) would have been a drastic step. In the absence of positive evidence that it was taken, it is safer to assume that it never was than to postulate an abolition (on the strength of an inconclusive piece of evidence)[44] and a subsequent unattested reimposition. But assuming that it was taken because Trajan was pursuing a vendetta against Jews inherited from his father is even more difficult than attributing it to pressing fiscal necessity.

Coming back to Vespasian, my colleague Gil Gambash has suggested to me that the Romans may have viewed the tax as a war indemnity of sorts, since the money collected from abroad must have been used to finance the rebellion. Of course, this was not an indemnity in any precise sense, for there was no claim that Jews in the Diaspora were guilty of anything. But Josephus makes Titus tell the Jews in Jerusalem, while enumerating the advantages of Roman rule (in order to stress the Jewish ungratefulness):

> And, as our greatest [favour], we permitted you to exact tribute to God and to collect offerings, without admonishing or hindering those who brought them – only that you might grow richer at our expense and prepare with our money to attack us! And then ... you turned your superabundance against the donors, and like untameable serpents spat your venom upon those who caressed you. (*BJ* 6.335–6)[45]

The claim that the money was a Roman 'donation' is, naturally, a rhetorical exaggeration; but from the Roman viewpoint, allowing it to be collected throughout the empire and sent to Jerusalem appears to have been a special privilege, not something merely technical or to be taken for granted. We know already from Cicero's *Pro Flacco* (28.67–9) that some took strong exception to it. From this viewpoint (coloured, no doubt, by the pressing need for money) it might have seemed reasonable that if Roman kindness had been abused in this way, Rome would help itself to this money from now on, even if the Diaspora contributors were not guilty of anything.

---

[44] This is acknowledged by Goodman in Goodman 2005: 176: 'the precise import of the legend ... is debated and debatable'.

[45] Cf. Tac. *Hist.* 5.8.1; 5.5.1 on the *immensa opulentia* of the Temple in Jerusalem and massive foreign contributions to it (referring to converts), mentioned with resentment.

3   The Temple in Jerusalem: Different Perspectives

It has been pointed out that the imposition of the Jewish tax implied a decision that the Temple in Jerusalem would not be rebuilt – or at least that it would not be allowed to enjoy its former status;[46] clearly, the tax created a strong financial disincentive for any such restoration. But the main thing about the Temple, from the Roman viewpoint, was, surely, that it had served as a military fortress during the rebellion, and in many ways as its epicentre;[47] that it had to be taken by storm; that its treasures must have financed the rebellion; and that, if rebuilt, it would again draw huge numbers of Jewish pilgrims into Jerusalem during especially sensitive periods. If considered by Roman authorities at all, the idea of rebuilding it must have seemed risky and unattractive.

Beyond direct considerations of public order, Romans were probably aware that Jewish rebels were influenced by 'hopes and memories which centred upon the Temple' which they viewed as 'God's House, that is, the palace of a supreme Jewish monarch who in no way could be considered a vassal to Rome'.[48] At this point, admittedly, the distinction between religion and politics becomes blurred. But even if the Flavians can be described as acting, in this matter, with the aim of neutralizing a certain aspect of the Jewish religion that had proved politically dangerous, it is still an exaggeration to say that they waged (or postured as waging) a war against Judaism. It was well known that the religious practices of the Jews were by no means confined to the Temple cult.[49]

---

[46] Rives 2005: 152–3.

[47] 'The Jewish Temple and its priests were inseparable from the revolt from the very onset of hostilities' – Gambash 2013: 186; cf. ibid. 184–7 on the destruction of the Temple as part of taking the city and the Temple by storm, compared with usual Roman practice. Josephus' claims that Titus tried to spare the Temple (*BJ* 6.241; 254–66) have been disbelieved by many. They do not prove that this was what actually happened, or the Flavian 'official version' of the events (cf. Barnes 2005: 144; Rives 2005: 145–50), although Josephus claims that Titus 'personally put his own stamp on my volumes and bade me publish them' – *Vit.* 363). They do, however, sit oddly with any claim that the Flavians waged an open war on Judaism and based their legitimacy on it; cf. note 56 and text.

[48] Schwartz 2005: 66.

[49] Cf. Rives 2005, contrasting the permanent suppression of the Temple cult with Vespasian's toleration of other aspects of 'what we would identify as Jewish religion' (165). Rives suggests that beyond considerations of public order and forestalling rebellion, the Temple cult had, in Vespasian's eyes, proven dangerous because it had made Diaspora Jewry 'to some extent a shadow *civitas*', identifying primarily with Jerusalem and its cult rather than with the city where they lived and with Rome (163). If Vespasian thought that suppressing the Temple cult would remove an obstacle to 'the integration of Jews into the empire', the Jewish tax had, naturally, the opposite effect, as Rives notes (165). It is probably safer to assume that more mundane considerations of money, public order and security were dominant.

According to Goodman,[50] there were less hurtful ways of coping with the threat of unrest posed by the Jewish Temple: 'It would be understandable if the Romans took greater care than they had before 66 to prevent the crowds at the great pilgrim festivals in Jerusalem getting out of hand, but that precaution would hardly require the Temple site to be left altogether in ruins. Treatment so harsh and unusual must have another explanation.'

But should it surprise us that Roman attitudes and policies on such matters did not correspond to modern notions of proportionality? And, moreover, how unusual and exceptional was Rome's conduct in this case? This, obviously, is a crucial element of Goodman's thesis:

> In the context of normal practice in the Roman Empire, the Jews' hopes [to see the Temple rebuilt] should not have been idle. Temples burned down through accident quite frequently in the ancient world. Romans took for granted that the obvious response was to rebuild. The great temple of Jupiter Capitolinus in Rome was burned down during the civil strife between Vespasian's supporters and those of Vitellius in 69; ... the first step towards the temple's restoration, took place on 21 June 70. But the Roman state was not to allow the Jerusalem Temple to be rebuilt in the same way, a refusal which may reasonably be seen as a major cause of the sixty-five years of conflict to come. It is worthwhile to emphasise the enormity of this refusal in the context of ancient religious practice, and the extent to which it revealed a special prejudice against the Jews.[51]

But one would have wished to find a closer parallel than Rome's decision to rebuild the temple of Jupiter on the Capitolium. How many examples do we have, in Roman history, and specifically in the decades preceding the Judaean rebellion, of a major enemy city taken by storm after a prolonged siege and sacked, and a major temple therein destroyed after it, too, had to be taken by storm, and then restored, within a short period of time, with Rome's permission? I cannot think of such an example.

All this does not mean that animosity to Jews – out of ethnic and religious prejudice, sheer vindictiveness, or the propagandistic needs of the regime – played no part in Roman policies towards Jews and Judaea under Vespasian and his successors. But there is no reason to assume that Roman policy was driven primarily by such feelings, or the political need to demonstrate them, rather than by conventional imperial policy considerations. These were indeed harsh, but not necessarily unusual.

---

[50] Goodman 2007: 464.   [51] Goodman 2007: 449.

This paper deals with the Roman perspective, not the Jewish one, but I would like to round it up with two observations on the latter. Firstly, what for the Roman state was perfectly rational imperial policy may well have been regarded by many Jews in the light suggested by Goodman. The Jewish tax was oppressive and offensive. If indeed it was earmarked for the temple of Jupiter, it must have been widely regarded by Jews as a religious insult.

In other respects, it should be stressed, Vespasian's policy towards Jewish religion was tolerant. It is surely an overstatement to say, that '[Vespasian and] Titus set about depicting the religion of the Jews as not worthy to exist'.[52] Nothing was done against Jewish religious observance in matters unconnected with the Temple. As Goodman notes, 'The only special and different aspect of Roman attitudes to Judaism compared to other provincial religions was the destruction of the Jerusalem Temple'.[53] The continued existence of Jews practicing their religion, freely and under state protection, throughout the empire, was conspicuous and well known enough to make any posture of treating Judaism as 'unworthy to exist', on the regime's part, quite meaningless. The Flavian patronage extended to Josephus and his writings, though its scope and Josephus' standing in Flavian Rome are debated,[54] seems hardly compatible with any consistent official posture of implacable hostility to Jews and Judaism. For all his Roman and Flavian loyalism, Josephus, in all his writings, is certainly a proud Jew.[55] 'His entire literary output was predicated on the indestruct-

---

[52] Goodman 2007: 439.

[53] Goodman 2007: 459. The closing of the Jewish temple in Leontopolis in Egypt was, like the Temple itself, an affair of local significance. It was provoked by the attempt of a group of *sicarii* who had escaped from Judaea to stir up trouble among the Jews in Alexandria; some of them had escaped 'into Egypt and the Egyptian Thebes' (Joseph. *BJ* 417). On receiving the report, Vespasian, 'suspicious of the interminable tendency of the Jews to revolution, and that they might again collect together in force and draw others away with them', ordered the Temple closed. The Roman reaction was certainly heavy-handed, and demonstrates Vespasian's unwillingness 'to take ... chances in allowing the revived Jewish temple cult' (anywhere) – Rives 2005: 154. But it was not an act of 'war on Judaism' in general.

[54] See, e.g., Cotton and Eck 2005 for a minimalistic view; contra, Bowersock 2005. Josephus' history of the war has often been described as 'Flavian propaganda' (see Barnes 2005: 142 with references; cf. Beard 2003: 556), though this may well be exaggerated; see next note.

[55] According to Goodman 2005: 172–3, 'Josephus' brave defence of his people's history and customs in the *Antiquitates* ... was produced in direct contradiction to the anti-Jewish ethos of the Flavian regime, but he also attests quite clearly the exceptional favour showered upon him by all three Flavian emperors (*Vit.* 425, 428–9)'. But Josephus would hardly be brave enough to write in direct contradiction to the ethos of the regime (as opposed to societal prejudice) on a matter that was, supposedly, of crucial importance to its very legitimacy, nor is it likely that Domitian's favours would have been showered upon someone as brave as this. Josephus' role as

ible value of Judaism'.[56] A comparison such as with 'the plight of the Jews in the early years of the Third Reich'[57] is out of place: there could have been no Flavius Josephus there.

For all that, Goodman may well be right to argue that in the first decades after the destruction of the Temple, the kind of post-Temple Judaism that was destined to develop was yet to emerge. Many must have hoped for a speedy restoration of the Temple, and were bitterly disappointed when this did not happen. Moreover, the very significance of the fact that the Temple was destroyed and lay in ruins, was, whatever the Romans' motives, much graver for the Jews than the case of a single sanctuary – one of many – being destroyed, and left unrestored, for other peoples of the empire.

On the other hand, it is worth noting that Vespasian is treated in the Jewish tradition with surprising leniency for someone who allegedly launched a war on Judaism and treated it as 'not worthy to exist'. Titus, the destroyer of the Temple, is naturally demonized, and so would be Hadrian. The non-demonization of Vespasian is surprising enough for someone who was, at any rate, an enemy, and that in a war that ended in the destruction of Jerusalem and the Temple. On the assumption that he then also, beyond imposing an oppressive tax in the aftermath of the suppression of the rebellion, waged what was perceived as a systematic war on Judaism, this non-demonization becomes very difficult to explain. Jewish tradition generally does not suffer from amnesia in such cases.

a 'prophet' of Vespasian's rise (Goodman 2005: 173) helps explain his special status but would hardly have allowed him to challenge the regime's 'ethos'.

[56] Rajak 2005: 83.

[57] Goodman 2005: 172. He notes that hostility, in the case of the Flavians, was not strictly racial and could be avoided by apostasy, citing the case of Tiberius Iulius Alexander.

12 | Between *ethnos* and *populus*

The Boundaries of Being a Jew

YOUVAL ROTMAN

In *Ethnic Groups and Boundaries* (1969), the Norwegian anthropologist Fredrik Barth has argued that it is impossible to find definite criteria for ethnicity and that ethnicity is rather the result of labelling.[1] Boundaries between so-called "ethnic groups" are created either by the group itself, or by others. So it may be that at one time the boundary marker is language, the other time it is religion, a third time it is a common history. Barth's perspective was adopted by scholars who were looking for ways to address the question of what forms a "collective identity." Barth suggested, however, that collective identities do not really exist but are fictions. In fact, we can moreover argue that the term identity itself, loaded with psychological significance, cannot so easily be translated from the psychological-individual sphere to the social-collective sphere.[2] Nonetheless both terms, ethnicity and collective identity, are used in all aspects of human life and serve as means to achieve real and often political objectives. Collective identities as demarcations between peoples, whether we define them as reality or fiction, are referred to for a reason.[3]

In what follows we shall examine what criteria can be adopted as defining features of a collective entity. We shall take here as a case study the very large definition of Jews in the Greco-Roman world and will focus on the ways in which certain Jews portrayed themselves to themselves as a collective group.[4] Having a single term to designate themselves, *Bney Israel* ("the sons of Israel"), they had to do without terms such as *ethnos*, *genos*, *laos*, *dēmos*, *populus*, *natio*, *polis*, and *civitas* when referring to themselves as an entity. The question is what kind of collective entity they were referring to, and whether their definition was kept unchanged.

To examine this question, this chapter proposes to focus on the border-line between what constituted a Jew and a Gentile by analyzing the way in which Jews included newcomers in their collectivity and excluded others. My main thesis will be that Jews referred to themselves as an entity by employing prisms to define political entities available to them in Greco-Roman antiquity. We shall use here the English term "the Jews" as

---

[1] Barth 1969.   [2] Erikson 1968.   [3] See for this Isaac 2004.   [4] See Jonker 2010.

a translation of the Hebrew *haYehudim* and of the Greek *hoi Ioudaioi*. The use of the English translation and its meaning, and the question of whether the translation should be Jews or Judaeans have been the center of a historiographical debate related to the modern definition of Judaism in antiquity.[5] Daniel Schwartz, for example, has addressed it and criticized the translation of *hoi Ioudaoi* as Judaeans instead of Jews affirming the religious aspect of the Greek term. This was recently challenged by Daniel Boyarin, who wished to dismiss the very notion of Judaism as a religion in antiquity.[6] Premodern Judaism, according to him, has very little to do with what we term today as religion.[7] In what follows we shall attempt to address the same question of ancient Jewish ethnicity by analyzing the use and meaning of the terms *haYehudim*, *hoi Ioudaioi*, and *Iudaei* to designate an entity. The question is what kind of entity these terms refer to. We shall employ here the English term "Jews" as a convenience without addressing directly the historiographical debate concerning Jews and Judaeans. In fact, this debate will be indirectly resolved by replacing the idea of a single meaning with that of an area of meanings, changeable in view of the political culture that those referring to themselves as Jews were exposed to. Our investigation begins with Classical times, albeit not with Greece itself but with the repercussions that its political culture had in Judaea under Persian rule.[8]

Methods of Political Exclusion in Achaemenid Judaea

In a paper dedicated to naming names, Benjamin Isaac has shown the dynamic use of what we term as ethnic for geographic and administrative concepts in Roman times.[9] He also revealed how this was used the other way around, namely how geographic concepts came to designate what we would term ethnicity.[10] We find this very process in the book of Ezra, which constructs the historical memory of the exiled Jews who returned to the land of Zion. They refer to themselves as both *Shavey Zion* (literally "the Returned to Zion") and *Yehudim*.

---

[5] And to a certain extent also to the definition of Judaism nowadays: Schwartz 2007: 3–27; Mason 2000: xi–xii; Schiffman 1985; Harvey 1996; Cohen 1999.

[6] Boyarin 2018.

[7] See Moore 2015, who proposes a much more sociological solution, taking as a case study the relation between Judaism and Hellenism and closely following Barth's analysis. See *infra*.

[8] A preliminary note: following Barth and Erikson (*supra* nn. 1–2) I refrain from using the terms "ethnicity" and "collective identity." In fact, my main objective here is to reveal the function of the construction of such concepts in the period under examination.

[9] Isaac 2013.   [10] Cf. La'da 2002, discussed later.

A lot has been written about the organization of *Yehud Medinata*, the Persian province of Judaea.[11] We can apply here Isaac's observation about a geographic name being used to create a group separated from all other descendants of the First Temple period. At its basis we find a political objective: defining the collectivity of *haYehudim* as a political entity. This term is never used here to refer either to the biblical Judah or to the land of Judaea, but it serves as a demarcation between the population that returned from the Babylonian exile to the land of Zion, and the local inhabitants of the land.[12] This demarcation is achieved for a reason: exclusion of the first from the second. The means are historical exclusivity, cultural exclusivity, and social exclusivity. These are recurrent themes in Ezra-Nehemiah. Historical exclusivity is achieved by a detailed documentation of the families who constitute the closed group of the Returned to Zion (Ezra 2, 8, 10:18–44, Nehemiah 7, 12), and by ignoring any reference that would connect them to those Israelites who were not exiled.[13] Their self-nomination as *haYehudim* serves here to make *haYehudim* a synonym to "the Returned Exiled" (i.e., a group separated from the Israelites who were not exiled or were exiled but did not return to Zion). The history of this group starts therefore from the moment of "the Return."

The cultural exclusivity of the group is achieved by the creation of an exclusive cult around the new temple in Jerusalem. The Returned refuse to allow the local peoples to share with them its financing and construction despite the eagerness of the second to participate in the enterprise (Ezra 4). This establishes a new cult to the God of the Returned. Finally, social exclusivity is achieved by a repeated prohibition on mixed marriage with women of local origin (i.e., women not from the group of *haYehudim* – the Returned; Ezra 9–10, Nehemiah 9, 13).[14] Genealogical enlisting of all the families who can prove their exile-return lineage (Ezra 2, 8, 10:18–44, Nehemiah 7, 12) enabled them to realize and control their designation as a distinct group. But what was the purpose of this exclusion?

Michael Heltzer compared the restrictions on mixed marriage defined by the Returned in Ezra-Nehemiah to the Athenian law of citizenship.[15] Fifth-century Judaea had very little to do with a Greek polis. Yet we would like to consider here the way in which the returning families designated themselves collectively as a means to construct a sense of a political entity akin to the way in which it was constructed in Greece in their time. In fact

---

[11] See more recently Lipschits et al. 2011; Heltzer 2008; Ro 2012.   [12] See Kalimi 2012.
[13] But see Nehemiah 8:14–18, 9:1–2, where the term *Bney Israel* is employed as synonym to "The Returned" (*haShavim*), thus rhetorically blurring the distinction between the two designations.
[14] See Dor 2011: 173–88; 2006; Olyabm 2004: 1–16.   [15] Heltzer 1990: 83–91.

"the Judaeans"/"the Jews" – *haYehudim* – can indeed serve here as the equivalent to *hoi Athenaioi*, *hoi Lakedaimonioi*, or *hoi Kares* (the latter being also under Persian rule). Through these denominations these people living in one place referred to themselves not as a group with a common origin but as a political group disassociated from all other descendants of a common origin. In the same way the term *haYehudim*, with the definite article, enabled the exiled who returned to the land of Zion to designate themselves politically. It reflected the same difference that the Greeks made between political and ethnic grouping, between "the Athenians" and "the Greeks." By referring to themselves as *haYehudim* they were able to completely ignore any common historical origin that they might have shared with others in favor of a political denomination that started from the moment of their Achaemenid return. In other words, and if we continue with the Greek parallelism, *haYehudim* was used in contrast to *Bney Israel* just as *hoi Athenaioi* was used in contrast to *hoi Hellenes*.[16]

Although we find the term *Yehudi* used in other documents of the Babylonian and Egyptian diasporas, it does not serve there as a collective denomination in the Ezra-Nehemiah form of *haYehudim*.[17] The epistles of the Jews from Elephantine to Jerusalem for example, concerning their relation with Jerusalem, reveal a demand to link their temple to the temple in Jerusalem in a manner similar to the way in which a Greek colony is attached in its cults to its metropolis.[18] However, this did not imply that they were in any way included in the political culture that developed in Judaea. In fact their unanswered appeals to Jerusalem to get help to rebuild their temple imply a deliberate ignorance on the part of Jerusalem.[19] *haYehudim* or *'am haYehudim* (literally "the people of the Judaeans/Jews") with its distinctive civic institutions such as the elders (Ezra 9:1, 10:8, Nehemiah 8:13), a general assembly (Ezra 3:1, 10:7, Nehemiah 4:8, 5:13, 8–9), a council and ministers (Ezra 4:3, 9:1, 10:5, 10:8, Nehemiah 2:16, 4:8, 5:7, 7:2, 11) and a head who is the juridical, economic and military authority (Ezra 7–9, Nehemiah 3–7, 10) evokes immediately a political entity that is constructed in contrast to any possible ethnic concept of a bygone Israelite past.[20] The same political objective determined the *realpolitik* of the Hasmoneans.

---

[16] This, however, is not definitive, as we would expect (for the exception, see supra, n. 13).

[17] Pearce and Wunsch 2014; Zadok 2002, 1988; Vukosavovic 2015; Porten and Yardeni 1986; Porten and Farber 2011.

[18] TAD A4.7, A4.8, A4.9, A4.10 Cowley 30–3 (Sachau Plates 1–4) (Porten 1986: B19-22) from 407 BCE.

[19] TAD A4.7 Cowley 30, verso l. 18 (Porten 1986: B19, p. 142).

[20] To this end even the adversaries in Ezra-Nehemiah may well be fictitious: Grätz 2013: 73–87.

The Hasmonean *Politeia* – Methods of Political Inclusion

In his book *The Beginnings of Jewishness: Boundaries, Varieties, Uncertainties* (1999) Shaye Cohen has presented a daring thesis regarding the definition of Judaism in Hasmonean time. According to his reading, Judaism acquired a new meaning as a religion to accommodate the Hasmonean policy, which separated the term from its previous ethnic meaning: to be Judaean. Cohen based his thesis on the definition of the religious process of conversion through which one can become a Jew: proselytism – *giyur*, and argued that this was used as a policy by the Hasmoneans in order to construct a new sense of collectivity for a new state.[21]

According to Cohen, "a Jew" has become whoever worships the God whose temple is in Jerusalem: a religious and mutable definition. Cohen sees this conversion through circumcision as a process of "Judaization." This was used as a strategy by the Hasmoneans, especially by John Hyrcanus and Judah Aristobulus in regard to the Idumeans and the Itureans.[22] "Judaization" has here a political meaning – to ally with the Hasmonean government.[23] Borrowing Polybius' description of the Achaean League, Cohen names the Hasmonean state "the Judaean League."[24] This complies much more to the mutability of a religious conversion than any ethnic definition of Judaism that preceded it. In his words a religious definition of Judaism replaced the ethnical definition as a means to construct an independent *politeia*. This thesis is based on a rigid separation between religion and ethnicity according to modern terminology, applied here to ancient sources. In a recent study on Jewish ethnicity in Hellenistic Egypt, Stewart Moore (2015), following Barth's threads of analysis, has proposed to consider religious attributes as boundary markers needed to construct a notion of ethnicity. His thesis invites us to consider the elasticity of ethnicity in Hellenistic politics, which was the subject of recent research.

In their studies about the way in which ethnic denomination functioned in Ptolemaic Egypt, Dorothy Thompson and Sylvie Honigman have shown that the so-called ethnic labels denoted juridical and fiscal statuses.[25] They revealed how a person's ethnic identity, in the words of Thompson, may

---

[21] Cohen 1999.   [22] Joseph. *AJ*, 13.254–8, 319. Cf. Strabo *Ge.*, 16.2.34.
[23] Cohen 1999, pp. 110–19.   [24] Cohen 1999, ch. 4, in particular pp. 127–9.
[25] Thompson 2001: 301–22; 1984: vol. 3, 1069–75. Honigman 2003: 61–102; 2002: 251–66. See also La'da 2002.

vary in different contexts.[26] *Hellenes*, for example, was a fiscal and a juridical status that could be applied to individuals and groups of various *ethnic* affiliation, like *Ioudaioi*. The term "Macedonians," on the other hand, designated a certain category of soldiers.[27] These denominative attributes were part of a social and political organization of the Ptolemaic state and provided a criterion to distinguish between its elite and any other population, in contrast to religion and culture. If religious cult may have offered a way of consolidation, military and juridical statuses provided a way to categorize society into groups of distinct civic statuses, under the jurisdiction of their particular archons.[28] But what do we mean by "civic status"?[29]

We are maybe too inclined to think in terms of Greek citizenship bestowed on members of *poleis* who were granted distinguished status. We should at the same time consider those who did not benefit from an equal status as also having a civic status, a *politeia*, different from the first and less privileged, but a status nonetheless. The analysis of the use in ethnic denominations in Hellenistic times reveals an array of statuses. It does not follow that these groups were separated by distinct laws. In fact, the Ptolemaic documents suggest that it was not the *nomos* itself that was necessarily different but the fact that it was used and controlled by different magistrates appointed for different groups. In other words, the main issue was not really the particular *politeia* of each group but the division into groups.

Benjamin Isaac has shown that categorization, especially in regard to origins, does not occur without a reason.[30] Indeed, the Ptolemaic categorization into "Macedonians," "Jews," "Egyptians," "Boeotians," "Idumeans," "Persians" and so on established a social stratification.[31] The fact that soldiers could move from one group to another according to not only

---

[26] Thompson 2001: 304.

[27] See Joseph. *AJ* 12.8, who affirms the civic equality (*isopolitai*) of the Jews and the Macedonians in Alexandria. See Honigman's (Honigman 2003) explanation about the origin of the Jewish *politeuma* in Alexandria in relation to this description. For the definition of the *politeuma* as a community of soldiers with a particular ethnic labeling and a particular juridical status controlled by particular archons or *politarches*, see previous note and Zuckerman 1985–8: 171–85.

[28] Honigman 2003: 62–4, 73; Coloru 2013: 37–56 (45–6). See all the same Mairs 2008: 19–43. What she terms "civic identity" is constructed from particular cultural identifiers. And see Moore 2015, who shows that religion had a major role to play as a marker of ethnic boundary in Egypt between Greeks, Jews and Egyptians.

[29] Cf. "civic identity," which Mairs 2008 uses in reference to the way in which Hellenic settlers in Bactria and Arachosia depicted their "Greekness."

[30] Particularly in Isaac 2004.

[31] Which was supported by an ideological system of separation (*supra* n. 28).

their origin but also their occupation (i.e., their status) created a civic status out of *ethnos*.[32] In regard to Hellenistic Syria too, recent studies by Omar Coloru, Laurent Capdetrey and Nathanael Andrade show the different ways in which ethnicity was used by the Seleucids in their social organization.[33] The separation into Macedonians, Carians, Syrians, Jews and Babylonians followed the same logic. It was not "us" and "them" (i.e., "Greeks" vs. "Syrians," or "Greeks" vs. "Egyptians," or "Greeks" vs. "Jews," or "Jews" vs. "Egyptians"), but an array of civil statuses realized through juridical distinction, military position or fiscal state.[34] The case of the Sidonians of Yavneh-Yam who applied to get a hereditary fiscal status from Antiochus V Eupater based on their military contribution in the time of Antiochus III exemplified it very well.[35] They asked for a distinct privileged fiscal status. In this way the Hellenistic ethnical array not only provided a sociopolitical structure but also allowed elasticity. We see this, for instance, in cases where persons move between these groups by acquiring a new ethnic name, thus acquiring a new civic status.[36] The same is also evident from juridical cases that were tried outside the court of their respective group.[37] This shows that ethnicity itself became elastic through its significance as a civic status.[38] The creation of the position of *ethnarch* as a juridical and fiscal magistrate, whose origin is still debatable, follows the same logic.[39]

In relation to the Jews of Egypt, Josephus cites Strabo in describing the great esteem in which Jews were held under Cleopatra III, who entrusted her armies to her generals Chelkias and Ananias, sons of Onias. Although "the majority of the Jews immediately went over to Ptolemy (Lathyrus, her son), only the Jews of the district named for Onias remained faithful to her because their fellow-*politai* (*hoi politai autōn*) Chelkias and Ananias were held in special favor by the queen."[40] What Strabo says has to do with the military organization of Ptolemaic Egypt, where different groups were

---

[32] Indeed, even "ethnicity by descent" (*epi epigonēs*) determined a status: Vandorpe 2008: 87–108.

[33] Coloru 2013; Capdetrey 2007: 91–111, 389–92; Andrade 2013: pt. I; in reference to the Iranians and the integration of some into the elite, see Briant 1985: 166–95 (173).

[34] This, however, does not dismiss religious identifiers as markers of such groups. Such was, for example, the observance of the Shabbat as a marker of the boundary between Jews and Egyptians, and the *horkos patrios*, the "ancestral oath," of the Jews as attested in the papyri of the Jewish *politeuma*: Moore 2015: 91–6.

[35] Isaac 1991: 132–44.   [36] Honigman 2003; Thompson 2001; Coloru 2013.

[37] Honigman 2003.   [38] Cf. the Greek–Syrian dynamics under the Romans: Andrade 2013.

[39] See *ethnarchēs* as the head of the soldiers' *politeuma* in Strabo *FGrHist* II, A91 F7 (Joseph. *AJ* 14.117), analyzed by Honigman 2003: 72–6. For the use of this position in Seleucid Syria: Wagner and Petzl 1976: 201–23. Cf. Sharon 2010: 472–93, discussed *infra*.

[40] Joseph. *AJ* 13.287. Hongiman (2003: 83–4) has emphasized this phrasing and connected it to the *politeumata* of the Jews.

defined using their so-called ethnic origin.[41] However, *ethnos* proved to be an identifier of status rather than the other way around. To put it differently, ethnicity seemed a means to construct civic statuses.[42] The main collective identity was civic and controlled by the Hellenistic state. The use of the denomination "Greeks" – *Hellenes* – and the naming of Greek names are extremely revealing, as Thompson and Clarysse have shown in relation to the Ptolemaic organization of Egypt.[43] Attributing a Hellenic status changed the fiscal and consequently the civic status.[44] If being a Greek became in that period a status, what about being a Jew? If a Persian, an Idumean or a Jew could become *Hellenēs* according to his position, can a Greek become a Jew by status? We have no evidence for that in the Egyptian sources, unless we turn to Hasmonean Judaea.[45]

Regarding the Hasmonean kingdom, we can maybe change the perspective of religion versus ethnos, so fixed in our mind. In view of the "elasticity of ethnicity" in the Hellenistic world, especially in relation to the status of Hellenes, we can consider the Hasmonean integration of the Idumeans and the Itureans not as a conversion to the Jewish faith, or simply as citizenship as Cohen would have it, but as their promotion to the ethnicity and civic status of Jews, their integration into the Hasmonean Jewish *politeia* depended on them becoming Jews. In a word, the elasticity of being a Jew under the Hasmoneans corresponded perfectly with the elasticity of being Greek in the Ptolemaic and the Seleucid kingdoms in the second century BCE.[46] Josephus emphasizes two things required from the Idumeans and Itureans: to live according to the laws of the Jews and circumcision.[47] Note that the worship of the one God and the temple in Jerusalem are not mentioned here. To live according to the laws of the Jews meant the laws

---

[41] Josephus employs fellow-*politai* (*hoi politai autōn*) in the same manner as he refers to the Jews and the Macedonians in Alexandria as *isopolitai* (Joseph. *AJ* 12.8). Cf. the colony of the Jews in Achaemenid Elephantine.

[42] See in particular the three distinct ways the Seleucids used ethnicity as explained by Capdetrey 2007: 91–111. He does not go so far as to recognize that *ethnos* itself has become a flexible term, but reveals nonetheless its necessity and functionality for the social organization of the kingdom.

[43] Thompson 2001; Clarysse and Thompson 2006: vol. 2, pp. 318–41.

[44] "When taxpayers are counted by occupation, persons with Greek and Egyptian names are listed separately with few exceptions: Hellenic status automatically eliminated an individual from registration under a 'real' occupation," *ibid.*, vol. 2, p. 319, and *ibid.*, vol. 2, pp. 39–52, 125, 205.

[45] For *Joseph and Aseneth*, a much later source, see *infra* n. 70. In any case a woman's ethnic identity was determined by her father or husband (Moore 2015: 87–8).

[46] Most of the evidence for the flexibility of ethnicity comes from that century: Clarysse and Thompson 2006.

[47] Joseph. *AJ*, 13.254–8, 319. For circumcision see *infra*. Grojnowski 2014: 165–83. See Shatzman 2005: 213–41; Rappaport 2009: 59–74.

of the Hasmonean state just as much as the Jewish ancestral law. It meant to be subject to the Hasmonean juridical system (i.e., to the Jewish juridical courts), with the result of "being Jews from that time on."[48]

Indeed, the Hasmoneans apply this policy of inclusion not only in regard to the Idumeans and Itureans. In his description of Alexander Jannaeus' conquests in Transjordan, Josephus narrates the incorporation of a list of cities, amongst which was the city of Pella. Pella was destroyed because its inhabitants refused to adhere to the ancestral customs of the Jews.[49] The authenticity of this description and the question why in this case Josephus did not mention circumcision were studied in depth by Daniel Schwartz.[50] Revealing the entire philological and historical background of Josephus' description and comparing it with the descriptions of the Idumeans and Itureans and the attitude toward circumcision of Gentiles in Qumranic texts, he concluded that Jannaeus did not apply circumcision in this case because of his adherence to the Sadducee attitude not to accept any form of integration of Gentiles by conversion. Schwartz brings Qumranic texts against circumcision of Gentiles and regards their conversion to Judaism in the same way Cohen does. However, conversion is not attested as a Halachic process for this period.[51] In fact, if we leave aside the definition of circumcision as conversion, we can consider it as a marker of integration into the Jewish *politeia*, not as citizenship but as receiving the status of Jews. Nonetheless, circumcision aimed to turn it into a permanent status. In all these cases the essential was adhering to the Jewish laws and judges, in a word, having the civic status of being a Jew meant to be a Jew. But why did the inhabitants of Pella refuse to become Jews if it simply meant having the status of Jews? In contrast to the Idumean and the Iturean cities, Pella was a Greek city.[52] Becoming Jews meant for them to stop being Greeks (i.e., stop having the civil Hellenistic status of Greeks). In Seleucid eyes, however, being *Hellenes* meant a higher civic status than being Jews. According to the Hasmonean perspective, incorporating Pella's inhabitants into their state as Jews was a civic promotion. In the Seleucid perspective, it meant demotion.

If being a Jew under the Hasmoneans was equivalent to being Greek under the Seleucids,[53] we can reflect in a new way on 2 Maccabees and the

---

[48] Joseph. *AJ* 13.258. That this was followed by their participation in Jewish rites is only logical (in contrast to both the Samaritans and the Qumranics, for example). Cf. the cultural integration into the Hellenistic elite in Bactria and Arachosia: Mairs 2008.

[49] Joseph. *AJ* 13.397.　　[50] Schwartz 2011: 339–59.　　[51] *Infra.*　　[52] Cohen 2006: 265–8.

[53] Although Cohen's argument is that being a Jew in the Hasmonean period was constructed in reference of being Greek. However, he sees this first and foremost as a cultural construct and not as a civic/juridical/fiscal status.

distinction that it establishes between the neologisms *ioudaismos* and *hellenismos*. Honigman has recently argued that these refer to two different political cultures and two different types of social organization, in sum to two distinct types of *politeia*, two distinct civil statuses. Jason's reforms aimed to politicize Jerusalem according to the Seleucid political culture with a Seleucid blessing.[54] And this meant enlisting Jews as Antiocheans (2 Mac. 4:9), or rather establishing a group of persons elevated to the status of Antiocheans, as an independent Seleucid *politeia* in Jerusalem. In Hellenistic terms this meant bestowing on them the highest civic status, as was done, for instance, in different cities in the kingdom.[55] But this also meant separating the Jews of Jerusalem through a distinct civic status from their fellow-*politai*, and the exclusion of many Jews, especially those living outside the city, who refused to accept being demoted. For the second it meant abiding to a new political culture in which their civic status would be inferior to a group of their co-patriots of the same civic rights, who now acquired new privileges at their expense.

The Hasmonean revolt came as a response to civic reforms that threatened to change the common civic status of the Jews who lived in Seleucid Judaea. Naturally being Greek meant adhering to Greek cultural and religious marks. The Hasmoneans, in contrast, used this situation to build their own *politeia* by considering as Jews whomever they wished to include in their *politeia*. The integration of the Idumeans and the Itureans meant strengthening the Hasmonean elite by joining them in. In times of internal strife, this was indeed much needed. In other words, the Hasmonean internal policy toward the Idumeans resembles very much the Seleucid policy in regard to the Jews of Jerusalem under Antiochus IV Epiphanes. In contrast to the Samaritans and the Greeks who were left outside the Hasmonean *politeia*, the Idumeans became proselytes who dwelled with the Jews, benefiting from the same civic status (i.e., Jews as the Hasmoneans defined them). Their so called "conversion," (i.e., their circumcision) meant *de facto* exactly what Josephus tells us: being Jews according to the *nomoi* of the Jews in the Hasmonean formula. We should consider circumcision not as a conversion ritual but as a marker of the *politeia* of the ruling class.[56] This process of inclusion opened the way to

---

[54] Honigman 2014.

[55] This was the case with the cities of Tyriaion in Phrygia, Alabanda in Caria ("the Antioch of the *ethnos* of the Chrysaorians") and Hanisa in Cappadocia: Capdetrey 2007: 104–5; Andrade 2013: 43ff.; Michels 2013: 283–307; Kirsch 2015: 24ff.

[56] Cf. the trepanation adopted as a marker of the social elite in Hellenistic Armenia of the same period: Khudaverdyan, 2011: 39–55.

power to Antipas' family. Whether they were considered Jews or not was a question that was debated in antiquity. But it was debated in a later period, when rabbinic conversion did exist.[57] In this way proselytism was not a religious conversion but exactly what the Greek word *prosēlutos* meant: arriving to dwell with (Hebrew: *ger*). In other words, the *prosēlutoi* that the Hasmoneans created were akin with those who became *Hellenes* under the Seleucids and the Ptolemies. Once the Hellenistic world was conquered by Rome, this ethnic elasticity was no longer in the hands of Greeks and Jews.

The Mutability of Being a Jew

Following the Roman conquests of the Near East, the civic organization moved to the hands of the Roman authorities, who used the elasticity of ethnicity to their benefit. The Romans managed to become a conquering state by expanding their definition of *civitas* to the people whom they conquered. Granting Roman citizenship to the inhabitants of Latium and to all the Italian peoples turned the Roman *civitas* from a city-state to a state, and made the definition of being Roman political and mutable. The Romans applied a politics of similar dynamics in regard to the people they subjugated.[58] Nathanael Andrade has recently shown how the civic markers of being Greek, Syrian and also Arab, and their political elasticity within the civic organization in Syria under the Romans were an essential element of the local Roman imperial strategy. "Being Greek" has gained even more elasticity as a status under the Romans. If we read the constant strife between Jews and Greeks in Roman Alexandria over civic privileges against the background of Andrade's analysis in contemporary Syria, it makes sense that what the Greek councils objected to was the Roman manipulation of their status.[59] In a word, under the Romans the civic status of a Greek was no more in the hands of Greeks. The Romans determined who was and who was not a Roman, a Greek, a Syrian and a Jew, and what de jure these terms meant.[60] This was an essential part of their imperialism.

Nadav Sharon, who argued for the Roman origin of a Jewish *ethnarch*, has revealed how it was used in Roman politics in Judaea. As is obvious from Josephus' descriptions, the Romans considered the *ethnarch* of the

---

[57] Thiessen 2011: ch. 4. For circumcision as a *sine qua non* in first-century proselytism, see Nolland 1981: 173–94.

[58] Isaac 2004: ch. 5.   [59] *CPJ* 153 (=P. Lond. 1912). Philo, *In Flaccum*.

[60] Cf. Walbank 1972: 145–68.

Jews (Hyrcanus II) as a juridical authority over the ethnos of the Jews.[61] Just like in Hasmonean times, this status also had religious aspects. Josephus quotes Claudius when he grants the Jews their high priest's vestments for reason of reverence and observance of their ancestral religious rites.[62] The Roman control of the jurisdiction of the *ethnarch* from a non-territorial to a territorial jurisdiction, if Sharon's interpretation is indeed correct, assured in every way that the Roman authorities determined who was under his jurisdiction. In the same way, the Roman authorities confirmed the civil rights of Jewish communities in different locations.[63] This also meant that Jews were entitled to perform their "divinatory practice," their *superstitio*, and to collect a special tribute to their temple in Jerusalem.[64] But could they decide who was a Jew and who was not? For this purpose, the equality between religion and juridical authority became essential.

Josephus puts in Claudius' mouth a definition of the Jewish ancestral ways (*ta patria*) as *eusebeia* and *thrēskia*. In fact, literally he says that everyone should observe the ancestral ways or practices.[65] The relation between the reverence of the religious cult (*eusebeia*), the way of living (*politeia*, *tōi patriōi politeuein nomōi*) and the *ethnos* is stressed in 4 Maccabees repeatedly (4 Mac. 3:20, 4:23, 5:16–18) as the essence of *hos ioudaismos* (4 Mac. 4:26).[66] This identification of religion with *politeia* opened for Jews the way to keep the elasticity of ethnicity in their hands. On the one hand, they could continue to perform their rites and customs even if they became Romans.[67] On the other hand, as Cassius Dio later states, they applied the term *Ioudaioi* also to people of alien descent who adopted their customs.[68] The Romans complied up to a point.

Cases of people, especially women, who adopted Jewish customs and religious rites are attested for the first century CE. The most famous of them was Helena, who was followed by her son Izates, the king of Adiabene. Josephus dedicates a long description to the event.[69] He narrates how everybody feared Izates' circumcision as the sign of the ultimate adoption of Jewish *sebeia* and *etē*, including the Jew who induced his mother. They feared

---

[61] Joseph. *AJ* 14.190–5, 20.244. Sharon 2010.   [62] Joseph. *AJ* 20.13.

[63] Rajak 1984 [2001]: 107–23 (repub. in Rajak 2001: 301–33).   [64] Isaac 2004: 448–9.

[65] Joseph. *AJ* 20.13: *to boulesthai hekastous kata ta patria thrēskeuein*.

[66] Note that circumcision is taken here as a mark of *politeuein tōi patriōi nomōi* not of *eusebeia* (4 Mac. 4:23–6).

[67] For this, see Philo's description of Augustus' handling of the Jews in Rome who were Roman citizens: although they kept their ancestral customs and prayer houses, he kept them as Romans and did not banish them from Rome nor deprive them of their Roman citizenship: Philo, *Leg.* 23 (155–17) (following Isaac 2004: 448).

[68] Dio. 67.141–3, following Isaac 2004: 460 and nn. 94–5.   [69] Joseph. *AJ* 20.34–53.

punishment as well as the refusal of his people to have a Jew as a king. Adoption of the Jewish faith and rite is also attributed to Roman women of status.[70] The fact that all of these cases were women was, of course, noted.[71] The only case where a possible punishment is mentioned is that of Izates. In contrast to the cases of women, his circumcision, which he performed privately with the help of his physician, was irreversible.[72] In any case, from a Roman point of view, a person could not independently take on what was considered a political act: joining the Jewish entity by becoming a Jew. In regard to women, their ethnicity was in any case determined by their male relatives.[73] Therefore, for women any independent act toward becoming a Jew was not really actualized within the political sphere, and had no political meaning. Yet Roman authors do mention proselytes and refer to their circumcision.[74] So the question should not be who was a Jew and who was not, but who determined who was a Jew and who was not?

The perception of proselytes as converts is related to the question of whether antique Judaism knew an equivalence of the early Christian missionary movement, or was even its archetype.[75] As I argued, the Judaization of the Idumeans and Itureans under the Hasmoneans was not related to a possible religious missionary movement but was a Hellenistic political measure. Although rabbinic sources were scrutinized in order to place the origin of *giyur* – proselytism as a religious conversion – in Judaism of the Hasmonean period, no specific process of conversion is attested for that period except of circumcision. The Mishnah does refer to proselytes (*ger*, *gioret*) but does not mention the process of conversion itself.[76] The Tosefta (*Shabbat* 15:9) on the other hand brings a Tannaic discussion and cites Shime'on ben El'azar in relation to the question of circumcision when the *ger* is already circumcised. Only in the Babylonian Talmud (*Yebamot* 47a-b) do we get a full definition of the process, in a passage that comprises a second-century *beraita*.[77] As was observed, no

---

[70] Matthews 2001; cf. the apocryphal story *Joseph and Aseneth*, shown to be of a much later date: Kraemer 1998; Chesnutt 1986; 1988: 21–48.

[71] Rabello 1999: 37–68 (repr. in Rabello 2000: pt. XIV).

[72] For Josephus' rhetoric see Grojnowski 2014.   [73] Moore 2015: 87–8.

[74] Isaac 2004: 453–60.

[75] Among the most thought-provoking theses: Cohen 2006; Goodman 1994; Will and Orrieux 1992; Feldman 2003: 115–56.

[76] Mishnah *Demai* 6:10, *Ḥalla* 3:6, *Psaḥim* 8:8, *Shkalim* 7:6, *Yevamot* 6:5, 8:2, 11:2, *Ktubot* 1:2, 1:4, 3:1–2, 4:3, 6:6, *Kiddushin* 4:6–7. Note that *ger toshav* is already distinguished from *ger* by the Mishnah: *Bava metzia* 9:12, *Makkot* 2:3. For the ambiguity of the Mishnah in the case of the *ger*'s status, see Porton 1994: ch. 2.

[77] And its elaborated version in the post-Talmudic tractate *Gerim*: Cohen 2006: ch. 7; Bamberger 1939.

anathema is mentioned here, but only the conviction of the candidate to abide by the law of the Jews with reference to immersion and circumcision. The text emphasizes particularly the fact that this process is invalid unless performed as a juridical act: in front of a juridical court or three witnesses. What the attitude of the Roman authority was to such a juridical conversion process is not mentioned. However, the legislation of the second and third centuries against circumcision should be taken here in consideration as a measure against proselytism.[78] In a word, if Jews found a way to define the mutability of their boundary as a people by employing a physical marker as a religious marker, and used it as a means to enlarging their civic definition of Jews to include Gentiles, especially Romans, the Roman authorities responded by prohibiting such mutability.[79] This should explain why the Tannatic collections do not refer to the process of *giyur* and why the actual definition of the process has survived in a Babylonian text. Such a process was illegal in the Roman Empire, and in any case not in the hands of Jews.[80] This could also explain the elaborate discussion on whether the status of being a Jew is matrilineal or patrilineal.[81] Such measures left, however, other forms of sharing in Jewish rites open for sympathizers and God-fearers, without going through an actual process of "conversion."[82] The act of conversion for which, it should be noted, we employ a modern term with a long history, could not be a legal Roman procedure since it contradicted the common perspective in antiquity that individuals cannot determine their ethnic/juridical/civic status themselves; that is, unless there could be yet another definition of *ethnos*.

In her book *Why This New Race: Ethnic Reasoning in Early Christianity*, Denise Kimber Buell has argued that a concept of fixed–fluid dialectic regarding ancient ethno-racial discourse can shed new light on the way early Christian authors have constructed the identity of Christianity as an *ethnos* and as a race (*genos*). In a Roman world that did not recognize new ethnicities, they invented a genealogy for an invented people and constructed its legitimacy *a contrario* to the legitimate genealogy of the

---

[78] Dig. 48.8.11 (Antoninus Pius); Paulus, *Sententiae* 5.22.3–4 (end of the third century); Linder 1987; Rabello 2000; Moga 2008: 95–111.

[79] In contrast to Dig 48.8.11, Paulus, *Sententiae* 5.22.3–4 refers explicitly to Roman citizens (all the Empire's inhabitants) and their slaves and also prohibited the circumcision of purchased slaves of *alienae nationis*. See Moga 2008.

[80] As noted by Cohen 2006: 213. It continued to be illegal also when the Empire became Christian: *CTh* 16.8.1 (=*Classical Journal* 1.9.3) from 329, *Constitutio Sirmondiana* 4 (from 335), *CTh* 16.9.2 (from 339) (Linder 1987: pp. 124–32, 138–50). Moga 2008.

[81] Cohen 2006: ch. 9.

[82] Wander 1998; Sim 2013: 9–27; Reynolds and Tannenbaum 1987; Bonz 1994: 281–99; Chaniotis 2002b: 209–26.

Jews.[83] To cut the cord that connected Jewish law to Jewish religiosity, Christians defined new interpretations of the law and made it universal. The means to create a new ethnos was conversion: the complete transformation of values. This was an individual psychological process of transformation, but it was at the same time a social and political act. Buell shows how Christian ideas of universalism were predicated on what she calls "ethnic reasoning."[84] Christians defined themselves as a new ethnos and a new *genos*, "the *genos* of the righteous" (*to genos tōn dikaiōn*), in contrast to two groups: the Jews and the *Hellenes*. *Hellenes* was the term used by pagans who adhered to Greek philosophy and religious rites.[85] Conversion became the means to move from one group to the other disregarding the Roman authority simply by portraying religion as ethnicity. Christians have positioned themselves as a political collectivity by using Roman ethnic terms to name themselves and by defining the ways to cross boundaries by themselves. Conversion was not only a form of cultural identity, it also enabled making Christianity a *politeia* whose marker was a newly created *superstitio*. In other words, the people who called themselves Christians took in their hands the Roman authority to revoke the status of being a Roman, which was a Roman juridical matter. Jews tried to do the same thing in order to keep the boundaries of their own *politeia* in their hands.

To Be a People *de jure*

Much attention was given in modern scholarship to the process of proselytism in Roman times, as both a halachic process and a historical phenomenon. We have proposed here to understand the meaning of proselytism against the background of the Roman strategy of incorporation of non-Romans into the Roman *civitas*. The transition period of civil war between the Republic and the Principate necessitated a change of a political character of the internal structure of the Roman state. For that purpose the term *populus* became a useful means. Giovannella Cresci Marrone and Alberto Grilli have shown how the rhetorical use of this term reflected the changes that the political structure of the Roman state underwent between the Republic and the early Principate.[86] If Caesar changed the status of the army in order to make an oppositional power to the authority of the Senate, Augustus did exactly the opposite. He used a new sense of *populus*, as it

---

[83] Buell 2005: ch. 1 for the Roman concept of religiosity and ethnicity.   [84] *Ibid.*, ch. 5.
[85] De Palma Digeser 2006: 36–57; 2011: 121–313.
[86] Marrone 2005: 157–72; Grilli 2005: 124–39.

were a *populus* "shared with the *princeps*," to challenge the power of the political Roman elite. The same political sense of Latin terminology is also apparent in the Roman writers from Cicero to Plutarch.[87] For them too, the term *populus romanus* came to designate the way in which they formulated their political thought. The means to control the definition of *populus romanus* was Roman law. Bestowing Roman citizenship to non-Romans and revoking it from others was handled by changing the juridical status. Bestowing and revoking a person's a juridical personality made him a Roman, and could stop him from being one. This was the case with criminals, traitors and prisoners of war. Having lost their Roman juridical personality, they were de jure "exterminated" in the sense of being placed outside (*ex*) the Roman *terminus*. Not having a Roman juridical personality meant that their marriage was declared null and void, and that they lost all property within the Empire. Rabbinic Judaism adopted the same perspective and put it into practice in order to create a political definition of who was a Jew and who was not by creating a new juridical term.

The Hebrew root *sh-m-d* provides a well-defined linguistic framework for the Jewish trope of extermination ever since the Bible. However, in the late antique rabbinic literature we find the same root used in the medial mode – *meshumad* – in reference to the apostate Jew. A priori, applying the term *meshumad* – the one who was exterminated – is a paradox: How can a person still be alive after an act of extermination – *hashmada*? This, however, makes sense if we consider Judaism to be a political term and a civic status that could be bestowed and revoked. In this way a person can be metaphorically exterminated from the point of view of the Jewish community, exterminated in the sense of the Latin meaning of extermination: the one who has gone out – *ex* of the Jewish *terminus* (i.e., excommunicated), in the same way that a Roman citizen could stop being Roman.[88] Nevertheless, the fact that this is a new term that was invented in a specific historical moment calls for an examination of the circumstances and rationale of this invention, which is connected to the political sense of being a Jew.

The first references to the use of the term *meshumad* are found in the Tosefta.[89] The *meshumadim* appear here next to the heretics (*minim*), betrayers (*moserot*), those who deny God (*epikorsin*), as well as those who denied the Torah (*sheKafru baTorah*), those who separate themselves from the community, those who deny the resurrection of the dead, and those who sinned and caused the public to sin. All these are not considered to be

---

[87] von Albrect 2005: 173–89.   [88] For excommunication, see *infra*.
[89] Tosefta (Zuckermandel), *Sanhedrin* 13:5.

part of the Jewish community. But who exactly were these *meshumadim*? One example that the Tosefta brings is Miryam from the Priest family of Blaga, who is called *mishtamedet* (here in the reflexive mode) because she married a Greek king.[90] All the other references to *meshumadim* (in the medial mode) are about Jews who disobeyed the Halakha. As an example we read in Tosefta *Horaiot*: "He who eats abominations – he is *meshumad*. He who eats pork and he who drinks libation-wine, he who desecrates the Shabbat, and he who draws up the foreskin. Rabbi Yose ben Rabbi Judah says: also he who is clothed in mixed species. Rabbi Shim'eon ben Ele'azar says: also he who does something after which his passion/drive does not lust."[91] In these cases, the actual Jewish faith in one God, the God of Israel, as well as apostasy from the Jewish faith are not mentioned. We can therefore conclude that the second- and third-century use of the term *meshumad* did not refer to renegades, Jews who left Judaism by converting to another religion, but simply to Jews who did not follow Jewish law. Whether they were forced to it under persecutions (*shmad*) or not, their acts of defying Jewish law excluded them from the Jewish way of life and the Jewish community, in sum the Jewish *politeia* along with betrayers, epicureans (i.e. people denying God's providence) and Christians. What all such cases have in common is disobedience to both Jewish law and rabbinic authority.

The measures taken against these *meshumadim* were therefore aimed to stop Jews from approaching other cults by defining them as "exterminated – *meshumadim* to the Jewish community." Whether such Jews really wanted to leave Judaism or not, any transgression of rabbinic authority in relation to the precepts was defined as their metaphoric extermination. This had a rationale within a pagan Roman world. In a civilization where a pagan could also be a God-fearer or sympathizer of the Jewish God, the denomination *meshumad* enabled the rabbis to stop the reverse phenomenon: by declaring that any Jew who disobeys their authority becomes "exterminated." With this juridical definition, the gray area of who was a Jew could be mapped and a clear demarcation set; whoever passed it stopped being a Jew.

Shlomo Pines pointed out the resemblance between the Hebrew root *sh-m-d* and the Syriac root *sh-m-t*, whose meaning is excommunication by curse: *ḥerem/nidui* (*shamta* being an evil spirit, demon).[92] We find this in

---

[90] Tosefta (Lieberman), *Suka* 4:28.
[91] Tosefta (Zuckermandel), *Horaiot* 1:5. This is the same rabbi Shim'eon whom the Tosefta (*Shabbat* 15:9) quotes in regard to the dispute about circumcision of someone who was born circumcised.
[92] Pines 1974: 205–13.

BT *Kidushin*, 72a, where rabbi Achai ben Rabbi Yoshiya excommunicates (*shametihu*) the Jews who fished in the pond on Shabbat, who, then, *ishtamud*. They thus become apostate because they are excommunicated by the local rabbi for not observing the Shabbat. In no way do we find here the issue of conversion to another religion, only the definition of transgression of Jewish law as apostasy. This makes much sense against the background of the historical circumstances following the suppression of the Judaean revolts. Jews no longer had a unifying cult, and more problematic, they did not have a state with either a political or a religious authority. The objective of the rabbis' jurisprudence was to set their law as the actual definition of who was a Jew and who was not. And the rabbinic authority decided that whoever transgresses it will no longer be a Jew. Of course, in the period under discussion, Christianity presented a concrete threat to the rabbinic authorities by attracting Jewish believers. The rabbis used excommunication for Jews who did not adhere to rabbinic law and rabbinic authority, but distinguished terminologically between a Jew who did it out of apostasy and became a Christian, and a Jew who did not convert but simply disobeyed rabbinic authority. The first was a *min*, the second a *meshumad*.

The distinction between *meshumad* and converted Jew is the subject of an elaborate discussion in the BT 'Aovdah Zara 26b. It concerns foreign cult and the way to draw a clear demarcation to separate Jews from it. The text comments on the distinction between *goyim* – Gentiles in general, and "Shepherds of small animals" (*ro'ei behemah daka*) on the one hand, and those considered as enemy. It states that in regard to foreigners, Jews should neither help them nor push them to death: "one should not raise them up from a pit (if they fall into it), nor throw/lower them into a pit." In contrast, in regard to the other group, which includes *minim* (Christians), *masorot* (traitors) and *meshumadim* ("exterminated"), Jews should take the opportunity to put them in risky situations: to lower them down into pits, and not help them by raising them from the pits into which they fall, clearly an act against enemies. This distinction between the two groups is followed by an elaborate discussion in the Babylonian Talmud about who is a *meshumad*. There are two types of *meshumad*, the Talmud says: the one who eats *nevelot* (dead animals that were not slaughtered and are forbidden to eat) because of an appetite for them (*leTeavon*), and the one who eats it to spite/in defiance (*leHakh'is*). The first is a *meshumad*, but the second is *min*, since he does what he does in order to defy the Torah. The Talmud then challenges this by bringing the case of a man who eats a flea or a mosquito and is called *meshumad*. How then, could he be considered eating a flea for pleasure (i.e., as a *meshumad*)? Shouldn't he be considered a *min*? Yet the Talmud settles this by saying that the one who eats a flea does it to taste a forbidden taste, and not in defiance. "Then, who is a *min*?" it is asked, and the reply: the one who practices a foreign cult. This is a clear indication that a *meshumad* is not a renegade or a convert, but the one who transgresses the law without adhering to a different faith. The rabbinic authority is nevertheless very severe and excommunicates him just as if he were a *min*. In fact, this should be considered as a means to execute a Jew de jure.

The fact that this was not just a theoretical discussion but a juridical practice is attested in a law promulgated in 392, in which Theodosius I, Arcadius and Honorius prohibit the readmission of Jews once "the Primates of their law (*legis suae primates*) banished (*proiciunt*) them."[93] I would like to relate this to Jews who were "exterminated" de jure (i.e., *meshumadim*) and who had no option but to turn to different judges in their matters. The law affirms that the authority of the primates is binding in matters of *religio*. In other words, the three Augusti declare here that the boundary of who is a Jew and who is not, is in the sole hands of the legal authorities. In other words, a *meshumad* remains with no juridical personality. He is "exterminated" de jure in reference not only to the rabbis' authority, but to any authority. Thus, the definition by the rabbis in the matter of life and death, although not in their hands, seems to find here a solution according to which they are authorized to revoke the juridical personality of a Jew, making him "exterminated" de jure. This means that being a Jew is kept a civic status, not just a juridical and a religious one. In fact, this law clearly connects the two by equating juridical authority to matters of the Jews' *religio*. The civic status is affirmed by the Roman delegation of this authority to the primates and to them only. In a word, the fact that a Jew has juridical personality, that he exists de jure, is completely in the hands of those who can determine if he is a Jew or not. To be a Jew is here to be, to exist de jure: to have a juridical personality of a Jew.

Conclusion

We have followed the ways in which certain groups of Jews designated themselves by defining their borderline, their *limes*. We have focused here on two sides of this definition: exclusion from the inside out and inclusion

---

[93] *CTh* 16.8.8 (Linder 1987: 186–9).

from the outside in. We did not refer to a global definition of Jews in the Greco-Roman world, but examined how certain groups referred to themselves as entities by employing the definition of who was a Jew and who was not as a political means. At the basis of all cases we find a political objective: a group of people who insist on defining themselves as a civic entity in order to become one, and to portray themselves as active agents, no matter what the circumstances are.

13 | Local Identities of Synagogue Communities in the Roman Empire

JONATHAN J. PRICE

A recently published volume of essays, under the title *Local Knowledge and Microidentities in the Imperial Greek World*,[1] explores an issue central to the theme of this volume, "Empire of Many Nations." The book examines, from different perspectives, what happened to Greek culture and "identities" when the lands of *paideia* were incorporated into the Roman Empire. Like many other books on ancient history, this one was inspired or suggested by current trends, in this case, globalization. The Roman Empire is viewed as an all-encompassing, globalizing, "translocal" or "supralocal" force. The collective argument of the essays is that the subsumption of the Greek world into the Roman Empire emphasized and sharpened local identities while at the same time providing material for Rome to build its own imperial identity, so that "the local and imperial are mutually reliant."[2] Aelius Aristides exalted the unity of a vast, diverse world under the rubric "Roman," but the imposition of Rome compelled local communities towards "an increased awareness, even questioning of, the power dynamics between the local and non-local." Thus local identities were "in constant dialogue with the translocal."[3]

The illuminating treatments of "micro-identities" in the volume do not include the Jews in the Roman Empire, either synagogues or predominantly Jewish settlements, as localized communities or identities.[4] There is no reason that the Jews had to be included. The essays in the collection are informed by the lingering issues from the furious debates about the Second Sophistic, and there should be no expectation that Jewish communities would find a natural place even in a composite study of different, particular manifestations of Greek cultural knowledge and localizations within the Roman sphere of influence. Moreover, Jewish status and identity in a "supralocal" context are inherently ambiguous, presenting both a strong, unifying, national/ethnic identity – their most-noticed feature

---

[1] Edited by Whitmarsh, 2010a.   [2] Whitmarsh 2010b: 16.   [3] Whitmarsh 2010b: 2, 3.
[4] Greg Woolf, in his conclusion to the volume, does mention the Jews in a list of examples of "difference but connectedness" (p. 192), but the Jews were significantly different from the other members of that list: Phoenicians, Greeks, Romans, Syrians.

in antiquity and also in most modern treatments – and widely varied local attachments and languages.[5]

It is this latter, less-studied element, *videlicet*, Jews' local identities in the Roman Empire, that is the subject of the present limited investigation, informed *inter alia* by the setting of the conference from which the present volume arose – Tel Aviv. Other chapters in the present volume deal with the Jews as an undifferentiated *ethnos* across the empire – with regard to "pluralism" (Gruen), law (Rotman), imperial policy (Yakobson), relations with emperors and Jewish attitudes to Romans (Shahar, Oppenheimer) – but the Jews' lived reality in their immediate settings in the city or countryside, in larger regional identities and in the Roman Empire itself would have forced Jewish communities – both in Iudaea/Palaestina and in the Diaspora – to face similar challenges of self-definition vis-à-vis their micro-environment (village, city) and larger regional environment.

Thus it may be asked – even if a full and detailed answer cannot be expected – whether individual, localized Jewish communities, without any obvious connection to each other across the ethnically, linguistically and religiously diverse Roman Empire,[6] can be said to have had, or displayed, a "micro-identity" in addition to their nonlocal ethnic one, or whether this feature, if not entirely absent in some cases, was indeed overshadowed by their shared history and ethnic origins.[7] Let me reveal at the outset that my answer to this question here is partial and inconclusive, but not entirely negative.

The question will be approached by concentrating on synagogues, which, as time went on, especially from the third century CE to the end of antiquity, were the focal point of whole Jewish communities – communities within cities and villages, or (most noticeably in Iudaea/Palaestina) the whole village itself – and not just ancillary buildings for worship or specific activities separate from civic life. Synagogues could represent the identity of a community, and were used, in addition to worship and study, for community gatherings and public meetings, schools, communal meals, courts and other legal procedures, rudimentary banking functions, lodging – everything

---

[5] Cohen 1999: 69–106 is fundamental. Two recent entries in the ongoing debate about Jewish identity (identities), the meaning of *Ioudaios*, etc., are "A 'Jew' by Any Other Name?" (Baker 2011: 153–80) and in the same volume, Schwartz 2011: 208–38. Schwartz's book (Schwartz 2001) argues that in Late Antiquity, Jewish identity formed in reaction to Christianity.

[6] Collar 2013; the complex networks that she hypothesizes are not convincing, being mostly based on rather loose evidence.

[7] This question is notably different from the questions motivating I. Gafni's useful essay, "At Home While Abroad: Expressions of Local Patriotism in the Jewish Diaspora of Late Antiquity," in Gafni 1997: 41–57.

connected with civic life, and even some aspects of private life.[8] A synagogue could be referred to as בית עם, lit. "house of the people" (bShabb. 32a).

While it is true that the synagogue buildings can be suggestive of the activities of communities and their extent – the presence of multiuse halls and side chambers, for example – the most useful evidence on the question of the localized or micro-identities of synagogues will be the several hundred inscriptions surviving from the floors, columns and walls of the ancient structures. This methodological choice is dictated not only by the real differences between literary and epigraphical attestations of synagogue communities. The inscriptions are the only unmediated written self-expression of the communities that built and used the synagogues. The inscriptions in synagogues are, despite their apparent public nature, directed to visitors to the synagogue, mostly (but not exclusively) Jews. They are valuable, internally focused evidence. Inscriptions are, moreover, the sole self-documentation of most Jewish communities otherwise undocumented in the literary sources. That is, the more than 200 surviving or partially surviving synagogue buildings from Roman antiquity (including those outside the bounds of direct Roman rule) represent the only evidence for almost all of those synagogal communities. Although there are hundreds, perhaps thousands of references to synagogues in literary sources (rabbinic and Christian literature), it is possible in only a very few instances to match up a literarily attested synagogal community to the actual physical remains of an ancient building (e.g., Beth She'an/ Scythopolis, Capernaum, possibly Caesarea and Sepphoris).[9] Occasionally, inscriptional evidence demonstrates that some synagogues served as focal points for whole regions, such as the building at Ḥammat Gader, which records donations and participation by individuals from Sepphoris, Capernaum, Arbel and other places – some of which places had their own synagogues. The relationship between the synagogues, and the affiliation or citizenship of individuals in each, can only be guessed, since the inscriptions are the only evidence for the synagogue at Ḥammat Gader.

Naturally, the authors of synagogue inscriptions – the texts are mostly dedications, vows and acclamations (e.g., *hyper soterias*), and labels for art – did not have the purpose of directly answering the questions asked here. It could be that community charter or rules were inscribed on the walls of some synagogues, as at Ein Gedi and Reḥov (see next). Even were it possible to translate "micro-identities" into Greek, Hebrew or Aramaic,

---

[8] Levine 2000: 357–86; 2012: 357–402. See also S. Safrai 1976: 942–4; and Z. Safrai 1995: 181–204.

[9] Despite the subtitle in his article, Stuart Miller deals with a different question, i.e., the problem of "pagan" imagery in synagogue art: 2004: 27–76.

no one in the ancient period would have understood it in the same way as the scholar equipped with (burdened by?) heavy modern theoretical apparatus.

This chapter will be primarily concerned with aspects of localized identities that can be assumed to have existed at a higher rate than they are actually found in the evidence. Yet one mark of localized identity can be said at the outset not to be found because it did not exist: a particular language or set of symbols, any kind of unique mode of expression that focuses or reflects how the members of community perceived themselves. As Woolf points out in the last essay in Whitmarsh's volume,[10] both isolation and connection can account for localism. There was no separate, Jewish epigraphic language in any region of the Roman Empire. As a rule, Jews adopted and adapted local epigraphic idioms in both their public and private inscriptions. Synagogues are identified by architectural elements, Jewish symbols, the content of the inscriptions rather than any peculiar idiom. Thus the distinctly local and imitative character of Jewish inscriptions can be interpreted both as the failure of the Jews in any particular place to create a localized linguistic idiom of their own, but also, on the contrary, their identification with and participation in the local epigraphic culture.[11]

We shall be paying close attention to an aspect of the evidence not normally noticed in discussions of ancient Jewish communities, highlighted in Whitmarsh's anthology: the origins of the communities, including foundation stories and myths. It has been well established, from the standard discussions,[12] that in Roman antiquity, synagogues and Jewish communities – which, as stated, were sometimes but not always coextensive – had internal structures, often particular laws and regulations, magistrates, treasuries, which made them communities within communities in every respect. It has been clearly demonstrated that the internal structures and magistracies of the Jewish communities mimicked those where the Jews lived, and synagogues have been compared to civic guilds, which accounted for so much of citizens' private and social lives.[13] What is less

---

[10] Whitmarsh 2010a: 189–200.

[11] Important discussion by Ameling 2007: 253–82; and see my "The Different Faces of Euergetism in Iudaea/ Palaestina and Syria in Late Antiquity: The Evidence of Synagogue Inscriptions," forthcoming in *Coping with Religious Change: Adopting Transformations and Adapting Rituals in the Late Antique Eastern Mediterranean*, edited by Eduard Iricinschi and Chrysi Kotsifo.

[12] For a summary of the ancient evidence and *status quaestionis* up to then, see Levine 2000: Ch. 10–11, "The Communal Dimension" and "Leadership."

[13] Ameling 1999.

clear is how Jews explained how and why they got to their particular location, and how important that explanation was to their identity.

The chosen corpus of evidence for this study presents a picture of inwardly focused communities, even for the more cosmopolitan synagogues like those along the coast of Iudaea/ Palaestina: most officials mentioned are those of the synagogue or Jewish community, and all benefactions mentioned are for Jews or the Jewish community at large. This may seem a self-evident fact; the point is that any contributions Jews made to the larger civic structures to which they belonged were recorded in other public places, not the synagogue.[14]

Mentions of synagogues in rabbinic literature seem routinely to assume that the population of a town and membership of the synagogue were coterminous.[15] Such cases would involve small towns with one synagogue and a predominantly or exclusively Jewish population, even if the leaders of the synagogues were different from a town's civic leaders. The impression in rabbinic sources of insular, self-sufficient and self-administered Jewish communities is reinforced by the exemptions from curial service given to some Jews in the Theodosian Code.[16]

Three Aramaic synagogue inscriptions – but strikingly, none in Greek – mention "the town" קרתה in which the synagogue is located, but not by name.[17] The large mosaic inscription at Ein Gedi contains sanctions against anyone who *inter alia* reveals "the secret of the town" רזה דקרתה to the Gentiles (CIIP IV, 3851); here the town seems to be coterminous with the synagogue community, especially in light of the second mosaic inscription from there (CIIP IV, 3852):

דכירין לטב כל בני קרתה דיהב גרמהון | וח<ז>קין כנישתה

> Be remembered for the good all the residents of the town who gave from their own property and support the synagogue.

The two entities are different, but the membership is the same, so that a prohibition published in the synagogue applies to all citizens of the town. The same picture emerges from the fragmentary chancel-screen inscriptions

---

[14] The dedications in synagogues to civic rulers are of course different, e.g., in Egypt, Horbury and Noy 1992: nos. 22, 24, 25, 27, 28, 117, 125; in Ostia, Noy 1993: no. 13; in Croatia, IJO I, Pan5; etc.

[15] See exx. in Levine 2000: 382–4.   [16] Linder 1987, 164–7; Nemo-Pekelman 2010: 30–7.

[17] In inscriptions, the use of the word קרתה seems not to veer from its regular usage in rabbinic literature, meaning just city or large town. In addition, the synagogue inscription from Horvat Ḥuqoq is restored by David Amit: בכל [| [וברוכי]ן | [כל בני העיר?] שהן | מתח[ז]קין]ן וואמ]ן ס[ל]ה] | [ש]ל]ום – מצות כן יהא | עמלכן ואמן ס[ל]ה] | [ש]ל]ום – see www.biblicalarchaeology.org/uncategorized/mosaic-inscription-from-a-synagogue-at-horvat-huqoq/.

in Susiya, which use identical language to commemorate "[members of] the holy congregation" (קה[לה קדישה דאתחזק]ין]) and "members of the town" ([דכיר]ין לטב [כ]ל בני קרתה [ד]מתחזק]ין]), synagogue and town being separate physical entities with the same membership.[18] And the same can be said for the blessing on all בני קרתה in the mosaic inscription at Ḥuseifa.[19] An extremely impressive example of a synagogue inscription that seems to represent an entire community tightly organized around a specific purpose and area is the halakhic inscription from Reḥov,[20] though naturally the community using the Reḥov synagogue was not the only one which strictly observed agricultural laws in the Land of Israel, and laws spelled out in the inscription had regional relevance and application. Roman citizenship, or really any form of participation in the Roman Empire, seems to have had little part in their identity and daily lives.

The formula דכיר לטב *dekir letav*, was not only the most prevalent formula in Jewish Aramaic dedications but also the most widespread dedicatory formula throughout the Aramaic-speaking world.[21] The formula is found in synagogue inscriptions in Batanea and Dura Europus in Syria and throughout Iudaea/Palaestina from north to south,[22] but its first use predates its first appearance in a Jewish text by centuries. The Jews' use of the formula differed from their surroundings in important respects: the target audience, for whom the dedicatee was meant to be remembered for the good, was the living community and not a deity, thus there are hardly any Jewish texts with דכיר לטב קדם plus a divine name, unlike, for example, Nabataean uses of the formula.[23] Moreover, the dedicatee in Jewish texts was a living person; the Jewish dedications were not, as in other non-Jewish contexts, memorials for the deceased.[24] The *dekir letav* synagogue dedications seem to reinforce the community from within, by commemorating, either by name or anonymously, contributions by particularly generous

---

[18] CIIP IV, 3878, 3880; parallels to "holy congregation" in Jericho, CIIP IV, 2806, and in Beth She'an, Naveh 1978: no. 46, see Levine 2000: 236–9. Barag's notion (1972: 453f.) that town and synagogue represented non-Jewish and Jewish entities is not supported by the evidence.

[19] Naveh 1978: no. 39.

[20] Naveh 1978: 79–85, and for a detailed discussion of the halakhic inscription, dealing primarily with agricultural laws, Y. Sussman 1973: 87–158; id. 1974: 193–5 (Hebr.); Vitto 1993: 1272–4. The painted inscriptions on the wall plaster from the synagogue are being prepared for publication by H. Misgav.

[21] Healey 2011: Chapter 20; Gudme 2011, citing abundant *comparanda*.

[22] IJO III Syr35, Syr91-92. There is a long list in Naveh 1978: index, p. 150; to these add the Aramaic dedications in the synagogue floor at Sepphoris, Weiss 2005: 199–208.

[23] A rare exception is in IJO III, Syr91 at Dura: (דכיר לטב קדם | מרי ש[מיא אמן]).

[24] See Gudme 2011. Again, there is one exception: Beth Guvrin (Naveh 1978: no. 71) ניח נפש. Sorek 2010 contends that the *dekir* inscriptions in synagogues regularly signified a memorial to a deceased donor rather than a dedication to a living patron; this thesis is untenable.

members of the community.[25] Jews' adaptation of the formula stressed *community* recognition of the dedicatee rather than *divine* confirmation; but a formula, even modified, is not a distinctive language, and the Jews' adaptation of it was similar throughout the East and cannot be read as a linguistic peculiarity of a particular city or region.

The commemorations of members of the town or congregation are collective and anonymous, stressing the importance of the community above the generosity of any individual, even if some anonymous benefactions are recorded together with named contributions, including another inscription at Ḥuseifa.[26] As Stemberger noted, "worship was a common responsibility of all members of the community."[27] The use of the formula *dekir letav* and the anonymity of a relatively large number of Aramaic dedications in synagogues are evidence of local knowledge, since the local community knew and recognized even their unnamed benefactors, but that local knowledge is not communicated to the outside world, or even to the next generations, in the inscriptions. The extent to which that knowledge was preserved in the oral tradition of the communities is a fascinating, unanswerable question.

Thus, according to the standard conception of Jewish communities under Roman rule, they could function as independent entities that provided and strengthened the Jews' local identity, their separation from but also connection to the larger urban or regional setting. This does not precisely answer the specific questions of micro-identities in the ancient equivalent of a globalizing imperial power. For that, we turn our attention to Jewish communities' account of their own origins and possibly distinctive features in their identity and self-accounting.

There is some evidence, if scrappy, suggesting that some Jewish communities had, aside from their shared national story of origins derived from the Bible, additional stories to explain how they got to their present location and why their community exists. In some cases, certainly more than the evidence shows, members of a synagogue would have had an interesting and unique answer to the question: Why are you in this particular spot?

Ancient synagogue communities, in contrast to the modern practice, did not inscribe their names or identities on their lintels or mosaic floors – at least,

---

[25] Cf. Schwartz 2004: 275–89: synagogue inscriptions (focusing on Roman Near East) reflect an egalitarian, self-enclosed community ideology, differing from pagan and Christian surroundings.

[26] Naveh 1978: no. 43; other combined named and anonymous contributions at Ḥamat Gader and Beth Alfa, Naveh 1978: nos. 33, 34. Anonymity is found only in inscriptions in Iudaea/Palaestina: in addition to those mentioned, Naʿaran CIIP IV, 2733; Maʿon (Naveh 1978: no. 57); Jericho (CIIP IV, 2806); Beth Sheʾan (Naveh 1978: nos. 46, 47 and Roth-Gerson 1987: no. 9).

[27] Stemberger 1998: 139.

no epigraphical instance has been found so far, although synagogues are given distinct names in literary sources, such as the Synagogue of Rebellion (כנישתא מרדתא דקיסרין) in Caesarea;[28] the name is suggestive of both "local knowledge" and "micro-community," but nothing is known beyond the evocative name. Slightly more insight – if very slightly more – may be gained from the synagogue names indicating origins elsewhere. The many epitaphs recovered from the Jewish catacombs in Rome mention synagogues with names suggesting communities,[29] such as the συναγωγή Τριπολειτῶν,[30] whose meaning seems straightforward, even if the foundational story is not revealed in the name, nor can it be known which Tripolis is referred to. Similarly, the synagogues Ἐλέας and Σεκηνῶν at Rome refer to places that can be variously identified.[31] In all such cases, one wonders how long, after the original founding of the synagogue by Tripolitans, Sekenoi, and others, the membership remained identified with their city of origin, or even ethnically insulated from Jews of other origins (was there a custom against "intermarriage" with Jews from different backgrounds, as in some ethnically tight Jewish communities today?). So far as this last point is concerned, the συναγωγή Αἰβρρέων (Ἑβρέων), as Leon suggests, possibly represents the first synagogue founded in Rome, therefore by Jews from Palestine, speakers of Aramaic and Hebrew, thus several generations before the date of the catacomb inscriptions.[32] A similar kind of chauvinism may be represented in συναγωγή Βερνάκλων (βερκακλησίων), which has been interpreted as an attempt to distinguish native-born Jews, vernaculi, from all the immigrant communities.[33]

Some of the questions arising from these mere mentions of communities, such as their age and longevity, could have been solved by the discovery of the actual buildings where they met, but not one physical structure identified as an ancient synagogue has been discovered in Rome.

In Iudaea/Palaestina, there is similar slight evidence for communities transplanted from abroad. I have recently explored this issue in print, and there is no need to repeat all of the arguments and evidence here.[34] I shall

---

[28] yBikk. 3,3,65d et al.
[29] The exact number is debated, but there are probably eleven discrete congregations mentioned; see index in Noy 1995: 539–40; Leon 1960: 135–66.
[30] Noy 1993: 166.   [31] Noy 1995: 406, 576, cf. Leon, 145–7; Noy 1993: 436.
[32] Noy, 1995: 2, 33, 578, 579. If Leon's conjecture is correct, then the self-named community celebrated their ethnic and linguistic origin, not the circumstances of their arrival there.
[33] Noy 1995: 106, 114, 117, maybe 540.
[34] Price 2015. The Theodotos synagogue inscription in Jerusalem does seem to represent a whole synagogal community transplanted from Italy or a western province, but the inscription itself indicates an openness of the institution rather than a closely self-identified "community."

only reiterate the conclusion that the literary and epigraphic data are ambiguous at best for any presumed micro-community other than in Jaffa, where one inscription testifies to a community of Cappadocians within the city, even though its origins and history are not revealed by the inscription. Other epitaphs in Jaffa document the presence of many Egyptian Jews in the city, although the history of that transplanted ethnic group is unknown – were they refugees from the second-century rebellion in Egypt, or opportunistic merchants who settled before then (or possibly even afterwards)? – and there is no indication that they organized into a micro-community within the Jewish population of Jaffa. We may suppose that the move of a Jewish community from one distinct different cultural and linguistic environment to another – like the move from Asia Minor or Alexandria to Iudaea/Palaestina – sharpened an idiosyncratic identity as well as their identity as Jews. Fully transplanted communities obviously had – like colonies – corresponding stories about the reasons and circumstances of their transplantation, and those stories would have been part of their particular identities in their specific location.

Another possible topos of origins involves a *ktistes* – or if not technically a *ktistes*, then an important and imposing figure who imprinted his personality on the building or community.[35] In the Greek world, a *ktistes* could be divine or semidivine, which is not possible in a Jewish context. Several synagogue inscriptions in fact use the word κτίστης or κτίζειν in connection with a person or persons, but the problem is that in none of the instances does the word mean "founder"; the meaning is, rather, "donor." This is clear in a dedication from the synagogue at Capernaum, in which the verb ἔκτισαν has a specific direct object: Ἡρώδης Μο[κί?]|μου καὶ Ἰοῦστος | υἱὸς ἅμα τοῖς | τέκνοις ἔκτι|σαν τὸν | κίονα.[36] Here, "founded the pillar" must mean "contributed towards construction of the pillar." In Dura Europus, the two Greek inscriptions on ceiling tiles using the same verb are to be interpreted in the same way:

– Σαμουὴλ | Εἰδδέου | πρεσβύτερος | τῶν Ἰουδέ|ων ἔκτισεν.
– Σαμουὴλ | Βαρσαφάρα | μνησθη ἐκ|[τ]ισεν ταῦ|τα οὕτως.[37]

The second of these texts has a direct object that is vague but nonetheless limiting the action of the verb: he did not "found" but contributed toward the construction of this or that element of the new building. Accordingly, the first Samuel was also one of many donors to the synagogue's construction. The main foundational inscription at Dura, set into the ceiling and

---

[35] Cf. Jones 2010: 111–24; for an outstanding example, Rogers 1991.
[36] Roth-Gerson 1987: no. 29.   [37] IJO III, Syr 86–7.

written on the same kind of tiles, is in Aramaic and records the specific date during which the entire building was constructed (244–5 CE), the distinguished individuals in charge of the work (the "building committee" in today's parlance), and blessings on all who worked on and contributed to the building.[38]

(A) This building was erected in the year five hundred and fifty six, which is the second year of Philip Julius Caesar, during the presbyterate of Samuel |5| the priest, son of Yedaya the archon. Now those who stood in charge of this work (were): Abraham [Abram] the treasurer, and Samuel son of Sphara, and . . . . the proselyte. With a willing spirit they began to build in the fifty-fifty-sixth year, and they sent to |10| . . .. and they made haste . . .. and they worked in . . . Blessing from the elders and from all the children of . . . they worked and toiled . . . Peace to them and their wives and all their children.

(B) And the 2nd (part). And like all those who worked were their brethren (in Dura?) . . . all of them who with their money . . . and in the eager desire of their souls . . . Their reward, all whatever . . . that the world which is to come . . . assured to them . . . on every Sabbath . . . spreading out their hands in it

(prayer?).

The date is determined by the Seleucid era, the regnal year of Philip Julius Caesar and the presbyterate of the priest Samuel son of Yedaya שמואל בר ידעי, who is obviously the Samuel in the first Greek inscription here. The Samuel in the second Greek inscription is named as one of those "who stood in charge of this work" (דקמו על עיבידה). Thus the two Samuels at Dura were members in the elite "founders' circle," as contemporary fundraisers would say, but they were not *ktistai*/founders of the community itself in the classical Greek sense, that is, they were not part of the foundational story of the community of people who used the new building; they were not the stuff of local legend or "local knowledge" that contributes to a community's unique identity.

The same interpretation of the noun κτίστης or verb κτίζειν is necessary for all but one of the remaining synagogue texts using those words. The many donors listed on one side of the inscribed stele at Aphrodisias are the collective subject of ἔκτισαν,[39] meaning that they were the ones who provided the necessary funds. In Ḥulda, the dedication to Εὐτυχῶς | Εὐστοχίῳ | καὶ Ἡσυχίῳ | καὶ Εὐαγρίῳ | τοῖς κτίσ|τες[40] records their

---

[38] IJO III, Syr 84, trans. Noy-Bloedhorn.   [39] IJO II, 14 A 7, with Ameling's commentary, p. 90.
[40] Roth-Gerson 1987: no. 13.

financial benefaction to the building; they could be either the exclusive, or just the major funders, but not "founders" in any other sense. In Daburra (Golan), ['Ρο]ύστικος ἔκτισεν[–?] is inscribed on a lintel underneath an Aramaic inscription recording that a certain Eleazar contributed some of the columns in the building.[41] Here, not only is Rusticus' inscription beneath Eleazar's dedication, and in smaller letters, but the missing part of the lintel could very well have recorded exactly what Rusticus donated.

All of these instances of *ktistai* as donors but not founders influence the interpretation of the complete inscription from the broken mosaic floor in Tiberias: Πρόκλος | Κρίσπου | ἔκτισεν.[42] Published translations of the text have Proclus son of Crispus as actual founder of the synagogue.[43] But in light of the many clear parallels, the inscription must indicate that Proclus contributed the funds for the mosaic, without the far-reaching implications of his being the founder of the building, much less the community. In fact, there is no word or expression in any surviving Greek synagogue inscription signifying "founding" in the sense required by the theory of local knowledge and micro-community.

Thus the κτίσται in synagogue inscriptions are major donors, and as such do not bring us any closer to discovering local knowledge or micro-identities. The same goes for the few instances of the individuals who claim responsibility in inscriptions for construction or renovation of a synagogue without being called κτίσται. A certain Leontis funded the lavish mosaic floor of the synagogue (or is it just a building next to the synagogue?) in Beth She'an and thereby purchased the right to advertise his benefaction in almost exclusive terms, but even if the building was known locally as "the Leontis synagogue," as it is in modern scholarship – perhaps even because it was in fact his private house? – that would describe the building and not the identity of the worshippers.

The most extravagant example of a single benefactor giving himself public credit for the synagogue building is, of course, the donation of Tiberius Claudius Polycharmus at Stobi.[44] That long text begins in this way:

[Κλ.] Τιβέριος Πολύ|χαρμος ὁ καὶ Ἀχύρι|ος ὁ πατὴρ τῆς ἐν | [5] Στόβοις συναγωγῆς. | ὃς πολιτευσάμε|νος πᾶσαν πολειτεί|αν κατὰ τὸν Ἰουδαῖ|σμὸν κτλ.

---

[41] Naveh's idea (1978: no. 7) that Rusticus was the craftsman cannot be right.

[42] Roth-Gerson 1987: no. 15.

[43] Roth-Gerson, ibid.; Milson 2007: 469; Hezser 2001: 402; Hachlili 2013: 476, "built or founded." L. Di Segni correctly translates the word as "built" = "had built" in 1988: 75 (Hebr.) and in 1998: 120.

[44] IJO I, Mac1 with bibliography; cf. commentary there for what follows.

There follows a list of the parts of the building that he subsidized, and provisions for keeping ownership within his family. In return for his benefaction, Polycharmos received the honorary title "Father of the synagogue in Stobi," obviously granted to him by the grateful, already existing community, which the wording suggests was organized around the only synagogue in Stobi. The expression πολιτευσάμενος πᾶσαν πολειτείαν κατὰ τὸν Ἰουδαϊσμὸν in ll. 5–8 means that he lived his entire public life according to the precepts of Judaism. Thus Polycharmos' rather typical and formulaic euergetistic inscription, if untypically long for a synagogue, perpetuates benefaction but does not represent or record the community's identity as such. It could even be said that, in contrast to other Jewish synagogue donor inscriptions, Polycharmos' does not contain explicit expressions of his personal devotion to the community but is really all about himself.

The one possible record of a Jewish *ktistes* as being a real founder is a dedicatory inscription from Sidibunda in Asia Minor.[45]

θεῷ ὑψίστωι καὶ | ἁγείᾳ καταφυγῇ | Ἀρτιμᾶς υἱὸς Ἀρ|τίμου Μομμίου | καὶ [Μ]αρκίας, ὁ αὐ|τὸς κτίστης, ἀ|νέστησεν καὶ | τὸν θυμιατίσ|τηρον καὶ κέον<α> | ἐκ τῶν ἰδίων

To the highest God and the holy refuge, Artimas son of Artimos Mommios and Markia, who himself is the founder (*ktistes*), donated the censer and column.

Here Artimas stresses that he is the κτίστης himself, and he uses an unrelated verb for the parts of the building he funded. There is not enough evidence in the short text to assert that Artimas' "foundation" gave the synagogue an exclusive identity or personal story, or that he really is not a κτίστης like Polycharmos and took special interest in these two components of the building; anything is possible, but not every possibility is likely. The inscription prima facie is a typical donor inscription, recording parts of the building for which Artimas provided all or most of the funds. This text is the only evidence of Jews in this city; but even its Jewishness is not certain.[46]

Before moving on to the next type of possible Jewish micro-community, we should briefly consider the basalt lintel from Dabbura, similar to the one cited previously, inscribed in Hebrew:[47]

זה בית | מדרשו | של רבי | אליעזר | הקפר

This is the *beth midrash* of Rabbi Eliezer Ha-Qappar.

---

[45] IJO II, 215.   [46] Ameling, ibid., and Schürer 1986: 32.
[47] Gregg and Urman 1996: 125–6, AF59; Naveh 1978: no. 6.

Here the rabbinic figure mentioned seems not to have been a founder but the main pedagogical or spiritual figure, and indeed the building could have been used exclusively by and identified with a small circle of R. Eliezer's students and followers. There is some doubt as to whether the rabbi of this inscription is the famous Talmudic sage,[48] but the question concerning us here is whether a school or academy is useful in consideration of a micro-community. A *beth midrash* was not a synagogue or a constituted community.[49] It is true that a teacher plus group of disciples could turn into a religio-social movement or the sort of "community" that provided its members a stronger sense of identity and belonging than their locality, city or Empire; Christianity is only the most obvious example. But a single *beth midrash* is not a religious movement, and furthermore it cannot be known from this single inscription how long the academy continued to function, with the strong identity of its intellectual leader, after his death. A stone building and carved inscription would presume such a continuation, no matter whether the foundation of the building, or the group that later moved into the building, can be dated to the lifetime of the sage. In this specific case, it seems the lintel is to be dated much later than the lifetime of the tanna R. Eliezer. But we are again poking around in the dark, and without further light from another source, the rabbi's academy remains an academy, not a full-blown community.

The cases adduced suggest that while some synagogues both in Iudaea/ Palaestina and the Diaspora may have had founders and founders' stories that afforded them a particular local identity distinguishing them both from their immediate surroundings and all other Jewish synagogues, no clear case emerges from any synagogue's self-documentation. The dim and partial picture is a matter of chance: fuller evidence, both epigraphical and literary, could reveal a wider, richer phenomenon. A few names of congregations and founders suggest that there were once many more, with their own unique stories.

Notably missing from the Jewish evidence – given the importance of Greek and Roman myths in the foundation of colonies and the identification of micro-identities in the Graeco-Roman world – is any connection between a certain Jewish community and a story or character from the Bible. It is true that the Jews of Babylonia traced their origins to the expulsion after the destruction of the First Temple in the sixth century BCE – a humble origin which became a mark of honor – and the Egyptian

---

[48] See discussion and previous bibliography in Miller 2014: 239–73. Cohen 1981: 11 and 14.
[49] Fine 2014: 123–37, who critiques Dan Urman's "oversized claims" that the southern Golan had become a Talmudic village by the fifth century.

Jews of the Hellenistic period, as well, related that the founding members of their large population were first brought to Egypt by the Persians and then by Ptolemy I.[50] So far as the Babylonian Jews are concerned, it would be instructive to have even one synagogue from there; there is no physical or epigraphical evidence for the phenomenon we seek. Egypt is a more complex case, not only because of the very clear, legitimizing aetiological legends involving as well the translation of the Bible into Greek, and the vigorously assertive Jewish community in Alexandria, but also because of the Jewish *politeumata*, which functioned more or less as independent or semi-independent communities, as well as the Temple of Onias at the center of a very particular self-defining community.[51] Yet we can preempt further discussion by noting that the Temple of Onias was destroyed in 73 CE, and the Jewish communities in Egypt were destroyed and dwindled to practically nothing in the second century CE, so that there is no real comparative evidence for the period under consideration here.

While much synagogue figurative art consists of nonlocalized images like the zodiac or – most prominently – depictions of shared national symbols like the Temple and its implements and symbols of Jewish holidays like the lulav and etrog, some synagogue floors and walls were illustrated with narrative scenes and figures from the Bible.[52] Do any of these figures or stories appear in a place connected with them in the Bible, thus providing a local connection to the national story? The answer is no. The usefulness of this observation is limited, since most surviving synagogue buildings are located in places not mentioned in the Bible, or where no important events occurred; and most important locations in the Biblical

---

[50] *Letter of Aristeas* 13 and 35, and see the commentary on these passages by Wright 2015.

[51] Schürer 1986: 47–8, 145–7; Gruen 1997: 47–70. On the Jewish *politeuma*, see now Sänger 2016: http://classics.oxfordre.com/view/10.1093/acrefore/9780199381135.001.0001/acrefore-9780199381135-e-8036?rskey=1tHUgO&result=1.

Aside from the *politeumata*, the inscriptions from the third- to second-century BCE synagogues in Egypt give no indication of the kind of thing we are looking for here; cf. Horbury and Noy 1992: nos. 9,13, 18, 20, 27, etc.

[52] Levine 2012: 350–4; Hachlili 2013: 389–434; Fine 2005: 57–134. Note Hachlili, 434: "The Jewish communities wanted to decorate their major religious and social structures with didactic, narrative illustrations expressing their religious and national tradition, their legacy and their shared experiences, evoking memories of past glory. The communities used folk tales based on biblical stories with additions taken from the world of legend, which found artistic expression in painted narrative scenes; the wall paintings of the third-century CE Dura Europus synagogue are the earliest evidence of this. Subsequently, this folk art would evolve and develop in synagogue mosaic pavements of the Byzantine period. The narrative scenes were considered historical events, yet they were also treated as parables and had symbolic implications." The richly decorated walls at Dura Europus and extensively inscribed walls at Reḥov serve as a sober warning about the mass of material that has been lost, and against attempting definitive conclusions about what was and was not.

patriarchal and monarchical narratives, such as they were identified in antiquity, do not have the remains of Jewish synagogues.[53] Nonetheless, it is interesting to note that the main figures, the primary formative moments and the famous instances of heroism in synagogue art – Abraham (the binding of Isaac), King David, Daniel in the lions' den, Noah, Samson, the investment of Aaron and the priests, the panoply of unique figures and scenes in the Dura Europus paintings – have no textual connection with their place. Samson, for example, is depicted in the Lower Galilee, in one scene even carrying the Gate of Gaza on his shoulders, but not in any surviving part of the Gaza floor.[54] David, who is depicted at Gaza, is not named in the long inscription at Ein Gedi; and other main locations of David's biblical story do not preserve the remains of synagogues.[55] It is just possible that the "Purim panel" in the Dura frescoes – a unique scene in synagogue art, placed significantly just to the left of the Torah shrine – highlights a presumed local association with the heroes Mordecai and Esther; some residents of Dura could very well have felt themselves to be more a part of Parthia/Persia than the Roman world, even at a great distance from the royal capital.[56] But since Dura is, of course, not mentioned in the Scroll of Esther, only a local text or tradition – not the Biblical one – would secure this connection.

This, of course, does not rule out for any synagogue some extrabiblical association with a figure, story or verse, such as a special association of the Sepphoris synagogue with priests, which could have been part of the community's local identity: the consecration of Aaron and his sons is portrayed there in a unique scene.[57] The locals knew.

In conclusion, this chapter took up a limited task within a limited set of evidence. It is somewhat artificial but nonetheless (hopefully) instructive to measure an aspect of ancient Judaism mainly by inscriptions in the ritual and civic centers in which they actually lived, without interference of partisan or particularistic literary sources. The phenomenon we are hunting probably had a stronger existence than what we have been able to uncover, but the evidence is too ambiguous – and the synagogal

---

[53] The situation is, of course, different for Samaritan synagogues, but they lie beyond the scope of the present inquiry.

[54] Magness 2013; Grey and Magness 2013.   [55] Barasch 1980.

[56] The Persian inscriptions in the building were written on that painted scene; this, however, was a sign of appreciation of visitors from Persia proper to the distant outpost IJO III, pp. 177–209. Sabar 2000: 154–63; Tawil 1979.

[57] Weiss 2005: 247–9; 2012: 91–111; Weiss downplays the actual role priests played in the synagogue in the period of the Sepphoris synagogue, but that does not rule out that a strong priestly presence contributed to the community's identity.

communities so uninterested in communicating it – that no clear and detailed instances can be added to the larger study of it. If you asked any Jewish community represented wholly by their synagogue – how did you get to this particular place? when were you founded, by whom and why? – they probably had answers, but none are advertised or perpetuated in mosaic or stone. The physical remains of Jewish synagogue communities show a connection to the shared Jewish story rather than any particularistic story connecting them to their actual location. When the members of the synagogues – or the synagogues themselves, as the collective donations show – erected inscriptions, they were talking more to themselves and perhaps other Jews and interested visitors than to random outsiders or the Roman authorities.

The cases of Ein Gedi and Reḥov reveal extremely inward-looking communities who saw fit to publish in their synagogue floors and walls regulations and laws regulating their local society, in a particular, nonformulaic language. This inward focus, this identification with, if anything, the collective Jewish identity, mean that Jewish synagogal communities did not react to Roman "globalization" in the same way as Greek cultural or political entities.

Roman Emperors in Talmudic Literature[*]

YUVAL SHAHAR

> R. Naḥman opened his discourse with the text, *Therefore fear thou not, O Jacob My servant* (Jer. xxx,10). This speaks of Jacob himself, of whom it is written, *And he dreamed, and behold, a ladder set up on the earth . . . and behold the angels of God ascending and descending on it* (Gen. xxviii,12). These angels . . . were the guardian princes of the nations . . . the Holy One, blessed be He, showed our father Jacob the prince of Babylon ascending seventy rungs of the ladder, the prince of Media fifty-two rungs, the prince of Greece one hundred and eighty, while the prince of Edom [= Rome] ascended till Jacob did not know how many rungs. Thereupon our father Jacob was afraid. He thought: is it possible that this one will never be brought down? Said the Holy One, blessed be He, to him: '*Fear thou not, O Jacob My servant.*' Even if he ascend and sit down by Me, I will bring him down from there![1]

This *midrash* clearly shows both the unique role of Rome in Jewish history in antiquity and the central place it occupies in Talmudic literature. A comprehensive study of Rome's role in the Talmudic literature would require us to collect, analyze and categorize all the sources referring to Rome, both directly and indirectly, as a collective political and cultural entity, through Rome as an empire (usually an evil one), down to details of toponomy in the place names from the city of Rome itself to the port of Brindisium, as well as the names of important Roman personae. As far as I know, there is at present no such comprehensive study, which would have to be vast. The present chapter is devoted to a narrow but important part of the Talmudic image of Rome: Roman emperors.

A methodological note: the Talmudic literature is ahistoric. It was created over a millennium, and even its earlier stages in Late Antiquity started at the beginning of the third century and continued to develop up to the seventh. There were two different centers – Palestine and Babylonia – which created two different Talmuds, and in Palestine especially rabbinic

---

[*] This chapter was given for the first time as a paper at the conference 'Rome – an empire of many nations', in honour of Benjamin Isaac (Tel Aviv University, May 2015). A different version of the present chapter was presented at the Oxford Centre for Hebrew and Jewish Studies, as part of the seminar on Jewish History and Literature in the Graeco-Roman Period, headed by Martin Goodman (November 2015).

[1] Va-Yiqra Rabbah, Emor 29, 2 (ed. Soncino, adapted).

literature branched out into different genres. Nevertheless, many narratives and anecdotes about historical events and personae, in our case Roman emperors, were described, related and repeated throughout all the Talmudic literature over many periods. This is why it is so essential to analyze each text carefully in its context. Jewish religious regulations (*halakhah*) have to be understood in their religious, cultural, sociological and political framework; and when analyzing a tale, our reading should address the different contexts of interpretation: literary, generic, comparative and historical. I cannot, of course, go into every detail of the development of the character of Hadrian, for instance, but only draw the bottom line – or rather lines – of what Jews told themselves about a named emperor, in Palestine on the one hand and in Babylonia on the other. In some cases, usually in the Palestinian literature, we can trace different chronological phases that shift and vary the profile and role of a particular Roman emperor. All the sources which we relate to are from the late second to the early third centuries up to the sixth century CE. The earliest are from the Palestinian tannaitic literature (i.e. up to the middle of the third century), while the rest were produced by the Palestinian Amoraim in the Jerusalem Talmud (which was redacted or came to an end in the seventies of the fourth century), and the early Palestinian *midrashei Aggadah, Bereshit Rabbah* and *Va-Yiqrah Rabbah* from the fifth or sixth century. From the other side of the Euphrates we can hear the Jewish Babylonian voice, through the Babylonian Talmud, mainly from the fourth to the sixth centuries.

There are nine named emperors in the whole of the Talmudic literature,[2] but two of these are barely mentioned and will not concern us: Augustus appears usually as a title,[3] and Tiberius is noted because of the city called

---

[2] Usually scholars identify gas*kalgas* גסקלגס with the emperor Gaius Caligula: T Sotah xiii,6 (ed. Lieberman: 232); JT Sotah ix 24b; BT Sotah 33a; Shir ha-Shirim Rabbah viii,9. This identification followed the medieval scholia of Megillat Taʾanit on 22nd Shvat (Noam 2003: 112–14. See also the discussion and previous literature, pp. 283–90; dating the various scholia, pp. 424–6, 386–91). However, all the Talmudic texts connect Gaskalgas with Shimoʾn haTzadiq, a figure from the Hellenistic, not the Roman, period. See especially Seder Olam Rabbah (Milikovski 2013: I, 323–4), which names Gaskalgas as one of the last Hellenistic kings מלכי יון who are separated from the wars against the Romans. Milikovski 2013: II, 550–1, came to the same conclusion concerning Seder Olam, but concluded that the Talmudic sources referred to Gaius Caligula, and even suggests, strangely, that these sources are dependent on the scholia of Megillat Taʾanit (n. 258, p. 551). See recently the discussion of Noam 2017: 453–84.

[3] JT Berakhot ix,12d; Shir ha-Shirim Rabbah i,19; Shir ha-Shirim Zuta i,6 (ed. Buber: 12); Esther Rabbah i,19; Aggadat Bereshit L,1 (ed. Buber: 101); Shmot Rabbah, be-Shalaḥ xxiii,1. There is only one occurrence of 'Augustus' referring to the first Roman Emperor in the Talmudic literature: Shir ha-Shirim Zuta i,12 (ed. Buber: 12). 'Augusta' is used several times as a title for the Biblical queen Vashti: Esther Rabbah iii,5 and 8; Shir ha-Shirim Zuta i,6 (ed. Buber: 12); Midrash Tehilim x,6 (ed. Buber: 96), xvii,11 (ed. Buber: 133).

after him.[4] This holds true also for Nero in the Palestinian literature, although in Babylonia his role is more significant and positive.[5] Thus, we are left with six emperors to deal with, who are categorized according to the Talmudic attitude to them and after Sergio Leone and Clint Eastwood, as the Good, the Bad (at times they are also ugly . . .) and the Middling. Historically, we should start with the Bad.

The Bad are those emperors who fought against and crushed the great Jewish revolts in Palestine and the Jewish diaspora during the first and second centuries CE: Vespasian, Titus, Trajan and Hadrian. I shall confine myself here to dealing only with Hadrian.[6]

Hadrian, like the 'bad' emperors who preceded him, opens his Talmudic career in the Palestinian literature with a terrible reputation based on very solid historical grounds: he crushed the Bar-Kokhva revolt, causing a great disaster for the Jewish people in their land in antiquity. His cruelty surpassed the deeds and character of Titus, and even those of Trajan and his bloodshed (in Egypt and Cyprus): Hadrian, we are told, devastated the land; killed hundreds of thousands of people; murdered infants; and profaned the bodies of the dead, forbidding their burial right up to his own death:

> R. Yose said . . . [that] Hadrian, the evil one, had come and devastated the entire land.[7]
>
> Said R. Yoḥanan, The voice [= orders] of Hadrian Caesar is killing 80,000 myriads in Beitar; they kept slaughtering [the Jews] until a horse sank into blood up to his nose; they found three hundred babies' skulls on a single rock; the evil Hadrian had a large vineyard, eighteen miles by eighteen miles. . . . They surrounded it by a wall made of those who were slain in Beitar. . . . And he did not decree that they could be buried, until another king came along and decreed that they may be buried.[8]

Unusually, the negative attitude towards Hadrian found its expression even in the halakhic field: Hadrianic earthenware is one of the things that belong to gentiles and is forbidden, and it is forbidden to have any benefit from it.[9]

---

[4] Bereshit Rabbah xxiii,17 (ed. Albeck and Theodor: 221).

[5] Yisraeli-Taran 1997: 24–8, including sources and previous studies.

[6] I prefer to deal with Hadrian because of three reasons: 1. Hadrian, as a Talmudic figure, has been discussed by scholars far less than the Talmudic Vespasian and Titus. 2. He is much more variegated through the various Talmudic compilations and layers than his 'bad' colleagues. 3. There are some interesting similarities between the portrayals of Hadrian in Talmudic and Roman literature.

[7] JT, Peah vii, 20a.   [8] JT, Ta'aniot iv, 68d–69a.

[9] M A'vodah Zarah ii,3; T A'vodah Zarah iv,8. It is interesting to note that the later Palestinian rabbis (at the end of the third century) attributed this ruling to Rabbi Meir, a distinguished figure from the first generation after the Bar Kokhva War, JT A'vodah Zarah ii 41b (= JT Orlah iii 63a).

Thus, fitting the punishment to the crime, Hadrian becomes the subject of the Talmud's most negative imprecation: 'May his bones be crushed!' A special sort of *damnatio memoriae*.[10]

But now comes a surprise. From the late fourth century on, both the Palestinian *midrashic* literature and the Babylonian Talmud delineate a new Hadrian, an intellectually curious man, who mixes with the mob and talks to ordinary people: 'Hadrian, may his bones be crushed, was walking on the paths of Tiberias and he saw an old man hew out an area in order to plant. Hadrian said to him: Old man, old man ...',[11] and in particular he converses patiently with rabbis. His conversation has a philosophical and theological aura: Hadrian wonders, how was the world created?[12] How was the human being created?[13] What is the nature of the water of the ocean (*okeanus*)?[14] In spite of the sharp change in the depiction of his character, this Hadrian is situated in the correct historical time, and usually his partner in dialogue is R. Yehoshua b. Hananiah. What brings this 'odd couple' together? Maybe this is a literary meeting between two moderate and enlightened figures, the very modest rabbi, a true successor of Rabban Yohanan ben Zakkai in the first two decades of the second century, and the enlightened emperor Hadrian, as he is depicted in the classical sources, at least during his first years, up to the middle of the third decade of the same century.[15]

The cruel Hadrian, 'may his bones be crushed', has not vanished but from now on he has a second face. The sole sign that we are dealing with the same person is the mutual epithet 'may his bones be crushed' for both the

[10] שחיק עצמות /שחיק עצמות/ שחוק עצמות /שחיק טמיא Bereshit Rabbah x (ed. Albeck and Theodor: 75–6), xxviii (ed. Albeck and Theodor: 261–2), lxv (ed. Albeck and Theodor: 740), lxxviii (ed. Albeck and Theodor: 916–8, and parallels); Va-Yiqra Rabbah, Qedoshim xxv (ed. Margaliot: 576–9, and parallels); Eikhah Rabbah i (ed. Buber: 82), iii (ed. Buber: 138–9), v (ed. Buber: 155–6); Qohelet Rabbah ii,2; Ruth Rabbah iii, and parallels; Tehilim Rabbah xii (ed. Buber: 104); Pesiqta Rabbati, Ten Commandments, Petihta (ed. Ulmer: 436–41).

[11] Va-Yiqra Rabbah, Qedoshim xxv (ed. Margaliot: 576–9, and parallels), and see the thorough discussion of Hasan-Rokem 2003: 87–137.

[12] Bereshit Rabbah x (ed. Albeck and Theodor: 75–6): Hadrian, may his bones be crushed, asked R. Yehoshua b. Hananiah how did the Holy One, blessed be He, create the world?

[13] Bereshit Rabbah xxviii (ed. Albeck and Theodor: 261–2, and parallels): Hadrian, may his bones be crushed, asked R. Yehoshua b. Hananiah, From what part will the Holy One, blessed be He, cause man to blossom forth in the future?

[14] Bereshit Rabbah xiii (ed. Albeck and Theodor: 118, and parallels): R. Eliezer and R. Yehoshua were once travelling on the Great Sea. ... they filled a barrel of water from there. When they arrived in Rome, Hadrian asked them, What is the nature of the water of the ocean?

[15] Hadrian as well educated and a promoter of culture is typical of all Roman writers, even those who are less positive towards him, such as Aurelius Victor in *De Caesaribus* xiv.

'wicked' and the 'enlightened'.[16] What is striking is the similarity between the two faces of the Talmudic Hadrian,[17] and the double face attributed to the emperor in Roman historiography, especially the *Vita Hadriani* in the *Historia Augusta*, which is dated either to the time of Diocletian or to the late fourth century.[18] The same characteristics of Hadrian are portrayed again and again throughout the second half of the fourth century up to the turn of the fourth and fifth centuries,[19] in other words, at the same time as the earliest Talmudic traditions of this other, positive face of Hadrian.

The *Vita Hadriani* characterizes Hadrian clearly as double-faced: 'He was, in the same person, austere and genial, dignified and playful, dilatory and quick to act, niggardly and generous, deceitful and straightforward, cruel and merciful, and always in all things changeable.'[20] In the words of Benario: 'even a cursory reading of the life reveals a curious mingling of two traditions, one favorable to the emperor, the other quite the opposite. The former is sober and detailed, the latter anecdotal and miscellaneous.'[21] At the turn of the fourth and fifth centuries, the *Epitome de Caesaribus* had the same impression: 'He was changeable, manifold, and multiform; as if a born arbiter with respect to vices and virtues, by some artifice he controlled intellectual impulse. . . . he simulated restraint, affability, clemency, and conversely disguised the ardor for fame with which he burned.'[22]

In two successive sentences the *Vita* relates to Hadrian's attitudes and manners towards both ordinary and learned people: (1) 'Most courteous in

---

[16] See the question of Kadushin 1987: 170, referring to Va-Yiqra Rabbah, Qedoshim xxv (ed. Margaliot: 576–9): 'The role played by the wicked Hadrian here is puzzling for his relations to the old man express the attitude of a pious man' (170).

[17] I call this 'two faces' because there is an (almost) total separation between the traditional 'bad' Hadrian, who is in charge of the destruction, massacre and persecutions, and the new 'enlightened' Hadrian. In Roman literature he has these two faces in each of his biographies.

[18] In the preface of the *Aelius* i1, Aelius Spartianus, the biographer, addresses Diocletian and informs him that he has already written a biography of Hadrian. Hermann Dessau challenged this and other 'alleged' dedications and the 'pretence' of six different biographers, and concluded that a single author wrote the whole of the *Historia Augusta* at the end of the fourth century. Up until now most scholars have accepted his conclusions. Recently, Renan Baker has vehemently criticized the common view and argued for different biographies composed by six different biographers; see Baker 2014, with detailed research history, especially his discussion of Spartianus/Separtianus: 260–6.

[19] Aurelius Victor, *De Caesaribus*, xiv; Eutropius, *Breviarium historiae Romanae*, viii, 6–7; *Epitome de Caesaribus*, xiv are only remnants of the vast fourth-century literature, now mainly lost, which retold the lives of earlier Roman emperors; see Bleckmann 1997.

[20] SHA, *Hadrianus* xiv, 11: *idem severus comis, gravis lascivus, cunctator, festinans, tenax liberalis, simulator simplex, saevus clemens, et semper in omnibus varius.*

[21] Benario 1980: 4.

[22] *Epitome de Caes.*, xiv, 6: *Varius multiplex multiformis; ad vitia atque virtutes quasi arbiter genitus, impetum mentis quodam artificio regens; . . . continentiam facilitatem clementiam simulans contraque dissimulans ardorem gloriae, quo flagrabat.*

his conversations, even with the very humble, he denounced all who, in the belief that they were thereby maintaining the imperial dignity, begrudged him the pleasure of such friendliness. (2) In the museum at Alexandria he propounded many questions to the teachers and answered himself what he had propounded.'[23] The first sentence matches the Talmudic Hadrian who walks through the fields of Tiberias and has a conversation with an old man. The second sentence fits Hadrian's philosophical and theological dialogues with R. Yehoshua – although here the emperor simply puts the questions and it is the rabbi who gives him the correct, meaningful answers.

The most interesting similarities between Hadrian both in the *Vita Hadriani* and in the *midrash* have been proposed and studied by Galit Hasan-Rokem.[24] Referring to Hadrian's generous gifts and his fondness for the public baths, the Roman biographer told a well-known bathing joke, in two scenes. In the first scene, Hadrian sees a veteran, known to him from military service, rubbing his back and the rest of his body on the wall. When he realizes that this is because he does not have a slave of his own, he presents him both with slaves and with the cost of their maintenance. In the second scene, on a different day, several old men imitate the veteran, rubbing themselves on the wall in order to arouse the emperor's generosity. But this time Hadrian orders them to be called out and rub each other down in turn.[25]

Midrash *Va-Yikra Rabbah* tells a similar story, also based on two opposed scenes. In the first scene, Hadrian sees an old man near Tiberias planting a young fig tree and asks him for whom is he planting this tree. The old man answers that if he is fortunate, he will eat the figs himself; if not, his descendants will eat them. Hadrian tells him: 'If you are fortunate enough to eat of them, let me know.' When the figs ripen, the old man fills a basket with figs and brings it to Hadrian. The emperor orders his servants to empty his basket and fill it with dinars. In the second scene, a neighbour of the old man, instigated by his wife, imitates the old man, comes before Hadrian and says: 'I have heard that the king loves figs and reimburses them with dinars.' Hadrian's reaction is very similar to his answer to the people in the bath house in the *Vita Hadriani*: he orders his servants 'to put him in front of the palace gate and whoever enters or exits should throw [a fig] in his face.'[26]

---

[23] *SHA, Hadrianus* xx, 1–2: (1) *In conloquiis etiam humillimorum civilissimus fuit, detestans eos qui sibi hanc voluptatem humanitatis quasi servantes fastigium principis inviderent.* (2) *apud Alexandriam in Museo multas quaestiones professoribus proposuit et proposuit ipse dissolvit.* Again, the same characteristic is delineated by the *Epitome de Caes.*, xiv, 7.

[24] Hasan-Rokem 2003: 135–6.   [25] *SHA, Hadrianus* xvii, 6–7.

[26] This *midrashic* story is much more developed and variegated than my simplistic reduction, but this should be sufficient for the current discussion. Hasan-Rokem (2003: 116) also points to the similarity between the 'fig story' and the 'fish anecdote' in the biography of Tiberius by

The Talmudic Hadrian, then, heads the Roman legions who destroy Palestinian Jewry, on the one hand, while on the other hand, holds philosophical dialogues with R. Yehoshua in the same narrative time. In this context we note that the *Historia Augusta* concludes its presentation of Hadrian's dual face with a nice anecdote about an argument between the emperor and the eminent philosopher and sophist Favorinus, which reveals the inequity of such disagreement. Although Favorinus is correct, he gives way to Hadrian, and when rebuked by friends, replies, 'You advise me badly, friends, since you do not permit me to believe that he who commands thirty legions is the most learned of all.'[27]

What is the historical background for the 'enlightened' Hadrian in Talmudic literature? Many scholars point to the early years of Hadrian's reign as a period of positive relationship between the new emperor and the Jews, at least with regard to some of his actions that were interpreted by the Jews as being in their favor.[28] This sounds logical at first glance, but in fact these scholarly conclusions totally neglect the clear distinction between two different chronological phases in the Talmudic literature which refer to Hadrian: both the *tannaitic* and *amoraic* literature up to the end of the Palestinian Talmud in the last quarter of the fourth century delineate only the wicked Hadrian; the enlightened Hadrian is a product of *aggadic midrashim* only from the early fifth century on.[29] There are some similarities between the enlightened Talmudic Hadrian and his depiction in fourth-century Roman literature, especially in his wide education and curiosity. Thus the Talmudic *midrashim* find him as the most convenient emperor to represent Rome in dialogues with Jewish rabbis of his generation, like Rabbi Yehoshua son of Ḥananiah.

To sum up: first of all, the 'wicked' Hadrian, 'may his bones be crushed', is a direct and immediate Jewish reaction to the historic role of this emperor in the most catastrophic event in Jewish antiquity. There is no

Suetonius (*Tiberius*, iii 60), and the possible association between the emperor (Tiberius) and the *midrashic* space (the town of Tiberias).

[27] SHA, *Hadrianus* xv, 12–13: (12) *et Favorinus quidem, cum verbum eius quondam ab Hadriano reprehensum esset, atque ille cessisset, arguentibus amicis, quod male cederet Hadriano de verbo quod idonei auctores usurpassent, risum iucundissimum movit.* (13) *ait enim: 'Non recte suadetis, familiares, qui non patimini me illum doctiorem omnibus credere, qui habet triginta legiones.'* I owe this reference to Benjamin Isaac.

[28] Especially Herr 1971: 123–5, 142–5; 1972: 91–3; Hengel 1984–5: 134, 155–60; a slightly different picture in Schäfer 1981: 242–4, but see Schäfer 1990, very similar to Herr's arguments. Alon 1989 (original Heb. 1955): 432–4, 453–4 already hints cautiously at this possibility.

[29] See the preliminary remark of Alon 1989: 437. Hasan-Rokem 2003: 121 proposes the same direction, but does not elaborate on it, and basically ignores the chronological difference between the two faces of Talmudic Hadrian.

connection between this phase of the Talmudic Hadrian and Roman historiography. On the contrary, Cassius Dio depicts Hadrian's reactions to the Jewish rebellion and the measures he takes as rational and very cautious. In fact, Hadrian's reign is usually remembered by the Romans as a period without wars. Secondly, Hadrian is already depicted in Roman literature as double-faced from the second and third centuries, but there is no positive hint about him at all in the contemporary Talmudic works. Thirdly, it is only from the early fifth century on, hundreds of years after the last revolt and its terrible consequences, that Jews could allow themselves to draw another Hadrian as well, an enlightened one, shown as a Roman representative who deals with the rabbis of his time, revealing, explicitly or tacitly, the advantage of Jewish culture and theology. Finally, there are similarities between the variegated and even unpredictable character of Hadrian in both the *Vita Hadriani* (and later fourth-century Roman history and biography) and the later Talmudic stories which were told from the early fifth century on.

We move now to consider the figure of **the good emperor** in the Talmudic literature. The one perfectly good emperor is called 'Antoninus', and he is usually identified with Caracalla.[30] He is presented as the intimate friend of Rabbi Judah ha-Nasi, the renowned Jewish patriarch of the late second and early third centuries (i.e. during the Severan period). Together they discuss business, politics and pleasure, to their mutual benefit, using biblical verses and hermeneutics. There are twenty-nine different Talmudic traditions, twenty-one Palestinian and eight Babylonian,[31] which characterize their very positive relationship and their dialogues, shaping 'Antoninus' as a clever, learned and moderate man and emperor.

Thematically there are three groups of traditions:

I. A concrete relationship, usually in the field of economics, where Rabbi benefits from the emperor.

II. Rabbi as the political advisor of Antoninus. The emperor consults him as to whether or not to go to Alexandria, how to fill his treasury, how to

---

[30] The main comprehensive studies of the 'Rabbi and Antoninus' Talmudic traditions are Krauss 1909/1910 (part two is devoted to scholarly opinions about the identity of Antoninus); Jacobs 1995: 125–54 (125–9, scholarly opinions, mainly the identification with Caracalla), who himself opposes methodologically and empirically any identification with a specific emperor; Meir 1999: 263–92, literary analysis and differentiation between the Palestinian traditions and the Babylonians; and Oppenheimer 2007: 43–50 (the identification with Caracalla, 47–50= Oppenheimer 2017: 48–8, as Caracalla, 54–8. See also Ch. 15 in this book).

[31] Meir 1999, Palestinian traditions: 263–77; Babylonian: 277–91.

manipulate the Roman aristocracy in order to achieve his goals, and so forth.

III. Philosophical and theological dialogues, where Antoninus is not only intellectually curious, learned, clever and witty, but also well versed in the Bible, Jewish regulations and hermeneutics.

Finally, one late Palestinian tradition even discusses the possibility that Antoninus became Jewish. This possibility is rejected, but Antoninus is still *the* non-Jew who nevertheless deserves the World to Come.[32]

Generally speaking, the earlier traditions are closer to the historical arena and characters. Antoninus seems to be much more of a political figure who benefits Rabbi as his client, and his interest in Judaism is very simplistic. Over time he becomes a true philosopher and in consequence nearly a Jewish sage. As I shall try to argue, his character, as depicted in the Talmudic sources, develops into a hybrid of two different emperors who were both called Antoninus, Caracalla and Elagabalus. I should note here, however, that there are some scholars who fiercely refute, both methodologically and empirically, any historical identification with any historical emperor.[33]

Now, within our very selective and narrow scope, I wish to point out another striking phenomenon: the way in which the Talmudic Antoninus (= Caracalla, as distinct from other candidates like Antoninus Pius and Marcus Aurelius) is the complete opposite of the portrait of this emperor in Roman historiography, mainly characterized by the epitome of Cassius Dio, and by Herodian, both of whom were active during the years of Caracalla's reign, and later on in the *Historia Augusta*. In these Roman sources, Antoninus Caracalla is capricious, cruel, bloodthirsty, anti-intellectual, and deaf to any advice and advisor.

Antoninus as Caracalla: There are at least three Talmudic traditions about Antoninus that have many resemblances to characteristics, anecdotes and events which are peculiar to the emperor Caracalla in the Roman historiography and biography of the third and fourth centuries.

The earliest traditions in the tannaitic Midrash known as the Mekhilta de-Rabbi Ishmael, redacted in the mid-third century (i.e. a short time after Rabbi's death),[34] associate Antoninus twice (out of four instances) with Alexandria, Egypt and Pharaoh.

---

[32] JT Megillah ii 72b, 74a, Sanhedrin x 29c, and see Cohen 2010. I shall come back to this later in this chapter.

[33] Jacobs 1995 (throughout the whole discussion and concluding on 153–4, 165), followed by Cohen 2010: 329. Meir 1994: 25 came to the same conclusions.

[34] The Mekhilta as the most ancient source for 'Antoninus' is also underlined by Meir 1999: 263–5; Cohen 2010: 357, n. 59.

> Antoninus asked our Holy Rabbi, I want to go to Alexandria, but will
> a king stand there and defeat me? He answered, I do not know, at any rate
> it is written that Egypt could not appoint a king or a minister.[35]

Rabbi gives Antoninus an indirect answer, and the whole issue appears
innocent. But according to the Roman historians, Antoninus turned
Alexandria into a bloodbath, as Dio writes:

> (1) Now Antoninus, in spite of the immense affection which he professed
> to cherish for Alexander, all but utterly destroyed the whole of his [i.e
> Alexander's] city. . . . (3) He slaughtered so many persons that he did
> not even venture to say anything about their number, but wrote to
> the senate that it was of no interest how many of them or who had died,
> since all had deserved to suffer this fate. 23,2: Antoninus was present at
> most of this slaughter and pillaging, both looking on and taking
> a hand.[36]

In the Mekhilta, Antoninus is afraid lest 'a king will stand there [in
Alexandria] and defeat me', which could be an echo to the story in Dio
that a short time before the assassination of Caracalla a certain Egyptian,
Serapio, had told the emperor that he would be short-lived and that
Macrinus would succeed him.[37]

Again, the Mekhilta, in the name of Rabbi himself, makes Antoninus the
true successor of Pharaoh, at least in chariot warfare.

> And shalishim over all of them [Shalishim means] that they were triply
> armed. Rabban Simon the son of Gamaliel says: It refers to the third man
> on the chariot. Formerly there had been only two who drove the chariot,
> but **Pharaoh** added one more so as to pursue Israel faster. **Rabbi says:**
> **Antoninus** added one more to them so that there were four.[38]

It is interesting to note here that Caracalla is the Roman emperor par
excellence who was portrayed as a Pharaoh, and four monumental

---

[35] Mekhilta de-Rabbi Ishmael, beShalah [Shirah] 6 (ed. Lauterbach: 201 adapted).
[36] Dio, lxxviii 22,1–3: Ὁ δὲ Ἀντωνῖνος, καίτοι τὸν Ἀλέξανδρον ὑπεραγαπᾶν φάσκων, τοὺς ἐκείνου
πολίτας μικροῦ δεῖν πάντας ἄρδην ἀπώλεσεν 3προσέτι καὶ τὰ τέγη προκατασχών. καὶ ἵνα τὰς
κατὰ μέρος συμφορὰς τὰς τότε κατασχούσας τὴν ἀθλίαν πόλιν παρῶ, τοσούτους κατέσφαξεν ὥστε
μηδὲ εἰπεῖν περὶ τοῦ πλήθους αὐτῶν τολμῆσαι, ἀλλὰ καὶ τῇ βουλῇ γράψαι ὅτι οὐδὲν διαφέρει
πόσοι σφῶν ἢ τίνες ἐτελεύτησαν· πάντες. 23.2 καὶ τούτων τὰ μὲν πλείω αὐτὸς ὁ Ἀντωνῖνος παρὼν
καὶ ὁρῶν.
   The Alexandrian massacre is a central issue in the main surviving Roman references to
Caracalla, Herodian iv 8.6–9.8; SHA, Caracalla vi, 2–3.
[37] Dio lxxix 4, 4–5.
[38] Mekhilta de-Rabbi Ishmael, beShalah [Va-yehi] 1 (ed. Lauterbach: 135, adapted).

'Pharaonic' statues of him have been discovered in Egypt.[39] This was due to the fact that his favourite deity was the Egyptian god Serapis, whose son or brother he claimed to be.

One tradition from the Babylonian Talmud also connects 'Antoninus son of Aseverus' with Egypt:

> R. Ḥama son of R. Ḥanina said: Three treasures did Joseph hide in Egypt: one was revealed to Korah; one to Antoninus the son of Aseverus; and the third is stored up for the righteous for the future time.[40]

If we can rely here upon the name of the Rabbi R. Ḥama son of R. Ḥanina, and the pure Hebrew language (i.e. not Aramaic) attributed to him, this would seem to be an original Palestinian tradition from the middle of the third century, the same time as the Mekhilta, and only one generation after the death of both Caracalla and Rabbi Judah the Prince.

In several Talmudic traditions, the background of Antoninus' consultations with Rabbi, as his political advisor and confidant, is the hostile relationship between the emperor and 'the prominent Romans' (i.e. the senators).[41] Thus one Babylonian tradition tells about a hidden tunnel through which Antoninus used to come secretly from his house in Rome to Rabbi's house in Palestine. In order to keep this completely secret, he would place two slaves, one at the Roman end of the tunnel, the other at the Jewish end, and when he accomplished his mission he would kill both of them.[42]

Dio tells a story about Caracalla with very similar elements: the emperor had a special relationship with the Scythians and Germans, whom he trusted more than his own soldiers. He often conversed with Scythian and German envoys when no one else but the interpreters were present,

---

[39] Petruccioli 2012: 153–64. Caracalla's portraits have been discovered in ten different sites along the Nile. For the Pharaonic statues, see Petrucioli 2012: vol. i 154, ii 110; vol. i 154–5, ii 111; vol. i 155, ii 113 – this was unearthed at the foot of a temple dedicated to Isis; vol. I 155, ii 112.

[40] BT Pesaḥim 119a (parallel in BT Sanhedrin 110a).

[41] Antoninus consulted Rabbi what to do with 'the prominent Romans' חשובי רומא who impeded him. Rabbi answered by pantomime that Antoninus should kill them one at a time (and not attack all of them at once). The answer of the Talmud to the question of why Rabbi did not whisper his answer is: 'Because it is written: *For a bird of the air shall carry the voice*', BT Avodah Zarah 10a. Thus both the enmity between the emperor and the Roman aristocracy, on the one hand, and the secret negotiations with Rabbi, his confidant, on the other side, are clearly essential parts of this Talmudic tradition.

[42] BT Avodah Zarah 10b. This is one of various traditions about Rabbi and Antoninus that are redacted together in BT Avodah Zarah 10a-11a. See also the previous note and the nice discussion of Meir 1999: 278–91.

and instructed them, in case anything happened to him, to invade Italy and march upon Rome.

'To prevent any inkling of his conversation from getting to **our** ears', writes Dio, adding his own personal voice and testament, 'he would immediately put the interpreters to death.'[43]

But contrary to the totally negative tone of Dio, the Talmudic tradition elaborates the 'secret tunnel' story into a very positive view of Antoninus and his attitude towards the Jews. Thus on one occasion, when Antoninus comes to meet Rabbi he found R. Ḥaninah b. Ḥama there. Antoninus sends him out to ask the sleeping slave outside to come in. The slave is, of course, already slain. R. Ḥaninah prays for him, he is restored to life, and Antoninus concludes: 'I am well aware that the least one among you can bring the dead to life, still, when I call, let no one be found with thee.'[44]

This is typical of the difference between the Roman stories, anecdotes and rumours about the most negative figure of Antoninus Caracalla and its mostly positive shift as seen in the Talmudic Antoninus.

In one Babylonian tradition, probably from the first half of the fourth century, Antoninus consults for the last time with his personal Jewish advisor,

> This was the case with Aseverus the son of Antoninus who reigned [in his father's place]. Antoninus once said to Rabbi: it is my desire that my son Aseverus should reign instead of me and that Tiberias should be declared a *colonia*. Were I to ask [the Senate] one of these things it would be granted, but both would not be granted. Rabbi thereupon brought a man, and having made him ride on the shoulders of another, handed him a dove bidding the one who carried him to order the one on his shoulders to liberate it. [Antoninus] perceived this to mean that he was advised to ask to appoint his son Aseverus to reign in his stead, and that subsequently he might get Aseverus to make Tiberias a *colonia*.[45]

What is interesting here is not only the question whether and when Tiberias became a Roman *colonia* (which is beyond the scope of this chapter),[46] but the problematic consequences of the end of Caracalla's life

---

[43] Dio, lxxix 6. The enmity between Caracalla and the Roman Senate is a central topic in the Roman literature: Dio lxxix 2,18; Herodian iv 3.4, 5.1, 5.7, 7.1, 11.6, v 2.1; SHA *Caracalla* 2.9; *Geta* 2.9, 6.2, 6.5, 7.3–6; *Macrinus* 2.3, 5.9–7.3; *Diadumenianus* 1.7.

[44] BT Avodah Zarah 10b. A similar story in Va-Yiqra Rabbah Tzav 10 (ed. Margalioth: 203–4).

[45] BT Avodah Zarah 10a.

[46] See the convincing discussion of Oppenheimer 1991: 72–8; 2005a: 30–46; 2017: 74–85; Ch. 15 in this book, and also Millar 2006: 167. For another view: Jacobs 1995: 133–6, 160–5. For the Severan urbanization, see Isaac 1992: 359–61; Millar 2006: 191–216.

and reign and the succession of the Severan dynasty. We can see here, once again, the tension between the emperor and the Senate. Caracalla was murdered by Macrinus, the Praetorian prefect, who did not belong to the Severan family. He deported the family of Avitus, Caracalla's cousin who later became the Emperor Elagabalus, to Emesa in Syria. From there his grandmother guided a successful campaign against Macrinus, which at last saw Avitus as Emperor. Now, Dio consistently calls Avitus/Elagabalus a false Antonine, and argues that the alleged connection between Caracalla/Antoninus and between Avitus, the false Antoninus, was simply propaganda from Avitus and his family.[47]

But who is 'Aseverus son of Antoninus' in our story? The most plausible identification is Severus Alexander. According to Herodian, when Maesa realized that Elagabalus could not serve as an emperor she persuaded him to adopt his cousin Alexienus/Alexander as a co-emperor and successor and 'invented' the story that not only Elagabalus but also Alexander was born to Caracalla.

> Alexianus changed his name from that inherited from his grandfather to Alexander, the name of the Macedonian so admired and honored by the alleged **father of the two cousins**. Both the daughter of Maesa, and the old lady herself, used to boast of the adultery of **Antoninus (Severus' son)**, to make the troops think **the boys were his sons** and so favour them.[48]

It is important to note that the classical Talmudic traditions about the Severii never confuse the dynastic sequence: the regnal years of (Septimius) [A]severus are counted as eighteen years; most traditions refer to Antoninus, whom the Babylonian Talmud calls twice 'Antoninus son of Aseverus', and finally we find 'Aseverus son of Antoninus'.[49]

---

[47] Dio, lxxix 2. Also Herodian 5.3.10; *SHA Caracalla* 9.2, *Macrinus* 7.5, 7.8, 8.4, *Elagabalus* 1.1, 2.4, 3.1–2 (unique argument that Antoninus was the real name of Elagabalus), and the *damnatio memoriae* of this 'Antoninus' 16.4. Later on, Aurelius Victor 23 and the *Epitome de Caesaribus* 23.1 present Elagabalus as the real son of Caracalla, in contrast to Dio; Eutropius 8.22, *SHA Elagabalus* 1.4 stresses that this was false propaganda.

[48] Herodian 5.7.3: μετονομάζεται δὲ ὁ Ἀλεξιανός, καὶ Ἀλέξανδρος καλεῖται, παραχθέντος αὐτῳ τοῦ παππῳου ὀνόματος ἐς τὸ τοῦ Μακεδόνος ὡς πάνυ τε ἐνδόξου καὶ τιμηθέντος ὑπὸ τοῦ δοκοῦντος **πατρὸς ἀμφοτέρων εἶναι· τὴν <γὰρ> Ἀντωνίνου τοῦ Σεβήρου παιδὸς μοιχείαν ἀμφότεραι** αἱ Μαίσης θυγατέρες αὐτή τε ἡ πρεσβῦτις ἐσεμνύνετο πρὸς τὸ τοὺς στρατιώτας στέργειν **τοὺς παῖδας, υἱοὺς ἐκείνου δοκοῦντας εἶναι**.

[49] Severus in Shir ha-Shirim Zuta 1, 6 (ed. Buber p. 12); Antoninus son of Severus, BT Pesaḥim 119a (parallel in BT Sanhedrin 110a), Avodah Zarah 10b; Severus son of Antoninus, Avodah Zarah 10a. Already in 1832 Jost, ii, p. 129 identified 'Antoninus' as Caracalla and Severus 'his son' as Severus Alexander. Even if we identified 'Antoninus' the father of Aseverus as Elagabalus, who adopted Severus Alexander as his colleague and successor, the latter remains the sole candidate for 'Aseverus son of Antoninus'.

Many Talmudic traditions point to the interest of Antoninus in Judaism, his knowledge about it, and his ability to follow hermeneutic discussions and even to contribute his own independent insight.[50] Over time he becomes the ideal and most prominent gentile figure, and the only Roman leader, who is said to deserve the 'World to come'. Again, it is the Babylonian Talmud that gives his full name: 'Antoninus son of Aseverus'.[51] But the next and last step is to be found quite surprisingly in the late Aramaic tradition, probably invented by the anonymous redactors of the Jerusalem Talmud, not earlier than the late fourth century.

> [There are some indications that Antoninus converted, and some that he did not convert] Antoninus said to Rabbi: Will you let me eat of the Leviathan in the world to come? He [R.] said to him: Yes. He [Ant.] said to him: From the Paschal lamb you will not let me eat, but you let me eat Leviathan? He [R.] said to him: What can I do for you, when concerning the Paschal lamb it is written (Ex. 12:48) *But no uncircumcised person may eat of it.* When he heard this, he [Ant.] went and was circumcised [אזל וגזר]. He [Ant.] came back to him (and) said to him: My master, look at my circumcision [חמי גזורתי]. He [R.] said to him: Never in my life have I looked at my own; (shall I look) at yours? And why was he [R.] called by the name 'Our holy master'? Because never in his life did he look at his circumcision [הביט במילתו].[52]

At this point, historians usually refer to a single sentence in the *Historia Augusta*'s life of Caracalla.

> Once, when a child of seven, hearing that a certain playmate of his had been severely scourged for adopting the religion of the Jews, he long refused to look at either the boy's father or his own, because he regarded them as responsible for the scourging.[53]

But this should be read carefully, because the context is the excessive humanity and tenderness of the younger Antoninus, who in the previous

---

50 Meir 1999, in the Palestinian sources: 265–71, 272–4, 276–7; in the Babylonian Talmud: 277–8, 285–7; general conclusions: 291–2. Cohen 2010. In Bereshit Rabbah xxxiv 10 (ed. Albeck and Theodor: 320–1) and BT Sanhedrin 91a, Rabbi admits the preference of Antoninus' hermeneutics and answer over his own.

51 BT Avodah Zarah 10b.

52 JT, Megillah i, 72b. See the thorough discussion of Cohen 2010, and his convincing conclusions that Antoninus was seen usually as a pious gentile and only the very last redaction phase of the Jerusalem Talmud raises the possibility of circumcision, esp. 357–60.

53 SHA *Caracalla* I,7: *septennis puer, cum conlusorem suum puerum ob Iudaicam religionem gravius verberatum audisset, neque patrem suum neque patrem pueri velut auctores verberum diu respexit.*

sentence cried whenever he saw criminals 'pitted against wild beasts', while in the next sentence he restores their ancient rights to the people of Antioch and Byzantium, after his father had punished them because they supported Niger.

Much more convincing is the plain circumcision that Dio related to Elagabalus, as showing what he saw as his absurd behavior, in both his religious policy and gender matters.

> Closely related to these irregularities was his [i.e. Elagabalus the emperor's] conduct in the matter of Elagabalus [i.e. the god]. The offence consisted, not in his [i.e the emperor] introducing a foreign god into Rome or in his exalting him [i.e. the god] in very strange ways, but in his placing him even before Jupiter himself and causing himself to be voted his priest, also in his circumcising himself and abstaining from swine's flesh, on the ground that his devotion would thereby be purer. He had planned, indeed, to cut off his genitals altogether, but that desire was prompted solely by his effeminacy; the circumcision which he actually carried out was a part of the priestly requirements of Elagabalus [i.e. the god], and he accordingly mutilated many of his companions in like manner.[54]

In the light of this, it seems to me that we can hear the sarcasm in the tone of the Talmudic account. The redactors of the Jerusalem Talmud do not seem to see the circumcision of Antoninus as a point in his favor, but they present it with much more gentle implied criticism than Dio.

If the comparison here between the Talmudic circumcision of 'Antoninus' and between the same action of Dio's 'false Antoninus' is valid, then we can point towards a hybrid Talmudic Antoninus, which combines Elagabalus with Caracalla.

Dio, and most Roman writers of the third and fourth centuries, sincerely lament the brutality of Antoninus against the Roman aristocracy, especially the senators;[55] at the same time, the Jewish aristocracy presents us with an

---

[54] Dio LXXX 11.1: Τῶν δὲ δὴ παρανομημάτων αὐτοῦ καὶ τὸ κατὰ τὸν Ἐλεγάβαλον ἔχεται, οὐχ ὅτι θεόν τινα ξενικὸν ἐς τὴν Ῥώμην ἐσήγαγεν, οὐδ' ὅτι καινοπρεπέστατα αὐτὸν ἐμεγάλυνεν, ἀλλ' ὅτι καὶ πρὸ τοῦ Διὸς αὐτοῦ ἤγαγεν αὐτόν, καὶ ὅτι καὶ ἱερέα αὐτοῦ ἑαυτὸν ψηφισθῆναι ἐποίησεν, ὅτι τε τὸ αἰδοῖον περιέτεμε, καὶ ὅτι χοιρείων κρεῶν, ὡς καὶ καθαρώτερον ἐκ τούτων θρησκεύσων, ἀπείχετο (ἐβουλεύσατο μὲν γὰρ παντάπασιν αὐτὸ ἀποκόψαι· ἀλλ' ἐκεῖνο μὲν τῆς μαλακίας ἕνεκα ποιῆσαι ἐπεθύμησε, τοῦτο δὲ ὡς καὶ τῇ τοῦ Ἐλεγαβάλου ἱερατείᾳ προσῆκον ἔπραξεν· ἐξ οὗ δὴ καὶ ἑτέροις τῶν συνόντων συχνοῖς ὁμοίως ἐλυμήνατο). See also Dio lxxx 16.7 where Elagabalus 'asked the physicians to contrive a woman's vagina in his body by means of an incision', and a similar expression in the *Epitome de Caesaribus*, Elagabalus 3: self-emasculation (*absciisque genitalibus*).

[55] Aurelius Victor, *De Caesaribus* 21 is the only one who praises the personality of Caracalla; see n. 3 of Bird on this passage.

elevated and enlightened Antoninus. Whose history is right? Whose history is it? Maybe the histories of Rome – an empire of many nations.

The middling emperor is represented by Diocletian. There are several Talmudic traditions, all of them in the Palestinian literature, which deal with this emperor. They give us information about the emperor, which usually ties in with other historical, epigraphical and archaeological data. I shall sum up the main points.

The Jerusalem Talmud notes that Diocletian was linked to the city of Tiberias, telling us that in his youth his name was Diclot, and he was a swineherd in Tiberias. He got the name Diocletian only when he was crowned:

> The children of R. Yehudah Nesiah scorned Diclot the swine[herd]. He became a king and went down to Paneas. He sent letters to the rabbis that they should be at his place immediately after the end of the Sabbath. . . . They said to him: **We treated Diclot**, the swine, with contempt. We do not treat **Di[o]cletianus, the king**, with contempt.[56]

All the historiographical sources agree that Diocletian's origins were lower class. See, for instance, the Anonymous Epitome about the Caesars (late fourth century):

> Diocletian of Dalmatia, a freedman of the senator Anulinus, ruled for twenty-five years. His mother and hometown were both called Dioclea, from which name he was called Diocles until he took power; when he took control of the Roman world, he converted the Greek name to the Roman fashion.[57]

Diocletian actually visited Tiberias in person on 31 May 286, and on 14 July in the same year, and again on 31 August when he and Maximianus were both consuls, namely in 287 or 290.[58] Two different Talmudic sources connect Diocletian with Paneas, the above-mentioned, and the following:

> Diocletian oppressed the people of Paneas. They told him: We will leave. A sophist said to him: They will not go, but if they do go they will return. If

---

[56] JT, Terumot viii, 46b-c. The parallel in Bereshit Rabbah lxiii (ed. Albeck and Theodor: 688–90) designates Diclot/Diocletian as a swineherd instead of the obscure חזירא in the JT.

[57] *Epitome de Caesaribus* 39.1: *Diocletianus Dalmata, Anulini senatoris libertinus, matre pariter atque oppido nomine Dioclea, quorum vocabulis, donec imperium sumeret, Diocles appellatus, ubi orbis Romani potentiam cepit, Graium nomen in Romanum morem convertit, imperavit annis viginti quinque.* See also Eutropius, *Breviarium* 19; Aurelis Victor, *De Caesaribus* 39, 40.12–13; Lactantius, *De mort. persec.* 9.11.

[58] *Cod. Jus.* iv 10.3 in Tiberias at 31 May 286 CE; i 51.1 at 14 July 286 CE; v 17.3 at 31 August in the consulate of Diocletian and Maximianus, namely 287 CE or 290 CE; see Barnes 1982: 50–1.

you want to check, bring deer and send them to a distant land; in the end they will return to their [original] places. He did so, brought deer, covered their antlers with silver, and sent them to Africa. At the end of thirteen years they returned to their places.[59]

There is no direct evidence that Diocletian was ever in Paneas, but there is an indirect link: inscriptions of the Tetrarchic land surveyors were discovered in the region of Paneas. As Millar has noted: 'The erection of these inscriptions clearly reflects the Tetrarchic taxation-reform of AD 297',[60] and it seems plausible that this tax reform is the background to the Talmudic statement: 'Diocletian oppressed the people of Paneas.'

Two Talmudic sources connect Diocletian to Tyre. One mentions an inscription of his, dedicated to his partner Maximianus, whose religious title was Herculius:

> R. Shimon b. Yoḥanan sent and asked R. Shimon b. Yoẓadak: Have you ever looked into the character of the fair held at Tyre? . . . He went up and found written there: I, Diocletian the king, have founded the fair of Tyre in honour of Herculi[u]s my brother, for eight days.[61]

Greenfield convincingly verifies the authenticity of this Talmudic passage as a reliable reflection of a formal inscription in Tyre.[62]

The other source mentions R. Hiyya, an important rabbi who was also a priest, who was so eager to see Diocletian in Tyre that he even went through a graveyard to get to him:

> R. Yannai said, A priest [may] defile himself in order to see a king. When King Diocletian came here, R. Hiyya was seen stepping over graves at Tyre in order to see him.[63]

Avi-Yonah, followed by Barnes, dates the visit of Diocletian to Tyre to the early years of his rule, prior to 293 CE; Greenfield tends to the later period, 296–302 CE, when Diocletian spent most of his time in the Roman East.[64]

---

[59] JT, Sheviit ix, 38d.

[60] Millar 1993: 535, and see the data and discussion there. Also Jacobs 1995: 158; Hadas-Label 2006: 202.

[61] JT, Avodah Zarah i, 39d.

[62] Greenfield 1991, suggests dating the fair to the twentieth anniversary of his reign (*vicennalia*), which began on 20 November 303 CE. See the interesting note of Hadas-Label 2006: 202 that maybe even the tetrarchy looked like a diarchy to the provincials. For the relationships between Palestinian Jewry and Tyre in Talmudic times, see Oppenheimer 2005b: 93–101.

[63] JT, Nazir vii, 56a.   [64] See Barnes 1982: 50, n. 25 and Greenfield 1991: 500.

Another source in the JT notes that Diocletian controlled the water source known as the lake of Emesa, probably the present-day Qattina lake on the Orontes to the south-west of Emesa:

> Seven seas surrounded the Land of Israel: the Great Sea, Lake Tiberias, Lake Semakho, the Salt Sea, Lake Ḥulata, Lake Sheliat, Lake Apamea. But is there not also a lake at Ḥomṣ? Diocletian dammed up rivers and created it.[65]

This is mentioned together with Hulata, Daphne of Antioch and the lake of Apamea. There is evidence that Diocletian was very active in this region: on 6 May 290 he was in Antioch, where he spent most of his time from 299 CE till 302 or 303, and four days later, on 10 May, he reached Emesa.[66]

In connection with monetary matters, the Jerusalem Talmud discusses different kinds of gold, and ends with the Diocletian denarius. This appears to refer to his reform of the currency, which stabilized the imperial coinage and fixed the denarius, instead of the sestertius, as the common coin. The first phase of the reform dates to 286 CE and does indeed apply to the gold coins.[67]

As an aside in a discussion about vows, the Talmud talks about a huge army headed by Diocletian, which it compares to the large number of Israelites who came out of Egypt in the biblical Exodus:

> This is a vain oath: ... if one said, (may I be punished) if I did not see walking on this road as many as went out of Egypt. ... When Diocletian went down there, one hundred twenty myriads went down with him.[68]

This may refer to Diocletian's campaign against the revolt in Egypt in 297–8 CE, which included a long siege of Alexandria.

Turning now to Diocletian's religious policy, the Jerusalem Talmud writes:

> R. Abbahu prohibited their [Samaritan] wine. ... When Di[o]cletian the king came up here, he issued a decree, saying, 'Every nation must offer

---

[65] JT, Kilayim ix, 32c, parallel JT, Ketubbot xii 35b. See the discussion of Grossmark 2014 with previous studies.

[66] Barnes 1982: 51, 55; Isaac 1992: 437.

[67] JT, Yoma, iv, 41c-d. For Diocletian's monetary reform as reflected in Talmudic literature, see Sperber 1991: esp. 36–7. See also Rees 2004: 40–1.

[68] JT, Shevu'ot, iii, 34d. The parallel in JT, Nedarim iii, 37d has 'Lulianus' instead of 'Diocletian', which could mean Julian the Apostate. Both led a huge army in the Middle East, but the literary context of 'walking on this road as many as went out of Egypt' fits nicely with Diocletian's campaign against Egypt; Eutropius, *Breviarium* 23, Barnes 1982: 54–5.

a libation, except for the Jews.' So the Samaritans made a libation, and [that is why] their wine was prohibited.[69]

This clearly refers to the anti-Christian persecutions, and it is very similar in wording to the original decrees, especially the Fourth Edict, which was published by Diocletian in spring 304 and reported by Eusebius in the long recension of the *Martyrs of Palestine*, composed in April 311 and preserved in a Syriac manuscript of 411:

> There came then again the second time edicts from the emperor, ... which compelled all persons equally: that the entire population of every city, both men and women, should sacrifice to dead idols, and a law was imposed upon them to offer libations to devils.[70]

The Jews alone were exempted from the pagan libation, while the Samaritans (or some of them) offered libations like the gentiles. What is striking here is the fact that the Talmudic passage does not even mention the Christians. I shall return to this point at the end of my chapter.

To sum up: Diocletian did nothing exceptional, either for or against the Jews.[71] Probably this is the reason why the Babylonian Talmud and the later Talmudic compilations ignore him almost completely. He is presented as the new broom who came to Palestine, restored order, initiated significant administrative, economic and fiscal reforms, and headed a huge army. He visited the local *polis* of Tiberias (probably a Roman colony), and the center of the most important Jewish institutions – the patriarchate and the central rabbinic academy – and stayed for a long time in the adjacent provinces. His name is carved on the coins and engraved in Greek, the *lingua franca* of the Roman East, on milestones and inscriptions of the land surveyors, so he left his mark on both urban centers and the rural environment. He is the middling Roman emperor of the Talmudic literature, between the 'bad' and the 'good'.

But 'middling' or moderate is also the proper adjective for the Talmudic voice which characterizes Diocletian. This emperor and his modern scholars are trapped between Christian anti-Diocletian historiography and between his admirers, the so-called pagan anti-Christian historians.[72] The Talmudic voice is much more temperate and moderate. In Tacitean mode, it is a good example of a tale told *sine ira et studio*.

Thus we come to the following preliminary conclusions.

---

[69] JT, Avodah Zarah 5, 44d. See the discussion in Shahar 2011, with details of earlier studies in n. 4.
[70] Eusebius, *History of the Martyrs in Palestine*, edited and translated into English by William Cureton (Paris 1891), 9–10; see also the short recension *MP* 3.1 (PG 20, 1469).
[71] Rabello 1984.   [72] Cameron 1993: 15; Rees 2004: 3–5, 86–7.

The Roman emperors mentioned by name in Talmudic literature belong to three different periods of relations between Judaea and Rome, from the late Second Temple period up to the early fourth century: the 'Bad' belong to the time of the great Jewish revolts (66–136 CE); the 'Good' reflect the honeymoon of the Severan period, with Rabbi and Antoninus/Caracalla; while the middling relations that were neither very bad nor very good are represented by Diocletian.

The shifts and changes in the Talmudic images of each emperor over the generations are the products of the political and social world of these different generations which retell and reshape the traditions. The 'Bad' emperors (with the exception of Titus) are usually presented much more positively in the Babylonian Talmud, as part of the agenda of the Babylonian amoraim discouraging Jewish rebellion. Over time, the Palestinian literature also softens the character of the 'Bad', as the contributors get further away from the revolts themselves and their harsh consequences.

The wording of the narrative may also be affected, probably indirectly, by stories about the emperors which were current throughout the empire, such as those which found their expression in the *Historia Augusta*.

Roman emperors who figure in the Talmudic literature are generally those who were very active and effective in the Jewish arena, especially in Palestine, but also, as in the case of Trajan, in the Hellenistic diaspora – Egypt and Cyprus. This is true in particular of emperors who came to the area in person, leaving their own mark on Jewish territory and the immediate vicinity.

Who are missing from the picture? First of all, the Julio-Claudians before Nero. At first glance, it seems as if the reason for this is the length of time which elapsed between Augustus and his successors, and the creation of the Talmudic literature. But the fact that Hellenistic kings and dramatic events at the end of the Hasmonean and early Roman periods found their expression in Talmudic literature makes this answer hardly satisfactory. It is more likely that their absence is due to the significant representation of the Herodian dynasty in the Talmudic literature. Thus this Roman client kingdom and its kings served as a membrane between the empire and the Jews, so that the emperors of their time, who had no direct contact with Jews, do not appear in Talmudic literature. It is when we come to the direct confrontation between the Roman legions headed by Vespasian and Titus, and the Jews that the future emperors came to the fore. Josephus' *Bellum Iudaicum* becomes the '*polemos* of Aspasianus' for the Mishnah and all the later Talmudic traditions. After Agrippa II dies (between 86/7 and 100 CE), there is direct contact between Judaea and Rome, and the cooperation or confrontation is headed by the emperor, on the Roman side, and by the Jewish patriarchate and central aristocracy and the rabbis, on the Jewish side. Thus all the other emperors who did not come into direct contact with Jews and did not legislate to affect the life of the Jewish community were of no interest to the compliers of the Talmudic literature. And this is true for the majority of the Roman emperors.

Most significant by their absence are the Christian emperors, especially Constantine. This silence is all the more noteworthy because the Constantinian revolution is contemporary with the late and very intensive phases of the creative process of the Palestinian Talmud. On the other hand, it suits the Talmudic references to the religious policies of Diocletian only as a background to the Jewish ban upon Samaritan wine, without mentioning the Christians, the true target of Diocletian's persecutions. There is a very strong scholarly tendency to search for any hint of Christians and Christianity in the Talmudic literature, especially the Palestinian literature, in order to stress their presence there, based on the supposition that Christians and Christianity played a significant role in the Jewish agenda. On the other side stand scholars who argue that the low profile of Christianity in the *Tannaitic* and *Amoraic* literature is a true representation of the limited role of Christians in the world of Palestinian Jewry during the third and fourth centuries.[73] I agree with this view, and the absence of Constantine and his successors from the Talmudic literature supports these conclusions.

---

[73] For the scholarly debate, see Schremer 2010, who tends to reduce the role of Christianity in the early Talmudic literature.

AHARON OPPENHEIMER

Rabbi Judah ha-Nasi's patriarchate was a golden age for Jewish life in Roman Palestine. The main reason for this was the excellent relationship with the Roman authorities. Before his time the Antonine emperors had been in power, and while they had allowed the leadership institutions to rehabilitate themselves after the persecutions which followed in the wake of the Bar Kokhba revolt, Roman policy in the province had still been a policy of repression. One of the factors leading to the improved relations between the Severan emperors and the Jews was presumably a result of the stance of the Jews in the struggle for the imperial throne which took place in the years 193–4, mainly in the east of the empire, between Septimius Severus and Pescennius Niger, the governor of Syria. In this struggle the Samaritans supported Niger. The two Roman legions stationed in Palestine at the time, the Tenth Fretensis and the Sixth Ferrata, also took an active part in the struggle between Severus and Niger. The Tenth Legion supported Niger, while the Sixth supported Severus. It was apparently as a result of this that Septimius Severus gave the Sixth Legion Ferrata the title of *fidelis constans*, true and firm. Similarly he took the status of *polis* away from Neapolis [Shechem], the city of the Samaritans.[1]

One of the results of the change of dynasty was mutual recognition between Jews and Romans. An example of this sort of recognition was the *de facto* permission for Rabbi Judah ha-Nasi to judge capital cases, even though this was not usually left in the hands of local leaders in the provinces. Roman recognition of the right to judge capital cases can be seen from the evidence of the Church Father Origen, in his letter to Julius Africanus, a Christian writer at the turn of the second and third centuries CE. Julius Africanus claimed that the story of Susannah and the Elders, an addition to the Book of Daniel in the Apocrypha, was a forgery. One of the reasons why Julius Africanus contends that it is a forgery is the fact that it

---

[1] There are some scholars who claim that, in contrast to the Samaritans who supported Pescennius Niger, the Jews supported Septimius Severus. See, e.g., Graetz 1908: 206. In the opinion of Menahem Stern, there is no mention of Jewish support for Septimius Severus, and the only evidence shows merely that the Sixth Legion joined Severus, while the Tenth Legion which was stationed in Jerusalem did not support him: Stern 1974–84: vol. II, 623; Ritterling 1925: 1592–3.

tells of a death sentence under foreign domination. Origen rejects this claim in his reply:

> And even now, under Roman rule, when the Jews pay the two dinars in tax, the ethnarch acts as the authority for the Jews, and, as it were with the connivance of the emperor, he is in no way different from a king over his people. For cases are tried surreptitiously according to the [Jewish] law, and people are even condemned to death, albeit not entirely openly, but certainly not without the knowledge of the emperor. Indeed we learned this and ascertained it when we lived in their land for many days.[2]

Origen, who came from Alexandria, stresses in his letter that he is relying on direct evidence obtained as a result of living in Palestine, and indeed we know that he was in the country during Rabbi's patriarchate, in the years 215–19. He gives evidence that in spite of the fact that the Jews were subject to the tax of two *denarii* after the destruction of the Temple,[3] the power of Rabbi Judah ha-Nasi was so great *de facto* that he could even enforce the death sentence. In spite of the many scholars who have doubted this testimony and proposed alternative explanations,[4] there is no real reason to doubt its reliability. This is contemporary evidence; and Rabbi's special status in relation to the Roman authorities and in relation to the Jews certainly fits the possibility that the authority given to the patriarch to judge capital cases was a sort of silent connivance,[5] especially since it was at this very time that the Romans granted permission to the free *poleis* to exact punishment. It is reasonable to suppose that this was a sort of kangaroo court, whose judges were perhaps aided by the sort of police force which was kept by the patriarch to carry out his death sentences.[6]

There is evidence of Jewish gratitude to Septimius Severus and his family from a Greek inscription found in Katziun in Eastern Upper Galilee (near

---

[2] Origen, *Ad Africanum de Historia Susannae*, 14 (*Patrologia Graeca*, xi, cols. 81–4).

[3] This tax was imposed on the Jews of Palestine and all the rest of the empire after the destruction of the Temple, and sent to the *fiscus Iudaicus*, the Jewish tax collection at Rome, in honour of Jupiter in place of the half shekel which Jews had paid to the Temple treasury, and was therefore perceived as especially insulting by the Jews.

[4] For scholars who have doubted the reliability of this evidence, see Habas Rubin: 64–71; 265–73; see discussion and a survey of scholarship on the issue in Jacobs 1995: 248–51 and bibliography *ad loc.*

[5] Alon 1977: 123–4.

[6] The Jewish origins for this sort of punishment without due legal process can be found in the 'sin of Baal Peor', when Pinchas, son of Eliezer son of Aaron the High Priest killed the Israelite Zimri b. Salu and the Mideanite Cozbi b. Zur with his spear, out of zeal for his God, and thus stopped the plague among the children of Israel (Numbers 25.1–15; Psalms 101.28–31).

present-day Rosh Pina) and dated to the end of the second century CE, which probably came from a synagogue:

> For the salvation of our lords, the rulers and emperors: Lucius Septimius Severus the pious, the strong, the august, and Marcus Aurelius Antoninus [known as Caracalla] and Lucius Septimius Geta his sons, for a vow, the Jews [dedicated this inscription].

On the left, there is a further part of the inscription, inside a wreath:

> And Iulia Domna, Augusta.[7]

This inscription is the only one of its kind from this time.[8] There can be no doubt that it was set up to show what was, from the Jewish point of view, the special network of relationships which developed between the Jews and their Roman rulers in the Severan period (i.e. in the days of Rabbi Judah ha-Nasi). It mentions three emperors, for the two sons of Septimius Severus, Caracalla and Geta, were co-emperors with their father during the years 198–211.

General imperial policy in the time of the Severans was to encourage leaders and institutions, especially in the east of the empire, which was the cradle of the Severan dynasty. Eastern religions, and sages and philosophers from the east enjoyed wide popularity in Rome. The cultural syncretism which was part of this all-embracing policy set as its goal the merging of the Greek east and the Roman west of the emperors. The peak of this policy came in 212, in a law which gave Roman citizenship to almost all the inhabitants of the empire. This was one of the legal initiatives of the emperor Caracalla. According to this law, known as the *constitutio Antoniniana*, Roman citizenship was granted to all the free inhabitants of the Roman Empire.[9] This can be seen as an important stage in the development of the legal status of the inhabitants of the empire, and a basis for unifying the Roman world.

In the Talmudic literature there are around a hundred traditions which tell of the close relations between Rabbi Judah ha-Nasi and the 'Emperor Antoninus'. It is true that there are also traditions about meetings of other rabbis with a Roman emperor or with the 'great men of Rome', such as, for example, the conversations between Joshua b. Ḥananiah and the Emperor Hadrian; or Rabbi Akiva and Tineius Rufus, the Roman governor of

---

[7] For an analysis of this inscription, see Roth-Gerson 1987: 125–9.

[8] There is a similar inscription from the fourth century found at Mughar. See Stepansky 2000: 169–71 (Heb.).

[9] *Digesta* 1, 5, 17; Cass. Dio, *Historia Romana*, LXXII 5; Pap. Giessen 40. See Jones 1936: 223 at seq.

Palestine; or Rabban Gamaliel and his colleagues who held talks during their visit to Rome with senators and people in power, but the accounts of these meetings can be summed up as vague expressions relating to the *Torah, halakhah* (religious law) and *aggadah* (narrative traditions). In contrast, in the traditions dealing with meetings between Rabbi and 'Antoninus', there are conversations on subjects where 'Antoninus' takes Rabbi's advice on business affairs, foreign and internal policy, and entertainment. These traditions are found in both the Palestinian and Babylonian Talmuds. No few scholars have spent much time and effort in debating the identity of 'Antoninus'. The general consensus is that this title refers to Marcus Aurelius Antoninus, known as Caracalla. The friendly relations between Caracalla and the Jews is clear from the commentary of the Church Father Jerome on a verse from the book of Daniel (11.34), *Now when they shall fall they shall receive a little help.* Jerome writes: 'There are Jews who relate this to Severus and his son Antoninus.'[10] It should be remembered that at this time Septimius Severus and Caracalla gave Jews the right to take significant positions on city councils. It is possible that Caracalla came to the East and even visited Palestine at least once. There is a tradition that 'Antoninus' converted to Judaism, and in the Jerusalem Talmud there is a tradition that he was circumcised.[11] In the eyes of the rabbis, the pagan 'Antoninus' is worthy of a place in the World to Come.[12] Another fantastic tradition mentions a tunnel which led from the house of 'Antoninus' in Rome to Rabbi's house. Every day, we are told, 'Antoninus' would come through it, to consult with Rabbi. 'Antoninus' set a slave at each opening to this tunnel, and each of them was killed after each visit so they could not reveal what had happened.[13]

A considerable part of the wealth of Rabbi Judah ha-Nasi, which enabled him to attain his special status among the Romans and also among the elite of Jewish society, came to him from the Romans themselves, and in particular from 'Antoninus'. There is no reason to cast doubt on the Talmudic sources which give evidence about the lands which Rabbi received from 'Antoninus' as a gift, or on lease (although it is possible, of course, that in some of the places where the Emperor is mentioned as bestowing the gift, in fact it was given by the governor or another high Roman official). Thus Rabbi owned the lands of Bet She'arim, and the lands of Mahlul (biblical Naḥalal). A tradition in the

---

[10] Com. in Dan. *PL* xxv, col 570 ed. Glorie, *CCSL* lxxv, p. 924.
[11] PT Megillah ii, 72b, col. 754; iii, 74a, col. 764; PT Sanhedrin x, 29c, col. 1326.
[12] PT Shevi'it vi, 36d, col. 199, Vatican MS p. 133.   [13] BT 'Avodah Zarah 10b.

Jerusalem Talmud notes that 'Antoninus gave Rabbi two pieces of fertile [lands] in Arisut'.[14]

From the context it appears that these lands were in the Golan. Rabbi also owned lands in the territory of Tiberias and in the Bashan, and in the area of Lod as well. Other texts give evidence that Rabbi had the right to grow *apharsimon*, balsam – a plant which produced an aromatic oil, called *opobalsamum*, when gashes were made in its bark. This was widely regarded as the best perfume. Growing balsam was generally an imperial monopoly, but it is clear that Rabbi Judah ha-Nasi had lands in the area of the Jordan valley or the Dead Sea which included balsam plantations. Another tradition tells us of Antoninus' thoroughbred cattle, which were brought in to fertilise Rabbi's herds.[15]

In contrast to these, there are other sources on the relations between Rabbi and 'Antoninus' which are clearly no more than legends and folk tales and do not belong to historical fact.[16]

Ulpian, one of the most outstanding Roman jurists, who originated in Tyre and was mostly active in the first quarter of the third century CE (i.e. in the time of Rabbi), notes legislation by Septimius Severus and Caracalla on the subject of the status of Jews in the cities, which has been preserved in the Digesta:

> The divine Severus and Antoninus allowed those who follow the customs of the Jewish religion to take offices, but they also subjected them to obligations, albeit ones that did not interfere with their religion.[17]

From this it is clear that until the permission given by Septimius Severus and Caracalla, official positions were closed to the Jews, and from the context it is clear that this referred to the city councils. In his time, Hadrian had organised the cities of Roman Palestine in order to keep Jews out of positions in the city leadership. By contrast, Septimius Severus and Caracalla ruled that Jews were allowed to serve in these positions, for example, to be a member of the city *boule*. In parallel, Jews

[14] PT Shevi'it vi, 36d, col 199. Vatican MS 133 does not have the word *alfin*, lands. These territories were apparently in the Golan, because of the discussion as to whether to absolve the Golan from the laws of the Sabbatical year. See on this: Klein 1939: vol. I, 26, *s.v.* Gevalan, Gavlona= Golan; Alon 1980: Vol. I, 206–52.

[15] *Antoninus' herds were passing by and they brought them to fertilise Rabbi's herds*: Genesis Rabbah 20, 6 (Albeck and Theodor 1903: 190).

[16] E.g. BT 'Avodah Zarah 10b: *Every day he [Antoninus] served Rabbi, fed him and brought him drink, and when Rabbi wanted to go to bed, he knelt down next to the bed and said to him: Get up on me to your bed*. Also, PT Megillah iii, 74a, col. 764 and parallels: *Antolinus* [sic] *converted* [to Judaism].

[17] *Digesta*, 50:2:3:3 (Mommsen and Krüger 1870: 896).

had to take upon themselves the liturgies (i.e. to fulfil certain civic demands), as long as it did not interfere with their religious practice.

According to the legislation of Septimius Severus and Caracalla, Jews could be members of the institutions of city leadership. As a result, in the cities where the majority of inhabitants were Jews, the leadership institutions were also manned by Jews. Both the Talmuds discuss a case where *aurum coronarium* was imposed on the institutions of the city leadership, apparently in Tiberias. This tax had originally been imposed when a new emperor succeeded to the throne, but over time it developed into a tax which was also imposed on other occasions. At first this tax was paid in the form of a golden crown given to the emperor, as its name implies, but over time it was changed to a sum of money like any other tax.[18] The *boule* and the *strategoi* were divided over whether each side had to pay half the sum, or the *strategoi*, who were also members of the *boule*, should pay half the tax, while the members of the *boule* should pay only one half of the sum. The case was brought before Rabbi Judah ha-Nasi, and he ruled that the members of the *boule* should pay half the sum required, while the *strategoi* should pay the other half.[19]

Many scholars have debated the question of what exactly the institution of the *strategoi* was. The word is not common in the Talmudic literature, so that it is necessary to examine the contexts in which it appears in the city administrations in other Roman provinces. This investigation reveals that *strategoi* was a Greek term parallel to the Latin *duoviri*, a term used for the two highest offices in the administration of a city which had acquired the status of a *colonia*. They were parallel to the two consuls who held the highest office in the city of Rome during the republic.[20] It is known that this governing body, the duovirate, existed in various different cities in the Roman provinces of Asia Minor. The term *strategos* is mentioned, for example, in an inscription from Gerasa across the Jordan, as well as in a basilica from the Severan period which was discovered in Sebaste, the central city in the Samarian hills, to which Septimius Severus granted the status of a *colonia*. *Strategoi* are also mentioned in connection with the cities of Gaza and Petra. When Tadmor/Palmyra became a *colonia*, they followed the accepted custom of appointing *duoviri*, and during the years 224–62 these two top city officials were called *strategoi*. The institution of *strategoi* is also mentioned in a document recording a sale written in Edessa

---

[18] Millar 1977: 139–44. [19] See PT Yoma i, 39a, col. 564.

[20] Mommsen 1871–88: vol. II; Gizewski 1997: 3, 20, cols. 843–5.

in north Mesopotamia, which was discovered in the excavations at Dura Europos.[21]

Given this peaceful atmosphere, the good economic situation and the autonomy given to the Jews in general and to their leadership institutions in particular under Severan rule, Rabbi Judah ha-Nasi felt that there was no longer any need to fast on the fast days commemorating the destruction of the Temple, even though the Temple had not been rebuilt, and the Jews did not have complete autonomy. His attempt to cancel the fasts of 17 Tammuz and 9 Av, which are an expression of mourning for the destruction of the Temple and the loss of Jerusalem, can be seen as a definitive expression of this political concept and the way in which he saw his own time as the 'beginning of the redemption', a vision which he wished to communicate to the people. Thus Rabbi gave a personal example, by going to bathe in the springs of Sepphoris on 17 Tammuz. Bathing is one of the enjoyments prohibited on a fast day, but in spite of this, Rabbi bathed in public on 17 Tammuz, the fast day which commemorates the breaching of the walls of Jerusalem by Titus.[22] Rabbi's attempt to cancel the fast of 9 Av as well was a reformatory move that was even more significant, for 9 Av is the day when, according the rabbis, Jewish suffering was redoubled: the fast commemorates the destruction of both the First Temple and the Second Temple as well. Rabban Shimon ben Gamaliel, Rabbi's own father, had said:

> [A]nyone who eats and drinks on 9th of Av, it is as if he had eaten and drunk on *Yom Kippur*, the Day of Atonement.[23]

The rabbis of the generation of Rabbi Judah ha-Nasi were not prepared to accept this ruling, and when he saw that he could not persuade them, he cancelled his own ruling. There is confirmation for the suggestion that the clement political climate of his time was one of the reasons behind Rabbi's attempted reformatory rulings. The Babylonian Talmud preserves a tradition that distinguishes between the days of *shemad* (repressive legislation) and the days of peace (political independence), and between the days when there is neither repression nor peace (i.e. foreign domination without repression). From this tradition – although it is cited in the name of Rav Papa, a Babylonian *amora* who lived in the mid fourth century – it is

---

[21] Oppenheimer 1991: 74, nos. 55–9.
[22] BT Megillah 5a-b: *Rabbi Elazar said Rabbi Hanina said: ... and he bathed in the spring of Sepphoris on the 17th Tammuz.*
[23] A *baraita* in BT Ta'anit 30b.

clear that the criterion for fasting or not fasting in memory of the destruction of the Temple was, in fact, the political situation.[24]

The Roman recognition of the Jewish courts in Palestine was expressed in the fact that the Roman authorities themselves were apparently also involved in the violent enforcement of legal sentences regarding personal status ruled by the Jewish courts, as is stated expressly in the Mishnah:

> A divorce given under duress – If it is a Jewish [court] it is valid, but if it is a non-Jewish court it is not valid. If the non-Jews beat him and say to him: Do what the Jews tell you, it is valid.[25]

From this we learn that there were cases where the Romans forced a husband to give his wife a divorce, according to the instructions of a Jewish court, and they were simply helping to carry out the sentence of the Jewish court.

The date of this law has not been ascertained, but a similar pattern of behaviour is seen also in a *baraita* which is clearly from Severan times – to be more exact, from the time of Rabbi Judah ha-Nasi, for it is stated by Rabbi Ḥiyya, a contemporary of Rabbi's:

> There is a *baraita* about Rabbi Hiyya: If non-Jews enforced the ruling of a Jewish law court – it is valid.[26]

The involvement of the Roman authorities in enforcing sentences dealing with personal status in Jewish courts is also seen in the following source:

> Ḥalitzah (release of a woman from marriage to her dead husband's brother) enforced in a Jewish court is valid. Among the non-Jews they beat him (the brother-in-law who refuses to release the widow) and say to him: Do what Rabbi So-and-So says to you.[27]

In his *Tosefta Kifshuta, ad loc.*, Lieberman discusses this passage, and distinguishes between *ḥalitzah* imposed by a Roman court, which is not allowed, and a case where the non-Jews violently force a Jew to release his brother's widow following a decision by the rabbis: in this case the *ḥalitzah* is permitted.

The emperors of the Severan dynasty were very active in raising the status of towns in the Eastern provinces (Asia Minor) and the North African provinces to the level of a *polis* or *colonia*. The founder of the dynasty, Septimius Severus, gave Lod [Lydda] the status of a *polis* in

---

[24] BT Rosh haShanah 18b.   [25] M Gittin ix 8, according to the Kauffman and Parma MSS.
[26] PT Gittin ix, 50d, col 1094.   [27] Tos. Yevamot xi, 13 (Lieberman 1955–73: 44).

the year 199/200,[28] and the city received the name Diospolis; Bet Guvrin received the name Eleutheropolis;[29] and apparently even before this the emperor gave Sebaste, which was already a *polis*, the status of a *colonia*. I have already noted how he temporarily lowered the status of Neapolis [Shechem] which lost its status as a *polis* because of its support for Pescennius Niger in 194, his rival in the struggle for the imperial throne. Elagabalus gave the status of *polis* to Emmaus, which received the name Nicopolis,[30] and the same status was granted to Antipatris.[31] Both of them raised the status of these cities in the time of Rabbi Judah ha-Nasi, but also acted similarly in other provinces.

It is possible that Tiberias was also granted the status of a *colonia*. There are a number of reasons for thinking so: the institution of the two *strategoi* which we have identified with the *duoviri* in Tiberias, and this was an institution which was found only in *coloniae*. One of the traditions in the Babylonian Talmud on the relations between Rabbi and 'Antoninus' appears in a legendary context which deals with making Tiberias a *colonia*.[32]

> And if it is a problem for you that one does not appoint a king's son as king, [such an appointment] would be made at [the king's] request, as was the case with Aseverus son of Antoninus who became the ruler. Antoninus said to Rabbi: I want my son Aseverus to reign after me, and Tiberias to be made a *colonia*, and if I ask them [the Senate] one of these, they will do it for me; if I ask them both things, they will not do it. [Rabbi] brought in a man riding on another man, and put a dove in the hand of the man on top, and said to the man below: Tell the man above to release the dove from his hand. [Antoninus] said, Understand from this, that he hinted to me as follows: You ask them for Aseverus my son to succeed me, and tell Aseverus that he should make Tiberias a *colonia*.[33]

Yaakov Meshorer, indeed, claimed that an inscription on one of the coins of Tiberias from the time of Elagabalus includes the letters COL, for *colonia*.[34] This would indeed have been enough to demonstrate that

---

[28] On Lod/Lydda, see Hill 1914: nos. 1–2; Rosenberger 1975: 28–31; id. 1977: 80; Kindler and Stein 1987: 96–9.

[29] On Bet Guvrin/Eleutheropolis, see Spijkerman 1972: 369–84, Pls. 1–4; Kindler and Stein 1987: 112–5.

[30] On Emmaus, see Jones 1971: 279, and n. 67; Schürer 1973: 512–3, n. 142; Kindler and Stein 1987: 177–9.

[31] There are seven types of coin known from Antipatris, all of them from the time of Elagabalus. See Hill 1914: 11, xv–xvi; van der Vliet 1950: 116–7, nos. 11–2; Meshorer 1984: 54, nos. 149–52; Kindler and Stein (n. 29), 41–2; Schürer 1979: 167–8.

[32] Krauss 1910: 52–5.   [33] BT 'Avodah Zarah 10a.   [34] Meshorer 1985: 35.

Tiberias did in fact become a *colonia*, and would have given it a date for when it occurred. Meshorer based himself on the Latin letters COL which he tried to identify on the coins, but these coins clearly have Greek letters on them. Thus this coin cannot be relied on for evidence that Tiberias was a *colonia* at the time it was minted, for in that case the whole inscription would have had to have been in Latin. The only place in which Tiberias is mentioned as a colony is a marriage contract from the year 1035, which was found in the Cairo Genizah, where there is a record which reads: *Medinta Tiberia Colon[ia]*.[35] This terminology would appear to show that there was a tradition that Tiberias had indeed been a *colonia* in earlier times.

The possibility that Tiberias did indeed receive colonial status in Severan times in the days of Rabbi Judah ha-Nasi goes some way to explain the reasons for, and the significance of the move of the Jewish leadership institutions from Diocaesaria (Sepphoris) to Tiberias in the first half of the third century. The leadership institutions – the patriarch and the *Bet Va'ad* (the rabbinical leadership) – grew in power, from their first rehabilitation in the little towns of Ushah and Shefar'am following the repressive legislation after the Bar Kokhba revolt, through their move to Bet She'arim and Sepphoris/Zippori in the days of Rabbi. The move to Bet She'arim, which was imperial land given to Rabbi, demonstrates the way he was recognised by the Roman authorities, while the move to Sepphoris, which was a *polis*, is evidence for the submission of the urban elite to his authority. This was the beginning of the settlement of the Jewish leadership in the cities. The final station of the Jewish leadership institutions was Tiberias, and after the city apparently received colonial status, it became the central and most important city in Galilee. The move to Tiberias happened after the process of separation between the patriarchate and the *Bet Va'ad*, which followed the death of Rabbi and took place in stages: first the *Bet Va'ad* moved to Tiberias in the middle of the third century, when it was headed by Rabbi Yoḥanan bar Napha. After this, the patriarchate moved as well, at the latest in the time of Rabbi Judah Nesia the second –the great-great-grandson of Rabbi Judah ha-Nasi. At any rate, in the time of Diocletian, who succeeded to the imperial throne in 284 CE, the patriarchate was already sited in Tiberias. Thus this gradual process, which had taken about a hundred years, came to an end, having begun in the little town of Usha and ending in Tiberias, the chief city of Galilee.

The increased number of cities appears to have changed the Roman administrative division of *Palaestina*. In the time of the Second Temple,

---

[35] See Friedman 1981: 207–12; Miller 1987: 7.

there was only one city in the territory of Judaea, Jerusalem, and even this status is not agreed on by scholars. In Galilee too there were few cities. A further city was Jaffa, which Vespasian made into an autonomous city called Flavia Ioppe. The province was divided into 24 toparchies, each centred on a settlement which did not necessarily have the status of a city. We know about these toparchies from Josephus, Pliny the Elder and the documents from the Judaean desert from the time of the Bar Kokhba revolt. Hadrian made Jerusalem into a *colonia*, and as a result, the city received the name of Aelia Capitolina. Hadrian also actively promoted the Hellenisation of the Galilean cities Tiberias and Sepphoris – which with its rise to city status appears to have received the name of Diocaesarea. In other words, he gave them a pagan character and transferred the city government from Jewish to pagan hands.

We have seen that the impetus for the process of urbanisation took place in the time of the Severans and that of Rabbi Judah ha-Nasi. We can understand the Roman administrative organisation of Palestine in their time from the *Onomasticon* of Eusebius, whose lists do not mention any villages belonging to the territories of other villages, but only villages in the territory of cities. The root of this administrative development in the context of which a city was the centre of each toparchy is based on the urban initiative of the time of the Severan emperors. In other words, at the time of this dynasty the process by which toparchies were set up centred on a village came to an end, and from now on territories were centred on cities only.

There is a considerable amount of overlap between the urbanisation policies of the Severans, and Rabbi's policies and halakhic rulings in relation to the cities. Thus he exempted cities with a Jewish minority of inhabitants from the religious obligations of tithes and the sabbatical year:

> Rabbi exempted Bet Shean, Rabbi exempted Caesarea, Rabbi exempted Bet Guvrin, Rabbi exempted Kfar Tzemah.[36]

Rabbi stressed that it was not his intention to remove these cities from the halakhic borders of the Land of Israel, and they were still subject to the purity laws of the halakhic Land of Israel. This step, therefore, was in order to encourage Jews from the countryside to settle in these cities, rather like the fact that in Israel today the inhabitants of Eilat are exempt from VAT, and people living in the countryside and the occupied territories have tax concessions. With these rulings Rabbi Judah ha-Nasi was cooperating with

---

[36] PT Demai ii, 22c, col. 121.

the urbanisation policies of the Severans, especially as one of the cities mentioned, Bet Guvrin, actually received the status of *polis* from Septimius Severus in the time of Rabbi himself. In his time the process began of granting Ascalon exemption from observing the religious obligations of tithes and the sabbatical year. It should be noted that Rabbi did not absolve his home city of Sepphoris from the observance of the commandments relating to the produce of the Land of Israel, nor Tiberias or Lod, because the majority of their inhabitants were Jews.

To conclude: In the time of Rabbi Judah ha-Nasi, there was a revolution in the relationship between the authorities and the Jews in Palestine. There can be no doubt that this revolution was linked with the special personality of Rabbi, and his way of leadership, as well as the succession of the Severan dynasty to the imperial throne, and Roman policy in the provinces in general in the time of the Severans. After the Severans came the imperial crisis, which left its mark especially on the eastern provinces, which were subjected to such a heavy economic burden that many Jews emigrated to Babylonia, the home of the largest Jewish diaspora community outside the borders of the Roman Empire.[37]

---

[37] For most of this period, the Jewish diaspora community in Babylonia was outside the circle of the direct influence of Hellenistic-Roman culture. Babylonian Jewry was the earliest community, and the only large one, outside the borders of the Roman Empire. The Jewish community in Babylonia had an identifiable influence not only on the rest of the Jewish diaspora, but also on the national centre in Palestine. Over the years, Babylonian Jewry and all its institutions took over the leadership of world Jewry, and its doctrines penetrated every corner of the Jewish world. For generations the Babylonian Talmud has been the basis for the patterns of Jewish life and Jewish belief in the Land of Israel and the diaspora up to and including the present day.

PART IV

Iudaea/Palaestina

16 | The Roman Legionary Base in Legio-Kefar 'Othnay – The Evidence from the Small Finds[*]

YOTAM TEPPER

Introduction

The Roman army in the eastern Roman Empire has been discussed extensively, including its military organization, camps, interaction with the local civilian population and policing and security actions.[1] Historical sources and epigraphical and archaeological finds attest to the presence of the Roman army in the Land of Israel, in *Provincia Syria-Palaestina*,[2] including the Roman legionary base of the Tenth Legion in Jerusalem.[3] With regard to the Roman military presence and the establishment of the Roman base at Legio-Kefar 'Othnay, Isaac and Roll argued that the soldiers of Legio II Traiana, who also built roads in the area between the legionary base and Akko-Ptolemais,[4] arrived first, and those of Legio VI Ferrata replaced them slightly thereafter.[5] Inscriptions found in Israel reveal that soldiers of both legions built the aqueducts to Caesarea.[6] The archaeological finds also show the presence of units of the Sixth Legion elsewhere throughout the country, and their bases in or near poleis such as Bet Guvrin-Eleutheropolis,[7] Samaria-Sebaste[8] and Tel Shalem near Bet She'an-Scythopolis (Fig. 16.1)[9] and other sites in Israel where the permanent presence of military units has been proven.[10]

[*] This research summarizes parts of the research for my M.A. thesis (Tepper 2003a), advised by Prof. Israel Roll, and my Ph.D. dissertation (Tepper 2014a), advised by Prof. Yoram Tsafrir and Dr. Yuval Shahar, both at Tel Aviv University. I would like to thank the many scholars and friends who assisted me in this work and to dedicate this chapter to the memories of Prof. Yoram Tsafrir and Prof. Israel Roll, who passed away before their time, and in honor of Prof. Benjamin Isaac, who has supported the research on Legio since the beginning.

[1] Isaac 1992.
[2] See Keppie 1986: 411–29; Isaac 1992: 427–35; Millar 1993: 27–111 and Chancey 2005: 43–70.
[3] Tsafrir 1975: 49–72, 286–301; Stiebel 1999: 68–103; Arubas and Goldfus 2005; and Wexler-Bdolach in this book.
[4] Isaac and Roll 1976: 9–14; 1979a: 54–66; 1979b: 149–56; see also Tepper 2007: 66.
[5] See in detail Cotton 2000: 351–7.
[6] Vilnay 1928: 108; Lifshitz 1960: 109–11; Negev 1964: 237–9. See also Lehmann and Holum 2000: nos. 45, 47, 49, 51–4; Eck 2003: 155–6.
[7] Iliffe 1933: 121.   [8] Reisner et al. 1924: 251.
[9] Tzori 1971: 53–4. See also Foerster 1985; Eck and Foerster 1999.   [10] Isaac 1992: 427–34.

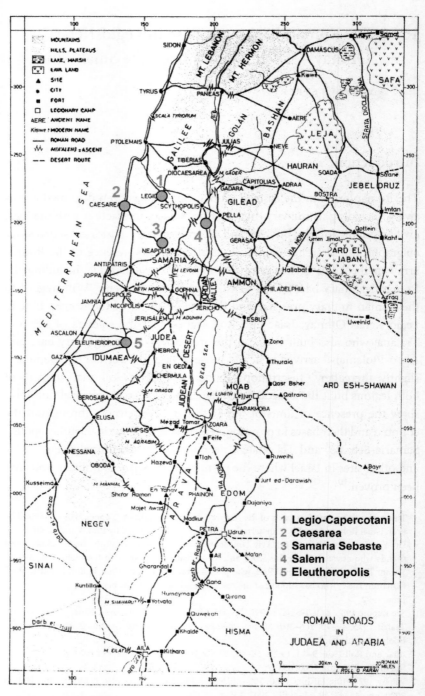

Figure 16.1 Map: Legio-Kefar 'Othnay and the sites in Palestine that mention Roman military presence, Roman roads and the activities of the soldiers of Legio II Traiana and Legio VI Ferrata (according to Roman Road map, Roll 1994).

This evidence has given rise to various theories about the size of the Roman legionary base and the period of time it was occupied by the soldiers of the Sixth Legion until its abandonment.[11] An archaeological survey in the Legio area proposed that the Roman legionary base at Legio-Kefar 'Othnay was situated on the northwestern part of the El Manakh hill.[12] A geophysical survey (2010–11)[13] and four excavation seasons (2013, 2015, 2017, 2019)[14] took place on the hill over the past decade, during which

[11] Ritterling 1925: 1587–96; and see also Barnes 2008b.

[12] During 1998–2000 a survey was carried out in the Legio-Megiddo region by the author, on behalf of the Department of Classical Studies and the Megiddo Excavation Expedition of Tel Aviv University. In the wake of this survey, identifications were proposed for the location of the ancient Jewish-Samaritan village of Kefar 'Othnay, the headquarters of the Roman Sixth Legion Ferrata and the city of Maximillianopolis. See Tepper 2002; 2003a; 2003b; 2007; 2014b.

[13] Ground-penetrating radar combined with electromagnetic sensitivity testing was carried out during 2010–11 in the northwestern part of El Manakh hill to identify subterranean architectural remains. The tests revealed a number of clear-cut anomalies including an artificial line running northeast–southwest, where in a previous survey an artificial depression and an earthen embankment were uncovered on the northwestern edge of the hill. See Pincus et al. 2013.

[14] The four excavations were carried out under the auspices of the Jezreel Valley Research Project (JVRP) on behalf of W. F. Albright Institute of Archaeological Research at Jerusalem. The first took place in the northwestern part of the base on the hill, and the second, third and fourth took place in the central part. The first three excavations seasons' excavations were directed by Yotam Tepper, Matthew J. Adams and Jonathan David, and the fourth by Matthew J. Adams, Susan Cohen and Yotam Tepper. In the northern excavation area a 125-meter-long archaeological trench was excavated from north to south, extending from the embankment on the edge of the hill to the upper part of the hill. At the top of the embankment a thick wall was uncovered on the inner side of which were dwellings, alleyways, the lines of water pipes and drainage channels in a complex identified as legionaries' barracks. In the upper part of the trench a rock-cut street was discovered, next to which were alleyways, drainage channels and more complexes of rooms. During the second through fourth seasons, two areas were excavated in the central part of the hill, one to the east and one to the west of a relatively level area where the winter rains had uncovered the tops of walls, floors and ashlar construction. The base's main street was uncovered in this central area, along which were the lines of clay water pipes and a central drainage channel, flanked by complexes built in an organized array. The tops of walls were uncovered west of the street, as well as a large, ashlar-built complex. In the western area, another street was discovered with a similar arrangement of water pipes and a drainage channel. Adjacent to it on a lower level a structure was discovered, partially ashlar-built and partially rock-cut. In one of the rooms of that structure a floor was found made of bricks bearing military stamps, along with an installation defined as a latrine. The identical orientation of the remains in all three areas, the use of clay pipes, the complex sanitation system and the small finds including weapons, tiles/bricks featuring military stamps and countermarked coins, support the identification of the remains with the Roman legionary base at Legio-Kefar 'Othnay. Moreover, in addition to the other remains described earlier, in the 2015, 2017 and 2019 seasons, we believe we unearthed the remains of the main street within the base, the *Via Principalis*. The location and details of the main structures in the base allow us to propose that remains of the principia (legionary headquarters) were located alongside the main street. A wide gate was exposed at the eastern lower part of the Principia and hewn and built rooms in the western upper part. Now we can estimate the base dimensions as 350 × 575 m. (20.125 ha). The findings from the excavations indicated that the Roman legionary base was abandoned in an organized and orderly manner, no later than the late third century through the beginning of the fourth century CE, and remained so for a long period (for the report of the first season's excavation, see Tepper et al. 2016; Adams et al. 2013;

architectural remains were uncovered. These support the identification of the legionary base at the site and enable us to relate archaeologically to the history of Roman military presence there in the second–third centuries CE. The findings also allow us to assess the area of the Roman legionary base, whose size resembles Roman legionary bases from the same period known in other parts of the empire.[15]

In this chapter we will survey the historical background of the Roman legionary base at Legio-Kefar 'Othnay and the small finds such as roof tiles/bricks with Roman military stamps and coins with countermarks as well as Roman weapons.[16] We will also discuss their contribution to understanding the Roman military presence at Legio-Kefar 'Othnay.

To begin with, we note that the Latin term *castra* may be the most suitable term to describe the legionary base. The term translates into English as "camp," "fort" or "fortress" depending on the usage in various periods. Webster proposed that the term "camp" was used to designate a temporary locale; "fort" was a more permanent station for a single unit, while "fortress" signified a permanent legionary base.[17] Nevertheless, this chapter will apply the term "legionary base" rather than "fortress" to the Roman legionary base at Legio, because this term attributes administrative characteristics to the site as well as those more typical of a permanent settlement than those associated with a fortified complex. We thank Professor Benjamin Isaac for his assistance in clarifying this issue.

Historical Background

The historical sources about Legio-Kefar 'Othnay, which were collected by Tsafrir, Di Segni and Green,[18] reveal evidence of three settlements at the site in the Roman period: a Jewish village (Kefar 'Othnay), a Roman army

---

for the report of the second and third seasons, see Adams et al. 2019); for similar abandonment of Roman military structures in that region, see Tepper and Di Segni 2006: 42–4).

[15] As noted, this chapter will not include detailed results of the archaeological excavations in the Roman legionary bases, nor of additional Roman remains found nearby, including an amphitheater, military fort, cemetery, enclosure atop Tel Megiddo, aqueducts and the Roman road system to and from the base (for more on these subjects, see Tepper 2014a; 2003a; 2003b; 2007). These findings underscore the evidence of the extent of Roman military presence at the site.

[16] Latin inscriptions that are also characteristic of a Roman military presence at the site will not be discussed here (see Eck and Tepper 2019). Burial fields in general and cremations in particular are characteristics of Roman military presence on the site; for urns finds, which also will not be discussed here, see Tepper 2007: 65–6.

[17] Webster 1969: 167.

[18] Tsafrir, Di Segni, and Green 1994: 170. Unless otherwise indicated, we use here the name Capercotani; see also Roman Road map, Roll 1994.

base (Legio-Capercotani) and a Roman–Byzantine city (Maximianopolis). In other sources, postdating the Byzantine period, the settlement is mentioned by the Arabic name El Lajjun and in Crusader sources is called La Leyun. These names preserve the name Legio, which in turn stems from the site's association with the Roman legionary base; it is the name by which the site is still known today.

Flavius Josephus describes Lower Galilee as encompassing the mountainous region only; his description did not include the "Great Plain" (the Jezreel Valley) to the south. The southern boundary of Galilee was marked at Exaloth (Iksal); no Jewish or other settlement is mentioned in the area between Exaloth in the north and Ginae (Jenin) in the south, on the northern border of Samaria.[19] The Mishnah also indicates that the valley was not included in Jewish Galilee.[20] By contrast, according to clear Talmudic tradition,[21] Kefar 'Othnay marks the southern halachic boundary of Galilee.

The name Kefar 'Othnay is not known in the Bible, and according to Elitsur, this form originated in *onomastica* of the Second Temple period.[22] Talmudic sources mention a locale by the name Kefar 'Othnay as early as the first generation after the destruction of the Second Temple, at the end of the first century CE.[23] This is the first mention of Kefar 'Othnay and the presence of Jews there; later on, Rabban Gamaliel, who was the Patriarch (*Nasi*) in the second generation after the destruction of the Temple (c. 85–115 CE), visited Kefar 'Othnay at the end of the first or early second century CE to confirm the divorce of a woman whose two required witnesses were *kutim* (Samaritans).[24] Further evidence about the site is found in the testimony of Gamaliel's son Simon, of the 'Usha generation' in the middle of the second century, who presented Kefar 'Othnay as an example of the produce of Samaritans.[25]

---

[19] Josephus, *Bellum Judaicum* 3.1.35–48.

[20] M. Shevi'it, 9, 2 and its parallels; Shahar 2004: 192–204.

[21] M. Gittin 7, 7 and its parallels in Tos. Gittin 5, 7 (ed. Lieberman: 266–7), and JT Ba.Maz. 7,11c, BT Gittin 76a.

[22] Elitsur 2009: 336, 433.

[23] Tos., Para, 10,2 (ed. Tzukermandel: 638); Gilat 1968: 243–4. Rabbi Eliezer ben Hyrkanos, who lived in the second half of the first century and until the second decade of the second century, said that his teacher, Yohanan ben Zakkai, allowed one Shemaya, from Kefar 'Othnay, to use *mei ḥatat* (a liquid applied to people who had been ritually defiled through contact with the dead).

[24] M. Gittin, 1, 5; Tos. Gittin, 1.4 (ed. Lieberman: 246–7); BT, Gittin 10b; Oppenheimer 1991: 26–8. This is certainly evidence of a Jewish settlement whose inhabitants lived according to the laws of the sages, and may also indicate that Jews and Samaritans lived there together.

[25] See Tos., Demai 5, 23 (ed. Lieberman: 92–3).

From the sources presented here, we may conclude that a settlement by the name of Kefar 'Othnay existed as early as the second half of the first century CE and in the second century CE; however, it is unclear from these sources whether Jews continued to live there in the third century and thereafter. The information here indicates that expansion of Jewish settlement in Galilee toward the Jezreel Valley, on the border of Samaritan country, accelerated after the first Jewish revolt (66–73 CE) and necessitated the updating of the halachic "map."

It is against this backdrop that we should examine the founding and growth of a Jewish village by the name of Kefar 'Othnay at this historical-geographical juncture and on the seam between the Jewish sphere in Galilee and the Samarian sphere in Samaria.[26] The mention of this settlement on the border of Galilee on the road from Galilee to Judea, with the same wording used to describe the location of Antipatris – on the border of Judaea and on the road from Judea to Galilee[27] – bolsters this assumption. Moreover, Rabban Gamaliel's journeys to Galilee and the mention of his visit to Kefar 'Othnay are consistent with the description of Kefar 'Othnay as a point on the southern boundary of Galilee for purposes of the laws governing divorce and as a settlement situated on the main road from Galilee to Judea. Not for nothing did Oppenheimer point out the similarity between the journeys of Rabban Gamaliel of Yavneh and those of Roman rulers of important cities.[28] It seems that this is another aspect attesting to the location and centrality of settlements on main roads in the Land of Israel in general and the centrality of the settlement at that spot in particular.

The name Kefar 'Othnay appears in its Latin form, Caporcotani, as a way station on the Peutinger Map (Fig. 16.2). The final version of that map is dated to the fourth century CE, although scholars agree that its sources concerning the Land of Israel date from the second century CE. The map places Capercotani midway between Caesarea and Scythopolis,[29] further evidence of its importance in the Roman imperial road network. The settlement is also mentioned as one of the cities of Galilee in the second-century *Geographia* by Claudius Ptolemy (καπαρκοτνεῖ).[30] The appearance of the name on the Peutinger Map and in *Geographia* shows that the Jewish-Samaritan village (Kefar 'Othnay) had given its name to the legionary base –

[26] Oppenheimer 1991: 66–71; Shahar 2004: 200.
[27] See the sources in n. 21 and Lieberman 1955–73: *Nashim*, 878–9.
[28] Oppenheimer 1991: 28–9. For the Roman governors' journeys, see Marshall 1966: 233–8.
[29] Tabula Peutingeriana, Weber 1976, Seg. X. See also Finkelstein 1979: 27–34.
[30] Claudii Ptolemae, *Geographia*, ed. Nobbe 1843–5, V, 16, 4.

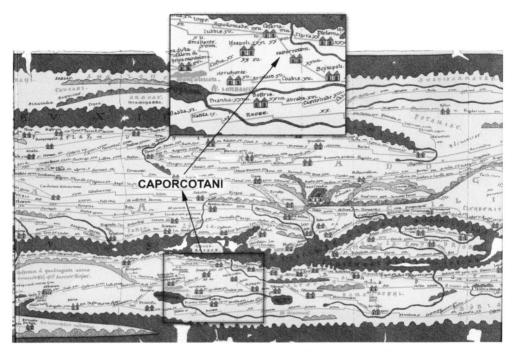

Figure 16.2 Peutinger Map – Caporcotani (Legio) along the Roman road between Caesarea and Bet She'an-Scythopolis (according to Weber 1976, Seg. X.).

Caporcotani/ Caparcotani.[31] Other than a lone reference in Josephus' writings to a commander of Legio VI Fretensis who was killed in the Battle of the Bet Ḥoron Ascent during Cestius Gallus' failed campaign in Judea in 66 CE,[32] we have no additional evidence, prior to the second century, of the presence in Judea of soldiers of the Sixth Legion, its commanders or headquarters.

The similarity between the name of the Roman legionary base and the name of the mixed Jewish and Samaritan village also emerges from burial inscriptions of soldiers of the Sixth Legion in their place of origin in Asia Minor. The name of the village in Latin appears on the Peutinger Map and in Ptolemy's *Geographia*. "Caparcotna" is also attested on inscriptions from Asia Minor.[33] One of the officers buried in Antioch of Pisidia is Gaius Novius Rusticus, son of Gaius Novius Prescus, who was consul from 165 to 168 CE. Thus, it seems that Gaius Novius served in Kefar 'Othnay

---

[31] Isaac 1992: 432–3.   [32] BJ, 2.19.7(544); and see also Tully 1998: 226–32.
[33] Ramsay 1916: 129–31; CIL III 6814–16; Levick 1958: 75–6; CIL. III: 6814; 6816.

sometime around the mid second century CE,[34] providing epigraphic confirmation of the historical information.

Furthermore, ancient milestones and inscriptions attest to the location of a legionary base on El Manakh hill at Legio,[35] showing that the Roman army did indeed reach Legio in the early second century CE.[36] According to a description by Cassius Dio, dating to the early third century CE, it appears that the Sixth Legion was still encamped in Judea at that time, in addition to the Tenth Legion,[37] and scholars concur that the Sixth Legion was indeed stationed at Kefar 'Othnay in Galilee (see next).[38] The Greek word cast[ron] ([ἀπό κάστ]ρων), engraved on a milestone found at the third mile from Legio, on the Legio-Scythopolis road, reconstructed by Isaac and Roll as "fortress" or "camp." According to Isaac and Roll, in the inscription on another milestone along the Roman road from Legio to Diocaesarea (Sepphoris, see next), the word "legion" ([ἀπό λ]εγεωνος) appears. Both inscriptions probably refer to the legionary base.

Thus, another Roman legion, in addition to the Tenth, was stationed in Provincia Judaea at the second decade of the second century CE. Isaac and Roll suggested that this legion was Legio II Traiana.[39] The promotion of a provincial governor from the rank of procurator to consul meant that the region received an additional legion. Indeed, an inscription dated to 120 CE was found at Caesarea, honoring Lucius Cossonius Gallus, the twenty-eighth governor of provincial Judaea and consul (approx. 117–18 CE, after the execution of Lusius Quietus). The inscription from Caesarea proves that Lucius Cossonius Gallus was already consul during Trajan's reign (117 CE).[40] With regard to Isaac and Roll's arguments (see aforementioned), it should be noted that Lucius Cossonius Gallus had served only shortly before as the commander of Legio II Traiana.[41]

---

[34] See n. 33; Levick 1958.   [35] Isaac and Roll 1982a: 10, 79–80, 86, nn. 23–7.

[36] Isaac and Roll 1979a; 1979b: 149–56; 1982a: 9; Rea 1980: 220–1; Cotton 2000: 351–7.

[37] Cassius Dio, *Historia*, 23, 25.   [38] Stern 1974–84: 363–4, n. 3.

[39] Isaac and Roll 1979a; 1979b; Isaac and Roll 1982a. In contrast, Shatzman (1983: 323–9) proposed two theories by which to double the legionary presence in Judea. The first was that the legion transferred from Syria to Judaea was either Legio III Gallica or Legio VI Ferrata. The second was that Legio III Cyrenaica was the legion transferred to Judaea from Egypt. Ancient sources document the legionary presence in Judaea during the Bar Kokhba Revolt. These sources were extensively surveyed by Shatzman, who noted that the Third Legions – Cyrenaica and Gallica – had been brought in their entirety to Judaea to suppress the revolt, and that parts of the Second Legion and others were also transferred here for that purpose.

[40] Regarding Lucius Cossonius Gallus' *cursus honorum*, see CIL III: 6813; on the Caesarea inscriptions, see Eck and Cotton 2001.

[41] Thanks to Yuval Shahar for the reference and possible connection mentioned earlier.

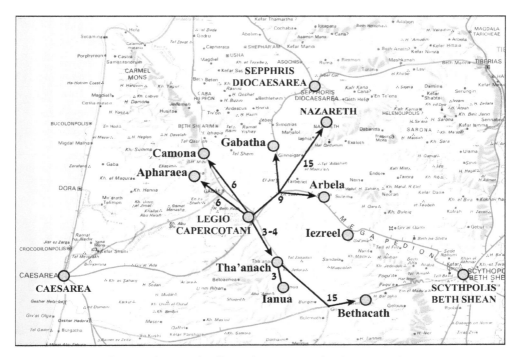

Figure 16.3 Map of sites in the Jezreel Valley and its environs showing connections to Legio, according to Eusebius (according to Roman Road Map, TIR 1994; Roll 1994; Eusebius, *Onomasticon*).

Thus, it would seem that the name Legio became entrenched as the name of the legionary base during the time the Roman legion was there; eventually this name replaced the name Caporcotani/Caparcotani, apparently at the beginning of the third century CE.[42] The site was also called Legio (λεγεών) by Eusebius in his *Onomasticon* at the end of the third century CE, where he notes it as a point from which distances to settlements in Galilee were measured (Fig. 16.3).[43] Because Eusebius' writings are evidence of the presence of military units in a number of settlements,[44] including Aila ('Aqaba) as the base of Legio X Fretensis,[45] it seems that his failure to mention the name of the unit that was based or present at Legio might indicate that in his time the legionary headquarters was no longer there. As to when the headquarters left Legio, a construction inscription of the Sixth Legion found in Udrukh, Arabia[46]

---

[42] Isaac 1992: 432–3.

[43] Eusebius, *Onomasticon*, 1, 140; 21, 116, 21, 100; 14, 108, 8; 100, 10; 98, 10; 70, 10.

[44] Eusebius, *Onomasticon*, 13, 25; 122–3, 128; 120–1, 96; 118, 7; 8, 4; 50, 3, 42, 3.

[45] Eusebius, *Onomasticon*, 6, 20; see also Tsafrir, Di Segni and Green 1994, 59–60.

[46] For the camp, see Gregory 1995–7: vol. 2, 383–9.

apparently attests that at the end of the third century the legion (or at least part of it) had moved eastward.[47] The absence of the name of the Sixth Legion from the legions posted in Palestine at the beginning of the fifth century CE[48] underscores the assumption that at that time the headquarters was no longer at Legio-Kefar 'Othnay. Ritterling claimed that the legion had already left by the time of Alexander Severus (222–35 CE),[49] and other assessments have been voiced for a later date for the departure of the Sixth Legion from Legio.[50]

Shatzman recently suggested that the small size of the bases in Udrukh and Al Lajjun (in Transjordan)[51] supports the evidence of the presence of soldiers of Legio VI Ferrata in Egypt[52] and attests that the legion was split when it was moved from the base in Judea and sent to two provinces, part to Arabia and part to Egypt.[53] Either way it is likely that by approximately the year 300 the legionary headquarters was no longer stationed at Kefar 'Othnay.

Hieronymus (342–420 CE), in his Latin translation of Eusebius' *Onomasticon*, calls Legio *oppido Legionis*,[54] which hints that a key civilian settlement developed at the site after the legion's departure from Legio or during the last stages of its presence there. The term *oppidum* indicates a regional administrative settlement center, not necessarily fortified, which under Roman influence gradually became an urban center of the type known in central and Western Europe.[55] In any case, during the Late Roman period, the name of the place was changed to Maximianopolis. Hence, even if until that time Legio had only the status of a regional settlement center, and assuming that it did not have the status of polis before then, the name change to Maximianopolis indicates that this status was granted to the settlement at that site. Abel suggested that the city was named after the Emperor Maximian Heraclius (286–304 CE).[56] Other scholars suggested that the name honored the Emperor Maximian Galerius (305 CE) at the latest.[57] Discussion of the regional urban center that developed at Legio in the Late Roman–early Byzantine period exceeds the boundaries of the matter at hand.

---

[47] Kennedy and Falahat 2008: 150–69; see also Tepper and Di Segni 2006: 42–54.
[48] The senior positions, Notitia Dignitatus, ed. Seeck 1962: 72–3; see also Tsafrir 1982: 362–71; Amit 2002: 798–805.
[49] Ritterling 1925: 1593.   [50] See, for example, Barnes 2008b: 62; Cotton 2000: 351.
[51] See Gregory 1995–7: vol. 2, 349–59.   [52] Rea 1996: vol. 63: 4359, 30–4.
[53] Shatzman, in press (pers. comm.)   [54] Hieronymus, *De situ.* 59,1; 15, 20.
[55] Jones 2001: 46; Woolf 1993a: 223–5; McIntosh 2009: 159.   [56] Abel 1938: 175.
[57] Avi-Yonah 1966: 122–3; see also Isaac and Roll 1982a: 11; Barnes 2008b: 64.

Lajjun, Kefar 'Othnay and the Legionary Base at Legio

The name Lajjun appears on the Schumacher map (1908) alongside a bridge over Naḥal Qeni (Fig. 16.4).[58] On Mandate maps,[59] the name Lajjun is given to the three central villages that existed in the area until the first half of the twentieth century. At the very beginning of scholarly research, the accepted opinion was that the Arabic name preserved the Latin word *legio* and thus preserved centuries-old traditions going back to the time the Roman legion built its base here.[60] This toponymic association was known to Eusebius (262–340 CE), author of the *Onomasticon*,[61] who notes distances from Legio (Legeon) to a number of settlements in Galilee (Fig. 16.3). As mentioned earlier, based on the distances between known milestones in the area around Legio, Isaac and Roll proposed identifying the location of the camp on El Manakh hill, north of Naḥal Qeni, northwest of the Megiddo Junction and southeast of Kibbutz Megiddo. The hill is mentioned by this name in both the Schumacher map (1908) and the Mandatory map,[62] and El Manakh according to Sharoni means "place of encampment" or "place of camel encampment" (Sharoni 1987: 1266). This may indicate an area that had previously been used as an encampment and perhaps that the memory of the legionary camp was preserved in the Arabic name of the hill, the way the name Legio-Lajjun (above)[63] was preserved.

As noted earlier, in historical sources dated to the mid second century CE, the legionary base was called Caporcotani, after the name of the village (Kefar 'Othnay) next to which it was established. We identify the rural site excavated within the Megiddo prison compound, south of Naḥal Qeni, as Kefar 'Othnay. In that excavation we uncovered remains of the rural village and evidence that the population was mixed – Jews, Samaritans and the families of Roman legionaries, some of whom were Christian.[64] According to the milestones, a Roman legionary base, although established earlier (and called Caporcotani, see previous discussion), was called Legio

---

[58] Schumacher 1908: 7.

[59] Palestine Grid: 1:20,000: Megiddo, S.S: 16–22. 1942; Umm El Fahm, S.S: 16–21. 1942; 'Afula, S.S: 17–22. 1942; Sīlat El Hārtīa, S.S: 17–21. 1942. 'Afula, S.S: 17–22. 1942; Sīlat El Hārtīa, S.S: 17–21. 1942.fula, S.S: 17–22. 1942; Sīlat El Hārtīa, S.S: 17–21. 1942.

[60] Guérin 1875: 232–5; Avi-Yonah 1949: 133–4; la Strange 1965: 380; Isaac and Roll 1982a: 79.

[61] Eus. *Onomasticon*, ed. Klostermann, 1904, passim.   [62] See n. 59.

[63] A similar phenomenon of the transfer of names appears at the site of Legeon in Transjordan. The site was called Betthoro, and following the establishment of the Fourth Roman Legion, Martia. Its name is preserved to this day as Lajjun, deriving from the Latin word *legio*. See Gregory 1995–7: 349–57; Parker 1993: 844–7.

[64] Tepper 2014a; Tepper and Di Segni 2006.

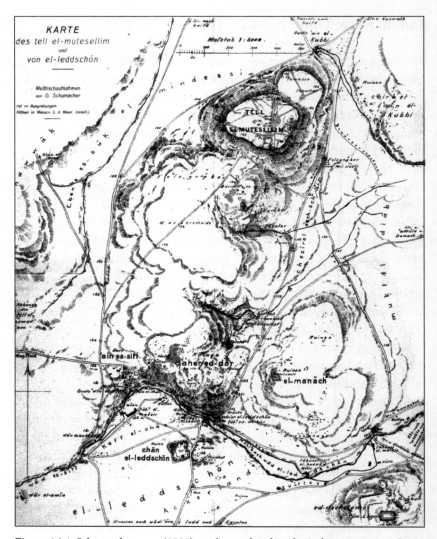

Figure 16.4 Schumacher map (1908), probes and archaeological excavations at Legio.

("legion") only after the beginning of the third century, and that was its name until the Roman legion left the site and the Byzantine polis was founded.

Roman military bases and fortifications, as well as Roman roads between main cities (*poleis*), are known as obvious elements of Roman state-sponsored construction in the Land of Israel.[65] The connection between the military camp and the nearby road network also manifests itself in the way standard Roman military bases were built. These legionary bases were usually

---

[65] Tsafrir 1984: 40–1.

built around an orthogonal network of streets, with the main street running the length of the base, the "headquarters road" or *via praetoria*, intersected in the center by the main road running its width, the "commanders' road" or *via principalis*. At the end of these main streets, in the middle of the base's walls, four gates were built to provide convenient access to roads leading to and from the base. According to Isaac, the Roman military legionary base in the Land of Israel served as the starting points of roads leading to the imperial road system, and only from the Severan period and onward did six main cities (*poleis*) in the province serve as starting points for Roman imperial roads.[66] According to Roll, this network reached its greatest extent during the third century CE.[67] At that time the legionary base was already situated at Kefar ʿOthnay, but served no more as *caput viae*.

From previous surveys conducted at the site and as-yet unpublished archaeological excavations,[68] we may suggest that this was a full-fledged legionary base of the type known in the Western Roman Empire, which we believe covered an area of at most 201.25 dunams (20.125 hectares). No Roman military base of this size from the second to third centuries CE has yet been documented in the eastern Roman Empire.

Roman Military Finds from Legio-Kefar ʿOthnay

Research on the material culture of the Roman army as reflected in archaeological findings in the Land of Israel shows that, in addition to legionary-stamped pottery objects (such as roof tiles, bricks and pipes) and Roman weapons, bread stamps, tableware and amphoras, stone masks, gems and jewelry, architecture, cultic objects and burials all enable us to identify Roman military presence in general.[69] The findings, of three main types – tiles and bricks with military-legionary stamps, counterstruck coins and weapons identified with the Roman army – will be discussed later. They will assist us in examining Roman military presence at the site.

Stamped Tiles and Bricks

In Jerusalem, where the Tenth Legion was stationed, military stamps, bricks and pipes were uncovered, as was a Roman military workshop, although opinions are divided as to the precise location of the military

---

[66] Isaac 1998a: 63–6. [67] Roll 1994; 2009. [68] Tepper 2003a; 2003b; 2014a; nn. 12–14.
[69] Rosenthal-Heginbottom 2008, 91*–107.

camp.[70] This contrasts with the paucity of finds documented so far of military stamps of the legions stationed at Legio. Recently published comparative research, however,[71] shows major differences in the quantity of military stamps among legionary sites throughout the empire. While in some cases legionary camps have produced a great many finds, excavations of other camps have unearthed no tiles or bricks with military stamps at all. At this stage of the research, therefore, it seems that no great significance should be attached to comparisons of the two sites in this regard.

Nevertheless, a number of tiles and bricks bearing Roman military stamps, or those of Legio VI Ferrata, have been documented from Legio. Schumacher (1908: 175) was the first to publish a tile with a Sixth Legion Ferrata stamp (LEG VI FER), which was found east of the theater at Legio. Other stamped tiles were discovered in Schumacher's excavations of the amphitheater south of the tell and in his excavations at e-Daher Hill.[72] Sixth Legion-stamped tiles were also found at Tel Ta'anach, south of Legio,[73] and an additional tile was found in the hiding complex at Har Hazon.[74] Adan-Bayewitz reported tiles bearing the Sixth Legion stamp from the excavations at Kefar Ḥananya, on the border of the Upper Galilee, where pottery kilns were also found.[75] A Sixth Legion-stamped tile was also found in the excavations of the Roman procurator's palace at Caesarea.[76] Tiles bearing military stamps have also been documented in private collections and in the possession of communities in the area.[77] Recently a number of military-stamped tiles were found in a number of archaeological excavations in the Legio area, among them on the edges of the legionary base hill,[78] in the Megiddo Prison compound[79] and in the JVRP excavations of the legionary base.[80] The findings include stamps of two legions, as well as numerous private stamps and stamps of other units. The latter will not be described here.

---

[70] For details and additional bibliography, see Barag 1967b: 168–82; Mazar 1971, 5; Arubas and Goldfus 1995: 95–107; Adler 2000: 117–32; Be'eri and Levy 2013. See Wexler-Bdolach in this book (Chapter 17).

[71] Kurzmann 2006: 26–9.   [72] Schumacher 1908: 182.   [73] Tepper 2003a: no. 68.

[74] Bahat 1974: 160–9.

[75] Adan-Bayewitz 1987: 178–9; 2009: 1909–11. It is interesting to point out a Talmudic source that links Kefar Ḥananya and Kefar 'Othnay by mentioning Sepphoris between them (Tos. Bekhorot 7.3, ed. Zuckermandel, p. 541).

[76] See Gleason 1998; Burrell 1996. My thanks to Or Fialkov for this information. The tiles are in the IAA storeroom in Bet Shemesh.

[77] Tepper 2003a: 63–8; 2014: 47–56.   [78] Tepper 2017.

[79] The excavations were conducted on behalf of the Israel Antiquities Authority (IAA) from 2003 to 2008. See Tepper 2006; Tepper and Di Segni 2006.

[80] See n. 14.

Roman Military Stamps of *Legio II Traiana*

Two stamps were found in excavations at the edges of El Manakh hill, identified as military stamps not of Legio VI Ferrata. In a preliminary report, it was proposed that they be identified as belonging to Legio II Traiana.[81] On one of the tiles, the following stamped inscription survived: LEGII[], which we propose reconstructing as LEGII[T].

The preliminary assumption, that these were tiles of the Second Legion (Traiana), relies on the fact that this legion is mentioned on the milestone dated to the year 120 CE found along the Roman road from Legio to Sepphoris/Acco.[82] The stamps on the tile found in the excavations at the edges of the hill are not intact, and we may propose reconstructing them as LEGIII[] or LEGII[]. This would mean the stamps could have belonged either to the Third Legion or the Second Legion (see discussion in the historical overview, n. 39). A new find of tiles of this type in the JVRP excavation of the legionary base,[83] of more intact stamps of Legio II Traiana, supports this proposal (Fig. 16.5).

Roman Military Stamps of *Legio VI Ferrata*

These stamps are divided into six main types. They are categorized typologically, and at this phase of the research it may be assumed that they were stamped at the site during the second to third centuries CE.

1. Well-executed, framed stamp. Top line: LEGVI (with a line above the number VI); bottom line: FERR (Fig. 16.6:1).
2. LEGVIF[ER], in a square frame.
3. LEGVIFE[R], in an elliptical frame.
4. LEGVIFE[R], with a line about the number VI.
5. LEGVIFER, carelessly executed, mostly mirror-stamped (negative; Fig. 16.6.2).
6. Tile with ligature (of the letters ERR) of the word Ferrata (Fig. 16.6.3).

Although a Roman military pottery kiln has not yet been found in the Legio area, the petrographic tests we conducted on a number of tiles bearing stamps of the two abovementioned legions revealed that they were all made from local

---

[81] Tepper and Di Segni 2006, 14. See also Tepper 2017.

[82] See Isaac and Roll 1979a; 1979b; Rea 1980; Isaac and Roll 1982b: 131–2.   [83] See n. 14.

Figure 16.5 Tile bearing the stamp of Legio II Traiana, from Legio-Kefar ʿOthnay (JVRP Excavation).

clay typical of Naḥal Qeni and the Megiddo area.[84] This is reasonable testimony to the presence of a workshop at the site, which would have operated to meet the construction needs in and near the legionary base, as shown by similar findings in Jerusalem[85] and elsewhere in the empire.[86]

---

[84] Tepper 2003a: 67; Tepper 2017; Shapiro 2017.　　[85] Arubas and Goldfus 1995: 95–107.
[86] Trilla 2000: 107; Arubas and Goldfus 1995: 102, n. 9.

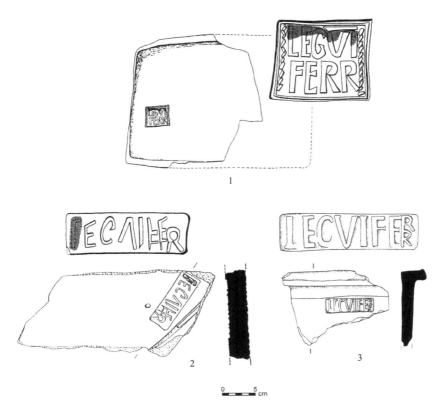

Figure 16.6 Stamps of Legio VI Ferrata stamps from Legio-Kefar 'Othnay (Tepper 2003).

The issue of whether this workshop operated parallel to a workshop not owned by the Roman army cannot be resolved at this time.[87] However, we note that the survey of the Legio area and in the excavations of Kefar 'Othnay revealed clay stands, which are typical of pottery workshop assemblages during the Roman period.[88] This demonstrates the existence of a local workshop here during the Roman period that would have also produced pottery objects. Another conclusion is that the production of materials for the Roman army at Legio, including bricks and tiles,[89] should

---

[87] See, e.g., Be'eri and Levy 2013: 203–10.   [88] See Be'eri and Levy 2013: 208.

[89] We have not yet found stamped pipes at Legio, or pipes with the VI Ferrata stamp elsewhere. Nevertheless, numerous pipes were found in the survey and excavations at Legio, including long pipes for aqueducts or water and drainage channels both inside and outside the legionary base (see nn. 12, 14, 15, 82). We assume that these pipes were also produced in a Roman army kiln that operated near the legionary base.

be dated to the first phase of the establishment of the camp at the site, in the second decade of the second century CE.

Countermarked Coins

Countermarked coins with legionary numbers or symbols were minted by the military authorities.[90] Thus, findings of this type can contribute to the identification of Roman presence at the site, as was also proposed with regard to the Tenth Legion Fretensis in Jerusalem.[91] Howgego mentioned eleven coins with countermarks of the Sixth Legion (LVIF). The seals in question were overstruck on coins originally minted from 5 BCE to 117 CE. Overstrikes were also found on coins minted in the time of Claudius (41–54 CE), Nero (54–68 CE) and Domitian (81–96 CE), as well as on one coin from the time of Agrippa II (48–95 CE)[92] from the same series, and Howgego posited that these coins were probably countermarked in Legio after the legion arrived there from Arabia.[93] In the Legio region survey, more than forty countermarked coins of the Sixth Legion were examined,[94] most of which were struck over worn coins. Of these, six coins could be identified as having been minted in Antioch, three from the time of Claudius, Domitian and Vespasian (69–79 CE), and two from the Iudaea Capta series, one of the latter from the time of Vespasian.

Our research confirms Howgego's conclusion that the VI Ferrata countermarks date no later than the second decade of the second century CE. We have found that the Sixth Legion stamps on the coins were divided into three groups: (1) stamps of the LVIF type; (2) stamps similar to the previous group, but with a line above the number VI (see Fig. 16.7); and (3) stamps of the FVI type. Their chronology is a subject for further study.

The letters on all the coins are very finely incised and clear. The average measurements are W: 0.5 mm; H: 2.0–2.5 mm. Of the additional dated countermarked coins, we note one from the time of Domitian and another from the time of Claudius. Interestingly, some of the coins revealed another, rectangular countermark, of a head facing right (see Fig. 16.7), measuring on average 3.5–5.0 mm. Among this type are additional coins

---

[90] See, extensively, Howgego 1985.   [91] Barag 1967a.

[92] According to a renewed assessment, there is no evidence of coins of Agrippa II after 86 CE; see Kushnir-Stein 2002: 123–31.

[93] Howgego 1985; 22, Ta. 1, 250–1; Pl. 27; see also Barag 1967a: 117, 121, n. 20, coin no. 25; Rosenberger 1978: 81, coin nos. 21–2.

[94] Tepper 2003a: Fig. 17; Tepper 2014: 62, 81–3.

Figure 16.7 Legio, Coin with two countermarks, the first of Legio VI Ferrata, the second of a head facing right (Tepper 2014a).

that do not feature the legion number; these will be discussed in a separate study. Furthermore, additional coins have recently been found bearing countermarks of the Sixth Legion in the excavations at Kefar ʿOthnay and of the legionary base (not yet published).[95] Those that can be dated will contribute greatly to the discussion of the characteristics of Roman military minting activities at the legionary base at Legio.

In recent years, coins have been found with the countermark of Legio VI Ferrata at Sepphoris[96] and at Kh. Hammam in eastern Galilee,[97] two sites that have been identified as Jewish. Although it has been suggested that the coins from Kh. Hammam are part of emergency hoards from the Bar Kokhba Revolt, it is possible that the coins from both sites are evidence of commerce between the legionaries from the base at Legio, or Roman troops throughout Galilee, and civilian settlements in the area of their operations.[98] The coins from Kh. Hammam might represent a life of peaceful commercial interaction before the violent events. As we know,

[95] See nn. 12 and 14.

[96] Porath 2010, pers. comm., unpublished. My thanks to L. Porath and D. Syon for their help.

[97] Leibner 2010; Leibner and Bijovsky 2014.

[98] See papyrus Muraba'at 114 (Cotton and Eck 2002), which mentions a Jewish man apparently living in one of the villages in the Jerusalem mountains who borrowed (money?) from a soldier who served in the Tenth Legion Fretensis. Cotton and Eck suggested dating the papyrus to the year 115 CE (but no later than 130 CE). See also Cotton 2007.

countermarks of different types, including those of the Sixth Legion, show extensive economic-monetary activity, which included the minting of worn coins with countermarks so as to put them back into circulation. It is reasonable to assume that this activity was carried out by a central authority, apparently in the context of the Sixth Legion at Legio. Furthermore, coins bearing the countermark of the Tenth Legion Fretensis, which were also found at Legio-Kefar 'Othnay,[99] enable us to deduce the existence of commerce among legionaries and/or the movement of merchandise between the two legions in the province.

Weapons

In the Legio area survey and the excavations at El Manakh hill, a number of metal and stone objects were found that were identified as weapons and legionaries' equipment (Fig. 16.8).[100] Next, we will discuss a small collection of the metal finds only.

Helmet carrying handle (Fig. 16.8:1): Such handles were attached at the center of the neck guard. Examples of such handles are known from Masada as well as from Western Europe.[101] They were also used at the time of the Republic.[102] Handles of this type also served as mirrors and medicine boxes in Roman times.

Items for suspension on a sword frog (Fig. 16.8:2–3): The Roman sword frog hung from leather strips from a soldier's belt. The strips were connected to a round, suspended element that was inserted in a slit in the belt. Two items that could not be dated are known from the Legio area. The first (Fig. 16.8:2) is decorated with a typical Eastern-style rosette, which is not previously known on a western weapon. The second (Fig. 16.8:3) was coated with gold, remnants of which can be seen on the round element.

Belt decoration (*cingulum, balteus*), resembling a tack, with a flat, silver-coated head (Fig. 16.8:4): This item apparently adorned the leather bands that hung from a Roman legionary's belt.[103] Parallels are known from many sites in Western Europe (e.g., Vindonissa, Switzerland).[104]

---

[99] Syon 2016.

[100] Tepper 2003a: 87–9; 2014: 64–70. The weapons were identified with the assistance of Guy Stiebel, Tel Aviv University.

[101] Allason-Jones and Miket 1984: 424–5, no. 3.   [102] Ulbert 1985: nos. 103–8.

[103] Bishop 1992: 96.   [104] Unz and Deschler-Erb 1997: nos. 2207–8, 2210–14.

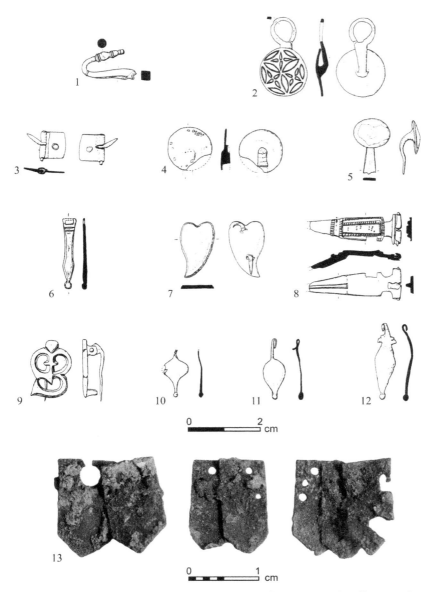

Figure 16.8 Legio, Roman military equipment: 1. Helmet carrying handle; 2–3. Object to be suspended from a sword frog; 4. Belt decoration; 5. Object from a segmented cuirass; 6. Strap terminals; 7. Belt mount; 8–9. Fibula; 10–12. Pendants; 13. Scale armor (Tepper 2003; no. 13 from JVRP excavation).

Belt buckle from a segmented cuirass (*lorica segmentata*: Fig. 16.8:5), used to attach chest and back bands of legionary armor,[105] dated according to parallels from Britain to the first and second centuries CE.[106]

Strap terminals (Fig. 16.8:6): Droplike, elongated objects attached to the fringes at the end of a Roman legionnaire's leather belt. Some have associated this item with a horse's reins.[107] Many parallels dated to the second and third centuries CE have been found in Romania, Germany, Spain and Britain.[108]

Belt mount (Fig. 16.8:7): Heart-shaped object apparently used as decoration on a legionary's belt or horse's bridle. Parallels from the fourth century CE are known from Spain[109] and Romania.[110]

Fibula (Fig. 16.8:8): Type of strip-bow brooch, dated to the first century CE. Parallels are known from Roman military assemblages in the West (e.g., from Germany).[111]

Fibula in trumpet design (Fig. 16.8:9). The fibula is dated by parallels from Morocco and Germany to the third and fourth centuries CE.[112] Earlier parallels are dated to the first and early second centuries CE, also documented in Britain.[113]

Pendant (Fig. 16.8:10–12), including a teardrop pendant, which decorated horses' bridles. Similar pendants, known from Gamla in the Kingdom of Agrippa II as well as from Britain and Romania, are dated to the first and second centuries CE.[114]

Also worthy of joining this assemblage of metal weapons are sixteen pieces of scale armor (*lorica squamata*) found on the eastern slope of Tel Megiddo.[115] The form of these scales is typical of scales from the Roman period that are dated to the second and third centuries CE.[116] Another group of similar scales (Fig. 16.8:13) were found in the JVRP excavations in 2013 in the northern part of the camp.[117]

[105] Bishop 1988: Figs. 22–4.   [106] Unz and Deschler-Erb 1997: 30–1, nos. 732–63, 765–90.
[107] Bishop 1992: 99.
[108] Dawson 1990: 7; Unz and Deschler-Erb 1997: 38: no. 1300; Lyne 1999: 51, 53, 76, 85; Oldenstein 1976: 142–4, nos. 291–304, Taf. 36, 47; Petculescu 1995: 115, Pl. 1: 3–4; Allason-Jones 1988: 213, 216, figs. 50b.2, 52a.9; Allason-Jones and Miket 1984: no. 3.3, 597.
[109] Fernández 1996: 105, pl. 6, figs. 4: 80–1, 10: 174–81.
[110] Dawson 1990: 7, 11, figs. 3, 11, n. 7.
[111] Ulbert 1959: 68, Taf. 15: 16, 60: 12; Ulbert 1969: 38–9, Taf. 25: 15.
[112] Boube-Piccot 1994: 88, 89–90, no. 125, Pl. 70, nos. 53–5 and 116–26, Pls. 5, 70; Oldenstein 1976: nos. 897–940, Pls. 69–70; Ulbert 1969: Taf. 36, 15.
[113] Brown 1986, 48–9, Figs. 31, 233.
[114] Bishop 1988: 98, 156, Table 6, Fig. 49; Unz and Deschler-Erb 1997: no. 1515, nos. 1408–34, 1548.
[115] Lamon and Shipton 1939: pl. 85:9–19, M 404/491.   [116] Robinson 1975: Fig. 159.
[117] See n. 14.

The variety of weapons and Roman military equipment described here dates from the first to the fourth centuries CE and includes objects that were part of the Roman legionary's equipment as well as from horses' bridles, which may also attest to the presence of a cavalry unit at or near the legionary base at Legio. The parallels to these items come also from sites in the eastern empire, but mainly from its western provinces, which is possible evidence of both the source of the manpower and the equipment of the legionaries stationed at the base at Legio-Kefar 'Othnay.

Summary

The evidence of Roman military presence in the area of Legio-Kefar 'Othnay found in roof tiles, coins and weapons augments the growing architectural-archaeological testimony from the excavation project of the legionary base at Legio-Kefar 'Othnay. Although we have not extended discussion to the detailed results of the excavations at the base, we can already propose that this was a legionary base whose plan and dimensions show that it was built in full Roman legionary style as it is known in the western Roman Empire.

The abovementioned military stamps on roof tiles and bricks reinforce the assessment that, during the lifetime of the base, two legions were stationed there, Legio II Traiana and Legio VI Ferrata, and they support Roll and Isaac's theory that Legio II Traiana was first to arrive there, followed by Legio VI Ferrata. We concur with their proposal that Legio II Traiana was there for only a short time, and that the Sixth Legion, which settled there only after the Second abandoned it, remained there until it was sent to Arabia at the end of the third century CE or the beginning of the fourth century CE, at the latest.

The weapons described here show the presence of Roman legionaries at the site from the end of the first century CE at the earliest and apparently more so only from the early second century until the end of the third century or the early fourth century at the latest. The dating of the evidence revealed by the weapons indicates a Roman military presence at the earliest before the permanent base at Legio was established and at the latest after the departure of most of the Roman forces from the site. This presence may have been in the form of relatively small units, stationed here because of the importance of the location both before and after the permanent base was built or abandoned.

Figure 16.9 Kefar 'Othnay – the northern panel of the mosaic in the Christian Prayer Hall. The floor was donated by Gaianus, a centurion (Tepper and Di Segni 2006).

The discovery of counterstruck coins in the Legio survey, the excavations of the base and the adjacent dwelling complex (see subsequent discussion) show commercial ties among the area's inhabitants, including between the population of Kefar 'Othnay and the Roman legionaries stationed in the base. The finding of these coins in other archaeological complexes in Galilee that are identified as Jewish settlements underscores this theory and expands the understanding of the legionary sphere of economic influence to additional areas of Galilee.

Additional evidence that reveals Roman military presence at the site emerged from a mosaic floor unearthed in the Megiddo Prison compound in salvage excavations by the Israel Antiquities Authority (2003–8; Fig. 16.9).[118] A wealthy dwelling uncovered at the edge of Kefar 'Othnay

---

[118] For the excavations, see n. 78. The Christian Prayer Hall, dating to the third century CE, with its colorful mosaic and three Greek inscriptions, has been published, including discussion of its dating and significance (Tepper and Di Segni 2006: 24–54). The site, buildings and mosaic were the subject of this author's Ph.D. dissertation (Tepper 2014a) and are now in preparation for final publication by the Israel Antiquities Authority.

revealed three inscriptions in Greek, one of which was dedicated to "the God Jesus Christ." Another inscription notes that a Roman centurion generously donated the floor. His name, Gaianus, indicates a Semitic (Arab) origin. Additional names documented on two bread stamps found in the structure are of Roman centurions; one of these names was apparently of Nabatean origin. We may reasonably posit that these individuals served in Legio VI Ferrata, thus revealing another source of that legion's manpower. The wealthy structure, whose inhabitants were Christian families of centurions in the Roman army, was built at the beginning of the third century CE and abandoned at the end of that century. We associate its abandonment with the departure of the legion from Legio-Kefar 'Othnay,[119] as was also clearly shown from the results of the archaeological excavation in the legionary base (n. 14).

The research presented in this chapter will be expanded in the future to include additional, still-unpublished findings from the excavation of the Christian structure in the Megiddo Prison compound and from the excavation of the legionary base (discussed earlier). These additional findings can shed new light on the complex relationship between legionaries and civilians in the eastern provinces in general and in the land of Israel in particular. Thus the current project enables a better understanding of the region of Legio-Kefar 'Othnay, where a Roman legionary camp coexisted with a civilian settlement, and Roman legionaries and civilians, including pagans, Jews, Samaritans and Christians, lived in close proximity to each other.

---

[119] Tepper and Di Segni 2006: 34–5; Stiebel 2006: 29–31.

17 | The Camp of the Legion X Fretensis and the Starting Point of Aelia Capitolina

SHLOMIT WEKSLER-BDOLAH

It is a great privilege to dedicate a chapter in honour of Prof. Benjamin Isaac, whose contribution to the studies of the Roman Army and Aelia Capitolina are well known. In recent years, as a result of archeological excavations in Jerusalem in which I was involved, and research discussing the main streets of Aelia Capitolina (under the supervision of Professor Yoram Tsafrir), I met and had long conversations and correspondence with Professor Benjamin Isaac. I would like to thank Professor Isaac for sharing his wide knowledge with me and answering my questions with detailed explanations. His opinion regarding several issues raised in our meetings contributed a lot to my views concerning the development of the Roman colony of Aelia Capitolina, near the camp of legio X Fretensis.

In his 'Roman Colonies in Judaea: The Foundation of Aelia Capitolina', Isaac asks: 'As regards Aelia, it seems quite certain that the legionary base was part of the city, but we have no evidence at all about the division of authority . . . and we know nothing of the territorial situation. What was the military territory and what belonged to the colony? Was there a division between the two or not?'[1] Mapping the archaeological remains of the Roman period that are known today in Jerusalem (and will be presented in short later) allows suggesting, with due caution, a possible solution to the territorial question raised by Isaac.

It is only natural to begin the present discussion with a quote from Isaac's *The Limits of Empire*: 'In 70 CE, the headquarters of the legion X Fretensis were established in Jerusalem to guard the former center of the revolt. This, is stated explicitly by Josephus on three occasions (Josephus, *BJ* 7.1–2, 5, 17; *Vita* 422); it follows from the text of a diploma of 93 CE (*ILS* 9059: "qui militaverunt Hierosolymnis in legione X Fretense"); and it is also clear from inscriptions found in the town'.[2]

In addition to the historical sources and the epigraphic finds – the bulk of military small finds, that were revealed in several sites around the Old City, indicate the presence of the X Fretensis in Jerusalem: Coins of Aelia

---

[1] Isaac 1998, 89–90, first published in 1980.
[2] Isaac 1990:280, footnote 3, now collected in *CIIP* I, 2, 721–7, 734–6, Isaac 2010, 10–26.

Capitolina, bearing symbols of the Tenth Legion; bread stamps of a military bakery, carrying the symbol of the *centuria* together with the names of the centurion and the baker-soldier, in Latin; and a wealth of construction materials, including clay pipes, roof tiles and bricks, bearing the stamps of the X Fretensis, are among these finds.[3] The kilns of the legion were recently exposed in Binyanei- ha'Ummah, adding important information.[4]

Legio X Fretensis retained its base in town until it was transferred to Aela on the Red Sea sometime in the second half of the third century, perhaps under Diocletian. Still later, in the late fourth century, the *Notitia* mentions a unit of *equites Mauri Illyriciani* as based in Aelia (*Notitia Dignitatum Orientis* xxxiv 21).[5]

Surprisingly, despite the long duration of military presence in Jerusalem, and although the ancient literatures insist on the fact that the Roman army never spent a single night without laying out a fortified camp (Josephus, *BJ* 3.76–84),[6] no archaeological remains were attributed with certainty to the military camp, and the site of the camp has not yet been identified.

Nevertheless, most researchers, relying on the testimony of Flavius Josephus and the topography of Jerusalem, propose identifying the legionary base in the area of the south-western hill – that is, the Upper City of the Second Temple period, and Herod's palace in its north-west corner.[7] The size of the camp is still a matter of disagreement. Tsafrir, and others, suggested it lay in the south-west quarter of the Old City – the current location of the Citadel and the Armenian Quarter; Wilson suggested it occupied the area of the Armenian and Jewish quarters in the south of the Old City, and Geva, recently followed by the author, suggested it stretched all over the summit of the upper city of the Second Temple period, including the areas of the Armenian and Jewish Quarters within the Old City, as well as Mount Zion outside the Ottoman walls. Vincent suggested the camp was larger in the beginning, occupying the areas of the Jewish and Armenian Quarters, and later reduced in size.

Since no architectural remains of the military camp were recognized with certainty in the south-western hill, other suggestions were offered in recent years. E. Mazar and Stiebel offered to identify the camp in the Temple Mount and its south-west footsteps.[8] Their proposal relied on

---

[3] For coins, see Meshorer 1989; for bread-stamps, see Di Segni and weksler-Bdolah 2012; for stamps of the Legio X Fretensis, see Geva 2003, *inter alia*.

[4] See Arubas and Goldfus 2008a,1828–30, Levi and Be'eri 2011, *inter alia*.

[5] Isaac 1990, 280, 427.   [6] For other sources, see Isaac 1990, 427, footnote 5.

[7] See Tsafrir 1999a, 124–35, and references there; Wilson 1905; Geva 1984; Weksler-Bdolah 2014a, 2020:19–42. Vincent and Abel 1914, planche 1.

[8] See Mazar 2011:1–8; Stiebel 1995.

findings that were exposed in B. Mazar's excavations, especially a Roman bathhouse, Roman latrines, and a group of ovens, identified as military facilities.[9] These structures were all located west of the Temple Mount, and in my opinion they constituted an integral part of Aelia Capitolina, with no boundary separating them from the eastern *cardo* and the *decumanus* – the main streets of the Roman city that delineate this area in the north and in the west.[10] Mazar, and Stiebel relied on, among other things, the fact that the floor of the hypocaust was built of bricks carrying the stamps of the Legio X Fretensis, and the ovens were made of broken pieces of bricks and fragments of roof tiles, some of which bear the stamp impressions of the Tenth Legion. However, building materials carrying the stamp of the Tenth Legion are not a rare find in Jerusalem. They are widespread in Roman sites throughout Jerusalem, and their wide distribution was explained as being produced by the military and sold to all in the markets of Aelia Capitolina.[11] The Legio X Fretensis stamped building materials should be taken as a chronological indicator of an occupation of the second through fourth centuries, more than an indication of a military possession. Abramovich suggested that the camp extended over the whole southern part of the Old City,[12] between the current western city wall, and the eastern Wall of the Temple Mount, including the area of the Ophel, to the south of the Temple Mount. He relied on findings that were exposed in recent excavations along the eastern *cardo* and the Great Causeway in the area of the Western Wall Plaza.[13] However, we suggested identifying the main remains as belonging to Aelia Capitolina, and not to the military camp. Alternatively, Bear suggested identifying the camp in the area of the Muristan and the Church of the Holy Sepulchre, but this is a hypothetical proposition. It is not based on historical evidence, and it is not substantiated by any archaeological findings. The area is identified by all as the central forum of Aelia Capitolina due to its central location near the intersection of the western *cardo* and the *decumanus* of Aelia Capitolina, and the substantial remains of the Roman period, including a public square, a decorative arch and monumental remains of public buildings.[14] Isaac reviewed the sources, noting that: 'After the first Jewish revolt the headquarters of the legion X Fretensis were established in the western part of the city, perhaps near the towers of Herod's

[9] See Mazar 2011: 11–84; 145–84; Reuven 2011; Stiebel 1995.

[10] Weksler-Bdolah 2011: 227–8.

[11] Tsafrir 1999a, 127–8; for a summary of the issue, see Weksler-Bdolah 2011: 301–7.

[12] Abramovich 2012.

[13] These excavations were directed by Onn and the author, and the findings shall be described, in short, in the following.

[14] See Bear 1993, 1994; Geva 1994b. For the archaeological remains, see summaries at Tsafrir 1999a: 151–2, Geva 1993:763; Mazor 2007, 118–19.

palace, that one of them still stands'. Alternatively, he suggested, the military base might have been at the Temple Mount, or in the northern part of the city, where no excavations were yet carried out. At Palmyra and Luxor, he added, the Roman army established a military headquarters in a former sanctuary.[15]

As mentioned earlier, I support the traditional identification of the south-western hill as the site of the Tenth Legion camp. In addition to the historical testimony of Josephus, it is important to note the advantageous topography of the south-western hill, which probably affected the choice of the army. The south-western hill's summit (heights) extends over an area of about 20 to 25 hectares. It is the highest hill of Jerusalem, and it has a more or less leveled and well drained surface, with the elevated podium of Herod's palace in the north-west (the Citadel, David's tower, and Armenian Garden today). Water supply was provided by the high-level and low-level aqueducts of the Second Temple period that were reconstructed and maintained throughout the Roman period. Thirty-one Latin inscriptions that were engraved on the conduits of the high-level aqueduct to Jerusalem – carrying a curvilinear sign, symbol of *centurio* or *centuria*, followed by the name of the centurion in command – provide the Roman dating and the military identity of the aqueduct's repair.[16]

These qualities of the south-western hill assured good sanitation and health to the soldiers and made it a site well suited to the needs of the army.

Without the archaeological evidence, however, it is not possible to certainly verify the location of the camp. And in this regard, I would like to add some notes.

In recent years, several archaeological remains of the Roman period, all dated between the late first and the fourth centuries, were exposed throughout the Old City of Jerusalem and in the Ophel. The new finds included segments of thoroughfares, a bridge that carried a street towards the Temple Mount, public buildings and private residences, all belonging to the civil colony of Aelia Capitolina, its extramural neighbourhoods, or the military entourage. Mapping down the remains that are now known allows a better understanding of the topography and chronology of the Roman city.

I would like to suggest identifying the site of the camp, not necessarily on the basis of its architectural remains (that are quite meager), but more on the basis of the clear differences between the layout of the remains in the suggested site of the camp, on one hand, and the remains within the limits of Aelia Capitolina on the other. The summit of the south-western hill was indeed settled in the Roman period, but it is almost bare of architectural remains and

[15] Isaac 1990:279–80; Isaac 1990:427.   [16] Vetrali 1968; Di Segni 2002:40–7.

has no urban characteristics whatsoever, while the area lying in the northern and south-eastern parts of the Old City, within the limits of Aelia Capitolina, is indicative of its orthogonal, well-developed urban layout.

Laying out the remains (of the late first to late fourth centuries) allows us to reconstruct the development of the military camp and Aelia Capitolina in four subsequent phases (Figs. 17.1–17.4):

1. In 70 CE the military camp was founded in the area of the former, Herodian, 'Upper City' (Fig. 17.1). A civilian settlement (*canabae legionis*) was probably established outside the walls of the fortress,[17] but its archaeological remains are unknown.
2. Around 120/130 the Roman city of Aelia Capitolina was founded next to the camp, in the northern and south-eastern areas of the Old City. The huge Temenos of the Temple Mount was included within the Roman city (Fig. 17.2).
3. Following the departure of the legio X Fretensis and the abandonment of the military camp, and especially following the Christianization of Jerusalem in the early fourth century in the Constantinian Age, the south-eastern extramural hill was inhabited, and several private courtyard houses were built.[18] The abandoned camp, in the south-western hill, remained walled and empty for several years (Fig. 17.3).
4. The abandoned camp in the south-western hill, now called 'Zion', was finally inhabited in the second half of the fourth century (Fig. 17.4). Several streets, churches and monasteries were built around the south-western hill, especially in the fifth and sixth centuries.[19] The 'emptiness' of Zion, due to its military past, made the Christian penetration easier, especially if compared to the rest of the city. Finally, around 400–50 CE, a city wall depicted in the Madaba map was built, encompassing the areas of the civil colony of Aelia Capitolina, the south-western hill of Zion, and the south-eastern hill. Scholars disagree on the date of the wall's construction, but do agree that the wide contour of the wall, as seen in the Madaba map, is Byzantine in date (that is, between Constantine and Justinian). The construction of the wall 'ended' the physical growth of the city's territory.

Following is a short description of the archaeological remains that allow such a reconstruction. Emphasis is given to the findings related to the camp and the Roman city. Remains that were described and discussed in research

[17] Wilson 1905, 141–2; and others.
[18] See: Gordon 2007, Ben Ami and Chachnowetz 2013, Crowfoot and Fitzgerald 1929 *inter alia*.
[19] See Tsafrir 1999b:303–21, 2012, Avigad 1980:228–46, Gutfeld 2012, *inter alia*.

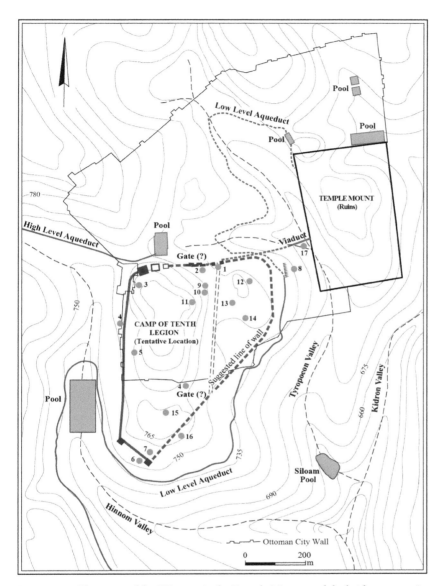

Figure 17.1 The camp of the X Fretensis, the Temple Mount, and the bridge connecting them in the early second century CE. The author's proposal. Drawing: Natalya Zak. Courtesy of the Israel Antiquities Authority.

literature in the past are described in short.[20] New findings are portrayed in greater detail.

[20] For comprehensive descriptions of the archaeological finds of the Roman period in Jerusalem, see Tsafrir 1999a, Geva 1993, Weksler-Bdolah 2020: 51–130, inter alia.

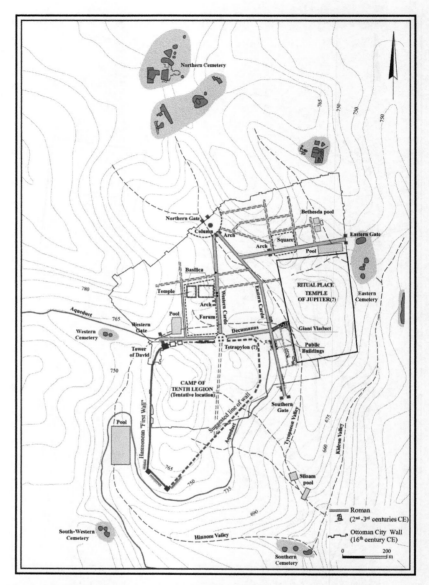

Figure 17.2 The city of Aelia Capitolina and the military camp in the second and third centuries CE. The author's proposal. Drawing: Natalya Zak. Based on data from Tsafrir 1999a, plan; Geva 1993, plan; Gordon 2007, fig. 1; Weksler-Bdolah 2014c, fig. 1. Courtesy of the Israel Antiquities Authority.

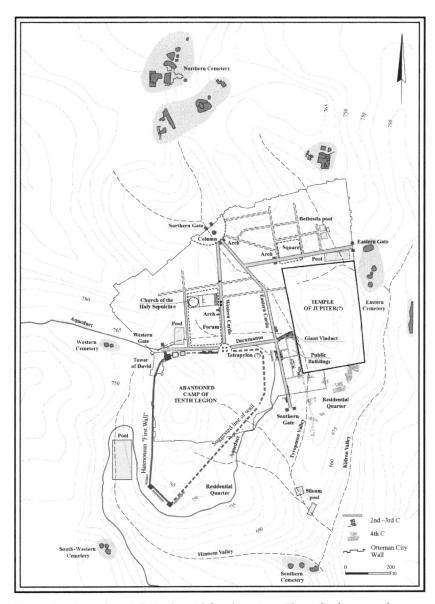

Figure 17.3 Jerusalem/Aelia in the mid fourth century. The author's proposal. Drawing: Natalya Zak. The south-eastern hill being settled with courtyard houses; the abandoned camp in the south-western hill is still walled. Courtesy of the Israel Antiquities Authority.

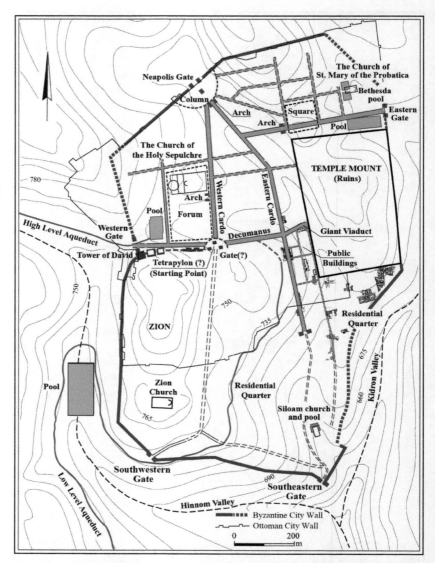

Figure 17.4 Jerusalem/Aelia around 450 CE. The author's proposal. Drawing: Natalya Zak. A wide circumference wall surrounds the city, encompassing the area of Aelia Capitolina, the south-western hill of Zion, and the south-eastern hill. The Martyrium and Anastasis (the Church of the Holy Sepulchre), the Church of Holy Zion, the Church of St. Mary of the Probatica and the Siloam Church were built. Courtesy of the Israel Antiquities Authority.

1   70 CE to Late Third Century: Legio X Fretensis Camp's Site (Fig. 17.1)

Permanent camps of the Roman army were preferably established in sites having topographic and strategic advantages, good water supply and good drainage, providing better health over time for the soldiers staying there. Indeed, the south-western hill of Jerusalem fits these requirements. The testimony of Josephus (BJ 7.1–2) further supports the western location, indicating that sections of the old fortifications in the western side of the city were left intact for the defense of the army.

The Camp's Fortifications and Related Structures

Identification of the camp's fortifications is a difficult challenge to the researchers of Jerusalem, and until now, no remains were attributed with certainty to these defenses. However, a re-examination of sections of walls, towers, a moat, steep natural cliffs and even the structure of a gate, described in the past along the route that I think delimited the camp, allows offering carefully that these remains are indeed contemporaneous and were incorporated into the line of defenses that surrounded the military camp. It is difficult to prove this assumption, though, as most of the remains were documented in the late nineteenth to early twentieth centuries, and there is no secure dating for them. Recent excavations in some nearby locations shed light on this issue.

The camp's fortifications in the north and west consisted of sections of earlier fortifications, the 'First Wall' of the Second Temple period, that were repaired and incorporated into a continuous line surrounding the camp area. Yet the northern line of the First Wall was abandoned several years before 70 CE, and the state of its remains in 70 CE is unknown.

A probable gate structure that was exposed in the past might be suggested as part of the Camp's northern gate. This is an arched entrance (3.2 m wide, 4.5 m high) that was exposed on the eastern side of Chabad Street, opposite its intersection with St. Mark Street (Fig. 17.1:1).[21] The opening is incorporated in a wall that continues from north to south and was interpreted as an indirect entrance gate, incorporated in a wall running from east to west. Warren identified it as the Second Temple period Gennath Gate, mentioned by Flavius Josephus (BJ 5.146), but most researchers believe that the gate was later than the Second Temple period,

---

[21] Wilson and Warren 1871, 274–86; Warren and Conder 1884, 234–5.

Figure 17.5 Café Bashourah: Four monolithic columns arranged in a square.
Photographed by the author.

and the estimated time of its construction was Roman or Byzantine. Wilson
suggested that it is not earlier than the fifth or sixth century CE, while
Vincent assumed that it is a tower gate in the wall of the camp of X Fretensis
when the camp extended over the whole summit of the south-western hill,
70–130 CE. Tsafrir suggested that the gate was an Early Islamic
construction.[22] The gate is sometimes referred as the Gennath Gate or
the café Bashoura Gate.

Cafe Bashourah is a square café hall (8 × 8 m) located in the center of the
Old City, near the intersection of David–es-Silsilah with Chabad–Jewish
Street. At the center of the café there are four monolithic columns arranged
in a square (4.5 × 4.5 m, Fig. 17.5) and it had been proposed that they
preserved a monument, presumably a *tetrapylon*, adorning the intersection
of the main streets of the Roman city.[23] A few meters to the south-south-
west of the café hall, on the east side of Chabad Street, the gate structure
discussed previously is located. Vincent rightly (in my view) identified it as
a northern gate of the X Fretensis military camp and considered the

---

[22] See Wilson 1906, 136–7; Vincent and Abel 1914, Planche 1; Vincent and Steve 1954, 54–6, Fig.
17; Tsafrir 1975, 60–5, 317–18. For a summary, see Gutfeld 2012, 23–5 and subsequent
discussion.
[23] See: Germer-Durand 1892, Tsafrir 1999a: plan of Jerusalem in the fourth century.

structure of the gate, and the café as belonging to one compound (25 ×
15 m), named in short 'The gate of Bashoura'.[24] Wilson too, in his suggested plan of the camp of the Tenth Legion at Jerusalem, placed the
northern gate of the camp exactly in this spot.[25]

The columns in the center of café Bashourah preserve, in my opinion,
a monument, possibly, as suggested before, a *tetrapylon*. However, I believe
that this monument was actually marking the 'starting point' of the ways
and roads that led out from the Camp's gate to the north, east and west.
Some of these roads were paved immediately after 70 CE (i.e., the road
leading north, the road leading east; see the following), and their starting
point was obviously connected to the camp of the X Fretensis. The monument under discussion (*tetrapylon*?) possibly stood in the center of a small
square outside the camp's gate. At first (after 70 CE), it was standing just
outside the northern gate of the military camp. Then (following the foundation of the Roman City), it stood in the intersection, between the military
camp and the civil city, and finally, after the soldiers abandoned the camp
grounds, and the area of the camp was attached to the civilian city, this spot
was located at the center of the city, at the intersection of the main streets –
the *cardo* and the *decumanus* (Fig. 17.2).

About 40 m west of the 'Bashoura Gate', in the Lutheran hostel, along
the northern side of St. Mark Street, two towers and a 30 m long wall
section between them were recorded in the late nineteenth century.[26] It was
believed that this section of wall and towers belongs to the Camp's northern
wall (Fig. 17.1:2).

Further to the west, near the north-western corner of the First Wall,
stands the Tower of David, now combined in the wall of the Citadel. The
Tower of David is usually recognized as either the Phazael or the
Hippicus Tower, two of the three towers built by King Herod north of
his palace, along the 'First Wall' (Josephus, *BJ* 5.161–9 176). The tower
might have been incorporated in the defense of the north-western
corner of the camp. South of the Tower of David, some sections of the
'First Wall' were revealed, with square towers protruding to the west.
The curved contour of the NW corner is typical of Roman military
camps. A thickening of the 'First Wall' that has been identified in the
Citadel might represent the Roman restoration of the First Wall, after 70
CE (Fig. 17.1:3).[27]

---

[24] Vincent and Steve 1954, 54–6, Fig. 17; Gutfeld 2012:24.   [25] Wilson 1905, 140.
[26] Vincent and Steve 1954, 54–6, Fig. 17; Tsafrir 1975, 55–60; Tsafrir 1999a, 131–2.
[27] Amiran and Eitan 1970, 15; Tsafrir 1999a, 131.

Other sections of the First Wall were discovered south of the Citadel, along the western side of the Ottoman city wall (Fig. 17.1:4),[28] and further south. In mount Zion, approximately 200 m south of the south-west corner of the old city wall, Maudsley documented a hewn cliff continuing from north to south, then turning south-east and continuing another 150 m along a straight axis, ending in a prominent tower in the south-east corner, (Fig. 17.1:6).[29] Hewn towers are protruding off the cliff's face, and fallen ashlars were documented along its foothills. The cliff and the towers were considered as belonging to a section of the 'First Wall' that was destroyed in 70 CE. A massive, towerlike structure (8 × 4 m), located a few meters away from the edge of the southern cliff of Mount Zion, slightly north of the southernmost tower (Bliss and Dickie's Tower AB), was recently re-excavated (Fig. 17.1:7).[30] This tower might be part of the fortifications of the camp. The structure was documented in the late nineteenth century by Conder, and again by Abel. The external southern wall (8 m long) and the western wall (4 m long) are built of large ashlars, some of which are reused Herodian stones, with drafted margins along their faces. The structure appears to be later than Herodian, and earlier than the Byzantine period, thus a Roman date may be suggested. The strategic advantage of its prominent location is clear.

From tower AB in the south-east, a hewn mote that was partly documented in the past is running north-east, around the summit of Mount Zion, disconnecting it from the lower slopes of the hill.[31] Bliss and Dickie, followed by others, suggested that the mote was of medieval age, but ditches and motes were used as defenses in many Roman camps, and there is a possibility that the mote is part of the camp's fortifications. The steep slopes of the south-western hill were recently revealed further north in an excavation conducted in the north-west of the Western Wall Plaza (Fig. 17.1:8).[32] It became evident that the natural steep slopes of the western hill were accentuated in quarrying operations during the First and the Second Temple periods. It would be reasonable to assume that the Roman Legion took advantage of this physical structure and settled

---

[28] Broshi and Gibson 1994.

[29] The remains were described by Conder 1875(1,2), plan opposite p. 82; and Bliss and Dickie 1898, 2–4, general plan no. 1.

[30] Conder 1875 (1); Abel 1911, 122–3, Angle de muraille, Fig. 1:B. The renewed excavations, on behalf of the IAA in December 2015, were directed by Neria Sapir (IAA weekly newsletter, no. 4615, 31.12.2015). I would like to thank Neria Sapir and Amit Reem of the IAA for the information.

[31] Bliss and Dickie 1898, Plan 1.   [32] Weksler-Bdolah 2014b.

over the hill, protected by the steep slopes. It seems that, as in the southern part, some kind of fortification was built in the head of the rock cliff, or slightly away from it, but the remains of such a wall were not revealed

In conclusion, the remains that might constitute the defenses of the camp include a possible gate tower in the center of the northern side, sections of walls, and towers, including the Tower of David in the northwest, a hewn cliff, and protruding towers in the south and steep cliffs along the eastern side. This line of fortifications enclosed the camp, and separated it from the city. The walls were not designed to defend the camp from enemies and were therefore not massive. Such a separation wall between camp and city is known from other sites in the eastern part of the Roman Empire, such as Dura Europos, Palmyra, and Bostra, sites in which the army was based near existing cities, or inside them.[33] The reasonable suggestion to identify the 'Wall of Sion' (*murum Sion*), in the itinerary of the Bordeaux Pilgrim (dated to 333 CE), with the Walls of the legionary camp[34] indicates that long sections of the walls of the camp were still standing long after the camp was abandoned in the late third century.

The outline of the south-western hill apparently dictated the irregular polygonal shape of the Tenth Legion camp. Following Wilson, most researchers prefer to restore the camp as a rectangle, relying on the usual outline of camps.[35] However, there are examples of polygon-shaped camps, which were established in accordance with the site's topography (e.g. Camp F of the Masada siege, and others)[36] – allowing such a reconstruction.

A difficulty arising from the reconstruction of the camp as extending around the whole summit of the south-western hill, including Mount Zion, relates to the view identifying Mount Zion as the holy center of the Jewish and Christian communities living outside Aelia Capitolina in the Roman period.[37] No church or synagogue could have been built here – had the area been included within the Legionary fortress.

However, recent excavations in the burial chamber of David's Tomb (below) showed the structure was not built prior to the late fourth century, excluding its identification with a synagogue mentioned in the early fourth-century sources.

---

[33] Isaac 1990,119–60 and references there.   [34] Hamilton 1952, 86; Tsafrir 1999a, 165.

[35] Wilson 1906, 142–5.

[36] For Camp F, see Arubas and Goldfus 2008b, 1938–9. For other polygonal camps, see Collingwood 1930, 7–9, fig. 1.

[37] See Tsafrir 1999a:159–60 and references there.

Structures, Roads and Installations inside the Camp

The camp site was presumably crossed by two roads, leading from the café Bashoura Gate in the north to south and from east to west (usually identified as the *via principalis* and the *via praetoria*). Wilson suggested reconstructing the longitude road, which he named *via principalis* along the route of the later Byzantine *Cardo*.[38] The remains of the military road are unknown today, but it is likely in my opinion that the southern section of the western *cardo* indeed followed the military route.

Poor remains of buildings and installations of the Roman period that were exposed in the areas of the south-western hill provide evidence that the hill was inhabited during the period in question. The finds were summarized in detail previously.[39] They include remains of a structure and clay pipes, bearing the stamp of the X Fretensis, in the courtyard of the Citadel (Fig. 17.1:3), and hundreds of broken pieces of roof tiles, pipes, and bricks bearing the legion's stamp in all excavated areas in the south-western hill, in the Armenian Garden (Fig. 17.1:5), and in the Jewish Quarter, indicating the existence of structures that were not preserved. [40]

A few remains that have been exposed in recent years add to our knowledge:

Short sections of two water canals that were dated to the Roman period (post 70 CE) were exposed in the Kishle Compound, immediately south of the Citadel, inside Jaffa Gate, near the remains of Herod's palace. According to the excavator, these canals might be part of the infrastructure of the Roman camp.[41]

The Assyrian Church of St. Mark

In the courtyard of the Assyrian Church of St. Mark, in the Armenian Quarter (Fig. 17.1:10, approximately 200 m east of the Citadel, 40 m west of the western *cardo*), two walls were partly exposed, apparently creating the north-western corner of a structure, or a room in a larger structure.[42] The walls (2–2.5 m in length, width unknown) were exposed along their inner

---

[38] Wilson 1905, 140.   [39] Tsafrir 1999a, 124–8, Geva 1993, 758–67.

[40] For the citadel, see Johns 1950; Amiran and Eitan 1970; Geva 1994a, 163. For the Armenian Garden, see Tushingham 1985, and for the Jewish Quarter, see Geva 2003.

[41] Re'em 2011, 100.

[42] I thank the excavator on behalf of the IAA, Ron Lavi, for the information and the authorization to cite it. The material is currently being processed and will be published in the future. The pottery was identified by Debora Sandhaus and Renate Rosenthal-Heginbottom.

faces only. They are built of roughly hewn fieldstones, arranged in homo-
genous courses, and were preserved to a height of more than a meter well
above their foundations. The walls were sealed by a thick white gravel-like
layer, containing potsherds of the fourth century. Below this layer, between
the walls, there was a stratified earthen fill, containing fragments of pottery
vessels from the Roman period, and at the bottom of the excavation, there
was a fill, mixed with ash, containing fragments of the Early Roman,
Second Temple period. The finds seem to date the walls to the Roman
period (second to fourth centuries). The limited size of the excavation does
not allow drawing a full plan of the building. However, the western wall of
the corner exposed now is located about 25 m to the south of a similar wall,
25 m long from north to south, that was exposed in Area R of Avigad's
excavations (Fig. 17.1:9).[43] Might these walls be part of the camp's
barracks?

Approximately 80 m south-west of the Assyrian Church of St. Mark,
an excavation inside a building on the southern side of Or HaHayim
Street, near Arrarat Street, revealed a Roman stratum consisting of short
segments of walls (along an east–west axis) and fragmented floor sections (Fig. 17.1:11). Earthen fills containing a multitude of potsherds
dating from the Roman period (second to third centuries CE) and roof
tiles bearing the stamp of the Legion X Fretensis were also recovered.[44]
The architectural remains were severely damaged during later periods.
Nevertheless, they indicate a Roman presence here in the second to
fourth centuries.

The Jewish Quarter

Another finding that highlights the presence of Romans, probably soldiers,
on the south-western hill in the late first/early second century is a group of
more than ten complete, or nearly complete pottery vessels that were
discovered in a cistern of the Second Temple period, in Area F of the
Jewish Quarter Excavations directed by Avigad (Fig. 17.1:14). Some of the
vessels, including bowls and oil lamps, were published by Avigad as
belonging to the Second Temple period. A re-examination of the vessels
by R. Rosenthal-Heginbottom revealed that some of them were made in the
kilns of the Tenth Legion in Binyanei-ha'Ummah, and others were similar
to those found at the Roman dump that was exposed below the pavement of

---

[43] For the plan, see Geva 1993, 730.
[44] The excavation (A-8088/2017), conducted on behalf of the Israel Antiquities Authority in
2017–18, was directed by the author. A report of the finds will be published in the *'Atiqot* series.

the Eastern *Cardo* (below). The date of the assemblage of vessels is between 70 and 130 CE.[45]

In area N in Avigad's excavations, east of the Hurva synagogue, about 50 m east of the western *cardo*, the corner of a large building whose nature is unknown was discovered (Fig. 17.1:13). The walls are 9.5 m long, and 1.7–2 m wide, with no internal division. Between the walls there was an earthen fill containing fragments of pottery vessels dating to the Roman period (second to fourth centuries). It may be assumed that the discussed corner is a foundation of a large building of the Roman period that was not preserved.[46]

In Omer St., in the Jewish Quarter, approximately 100 m east of the axis of the western *cardo*, a part of a plastered, large installation, presumably a pool, with a bench built along its side, was exposed (Fig. 17.1:12).[47] The excavators suggested it was possibly part of a bathhouse. A ceramic pipe covered with tiles bearing the stamp of the Tenth Legion was part of the construction of the pool, dating its construction to the period of Aelia Capitolina, second to fourth centuries CE.

Roman Refuse Dump on the Slopes of the South-Western Hill

An indirect evidence regarding the presence of Roman soldiers west of the Temple Mount, possibly at the south-western hill, was recently revealed in the excavations along the eastern *cardo*, in the north-west part of the Western Wall Plaza (Fig. 17.6). The *cardo*'s course here was hewn across the slopes of the south-western hill, along a north–south direction (Fig. 17.7). The excavations exposed an accumulation of refuse dump in a deep abandoned quarry pit (extending over an area of approximately 9 × 5 meters, 3.5 m deep) that was located along the route of the street and had to be filled up and leveled prior to the paving itself. The filling material (i.e. the dump) was presumably brought from a nearby military dump, containing organic material that was burned on the site itself. The dump was rich in artifacts that possibly originated in the military camp. The main findings were three military bread-stamps, two complete and one broken (Fig. 17.8), and a very rich and varied assemblage of broken pottery vessels (Fig. 17.9:1–3). Many vessels were produced in the kilns of the X Fretensis in Binyanei-ha'Ummah, and along with them there were vessels made in the local traditions prevalent in Jerusalem before the destruction of the Second Temple, as well as imported vessels, including amphorae, lamps and fine tableware. Of the

---

[45] Avigad 1980: illustrations 233, 252; Rosenthal-Heginbottom 2015, Figs. 1b, 5, inter alia. For the plan see Geva 1993, 730.

[46] Geva 2014, 100–6, Str. 1b.   [47] Sion and Rapuano 2014; Rapuano 2014, 428–31.

Figure 17.6 Eastern *Cardo* in the Western Wall Plaza, looking northeast. January 2009. In lower part – flagstones of the *cardo*. In lower left – remains of a seventh century BCE (Iron Age) building, sealed beneath the Roman street's pavement. Photographed by the author. Courtesy of the Israel Antiquities Authority.

faunal remains, pigs constitute the most common species, constituting over 60 per cent of the finds, and the bones were assigned to domesticated piglets – a hallmark of Roman military diet. The dump, dated to 70–130 CE, obviously belonged to Roman soldiers, indicating their presence in the vicinity of the find spot. The importance of the finding stems from the fact that this was the first time that a sealed assemblage of finds clearly attributed to the Roman army, and dated to 70–130 CE, was unearthed in Jerusalem.[48]

Aside from the Roman findings, the dump contained also findings that derived from private houses (e.g. fragments of stone vessels and fragments of frescoes), typical of the Herodian houses of the Upper City. It can therefore be assumed that the findings derived from the clearing of collapsed buildings of the Second Temple period, along with refuse of soldiers and officers who stayed on the summit of the south-western hill.

---

[48] See Weksler-Bdolah 2014b, 54–6. For the bread-stamps, see Di Segni and Weksler-Bdolah 2012; for the pottery finds, see Rosenthal-Heginbottom 2015; 2019; Weksler-Bdolah and Rosenthal-Heginbottom 2014, 48–58; for the faunal finds, see Kolska-Horwitz in press.

Figure 17.7 Eastern *Cardo* in the Western Wall Plaza, looking south-west. A rock-hewn cliff runs along the west side of the street. Hewn cells (probably shops) are carved at the bottom of the cliff, and structures of the Jewish Quarter are built atop it. In the lower-right corner – remains of a seventh century BCE (Iron Age) building, sealed under the Roman street's pavement. Left – flagstones and portico of the Roman *cardo*. Photographed by the author. Courtesy of the Israel Antiquities Authority.

The dump was probably brought to the abandoned quarry from a nearby dump site of the military camp, possibly located on the slopes of the south-western hill. If this is so, it sheds light on the probable location of the camp itself up the hill.

Mount Zion: David's Tomb (Fig. 17.1:15)

Limited excavations were undertaken recently by the Israel Antiquities Authority in the burial chamber of 'David's Tomb' in Mount Zion. A coin of the late fourth century in the core of the external wall of the building, as well as potsherds of a similar date, that were exposed under the lower floor that abutted the wall, allow establishing a late fourth century *terminus post quem* for the construction of the building. In the opinion of the excavator, the

(a)

(b)

Figure 17.8 Bread stamp from the Roman dump: (Centuria) Caspe(rii), (Opus) Canin(ii). (Century) of Casperius. (Work) of Caninius (photos by Clara Amit; reading by Leah Di Segni): (a) stamp's sealing surface; (b) stamp's long side. Courtesy of the Israel Antiquities Authority.

building was probably related to the Church of Hagia Sion in the Byzantine period, but some architectural elements (fragments of columns and a Corinthian capital) that were exposed in the excavation in a secondary use might originate in a Roman structure that stood nearby and was not preserved.[49]

Other remains of the Roman period (second to fourth centuries), including small segments of a floor of rectangular stone slabs and a set of drainage channels, were recently discovered approximately 60–70 m south-east of the tomb of David, in the Mount Zion lower parking lot (Fig. 17.1:16).[50] The remains were dated to the Roman period, but it was not possible to determine whether they were part of a private residence, or anything public.

[49] Reem 2013, 240.   [50] Sapir 2015.

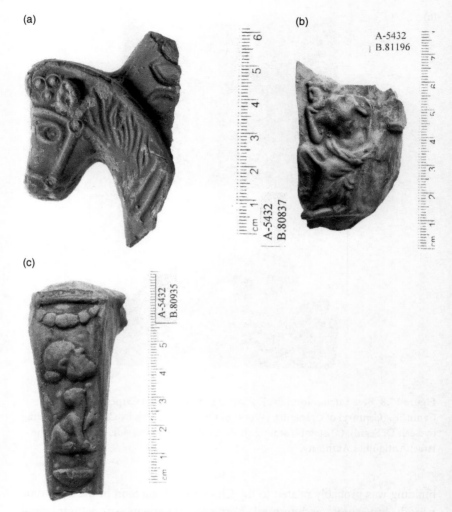

Figure 17.9 Finds from the Roman dump along the Eastern *Cardo* (photos by Clara Amit): (a) fragment of Broneer Type XXI lamp, with left-harnessed horse-head volute preserved; (b) wall fragment of drinking vessel, showing seated male figure in a pensive mood, identified as Saturn; (c) fragment of mold-made jug handle, decorated with Dionysiac motifs: the head of an old satyr, a panther and a bowl of fruit. After Rosenthal-Heginbottom 2019, Cat. nos 747(a), 828(b), 841(c). Courtesy of the Israel Antiquities Authority.

A Roman Bridge Connecting the Slopes of the South-Western Hill and the Temple Mount

The Great Causeway, whose remains were investigated recently, is a long, arched Roman bridge, lying under es-Silsilah Street, west of the Temple

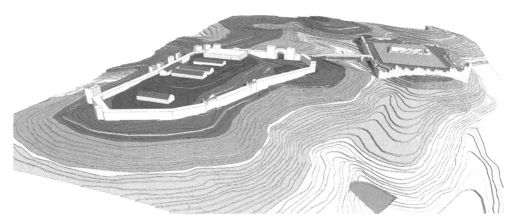

Figure 17.10 Author's proposed reconstruction of the military camp, the ruins of the Temple Mount and the bridge connecting them in the early second century CE. The outline of the bridge is generally based on the findings of the excavations. The restoration of the camp and the Temple Mount are for illustration purposes only. Drafting: Yaakov Shmidov. Courtesy of the Israel Antiquities Authority.

Mount.[51] The findings that were revealed may suggest that as early as the late first century, or the early second century, and even before the founding of Aelia Capitolina during Hadrian's reign, a narrow, long, arched bridge (the northern row of arches in the structure of the Great Causeway) was constructed west of the Temple Mount.[52] The entire structure of the Great Causeway includes the monumental Wilson's Arch that is integrated in the Western Wall of the Temple Mount, and two rows of arches that were built west of Wilson's Arch: the northern row was built first, and the southern row later, abutting it. Both rows are founded on a 14 m-wide dam wall that was built across the Tyropoeon valley in the Second Temple period. The northern bridge (some 80 m long, about 6 m wide) ran across the Tyropoeon Valley and was presumably incorporated into a narrow road that connected the slopes of the south-western hill, with the ruins of the Temple Mount (Figs. 17.1:17, 17.10). The construction of the bridge was dated between 70 and 130 CE, indicating that immediately after 70 CE, soldiers started cleaning and leveling the surface of the wide dam wall in order to construct the bridge upon it. Fallen stones, broken stone vessels, and potsherds of the Second Temple period, the remains of the destruction of 70 CE, were removed into plastered installations of the Second Temple period (one of which was identified as a ritual bath) that were hewn into the surface of the dam wall, probably during the Great Revolt of the Jews against the

---

[51] Onn, Weksler-Bdolah and Bar Nathan 2011.   [52] Weksler-Bdolah 2014c, 192–5, fig. 2.

Romans. Two Roman furnaces, perhaps used for smelting metal, that were constructed on top of the dam wall, after its surfaces were cleared and leveled, are testimony to the type of activity carried out on the spot.

It seems that at this stage, when the Tenth Legion established its camp on the south-western hill, soldiers began clearing the area around the camp and installing access roads to and from the camp. One road that the bridge in question was incorporated into ran across the Tyropoeon Valley leading east to the Temple Mount. Another road was presumably paved at the same stage, as indicated by the two Flavian milestones, carrying the names of Vespasian and Titus, that were discovered, in secondary use, near Robinson's Arch.[53]

The construction of the bridge indicates the importance of the Temple Mount in the eyes of the Roman soldiers despite the fact that the Jewish Temple was destroyed, and parts of the Temenos walls dismantled. Possible reasons for that could be the following:

1. Obviously, the Temple Mount was still rising high and noticeable above its surroundings. From the heights of the complex, and certainly from the south-east corner there was a good strategic control of the environment, especially towards the East. It is likely that the soldiers were patrolling the Temple Mount regularly, perhaps even establishing a military outpost for observation somewhere on the mountain.

2. In addition, it is unlikely that the Romans ignored the ruins of the Jewish Temple that were still standing in the center of the compound and attracted visitors (Jews and others). Under these conditions, it is conceivable that the Romans sought to demonstrate their presence in the Temple Mount, if only to highlight their victory and supremacy.

3. Another option with due caution is that the Roman presence on the Temple Mount was also associated with the recognition of the site as holy, if only because of tradition identifying it as such for over a thousand years. In this context it is possible to suggest that the decision of Hadrian, a few years later, to build a temple to Jupiter on the Temple Mount (Cassius Dio, *Roman History*, 69, 12), was due to the same reasons. In Carthage, too, the Roman Capitolium was constructed on the ruins of the Punic Temple.[54]

All in all – the findings that are known around the south-western hill allows the conclusion that the south-western hill was indeed inhabited, and fortified soon after the destruction of the Upper City of Herodian Jerusalem, in

[53] Isaac and Gichon 1974; Reich and Bilig 2003.   [54] Rakob 2000, 79.

70 CE. Interestingly, no structures in good state of preservation were preserved on the summit of the hill and the whole appearance of the area seems quite poor, standing in contrast to the orthogonal, well preserved state of the Roman city (below).

2　Aelia Capitolina (Second to Third/Early Fourth Century)

By the time that Aelia Capitolina was founded, the south-western hill was already occupied by the military camp, and the Roman city was built north and east of the camp, in relatively moderate areas (Fig. 17.2). As noted earlier, it is likely that the military camp was surrounded by a wall, while the limits of the city were marked with freestanding city gates, set along the roads that led out from the military camp.[55] The starting point of these roads was probably located immediately outside the northern gate of the camp and marked by a *tetrapylon* (described previously in the café Bashoura area). That monument was now set in the center of Aelia Capitolina (below).

The orthogonal layout of Aelia Capitolina was shaped with a grid network of streets that were parallel and perpendicular to each other. The main, central streets were somewhat wider than the rest and had porticos along their sides. The orthogonal layout of the Roman city is reflected in the Madaba mosaic map of the sixth century,[56] and is actually preserved in the urban topography of the old city of Jerusalem to our own days.

Two colonnaded thoroughfares, identified as the eastern and western *cardines* of the Roman city, run across the city in a north–south axis. Both streets start in an oval square that is partly known today inside and under the Ottoman Damascus Gate. The eastern *cardo* (its flagstones were revealed in many places along el-Wad, ha'Gai Street) runs along the Tyropoeon valley, in a north-west–south-east direction, and approximately opposite the corner of the Temple Mount, it turns south and continues in a straight line, parallel to the western wall of the Temple enclosure, towards a presumed gate in the area of the current Dung Gate. The western *cardo*, whose remains were documented 400 m along Khan ez-Zeit Street (Fig. 17.11), runs from the oval square inside the Damascus Gate directly south, towards the presumed northern gate of the military camp, in the area of the Café Bashoura, located today in the center of the Old City.[57] The *decumanus* runs from the western city gate, in the area of Jaffa Gate, eastward. It

---

[55]　Mazor 2004, 112–19; 2007, 120–2.　　[56]　Avi-Yonah 1954.
[57]　Johns 1948:94; Weksler-Bdolah 2011, 56–8, figs. 52–8.

Figure 17.11 Flagstones of the Western *Cardo* along Khan ez-Zeit street, looking south (Source: Archives of the Israel Antiquities Authority, the British Mandate files, 1947. Jerusalem, Muslim quarter A2, Volume 101, photograph 38812). Courtesy of the Israel Antiquities Authority.

runs along David street (towards Café Bashoura), and from there, along el-Silsila street, towards the Temple Mount. North of the Temple Mount, remains of another street were exposed in the route of the Via Dolorosa. Some identify it as the northern *decumanus*, running from the Eastern gate, in the site of the Lion's Gate, towards the eastern *cardo* in the west.

Along the main streets, remains of urban squares, monumental arches decorating the squares, and a variety of buildings typical of a Roman city are known (Fig. 17.2 and subsequent discussion).[58] The monumental appearance of the Roman city, and the good state of its preservation, are exhibited in the findings of the eastern *Cardo* that was exposed along the north-western side of the Western Wall Plaza; and the Great Causeway – the bridge that carried the *decumanus*, from the west, eastwards towards the Temple Mount, and was recently investigated along the northern side of the same Plaza (Fig. 17.12).[59]

[58] See Tsafrir 1999a; Geva 1993, *inter alia*.
[59] For the *cardo*, see Weksler-Bdolah 2014b, 2020:74–96; for the causeway, see Onn, Weksler-Bdolah, and Bar-Nathan 2011, Weksler-Bdolah 2020:97.

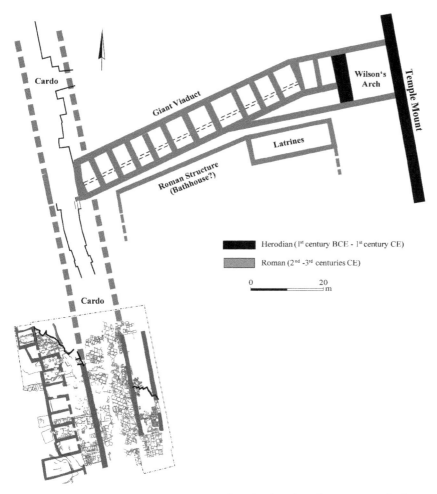

Figure 17.12 Great Causeway – Eastern *Cardo* – plan based on the excavation findings. Drafting: Vadim Essman, Natalya Zak. Courtesy of the Israel Antiquities Authority.

A 50 m-long segment of the eastern *cardo* was exposed in the Western Wall Plaza (Figs. 17.6, 17.7). The colonnaded street consisted of a carriageway (8 m wide), lined on both sides with an elevated sidewalk (1.5 m wide), and a further elevated portico (6.5 m wide). The carriageway was paved with large flagstones of the local *Mizzi Hilu* limestone, laid diagonally across the street's route. The sidewalks were paved with similar flagstones, laid parallel along the street. The appearance of the 24 m-wide street is monumental. The latest coin from beneath the pavement of the street was Hadrianic, indicating that the street was not paved prior to the Hadrianic reign. Along the western side of the street, there was a row of

Figure 17.13 Great Causeway, carrying the *decumanus*, and the Eastern *Cardo*, reconstruction based on the excavation findings. Drafting: Yaakov Shmidov. Courtesy of the Israel Antiquities Authority.

shops, and along its eastern side, remains of two streets heading east. A monumental gateway (*propylaea*) between these two streets is probably part of a public building that was not exposed.

In the section that was exposed now, the *cardo*'s route ran across the slope of the south-western hill, paralleling the Western Wall of the Temple Mount. Its surface sloped gently from north to south. The route of the *cardo* was hewn and lowered to adjust the street's level, creating a vertical cliff, 11 m high, along the western side of the street. This cliff separated the hill, where the military supposedly camped, from the civilian sphere of the colonnaded street. In the northern section of the street exposed now, the flagstones were laid on top of remains of older buildings (i.e. an Iron Age building), as well as on top of the Roman dump that was brought to the site in order to fill the pit of an abandoned quarry (described previously).

North of the Western Wall Plaza, the investigation of the Great Causeway revealed that during the Hadrianic reign, or slightly later, the narrow bridge that was constructed between the slopes of the south-western hill and the Temple Mount in 70–130 CE was widened with another row of arches. The later, southern row of arches abutted the northern row, and on top of both rows, flagstones of a street were laid. The street, recognized as the *decumanus*, a main street in the new Roman City, ran across the Tyropoeon valley and above the eastern *cardo*, leading towards the Temple Mount (Figs. 17.12, 17.13).

Recent excavations enabled a glimpse into the buildings that adorned the Roman city. Remains of a well-built, large complex of public buildings of the Roman period were exposed south of the Great Causeway, extending all the way between the Temple Mount and the eastern *cardo*. The walls of the Roman buildings are standing at present 10 m high. The eastern section of the building contained a public latrine of the Roman period, which might have been part of a larger Roman bathhouse (Fig. 17.12).[60]

The western section of the Roman building (Fig. 17.12) was partly excavated recently. One of the stones of its northern wall (facing north) carries an inscription of the X Fretensis. Bahat thought that the stone was in a secondary use,[61] while Eck suggested it was in situ (*CIIP*, 1, 2, 725). The inner parts of this section are constructed of hewn ashlars with a monumental appearance. The date of this building is not known yet, though a Roman date might be postulated (the excavations reached a secondary, Early Islamic stratum inside this building, and did not proceed further).[62]

In the northern part of the Old City, about 20 m north of Via Dolorosa St. and 50 m east of the eastern *cardo*'s route (el-Wad street), within the current compound of the 'Austrian Hospice', the upper part of walls and arches that supported a flat roof – belonging, presumably, to a square courtyard of a building, surrounded by rooms – were exposed.[63] The small finds within the fills that sealed the building were dated to the fourth century, implying that the building, possibly a private building in Aelia Capitolina, was built not later than the fourth century.

Summing up, the examination and mapping of all known remains of the Roman period in the area of the Old City show that the Roman city was designed according to the Roman orthogonal tradition. However, prominent remains of the Herodian city, such as the Temple Mount, were integrated in the urban plan.

Discussion

A re-examination of the remains of the Roman period that are known around the Old City of Jerusalem at present shows chronological

---

[60] Bahat 2013, 169, plan 6.06; 174, Fig. 6.21; Onn, Weksler-Bdolah, and Bar Nathan 2011.

[61] Bahat 2013, 43.

[62] I wish to thank the excavators, Peter Gendelman and Ortal Chalaf of the IAA, for the information. A general description was published in the IAA weekly newsletter, no. 3615, for October 11–15, 2015.

[63] Kisilevitz and Greenwald 2012, 143–7.

differences that allow us to recover several stages in the development of Aelia Capitolina after 70 CE.

Earlier, we concentrated on remains in the south-western hill of Jerusalem that are related to the military camp of the Tenth Legion, and remains in the northern and south-eastern parts of the Old City that are related to Aelia Capitolina. The marked difference between these areas require a further discussion. Presented here are a few matters that arose from this study:

1. All of the remains of the Roman period (that are dated between the late first and the late third/early fourth century) are located more or less in the area of the Old City, supporting the view that the Old City, in general, preserves the remains of Aelia Capitolina, including the camp of Legio X Fretensis. The summit of Mount Zion, lying today outside the Ottoman Walls, might have been included within the limits of the camp, although this cannot be verified at present.

2. The Herodian Temenos of the Temple Mount was obviously included within the limits of Aelia Capitolina.[64] The Great Causeway carried the eastern section of the *decumanus* toward the main western gate of the enclosure.

3. The bridge, connecting the Temple Mount with the south-western hill at first, and with Aelia Capitolina, later, indicates the importance of the Temple Mount to the Romans. It was offered, with due caution, that its significance was not only due to strategic reasons, but also a result of the tradition identifying the Temple Mount as a holy site.

4. Mapping the remains of the Roman period in Jerusalem shows marked differences between the orthogonal layout of the remains in the northern and south-eastern parts of the Old City that seem to represent the Roman colony of Aelia Capitolina, and the 'quite empty' area of the south-western hill, which probably represents the military camp. The streets and the monumental buildings of Aelia Capitolina are well preserved in many places throughout the Old City of Jerusalem. Paving stones of Roman streets were exposed below the routes of several main streets of the Old City,[65] and the original drainage channels that run below their level have been used continually until the twentieth century. Monumental buildings of Aelia Capitolina, such as the arch of the 'Ecce Homo', are still standing high above the surface, decorating the cityscape of the Old City, and other structures are preserved to

---

[64] For another opinion, see Eliav 1997, 131–3; 2005, 107–24.
[65] See a summary of all the known street remains in Weksler-Bdolah, 2020:65–110.

significant heights below ground level (such as the northern Roman city gate below the Damascus gate, or the latrine building near the Great Causeway). All in all, it is possible to suggest that the colony of Aelia Capitolina is indeed preserved in the Old City of Jerusalem, streets and structures alike.

5. The meager nature of the remains in the south-western hill requires discussion. Most scholars believe that the Roman military camp in Jerusalem was similar in shape to other military camps throughout the Empire. Lack of remains of the camp and the least amount of building inscriptions is surprising, and different explanations have been proposed.[66] In my opinion, the absence of the remains might be related to the mode of the camp's evacuation and the fate of the abandoned camp thereafter. Polybius (*Histories*, VI, 40, 1–3); and Josephus (*BJ* 3, 89–92) indicated that the evacuation of a military camp during the battle is done according to a proper procedure.[67] It is likely that the evacuation of a permanent camp also followed an established procedure, although no descriptions are preserved in the historical sources. In this scenario, most of the buildings were probably dismantled, building materials collected in piles, and lightweight materials that could be utilized to build the next camp (wooden beams, furniture, perhaps even intact roof tiles) loaded on wagons and taken with the soldiers. It is likely that the heavy building materials, ashlars, for example, that were left in piles in the area of the camp, were later 'robbed' and utilized for construction of buildings around the city. Indeed, stones carrying fragments of Latin inscriptions, including inscriptions of the Legio X Fretensis, were reused as building stones in later buildings throughout the city, and their origin might have been the dismantled buildings of the camp.[68]

The camp, therefore, remained mostly empty. However, large structures, such as the Tower of David, were not dismantled but probably used by the units of the army that continued to be present in the city long after the Legion was transferred to Aelia (above, *Notitia Dignitatum Orientis* xxxiv 21).

6. The historical sources and the archaeological finds indicate that the abandoned campsite that became known as Zion in the Byzantine

---

[66] Tsafrir 1999a, 129, note 39; Geva 1984 and others.

[67] 'The following is their manner of breaking up camp. Immediately upon the signal being given they take down the tents and every one packs up. No tent, however, may be either taken down or set up before those of the tribunes and consul. On the second signal they load the pack animals, and on the third the leaders of the column must advance and set the whole camp in movement' (Polybius, *The Histories*, VI, 40:1–3, in: Loeb Classical Library III).

[68] See, for example, *CIIP* I, 2, 726, 727, 729.

period remained walled and mostly empty of structures long after the departure of the Legion (above). The south-western hill did not enjoy urban development like other parts of the city, and especially in relation to the extramural, south-eastern hill, where large private courtyard houses were built from the early fourth century onward.[69] It follows that the abandoned campsite remained a military zone for several decades after the legion was transferred to Aela. It was eventually inhabited, mainly by churches and monasteries, several decades later. A similar phenomenon, of campsites staying uninhabited for several decades after their abandonment, was observed in Legio and Rapidum, too.[70]

Summary: The X Fretensis Camp and the Roman City of Aelia Capitolina

The historical evidence and the archaeological remains enable the following reconstruction: After the destruction of Jerusalem in 70 CE, the Legio X Fretensis camped on the south-western hill. The defenses of the camp included sections of the First Wall in the north and the west, the Herodian Tower of David in the NW corner, a hewn cliff, and protruding towers in the south and steep cliffs along the eastern side. The camp extended over an area of approximately 20–25 hectares and housed, apparently, the Legion headquarters and some of the units (Fig. 17.1).

Inside the camp there were presumably different structures, including the headquarters (*principia*) and barracks. Epigraphic finds indicate the existence of stables, too. Outside the camp, on the eastern slopes of the camp's hill, artifacts originating from the camp's refuse dump were recently discovered, and the remains of a long bridge that connected the camp with the Temple Mount were revealed.

Fifty to sixty years later, Hadrian built a new city on the ruins of Jerusalem, naming it Aelia Capitolina. The Roman city was built north and east of the camp's hill, 'wrapping' the camp and maintaining a prominent border between the territory of the camp and the city. The city's orthogonal plan abutted the camp, so that its main streets were leading to the north gate of the camp (Fig. 17.2). This intersection of the

---

[69] See Gordon 2007; Ben-Ami and Tchaknowetz 2013; Crowfoot and Fitzgerald 1929, 41–3; Macalister and Duncen 1926, 105–11.

[70] I thank Yotam Tepper for the information in regard to Legio; for Rapidum, see Le-Bohec 1994, XXXVII, pl. 38.

camp and the city became the starting point of the roads that led from the city in all directions.

Following the departure of the Tenth Legion to Aela, and the abandonment of the camp, and even more so after the Christianization of Jerusalem in the early fourth century, the abandoned campsite remained a close military zone, empty and fortified, while the rest of the city, and especially the extramural area of the south-eastern hill, was developed and settled densely (Fig. 17.3). Finally, between the late fourth and the mid fifth centuries, the camp's hill that was now called Zion was inhabited and settled, and a wide-circumference city wall, encompassing the area of Aelia Capitolina together with the south-western hill and the south-eastern hill, was built (Fig. 17.4). As noted earlier, the relative emptiness of the south-western hill until comparatively late – a result of its being the former site of the Roman legionary camp – might have been among the factors that enabled the extensive construction of churches and monasteries across the hill in the Byzantine period, when the hill was named Zion.

Bibliography

Abdelwahed, Y. 2016. 'Two Festivals of the God Serapis in Greek Papyri', *Rosetta* 18: 1–15.

Abel, F. -M. 1911. 'Petites découvertes au quartier du cénacle a Jérusalem', *Revue Biblique* 20: 119–25.

　1938. *Géographie de la Palestine*, Vol. II. Paris: J. Gabalda.

Abramovich, A. 2012. 'A New Suggestion for the Location of the Tenth Legion', in E. Baruch, Y. Levin and A. Levy-Reifer (eds.), *New Studies on Jerusalem* 18: 317–32 (Heb., English summary 57*–58*).

Adams, J. N. 1999. 'The Poets of Bu Njem: Language, Culture and the Centurionate', *Journal of Roman Studies* 89: 109–34.

　2003. *Bilingualism and the Latin Language*. Cambridge University Press.

Adams, M. J., Cradic, M., Farhi, Y., Peers, M. and Tepper, M. 2018–19. A Betyl with a Decorated Base from the Principia of the Roman VIth Ferrata Legionary Base, Legio, Israel. *Israel Museum Studies in Archaeology* 9: 69–82.

Adams, M. J., David, J. and Tepper, Y. 2013. 'Legio, Excavations at the Camp of the Roman Sixth Ferrata Legion in Israel', *Bible History Daily*: www .biblicalarchaeology.org/daily/biblical-sites-places/biblical-archaeologysites /legio/

Adan-Bayewitz, D. 1987. 'Kefar Hananya, 1986', *Israel Exploration Journal* 37: 178–9.

　2008. 'Kefar Hananya', in E. Stern, H. Geva, A. Paris and J. Aviram (eds.), *The New Encyclopedia of Archaeological Excavations in the Holy Land* 5, Supplementary Volume. Jerusalem: Israel Exploration Society and Carta. 1909–11.

Adler, N. 2000. 'Stamped Tiles and Bricks of the Tenth Legion from the Temple Mount Excavations', *New Studies on Jerusalem* 6: 117–32 (Heb.).

Albeck, C. and Theodor, J. (eds.) 1903. *Midrash Bereshit rabbah*. Berlin: Bi-defus Ts. H. Itskovski.

Alcock, S. E., T. D'Altroy, K. Morrison and C. Sinopoli (eds.) 2001. *Empires: Perspectives from Archaeology and History*. Cambridge: Cambridge University Press.

Alföldi, A. 1947. 'On the Foundation of Constantinople: a Few Notes', *Journal of Roman Studies* 37: 10–16.

　1976. *Oktavians Aufstieg zur Macht*. Bonn: Habelt.

Allason-Jones, L. 1988. 'Small Finds from Turrets on Hadrian's Wall', in J. C. N. Coulston (ed.), *Military Equipment and the Identity of Roman Soldiers. Proceeding of the Fourth Roman Military Equipment Conference.* Oxford: B.A.R. 197–233.

Allason-Jones, L. and Miket, R. 1984. *The Catalogue of Small Finds from South Shields Roman Fort.* Newcastle upon Tyne: Society of Antiquaries.

Alon, G. 1977. 'On Philo's Halakha', in *Jews, Judaism and the Classical World.* Jerusalem: Magnes.

  1980–4. *The Jews in Their Land in the Talmudic Age (70–640 C.E.)* Jerusalem: Magnes.

  1989. *The Jews in Their Land in the Talmudic Age (70–640 C.E.).* Translated and edited by Gershon Levi. Cambridge, MA: Harvard University Press.

Alvar, J. 2007. *Romanising Oriental Gods. Myth, Salvation, and Ethis in the Cults of Cybele, Isis, Serapis, and Mithras.* Leiden: Brill.

Ameling, W. 1999. 'Ein Verehrer des Θεὸς Ὕψιστος in Prusa ad Olympum (IK 39, 115)', *Epigraphica Anatolica* 31: 105–8.

  2007. 'Der jüdische Diaspora Kleinasiens und der "Epigraphic Habit"', in J. Frey, D. R. Schwartz and S. Gripentrog (eds.), *Jewish Identity in the Greco-Roman World.* Leiden: Brill. 253–82.

  et al. (eds.) 2010–. *CIIP.* Berlin and Boston: De Gruyter.

Amiran, R. and Eitan, A. 1970. 'Excavations in the Courtyard of the Citadel, Jerusalem, 1968–1969: Preliminary Report', *Israel Exploration Journal* 20: 9–17.

Amit, M. 2002. *A History of the Roman Empire.* Jerusalem: Magnes (Heb.).

Andermahr, A. M. 1998. *Totus in praediis. Senatorischer Grundbesitz in Italien in der fruhen und hohen Kaiserzeit,* Bonn: Habelt.

Anderson, J. G. C. 1898. 'A Summer in Phrygia. II', *Journal of Hellenic Studies* 18: 81–128.

Ando, C. 2000. *Imperial Ideology and Provincial Loyalty in the Roman Empire.* Berkeley, Los Angeles and London: University of California Press.

  2008. *The Matter of the Gods: Religion and the Roman Empire.* Berkeley: University of California Press.

  2013. *L'Empire et le Droit.* Paris: Editions Odile Jacob.

Andrade, N. J. 2013. *Syrian Identity in the Greco-Roman World.* Cambridge University Press.

Arcella, S. 2002. *I misteri del sole; il culto di Mithra nell'Italia antica.* Naples: Controcorrente.

Arubas, B. and Goldfus, H. 1995. 'The Kilnworks of the Tenth Legion Fretensis', *Journal of Roman Archaeology* 14: 95–107.

  (eds.) 2005. *Excavations on the Site of the Jerusalem International Convention Center (Binyanei Ha'uma): A Settlement of the First to Second Temple Period, The Tenth Legion's Kilnworks, and the Byzantine Monastic Complex. The*

Pottery and Other Small Finds (*Journal of Roman Archaeology.* Supplementary series 60). Portsmouth: Journal of Roman Archaeology.

2008a. 'The Jerusalem International Convention Center', in E. Stern, H. Geva, A. Paris and J. Aviram (eds.), *The New Encyclopedia of Archaeological Excavations in the Holy Land* 5, Supplementary Volume. Jerusalem: Israel Exploration Society & Carta. 1828–30.

2008b. 'Masada – The Roman Siege Works', in E. Stern, H. Geva, A. Paris and J. Aviram (eds.), *The New Encyclopedia of Archaeological Excavations in the Holy Land* 5, Supplementary Volume. Jerusalem: Israel Exploration Society & Carta. 1937–40.

Aupert, M.-F. 2004. 'Torches et candélabres dans les terres cuites de l'Égypte gréco-romaine', *Chronique d'Égypte* 79: 305–19.

Aupert, P. and Masson, O. 1979. 'Inscriptions d'Amathonte, I', *Bulletin de Correspondance Hellénique* 103: 361–89.

Avi-Yonah, M. 1949. *A Historical Geography of the Land of Israel from the Return to Zion to the Beginning of the Arab Conquest*, Jerusalem: Mosad Bialik (Heb.).

1954. *The Madaba Mosaic Map: with Introduction and Commentary by Michael Avi-Yonah.* Jerusalem: Israel Exploration Society.

1966. *The Holy Land, from the Persian to the Arab Conquest.* Grand Rapids: Baker Book House.

Avigad, N. 1980. *Discovering Jerusalem*, Nashville: T. Nelson.

Avni, G. (ed.) 2015. *The Lod Mosaic. A Spectacular Mosaic Floor.* Jerusalem: Israel Antiquities Authority.

Badian, E. 1968. *Roman Imperialism in the Late Republic.* Ithaca, NY: Cornell University Press. Second edition.

Bahat, D. 1974. 'A Roof Tile of the Legio VI Ferrata and Pottery Vessels from Horvat Hazon', *Israel Exploration Journal* 24: 160–9.

2013, *The Jerusalem Western Wall Tunnel.* Jerusalem: Israel Exploration Society.

Baker, C. 2011. 'A "Jew" by Any Other Name?', *Journal of Ancient Judaism* 2: 153–80.

Baker, R. 2014. *A Study of A Late Antique Corpus of Biographies [Historia Augusta]*, Ph.D. thesis, Wolfson College, University of Oxford.

Barag, D. 1967a. 'The Countermarks of the Legio Decima Fretensis', in A. Kindler (ed.), *The Patterns of Monetary Development in Phoenicia and Palestine in Antiquity* (Proceedings of International Numismatic Convention Jerusalem, 27–31 December 1963). Tel Aviv: Schocken. 117–25.

1967b. 'Brick Stamp Impressions of the Legio X Fretensis', *Eretz-Israel* 8 (Sukenik Volume): 168–82 (Heb.).

1972. 'QRTH in the Inscriptions from the Synagogue of En-Gedi', *Tarbiz* 41: 453–4 (Heb.).

Barasch, M. 1980. 'The David Mosaic of Gaza', *Assaph* 1: 1–41.

Barnes, T. D. 1982. *The New Empire of Diocletian and Constantine.* Cambridge, MA and London: Harvard University Press.

2005. 'The Sack of the Temple in Josephus and Tacitus', in J. Edmondson, S. Mason and J. B. Rives (eds.), *Flavius Josephus and Flavian Rome*. Oxford University Press. 129–44.

2008a. 'The Date of Ignatius', *The Expository Times* 120.3: 119–30.

2008b. 'Eusebius and Legio', *Scripta Classica Israelica* 27: 59–66.

Barth, F. 1969. *Ethnic Groups and Boundaries: The Social Organization of Culture Difference*. Oslo: Universitetsforlaget.

Barton, C. A. and D. Boyarin. 2016. *Imagine No Religion*. New York: Fordham University Press.

Baslez, M.-F. 2004. 'Les notables entre eux. Recherches sur les associations d'Athènes à l'époque romaine', in S. Follet (ed.), *L'hellénisme d'époque romaine. Nouveaux documents, nouvelles approches (1er s. a.C. – IIIe s. p. C.). Actes du colloque international à la mémoire de Louis Robert, Paris, 7–8 juillet 2000*. Paris: Editions De Boccard. 105–20.

Battistoni, F. 2010. *Parenti dei Romani. Mito Troiano e Diplomazia*. Bari: Edipuglia.

Beacham, R. C. 1999. *Spectacle Entertainments of Early Imperial Rome*. New Haven and London: Yale University Press.

Bear, D. 1993. 'The Southern Boundary of Aelia Capitolina and the Location of the Tenth Roman Legion's Camp', *Cathedra* 69: 37–56 (Heb.), 183 (English abstract).

1994. 'A Response', *Cathedra* 73: 187 (Heb.).

Beard, M. 2003. 'The Triumph of Flavius Josephus', in A. J. Boyle and W. J. Dominik (eds.), *Flavian Rome: Culture, Image, Text*. Leiden and Boston: Brill. 543–58.

Beard, M., North, J. and Price, S. 1998. *Religions of Rome*. Cambridge University Press.

Beck, R. 1984. 'Mithraism since Franz Cumont', *Aufstieg und Niedergang der römischen Welt* 2.17.4: 2002–115.

Becker, M. 2013. 'Nacht (Dunkelheit)', *Reallexikon für Antike und Christentum* 25: 565–94.

Be'eri, R. and Levy, D. 2013. 'Excavation at the Crowne Plaza Hotel (Binyanei Ha'uma) in Jerusalem', *New Studies on Jerusalem* 18: 203–10 (Heb.).

Below, K. H. O. 1953. *Der Arzt im römischen Recht*. Munich: Beck.

Bamberger, B. J. 1939. *Proselytism in the Talmudic Period*. New York: Ktav.

Ben Ami, D. and Tchaknowetz, Y. 2013. 'A Roman Mansion Found in the City of David', *Israel Exploration Journal* 63: 164–73.

Ben Zeev, M. P. 1998. *Jewish Rights in the Roman World: The Greek and Roman Documents Quoted by Josephus Flavius*. Tübingen: Mohr.

Bénabou, M. 1976. *La résistance africaine à la Romanisation*. Paris: F. Maspero.

Benario, H. W. 1980. *A Commentary on the Vita Hadriani in the Historia Augusta*. Chico, CA: Scholars Press.

Berkowitz, B. A. 2012. *Defining Jewish Difference from Antiquity to the Present*. Cambridge University Press.

Berrendonner, C. 2002. 'Les cultures épigraphiques de l'Italie républicaine: les territoires de langue étrusque et les territoires de langue osque', *Mélanges d'archéologie et d'histoire de l'École française de Rome* 114.2: 817–60.

Berthelot, K. 2003. *Philanthropia Judaica: Le débat autour de la 'misanthropie' des lois juives dans l'antiquité.* Leiden: Brill.

Berthelot, K. and J. J. Price (eds.) 2019. *In the Crucible of Empire: The Impact of Roman Citizenship upon Greeks, Jews and Christians.* Leuven: Peeters.

Bettini, M. 2006. 'Homéophonies magiques? Le rituel en l'honneur de Tacita dans Ovide, Fastes 2, 569 sq.', *Revue de l'histoire des religions* 223.2: 149–72.

Birley, A. R. 1982 [1984]. 'Senatores from Britain?', in Panciera (ed.), Vol. II, 531–8.

Birnbaum, E. 1996. *The Place of Judaism in Philo's Thought: Israel, Jews, and Proselytes.* Atlanta: Scholars' Press.

Bishop, M. C. 1988. 'Cavalry Equipment of the Roman Army in the First Century AD', in J. C. N. Coulston (ed.), *Military Equipment and the Identity of Roman Soldiers. Proceeding of the Fourth Roman Military Equipment Conference.* Oxford: B.A.R. 67–195.

1992. 'The Early Imperial "Apron"', *Journal of Roman Military Equipment Studies* 3: 81–104.

Bleckmann, B. 1997. 'Überlegungen zur Enmannschen Kaisergeschichte und zur Formung historischer Traditionen in tetrarchischer und konstantinischer Zeit', in G. Bonamente and K. Rosen (eds.), *Historiae Augustae Colloquium Bonnense.* Bari: Edipuglia. 11–37.

Bliss, F. J. and Dickie, A. C. 1898. *Excavations in Jerusalem 1894–1897.* London: Committee of the Palestine Exploration Fund.

Bonner, S. F. 1977. *Education in Ancient Rome.* London: Methuen.

Bonniard, F. 1934. *La Tunisie du Nord: Le Tell septentrionale, étude de géographie régionale,* 2 vols. Paris: Paul Geuthner.

Bonz, M. P. 1994. 'The Jewish Donor Inscription from Aphrodisias: are they both third-century, and who are the Theosebeis?', *Harvard Studies in Classical Philology* 96: 281–99.

Booth, A. D. 1979. 'The schooling of slaves in first century Rome', *Transactions of the American Philological Association* 91: 11–19.

Borchhardt-Birbaumer, B. 2003. *Imago noctis. Die Nacht in der Kunst des Abendlandes. Vom Alten Orient bis ins Zeitalter des Barock.* Vienna: Böhlau.

Borgognoni, R. 2010. 'No Animals in the New Paradise? The "Hall of Philia" from Antioch and the Patristic Exegesis of Isaiah's "Peaceable Kingdom",' in J. Baun, A. Cameron, M. Edwards and M. Vinzent (eds.), *Studia Patristica vol. XLIV.* Leuven: Peeters Publishers. 21–6.

Botermann, H. 1996. *Das Judenedikt des Kaisers Claudius: Römischer Staat und Christiani im 1. Jahrhundert.* Stuttgart: F. Steiner.

Boube-Piccot, C. 1994. *Les bronzes antiques du Maroc, IV. L'équipement militaire et l'armenent.* Paris: Éditions Recherche sur les Civilisations.

Bourdin, P. (ed.) 2013. *Les nuits de la Revolution française*, Clermont-Ferrand: Presses Universitaires Blaise Pascal.

Bowersock, G. W. 1969. *Greek Sophists in the Roman Empire*. Oxford: Clarendon Press.

   1982a [1984]. 'Roman Senatores from the Near East: Syria, Judaea, Arabia, Mesopotamia', in Panciera (ed.), Vol. 2, 651–68.

   1982b [1984]. 'No Senators from Cyprus', in Panciera (ed.), Vol. 2, 669–70.

   2005. 'Foreign Elites in Rome', in J. Edmondson, S. Mason and J. B. Rives (eds.), *Flavius Josephus and Flavian Rome*. Oxford University Press. 53–62.

Boyarin, D. 2018. *Judaism: The Genealogy of a Modern Notion*. New Brunswick, NJ: Rutgers University Press.

Bréhier, L. 1915. 'Constantin et la fondation de Constantinople', *Revue Historique* 119: 241–72.

Brélaz, C. 2005. *La sécurité publique en Asie Mineure sous le Principat (Ier-IIIème s. ap. J.-C.). Institutions municipales et institutions impériales dans l'Orient romain*. Basel: Schwabe.

   2011. 'Aelius Aristide (Or. 50.72–93) et le choix des irénarques par le gouverneur: à propos d'une inscription d'Acmonia', in N. Badoud (ed.), *Philologos Dionysios. Mélanges offerts au professeur Denis Knoepfler*. Geneva: Droz. 603–37.

   2015. 'La langue des *incolae* sur le territoire de Philippes et les contacts linguistiques dans les colonies romaines d'Orient', in F. Colin, O. Huck and S. Vanséveren (eds.), *Interpretatio. Traduire l'altérité culturelle dans les civilisations de l'Antiquité*. Paris: Editions de Boccard. 371–407.

   2016. 'Des communautés de citoyens romains sur le territoire des cités grecques: statut politico-administratif et régime des terres', in F. Lerouxel and A.-V. Pont (eds.), *Propriétaires et citoyens dans l'Orient romain*. Bordeaux: Ausonius. 69–85.

   2017a. 'Auguste, (re)fondateur de cités en Asie Mineure: aspects constitutionnels', in L. Cavalier, M.-C. Ferriès and F. Delrieux (eds.), *Auguste et l'Asie Mineure*. Bordeaux: Ausonius. 75–90.

   (ed.) 2017b. *L'héritage grec des colonies romaines d'Orient: interactions culturelles dans les provinces hellénophones de l'empire romain*. Paris: Editions De Boccard.

Bresson, A. 1996. 'L'onomastique romaine à Rhodes', in A. D. Rizakis (ed.), *Roman Onomastics in the Greek East. Social and Political Aspects*. Athens: Diffusion de Boccard. 225–38.

Briant, P. 1985. 'Les Iraniens d'Asie Mineure après la chute de l'Empire achéméide (A propos de l'inscription d'Amyzon)', *Dialogues d'histoire ancienne* 11: 166–95.

Bricault, L. 2005. *Recueil des inscriptions concernant les cultes isiaque*. Paris: Académie des Inscriptions et Belles-Lettres.

Bronfen, E. 2008. *Tiefer als der Tag gedacht. Eine Kulturgeschichte der Nacht.* Munich: Carl Hanser Verlag.

Broshi, M. and Gibson, S. 1994. 'Excavations along the Western and Southern Walls of the Old City of Jerusalem', in H. Geva (ed.), *Ancient Jerusalem Revealed.* Jerusalem: Israel Exploration Society. 147–55.

Broughton, T. R. S. 1935. 'Some Non-colonial Coloni of Augustus', *Transactions and Proceedings of the American Philological Association* 66: 18–24.

Brown, R. A. 1986. The Iron Age and Romano-British Settlement at Woodcock Hall, Saham Tony, Norfolk. *Britannia* 17: 1–52.

Bru, H. in press. 'Implantations coloniales et identités culturelles en Phrygie Parorée et Phrygie pisidienne aux époques hellénistique et romaine', in H. Bru, A. Dumitru and N. Sekunda (eds.), *Colonial Geopolitics and Local Cultures in the Hellenistic and Roman East (3rd century B.C.E. – 3rd century C.E.).* Gdańsk: Akanthina.

Brubaker R. 2004. *Ethnicity without Groups.* Cambridge, MA: Harvard University Press.

Bruhl, A. 1953. *Liber Pater: origine et expansion du culte dionysiaque à Rome et dans le monde romain.* Paris: E. De Boccard.

Bryce, T. R. 2006. *The Trojans and Their Neighbours.* London and New York: Routledge.

Buell, D. K. 2005. *Why This New Race: Ethnic Reasoning in Early Christianity.* New York: Columbia University Press.

Burnett, A. et al. (eds.) 1992–. *RPC.* London–Paris: British Museum Press.

Burrell, B. 1996. 'Palace to Praetorium: The Romanization of Caesarea', in A. Raban and K. G. Holum (eds.), *Caesarea Maritima, A Retrospective after Two Millennia.* Leiden, New York and Köln: Brill. 241–7.

Burstein, S. M. (ed.) 1985. *Translated Documents of Greece and Rome, III: The Hellenistic age from the Battle of Ipsos to the Death of Kleopatra VII.* Cambridge University Press.

Burton, P. J. 1996. 'The Summoning of the Magna Mater to Rome (205 BC)', *Historia* 45: 36–63.

Busine, A. 2005. *Paroles d'Apollon. Pratiques et traditions oraculaires dans l'Antiquité tardive (IIe–VIe siècles).* Leiden: Brill.

Caballos, A. 1990. *Los senadores hispanorromanos y la romanización de Hispania (Siglos I–III). I: Prosopografía,* Écija: Ed. Gráficos Sor.

Cabantoux, A. 2009. *Histoire de la nuit (XVIIe–XVIIIe siècles).* Paris: Fayard.

Cagnat, R. et al. (eds.) 1888–. *AE.* Paris: Presses Universitaires de France. 1892. *BCTH.* Paris: Impr. nationale.

Cagnat, R. et al. (eds.) 1906–. *IGR.* Roma: 'L'Erma' di Bretschneider.

Caldelli, M. L. and Gregori, G. L. (eds.) 2014. *Epigrafia e Ordine Senatorio 30 anni dopo.* Roma: Edizioni Quasar.

Calder, W. M. 1956. 'A Hellenistic Survival at Eucarpia', *Anatolian Studies* 6: 49–51.

Calder, W. M. et al. (eds.) 1928–. *MAMA*. Manchester University Press.

Cameron, A. 1970. *Agathias*. Oxford: Clarendon Press.

   1993. *The Later Roman Empire, A.D. 284–430*. London: Fontana Press.

Camps, G. 1960. *Massinissa ou les débuts de l'histoire. Libyca* 8.

   1993a. 'A la recherche des Misiciri: cartographie et inscriptions libyques', in J. Drouin & J. Martinet (eds.), *A la croisée des études libyco-berbères: Mélanges offerts à Paulette Galand-Pernet et Lionel Galand*. Paris: Paul Geuthner. 113–26.

   1993b. 'La Cheffia', *Encyclopédie berbère* 12: 1892–3.

   2002. 'La main et la segmentation quinaire chez les Berbères', *Antiquités Africaines* 37: 141–7.

Cancik-Lindemaier, H. 1996. 'Der Diskurs Religion in Senatsbeschluss über die Bacchanalia von 186 v. Chr. und bei Livius (B. XXXIX)', in H. Cancik, *Geschichte-Tradition-Reflexion: Festschrift für Martin Hengel zum 70 Geburtstag* 2. Tübingen: Mohr. 77–96.

Cañizar Palacios, L. 2014. 'From Vetus Byzantium (Amm. 22.8.8) to Urbs Regia: Representation of Constantinople in Late Roman Empire Laws', in A. de Franciso Heredro, D. H. Hernández de la Fuente and S. Torres Prieto (eds.), *New Perspectives on Late Antiquity in the Eastern Roman Empire*. Newcastle: Cambridge Scholars Publishing. 280–310.

Capdetrey, L. 2007. *Le pouvoir séleucide: Territoire, administration, finances d'un royaume hellénistique (312–129 avant J.-C.)*. Rennes: Presses Universitaires de Rennes.

Cappelletti, L. 2011. 'Le magistrature italiche. Problemi e prospettive', *Index* 39: 323–38.

Carlà-Uhink, F. 2018. 'Nocturnal Religious Rites in the Roman Religion and in Early Christianity', in Chaniotis (ed.), 331–60.

Casabonne, O. 2006. 'Buffles et zébus au Proche-Orient ancient', *Colloquium Anatolicum* 5: 71–84.

Casali, S. 2010. 'Autoreflessività onirica nell' Eneide e nei successori epici di Virgilio', in Scioli and Walde (eds.), 119–42.

   2018. 'Imboscate notturne nell'epica romana', in Chaniotis (ed.), 209–37.

Chabot, J.-B. (ed.) 1940. *RIL*. Paris: Imprimerie nationale.

Champlin, E. 1980. *Fronto and Antonine Rome*. Cambridge, MA: Harvard University Press.

Chancey, M. A. 2005. *Greco-Roman Culture and the Galilee of Jesus*. Cambridge University Press.

Chaniotis, A. 2002a. 'Old Wine in a New Skin. Tradition and Innovation in the Cult Foundation of Alexander of Abonouteichos', in E. Dabrowa (ed.), *Tradition and Innovation in the Ancient World (Electrum 6)*. Krakow: Archeobooks. 67–85.

   2002b. 'The Jews of Aphrodisias: New Evidence and Old Problems', *Scripta Classica Israelica* 21: 209–26.

2009. 'The Dynamics of Rituals in the Roman Empire', in O. Hekster, S. Schmidt- Hofner, and C. Witschel (eds.), *Ritual Dynamics and Religious Change in the Roman Empire. Proceedings of the Eighth Workshop of the International Network Impact of Empire (Heidelberg, July 5-7, 2007)*. Leiden: Brill. 3–29.

2011. 'Emotional Community through Ritual. Initiates, Citizens, and Pilgrims as Emotional Communities in the Greek World', in A. Chaniotis (ed.), *Ritual Dynamics in the Ancient Mediterranean: Agency, Emotion, Gender, Representation*. Stuttgart: Franz Steiner. 264–90.

2017. 'Violence in the Dark: Emotional Impact, Representation, Response', in M. Champion and L. O'Sullivan (eds.), *Cultural Perceptions of Violence*. London: Routledge. 100–15.

(ed.) 2018a. *La nuit. Imaginaire et réalités nocturnes dans le monde gréco-romain (Entretiens Hardt, 64)*. Geneva: Droz.

2018b. 'Nessun Dorma! Changing Nightlife in the Hellenistic and Roman East', in Chaniotis (ed.), 1–49.

2018c. 'The Polis after Sunset. What Is Hellenistic in Hellenistic Nights?', in H. Börm and N. Luraghi (ed.), *The Polis in the Hellenistic World*. Stuttgart: Franz Steiner. 181–208.

2019, in press. 'The Epigraphy of the Night', in N. Papazarkadas and C. Noreña (eds.), *From Document to History: Epigraphic Insights into the Greco-Roman World*. Leiden: Brill, 13–36.

Chaniotis, A. et al. (eds.) 1923–. *SEG*. Leiden: Brill.

Chankowski, A. S. 2010. 'Les Cultes des Souverains Hellénistiques après la Disparition des Dynasties: Formes de Survie et d'extinction d'une institution dans un contexte civique', in I. Savalli-Lestrade and I. Cogitore (eds.), *Des Rois au Prince. Pratiques du Pouvoir Monarchique dans l'Orient Hellénistique et Romain (IVe siècle avant J.-C. – IIe siècle après J.-C.)*. Editions littéraires et linguistique de l'université de Grenoble. 271–90.

Chapot, F. and Laurot, B. (ed.) 2001. *Corpus de prières grecques et romaines*. Turnhout: Brepols.

Chesnutt, R. D. 1986. *Conversion in Joseph and Aseneth: Its Nature, Function, and Relation to Contemporaneous Paradigms of Conversion and Initiation*, Ph.D. thesis, Duke University.

1988. 'The Social Setting and Purpose of Joseph and Aseneth', *Journal for the Study of the Pseudepigrapha* 2: 21–48.

Christopoulos, M., Karakantza, E. D. and Levaniouk, O. (eds.) 2010. *Light and Darkness in Ancient Greek Myth and Religion*. Lanham: Lexington Books.

Clarke, M. L. 1971. *Higher Education in the Ancient World*. London: Routledge & Kegan Paul.

Clarysse, W. and Thompson, D. J. 2006. *Counting the People in Hellenistic Egypt*, 2 vols. Cambridge University Press.

Clauss, M. 1990. *Mithras. Kult und Mysterien*. Munich: C. H. Beck.

Cody, J. M. 2003. 'Conquerors and Conquered on Flavian Coins', in A. J. Boyle and W. J. Dominik (eds.), *Flavian Rome: Culture, Image, Text*, Leiden and Boston: Brill. 103–24.

Cohen, G. M. 2006. *The Hellenistic Settlements in Syria, the Red Sea Basin, and North Africa*. Berkeley: University of California Press.

Cohen, S. J. D. 1981. 'Epigraphical Rabbis', *Jewish Quarterly Review* 72: 1–17.

   1999. *The Beginnings of Jewishness: Boundaries, Varieties, Uncertainties*. Berkeley: University of California Press.

   2010. 'The Conversion of Antoninus', in S. J. D. Cohen, *The Significance of Yavneh and Other Essays in Jewish Hellenism*. Tübingen: Mohr Siebeck. 329–60 (originally in 1998. P. Schäfer (ed.), *The Talmud Yerushalmi and Greco-Roman Culture*, vol. I, Tübingen: Mohr Siebeck. 141–71).

Cohn, R. L. 1994. 'Before Israel: The Canaanites as Other in Biblical Tradition', in L. Silberstein and R. L. Cohn (eds.), *The Other in Jewish Thought and History*. New York University Press. 74–90.

Cohn-Haft, L. 1956. *The Public Physicians of Ancient Greece*. Northampton: Department of History of Smith College.

Cole, S. G. 1984. *Theoi Megaloi. The Cult of the Great Gods at Samothrace*. Leiden: Brill.

Collar, A. 2013. *Religious Networks in the Roman Empire: the Spread of New Ideas*. Cambridge University Press.

Collin-Boufriet, S. 2008. 'Organisation des territoires grecs antiques et gestion de l'eau', in E. Hermon (ed.), *Vers une gestion intégrée de l'eau dans l'Empire romain. Actes du Colloque International, Université Laval, octobre 2006*. Rome: L'Erma di Bretschneider. 41–53.

Collingwood, R. G. 1930. *The Archaeology of Roman Britain*. London: Methuen.

Collingwood, R. G. et al. (eds.) 1965–. *RIB*. Oxford: Clarendon Press.

Coloru, O. 2013. 'Seleukid Settlements: Between Ethnic Identity and Mobility', *Electrum* 20: 37–56.

Conder, C. R. 1875a. 'The Zion Scarp', *Palestine Exploration Fund, Quarterly Statement* 8: 7–10.

   1875b. 'The Rock Scarp of Zion', *Palestine Exploration Fund, Quarterly Statement* 8: 81–9.

Cook, J. M. 1973. *The Troad. An Archaeological and Topographical Study*. Oxford: Clarendon Press.

Corbeill, A. 2010. 'Dreams and the Prodigy Process in Republican Rome', in Scioli and Walde (eds.), 81–101.

Corbier, M. 1982 [1984]. 'Les familles clarissimes d'Afrique proconsulaire', in Panciera (ed.), vol. II, 685–754.

Cornell, T. J. 1995. *The Beginnings of Rome. Italy and Rome from the Bronze Age to the Punic Wars (c. 1000–264 BC)*. London and New York: Routledge.

Cotton, H. M. 2000. 'The Legio VI Ferrata', in Y. Le Bohec (ed.), *Las legions de Rome sous le Haut-Empire: Proceedings of Deuxième congrès de Lyon sur Làrmée romaine 17–19 September 1988*. Paris: De Boccard. 351–7.

2007. 'The Administrative Background to the New Settlement Recently Discovered near Giv'at Shaul, Ramallah-Shuafat Road', in J. Patrich and D. Amit (eds.), *New Studies in the Archaeology of Jerusalem and Its Region*, Jerusalem: Israel Antiquities Authority Jerusalem Region. 16*–18*.

Cotton, H. M. and Eck, W. 2002. 'P. Murabba 'at 114 und die Anwesenheit römischer Truppen in den Höhlen des Wadi Murabba'at nach dem Bar Kochba Aufstand', *Zeitschrift fur Papyrologie und Epigraphik* 138: 173–83.

2005. 'Josephus' Roman Audience: Josephus and the Roman Elites', in J. Edmondson, S. Mason and J. B. Rives (eds.), *Flavius Josephus and Flavian Rome*. Oxford University Press. 37–52.

Crawford, M. H. (ed.) 1996. *Roman Statutes*, 2 vols. University of London.

Cribiore, R. 2005. *Gymnastics of the Mind: Greek Education in Hellenistic and Roman Egypt*. Princeton: Princeton University Press.

Croke, B. 1983. 'A.D. 476: The Manufacture of a Turning Point', *Chiron* 13: 81–119.

Crowfoot, J. W. and Fitzgerald, G. M. 1929. *Excavations in the Tyropoeon Valley 1927*. London: Palestine Exploration Fund.

Dąbrowa, E. 2004. 'Roman Military Colonisation in Anatolia and the Near East (2nd–3rd c. AD): The Numismatic Evidence', in G. Salmeri, A. Raggi and A. Baroni (eds.), *Colonie Romane nel Mondo Greco*. Rome: L'Erma di Bretschneider. 211–31.

2012. 'Military Colonisation in the Near East and Mesopotamia under the Severi', *Acta Classica* 55: 31–42.

Dagron, G. 1984. *Naissance d'une capitale, Constantinople et ses institutions de 330 à 451*. Paris: Presses Universitaires.

Dana, D. 2011. 'Les Thraces dans les armées hellénistiques: essai d'"histoire par les noms"', in J.-C. Couvenhes, S. Crouzet and S. Péré-Noguès (eds.), *Pratiques et identités culturelles des armées hellénistiques du monde méditerranéen*. Bordeaux: Ausonius. 87–115.

D'Arms, J. 1990. 'The Roman Convivium and the Idea of Equality', in O. Murray (ed.), *Sympotica: A Symposium on the Symposion*. Oxford University Press. 308–20.

Davies, C. 1982. 'Ethnic Jokes, Moral Values and Social Boundaries', *The British Journal of Sociology* 33(3): 383–403.

Dawson, M. 1990. 'Roman Military Equipment on Civil Sites in Roman Dacia', *Journal of Roman Military Equipment Studies* 1: 7–15.

De Palma Digeser, E. 2006. 'Christian or Hellene? The Greek Persecution and the Problem of Christian Identity', in E. De Palma Digeser and R. M. Frakes (eds.), *Religious Identity in Late Antiquity*. Toronto: Edgar Kent. 36–57.

2011. 'Hellens, Barbarians, and Christians: Religion and Identity Politics in Diocletian's Rome', in R. W. Mathisen and D. Shanzer (eds.), *Romans,*

Barbarians, and the Transformation of the Roman World: Cultural Interaction and the Creation of Identity in Late Antiquity. Aldershot: Ashgate. 121–313.

De Temmerman, K. 2014. *Crafting Characters. Heroes and Heroines in the Ancient Greek Novel*. Oxford University Press.

2018. 'Novelistic Nights', in Chaniotis (ed.), 257–85.

De Vaux, R. 1938. 'Une mosaïque byzantine à Ma'in (Transjordanie)', *Revue biblique* 47: 227–58.

Degrassi, A. 1963. *Inscriptiones Italiae. XIII. 2. Fasti anni Numani et Iuliani*. Rome: Istituto Poligrafico dello Stato.

Dekkers, E. et al. (eds.) 1953–. *CCSL*. Tornhout: Typographi Brepols.

Delattre, S. 2000. *Les douze heures noires. La nuit à Paris au XIXe siècle*. Paris: Albin Michel.

Delrieux, F. 2012. 'Séismes et reconnaissance civique dans l'Ouest de l'Asie Mineure. La représentation monétaire des Empereurs romains restaurateurs de cités', in K. Konuk (ed.), *Stephanèphoros: De l'économie antique à l'Asie Mineure. Hommages à Raymond Descat*. Bordeaux: Ausonius. 261–74.

Deman, A. et al. (eds.) 1985–. *ILB*. Editions de l'Universite de Bruxelles.

Demougin, S. 1988. *L'ordre équestre sous les Julio-Claudiens (43 av. J.C. – 70 ap. J. C.)*. Rome: École française de Rome.

Derks, T. 1998. *Gods, Temples and Ritual Practices: The Transformation of Religious Values in Roman Gaul*. Amsterdam University Press.

2012. 'Les rites de passage dans l'empire romain: esquisse d'une approche anthropologique', in P. Payen and E. Scheid-Tissinier (eds.), *Anthropologie de l'antiquité. Anciens objets, nouvelles approches* (Antiquité et sciences humaines, vol. 1). Turnhout: Brepols. 43–80.

Desanges, J. 1998. 'Gétules', *Encyclopédie berbère* 20: 3063–5.

2005. 'Ketiani', *Encyclopédie berbère* 27: 4188.

Desanges, J., Duval, N., Lepelley, C. and Saint-Adams, S. 2010. *Carte des routes et des cités de l'est de l'Africa à la fin de l'Antiquité*. Turnhout: Brepols.

Despois, J. and Raynal, R. 1967. *Géographie de l'Afrique du Nord-Ouest*, Paris: Payot.

Dessau, H. (ed.) 1892–1916. *ILS*. Berlin.

Deutsche Akademie der Wissenschaften zu Berlin. 1873–. *IG*. Berolini: Apud G. Reimerum.

Deutsches Archäologisches Institut. 1904–. *BRGK*. Frankfurt am Main: J. Baer & Co.

Di Segni, L. 1988. 'The Inscriptions of Tiberias', in Y. Hirschfeld (ed.), *Tiberias – From Establishment till The Muslim Conquest*, Jerusalem: Yad Yitzhak Ben Zvi. 70–96 (Heb.) = 1998, in F. Israel, A. M. Rabello and A. M. Somekh (eds.), *Hebraica: Miscellanea di Studi in Onore di Sergio J. Sierra per il suo 75. Compleanno*. Torino: Instituto di Studi Ebraici / Scuola Rabbinica. 115–63.

2002. 'The Water Supply of Roman and Byzantine Palestine in Literary and Epigraphical Sources', in D. Amit, J. Patrich and Y. Hirschfeld (eds.), *The Aqueducts of Israel (Journal of Roman Archaeology* Suppl. 46). Portsmouth: Journal of Roman Archaeology. 37–67.

Di Segni, L. and Weksler-Bdolah, S. 2012. 'Three Military Bread Stamps from the Western Wall Plaza Excavations, Jerusalem'. *Atiqot* 70: 21*–31*.

Diels, H. 1890. *Sibyllinische Blätter*. Berlin: Georg Reimer.

Dietze-Mager, G. 2009. 'Der Begriff κολων(ε)ία in den ägyptischen Papyri', *Ancient Society* 39: 111–20.

Dimitrova, N. M. 2008. *Theoroi and Initiates in Samothrace. The Epigraphic Evidence*. Princeton: The American School of Classical Studies at Athens.

Dittenberger, W. and Purgold, K. 1896. *IvO*. Berlin: Asher.

Dittmann-Schöne, I. 2001. *Die Berufsvereine in den Städten des kaiserzeitlichen Kleinasiens*. Regensburg: Roderer.

Dmitriev, S. 2005. *City Government in Hellenistic and Roman Asia Minor*. Oxford University Press.

2009. 'The Rise and Quick Fall of the Theory of Ancient Economic Imperialism', *The Economic History Review, New Series* Vol. 62, No. 4, 785–801.

Domenicucci, P. 1996. *Astra Caesarum: Astronomia, astrologia, e catasterismo da Caesare a Domiziano*. Pisa: ETS.

Donahue, J. F. 2017. *The Roman Community at Table during the Principate*. Ann Arbor: University of Michigan Press (1st ed., 2004).

Dor, Y. 2006. *Have the 'Foreign Women' Really Been Expelled? Separation and Exclusion in the Restoration Period*. Jerusalem: Magnes (Heb.).

2011. 'The Rite of Separation of the Foreign Wives in Ezra-Nehemiah', in Lipschits et al. (eds.), 173–88.

Dossey, L. 2018. 'Shedding Light on the Late Antique Night', in Chaniotis (ed.), 293–322.

Doukellis, P. N. 2009, 'Hadrian's Panhellenion: A Network of Cities?', in I. Malkin, C. Constantakopoulou and K. Panagopoulou (eds.), *Greek and Roman Networks in the Mediterranean*. London and New York: Routledge. 285–98.

Dowden, K. 2010. 'Trojan Night', in Christopoulos et al. (eds.), 110–20.

Dräger, P. 2004. 'Homer und Lukrez an der Mosel oder: die Furcht vor dem Dativ? Eine griechisch-lateinische Weihinschrift an den keltischen Gott Lenus Mars', in *Göttinger Forum für Altertumswissenschaft* 7: 185–201.

Drew-Bear, T., Eck, W. and Herrmann, P. 1977. 'Sacrae Litterae', *Chiron* 7: 355–83.

du Bouchet, J. and Chandezon, C. (eds.) 2012. *Études sur Artémidore et l'interprétation des rêves*. Nanterre: Presses Universitaires de Paris.

Dueck, D. 2004. 'Bird's Milk in Samos: Strabo's Use of Geographical Proverbs and Proverbial Expressions', *Scripta Classica Israelica* 23: 41–56.

2016. 'Graeco-Roman Popular Perception of Africa – the Proverbial Aspect', in D. Schaps, U. Yiftach-Firanko and D. Dueck (eds.), *When West Met East: The Encounter of Greece and Rome with the Jews, Egyptians and Others,*

Papers Presented to Ranon Katzoff on his Jubilee, Edizioni Università di Trieste. 204–16.

2021. *Illiterate Geography in Classical Athens and Rome*. London: Routledge.

Dunbabin, K. M. D. 2003. *The Roman Banquet. Images of Conviviality*. Cambridge University Press.

Duncan-Jones, R. 1982. *The Economy of the Roman Empire*, 2nd ed. Cambridge University Press.

Eck, W. 1980. 'Die Präsenz senatorischer Familien in den Städten des Imperium Romanum bis zum späten 3. Jahrhundert', in W. Eck, H. Galsterer and H. Wolff (eds.), *Studien zur antiken Sozialgeschichte, Festschrift F. Vittinghoff*. Cologne: Böhlau. 283–322.

1981. 'Miscellanea prosopographica', *Zeitschrift fur Papyrologie und Epigraphik* 42: 227–56.

1982 [1984]. 'Senatoren aus Germanien, Raetien, Noricum?', in Panciera (ed.), vol. II, 539–52.

1991a/1995. 'Die Umgestaltung der politischen Führungsschicht – Senatorenstand und Ritterstand', in A. Schiavone, *Storia di Roma II.2*, Turin: Einaudi. 73–118. = repr. in W. Eck (ed.), *Die Verwaltung des römischen Reiches in der Hohen* Kaiserzeit. *Ausgewählte und erweiterte Beiträge*. Basel: F. Reinhardt.

1991b. 'Die Struktur der Städte in den nordwestlichen Provinzen und ihr Beitrag zur Administration des Reiches', in W. Eck and H. Galsterer (eds.), *Die Stadt in Oberitalien und in den nordwestlichen Provinzen des Römischen Reiches: deutsch-italienisches Kolloquium im Italienischen Kulturinstitut, Köln*. Mainz: Von Zabern. 73–84.

2003. 'Hadrian, the Bar Kokhba Revolt, and the Epigraphic Transmission', in P. Schäfer (ed.). *Bar Kokhba Reconsidered*. Tübingen: Mohr. 153–70.

2004. *Köln in römischer Zeit. Geschichte einer stadt im Rahmen des Imperium Romanum*. Cologne: Greven.

2007. *Rom und Judaea. Fünf Vorträge zur römischen Herrschaft in Palaestina*. Tübingen: Mohr Siebeck.

2008. 'Die Verteilung des Mangels: Die landwirtschaftliche Bewässerung in römischer Zeit', in C. Ohlig (ed.), *Cura aquarum in Jordanien. Beiträge des 13. Internationalen Symposiums zur Geschichte der Wasserwirtschaft und des Wasserbaus im Mediterranen Raum, Petra/Amman 31.03–09.04.2007*. Siegburg: DWhG. 227–38.

2009/2014. 'The Presence, Role and Significance of Latin in the Epigraphy and Culture of the Roman Near East', in H. M. Cotton, R. G. Hoyland, J. J. Price and D. J. Wasserstein (eds.), *From Hellenism to Islam. Cultural and Linguistic Change in the Roman Near East*. Cambridge University Press. 15–42. = repr. in W. Eck, *Judäa – Syria Palästina. Die Auseinandersetzung einer Provinz mit römischer Politik und Kultur*. Tübingen: Mohr Siebeck. 125–49.

2010. 'Emperor and Senatorial Aristocracy in Competition for Public Space', in B. C. Ewald and C. F. Noreña (eds.), *The Emperor and Rome: Space, Representation, Ritual*. Cambridge University Press. 89–110.

2016a. 'Fragmente eines neuen Stadtgesetzes – der lex coloniae Ulpiae Traianae Ratiariae', *Athenaeum* 104: 538–44.

2016b. 'Die lex Troesmensium: ein Stadtgesetz für ein municipium civium Romanorum. Publikation der erhaltenen Kapitel und Kommentar', *Zeitschrift fur Papyrologie und Epigraphik* 200: 565–606.

2016c. 'Die Wirksamkeit des römischen Rechts im Imperium Romanum und seinen Gesellschaften', in Elio Lo Cascio (ed.), *Diritto romano e economia. Due modi di pensare e organizzare il mondo (nei primi tre secoli dell'Impero)*. Pavia University Press.

2016d. 'Ordo senatorius und Mobilität: Auswirkungen und Konsequenzen im Imperium Romanum', in A. Giardina, E. Lo Cascio and R. Tacoma (eds.), *Mobility and Migration in the Roman World, Impact of Empire (Rome, June 17–19, 2015)*. Leiden: Brill. 100–15.

2017. 'Ein Zeichen von senatorischer Identität: Statuenehrungen für Kaiser mit lateinischen Inschriften aus Messene', *Zeitschrift fur Papyrologie und Epigraphik* 202: 255–62.

Eck, W. and Cotton, H. M. 2001. 'Governors and their Personnel on Latin Inscriptions from Caesarea Maritima', *Proceedings of the Israel Academy of Sciences and Humanities* 7: 219–23.

Eck, W. and Foerster, G. 1999. 'Ein Triumphbogen fur Hadrian im Tal von Beth Shean bei Tel Shalem', *Journal of Roman Archaeology* 12: 294–313.

Eck, W. and Navarro, F. J. 1998. 'Das Ehrenmonument der Colonia Carthago für L. Minicius Natalis Quadronius Verus in seiner Heimatstadt Barcino', *Zeitschrift fur Papyrologie und Epigraphik* 123: 237–48.

Eck, W. and Tepper, Y. 2019. Latin Inscriptions of the Legio VI Ferrata from Legio / Lajjun and Its Vicinity. *Scripta Classica Israelica* 38; 117–28.

Edmondson, J. 2005. 'Introduction: Flavius Josephus and Flavian Rome', in J. Edmondson, S. Mason and J. B. Rives (eds.), *Flavius Josephus and Flavian Rome*. Oxford University Press. 1–33.

Egelhaaf-Gaiser, I. 2002. *Religiöse Vereine in der römischen Antike. Untersuchungen zu Organisation, Ritual und Raumordnung*. Tübingen: Mohr Siebeck.

Egger, R. 1957. 'Zu einem Fluchtäfelchen aus Blei', in W. Krämer (ed.), *Cambodunum forschungen 1953. 1. Die Ausgrabungen von Holzhäusern zwischen der 1. und 2. Querstraße* (Heft 9, Materialhefte zur bayrischen Vorgeschichte), Kallmünz: Michael Lassleben.

Eilers, C. 2002. *Roman Patrons of Greek Cities*. Oxford Clarendon Press.

Ekirch, A. R. 2005. *At Day's Close: Night in Times Past*. New York and London: W. W. Norton & Company.

Eliav, Y. Z. 1997. 'Hadrian's Actions in the Jerusalem Temple Mount According to Cassius Dio and Xiphilini Manus', *Jewish Studies Quarterly* 4: 125–44.

2005. *God's Mountain, The Temple Mountain in Time, Place and Memory.* Baltimore: Johns Hopkins University Press.

Elitsur, Y. 2009. *Ancient Place Names in the Holy Land: Preservations and History.* Jerusalem: Magnes (Heb.).

Engels, I. J. 1998a. 'Aeneas', in W. P. Gerritsen and A. G. van Melle, *A Dictionary of Medieval Heroes. Characters in Medieval Narrative Traditions, and Their Afterlife in Literature, Theatre and the Visual Arts.* Tr. from the Dutch by T. Guest. Woodbridge: Boydell Press. 9–12.

1998b. 'Hector', in W. P. Gerritsen and A. G. van Melle, *A Dictionary of Medieval Heroes. Characters in Medieval Narrative Traditions, and Their Afterlife in Literature, Theatre and the Visual Arts.* Tr. from the Dutch by T. Guest. Woodbridge: Boydell Press. 139–45.

Engesser, F. 1957. *Der Stadtpatronat in Italien und den Westprovinzen des römischen Reiches bis Diokletian,* thesis, Albert-Ludwigs-Universität Freiburg im Breisga.

Engle, A. 1987. Light. *Lamps and Windows in Antiquity.* Jerusalem: Phoenix Publications.

Erikson, E. H. 1968. *Identity, Youth and Crisis.* New York: W. W. Norton.

Erkelenz, D. 2003. *Optimo praesidi.* Bonn: Habelt.

Erskine, A. 2001. *Troy between Greece and Rome: Local Tradition and Imperial Power.* Oxford University Press.

Esch, T. 2008. 'Zur Frage der sogenannten Doppelgemeinden. Die caesarische und augusteische Kolonisation in Kleinasien', in E. Winter (ed.), *Vom Euphrat bis zum Bosporus. Kleinasien in der Antike. Festschrift für Elmar Schwertheim zum 65. Geburtstag.* Bonn: Habelt. 188–216.

Everaert, M., van der Linden, E. J., Schenk, A. and Schreuder, R. (eds.) 1995. *Idioms: Structural and Psychological Perspectives.* New York and London: Psychology Press.

Fabrizi, V. 2012. *Mores veteresque novosque: rappresentazioni del passato e del presente di Roma negli Annales di Ennio.* Pisa: ETS.

Fagan, G. G. 1999. *Bathing in Public in the Roman World.* Ann Arbor: University of Michigan Press.

Farrington, A. 1999. 'The Introduction and Spread of Roman Bathing in Greece', in J. DeLaine and D. E. Johnston (eds.), *Roman Baths and Bathing. Proceedings of the First International Conference on Roman Baths Held at Bath, England, 30 March– 4 April 1992. Part 1: Bathing and Society (Journal of Roman Archaeology* Suppl. 37). Portsmouth: Journal of Roman Archaeology. 57–66.

Feldman, L. H. 1991. 'Pro-Jewish Intimations in Tacitus' Account of Jewish Origins', *Revue des études juives* 150: 331–60.

1993. *Jew and Gentile in the Ancient World.* Princeton University Press.

2003. 'Conversion to Judaism in Classical Antiquity', *Hebrew University Colloquium Annalium* 74: 115–56.

Fentress, E. W. B. 1982. 'Tribe and Faction: the Case of the Gaetuli', *Mélanges d'archéologie et d'histoire de l'École française de Rome* 94: 325–34.

Ferguson, J. 1970. *The Religions of the Roman Empire*. Ithaca: Cornell University Press.

Fernández, J. A. 1996. 'Bronze Studs from Roman Spain', *Journal of Roman Military Equipment Studies* 7: 97–146.

Fiema, Z. T., Kanellopoulos, C., Schick, R. and Waliszewski, T. 2001. *The Petra Church*. Amman: American Center of Oriental Research.

Fine, S. 2005. *Art and Judaism in the Greco-Roman World*. Cambridge University Press.

  2014. *Art, History and the Historiography of Judaism in Roman Antiquity*. Leiden: Brill.

Finkelberg, M. 2012. 'Canonising and Decanonising Homer: Reception of the Homeric Poems in Antiquity and Modernity', in M. Niehoff (ed.), *Homer and the Bible in the Eyes of Ancient Interpreters*. Leiden: Brill. 15–28.

Finkelstein, I. 1979. 'The Holy Land in the Tabula Peutingeriana: A Historical Geographical Approach', *Palestine Exploration Quarterly* 111: 27–34.

Fishwick, D. and Shaw, B. D. 1976. 'Ptolemy of Mauretania and the Conspiracy of Gaetulicus', *Historia* 25: 491–4.

Flower, H. 2000. 'Fabula de Bacchanalibus: The Bacchanalian Cult of the 2nd Century BC and Roman Drama', in G. Manuwald (ed.), *Identität und Alterität in der frührömischen Tragödie*. Würzburg: Ergon Verlag. 23–35.

Foerster, G. 1985. 'A Cuirassed Bronze Statue of Hadrian', *'Atiqot* 27: 139–57.

Förster, H. and Sänger, P. 2014. 'Ist unsere Heimat im Himmel? Überlegungen zur Semantik von πολίτευμα in Phil 3,20', *Early Christianity* 5: 149–77.

Franken, N. 2002. 'Lampen für die Götter. Beobachtungen zur Funktion der sogenannten Vexillumaufsätze', *Mitteilungen des Deutschen Archäologischen Instituts (Abt. Istambul)* 52: 369–81.

Freeman, P. W. M., 1997. 'Mommsen to Haverfield: The Origins of Studies in Romanization in Late 19th-c. Britain', in D. J. Mattingly, ed., *Dialogues in Roman Imperialism*, Portsmouth, RI, 27–50.

Friedman, M. A. 1981. *Jewish Marriage in Palestine*, vol. 2. Tel Aviv and New York: Chaim Rosenberg School of Jewish Studies.

Frisch, P. (ed.) 1975. *Inschriften von Ilion*. Bonn: Habelt.

Fröhlich, P. and Hamon, P. (eds.) 2013. *Groupes et associations dans les cités grecques (IIe siècle a. J.-C.-IIe sècle apr. J.-C.)*. Geneva: Droz.

Fuhrmann, C. J. 2012. *Policing the Roman Empire. Soldier, Administration, and Public Order*. Oxford University Press.

Gabba, E. 1991. *Dionysius and the History of Archaic Rome*. Berkeley: University of California Press.

Gabrielsen, V. and Thomsen, C. A. (eds.) 2015. *Private Associations and the Public Sphere: Proceedings of a Symposium Held at the Royal Danish Academy of*

Sciences and Letters, 9–11 September 2010. Copenhagen: Det Kongelige Danske Videnskabernes Selskab.

Gafni, I. 1997. *Land, Center and Diaspora: Jewish Constructs in Late Antiquity.* Sheffield Academic Press. 41–57.

Galand, L. 1966. 'Inscriptions Libyques', in Galand et al. (eds.), 9–77.

Galand, L., Février, J. G. and Vajda, G. (eds.) 1966–. *IAM.* Paris: Editions du Centre national de la recherche scientifique.

Galinsky, G. K. 1969. *Aeneas, Sicily, and Rome.* Princeton University Press.

Gambash, G. 2013. 'Foreign Enemies of the Empire: The Great Jewish Revolt and the Roman Perception of the Jews', *Scripta Classica Israelica* 32: 173–94.

Gambash, G., Gitler, H. and Cotton, H. M. 2013. 'Iudaea Recepta', *Israel Numismatic Research* 8: 89–104.

Garnsey, P. 1984. 'Religious Toleration in Classical Antiquity', in W. J. Sheils (ed.), *Persecution and Toleration.* Oxford: Blackwell. 1–27.

Gascou, J. 1969. 'Inscriptions de Tébessa', *Mélanges d'Archéologie et d'Histoire de l'École Française de Rome* 81: 537–99.

 1970. 'Le cognomen Gaetulus, Gaetulicus en Afrique romaine', *Mélanges d'Archéologie et d'Histoire de l'École Française de Rome* 82: 723–36.

 1972. *La politique municipale de l'empire romain en Afrique proconsulaire de Trajan à Septime-Sévère.* École française de Rome.

 1982. 'La politique municipale de Rome en Afrique du Nord, II: Après la mort de Septime-Sévère', *Aufstieg und Niedergang der römischen Welt* 2.10.2: 230–320.

Gellner, E. 2006. *Nations and Nationalism,* 2nd ed., Malden, MA: Blackwell.

Germer-Durand, J. 1892. 'Aelia-Capitolina', *Revue Biblique* 1: 369–87.

Geva, H. 1984. 'The Camp of the Tenth Legion in Jerusalem: An Archaeological Reconsideration', *Israel Exploration Journal* 34: 239–54.

 1993. 'Jerusalem, the Roman Period', in E. Stern (ed.), *The New Encyclopedia of Archaeological Excavations in the Holy Land 2.* Jerusalem: Israel Exploration Society & Carta. 758–67.

 1994a. 'Excavations in the Citadel of Jerusalem, 1976–1980', in H. Geva (ed.), *Ancient Jerusalem Revealed.* Jerusalem: Israel Exploration Society. 156–67.

 1994b. 'The Tenth Roman Legion *Did* Camp on the Southwest Hill', *Cathedra* 73: 181–6 (Heb.).

 2003. 'Stamp Impressions of the Legio X Fretensis', in H. Geva, *Jewish Quarter Excavations in the Old City of Jerusalem. Conducted by Nahman Avigad 1969–1982. Volume II: The Finds from Areas A, W and X-2. Final Report.* Jerusalem: Israel Exploration Society. 405–22.

 2014. *Jewish Quarter Excavations in the Old City of Jerusalem. Conducted by Nahman Avigad 1969–1982. Volume VI: Areas J, N, Z and Other Studies. Final Report.* Jerusalem: Israel Exploration Society.

Gilat, Y. D. 1968. *The Teachings of R. Eliezer Ben Hyrcanus.* Tel Aviv: Dvir (Heb.).

Gizewski, C. 1997. 'Duoviri Duumviri', in *Der neue Pauly*, 3, 20. Stuttgart and Weimar: Metzler. cols. 843–5.

Gleason, K. L. 1998. 'The Promontory Palace at Caesarea Maritima: Preliminary Evidence for Herod's "Praetorium"', *Journal of Roman Archaeology* 11: 23–52.

Glucksberg, S. 2001. *Understanding Figurative Language: From Metaphors to Idioms*. Oxford University Press.

Goodman, M. 1989. 'Nerva, the *Fiscus Iudaicus*, and Jewish Identity', *Journal of Roman Studies* 79: 40–4.

1994. *Mission and Conversion: Proselytizing in the Religious History of the Roman Empire*. Oxford: Clarendon Press.

2005. 'The *Fiscus Iudaicus* and Gentile Attitudes to Judaism in Flavian Rome', in J. Edmondson, S. Mason and J. B. Rives (eds.), *Flavius Josephus and Flavian Rome*. Oxford University Press. 167–80.

2007. *Rome and Jerusalem: The Clash of Ancient Civilizations*. London: Allen Lane; New York: A. A. Knopf.

Gordon, B. 2007. 'The Byzantine Quarter South of the Temple Mount Enclosure', in E. Mazar, *The Temple Mount Excavations in Jerusalem 1968–1978 Directed by Benjamin Mazar. Final Reports Volume III. The Byzantine Period*. Hebrew University of Jerusalem, Institute of Archaeology. 201–15.

Gose, E. 1972. *Der gallo-römische Tempelbezirk im Altbachtal zu Trier*. Mainz: Von Zabern.

Graetz, H. 1908. *Geschichte der Juden*, IV. Leipzig: O. Leiner.

Graf, D. F. 1978. 'The Saracens and the Defence of the Arabian Frontier', Bulletin of the American Schools of Oriental Research 229: 1–26.

Graf, F. 1996. *Gottesnähe und Schadenzauber. Die Magie in der griechisch-römischen Antike*. Munich: C. H. Beck.

2010. 'Dreams, Visions, and Revelations: Dreams in the Thought of the Latin Fathers', in Scioli and Walde (eds.), 211–29.

Grandjean, C., Hugoniot, C. and Lion, B. (eds.) 2013. *Le banquet du monarque dans le monde antique*. Presses Universitaires de Rennes.

Grätz, S. 2013. 'The Adversaries in Ezra/Nehemiah – Fictitious or Real? A Case Study in Creating Identity in Late Persian and Hellenistic Times', in R. Albertz and J. Wöhrle (eds.), *Between Cooperation and Hostility: Multiple Identities in Ancient Judaism and Interaction with Foreign Powers*. Göttingen: Vandenhoech & Ruprecht. 73–87.

Greenfield, J. C. 1991. 'An Aramaic Inscription from Tyre from the Reign of Diocletion Preserved in the Palestinian Talmud'. *Atti del II Congresso Internazionale di Studie Fenici e Punici* 2: 499–502.

Gregg, R. C. and Urman, D. 1996. *Jews, Pagans and Christians in the Golan Heights*. Atlanta: Scholars Press.

Gregory, S. 1995–7. *Roman Military Architecture on the Eastern Frontier*, vols. 1–3. Amsterdam: Hakkert.

Grey, M. J. and Magness, J. 2013. 'Finding Samson in Byzantine Galilee: The 2011–2012 Archaeological Excavations at Huqoq', *Studies in the Bible and Antiquity* 5: 1–30.

Griffiths, J. G. 1975. *Apuleius of Madauros. The Isis-Book (Metamorphoses, Book XI). Edited with an Introduction, Translation, and Commentary*. Leiden: Brill.

Grig, L. and Kelly, G. (eds.) 2012. *Two Romes: Rome and Constantinople*. Oxford University Press.

Grilli, A. 2005. 'Populus in Cicerone', in G. Urso (ed.), *Popolo e potere nel mondo antico, Cividale del Friuli, 23–25 settembre* 2004. Pisa: ETS. 124–39.

Grojnowski, D. 2014. 'Can a Body Change? Josephus's Attitude to Circumcision and Conversion', in J. E. Taylor (ed.), *The Body in Biblical, Christian and Jewish Texts*. London: Bloomsbury T & T Clark. 165–83.

Grossmark, T. 2014. 'Diocletian and the Construction of the Homs Dam', *Mediterranean Chronicle* 4: 27–41.

Gruen, E. S. 1990. *Studies in Greek Culture and Roman Policy*. Leiden: Brill.

1992. *Culture and National Identity in Republican Rome*. Ithaca: Cornell University Press.

1997. 'The Origins and Objectives of Onias' Temple', *Scripta Classica Israelica* 16: 47–70.

2002a. 'Roman Perspectives on the Jews in the Age of the Great Revolt', in A. M. Berlin and J. A. Overman (eds.), *The First Jewish Revolt: Archeology, History and Ideology*. London and New York: Routledge. 27–42.

2002b. *Diaspora: Jews amidst Greeks and Romans*. Cambridge, MA: Harvard University Press.

2011. *Rethinking the Other in Antiquity*. Princeton University Press.

2012. 'Caligula, the Imperial Cult, and Philo's Legatio,' *Studia Philonica Annual*, 24, 135–47.

2020. *Ethnicity in the Ancient World – Did It Matter?* Berlin: De Gruyter.

Gsell, S. et al. 1922–. *ILAlg*.

Gudme, A. K. de H. 2011. *Before the God in This Place for Good Remembrance: An Analysis of the Votive Inscriptions from Mount Gerizim*, Ph.D. thesis, University of Copenhagen.

Guerber, E. 2010. *Les cités grecques dans l'Empire romain. Les privilèges et les titres des cités de l'Orient hellénophone d'Octave Auguste à Dioclétien*, 2nd ed. Presses Universitaires de Rennes.

2013. 'La fondation de Nicopolis par Octavien: affirmation de l'idéologie impériale et philhellénisme', in A. Gangloff (ed.), *Lieux de mémoire en Orient grec à l'époque impériale*. Bern: Lang. 255–77.

Guérin, V. 1875. *Description Géographique, Historique et Archéologique de la Palestine*, vol. II: Samarie. Paris: Impr. Nationale.

Gustafsson, G. 2000. *Evocatio Deorum: Historical and Mythical Interpretations of Ritualized Conquests in the Expansion of Ancient Rome.* Uppsala: Coronet Books Inc.

Gutfeld, O. 2012. *Jewish Quarter Excavations in the Old City of Jerusalem. Conducted by Nahman Avigad, 1969–1982. Volume V: The Cardo and the Nea Church. Final Report.* Jerusalem: Israel Exploration Society.

Haack, M.-L. 2003. *Les haruspices dans le monde romain.* Paris: E. De Boccard.

Habas Rubin, E. 1991. *The Patriarch in the Roman-Byzantine Era – The Making of a Dynasty,* Ph.D. thesis, Tel Aviv University (Heb.).

Habicht, C. 1969. *Deutsches Archäologisches Institut. Altertümer von Pergamon, VIII, 3: Die Inschriften des Asklepieions.* Berlin: De Gruyter.

Hächler, N. 2019. *Kontinuität und Wandel des Senatorenstandes im Zeitalter der Soldatenkaiser. Prosopographische Untersuchungen zu Zusammensetzung, Funktion und Bedeutung des amplissimus ordo zwischen 235–284 n. Chr. Leiden: Brill.*

Hachlili, R. 2013. *Ancient Synagogues – Archaeology and Art: New Discoveries and Current Research.* Leiden: Brill.

Hadas-Label, M. 2006. *Jerusalem against Rome.* Leuven: Peeters.

Halfmann, H. 1979. *Die Senatoren aus dem östlichen Teil des Imperium Romanum bis zum Ende des 2. Jahrhunderts n.Chr.,* Göttingen: Vandenhoeck und Ruprecht.

    1982 [1984]. 'Die Senatoren aus den Kleinasiatichen Provinzenm des römischen Reices vom 1. bis 3. Jahrhundert (Asia, Pontus-Bithynia, Lycia-Pamphylia, Galatia, Cappadocia, Cilicia)', in Panciera (ed.), Vol. II, 603–50.

Halsall, G. 2007. *Barbarian Migrations and the Roman West, 376–568.* Cambridge University Press.

Hamilton, R. W. 1952. 'Jerusalem in the Fourth Century', *Palestine Exploration Quarterly* 84: 83–90.

Harland, P. A. 2003. *Associations, Synagogues, and Congregations. Claiming a Place in Ancient Mediterranean Society.* Minneapolis: Fortress Press.

    2014. *Greco-Roman Associations: Texts, Translations, and Commentary. II. North Coast of the Black Sea, Asia Minor.* Berlin: De Gruyter.

Harris, W. V., 1979. *War and Imperialism in Republican Rome, 327–70 BC.* Oxford: Oxford University Press.

    1989. *Ancient Literacy.* Cambridge, MA: Harvard University Press.

    2009. *Dreams and Experience in Classical Antiquity.* Cambridge, MA: Harvard University Press.

    2016. *Roman Power: A Thousand Years of Empire.* Cambridge: Cambridge University Press.

Harris-McCoy, D. 2012. *Artemidorus' Oneirocritica. Text, Translation, and Commentary.* Oxford University Press.

Harrison, J. 2013. *Dreams and Dreaming in the Roman Empire. Cultural Memory and Imagination.* London: Bloomsbury.

Harvey, G. 1996. *The True Israel: Uses of the Names Jew, Hebrew and Israel in Ancient Jewish and Early Christian Literature*. Leiden: Brill.

Hasan-Rokem, G. 2003. 'The Evasive Center, Hadrian, the Old Man, the Neighbor, and the Rabbinic Rhetoric of the Empire', in G. Hasan-Rokem, *Tales of the Neighborhood*, Berkely, Los Angeles, London: University of California Press. 87–137.

Hatzopoulos, M. B. 2016. Νεότης γεγυμνασμένη. *Macedonian Lawgiver Kings and the Young*. Athens: Hellenike Epigraphike Hetaireia.

Hauken, T. 1998. *Petition and Response. An Epigraphic Study of Petitions to Roman Emperors 181–249*. Bergen: The Norwegian Institute at Athens.

Healey, J. 2011. *Law and Religion between Petra and Edessa: Studies in Aramaic Epigraphy on the Roman Frontier*. Surrey and Burlington: VT.

Heller, A. 2006. *'Les bêtises des Grecs'. Conflits et rivalités entre cités d'Asie et de Bithynie à l'époque romaine (129 a.C.–235 p.C.)*. Bordeaux: Ausonius.

— 2013. 'Les institutions civiques grecques sous l'Empire: romanisation ou aristocratisation?', in P. Schubert (ed.), *Les Grecs héritiers des Romains*. Geneva-Vandoeuvres: Fondation Hardt. 201–40.

Heltzer, M. 1990. 'A New Perspective on the Problem of "the Foreign Women" in the Books of Ezra and Nehemiah', *Shnaton: an Annual for Biblical and Ancient Near Eastern Studies* 10: 83–91 (Heb.).

— 2008. *The Province Judah and Jews in Persian Times*. Tel Aviv: Archaeological Center Publications.

Hengel, M. 1984–5. 'Hadrians politik gegenüber Juden und Christen', *Journal of the Ancient Near Eastern Society* 16/17: 153–82.

Hennig, D. 2002. 'Nyktophylakes, Nyktostrategen und die παραφυλακή τῆς πόλεως', *Chiron* 32: 281–95.

Herr, M. D. 1971. 'The Historical Significance of the Dialogues between Jewish Sages and Roman Dignitaries', in J. Heinemann and D. Noy (eds.), *Studies in Aggadah and Folk-Literature, Scripta Hierosolymitana*, Vol. XXII, Jerusalem: Magnes. 123–50.

— 1972. 'Persecutions and Martyrdom in Hadrian's Days', in D. Asheri and I. Shatzman (eds.), *Studies in History, Scripta Hierosolymitana*, Vol. XXIII, Jerusalem: Magnes. 85–125.

Hertel, D. 2003. *Die Mauern von Troia. Mythos und Geschichte im antiken Ilion*. Munich: C. H. Beck.

Herzog, R. 1935. 'Urkunden zur Hochschulpolitik der römischen Kaiser', *Sitzungsberichte der preussischen Akademie der Wissenschaft*, phil.-hist. Klasse. Berlin: Verl. d. Akad. d. Wissenschaften. 967–1019.

Hezser, C. 2001. *Jewish Literacy in Roman Palestine*. Tübingen: Mohr.

Hill, G. F. (ed.) 1914. *BMC Palestine*. London: British Museum.

Hingley, R. 2005. *Globalizing Roman Culture: Unity, Diversity and Empire*. London: Routledge.

Homoth-Kuhs, C. 2005. *Phylakes und Phylakon-Steuer im griechisch-römischen Ägypten. Ein Beitrag zur Geschichte des antiken Sicherheitswesens.* Munich: Saur.

Honigman, S. 2002. 'The Jewish *"politeuma"*at Heracleopolis', *Scripta Classica Israelica* 21: 251–66.

  2003. '*Politeuma* and Ethnicity in Ptolemaic and Roman Egypt', *Ancient Society* 33: 61–102.

  2014. *Tales of High Priests and Taxes: the Books of the Maccabees and the Judean Rebellion againt Antiochos IV.* Berkeley: University of California Press.

Hooper, R. W. 1999. *The Priapus Poems: Erotic Epigrams from Ancient Rome.* University of Illinois Press.

Horbury, W. and Noy, D. (eds.) 1992. *Jewish Inscriptions of Graeco-Roman Egypt.* Cambridge University Press.

Horden, P. and N. Purcell 2000. *The Corrupting Sea: A Study of Mediterranean History.* Oxford: Oxford University Press.

Hornblower, S. 2015. *Lycophron: Alexandra. Greek Text, Translation, Commentary, and Introduction.* Oxford University Press.

Hošek, A.-R. 2017. 'De Berytus à Héliopolis: nouvelles identités et recompositions territoriales', in C. Brélaz (ed.), L'héritage grec des colonies romaines d'Orient: interactions culturelles dans les provinces hellénophones de l'empire romain. Paris: Editions De Boccard, 311–30.

Howgego, C. J. 1985. *Greek Imperial Countermarks.* London: Royal Numismatic Society.

Hurlet, F. 1993. 'La *Lex de imperio Vespasiani* et la légitimité augustéene', *Latomus* 52: 261–80.

Huxley, G. L. 1981. 'Stories Explaining Origins of Greek Proverbs', *Proceedings of the Royal Irish Academy* 81 c: 331–43.

Iliffe, J. H. 1933. 'Greek and Latin Inscriptions in the Museum', *Quarterly of the Department of Antiquities in Palestine* 2: 120–6.

Ingledew, F. 1994. 'The Book of Troy and the Genealogical Construction of History: The Case of Geoffrey of Monmouth's *Historia regum Britanniae*', *Speculum* 69: 665–704.

Isaac, B. 1980–1. 'Roman Colonies in Judaea: The Foundation of Aelia Capitolina', *Talanta* 12–13:31–53.

  1986. *The Greek Settlements in Thrace until the Macedonian Conquest.* Leiden: Brill.

  1990. *The Limits of Empire: The Roman Army in the East.* Oxford: Clarendon Press.

  1991. 'A Seleucid Inscription from Jamnia-on-the-Sea: Antiochus V Eupator and the Sidonians', *Israel Exploration Journal* 41: 132–44.

  1992. *The Limits of Empire: The Roman Army in the East,* 2nd ed. Oxford: Clarendon Press.

  1998a. 'Roman Colonies in Judaea: The Foundation of Aelia Capitolina', in B. Isaac, *The Near East under Roman Rule. Selected Papers.* Leiden: Brill. 87–111 (repr. of 1980–1).

1998b. 'Milestones in Judaea: from Vespasian to Constantine', in B. Isaac, *The Near East under Roman Rule, Selected Papers*. Leiden: Brill. 48–75.

2004. *The Invention of Racism in Classical Antiquity*. Princeton University Press.

2009. 'Latin in Cities of the Roman Near East', in H. M. Cotton, R. G. Hoyland, J. J. Price and D. J. Wasserstein (eds.), *From Hellenism to Islam. Cultural and Linguistic Change in the Roman Near East*. Cambridge University Press. 43–72.

2010. 'Jerusalem – an Introduction', *CIIP*, vol. I, Jerusalem, Part 1: 1–37.

2013. 'Names: Ethnic, Geographic and Administrative', delivered at *The Future of Rome: Roman, Greek, Jewish and Christian Perspective*, Tel Aviv University (October 2013).

2017a. 'Roma Aeterna', in B. Isaac, *Empire and Ideology in the Graeco-Roman World: Selected Papers*, Cambridge University Press, 33–44.

2017b. 'Core-Periphery Notions', in B. Isaac, *Empire and Ideology in the Graeco-Roman World: Selected Papers*, Cambridge University Press, 99–121.

Isaac, B. and Gichon, M. 1974. 'A Flavian Inscription from Jerusalem', *Israel Exploration Journal* 24: 117–23.

Isaac, B. and Roll, I. 1976. 'A Milestone of A.D. 69 from Judaea', *Journal of Roman Studies* 56: 9–14.

1979a. 'Judaea in the Early Years of Hadrian`s Reign', *Latomus* 38: 54–66.

1979b. 'Legio II Traiana in Judaea', *Zeitschrift fur Papyrologie und Epigraphik* 33: 149–56.

1982a. *Roman Roads in Judaea, I. The Legio – Scythopolis Road*. Oxford: B.A.R.

1982b. 'Legio II Traiana in Judaea – a Reply', *Zeitschrift fur Papyrologie und Epigraphik* 47: 131–2.

Isaac, B., Rotman, Y. and Bowersock, G. 2011. 'Interview with Professor Glen Bowersock', *Historia. Journal of the Historical Society of Israel* 27: 5–28 (Heb.).

Israelowich, I. 2014. 'Identifications of Physicians during the High Empire', in M. Depauw and S. Coussement (eds.), *Identifiers and Identification Methods in the Ancient World*. Leuven: Peeters. 233–52.

2015. *Patients and Healers in the Roman Empire*. Baltimore: Johns Hopkins University Press.

2016. 'Aristides as a Teacher: Rhetorical Means for Self-Promotion in the Fourth Sacred Tale', In L. Pernot, G. Abbamonte and M. Lamagna (eds.) *Aelius Aristide écrivain*. Brussels: Brepols. 236–47.

Jacobs, M. 1995. *Die Institution des jüdischen Patriarchen*. Tübingen: J. C. B. Mohr.

Jalabert, L. et al. (eds.) 1929–. *IGLS*. Paris.

James, E. 1988. *The Franks*. Oxford: Blackwell.

Johns, C. N. 1948. 'Discoveries in Palestine since 1939'. *Palestine Exploration Quarterly* 80: 81–101.

1950. 'The Citadel, Jerusalem. A Summary of Work since 1934', *Quarterly of the Department of Antiquities in Palestine* 14: 121–90.

Johnston, A. 1985. 'The So-Called 'Pseudo-Autonomous' Greek Imperials', *American Numismatic Society Museum Notes* 30: 89–112.

Johnston, S. I. 2010. 'Sending Dreams, Restraining Dreams: Oneiropompeia in Theory and Practice', in Scioli and Walde (eds.), 1–18.

Jones, A. H. M. 1936. 'Another Interpretation of the Constitutio Antoniniana', *Journal of Roman Studies* 26: 223–35.

   1971. *The Cities of the Eastern Roman Provinces* (2nd ed.). Oxford: Clarendon Press.

Jones, A. H. M. et al. (eds.) 1970/1980–92. *PLRE*. Cambridge University Press.

Jones, C. P. 1999. *Kinship Diplomacy in the Ancient World*. Cambridge, MA: Harvard University Press.

   2010. 'Ancestry and Identity in the Roman Empire', in Whitmarsh (ed.), 111–24.

   2011. 'An Inscription Seen by Agathias', *Zeitschrift fur Papyrologie und Epigraphik* 179: 107–15.

   2015. 'The Earthquake of 26 BCE in Decrees of Mytilene and Chios (with S. Prignitz)', *Chiron* 45: 101–22.

   2016. 'The Greek Letters Ascribed to Brutus', *Harvard Studies in Classical Philology* 108: 195–244.

Jones, S. 2001. *Deconstructing the Celts: a Skeptic's Guide to the Archaeology of the Auvergne*. Oxford: B.A.R.

Jongeling, K. 2008. *Handbook of Neo-Punic Inscriptions*. Tübingen: Mohr-Siebeck.

Jongeling, K. and Kerr, R. M. 2005. *Late Punic Epigraphy: an Introduction to the Study of Neo-Punic and Latino-Punic Inscriptions*. Tübingen: Mohr Siebeck.

Jonker, L. (ed.) 2010. *Historiography and Identity: (Re)Formulation in Second Temple Historiographical Literature*. New York: T & T Clark.

Jost, I. M. 1832. *Allgemeine Geschichte der Israel Volkes*, II, Berlin: G. Grote.

Kadushin, M. 1987. *A Conceptual Commentary on Midrash Leviticus Rabbah, Value Concepts in Jewish Thought*. Atlanta: Scholars' Press.

Kalimi, I. (ed.) 2012. *New Perspectives on Ezra-Nehemiah: History and Historiography, Text, Literature, and Interpretation*. Winona Lake, IN: Eisenbrauns.

Kalinka, E. et al. (eds.) 1901–. *TAM*. Vindobonae: apud Academiam Scientiarum Austriacam.

Karabatsou, E. D. 2010. Ἀπὸ τῆ Ρώμη στὴν Ἀστυπάλαια. Μιὰ ἀθωωτικὴ ἀπόφαση τοῦ Αὐγούστου', Ἐπετηρὶς τοῦ Κέντρου Ἐρεύνης τῆς Ἱστορίας τοῦ Ἑλληνικοῦ Δικαίου 42: 95–109.

Kaster, R. A. 1995. *De grammaticis et rhetoribus*. Oxford University Press.

Katsari, C. and Mitchell, S. 2008. 'The Roman Colonies of Greece and Asia Minor. Questions of State and Civic Identity', *Athenaeum* 96: 221–49.

Kenaan, V. L. 2010. 'The Ancient Road to the Unconscious: On Dream Narratives and Repressed Desires in Ancient Fiction', in Scioli and Walde (eds.), 165–84.

Kennedy, D. L. and Falahat, H. 2008. 'Castra Legionis VI Ferratae: a Building Inscription for the Legionary Fortress at Udruh near Petra', *Journal of Roman Archaeology* 21: 151–69.

Kenyon, F. G. and Bell, H. I. (eds.) 1893–1917. *P.Lond.* London: British Museum.

Keppie, L. 1986. 'Legions in the East from Augustus to Trajan', in P. Freeman and D. Kennedy (eds.), *The Defence of the Roman and Byzantine East*, vol. 2. Oxford: B.A.R. 411–29.

Ker, J. 2004. 'Nocturnal Writers in Imperial Rome. The Culture of *lucubratio*', *Classical Philology* 99: 209–42.

Ker, J. and Wessels, A. (eds.) 2020. *The Values of Nighttime in Classical Antiquity.* Leiden: Brill.

Kerr, R. M. 2008. 'Some Thoughts on the Origins of the Libyco-Berber Alphabet', *Etudes berbères 5: Essais sur des variations dialectales*: 41–68.

2010. *Latino-Punic Epigraphy: a Descriptive Study of the Inscriptions.* Tübingen: Mohr Siebeck.

Khudaverdyan, A. 2011. 'Trepanation and Artificial Cranial Deformations in Ancient Armenia', *Anthropological Review* 74: 39–55.

Kienast, D. 2014. *Augustus. Prinzeps und Monarch.* Darmstadt: Von Zabern.

Kim, L. Y. 2010. *Homer between History and Fiction in Imperial Greek Literature.* Cambridge University Press.

Kindler, A. and Stein, A. 1987. *A Bibliography of the City Coinage of Palestine.* Oxford: B.A.R.

Kindstrand, J. F. 1978. 'The Greek Concept of Proverbs', *Eranos* 76: 71–85.

King, K. C. 1987. *Achilles. Paradigms of the War Hero from Homer to the Middle Ages.* Berkeley: University of California Press.

2011. 'Reception, in Latin Middle Ages', in M. Finkelberg (ed.), *The Homer Encyclopedia.* Malden, MA/Oxford: Wiley-Blackwell. 720–2.

Kirbihler, F. 2012. 'César, Auguste et l'Asie: continuités et évolutions de deux politiques', in O. Devillers and K. Sion-Jenkins (eds.), *César sous Auguste.* Bordeaux: Ausonius. 125–44.

2014. 'Un complot Italo-Asiatique contre Commode en 191/192?', in C. Bertraud- Dagenbach and F. Chausoon (eds.), *Historiae Augustae Colloquium Nanceiense. Atti dei Convegni sulla Historia Augusta XII.* Bari: Edipuglia. 279–315.

2017. 'Les problèmes d'une mission publique entre République et Empire: P. Vedius Pollio en Asie', in L. Cavalier, M.-C. Ferriès and F. Delrieux (eds.), *Auguste et l'Asie Mineure.* Bordeaux: Ausonius. 129–51.

Kirsch, K. A. 2015. *Asylia and Peer Polity Interaction in the Hellenistic Period*, a M. A. thesis, San Jose State University: http://scholarworks.sjsu.edu/cgi/view content.cgi?article=8095&context=etd_these

Kisilevitz, S. and Greenwald, R. 2012. 'New Discoveries in the via Dolorosa – Excavation and a Survey in the Austrian Hospice and at the Vicinity of the "Ecce Homo" Arch', in D. Amit, G. D. Stiebel, O. Peleg-Barkat and D. Ben-Ami (eds.), *New Studies in the Archaeology of Jerusalem and Its Region*, Collected Papers 6. Jerusalem: Israel Antiquities Authority. 136–48 (Heb.).

Klebs, E. et al. (eds.) 1897–8/1933–. *PIR.* Berlin.

Klein, S. (ed.) 1939. *Sefer haYishuv*. Jerusalem: Bialik Institute.

Kloppenborg, J. S. and Ascough, R. S. 2011, *Greco-Roman Associations: Texts, Translations, and Commentary. I. Attica, Central Greece, Macedonia, Thrace*. Berlin: De Gruyter.

Kloppenborg, J. S. and Wilson, S. G. (eds.) 1996. *Voluntary Associations in the Graeco- Roman World*. London and New York: Routledge.

Kneissl, P. 1994. 'Die fabri, fabri tignuarii, fabri subaediani, centonarii und dolabrarii als Feuerwehr in den Städten Italien und der westlichen Provinzen', in R. Günther and S. Rebenich (eds.), *E fontibus haurire. Beiträge zur römischen Geschichte und zu ihren Hilfswissenschaften*. Paderborn: F. Schöningh. 133–46.

Knibbe, D. 1981. 'Quandocumque quis trium virum rei publicae constituendae . . . : Ein neuer Text aus Ephesos', *Zeitschrift fur Papyrologie und Epigraphik* 44: 1–10.

    1981–2. 'Neue Inschriften aus Ephesos VIII', *Jahreshefte des Österreichischen Archäologischen Instituts* 53: 87–150.

Kolska-Horwitz, L. in press. 'Fauna from the Roman Deposits at the Cardo', in S. Weksler-Bdolah and A. Onn, *Jerusalem, the Western Wall Plaza Excavations, the Eastern Cardo* (Israel Antiquities Authority Reports). Jerusalem: Israel Antiquities Authority.

König, J. 2012. *Saints and Symposiasts: The Literature of Food and the Symposium in Greco-Roman and Early Christian Culture*. Cambridge University Press.

Koslofsky, C. 2011. *Evening's Empire: A History of the Night in Early Modern Europe*. Cambridge University Press.

Kraemer, R. S. 1998. *When Aseneth Met Joseph: A Late Antique Tale of the Biblical Patriarch and His Egyptian Wife, Reconsidered*. Oxford University Press.

Krauss, S. 1910. *Antoninus und Rabbi*. Wien: Verlag der Israel.-Theol. Lehranstalt.

Krautheimer, R. 1980. *Rome: Profile of a City, 312–1308*. Princeton University Press.

Krieckhaus, A. 2006. *Senatorische Familien und ihre 'patriae' (1./2. Jahrhundert n. Chr.)*. Hamburg: Kovac.

Kümmel, A. 1904. *Karte der Materialien zur Topographie des Alten Jerusalem*. Leipzig: Deutsche Palästina-Vereins.

Kurzmann, R. 2006. *Roman Military Brick Stamps: A Comparison of Methodology*. Oxford: B.A.R.

Kushnir-Stein, A. 2002. 'The Coinage of Agrippa II', *Scripta Classica Israelica* 21: 123–31.

La'da, C. A. 2002. *Foreign Ethnics in Hellenistic Egypt*. Leuven: Peeters.

Labarre, G. 2016. 'Distribution spatiale et cohérence du réseau colonial en Pisidie à l'époque augustéenne', in H. Bru, G. Labarre and G. Tirologos (eds.), *Espaces et territoires des colonies romaines d'Orient*. Besançon: Presses Universitaires de Franche-Comté. 45–69.

Lamon, R. S. and Shipton, G. M. 1939. *Megiddo I, Seasons of 1925–34, Strata I–V*. University of Chicago Press.

Lampe, G. W. H. (ed.) 1961. *A Patristic Greek Lexicon*. Oxford: Clarendon Press.

Lassère, J. -M. 1973. 'Recherches sur la chronologie des épitaphes païennes de l'Africa', *Antiquités africaines* 7: 7–152.

    1994. 'La cohorte des Gétules', in Y. Le Bohec (ed.), *L'Afrique, la Gaule, la Religion à l'époque romaine. Mélanges à la mémoire de Marcel Le Glay*. Brussels: Latomus. 244–53.

Launey, M. 1949. *Recherches sur les armées hellénistiques*, 2 vols. Paris: de Boccard.

Laurent, D. et al. 2008. 'Bulletin épigraphique', *Revue des Études Grecques* 121: 571–770.

Lavan, M. 2016. 'The spread of Roman Citizenship, 14–212 CE: Quantification in the Face of High Uncertainty', *Past & Present* 230: 3–46.

Le Bohec, Y. 1989. *La troisième légion Auguste*. Paris: CNRS.

    1994. *The Imperial Roman Army*, tr. R. Bate. London: Batsford.

Le Glay, M. 1982 [1984]. 'Senateurs de Numidie et des Mauretanies', in Panciera (ed.), vol. 2, 755–81.

Le Roy, C. 2000. 'Pisidiens en Lycie et Lyciens en Pisidie', in C. Işık (ed.), *Studien zur Religion und Kultur Kleinasiens und des ägäischen Bereiches. Festschrift für Baki Öğün zum 75. Geburstag*. Bonn: Habelt. 255–66.

Le Strange, G. 1965. *Palestine under the Moslems. A Description of Syria and the Holy Land from A.D. 650 To 1500*. Beirut: Khayat's.

Lehmann, C. and Holum, K. K. 2000. *Greek and Latin Inscriptions of Caesarea Maritima. Joint Expedition to Caesarea Maritima Excavetions*, Report 5. Boston: American Schools of Oriental Research.

Leibner, U. 2010. 'Excavations at Khirbet Wadi Hamam (Lower Galilee): The Synagogue and the Settlement', *Journal of Roman Archaeology* 23: 220–38.

Leibner, U. and Bijovsky, G. 2014. 'Two Hoards from Khirbet Wadi Hamam and the Scope of the Bar Kokhba Revolt', *Israel Numismatic Research* 8: 109–34.

Leon, H. 1960. *The Jews of Ancient Rome*. Philadelphia: Jewish Publication Society of America.

Lepelley, C. 1981. *Les cités de l'Afrique romaine au Bas-Empire, vol. 2: Notices d'histoire municipale*. Paris: Etudes Augustiniennes.

Leschhorn, W. 1993. *Antike Ären. Zeitrechnung, Politik und Geschichte im Schwarzmeerraum und in Kleinasien nördlich des Tauros*. Stuttgart: Steiner.

Leutsch, E. L. and Scheidewin, F. G. (eds.) 1965. *CPG*. Hildesheim: G. Olms (Originally pr. 1839).

Leveau, P. 1984. *Caesarea de Maurétanie. Une ville romaine et ses campagnes*. École Française de Rome.

Levi, D. 1947. *Antioch Mosaic Pavements*. Princeton University Press.

Levi, D. and Be'eri, R. 2011. 'Jerusalem, Binyane Ha-'Umma: Preliminary Report', *Hadashot Arkheologiyot, Excavations and Surveys in Israel* 123: www .hadashot-esi.org.il/report_detail_eng.aspx?id=1813&mag_id=118

Levick, B. 1958. 'Two Pisidian Colonial Families', *Journal of Roman Studies* 48: 75–8.

    1967. *Roman Colonies in Southern Asia Minor*. Oxford: Clarendon Press.

1999. *Vespasian*. London and New York: Routledge.

Levine, L. I. 2000. *The Ancient Synagogue: The First Thousand Years*. New Haven and London: Yale University Press.

2012. *Visual Judaism in Late Antiquity*. New Haven and London: Yale University Press.

Lieberman, S. M. 1955–73. *Tosefta Ki-Feshutah*. New York: Jewish Theological Seminary (Heb.).

Lieu, J. 2004. *Christian Identity in the Jewish and Graeco-Roman World*. Oxford University Press.

Lifshitz, B. 1960. 'Sur Le date du transfert de la Legio VI Ferrata en Palestine', *Latomus* 19: 109–11.

Linder, A. 1987. *Jews in Roman Imperial Legislation*. Detroit: Wayne State University Press.

Lipschits, O., Knoppers, G. N. and Oeming, M. (eds.) 2011. *Judah and the Judeans in the Achaemenid period: Negotiating Identity in an International Context*. Winona Lake, IN: Eisenbrauns.

Loar, M., C. MacDonald and D. Padilla Peralta (eds.) 2018. *Rome, Empire of Plunder: The Dynamics of Cultural Appropriation*. Cambridge and New York: Cambridge University Press.

Lopez, D. forthcoming. *The Flavians and the Jews: The Policy of the Flavian Emperors towards Jews and Judaism after the Destruction of the Second Temple*, Ph.D. thesis, Hebrew University of Jerusalem.

Luttwak, E. N. 1976. *The Grand Strategy of the Roman Empire: From the First Century CE to the Third*. Baltimore: Johns Hopkins University Press. Rev. 2016.

Lyne, M. 1999. 'Fourth Century Roman Belt Fittings from Richborough', *Journal of Roman Military Equipment Studies* 10: 103–13.

Macalister, R. A. S. and Duncan, J. G. 1926. *Excavations on the Hill of Ophel, Jerusalem 1923–1925*. London: Palestine Exploration Fund.

MacBain, B. 1982. *Prodigy and Expiation: A Study in Religion and Politics in Republican Rome*. Brussels: 60 rue Colonel Chaltin.

MacMullen, R. 1984/90. 'The Legion as Society', *Historia* 33: 440–56 = in MacMullen, R. (ed.), *Changes in the Roman Empire: Essays in the Ordinary*. Princeton University Press. 236–49.

Magie, D. 1950. *Roman Rule in Asia Minor to the End of the Third Century after Christ*, 2 vols. Princeton University Press.

Magness, J. 2013. 'Samson in the Synagogue', *Biblical Archaeology Review* 39: 32–9.

Mairs, R. 2008. 'Greek Identity and the Settler Community in Hellenistic Bactria and Arachosia', *Migrations and Identities* 1: 19–43.

Malaise, M. 1972. *Les conditions de pénétration et de diffusion des cultes égyptiens découvertes en Italie*. Leiden: Brill.

Malkin, I. and Shmueli, N. 1988. '"The City of the Blind" and the Founding of Byzantium', *Mediterranean Historical Review* 3/1: 21–36.

Mango, C. 1980. *Byzantium: The Empire of the New Rome*. London: Weidenfeld and Nicolson.

Mango, C. and Scott, R. 1997. *The Chronicle of Theophanes Confessor: Byzantine and Near Eastern History, AD 284–813*. Oxford: Clarendon Press.

Marotta, V. 2009. *La cittadinanza romana in età imperiale: (secoli I–III d.C.): una sintesi*. Torino: Giappichelli.

Marrone, G. C. 2005. '"voi che siete popolo . . ." Popolo ed esercito nella concezione cesariana ed augustea', in G. Urso (ed.), *Popolo e potere nel mondo antico, Cividale del Friuli, 23–25 settembre 2004*. Pisa: ETS. 157–72.

Marrou, H. I. 1956. *History of Education in Antiquity*. London: Sheed & Ward.

Marshall, A. 1966. 'Governors in the Roman World', *Phoenix* 22: 231–46.

Martin, K. 2013. *Demos, Boule, Gerousia. Personifikationen städtischer Institutionen auf kaiserzeitlichen Münzen aus Kleinasien*. Bonn: Habelt.

Martzavou, P. 2012. 'The Aretalogies of Isis as a Source for the Socio-cultural Construction of Emotions in the Greek World', in A. Chaniotis (ed.), *Unveiling Emotions. Sources and Methods for the Study of Emotions in the Greek World*. Stuttgart: Franz Steiner. 267–91.

Mason, S. 2000. 'Series Preface', in L. H. Feldman, *Judean Antiquities, 1–4, Flavius Josephus: Translation and Commentary*, vol. 3. Leiden: Brill. xi–xii.

2005. 'Figured Speech and Irony in T. Flavius Josephus', in J. Edmondson, S. Mason and J. B. Rives (eds.), *Flavius Josephus and Flavian Rome*. Oxford University Press. 243–88.

2007. 'Jews, Judaeans, Judaizing, Judaism: Problems of Categorization in Ancient History,' *Journal for the Study of Judaism*, 38, 457–512.

Mastino, A. and Ibba, A. 2014. 'I senatori Africani: Aggiornamenti', in Caldelli and Gregori (eds.), 353–86.

Mathisen, R. 2018. '"Roman' Identity in Late Antiquity, with Special Attention to Gaul,"in W. Pohl, C. Gantner, C. Grifoni and M. Pollheimer-Mohaupt eds., *Transformations of Romanness: Early Medieval Regions and Identities*. Berlin-Boston: De Gruyter. 255–74.

Matthews, S. 2001. *First Converts: Rich Pagan Women and the Rhetoric of Mission in Early Judaism and Christianity*. Stanford University Press.

Mattingly, D. J. 2011. *Imperialism, Power, and Identity: Experiencing the Roman Empire*.

Maxfield, V. A. 1981. *The Military Decorations of the Roman Army*. London: Batsford.

Mazar, B. 1971. 'The Excavations in the Old City of Jerusalem Near the Temple Mount –Second Preliminary Report, 1969–70 Seasons', *Eretz-Israel* 10 (Shazar Volume): 1–33 (Heb.).

Mazar, E. 2011. *The Temple Mount Excavations in Jerusalem 1968–1978 Directed by Benjamin Mazar, Final Reports Volume IV, The Tenth Legion in Aelia Capitolina*. Hebrew University of Jerusalem, Institute of Archaeology.

Mazor, G. 2004. *Free Standing City Gates in the Eastern Provinces During the Roman Imperial Period.* Ph.D. thesis. Bar-Ilan University, Ramat-Gan (Heb.).

2007. 'Concerning the Urban Plan of Aelia Capitolina: Colonnaded Streets, Monumental Arches and City Gates', *Eretz-Israel* 28: 116–24 (Heb., English Summary, 13*).

McGill, S. 2014. 'Ausonius at Night', *American Journal of Philology* 135: 123–48.

McIntosh, J. 2009. *Handbook of Life in Prehistoric Europe.* Oxford University Press.

McRae, R. M. 2011. 'Eating with Honor: The Corinthian Lord's Supper in Light of Voluntary Association Meal Practices', *Journal of Biblical Literature* 130: 165–81.

McCrum, M. and Woodhead, A. G. (eds.) 1961. *Documents of the Principates of the Flavian Emperors, A.D. 68–96.* Cambridge University Press.

Meir, O. 1994. 'ha-teruma ha-historit shell aggadot ḥaza'l leor aggadot Rabbi ve-Antoninus', *Maḥanyim* 7: 5–28 (Heb.).

1999. *Rabbi Judah the Patriarch, Palestinian and Babylonian Portrait of a Leader.* Tel Aviv: Ha-Kibbutz Ha-Me'uḥad (Heb.).

Melbin, M. 1978. 'Night as Frontier', *American Sociological Review* 43.1: 3–22.

1987. *Night as Frontier. Colonizing the World after Dark.* New York: Free Press.

Melville-Jones, J. R. 2014. 'Constantinople as "New Rome",' *Byzantina Symmeikta* 24: 247–62.

Merkle, S. 1996. 'The Truth and Nothing but the Truth: Dictys and Dares', in G. Schmeling (ed.). *The Novel in the Ancient World.* Leiden: Brill. 563–80.

Merle, H. 1916. *Die Geschichte der Städte Byzantion und Kalchedon: von ihrer Gründung bis zum Eingreifen der Römer in die Verhältnisse des Ostens.* Kiel: H. Fiencke.

Merlin, G. (ed.) 1944. *ILTun.* Paris, Presses Universitaires de France.

Meshorer, Y. 1984. *Coins of the Cities of the Land of Israel and Trans-Jordan.* Jerusalem: Israel Museum.

1985. *City-Coins of Eretz Israel and the Decapolis in the Roman Period.* Jerusalem: Israel Museum.

1989. *The Coinage of Aelia Capitolina. Israel Museum's Catalogues* 301. Jerusalem: Israel Museum.

Michels, C. 2013. 'The Spread of Polis Institutions in Hellenistic Cappadocia and the Peer Polity Interaction Theory', in E. Stavrianopoulou (ed.), *Shifting Social Imaginaries in the Hellenistic Period: Narrations, Practices, and Images.* Leiden: Brill. 283–307.

Mieder, W. 2004. *Proverbs: A Handbook.* Westport and London: Greenwood.

Mieder, W. and Dundes, A. (eds.) 1994. *The Wisdom of Many: Essays on the Proverb.* Madison: University of Wisconsin Press.

Mihailov, G. (ed.) 1970. *IGBulg.* Sofia: In Aedibus Typog. Academiae Litterarum Bulgaricae.

Milikovski, H. 2013. *Seder olam: Critical Edition, Commentary, and Introduction.* Jerusalem: Yad Izhak Ben Zvi Institute (Heb.).

Millar, F. 1977. *The Emperor in the Roman World.* London: Duckworth.

1990. 'The Roman Coloniae of the Near East: a Study of Cultural Relations', in H. Solin and M. Kajava (eds.), *Roman Eastern Policy and Other Studies in Roman History.* Helsinki: The Finnish Society of Sciences and Letters. 7–58.

1993. *The Roman Near East, 31BC–AD 337.* Cambridge, MA and London: Harvard University Press.

2005. 'Last Year in Jerusalem: Monuments of the Jewish War in Rome', in J. Edmondson, S. Mason and J. B. Rives (eds.), *Flavius Josephus and Flavian Rome.* Oxford University Press. 101–28.

2006. 'The Roman Coloniae of the Near East: a Study of Cultural Relations', in H. M. Cotton and G. M. Rogers (eds.), *Rome the Greek World and the East, Vol. III: The Greek World, the Jews, and the East.* Chapel Hill, NC and London: University of North Carolina Press. 164–222.

Miller, D. M. 2010. 'The Meaning of *Ioudaios* and its Relationship to Other Group Labels in Ancient "Judaism",' *Currents in Biblical Research* 9: 98–126.

2012. 'Ethnicity Comes of Age: An Overview of Twentieth Century Terms for *Ioudaios*', *Currents in Biblical Research* 10: 293–311.

2014. 'Ethnicity, Religion, and the Meaning of *Ioudaios* in Ancient Judaism', *Currents in Biblical Research* 12: 216–65.

Miller, S. S. 1987. 'Intercity Relations in Roman Palestine: The Case of Sepphoris and Tiberias', *Association for Jewish Studies Review* 12: 1–24.

2004. '"Epigraphical"Rabbis, Helios, and Psalm 19: Were the Synagogues of Archaeology and the Synagogues of the Sages One and the Same?', *Jewish Quarterly Review* 94: 27–76.

2014. '"This Is the Beit Midrash of Rabbi Eliezer ha-Qappar" (Dabbura Inscription) – Were Epigraphical Rabbis Real Sages or Nothing More Than Donors and Honored Deceased?', in S. Fine and A. Koller (eds.), *Talmuda de-Eretz Israel: Archaeology and the Rabbis in Late Antique Palestine.* Berlin: de Gruyter. 239–73.

Millis, B. W. 2010. 'The Social and Ethnic Origins of the Colonists in Early Roman Corinth', in S. J. Friesen, D. N. Schowalter and J. C. Walters (eds.), *Corinth in Context. Comparative Studies on Religion and Society.* Leiden and Boston: Brill. 13–35.

Milson, D. 2007. *Art and Architecture of the Synagogue in Late Antique Palestine.* Ledien: Brill.

Minchin, E. 2012. 'Commemoration and Pilgrimage in the Ancient World: Troy and the Stratigraphy of Cultural Memory', *Greece and Rome* 59: 76–89.

Mitchell, S. 1978. 'Roman Residents and Roman Property in Southern Asia Minor', in E. Akurgal (ed.), *The Proceedings of the Xth International Congress of Classical Archaeology.* Ankara: Türk Tarih Kurumu. 311–18.

1979. 'Iconium and Ninica. Two Double Communities in Roman Asia Minor', *Historia* 28: 409–38.

2010. 'Further Thoughts on the Cult of Theos Hypsistos', in S. Mitchell and P. van Nuffelen (eds.), *One God. Pagan Monotheism in the Roman Empire*. Cambridge University Press. 167–208.

Modéran, Y. 2003. *Les Maures et l'Afrique romain (IVe–VIIe siècle)*. École française de Rome.

2004. 'Les Maures de l'Afrique romaine dans l'Antiquité tardive', *Revue des études latines* 82: 249–69.

2008. 'Des Maures aux Berbères: identité et ethnicité en Afrique du Nord dans l'Antiquité tardive', in V. Gazeau, P. Bauduin and Y. Modéran (eds.), *Identité et ethnicité: concepts, débats historiographiques, exemples (IIIe–XIIe siècle)*. Caen: Publications du CRAHM. 91–134.

Moga, I. 2008. 'The Legal Rights of the Jews from Hadrian to Theodosius I', *Journal for Interdisciplinary Research on Religion and Science* 3: 95–111.

Momigliano, A. 1973. 'La caduta senza rumore di un impero nel 476 d.C.', in V. Branca (ed.), *Concetto, storia, miti e immagini del Medio Evo*. Florence: Sansoni. 409–28.

1975. *Alien Wisdom*. Cambridge University Press.

Mommsen, T. 1871–88. *Römisches Staatsrecht*. Leipzig: S. Hirzel.

Mommsen, T. et al. (eds.) 1853–. *CIL*. Deutsche Akademie der Wissenschaften zu Berlin.

Mommsen, T. and Krüger, P. (eds.) 1870. *Digesta Iustiniani Augusti*. Berolini: apud Weidmannos.

Moore, S. 2015. *Jewish Ethnic Identity and Relations in Hellenistic Egypt*. Leiden: Brill.

Morey, C. R. 1938. *The Mosaics of Antioch*. London: Longmans, Green and Co.

Morgan, J. R. 1985. 'Lucian's True Histories and the Wonders beyond Thule of Antonius Diogenes', *Classical Quarterly* 35: 475–90.

Morgan, T. J. 1998. *Literate Education in the Hellenistic and Roman Worlds*. Cambridge University Press.

Morris, I. and W. Scheidel (eds.) 2009. *The Dynamics of Ancient Empires: State Power from Assyria to Byzantium*. Oxford and New York: Oxford University Press.

Müller, C. et al. (eds.) 1841–70. *FHG*. Paris: Ambrosio Firmin Didot.

Murray, O. 2000. 'Ancient History 1872–1914.' In M. G. Brock and M. C. Curthoys, eds., *The History of the University of Oxford*, vol. 7. Oxford: Oxford University Press, 330–60.

Mutschler, F.-H. and A. Mittag (eds.) 2008. *Conceiving the Empire: China and Rome Compared*. Oxford and New York: Oxford University Press.

Mylonopoulos, I. 2018. '"Brutal Are the Children of the Night"! Nocturnal Violence in Greek Art', in Chaniotis (ed.), 173–200.

Nadeau, R. 2010. 'Les pratiques sympotiques à l'époque impériale', *Ktema* 35: 11–26.

Näf, B. 2010. 'Artemidor – ein Schlüssel für das Verständnis antiker Traumberichte?', in Scioli and Walde (eds.), 185–209.

Nathan, G. 1992. 'The Last Emperor: The Fate of Romulus Augustulus', *Classica et Mediaevalia* 43: 261–71.

Naveh, J. 1978. *On Stone and Mosaic*. Tel Aviv: Israel Exploration Society.

Negev, A. 1964. 'The High Level Aqueduct at Caesarea', *Israel Exploration Journal* 14: 237–49.

Nemo-Pekelman, C. 2010. *Rome et ses citoyens juifs*. Paris: Champion.

Nickel, C., Oelschlägel, C. and Haffner, A. (eds.). 2008. *Martberg. Heiligtum und Oppidum der Treverer. I. Der Kultbezirk. Die Grabungen 1994–2004*. Koblenz: Direktion Archäologie, Aussenstelle Koblenz.

Nicolet, C. 1966/74. *L'ordre équestre à l'époque républicaine, 312–43 av. J.-C*. Paris: De Boccard.

Nicols, J. 2014. *Civic Patronage in the Roman Empire*. Leiden and Boston: Brill.

Nielsen, I. 1999. 'Early Provincial Baths and Their Relations to Early Italic Baths', in J. DeLaine and D. E. Johnston (eds.), *Roman Baths and Bathing. Proceedings of the First International Conference on Roman Baths Held at Bath, England, 30 March– 4 April 1992. Part 1: Bathing and Society (Journal of Roman Archaeology* Suppl. 37). Portsmouth: Journal of Roman Archaeology. 35–43.

Nigdelis, P. M. 2010. '"Voluntary Associations"in Roman Thessalonike: In Search of Identity and Support in a Cosmopolitan Society', in L. Nasrallah, C. Bakirtzis and S. J. Friesen (eds.), *From Roman to Early Christian Thessalonike. Studies in Religion and Archaeology*. Cambridge, MA: Harvard University Press. 13–47.

Nippel, W. 1995. *Public Order in Ancient Rome*. Cambridge University Press.

Nissin, L. 'Sleeping Culture in Roman Literary Sources', *Arctos* 49, 95–133.

Noam, V. 2003. *Megillat Ta'anit: Versions Interpretation History*. Jerusalem: Yad Izhak Ben Zvi Institute (Heb.).

　　2017. 'A Statue in the Temple', in T. Illan and V. Noam (eds. in collaboration with M. Ben Shahar, D. Baratz and Y. Fisch), *Josephus and the Rabbis, I, The Lost Tales of the Second Temple Period*. Jerusalem: Yad Yitzhak Ben Zvi. 453–84.

Nolland, J. 1981. 'Uncircumcised Proselytes?', *Journal for the Study of Judaism* 12: 173–94.

Noreña, C. F. 2003. 'Medium and Message in Vespasian's Templum Pacis', *Memoirs of the American Academy in Rome* 48: 25–43.

North, J. 2000. *Roman Religion*. Oxford University Press.

　　2013. 'Caesar on *religio*', *Archiv für Religionsgeschichte* 15: 187–200.

Noy, D. (ed.) 1993. *Jewish Inscriptions of Western Europe*. Cambridge University Press.

1995. *Jewish Inscriptions of Western Europe II, the City of Rome*. Cambridge University Press.

Noy, D. et al. (eds.) 2004–. *IJO*. Tubingen: Mohr Siebeck.

Nutton, V. 1977. 'Archiatri and the Medical Profession', *Papers of the British School at Rome* 32: 191–226.

1981. 'Continuity or Rediscovery?: The City Physician in Classical Antiquity and Medieval Italy', in A. W. Russell (ed.), *The Town and State Physician in Europe from the Middle Ages to the Enlightenment*. Wolfenbüttel: Herzog August Bibliothek. 9–46.

Olbrich, K. 2006. 'Constantiniana Daphne: Die Gründungsmythen eines anderen Rom?', *Klio* 88: 483–509.

Oldenstein, J. 1976. 'Zur Ausrüstung römischer Auxiliareinheiten: Studien zu Beschlägen und Zierat an der Ausrüstung der römischen Auxiliareinheiten des obergermanisch-raetischen Limesgebietes aus dem zweiten und dritten Jahrundert n. Chr', *Berichte der Römisch-Germansichen Kommission* 57: 49–284.

Oliver, J. 1989. *Greek Constitutions of Early Roman Emperors from Inscriptions and Papyri*. Philadelphia: Amer Philosophical Society.

Olyabm, S. M. 2004. 'Purity Ideology in Ezra-Nehemiah as a Tool to Reconstitute the Community', *Journal for the Study of Judaism* 35.1: 1–16.

Onn, A., Weksler-Bdolah, S. and Bar-Nathan, R. 2011. 'Jerusalem, the Old City, Wilson's Arch and the Great Causeway, Preliminary Report', *Hadashot Arkheologiyot, Excavations and Surveys in Israel* 123: www.hadashot-esi.org.il/report_detail_eng.asp?id=1738&mag_id=118.

Oppenheimer, A. 1991. *The Galilee in the Mishnaic Period*. Jerusalem: The Zalman Shazar Center for Jewish History (Heb.).

2005a. 'Urbanisation and City Territories in Roman Palestine', in A. Oppenheimer, *Between Rome and Babylon*. Tübingen: Mohr Siebeck. 30–46.

2005b. 'Tyrus, Phönizien und Galiläa', in A. Oppenheimer, *Between Rome and Babylon*. Tübingen: Mohr Siebeck. 93–101.

2007. *Rabbi Judah Ha-Nasi*, Jerusalem: The Zalman Shazar Center for Jewish History (Heb.).

2017. *Rabbi Judah ha-Nasi: Statesman, Reformer, and the Redactor of the Mishnah*, Tübingen: Mohr Siebeck.

Orlin, E. M. 1997. *Temples, Religion and Politics in the Roman Republic*. Leiden: Brill.

2010. *Foreign Cults in Rome: Creating a Roman Empire*. New York: Oxford University Press.

Otto, A. 1890/1962. *Die Sprichwörter und sprichwörtlichen Redensarten der Römer*, Leipzig: Teubner. = repr. in Hildesheim: G. Olms.

Otto, A. 1890/1964. *Die Sprichwörter und sprichwörtlichen Redensarten der Römer*. Leipzig: Teubner. = repr. in Hildesheim: G. Olms.

Overman. J. A. 2002. 'The First Revolt and Flavian Politics', in A. M. Berlin and
    J. A. Overman (eds.), *The First Jewish Revolt: Archeology, History and
    Ideology*. London and New York: Routledge. 213–20.

Pagan, V. 2005. *Conspiracy Narratives in Roman History*. Austin: University of
    Texas Press.

Pailler, J. M. 1988. *Bacchanalia. La répression de 186 av. J.-C. à Rome et en Italie*.
    École française de Rome.

    1998. 'Les Bacchanales, dix ans après', *Pallas* 48: 67–86.

Paleothodoros, D. 2010. 'Light and Darkness in Dionysiac Rituals as Illustrated on
    Attic Vase Paintings of the 5th Century BCE', in Christopoulos et al. (eds.),
    237–60.

Panciera, S. (ed.), 1982 [1984]. *Epigrafia e Ordine Senatorio*. Roma: Edizioni di
    storia e letteratura.

Papageorgiadou-Bani, H. 2004. *The Numismatic Iconography of the Roman
    Colonies in Greece. Local Spirit and the Expression of Imperial Policy*.
    Athens: National Hellenic Research Foundation.

Papazoglou, F. 1986. 'Oppidum Stobi civium Romanorum et municipium
    Stobensium', *Chiron* 16: 213–37.

Parisinou, E. 2000. *The Light of the Gods. The Role of Light in Archaic and Classical
    Greek Cult*. London: Bristol Classical Press.

Parker, S. T. 1993., 'El-Lejjun', in E. Stern (ed.), *The New Encyclopedia of
    Archaeological Excavations in the Holy Land*, Vol. 3. Jerusalem: Israel
    Exploration Society & Carta. 913–5.

Parsons, P. J. 1976. 'Petitions and a Letter; the Grammarian's Complaint', in
    A. E. Hanson (ed.), *Collectanea Papyrologica. Texts Published in Honour of
    H. C. Youtie*. Bonn: Habelt. 409–46.

Patera, I. 2010. 'Light and Lighting Equipment in the Eleusinian Mysteries.
    Symbolism and Ritual Use', in Christopoulos et al. (eds.), 261–75.

Patterson, L. 1991. *Chaucer and the Subject of History*. Madison: University of
    Wisconsin Press.

Pearce, L. E. and Wunsch, C. 2014. *Documents of Judean exiles and West Semites in
    Babylonia in the Collection of David Sofer*. Bethesda, MD: CDL Press.

Pedersen, P. 2009. 'Report of the Turkish-Danish Investigations at Ancient
    Halikarnassos (Bodrum) in 2008', *Araştırma Sonuçları Toplantısı* 27.3: 250.

Peek, W. (ed.) 1955. *GV*. Berlin: Akademie-Verlag.

Pernot, L. 2008. 'Aelius Aristides and Rome', in W. V. Harris and B. Holmes (eds.),
    Aelius Aristides between Greece, Rome, and the Gods. Leiden—Boston: Brill.
    175–201.

Petculescu, L. 1995. 'Military Equipment Graves in Roman Dacia', *Journal of
    Roman Military Equipment Studies* 6: 105–45.

Petruccioli, G. 2012. *The Portraiture of Caracalla and Geta: Form, Context,
    Function*. Ph.D. thesis, St. Cross College, Oxford.

Petzl, G. (ed.) 1987. *Inschriften griechischer Städte aus Kleinasien, XXIV,1: Die Inschriften von Smyrna*, II,1. Bonn: Habelt.

Piccirillo, M. 1993. *The Mosaics of Jordan*. Amman: American Center of Oriental Research.

Pincus, J. A., de Smet, T. S., Tepper, Y. and Adams, M. J. 2013. 'Ground Penetrating Radar and Electromagnetic Archaeogeophysical Investigations at the Roman Legionary Camp at Legio, Israel', *Archaeological Prospective* 30.3: 175–88.

Pines, S. 1974. 'Notes on the Existing Equivalence between Syriac Terms and Terms of Ḥazal Language', in S. Pines (ed.), *In memory to Jacob Friedman*. Jerusalem: Institute of Jewish Studies. 205–13.

Pirenne-Delforge, V. 2018. 'Nyx est, elle aussi, une divinité. La nuit dans les mythes et les cultes grecs', in Chaniotis (ed.), 131–65.

Podvin, J. -L. 2011. *Luminaire et cultes isiaques*. Montagnac: M. Mergoil.

2014. 'Illuminer le temple: la lumière dans les sanctuaires isiaques à l'époque gréco-romaine', *Revue des études anciennes* 116: 23–42.

2015. 'La lumière dans les fêtes isiaques', *Revista Transilvania* 10: 35–42.

Pohl, W. 1998. 'Telling the Difference: Signs of Ethnic Identity', in W. Pohl and H. Reimitz (eds.), *Strategies of Distinction: The Construction of Ethnic Communities, 300–800*. Leiden-Boston: Brill. 17–69.

Pont, A.-V. 2007. 'L'empereur "fondateur": enquête sur les motifs de la reconnaissance civique', *Revue des études grecques* 120: 526–52.

Poole, R. S. et al. (eds.) 1923–. *BMCRE*. London.

Porat, L. 2010. 'Zippori (Southeast) Preliminary Report (2.6.2010)'. *HA-ESI* 122: www.hadashot-esi.org.il/Report_Detail_Eng.aspx?id=1403&mag_id=117.

Porten, B. and Farber, J. J. 2011. *The Elephantine Papyri in English: Three Millennia of Cross-cultural Continuity and Change*. Atlanta: Society of Biblical Literature.

Porten, B. and Yardeni, A. (eds. and trans.) 1986. *Textbook of Aramaic Documents from Ancient Egypt*, 4 vols. in 8 pts. Jerusalem: Akademon.

Porton, G. G. 1994. *The Stranger within Your Gates: Converts and Conversion in Rabbinic Literature*. The University of Chicago Press.

Potter, D. 2006. 'Introduction: The Shape of Roman History: The Fate of the Governing Class' in D. Potter, ed., *A Companion to the Roman Empire*, Cambridge: Cambridge University Press, 1–19.

Price, J. J. 2015. 'Transplanted Communities in Iudaea/Palaestina: The Epigraphic Evidence', *Scripta Classica Israelica* 34: 27–40.

forthcoming. 'The Different Faces of Euergetism in Iudaea/Palaestina and Syria in Late Antiquity: The Evidence of Synagogue Inscriptions', in E. Iricinschi and C. Kotsifo (eds.), *Coping with Religious Change: Adopting Transformations and Adapting Rituals in the Late Antique Eastern Mediterranean*.

'2020. 'The Future of Rome in Three Greek Historians of Rome,' in J. J. Price and K. Berthelot (eds.), *The Future of Rome: Roman, Greek, Jewish and Christian Visions*, Cambridge: Cambridge University Press, 85–111.

Purcell, N. 1983. 'The Apparitores: a Study in Social Mobility', *Papers of the British School at Rome* 51: 125–73.

Rabello, M. A. 1984. 'On the Relations between Diocletian and the Jews', *Journal of Jewish Studies* 35: 147–67.

1999/2000. 'The Attitude of Rome towards Conversions to Judaism (Atheism, Circumcision, Proselytism)', in A. Gambaro and A. M. Rabello (eds.), *Towards a New European Ius Commune, Essays on European, Italian and Israeli Law in Occasion of 50 Years of the EU and of the State of Israel*. The Harry and Michael Sacher Institute for Legislative Research and Comparative Law in the Hebrew University of Jerusalem. 37–68. = repr. in A. M. Rabello, *The Jews in the Roman Empire: Legal Problems, from Herod to Justinian*. Aldershot: Ashgate Variorum. pt. XIV.

Raepsaet, G. 2013. 'L'ethnogenèse de la civitas Tungrorum et la formation de la Province de Germanie', *L'Antiquité Classique* 82: 111–48.

Rajak, T. 1984/2001. 'Was There a Roman Charter for the Jews', *Journal of Roman Studies* 74: 107–23. = repub. in Rajak, T. *The Jewish Dialogue with Greece and Rome*. Leiden: Brill. 301–33.

2005. 'Josephus in the Diaspora', in J. Edmondson, S. Mason and J. B. Rives (eds.), *Flavius Josephus and Flavian Rome*. Oxford University Press. 79–100.

Rakob, F. 2000. 'The Making of Augustan Carthage', in E. Fentress (ed.), *Romanization and the City: Creation, Transformations and Failures* (*Journal of Roman Archaeology* Suppl. 38). Portsmouth: Journal of Roman Archaeology. 73–82.

Ramsay, W. M. 1916. Colonia Caesarea (Pisidian Antioch) in the Augustan Age. *JRS* 6; 83–134.

Rantala, J. 2013. *Maintaining Loyalty, Declaring Continuity, Legitimizing Power. Ludi Saeculares of Septimius Severus as a Manifestation of the Golden Age.* Tampere University Press.

2017. *The Ludi Saeculares of Septimius Severus. The Ideologies of the New Roman Empire.* London: Routledge.

Rappaport, U. 2009. 'The Conversion of the Idumaeans under John Hyrcanus', in J. Geiger, H. M. Cotton and G. D. Stiebel (eds.), *Israel's Land: Papers Presented to Israel Shatzman on His Jubilee.* Raanana: The Open University of Israel. 59–74 (Heb.).

Rapuano, Y. 2014. 'The Pottery from the Pool from the Period of Aelia Capitolina in the Jewish Quarter of Jerusalem', in Geva, Appendix 1: 427–36.

Rea, J. R. 1980. 'The Legio II Trajana in Judaea?', *Zeitschrift fur Papyrologie und Epigraphik* 38: 220–2.

1996. *The Oxyrhynchus Papyri, 63.* London: Egypt Exploration Society.

Rebillard, E. 2012. *Christians and Their Many Identities in Late Antiquity: North Africa, 200–450 CE*. Ithaca-London: Cornell University Press.

Rebuffat, F. 1986. 'Alexandre le Grand et Apollonia de Pisidie', *Revue numismatique* 28: 65–71.

1997. *Les enseignes sur les monnaies d'Asie Mineure. Des origines à Sévère Alexandre*. Ecole Française d'Athènes.

Rebuffat, R. 1974–75. 'Graffiti en "Libyque"de Bu Njem (Notes et documents VII)', *Libya antiqua* 11–12: 165–87.

1995. 'Le centurion M. Porcius Iasucthan à Bu Njem (notes et documents XI)', *Libya antiqua* n.s. 1: 79–123.

2005. 'Le vétéran gétule de Thullium', in C. Briand-Ponsart (ed.), *Identités et culture dans l'Algérie antique*. Publications de l'Université de Rouen et du Havre. 193–233.

2006. 'Aires sémantiques des principaux mots libyques', *Mélanges d'archéologie et d'histoire de l'École française de Rome* 118.1: 267–95.

2007. 'Pour un corpus de bilingues punico-libyques et latino-libyques', in M. H. Fantar (ed.), *Osmose Ethno-culturelle en Méditerranée*. Université de Tunis El Manar. 183–242.

Re'em, A. 2011. 'First Temple Period Fortifications and Herod's Palace in the Kishle Compound', *Qadmonioit* 140: 96–101.

2013. 'King David's Tomb on Mount Zion: Theories vs. the Archaeological Evidence', in G. D. Stiebel, O. Peleg-Barkat, D. Ben-Ami, S. Weksler-Bdolah and Y. Gadot (eds.), *New Studies in the Archaeology of Jerusalem and Its Region*, Collected Papers 7. Jerusalem: Israel Antiquities Authority. 221–42 (Heb.).

Rees, R. 2004. *Diocletian and the Tetrarchy*. Edinburgh University Press.

Reich, R. and Bilig, Y. 2003. 'Another Flavian Inscription near the Temple Mount of Jerusalem', *'Atiqot* 44: 243–7.

Reichmann, C. 1991. 'Das Heiligtum in Krefeld-Elfrath', *Die Heimat* 62: 1–30.

Reisner, G. A., Fisher, C. S. and Lyon, D. G. 1924. *Harvard Excavations at Samaria, 1908–1910*. Cambridge, MA: Harvard University Press.

Reiter, F. 2005. 'Symposia in Tebtynis. Zu den griechischen Ostraka aus den neuen Grabungen', in S. Lippert and M. Schentuleit (eds.), *Tebtynis und Soknopaiu Nesos. Leben im römerzeitlichen Fajum. Akten des Internationalen Symposions vom 11. bis 13. Dezzember 2003 in Sommerhausen bei Würzburg*. Wiesbaden: Harrassowitz. 131–40.

Renberg, G. 2006. 'Was Incubation Practiced in the Latin West?', *Archiv für Religionsgeschichte* 8: 105–47.

2010. 'Dream-Narratives and Unnarrated Dreams in Greek and Latin Dedicatory Inscriptions', in Scioli and Walde (eds.), 33–61.

2015. 'The Role of Dream-Interpreters in Greek and Roman Religion', in Weber (ed.), 233–62.

2016. 'I.GrEgLouvre 11 and the Lychnaption: A Topographical Problem at Saqqara', *Zeitschrift fur Papyrologie und Epigraphik* 200: 215–18.

2017. *Where Dreams May Come. Incubation Sanctuaries in the Greco-Roman World.* Leiden: Brill.

Reuven, P. 2011. 'A Comparative Analysis of the Bathhouse Plan', in Mazar, 119–30.

Reynolds, J. 1982 [1984]. 'Senatores Originating in the Provinces of Egypt and of Crete and Cyrene', in Panciera (ed.), vol. 2, 671–83.

Reynolds, J. and Tannenbaum, R. 1987. *Jews and God-Fearers at Aphrodisias: Greek Inscriptions with Commentary.* Cambridge Philological Society.

Rigsby, K. J. 2010. 'Meros the Founder: I. Olympia 53', *Zeitschrift fur Papyrologie und Epigraphik* 173: 89–90.

Ritterling, C. 1925. 'Legio VI Ferrata', in A. F. Pauly and G. Wissowa (eds.), *Pauly Wissova – Realencyclopädie der klassischen Altertumswissenschaft*, Vol. 12.2: Stuttgart: Metzler. 1587–96.

Rives, J. 2006. 'Interdisciplinary Approaches', in D. Potter, ed., *A Companion to the Roman Empire*, Cambridge: Cambridge University Press, 98–112.

2005. 'Flavian Religious Policy and the Destruction of the Jerusalem Temple', in J. Edmondson, S. Mason and J. B. Rives (eds.), *Flavius Josephus and Flavian Rome.* Oxford University Press. 145–66.

2007. *Religion in the Roman Empire.* Oxford University Press.

Rizakis, A. D. 2004. 'La littérature gromatique et la colonisation en Orient', in G. Salmeri, A. Raggi and A. Baroni (eds.), *Colonie romane nel mondo Greco.* Rome: L'Erma di Bretschneider. 69–94.

Ro, J. U. (ed.) 2012. *From Judah to Judaea: Socio-economic Structures and Processes in the Persian Period.* Sheffield: Sheffield Phoenix Press.

Robert, J. and Robert, L. 1954. *La Carie. II. Le plateau de Tabai et ses environs.* Paris: Adrien-Maisonneuve.

Robert, L. 1948. *Hellenica V.* Paris: Librairie d'Amérique et d'Orient, Adrien-Maisonneuve.

Robinson, H. R. R. 1975. *The Armour of Imperial Rome.* London: Arms and Armour Press.

Rochette, B. 1997. *Le latin dans le monde grec. Recherches sur la diffusion de la langue et des lettres latines dans les provinces hellénophones de l'Empire romain.* Brussels: Peeters Publishers.

Rogers, G. 1991. *The Sacred Identity of Ephesos: Foundation Myths of a Roman City.* London and New York: Routledge.

Roll, I. 1994. 'Roman Roads', in Tsafrir et al., 21–2.

2009. 'Between Damascus and Megiddo: Roads and Transportation in Antiquity across the Northeastern Approaches to the Holy Land', in L. Di Segni, Y. Hirschfeld, J. Patrich and R. Talgam (eds.), *Man Near a Roman Arch – Studies Presented to Prof. Yoram Tsafrir.* Jerusalem: Israel Exploration Society. 1*–20*.

Roller, L. E. 1999. *In Search of God the Mother: The Cult of Anatolian Cybele.* Berkeley: University of California Press.

Rose, C. B. 2011. 'Troy VIII–IX', in M. Finkelberg (ed.), *The Homer Encyclopedia.* Malden, MA and Oxford: Wiley-Blackwell. 902–5.

Rosenberger, M. 1975. *City Coins of Palestine II.* Jerusalem: Rosenberger.

1977. *City Coins of Palestine III.* Jerusalem: Rosenberger.

1978. *The Coinage of Eastern Palestine.* Jerusalem: Rosenberger.

Rosenthal-Heginbottom, R. 2008. 'The Material Culture of the Roman Army', in O. Guri- Rimon, *The Great Revolt in the Galilee.* Haifa: Hecht Museum. 91*–108*.

2015. 'The Kiln Works of the Legio Decima Fretensis: Pottery Production and Distribution', in L. Vagalinski and N. Sharankov (eds.), *Limes XXII, Proceedings of the 22nd International Congress of Roman Frontier Studies, Ruse, Bulgaria, September 2012.* Sofia: National Archaeological Institute with Museum Bulgarian Academy of Sciences. 611–18.

2019. Jerusalem, Western Wall Plaza Excavations, Volume II, the Pottery from the Eastern Cardo, IAA Reports 64. Jerusalem: Israel Antiquities Authority.

Roth-Gerson, L. 1987. *The Greek Inscriptions from the Synagogues in Eretz-Israel.* Jerusalem: Yad Izhak Ben Zvi Institute (Heb.).

Rothe, G. 2012. 'Romanization', in R. Bagnall et al., eds., *The Encyclopedia of Ancient History,* Wiley-Blackwell online, 5875–81.

Roueché, C. 1993. *Performers and Partisans at Aphrodisias in the Roman and Late Roman Periods.* London: Society for the Promotion of Roman Studies.

Roxan, M. M. and Holder, P. (eds.) 1978–2006. *RMD.* University of London.

Rüger, C. 1987. 'Beobachtungen zu den epigraphischen Belegen der Muttergottheiten in den lateinischen Provinzen des Imperium Romanum', in G. Bauchhenß and G. Neumann (eds.), *Matronen und verwandte Gottheiten. Ergebnisse eines Kolloquiums veranstaltet von der Göttinger Akademiekommission für die Altertumskunde Mittel- und Nordeuropas.* Bonn: Habelt. 1–30.

Rüpke, J. 1995. *Kalender und Öffentlichkeit: Die Geschichte der Repräsentation und religiösen Qualifikation von Zeit in Rom (Religionsgeschichtliche Versuche und Vorarbeiten 40).* Berlin: De Gruyter.

2001. *Die Religion der Römer .* Munich: C. H. Beck Verlag.

2012. *Religion in Republican Rome: Rationalization and Ritual Change.* Philadelphia: University of Pennsylvania Press.

2014. *From Jupiter to Christ. On the History of Religion in the Roman Imperial Period,* tr. by D. M. B. Richardson. Oxford University Press.

Ruscu, L. 2006. 'Actia Nicopolis', *Zeitschrift fur Papyrologie und Epigraphik* 157: 247–55.

Russo, J. 1997. 'Prose Genres for the Performance of Traditional Wisdom in Ancient Greece: Proverb, Maxim, Apothegm", in L. Edmunds and

R. W. Wallace (eds.), *Poet, Public, and Performance in Ancient Greece*. Baltimore and London: Johns Hopkins University Press. 49–64.

Sabar, S. 2000. 'The Purim Panel at Dura: A Socio-Historical Interpretation', in L. I. Levine and Z. Weiss (eds.), *From Dura to Sepphoris: Studies in Jewish Art and Society in Late Antiquity*. Portsmouth: Journal of Roman Archaeology. 154–63.

Sablayrolles, R. 1996. *Vigiles. Libertinus miles. Les cohortes de vigiles*. École française de Rome.

Sacerdoti, A. 2014, '*Quis magna tuenti somnus?* Scenes of Sleeplessness (and Intertextuality) in Flavian Poetry', in A. Augoustakis (ed.), *Flavian Poetry and its Greek Past*. Leiden: Brill. 13–29.

Safrai, S. 1976. 'The Synagogue', in S. Safrai and M. Stern (eds.), *The Jewish People in the First Century*. Assen/Amsterdam: Van Gorcum. 908–44.

Safrai, Z. 1995. 'The Communal Functions of the Synagogue in the Land of Israel in the Rabbinic Period', in D. Urman and P. V. M. Flesher (eds.), *Ancient Synagogues*. Leiden: Brill. 181–204.

Sage, M. 2000. 'Roman Visitors to Ilium in the Roman Imperial and Late Antique Period: The Symbolic Functions of a Landscape', *Studia Troica* 10: 211–32.

Salvo, I. 2012. 'Romulus and Remus at Chios Revisited: A Re-examination of SEG XXX 1073', in P. Martzavou and N. Papazarkadas (eds.), *Epigraphical Approaches to the Post-Classical Polis, Fourth Century BC to Second Century AD*. Oxford University Press. 125–37.

Sänger, P. 2016. 'Heracleopolis, Jewish *politeuma*', in the new online OCD, publ.: http://classics.oxfordre.com/view/10.1093/acrefore/9780199381135.001.00 01/acrefore-9780199381135-e-8036?rskey=1tHUgO&result=1

Sapir, N. 2015. 'Jerusalem, Mount Zion', *Hadashot Arkheologiyot, Excavations and Surveys in Israel* 127: www.hadashot-esi.org.il/Report_Detail_Eng.aspx? id=24863&mag_id=122

Sartre, M. 2001a. *D'Alexandre à Zénobie. Histoire du Levant antique. IVe siècle av. J.-C. – IIIe siècle ap. J.-C.* Paris: Fayard.

  2001b. 'Les colonies romaines dans le monde grec. Essai de synthèse', in E. Dąbrowa (ed.), *Roman Military Studies*. Kraków: Jagiellonian University Press. 111–52.

  2011. 'Brigands, colons et pouvoirs en Syrie du Sud au Ier siècle de notre ère', *Anabases* 13: 207–45.

Sartre-Fauriat, A. 2001. *Des tombeaux et des morts: Monuments funéraires, société et culture en Syrie du Sud du Ier S. av. J.-C. au VIIe S. apr. J.-C.* Beirut: Institut Français d'Archéologie du Proche-Orient.

Šašel, J. 1982 [1984]. 'Senatori ed appartenenti all'ordine senatorio provenienti dalle province romane di Dacia, Tracia, Mesia, Dalmazia, Pannonia', in Panciera (ed.), vol. 2, 553–81.

Schäfer, P. 1981. *Der Bar Kokhba – Aufstand*, Tübingen: J. C. B. Mohr.

1990. 'Hadrian's Policy in Judaea and the Bar Kokhba Revolt: a Reassessment', in P. R. Davies and R. T. White (eds.), *A Tribute for Geza Vermes*. Sheffield: JSOT Press. 291–7.

1997. *Judeophobia*. Cambridge, MA: Harvard University Press.

Scheid, J. 1991. 'Sanctuaires et territoire in la Colonia Augusta Treverorum', in J.-L. Brunaux (ed.), *Les sanctuaires celtiques et le monde méditerranéen* (Dossiers de Protohistoire n° 3). Paris: Éd. Errance. 42–57.

1998. *Recherches archéologiques à la Magliana: Commentarii fratrum Arvalium qui supersunt: les copies épigraphiques des protocoles annuels de la confrérie arvale: (21 av.-304 ap. J.-C.)*. Soprintendenza archeologica di Roma.

1999. 'Aspects religieux de la municipalisation. Quelques réflexions générales', in M. Dondin-Payre, M.-T. Raepsaet-Charlier (eds.), *Cités, municipes, colonies. Les processus de municipalisation en Gaule et en Germanie sous le Haut-Empire*. Paris: Publ. de la Sorbonne. 381–423.

2012. 'Les métamorphoses dans l'Antiquité grecque et romaine. Autour des Métamorphoses d'Ovide', in J.-P. Changeux (ed.), *La Vie des formes et les formes de la vie*. Paris: Ed. Odile Jacob. 150–71.

Scheid J. and Svenbro, J. 2004. 'Le mythe de Vertumne', *Europe* 82: 176–90.

Scheidel, W. (ed.). 2009. *Rome and China: Comparative Perspectives on Ancient World Empires*. New York and Oxford : Oxford University Press.

Schiffman, L. H. 1985. *Who Was a Jew? Rabbinic and Halakhic Perspectives on the Jewish-Christian Schism*. Hoboken, NJ: Ktav.

Schilling,R. 1954. *La religion romaine de Venus, depuis les origines jusqu' au temps d'Auguste*. Paris: E. De Boccard.

Schivelbusch, W. 1988. *Disenchanted Night: The Industrialization of Light in the Nineteenth Century*, tr. by Angela Davies. Berkeley: University of California Press.

Schlesier, R. 2018. 'Sappho bei Nacht', in Chaniotis (ed.), 91–121.

Schmidt, M. 2003. *'Wie einem Becher der Liebe . . .': Fallstudien zur Frage ethnischer Identitäten in hellenistischer Literatur und den synoptischen Evangelien*. Ph.D. dissertation, Hebrew University of Jerusalem.

Schmitt Pantel, P. 1992. *La cité au banquet. Histoire des repas publics dans les cités grecques*. École Française de Rome.

Schnurbusch, D. 2011. *Convivium: Form und Bedeutung aristokratischer Geselligkeit in der romischen Antike*. Stuttgart: Franz Steiner.

Schremer, A. 2010. *Brothers Estranged: Heresy, Christianity, and Jewish Identity in Late Antiquity*. Oxford University Press.

Schuler, C. 1998. *Ländliche Siedlungen und Gemeinden im hellenistischen und römischen Kleinasien*. Munich: C. H. Beck.

Schumacher, G. 1908. *Tell el-Mutesellim*, 1. Leipzig: Haupt.

Schürer, E. 1973. *The History of the Jewish People in the Age of Jesus Christ*, I. (rev. and ed. by G. Vermes, F. Millar and M. Black). Edinburgh: Clark.

1979. *The History of the Jewish People in the Age of Jesus Christ*, II. (rev. and ed. by G. Vermes, F. Millar and M. Black). Edinburgh: Clark.

1986. *The History of the Jewish People in the Age of Jesus Christ*, III (rev. and ed. by G. Vermes, F. Millar and M. Black). Edinburgh: Clark.

Schwartz, D. R. 2005. 'Herodians and *Ioudaioi* in Flavian Rome', in J. Edmondson, S. Mason and J. B. Rives (eds.), *Flavius Josephus and Flavian Rome*. Oxford University Press. 63–78.

2007. '"Judeans"or "Jew"? How should we translate *ioudaios* in Josephus?', in J. Frey, D. R. Schwartz and S. Gripentrong (eds.), *Jewish Identity in the Greco-Roman World: Jüdische Identität der greichisch-römischen Welt*. Leiden: Brill. 3–27.

2011. 'Yannai and Pella', *Dead Sea Discoveries* 18: 339–59.

2014. *Judeans and Jews: Four Faces of Dichotomy in Ancient Jewish History*. University of Toronto Press.

Schwartz, R. M. 1997. *The Curse of Cain*. University of Chicago Press.

Schwartz, S. 2001/2004. *Imperialism and Jewish Society, 200 B.C.E. to 640 C.E.* Princeton University Press.

2011. 'How Many Judaisms Were There?', *Journal of Ancient Judaism* 2: 208–38.

Scioli, E. and Walde, C. (eds.) 2010. *Sub imagine somni: Nighttime Phenomena in Greco- Roman Culture*. Pisa: ETS.

Seidel, Y. 2012. *Künstliches Licht im individuellen, familiären und öffentlichen Lebensbereich*. Vienna: Phoibos.

Sevenster, J. N. 1975. *The Roots of Anti-Semitism in the Ancient World*. Leiden: Brill.

Sfameni Gasparro, G. 1999. 'Alessandro di Abonutico, lo "pseudo-profeta"ovvero come construirsi un'identità religiosa. II. L'oracolo e i misteri', in C. Bonnet and A. Motte (eds.), *Les syncrétismes religieux dans le monde méditérranéen antique. Actes du colloque international en l'honneur de Franz Cumont*. Brussels and Rome: Brepols. 275–305.

Shahar, Y. 2004. *Josephus Geographicus: The Classical Context of Geography in Josephus*. Tübingen: Mohr Siebeck.

2011. 'Imperial Religious Unification Policy and Its Decisive Consequences: Diocletian, the Jews and the Samaritans', in R. Mathisen and D. R. Shanzer (eds.), *Romans, Barbarians, and the Transformation of the Roman World: Cultural Interaction and the Creation of Identity in Late Antiquity*. Aldershot: Ashgate. 109–20.

Shapiro, A. 2017. 'Petrographic Examination of Tiles, Bricks and Mortaria from Legio', *'Atiqot* 89: 41–7.

Sharon, N. 2010. 'The Title Ethnarch in Second Temple Period Judea', *Journal for the Study of Judaism* 41: 472–93.

Sharoni, A. 1987. *The Comprehensive Arabic-Hebrew Dictionary*. Israeli Defence Force, Intelligence Corps, Ministry of Defence Publishing House and Tel Aviv University (Heb.-Arab.).

Shatzman, I. 1983. 'The Military Confrontation between Rome and the Jews', in U. Rappaport (ed.), *Judaea and Roma – the Jewish Revolts*. Tel Aviv: Am-Oved. 300–29 (Heb.).

1994. Review of Isaac 1990, *IEJ* 44, 1994, 129–34.

2005. 'On the Conversion of the Idumaeans', in M. Mor (ed.), *For Uriel: Studies in the History of Israel in Antiquity Presented to Professor Uriel Rappaport*. Jerusalem: Zalman Shazar Center. 213–41 (Heb.).

Shaw, B. D. 1983. 'Soldiers and Society: The Army in Numidia', *Opus* 2: 133–59.

1991. 'The Structure of Local Society in the Early Maghrib: The Elders', *The Maghrib Review* 16: 18–55.

2003. 'A Peculiar Island: Maghrib and Mediterranean', *Mediterranean Historical Review* 18: 93–125.

2005. 'The Invention of Racism in Classical Antiquity' (Review), *Journal of World History* 16: 230–1.

2011. *Sacred Violence: African Christians and Sectarian Hatred in the Age of Augustine*. Cambridge University Press.

2013. *Bringing in the Sheaves: Economy and Metaphor in the Roman World*. University of Toronto Press.

2014. 'Who Are You? Africa and Africans', in J. McInerney (ed.), *A Companion to Ethnicity in the Ancient Mediterranean*. Oxford: Blackwell. 527–40.

Sherwin-White, A. N. 1967. *Racial Prejudice in Imperial Rome*. Cambridge University Press.

1973. *The Roman Citizenship*, 2nd ed., Oxford: Clardendon Press.

Siegert, F. 1973. 'Gottesfürchtige und Sympathisanten', *Journal for the Study of Judaism* 4: 109–64.

Sim, D. C. 2013. 'Gentiles, God-Fearers and Proselytes', in D. C. Sim and J. S. McLaren (eds.), *Attitudes to Gentiles in Ancient Judaism and Early Christianity*. London: Bloomsbury. 9–27.

Simpson, J. 1998. 'The Other Book of Troy: Guido delle Colonne's *Historia destructionis Troae* in Fourteenth- and Fifteenth-Century England', *Speculum* 73: 397–423.

Sion, O. and Rapuano, Y. 2014. 'A Pool from the Period of Aelia Capitolina in the Jewish Quarter of Jerusalem', in Geva, 414–27.

Sion-Jenkis, K. 2010. 'La perception du pouvoir impérial en Asie Mineure à l'époque julio-claudienne: l'exemple d'Aphrodisias', in L. Callegarin and F. Réchin (eds.), *Espaces et Sociétés à l'époque romaine: entre Garonne et Ebre*. Pau: Université de Pau et des Pays de l'Adour. 69–95.

Slingerland, H. D. 1997. *Claudian Policymaking and the Early Imperial Repression of Judaism at Rome*. Atlanta: Scholars Press.

Smallwood, E. M. 1981. *The Jews under Roman Rule: From Pompey to Diocletian: A Study in Political Relations*. Leiden: Brill.

Sokolowski, F. 1955. *LSAM*. Paris: E. de Boccard.

Sonnabend, H. 1986. *Fremdenbild und Politik: Vorstellungen der Römer von Ägypten und dem Partherreich in der späten Republik und frühen Kaiserzeit.* Frankfurt: Lang.

Sorabella, J. 2010. 'Observing Sleep in Greco-Roman Art', in Scioli and Walde (eds.), 1–31.

Sorek, S. 2010. *Remembered for Good: A Jewish Benefaction System in Ancient Palestine.* Sheffield: Phoenix.

Spaeth, B. S. 2010. '"The Terror That Comes in the Night". The Night Hag and Supernatural Assault in Latin Literature', in Scioli and Walde (eds.), 231–58.

Spaul, J. 1994. *ALA2. The Auxiliary Cavalry Units of the Pre-Diocletianic Imperial Roman Army.* Andover: Nectoreca Press.

Spawforth, A. 2006. '"Macedonian Times": Hellenistic Memories in the Provinces of the Roman Near East', in D. Konstan and S. Saïd (eds.), *Greeks on Greekness. Viewing the Greek Past under the Roman Empire.* Cambridge Philological Society. 1–26.

Sperber, D. 1970. 'On Pubs and Policemen in Roman Palestine', *Zeitschrift der Deutschen Morgenländischen Gesellschaft* 120: 257–63.

1991. *Roman Palestine 200–400 Money and Prices* (2nd ed. with suppl.). Ramat-Gan: Bar-Ilan University.

Spijkerman, F. A. 1972. 'The Coins of Eleutheropolis Iudaeae', *Liber Annuus* 22: 369–84.

Stavrianopoulou, E. 2009. 'Die Bewirtung des Volkes: Öffentliche Speisungen in der römischen Kaiserzeit', in O. Hekster, S. Schmidt-Hofner, and C. Witschel (eds.), *Ritual Dynamics and Religious Change in the Roman Empire. Proceedings of the Eighth Workshop of the International Network Impact of Empire (Heidelberg, July 5–7, 2007).* Leiden: Brill. 159–85.

Stein-Hölkeskamp, E. 2005. *Das römische Gastmahl. Eine Kulturgeschichte.* Munich: C. H. Beck.

Stemberger, G. 1998. 'Jewish-Christian Contacts in Galilee (Fifth to Seventh Centuries)', in A. Kofsky and G. Strousma (eds.), *Sharing the Sacred.* Jerusalem: Yad Izhak Ben Zvi. 131–46.

Stepansky, Y. 2000. 'Archaeological Discoveries in Mughar', *Cathedra* 97: 169–71 (Heb.).

Stern, M. 1974–1984. *Greek and Latin Authors on Jews and Judaism.* Jerusalem: The Israel Academy of Sciences and Humanities.

Stiebel, G. D. 1995. 'The Whereabouts of the Xth Legion and the Boundaries of Aelia Capitolina', in A. Faust and E. Baruch (eds.), *New Studies on Jerusalem: Proceedings of the Fifth Conference.* Ramat-Gan: Bar-Ilan University. 68–103 (Heb.).

2006. 'Roman Military Artifacts', in Tepper and Di Segni, 29–31.

Stone, D. 1998. 'Culture and Investment in the Rural Landscape: the Bonus Agricola', *Antiquités africaines* 34: 103–13.

Sussman, Y. 1973. 'A Halakhic Inscription from the Beth-Shean Valley', *Tarbiz* 43: 88–158 (Heb.).

    1974. 'Additional Notes to 'A Halakhic Inscription from the Beth-Shean Valley', *Tarbiz* 44: 193–5 (Heb.).

Sweetman, R. J. 2007. 'Roman Knossos: Nature of a Globalized City', *American Journal of Archaeology* 111, 61–81.

Syme, R. 1939. *The Roman Revolution*. Oxford: Clarendon Press.

Syon, D. 2016. 'Legio and 'Kefar Otnai: The Coins', *HA-ESI* 128 (Heb.): www .hadashot-esi.org.il/Report_Detail_Eng.aspx?id=24904&mag_id=124

Takács, S. 1995. *Isis and Sarapis in the Roman World*. Religions in the Graeco-Roman World, vol. 124, Leiden: Brill.

    2000. 'Politics and Religion in the Bacchanalian Affair of 186 B.C.', *Harvard Studies in Classical Philology* 100: 301–10.

Talamanca, M. 2006. 'Aulo Gellio ed i "municipes". Per un'esegesi di "Noctes Atticae" 16.13', in L. Capogrossi Colognesi and E. Gabba (eds.), *Gli Statuti Municipali*. Pavia: IUSS Press. 443–513.

Talbert, R. J. A. 1984. *The Senate of Imperial Rome*. Princeton University Press.

Talgam, R. 2014. *Mosaics of Faith*. University Park: Pennsylvania State University Press.

Tawil, D. 1979. 'The Purim Panel in Dura in the Light of Parthian and Sasanian Art', *Journal of Near Eastern Studies* 38: 93–109.

Tcherikover, V. A., Fuks, A. and Stern, M. (eds.) 1957–64. *CPJ*. Cambridge, MA: Published for the Magnes Press, Hebrew University [by] Harvard University Press.

Tepper, Y. 2002. 'Lajjun–Legio in Israel: Results of a Survey in and around the Military Camp Area', in P. Freeman, J. Bennett, Z. T. Fiema and B. Hoffmann (eds.), *Limes XVIII: Proceedings of the 18th International Congress of Roman Frontier Studies*, Amman, September 2000. Oxford: Archaeopress. 231–42.

    2003a. *Survey of the Legio Area near Megiddo – Historical Geographical Research*, M.A. thesis, Tel Aviv University (Heb.).

    2003b. 'Survey of the Legio Region', *HA-ESI* 115: 29*–31*.

    2006. 'Legio, Kefar 'Othnai', *HA-ESI* 118: www.hadashot-esi.org.il/report_detail .aspx?id=363&mag_id=111

    2007. 'The Roman Legionary Camp at Legio, Israel: Results of an Archaeological Survey and Observations on the Roman Military Presence at the Site', in A. S. Lewin and P. Pellegrini, *The Late Roman Army in the East from Diocletian to the Arab Conquest, Proceedings of a Colloquium Held at Potenza, Acerenza and Matera, Italy (May 2005)*. Oxford: Archaeopress. 57–71.

    2014a. *Legio in the Roman Period: a Historical and Archeological Study with an Emphasis on the Ethnic, Social and Religious Components*, Ph.D. thesis, Tel Aviv University (Heb.).

2014b. 'The Tomb of Ephraim Bar-Shimon from Kefar 'Othnay and the Identity of the Site's Population in the Roman and Byzantine Periods'. In G. C. Bottini., L. D. Chrupcata and J. Patrich (eds.), *Knowledge and Wisdom. Studium Biblicum Franciscanum, 54*. Milano: 295–303.

2017. 'Legio: Tiles and Bricks Bearing Seal Prints of Roman Legionary Stamps from Legio', *'Atiqot* 89: 133*–144* (Heb.; English summary: 123).

Tepper, Y. and Di Segni, L. 2006. *A Christian Prayer-Hall of the Third Century CE at Kefar 'Othnay (Legio). Excavations at the Megiddo Prison 2005*. Jerusalem: Israel Antiquities Authority.

Tepper, Y., David, J. and Adams, M. J. 2016. 'The Roman VIth Legions Ferrata at Lagio (el-Lajjun) Israel: Preliminary Report of the 2013 Excavation', *Strata* 34: 91–123.

Terpstra, T. T. 2013. *Trading Communities in the Roman World. A Micro-Economic and Institutional Perspective*. Leiden and Boston: Brill.

Thiessen, M. 2011. *Contesting Conversion: Genealogy, Circumcision, and Identity in Ancient Judaism and Christianity*. Oxford University Press.

Thompson, D. J. 1984. 'The Idumaeans of Memphis and the Ptolemic "Politeumata"', in *Atti XVII Congresso Internazionale di Papirologia*, vol. 3. Naples: Centro internaz. per lo stud. dei papiri ercol. 1069–75.

2001. 'Hellenistic Hellenes: the Case of Ptolemaic Egypt', in I. Malkin (ed.), *Ancient Perceptions of Greek Ethnicity*. Cambridge, MA: Harvard University Press. 301–22.

Thonemann, P. 2011. *The Maeander Valley. A Historical Geography from Antiquity to Byzantium*. Cambridge University Press.

2012. 'Abercius of Hierapolis. Christianization and Social Memory in Late Antique Asia Minor', in B. Dignas and R. R. R. Smith (eds.), *Historical and Religious Memory in the Ancient World*. Oxford University Press. 257–82.

2015. 'The Calendar of the Roman Province of Asia', *Zeitschrift fur Papyrologie und Epigraphik* 196: 123–41.

Touratsoglou, I. 1987. 'Macedonia', in A. M. Burnett and M. H. Crawford (eds.), *The Coinage of the Roman World in the Late Republic*. Oxford: B.A.R. 53–78.

Traill, D. 1995. *Schliemann of Troy. Treasure and Deceit*. London: John Murray Publishers.

Trilla, J. T. 2000. *Industria y artesando cerémico de época romana en el nordeste de Cataluna*. Oxford: J. and E. Hedges.

Triolaire, C. 2013. 'Faire la nuit. Révolution de jeux de lumières sur les scènes théâtrales', in Bourdin (ed.), 269–89.

Tsafrir, Y. 1975. *Zion – The Southwestern Hill of Jerusalem and Its Place in the Urban Development of the City in the Byzantine Period*. Ph.D. thesis. Hebrew University, Jerusalem (Heb.).

1982. 'The Provinces in the Land of Israel – Names, Borders and Administrative Boundaries', in Z. Baras, S.Safrai, Y. Tsafrir and M. Stern (eds.), *Eretz Israel from the Destruction of the Second Temple to the Muslim Conquest*, vol. 1. Jerusalem: Izhak Ben-Zvi Institute. 350–86.

1984. *Eretz Israel from the Destruction of the Second Temple to the Muslim Conquest*, vol. 2: *Archaeology and Art*. Jerusalem: Izhak Ben-Zvi Institute (Heb.).

1999a. 'The Topography and Archaeology of Aelia Capitolina', in Y. Tsafrir and S. Safrai (eds.), *The History of Jerusalem, The Roman and Byzantine Periods (70–638 CE (70–638 CE)*, Jerusalem: Yad Izhak Ben Zvi Institute. 115–66 (Heb.).

1999b. 'The Topography and Archaeology of Jerusalem in the Byzantine Period', in Y. Tsafrir and S. Safrai (eds.), *The History of Jerusalem, the Roman and Byzantine Periods (70–638 CE)*, Jerusalem: Yad Izhak Ben Zvi Institute. 281–351 (Heb.).

2012. 'Between David's Tower and Holy Zion: Peter the Iberian and His Monastery in Jerusalem', in L. D. Chrupcala (ed.), *Christ Is Here! Studies in Biblical and Christian Archaeology in Memory of Michele Piccirillo, ofm*. Milano: Edizioni Terra Santa. 247–64.

Tsafrir, Y., Di Segni, L. and Green, J. 1994. *Tabula Imperii Romani. Iudaea-Palaestina*. Jerusalem: Israel Academy of Sciences and Humanities.

Tully, G. D. 1998. 'The Στραταρχης of Legio VI Ferrata and the Employment of Camp Perfects as Vexillation Commanders', *Zeitschrift fur Papyrologie und Epigraphik* 120: 226–32.

Turcan, R. 1996. *The Cults of the Roman Empire*. Oxford: Blackwell.

Tushingham, A. D. 1985. 'Excavations in the Armenian Garden on the Western Hill', in *Excavations in Jerusalem 1961–1967*, vol. 1. Toronto: Royal Ontario Museum. 60–107.

Tzori, N. 1971. 'An Inscription of the Legion VI Ferrata from the Northern Jordan Valley', *Israel Exploration Journal* 21: 53–4.

Ulbert, G. 1959. *Die Römischen Donau-Kastelle Aislingen und Burghöfe*. Berlin: Mann.

1969. *Das Frührömische Kastell Rheingönheim*. Berlin: Mann.

1985. *Cáceres el Viejo, Ein Spätrepublikanisches Legio lager in Spanisch Extremadura*. Mainz: Von Zabern.

Unz, C. and Deschler-Erb, E. 1997. *Katalog der Militaria aus Vindonissa*. Brugg: Gesellschaft Pro Vindonissa.

Ustinova, Y. 2005. '*Lege et consuetudine*. Private Cult Associations in the Greek Law', in V. Dasen and M. Piérart (eds.), Ἰδίᾳ καὶ δημοσίᾳ. *Les cadres 'privés' et 'publics' de la religion grecque antique* (*Kernos* Suppl. 5). Presses universitaires de Liège. 177–90.

Vahlen, J. et al. (eds.) 1866–. *CSEL*. Vienna: Tempsky.

Van Andringa, W. 2003. 'Cités et communautés d'expatriés installées dans l'empire romain: le cas des cives Romani consistentes', in N. Belayche and

S. C. Mimouni (eds.), *Les communautés religieuses dans le monde gréco-romain. Essais de définition*, Turnhout: Brepols. 49–60.

2009. *Quotidien des dieux et des hommes: la vie religieuse dans les cités du Vésuve à l'époque romaine*. École Française de Rome.

van Bremen, R. 2011. 'Day and Night at Stratonikeia', in L. Karlsson and S. Carlsson (eds.), *Labraunda and Karia. Proceedings of the International Symposium Commemorating Sixty Years of Swedish Archaeological Work in Labraunda*. Uppsala Universitet. 307–29.

van Dam, R. 2010. *Rome and Constantinople: Rewriting Roman History during Late Antiquity*. Waco: Baylor University Press.

van der Vliet, N. 1950. 'Monnaies inédites ou très rares du médaillier de sainte Anne de Jérusalem', *Revue Biblique* 57: 110–29.

van Nijf, O. M. 1997. *The Civic World of Professional Associations in the Roman East*. Amsterdam: J. C. Gieben.

2002. 'Collegia and Civic Guards: Two Chapters in the History of Sociability', in W. Jongman and M. Kleijwegt (eds.), *After the Past. Essays in Ancient History in Honour of H. W. Pleket*. Leiden: Brill. 305–39.

Vandorpe, K. 2008. 'Persian Soldiers and Persians of the Epigone: Social Mobility of Soldiers-Herdsmen in Upper Egypt', *Archiv für Papyrusforschung und verwandte Gebiete* 54: 87–108.

Vasta, M. 2007. 'Flavian Visual Propaganda: Building a Dynasty', *Constructing the Past* 8.1: 107–38.

Verboven, K. 2017. 'Guilds and the Organization of Urban Populations during the Principate', in K. Verboven and C. Laes (eds.), *Work, Labour, and Professions in the Roman World*. Leiden: Brill. 173–202.

Vermeule, C. C. 1995. 'Neon Ilion and Ilium Novum: Kings, Soldiers, Citizens, and Tourists at Classical Troy', in J. B. Carter and S. P. Morris (eds.), *The Ages of Homer. A Tribute to Emily Townsend Vermeule*. Austin: University of Texas Press. 467–82.

Versnel, H. S. 1994. *Transition and Reversal in Myth and Ritual*. Leiden: Brill.

Vetrali, L. 1968. 'Le iscrizioni dell'acquedotto romano presso Betlemme', *Liber Annuus* 17: 149–61.

Vetters, H. et al. 1979–84. *Die Inschriften von Ephesos*. Bonn: R. Habelt.

Veyne, P. 1999/2005. 'L'identité grecque devant Rome et l'empereur', *Revue des études grecques* 112: 510–67. = 'L'identité grecque contre et avec Rome: "collaboration" et vocation supérieure', in P. Veyne, *L'Empire gréco-romain*. Paris: Seuil. 163–257.

Vilnay, Z. 1928. 'Another Roman Inscription from the Neighborhood of Caesarea', *Palestine Exploration Fund, Quarterly Statement* 60: 108–9.

Vincent, L. H. and Abel, F. M. 1914. *Jérusalem: Recherches de topographi, d'archeologie et d'histoire, II, Jérusalem nouvelle*. Paris: J. Gabalda.

Vincent, L. H. and Steve, A. M. 1954. *Jerusalem de l'Ancien Testament*. Paris: J. Gabalda.

Vittinghoff, F. 1952. *Römische Kolonisation und Bürgerrechtspolitik unter Caesar und Augustus*. Wiesbaden: Steiner.

1994. *Civitas Romana. Stadt und politisch-soziale Integration im Imperium Romanum der Kaiserzeit*. Stuttgart: Klett-Cotta.

Vitto, F. 1993. 'Rehob', in E. Stern, *New Encyclopedia of Archaeological Excavations in the Holy Land* 4. Jerusalem: Israel Exploration Society & Carta. 1272–4.

von Albrect, M. 2005. 'Populus: la testimonianza dei poeti augustei', in G. Urso (ed.), *Popolo e potere nel mondo antico, Cividale del Friuli, 23–25 settembre 2004*. Pisa: ETS. 173–89.

von Ehrenheim, H. 2015. *Greek Incubation Rituals in Classical and Hellenistic Times*. Presses Universitaires de Liège.

Vössing, K. 2004. *Mensa regia: das Bankett beim hellenistischen König und beim römischen Kaiser*. Munich and Leipzig: Saur.

Vukosavovic, F. 2015. *By the Rivers of Babylon: the Story of the Babylonian Exile*, trans. and ed. O. Meiri and R. Elitzur-Leiman. Jerusalem: Bible Lands Museum.

Wachter, R. 1998. '"Oral Poetry" in ungewohntem Kontext: Hinweise auf mündliche Dichtungstechnik in den pompejanischen Wandinschriften', *Zeitschrift fur Papyrologie und Epigraphik* 121: 73–89.

Wagner, J. and Petzl, G. 1976. 'Eine neue Temenos-Stele des König Antiochos I. Von Kommagene', *Zeitschrift fur Papyrologie und Epigraphik* 20: 201–23.

Walbank, F. W. 1972. 'Nationality as a Factor in Roman History', *Harvard Studies in Classical Philology* 76: 145–68.

Wander, B. 1998. *Gottesfürchtige und Sympathisanten*. Tübingen: Mohr.

Wardle, D. 1998. *Valerius Maximus, Memorable Deeds and Sayings, Book 1*. Oxford: Clarendon Press.

Warren, C. and Conder, C. R. 1884. *The Survey of Western Palestine III, Jerusalem*. London: Committee of the Palestine Exploration Fund. 193–209.

Waswo, R. 1995. 'Our Ancestors, the Trojans: Inventing Cultural Identity in the Middle Ages', *Exemplaria* 7: 269–90.

Weber, E. 1976. *Peasants into Frenchmen: the Modernization of Rural France, 1870–1914*. Stanford University Press.

Weber, G. 2005/06. 'Träume und Visionen im Alltag der römischen Kaiserzeit. Das Zeugnis der Inschriften und Papyri', *Quaderni Catanesi NS* 4/5: 55–121.

Weber, G. (ed.) 2015. *Artemidor von Daldis und die antike Traumdeutung. Texte – Kontexte – Lektüren*. Berlin: De Gruyter.

Webster, G. 1969. *The Roman Imperial Army of the First and Second Centuries A.D.* London: Adam & Charles Black.

Webster, J. 2001. 'Creolizing the Roman Provinces', *American Journal of Archaeology* 105, 209–25.

Wecowski, M. 2014. *The Rise of the Greek Aristocratic Banquet*. Oxford University Press.

Weiß, P. 2015. 'Eine *honesta missio* in Sonderformat. Neuartige Bronzeurkunden für Veteranen der Legionen in Germania superior unter Gordian III', *Chiron* 45: 23–75.

Weiss, Z. 2005. *The Sepphoris Synagogue*. Jerusalem: Israel Exploration Society.

　　2012. 'Were Priests Communal Leaders in Late Antique Palestine? The Archaeological Evidence', in D. R. Schwartz and Z. Weiss (eds.), *Was 70 CE a Watershed in Jewish History? On Jews and Judaism before and after the Destruction of the Second Temple*. Leiden: Brill. 91–111.

Weksler-Bdolah, S. 2011. *The Main Streets in Southeastern Jerusalem in the Roman Period and Their Role in the Development of Aelia Capitolina in the Second to Fourth Centuries CE, Focusing on the Excavations along the Eastern Colonnaded Street and the 'Wilson Bridge' ('Great Causeway')*. Ph.D. thesis, Hebrew University of Jerusalem (Heb.).

　　2014a. 'The Tenth Legion Camp – Nonetheless on the Southwestern Hill', in E. Baruch and A. Faust (eds.), *New Studies on Jerusalem*, Collected Papers 20: 219–38 (Heb.; English summary, 48–50).

　　2014b. 'The Foundation of Aelia Capitolina in Light of New Excavations along the Eastern *Cardo*', *Israel Exploration Journal* 64: 38–62.

　　2014c. 'The Environs of the Temple Mount between its Destruction in 70 CE and Madaba Map: The Archaeological Evidence from Southeastern Jerusalem', in G. D. Stiebel, O. Peleg-Barkat, D. Ben-Ami and Y. Gadot (eds.), *New Studies in the Archaeology of Jerusalem and Its Region*, Collected Papers 8. Jerusalem: Israel Antiquities Authority. 190–209 (Heb.).

Weksler-Bdloah, S. 2020. Aelia Capitolina – Jerusalem in the Roman Period, in Light of Archaeological Research. Leiden/ Boston: Brill.

Weksler-Bdolah, S. and Rosenthal-Heginbottom, R. 2014. 'Two Aspects of the Transformation of Jerusalem into the Roman Colony of Aelia Capitolina', in J. Patrich (ed.), *Knowledge and Wisdom Archaeological and Historical Essays in Honour of Leah Di Segni*. Milano: Edizioni Terra Santa. 43–61.

Wells, C. 1984. *The Roman Empire*. London: Fontana Paperbacks.

Wesseling, A. 1993. 'Are the Dutch Uncivilized? Erasmus on the Batavians and His National Identity', *Erasmus of Rotterdam Society Yearbook* 13(1): 68–102.

Whitmarsh, T. (ed.) 2010a. *Local Knowledge and Microidentities in the Imperial Greek World*. Cambridge University Press.

　　2010b. 'Thinking Local', in Whitmarsh (ed.), 1–16.

　　2010c. 'Prose Fiction', in J. J. Clauss and M. Cuypers (eds.), *A Companion to Hellenistic Literature*. Malden, MA/Oxford: Wiley-Blackwell. 395–411.

Wilhelm, A. 1913. *Neue Beiträge zur griechischen Inschriftenkunde III (Sitzungsberichte der philosophisch-historischen Klasse der Österreichischen Akademie der Wissenschaften 175.1)*. Vienna: Hölder.

Will, E. and Orrieux, C. 1992. '*Prosélytime juif?* Histoire d'une erreur. Paris: Les Belles Lettres.

Williams, M. 2010. 'The Disciplining of the Jews of Ancient Rome: Pure Gesture Politics?' in C. Deroux, *Studies in Latin Literature and Roman History*, XV, 323, 79–100.

Wills, L. M. 2008. *Not God's People*. Lanham, MD: Rowman & Littlefield Publishers.

Wilson, A. 2018. 'Roman Nightlife', in Chaniotis (ed.), 59–81.

Wilson, C. W. 1905. 'The Camp of the Tenth Legion at Jerusalem and the City of Aelia', *Palestine Exploration Fund, Quarterly Statement* 37: 138–44.

   1906. *Golgotha and the Holy Sepulchre*. London: Kessinger Publishing.

Wilson, C. W. and Warren, C. 1871. *Recovery of Jerusalem*. London: R. Bentley.

Wilson, K. 2020. 'The Astronomer-Poet at Night: the Evolution of a Motif', in Ker and Wessels (eds.), 131–49.

Wiseman, T. P. 1971. *New Men in the Roman Senate*. Oxford University Press.

   1995. *Remus. A Roman Myth*. Cambridge University Press.

Wishnitzer, A. 2014. 'Into the Dark: Power, Light, and Nocturnal Life in 18th-Century Istanbul', *International Journal of Middle East Studies* 46: 513–31.

Woolf, G. 1993a. 'Rethinking the Oppida', *Oxford Journal of Archaeology* 12: 223–34.

   1993b. 'Roman Peace', in J. Rich and G. Shipley (eds.), *War and Society in the Roman World*. New York: Routledge. 171–94.

   1998. *Becoming Roman: The Origins of Provincial Civilization in Gaul*. Cambridge University Press.

   2010. 'Afterword: the Local and the Global in the Graeco-Roman East', in Whitmarsh (ed.), 189–200.

   2012. *Rome: An Empire's Story*. Oxford: Oxford University Press.

Woytek, B. E. 2011. 'The Coinage of Apamea Myrlea under Trajan and the Problem of Double Communities in the Roman East', *Numismatic Chronicle* 171: 121–32.

Wright, B. G. (ed.) 2015. *The Letter of Aristeas: 'Aristeas to Philocrates' or 'On the Translation of the Law of the Jews'*. Berlin: De Gruyter.

Wypustek, A. 2012. *Images of Eternal Beauty in Funerary Verse Inscriptions of the Hellenistic and Greco-Roman Periods*. Leiden: Brill.

Yisraeli-Taran, A. 1997. *The Legends of the Destruction*. Tel Aviv: Ha-Kibbutz Ha-Me'uḥad (Heb.).

Youtie, H. 1964. 'A Reconsideration of P. Oxy. 1.40', in H. Braunert (ed.), *Studien zur Papyrologie und Antiken Wirtschaftgeschichte*. Bonn: Habelt. 20–9.

Zadok, R. 1988. *The pre-Hellenistic Israelite Anthroponymy and Prosopography*. Leuven: Peeters.

   2002. *The Earliest Diaspora: Israelites and Judeans in Pre-Hellenistic Mesopotamia*. Tel-Aviv: Diaspora Research Institute.

Zeitlin, F. I. 2001. 'Visions and Revisions of Homer', in S. Goldhill (ed.), *Being Greek under Rome. Cultural Identity, the Second Sophistic and the Development of Empire*. Cambridge University Press. 195–266.

Zelle, M. 2006. *Die römischen Wand- und Deckenmalereien in Gelduba*. Schwelm: Archaea.

Zimmermann, C. 2002. *Handwerkervereine im griechischen Osten des Imperium Romanum*. Mainz: RGZM.

Zucca, R. 2014. 'Senatori nella Sardinia', in Caldelli and Gregori (eds.), 341–52.

Zuckerman, C. 1985–8. 'Hellenistic *Politeumata* and the Jews: A Reconsideration', *Scripta Classica Israelica* 8–9: 171–85.

General Index

Aaron, Biblical character, 237
Abdera, 44, 47
Abel, Félix-Marie, 284
Abonou Teichos, 159
Abraham, Biblical character, 175, 237
Achaia, 33
Achilles, 21, 90, 95, 96–97
Achilles Tatius, 149, 159
Achilleum, 91
Actium, 100, 104, 106, 148, 192, 194–195
Adan-Bayewitz, David, 288
Adiabene, 214
Aegean, 92, 179
Aegyptus. *See* Egypt
Aelia Capitolina, 110, 270
Aelius Aristides Theodorus, P., 101, 113, 140–141, 223
Aelius Coeranus, P., 33
Aelius Donatus, 46
Aelius Stilo Praeconius, L., 137
Aeneas, 20, 87, 89, 93, 95–97, 171
Aesculapius, 122
Africa, 32, 33–35, 37, 40, 46, 55, 148, 178, 255, 267
Agamemnon, 89–90
Agathias, 105
Agrippa II, 258, 292, 296
Aila ('Aqaba), 283
Ajax, 24, 96
Akko, 289
Akko-Ptolemais, 275
Al Lajjun (Transjordan), 284
Albanum, 157
Alcibiades, 47
Alcmene, 126–127
Alexander the Great, 92, 98, 108, 148, 158, 248
Alexandria, 19–20, 24, 33, 143, 191, 213, 231, 236, 244, 246, 247–248, 256, 261
Alexianus. *See* Severus Alexander
Algeria, 46, 110
Alps, 33, 194
Altbach valley, 130
Altbachtal, 126–127

Amphipolis, 162
Amsterdam, 17
Amyntas, king of Galatia, 109
Ananias, 209
Anatolia, 23, 106, 114, 179
Anchises, 87, 90
Ando, Clifford, 134
Andrade, Nathanael, 209, 213
Annaeus Seneca, L. (Minor), 38, 87, 151, 164, 183
Annius Milo, T., 54
Antamonides, 45
Antioch, 20, 24–25, 111, 253, 256, 292
Antioch (Pisidia), 32, 109, 113, 281
Antiochus III, 209
Antiochus IV Epiphanes, 212
Antiochus V Eupater, 209
Antipater the Idumaean (Antipas), 213
Antipatris, 268, 280
Antistius Rusticus, L., 32
Antium, 20
Antius A. Iulius Quadratus, C., 32, 34, 37
Antoninus, 246–254, 258, 262–264, 268,
    See also Caracalla *and* Elagabalus
Antoninus Pius, 37, 136, 139, 144, 247
Antonius Diogenes, 151
Antonius, M., 19–21, 195
Apamea, 32, 108
Apamea, lake, 256
Aphrodisias, 114, 177, 232
Aphrodite, 161, *See also* Venus
Apollo, 117–118, 122, 125, 127, *See also*
    Phoebos
  Apollo Klarios, 160
Apollonia, 106–109, 113, 115
Apollonius of Tyana, 114
Appian, 152
Apuleius Madaurensis, L., 159, 184
Aquileia, 24
Aquitania, 141
Arabia, 33, 38, 110, 283–284, 292, 297
Arbel, 225
Arcadius, 221

Index Locorum

The Bible
Jewish Bible

For EU product safety concerns, contact us at Calle de José Abascal, 56–1°,
28003 Madrid, Spain or eugpsr@cambridge.org.

www.ingramcontent.com/pod-product-compliance
Ingram Content Group UK Ltd.
Pitfield, Milton Keynes, MK11 3LW, UK
UKHW051048150625
459647UK00017B/1817